WRISTWATCH ANNUAL

2020

THE CATALOG

of

PRODUCERS, PRICES, MODELS,

and

SPECIFICATIONS

BY PETER BRAUN

WITH MARTON RADKAI

ABBEVILLE PRESS PUBLISHERS

New York   London

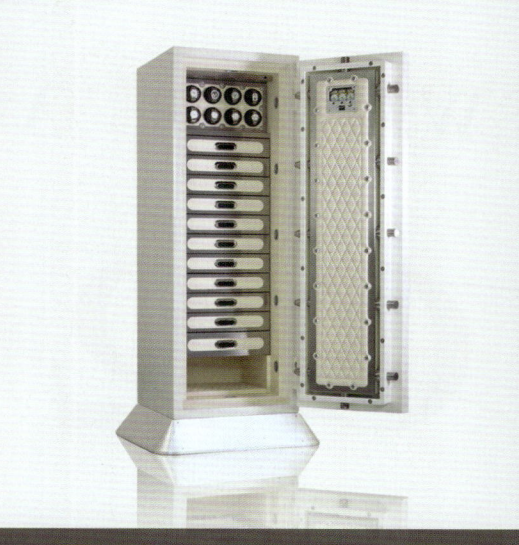

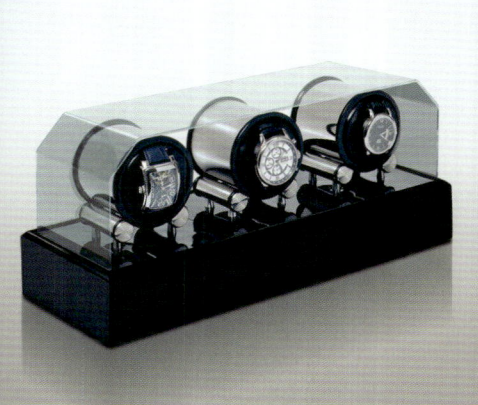

STYLE
SOPHISTICATION
SECURITY

High-security luxury safes and watch winders expertly crafted to keep your collection securely organized and running in top form.

View the complete collection of fine watchwinders at *Orbita.com* & visit *BrownSafe.com* for a full lineup of high-security luxury safes featuring Orbita watchwinders.

BROWN SAFE
Ph.(760) 233-2293
www.BrownSafe.com

ORBITA WATCHWINDERS
Ph.(800) 800-4436
www.Orbita.com

When you've been making watches for as long as we have, some things just come naturally.

#GoYourOwnWay

**Big Crown
ProPilot X Calibre 115**

CONTENTS

A
A. Lange & Söhne ... 48
Alexander Shorokhoff ... 54
Alpina ... 56
Angelus ... 57
Anonimo ... 58
Aristo ... 59
Armin Strom ... 60
Arnold & Son ... 62
ArtyA ... 64
Audemars Piguet ... 66
AVeritas ... 71
Azimuth ... 72

B
Ball Watch Co. ... 74
Baume & Mercier ... 78
Bell & Ross ... 80
Blancpain ... 82
Borgward ... 86
Bovet ... 88
Breguet ... 90
Breitling ... 94
Bremont ... 98
BRM ... 100
Carl F. Bucherer ... 106
Bulgari ... 102

C
Carl F. Bucherer ... 106
Cartier ... 110
Casio ... 114
Chanel ... 115
Chopard ... 116
Christophe Claret ... 121
Chronoswiss ... 122
Claude Meylan ... 125
Frédérique Constant ... 148
Corum ... 126
Cuervo y Sobrinos ... 130
Czapek & Cie. ... 131

D
Davosa ... 132
Deep Blue ... 134
Detroit Watch Co. ... 135
Doxa ... 136
Roger Dubuis ... 270
duManège ... 137

E
Eberhard & Co. ... 138
Eterna ... 140

F
Fabergé ... 142
Laurent Ferrier ... 201
F.P. Journe ... 144
Franck Muller ... 146
Frédérique Constant ... 148

G
Paul Gerber ... 254
Girard-Perregaux ... 150
Glashütte Original ... 154
Graham ... 159
Grand Seiko ... 160
Greubel Forsey ... 162

H
H. Moser & Cie. ... 164
Habring² ... 166
Hager Watches ... 168
Hamilton ... 169
Hanhardt ... 171
Harry Winston ... 172
Hautlence ... 174
Hermès ... 176
Hublot ... 178
HYT ... 181

I
Itay Noy ... 182
IWC ... 184

J
Jaeger-LeCoultre ... 188
Jaquet Droz ... 194
Jörg Schauer ... 195
F.P. Journe ... 144
JS Watches ... 196
Junghans ... 197
Urban Jürgensen & Sønner ... 311

K
Kobold ... 199
Kudoke ... 200

L
A. Lange & Söhne ... 48
Maurice Lacroix ... 210
Laurent Ferrier ... 201
Longines ... 202
Louis Moinet ... 205
Louis Vuitton ... 206
Luminox ... 208

M
Manufacture Royale ... 209
Maurice Lacroix ... 210
MB&F ... 213
MeisterSinger ... 214
Claude Meylan ... 125
Mido ... 216
Richard Mille ... 268
Ming ... 218
Mk II ... 219
Louis Moinet ... 205
Mondaine ... 220
Montblanc ... 221
H. Moser & Cie. ... 164
Mühle-Glashütte ... 225
Franck Muller ... 146

N
Ulysse Nardin ... 308
Nivrel ... 227
Nomos ... 228
Itay Noy ... 182

O
Omega ... 232
Oris ... 236

P
Panerai ... 239
Parmigiani ... 242
Patek Philippe ... 246
Paul Gerber ... 254
Piaget ... 256
Porsche Design ... 260
Pramzius ... 262

R
Rado ... 263
Reservoir ... 264
Ressence ... 265
RGM ... 266
Richard Mille ... 268
Roger Dubuis ... 270
Rolex ... 274

S
Jörg Schauer ... 195
Schaumburg Watch ... 280
Schwarz Etienne ... 281
Seiko ... 282
Alexander Shorokhoff ... 54
Sinn ... 284
Speake-Marin ... 287
Stowa ... 288
Armin Strom ... 60

T
TAG Heuer ... 290
Temption ... 294
Tissot ... 296
Tourby ... 298
Towson Watch Company ... 300
Tudor ... 302
Tutima ... 305

U
Ulysse Nardin ... 308
Urban Jürgensen & Sønner ... 311
Urwerk ... 312
UTS ... 313

V
Vacheron Constantin ... 314
Van Cleef & Arpels ... 320
Vortic ... 321
Vostok-Europe ... 322
Louis Vuitton ... 206

W
Wempe Glashütte I/SA ... 324
Harry Winston ... 172

Z
Zeitwinkel ... 326
Zenith ... 327

Movement manufacturers
Concepto ... 332
ETA ... 334
Ronda ... 338
Sellita ... 340

Editorial
Letter to the Reader ... 6
Independent Watchmaking:
The Independent Scene 2019 ... 10
Masters and Mavericks:
Engineering Emotion ... 20
Watch Tech:
For Beauty's Sake ... 38
Watch Your Watch ... 342
Glossary ... 344
Masthead ... 352

Advertisers
Abbeville
Alexander Shorokhoff
Brillier
Casio
Claude Meylan
Deep Blue
Detroit Watch Company
Franck Muller
Hager
Island Watch
Itay Noy
Junghans
Luminox
Maurice Lacroix
MeisterSinger
Ming
Mk II
Mühle Glashütte
Old Northeast Jewelers
Orbita
Oris
Parmigiani
Paul Forrest
Quill & Pad
Sturmanskie
Tourby
Towson Watch Company
Vortic Watch Company
William Henry
Wolf

AMERICANA CHAPTER III
"BUILT BETTER IN THE USA"

TYPE: STANDARD ISSUE "INFANTRY"

SERIAL NO: AMCH3

MOVEMENT: AMERIQUARTZ CALIBER 7M21 DAY / DATE MOVEMENT

STRAP: HORWEEN LEATHER MADE IN USA

MARKING: GENUINE BRONZE MINUTE COUNTER RING

FINAL ASSEMBLY AND CALIRATION: FOUNTAIN HILLS, AZ USA

www.Brillier.com

PRESERVING AMERICAN HISTORY ONE WATCH AT A TIME

FORT COLLINS, CO

www.vorticwatches.com

LETTER TO THE READER

Dear Reader,

Luxury is an elastic term, not to say indefinable. Is it a thing? A process? Is it big? Or small? Two- or three-dimensional? For some, it might mean adding to, or completing, a beautiful collection of objects, be they watches, artworks, vintage cars, stamps. For others, it's diving into a mountain lake after a long hike in the heat of summer. Luxury can simply mean spending industrial quantities of money on a superyacht, or eating beluga caviar by the shovelful. It can also mean buying oneself, or receiving, a gift in memory of a special occasion, a marriage anniversary, or graduation.

All too often, though, luxury is in fact connected with price and expense, which is, in turn, linked to exclusivity, because it implies that fewer people can have the object of desire, so it becomes more valuable. . . . It's a strange syllogism based on the classic supply-and-demand economics of Dr. Seuss's *Sneetches*, only at a very high level.

In the final analysis, for the consumer, luxury and luxuriousness are a very personal matter. To use the old platitude, it's in the mind of the beholder. The object, whatever it may be, must possess the quality of rarity for the receiver, but not necessarily for the world at large. It must and will engage in a relationship that can change over time and even end.

For brands, however, especially in the so-called luxury industries, it tends to be all about the products. These must trigger enough desire in a vast array of individuals to result in purchase, regardless of the reason. In the case of watches, Yvan Arpa, founder and creative head of ArtyA, often points out that time-telling is ubiquitous thanks to the mobile phone, so a watch—our industry, if you will—has no other purpose than to generate an emotional or intellectual bond. It can be knowledge of the technical hijinks inside—a Greubel Forsey is an almost ecstatic-religious experience for the true connoisseur—or it may be something as simple as the materials of the case: warm golds, icy clear platinum and steel, brittle and light titanium, techy-techy carbon and PVD coatings, diamonds, rubies, emeralds, and sapphires. The one unifying factor, however, will be how this is all put together and packaged, namely the design. That is what delivers the first wow when looking at the piece, or what the French call the *coup de foudre* (love at first sight).

LETTER TO THE READER

This edition of *Wristwatch Annual*, my tenth, almost inadvertently gravitated toward watch design topics. The article "Engineering Emotion" (page 20) takes a look at Germany's industrial design norms through the watches from Glashütte, which is celebrating 175 years of horological history in 2020. The Watch Tech section (page 38) examines the tourbillon, a *grande complication* invented for pocket watches that no longer serves any real engineering purpose, say some, but has become a bit of kinetic art.

The periphery of a watch also makes demands on designers. Winders, shops, storage facilities, even testers and loupes all need a shape that will be attractive to the user. So this year, *Wristwatch Annual* once again takes a brief look at the industry the watch industry has spurred, from analyzers to display cases.

As for brands, there are 126 being presented. Between the pages devoted to the Big Names, like Patek (whose Nautilus might be phased out), Rolex, and several Swatch brands, you'll find many new models of existing brands and a couple of newcomers to the book and to the industry, like Ming, from Kuala Lumpur, Angelus, AVeritas, Reservoir, and more. A chance meeting with Erdal Yildiz at Baselworld resulted in a chapter on his brand, Tourby. U.S. brands are, as usual well represented, so do not miss the grandmaster from Pennsylvania Roland Murphy's spread at RGM, or the Americana redux watches of Vortic, which successfully fought off an injunction by a modern brand with an old name against the nineteenth-century dials he had been using. Deep Blue is back, too, with more diving watches.

Wristwatch Annual prides itself on giving space to the smaller brands, sometimes the unknown and independent ones. This is all the more tempting, as the bigger brands and groups seem to be playing harder and harder to get. That is one of the reasons we always publish Elizabeth Doerr's insightful review of the Independent Scene, this year scanning such great watchmakers as Aaron Becsei, Beauregard, and Singer Reimagined, and more.

Our book couldn't be completed without the advertisers, who understand that a book of paper filled with nice, durable images is a boost not only for the brand but for the industry as a whole, especially in this age of ephemeral electronic communication. Thanks go to them, and to the people who put the whole book together, notably Ginny Carroll, who proofreads the manuscript in record time. Errors do occur, and if you run into one, please make gentle note of it and enjoy everything else. We'd love to hear from you.

By the way, my little luxury, when this annual project ends, is a fresh bottle of fine ink for my pens. What is yours?

Marton Radkai

This year's *Wristwatch Annual* features a special GMT watch, the 19.02 Worldtimer, by the young horologer MING from Kuala Lumpur. For improved readability, the reference cities, including Kuala Lumpur, are static and printed on the underside of the graduated black sapphire dial. A 24-hour titanium disk rotates to display the different time zones, and crosshairs on the dial facilitate indexing and time reading. Inside the watch beats a microrotor automatic Schwarz Etienne ASE220.1 movement custom-modified for MING, notably with a skeletonized barrel cover, which acts as a power reserve indicator.

TOURBY
Hagen in Westfalen

we build your watch

Art Deco Sector Dial 40
Diameter 40 mm
Height 11.6 mm
Domed sapphire crystal
Transparent case back
Swiss-made movement
Hand wound
Genuine Louisiana alligator
Price $ 1,850.00

www.tourbywatches.com

Tourby Watches - Königstr. 78 - 58300 Wetter an der Ruhr (Hagen in Westfalen) - GERMANY - Tel. +49 2335 8463447

THE INDEPENDENT SCENE 2019: KEEP WATCHING

ELIZABETH DOERR

News from the world of independent watchmakers has been very positive. The segment has been growing steadily, and the diversity of creations, strategies, directions, and personalities in this milieu has certainly reached an all-time high.

1 Singer Reimagined, a chronograph that is retro, yet not.

2 The new brand Genus reveals all, including time.

While some independents such as **Singer Reimagined** find continued success with new variations on one watch—in this case, the fantastic **Track 1** chronograph—others like Ming have emerged with a variety of watches in a range of price classes (see page 218). And not only have the independents come out in droves at high-profile events like Only Watch and Grand Prix d'Horlogerie de Genève (GPHG) in 2019, they have taken home some of the big prizes at these events: At the 2019 GPHG, for example, independents clinched seven of the eighteen prizes awarded.

One of these is newcomer **Genus**, awarded the Mechanical Exception Prize for its very first commercial offering: the visually captivating **GNS1.2**, which—despite its very complex dial revealing everything of the mechanics inside—"only" displays hours and minutes. Founded by Sébastien Billières and Catherine Henry, this small Genevan company is definitely one to keep tabs on.

INDEPENDENT WATCHMAKING

Beauregard is another we should be watching carefully. Jeweler Alexandre Beauregard has drawn the attention of the watch world with a number of particularly captivating timepieces. Hailing from Montreal, Beauregard does not have the usual view on watchmaking—and his creations positively reflect that. Thus far, the round **Dahlia** with central flying tourbillon has emerged as a kind of flagship watch Beauregard and his small team use as the starting point for the made-to-measure pieces of lapidary art crafted from precious and semiprecious stones.

Trilobe's first collection, **Les Matinaux**, is the brainchild of young Gautier Massonneau and watch industry technician *par excellence* Jean-François Mojon. At the age of 28, Massonneau gave up his comfy job as a banker and followed his dream of creating a special way of displaying the time. With much passion and an eye for esthetics, the philosophical young man searched out the best watchmaker he could . . . and the special disks leading to philosophical meanderings in the mind of the wearer became reality.

1 Alexandre Beauregard from Montréal, and his fascinating Dahlia with central flying tourbillon.

2 Gautier Massonneau joined Jean-François Mojon to create a watch without hands.

STURMANSKIE
THE FIRST IN SPACE

Only one watch company holds the distinction of being the first watch in space - Sturmanskie

It is rare when the phrase "own a piece of history" has real meaning. In the case of the Sturmanskie Yuri Gagarin commemorative edition it is not hyperbole.

Inspired by the original watch Gagarin wore during his historic 1961 flight, the watch is the only timepiece in the world authorized to use Gagarin's likeness. Hand assembled in Moscow, the watch uses the same Poljot movement as the original and truly brings the history of space travel to your wrist.

Detente Watch Group, 244 Upton Road, Suite 4, Colchester, CT 06415.
877-486-7865. sales@detentewatches.com

INDEPENDENT WATCHMAKING

MICRO BRANDS OR INDEPENDENTS?

One energizing factor in the industry is the growing presence and, perhaps, influence of newcomers who are simply enthusiasts, like AnOrdain and Ming. At the beginning of these two small companies' existences I might have wanted to categorize them each as micro brands—small, typically independently owned brands manufacturing on a small scale using supplied parts to make reasonably priced timepieces—but with time I have come to realize they both operate more along the lines of independent watchmakers, albeit perhaps on a different plane than, say, the A.H.C.I.

Ming Thein is a well-known figure in the inside world of haute horlogerie: As an avid watch collector he had built numerous relationships. A commercial photographer by trade, his watch photos were also legendary. But Thein has also emerged as a discerning perfectionist; thus, the quest for the perfect watch is the premise for the founding of **Ming**. Since its establishment, Thein and his team have launched a number of watches in varying price categories powered by ETA or Schwarz Etienne movements, but what is so fascinating about these watches is the absurd amount of thought and attention to detail that have very obviously gone into every single component and feature. Ming was rewarded for this work by winning the Horological Revelation prize at the 2019 Grand Prix d'Horlogerie de Genève for the **17.06 Copper**.

---

1 AnOrdain: Success with the basics.

2 Ming Thein: photographer and committed watch enthusiast.

3 Ming's Copper 17.06, warm shades and riveting pattern.

MAURICE Ⓜ LACROIX
Manufacture Horlogère Suisse

YOUR TIME IS NOW.

AIKON MERCURY 44MM
AI6088-SS001-030-1

#BE**YOUR**AIKON

DISTRIBUTED BY
DKSH Luxury & Lifestyle North America
9-D Princess Road
Lawrenceville, NJ 08648
(609) 750-8800
www.mauricelacroix.com • @mauricelacroix

INDEPENDENT WATCHMAKING

AnOrdain's claim to fame is the genuine enamel dials made right in the heart of Glasgow. Founded by a young group of designers—architects and product designers as well as jewelers, a photographer, and, of course, a watchmaker—the small brand's MO sounds very much like micro brand material. But as I've gotten to know them over the last couple of years, I realize that this band of merry creators is here for the long run, discovering a passion for the subject even though they are not from any part of the traditional horological world.

A.H.C.I.

The heart piece of the independent scene is the A.H.C.I. (Académie Horlogère des Créateurs Indépendents/Horological Academy of Independent Creators), a group of independent creators founded in 1985. The way of these individualistic watchmaker-inventors is indeed anachronistic, and though the products that emerge may not be everyone's cup of tea all of the time, they do attract the attention of collectors of rare taste who follow not only the horological escapades of these thirty or so extraordinary men—and women—of varying age and nationality, but also the passion and personality that go into each extremely limited timepiece.

Kari Voutilainen is undoubtedly one of the most popular members of this group, and his extremely limited releases always seize the attention of horophiles—his 2019 release, the **28ti**, perhaps even more so due to the fact that the Finnish watchmaker living in Switzerland has flipped his Vingt-8 movement to make it visible through the front of the watch. A "turn" that collectors have long asked for, the execution was rewarded with the Men's prize at the 2019 Grand Prix d'Horlogerie de Genève.

A.H.C.I. co-founder **Svend Andersen**'s brand-new **Art & Culture Collection** kicks off with a watch that honors the art of winemaking by depicting the various stages involved in the winemaking process, and by celebrating and drawing attention to winemakers and wine lovers. Specifically, this automatic features a center dial made of 21-karat blue gold with an upper arched section with a miniature painting depicting scenes of the applicable work done on the vineyard throughout the year. This section makes one complete rotation over the course of a full year showing the task that is done at each period in

1 Voutilainen's 28ti turns the movement back to front for fans.

2 Days of wine and watches . . . by Svend Andersen.

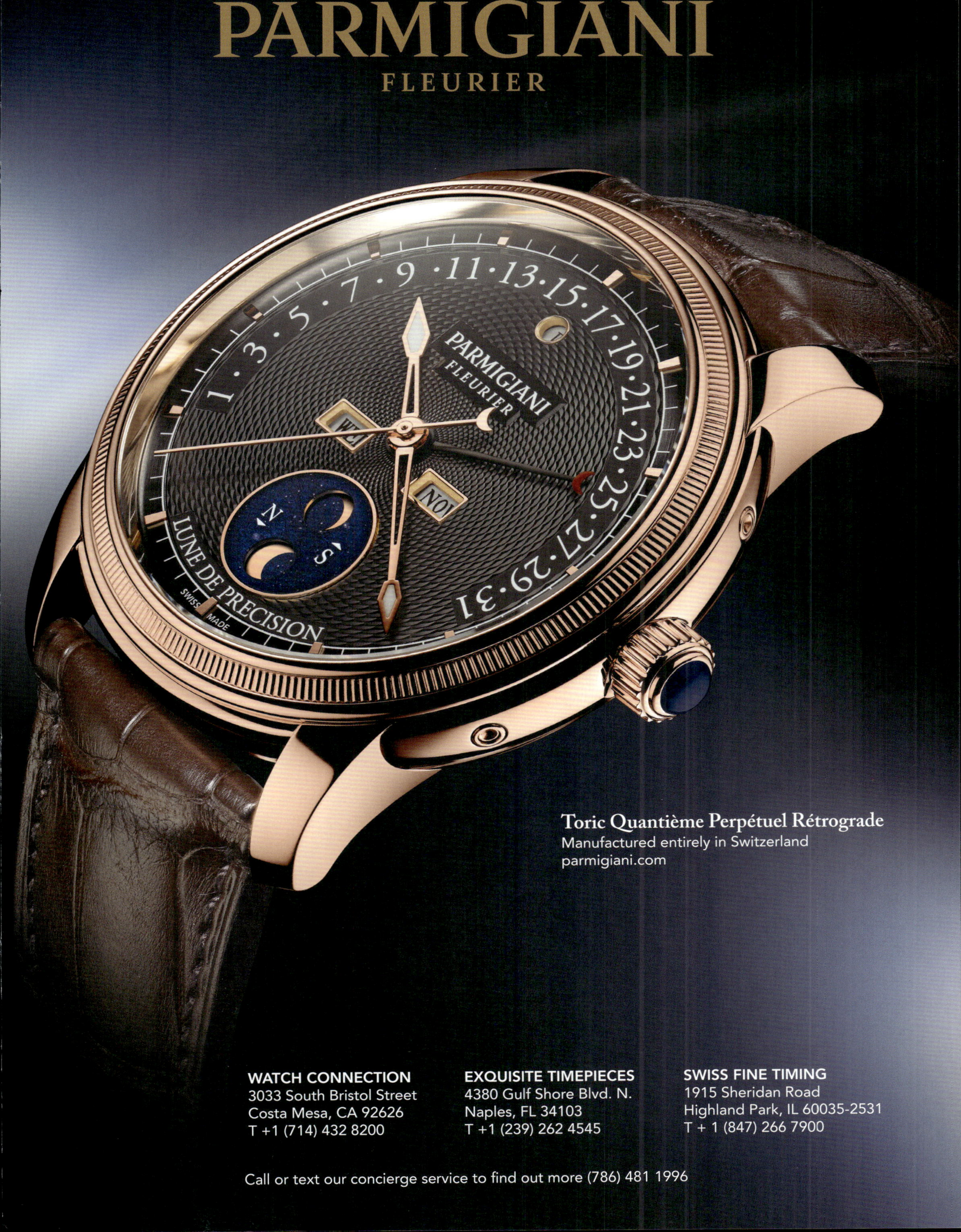

PARMIGIANI
FLEURIER
PARMIGIANI
FLEURIER
LUNE DE PRECISION
Toric Quantième Perpétuel Rétrograde
Manufactured entirely in Switzerland
parmigiani.com
WATCH CONNECTION
3033 South Bristol Street
Costa Mesa, CA 92626
T +1 (714) 432 8200
EXQUISITE TIMEPIECES
4380 Gulf Shore Blvd. N.
Naples, FL 34103
T +1 (239) 262 4545
SWISS FINE TIMING
1915 Sheridan Road
Highland Park, IL 60035-2531
T + 1 (847) 266 7900
Call or text our concierge service to find out more (786) 481 1996

INDEPENDENT WATCHMAKING

Switzerland. While the winemaker's work in various wine regions of the world is the same, those tasks are not performed at the same time (in Argentina the seasons are opposite, and in Bordeaux grapes are harvested earlier than those in Switzerland). The 42.5- × 11-mm fluted case in white and red gold is made traditionally, meaning without the help of CNC machinery.

Two other 2019 timepieces from A.H.C.I. candidates that deserve mentioning are from the workshop of Czech independent **Ludek Seryn**. The **Karel Rotation** includes two symmetrical movements making one full 360-degree rotation every eight hours. The mechanics, realized without the aid of CNC machinery, are placed within a fully transparent case measuring 45 × 20 mm so that the unique movement can be enjoyed from every angle. German independent watchmaker and self-taught engraver **Stefan Kudoke**, on the other hand, shows little of his new Kaliber 1 (based on the Habring A11B) on the dial side of his first two watches to house it: **Kudoke 1** (a three-hand watch with frosted dial) and **Kudoke 2** (with special day/night indication that puts his engraving skills on display). This is almost a shame, as the movement is beautifully decorated with hand-engraving, traditional frosting, and blued screws breaking up the full base plate, putting the balance and its hand-engraved cock center stage. The Kudoke 2 justifiably took home the Petite Aiguille prize at the 2019 Grand Prix d'Horlogerie de Genève.

Elizabeth Doerr is a freelance journalist specializing in watches and was senior editor of Wristwatch Annual *until the 2010 edition. She is now the editor in chief of* Quill & Pad, *an online magazine that keeps a watch on time (www.quillandpad.com).*

1 The movement of Ludek Seryn's Karel Rotation floats and gyrates in space.

2 Traditional crafts were used by Stefan Kudoke for his Kudoke 1.

3 German independent Stefan Kudoke, winner of the Petite Aiguille at the GPHG 2019.

4 The Kudoke 2: a plain backdrop back and front highlights the salient features.

MASTERS AND MAVERICKS

ENGINEERING EMOTION

MARTON RADKAI

Germans like to see themselves as a people of "poets and thinkers." This combination of rationalism, empiricism, and emotion may explain the nation's success in engineering and industrial design, including watchmaking. In 2020, the town of Glashütte is celebrating its 175th anniversary as a hub of horology. Much of its success is due to the subtle poetry they inject into design.

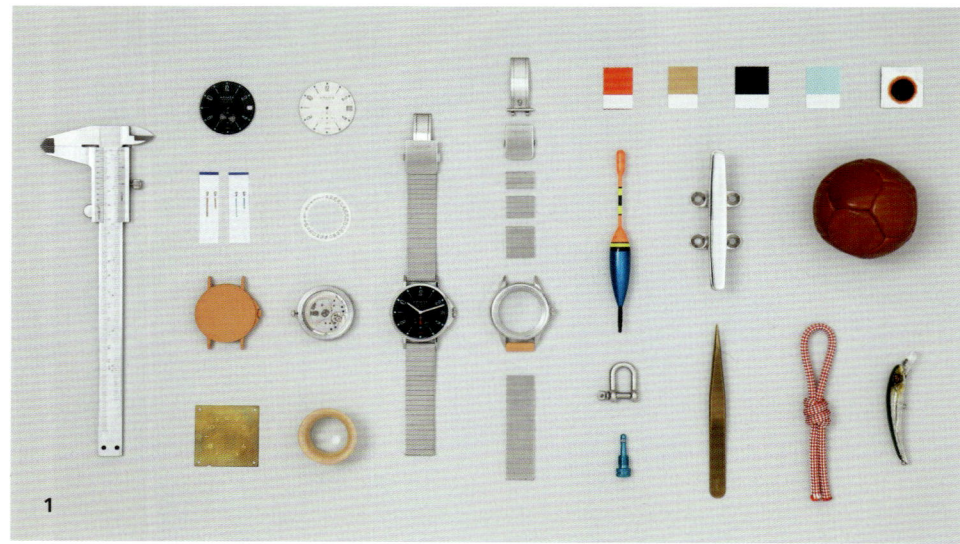

1 The eclectic inspiration on a Nomos mood board.

2 Surprising date at 4 o'clock on the Ludwig Neomatik.

3 Michael Paul, qualified designer at Nomos.

In 2008, I attended my first Baselworld Fair. This was a few months before Lehman Brothers' collapse, and the overheated atmosphere was almost oppressive. Among the booths that stood out for being counterintuitively calm, however, was one nestled on the edge of one of the big halls. The display case was simple and humorous, though I cannot remember the details; the representatives were friendly and relaxed, and highly informative, or *sachlich,* as the Germans say, down to earth. They never seemed to be actually selling their product.

Their watches were in a similar vein: They wooed the observer by leaving space for the eye to explore and find subtle details. Everything appeared organic, from the neat case, the slightly off-white or gray dial, the needle-thin second hand, to the discreet lugs. The company was Nomos Glashütte, launched in 1992 by photographer and IT specialist Roland Schwertner. The main models making the rounds that year were the Tangente, Orion, Ludwig, and Tetra, all thin two-handers with subsidiary seconds at 6 o'clock. Three were round; the Tetra square, like a window. It was in sharp contrast to the brash, 45-millimeter-plus behemoths weighing down so many wrists at that fair.

JUST IN TIME

The Tangente is, in a some ways, the watch carrying all the Nomos chromosomes, says Michael Paul, designer at Berlinblau, a wholly-owned subsidiary of Nomos in charge of design and brand communication—a revealing coupling of tasks. "These models have been around for twenty years and they still look

A BRIEF HISTORY OF THE TOWN THAT TIME FOUND

Twenty-five miles south of Dresden, in the Ore Mountains (Erzgebirge) of eastern Germany, is a narrow valley irrigated by the Müglitz river. It's there that you'll find Glashütte i/SA, a town of about 7,000 inhabitants, whose lives, for generations, have been governed by watchmaking. The name of the town, and its coat of arms with the two crossed hammers, reveals a history of mining going back to the late Middle Ages: -hütte suggests a place where ore is processed, as the name of the surrounding mountains indicates, and Glas-, well, glass. As for the "i/SA," it refers to the Land of Saxony, since there are a number of places in Germany and Austria bearing the same name.

By the mid-nineteenth century, the volume of ore mined had diminished and the region was feeling a serious economic pinch. Ferdinand Adolph Lange, a watchmaker from Dresden, who had traveled to Paris and Switzerland, sought and, after several attempts, received financial assistance from the Saxon government to launch a greenfield project in the little town.

The time was ripe. The German Customs Union of 1834 and the spreading railway system had boosted the economy, creating a new consumer class, and watches were a prized and now more affordable object. Lange was soon joined by Adolph Schneider, a fellow student of the great Johann Gutkaes, and he hired two young watchmakers, Carl Moritz Grossmann and Julius Assmann. All four went on to found and nurture a dynamic industry in Glashütte, producing not only watches, but also tools, machines, gauges, measuring devices, a publishing house, and, most important, a school that produced even more watchmakers. It was what author Charlotte Steffen called a "networked environment." And it thrived as competition to the Swiss industry, ironically in a region that earlier had been named "Saxon Switzerland" by two eighteenth-century Swiss painters.

Glashütte survived numerous ups and downs, of course: When inflation hit in the 1920s, the Bank of Saxony came to the rescue and financed two new companies, UFAG for assembling wristwatches, and UROFA for manufacturing movements. It was bombed a day before the end of the war on the eastern front, and the Soviet occupiers then took away most of the machines. Then came the years of nationalization under Communism. But the town continued to produce, thereby maintaining a vital supply of trained watchmakers. After the fall of the Iron Curtain in 1989, the Glasshütter Uhrenbetriebe (GUB) conglomerate was dissolved. Many brands were revived and resumed production of a wide range of high-end watches that have given Glashütte an outstanding global reputation.

Images: © German Watch Museum Glashütte

MASTERS AND MAVERICKS

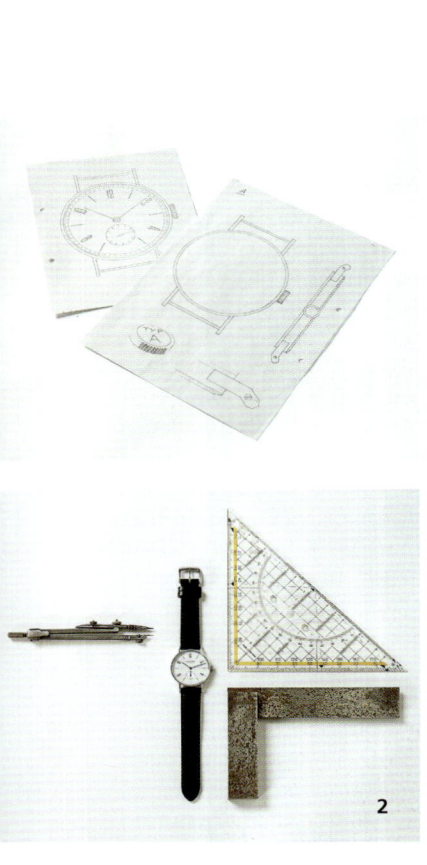

1 Entertaining marketing: the simple Tetra as a petit four.

2 Basic geometry, the secret to the pure design of the Tangente.

fresh and contemporary," he points out. His explanation is simple: "The main function of a watch is to tell time and be reliable." It's a platitude, of course, but not when considering the very real consequences the statement has for design and technology.

Nomos is ancient Greek for a natural law applying to all living beings, and there are a few unifying codes behind the brand's products, such as restraint and fun. "We don't think in terms of collections, the way a fashion company might think," says Paul. "The Tangente started as a 35-millimeter watch, and became a classic, the face of Nomos, and we move on from there." Indeed, it then became a 33-millimeter watch for finer wrists, and a larger watch for those who like it that way.

The company is disruptive, but without being obvious about it. They avoid using focus groups, or the siren call of the market to find trends they can then underscore or break. "It's dangerous to think that you know what other people want, or to think cockily that at some point your watch will sell, anyway," Paul points out ominously. "You really have to believe in your watch." Zeitgeist can have an impact, he says: "You might be walking through the city, and you'll suddenly noticed that brown is a great color. And then you ask and talk to others and they also find the brown is good, so you look into it . . ."

How the designers come up with inspiration for shapes and colors is serendipitous, as described above, or spontaneous. The 20th anniversary of the fall of the Berlin Wall engendered the Zürich model with a cement-gray dial. The Ahoi, a swimmer's watch, comes with an additional nylon strap, the kind used at German pools to tie your locker key to your wrist. And because humor lightens up the mood, it can be found throughout the Nomos portfolio and the communication. It tells curious onlookers: "We are not crazy, just a bit different."

KEEP IT SIMPLE

Nomos's visual codes, like those of most Glashütte or German brands, can be traced back to the Deutscher Werkbund, an association of architects, designers, and artists, and the Bauhaus, which celebrated its 100th anniversary in 2019. Both made simplicity and functionality absolute virtues. Michael Paul sees in this understated style an expression of "Protestant austerity" as well, which is surprising when considering the more ostentatious timekeepers produced in Geneva, Switzerland, the very fountainhead of dour Calvinism.

MASTERS AND MAVERICKS

No watch escapes this esthetic guideline. Instead of having lots of whirling dials, the company's most expensive watch, the Lambda, has a large power reserve indicator on the upper half of the dial. It shows eighty-four hours, a reminder of the double barrel unwinding inside. The transparent case back opens onto a radiant sunburst ribbing on the three-quarter plate furrowed by a trail of gold chatons, typical Glashütte features (see box page 29).

Perhaps the most "complicated" dials to date are the world timers of the Tangomats and Zürichs. The reference city on the former appears in a small window at 9 o'clock and can be moved, along with the hour hand, thanks to a pusher at 2 o'clock. The home time appears in a cutout at 3 o'clock. The automatic DUW 5201 driving the watch is also used for a Zürich GMT, though the ring bearing the reference cities turns around the dial center on a lower-level dial, thus leaving much-needed space. The effect is one of a well-tidied room.

Even the Autobahn, which was designed by Werner Aisslinger, stays within the norms. The subsidiary seconds dial is concave, and the blue line running from 4 to 8 o'clock, like the guiding line of an odometer, keeps some order on the dial. Aisslinger, whose installations or furnishings are never really spartan, managed to toe the Nomos line—with a little help from the Nomos designers, I suspect.

A LIFE WITHIN

Yet design does not exist for its own sake. Rather, there is a healthy, cross-pollinating dialectic in this brand that may well be unique in the industry. The designers live and work in buoyant, garrulous Berlin, a city with some impressive (and beautifully restored) industrial and residential buildings, like the ones along the Landwehr canal where Berlinblau rents space. All the hard technical work, the polishing, the beveling, the assembling, is done at the Nomos headquarters in rural Glashütte, some 150 miles to the south (see page 21). A staff of top-drawer watchmakers there allowed the company to wean itself from the Swiss ETA movements it started with in 1992. In 2005, it released the tight little 17-jewel Alpha, which fit perfectly inside the small Tangente and some of its siblings, like the Ludwig.

The Alpha has since been joined by ten more movements, including the Epsilon, the Zeta, and a series of automatic and hand-wound movements that begin with the acronym DUW (Deutsche Uhrenwerke, German Movements), some featuring the in-house "swing system," released in 2014 and present in models like the Tangente Neomatik. This verticalization of the manufacturing process was not only for the sake of independence, says Paul. "Because we build our own movements, we can begin designing early on in the process. When we added a large date to the Tangente, we wanted to place it as far to the edge of the dial as possible. You can't do this with a standard movement."

1 Werner Aisslinger, designer of the Autobahn. (l.)

2 Tangomat and Zürich GMT: the simplest possible solution.

3 The Nomos Lambda's radiant movement landscape.

4 Let there be light: the Nomos HQ in Glashütte.

SEIKO   *Laco*   ORIENT

CITIZEN   SQUALE   TIMEX

ISLAND Watch

LONGISLANDWATCH.COM
AFFORDABLE QUALITY TIMEPIECES ONLINE
SINCE 2003

MASTERS AND MAVERICKS

MACHINES THAT CAN

Nomos, one of nine current Glashütte brands (see box, pages 30–31) is perhaps the most "modern." It consciously seeks to give time without imposing all the microengineering wizardry on the wearer. A strong contrast to this Mozartian approach to watchmaking is A. Lange & Söhne, located in the original building that Herr Lange himself occupied after founding his company in 1845 (see History box, page 21), which launched the watchmaking industry in Glashütte. The old house is now just part of a large complex of buildings that straddles one of the main streets running through town.

At Lange, the watches are divided up into collections in different price ranges and with distinct features, though some, like the large date, are occasionally shared. What counts a lot, though, is what's inside.

"The ratio of design to technical is usually about eighty to twenty percent with most brands," says Product Development Director Anthony de Haas. "At Lange it's about fifty-fifty, so we try to design in our own way." One example he gives is a Lange one, whose dial at first glance looks strangely asymmetrical: A two-hand clock occupies much of the left half of the dial, while the right-hand side is occupied from 1 to 5 o'clock by the large date, the power reserve, and subsidiary seconds. It would leave a small blank segment around 7 o'clock, but the designers simply inscribed *Doppelfederhaus* (double spring barrel) there to balance out the visual topography.

Still, most Lange models reflect a deep understanding and kinship with a tradition of extreme engineering. The mere fact that Lange is willing to make its own mainsprings says a lot—notably why the watches are costly. As with Nomos, it's not just for the sake of independence, but rather to have full control. The company's know-how and determination to create technical art are perhaps best expressed in the Zeitwerk collection, which was inspired by the five-minute clock in the Semper opera house in nearby Dresden: The hours and minutes appear as digits in two separate windows.

Trying to replicate a digital time display in a mechanical watch seemed absurd at first. "Whenever you hear that this has never been done, you should think about *why* it has never been done," says Anthony de Haas, with a Cheshire cat smile. "Everything becomes more complicated, and more and more expensive." There is an additional problem that Arnd Einhorn, Director of Public Relations, points out: The market defines the price, basically, and you can never be sure where the market will be when, after years of development, the product becomes reality. The first Zeitwerk was released in 2009, when the world economy was crashing and money for luxuries was vanishing. And yet it became an icon, a stunningly fancy steam locomotive of sorts, filled with luscious engineering expressed with a stately dial using various alloys and decorative techniques, such as untreated or rhodium-plated German silver, block polishing, and so on.

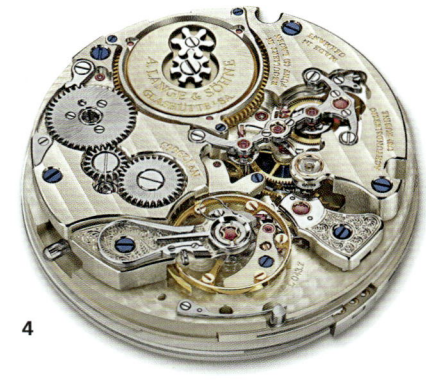

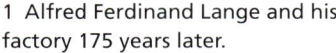

1 Alfred Ferdinand Lange and his factory 175 years later.

2 The Lange 1, a balanced dial.

3 Design and engineering get equal time at Lange.

4 The complex Zeitwerk movement.

JUNGHANS
GERMANY. SINCE 1861

Passion
has priority.

Live your style.

Since the 1930s the finest watches of the company have borne the Meister appellation. They continue to feature a skilful blend of the fascination with watchmaking and aesthetic design. Junghans Meister Driver Chronoscope: Self-winding movement, stop function, water-resistant up to 3 bar.   www.junghans.de

---

DISTRIBUTED BY
DKSH Luxury & Lifestyle North America Inc
9-D Princess Road · Lawrenceville, NJ 08648 · Tel: +1 609.750.8800 · sales@dksh.com · www.junghansus.com · IG @junghansgermany

MASTERS AND MAVERICKS

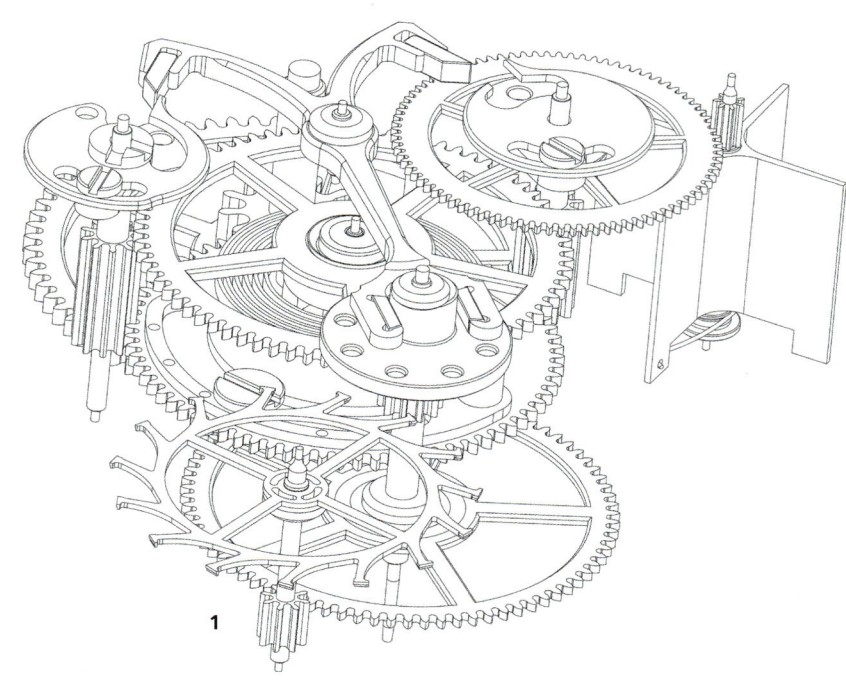

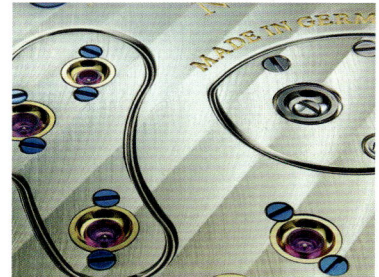

POWER TIME

The instantaneously and precisely jumping hours and minutes produced a chain of difficult challenges. "The three printed rings, two for the minutes, one for the hour, are layered on top of one another with a tolerance of 0.2 millimeters," says Jens Knospe, who heads the fifteen-strong unit working on the Zeitwerk. The rings have to be kept absolutely plane even while they move and "jump." Moving these rings requires a lot of energy, which called for an extra-strength mainspring. This generated a long chain of problems: "The torque was far too great for such a filigree movement," Knospe points out. "It would damage the escapement and affect precision." And so the Lange engineers set about building what would become a patented constant-force mechanism just for the Zeitwerk. It is made up of two wheels with a hairspring in between. The one wheel picks up the energy from the mainspring and passes it on to the second wheel in little bursts. The extra momentum from the mainspring is passed off onto a tiny vane that spins it out, a little like the flare stacks burning off flammables in industrial plants.

The first Zeitwerk was relatively simple, compared with the follow-up models, because watchmakers like challenges, the way mountain climbers like steep cliffs. In 2010, for example, the company added a minute repeater with a pusher that stops the mechanism. The case was in a special "honey gold." In 2012, the Zeitwerk's dial featured a special decorating technique known as *tremblage*, a dense network of tiny squiggly lines, which has to be done by hand. The latest offspring gives the date in red on a ring at the edge of the dial, which involves a whole new set of engineering problems.

It's hard to think of inanimate objects expressing emotion of some sort, and especially being able to connect on an emotional level to consumers. But they have to, as marketing managers will tell you, and they do. Nomos and Lange—and all successful brands—do it in different ways, even if one focuses more on the design side, and the other revels in the technology behind the dial. To broadcast their great news, though, many brands spend a king's ransom on advertising, funding extreme sports events, expensive cars, round-the-world flights in old aircraft, daredevils jumping to earth from the ionosphere, and so forth. And there are the internationally famous ambassadors from the world of film or sports. But none of this can really deflect from the need, in one way or another, for coherent design and excellent technology.

In the Glashütte watches, and many other German brands, the attraction of the design seems to be the questions left in the eye of the beholder that whet the appetite and allow a relationship between wearer and watch. Let's face it, love at first sight seldom has to do with instant gratification, but rather a certain hunger for discovering more. Through the coating, or the design, the "precise and brutal" gestures of technology, to quote Adorno in *Minima Moralia*, can become romantic, nostalgic, joyful, intriguing, mysterious, or simply pleasing. It can even enhance the workings below, or turn them into transparent and fascinating pieces of kinetic art, as in skeleton watches. In the final analysis, then, design tames what Adorno once called the "implacable, as it were ahistorical demands of objects."

1 A special constant force escapement controls the output of a powerful mainspring.

2 The angel in the detail: fine finishing on the movement.

3 The Zeitwerk with *tremblage*, and in honey gold with striking mechanism.

THE MAKINGS OF A GLASHÜTTE WATCH

The Glashütte Rule states, basically, that most of the watch's value creation must be from Glashütte, which leaves enough room for the use, occasionally, of Swiss parts and even movements, which are then modified. Lange, Glashütte Original, Moritz Grossmann, and Nomos manufacture their own movements. There are, however, some very special features on a Glashütter. They usually appear on the back of the watch and are visible if through the transparent case back.

1. The **three-quarter plate** is the most obvious feature. It was invented by Lange himself as a way to hold the gear train, spring barrel, and winding mechanism firmly against the mainplate. It does not cover the escapement, however, so the watch can be adjusted easily. The plate is usually made of untreated German silver, an alloy of copper, nickel, and zinc. Mühle calls this large plate a three-fifths plate.

4. Screw-mounted gold chatons are used as the jewel bearings. The jewels hold the pinions in place. The screws are usually heat-blued, giving additional touches of color and a high-end look and feel to the watch.

2. The escapement is held in place by a balance cock that can be highly decorated. Lange uses untreated German silver. Customers can choose an engraving or engraver and have their balance cocks (*Unruhkloben*) personalized.

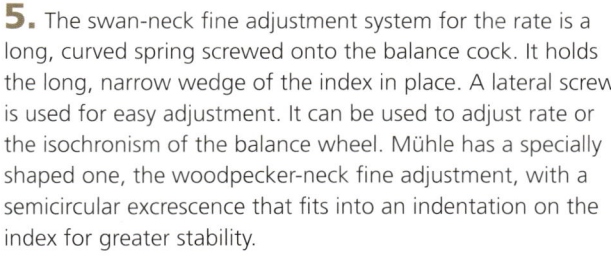

5. The swan-neck fine adjustment system for the rate is a long, curved spring screwed onto the balance cock. It holds the long, narrow wedge of the index in place. A lateral screw is used for easy adjustment. It can be used to adjust rate or the isochronism of the balance wheel. Mühle has a specially shaped one, the woodpecker-neck fine adjustment, with a semicircular excrescence that fits into an indentation on the index for greater stability.

3. The large ratchet wheel(s) and the crown wheel visible through the transparent case back are decorated using a sunburst pattern (*Sonnenschliff*) that is polished onto the wheel. The côtes de Genève–like decoration on the three-quarter plate or bridges—is called Glashütte ribbing.

6. The Glashütte click (*Gesperr*) is a long, narrow spring that presses a lock into the barrel gear to prevent overwinding and the mainspring from unwinding, here clearly visible on the Patria by Tutima.

MASTERS AND MAVERICKS

GLASHÜTTE'S BRANDS

A. LANGE & SÖHNE:
Watchmaking in Glashütte began officially on December 7, 1845, when Adolph Ferdinand **Lange** set fifteen apprentices to work in his new company. On December 7, 1990, exactly 145 years after the original founding, Lange's great-grandson Walter Lange and IWC head Günter Blümlein re-founded the company following the fall of the Iron Curtain. The company joined Richemont Group in 2000. Lange collections include Saxonia, Lange 1, Richard Lange, and Zeitwerk, all with in-house movements.

GLASHÜTTE ORIGINAL
was constituted in 1994 out of the ruins of the state-run East German conglomerate GUB and had a collection in stores by 1995. In 2000, it—and its associate, Union Glashütte—was purchased by Swatch Group, which poured money into expanding capacity. The main lines are the complicated Senator and Pano collections. In 2019, a new collection, Spezialist, debuted with the SeaQ, a diver's watch.

BRUNO SÖHNLE UHRENATELIER GLASHÜTTE/SA,
was originally a distributor for Swiss watches in Germany. In 2000, it began making quartz watches, followed in 2008 by a hand-wound series, the Mechanik Edition, and an automatic movement in 2010. The watch depicted is a Stuttgart model (in honor of the family's origins in Swabia), released in 2016. It runs on the in-house caliber BS 283, a modified Unitas 6498.

MORITZ GROSSMANN:
In 2008, Christine Hutter from Munich, watchmaker and veteran of many big brands, boldly launched the brand named after one of Glashütte's most eminent personalities. First came the Benu, named after an ancient Egyptian bird symbolizing rebirth. It was followed by the Atum and the Tefnut, watches that combine technical prowess with a definite feeling for visual playfulness. In 2012, the brand invested a fascinating new building in Glashütte that combines geometric shapes and light in Bauhaus style.

MASTERS AND MAVERICKS

MÜHLE GLASHÜTTE:

The full name of this family business is *Mühle-Glashütte GmbH nautische Instrumente und Feinmechanik*. It recalls the origins of this company, now run by the fifth generation of real Glashütte Mühles, as a manufacturer of machines, gauges, speedometers, etc. It was Hans-Jürgen Mühle who was put in charge of privatization and revived his brand, which started making very classic watches like the Teutonia and S.A.R. series, or the elegant Robert Mühle and Lunova collections. These sportive watches are known for their especially robust woodpecker-neck regulator, which holds the index firmly in place.

NOMOS GLASHÜTTE:

The company has grown exponentially since it was founded by Roland Schwertner, a photographer, in 1992. Its minimalist, urbane esthetics makes it stand out in the Glashütte constellation. The brand has grown its portfolio from a basic model, the Tangente and a few "siblings," into a wide array of visually related branches. Nomos also builds its own movements at its large and modern premises in Glashütte.

UNION GLASHÜTTE,

launched as the manufacturing division of Johannes Dürrstein's Dresden-based wholesale business, went under in 1936. It was revived in 1997 as a subsidiary of Glashütte Original, and finally became a separate entity in 2008. It produces a range of affordable watches with in-house movements and a slightly vintage look (like the Noramis and the Viro). The 1893 Johannes Dürrstein Edition Moon Phase in gold, for example, is under $10,000.

TUTIMA GLASHÜTTE:

Founded in 1927, Tutima (meaning "safe, secure" in Latin) subscribes to the genuine Bauhaus idea of "form follows function," says designer Alexander Phillipp, which accounts for the bold application of luminous mass on the hands and indices. "Even the case shape has a function," he says, about the NATO Chronograph. "It has been rounded off so that no edges get in the way of user-friendliness, and the large pushers have a neoprene insert for better grip." Tutima manages to be modern, as in the Seven Seas M2 diver, and elegant with a hint of vintage, as in the Patria collection. A special model is the Tempostopp: "It recalls the Urofa Caliber 59 from the 1940s developed for the legendary Tutima pilot chronographs and became the first German chronograph with a flyback function and additive stopping," says Phillipp.

WEMPE GLASHÜTTE

is a family-run business, now in the fourth generation. Founder Gerhard D. Wempe, a man with an uncanny sense for marketing, started the business in 1878 as a shop in Elsfleth, Germany, later expanding to Oldenburg and Hamburg. Today Wempe sells major brands worldwide. It was Wempe's grandson Hellmut Wempe who launched the Zeitmeister line of watches in the 1950s. His daughter, CEO Eva-Kim Wempe, took the bold step of purchasing the old observatory above Glashütte and turning it into a manufactory for the high-end Chronometerwerke line, which boasts its own movements.

THE AFTERMARKET

COLLECTOR'S CORNER

MARTON RADKAI

These days, it's not enough to have a collection of beautiful watches to show off on your wrist—rightfully. For the serious collector, the devices and objects on the periphery, from safes to screwdrivers, are just as important to present, preserve, observe, and enhance the watches in your collection. And they require design to attract attention.

The ultimate aim of collecting, whether avid or casual, is to turn necessities and practicalities into luxuries, and that, often, to a delightfully absurd degree. It's the unfettered world of artistic engineering and marketing that then turns these into lifestyle paraphernalia by developing a host of products to cater to the collectors' passions. The products, however, must differentiate themselves through design, even if the function more often than not defines the form. The products must touch the buyers' heartstrings, and at times meet a retailers' esthetic needs. This slightly cryptic musing relates perfectly to the world of watches, which not only is dominated by manufacturers of watches, but has also produced a wide spectrum of gadgets, gizmos, and other thingamajigs that the collector might need for a holistic watch experience that will adapt to his or her overall style. These products are just as through-designed as the watches themselves, or at least they should be.

TESTING, TESTING

Automobile owners concerned with the health of their car, or of a prospective one, will be equipped with all sorts of little gadgets designed to analyze the condition of a vehicle, from pressure gauges to battery testers. The situation for the watch lover is similar, but simpler, since several companies that manufacture tools for watchmakers and retailers have also thought of the end-customer.

Anyone who has visited a watchmaker's workshop knows of the Witschi, a gadget which, in its older incarnation, resembled a kind of kinetic artwork. Witschi is actually the name of a well-established company making precision measurement tools for the watch industry. The modern Chronoscope and the WisioScope S measure all sorts of other vital signs of an escapement optically and acoustically using lasers and cameras and LCD screens. They are built for the workbench, however, so Witschi produced the ChronoCube, a very simple cube-shaped tabletop device in three basic colors. It is easy to use: Strap in the watch and press the button. Like modern analyzers, the device uses the watch's own acoustic signal (the ticktocking) and vibrations to generate data. These are then passed onto an app, which translates them into accuracy, rate variation, amplitude, beat error, and lift angle, the distance the balance wheel travels between the first tick and the last (there are actually three ticks, but one is not audible to the human ear).

Watch fans are mobile and apt to scour all sorts of places from eBay to the local pawnshop in search of that diamond in the rough. So what happens if you fall in love with a watch but you're not sure of its state of health? **Lepsi**, founded in 2014 by three Genevans—Alexandre Vauchel, David Pillet, and Stéphane Caregnato—thought of this when designing a convenient tester that fits in a pocket and will not incur a surcharge when flying. The Watch Chrono is a small, round device measuring 36 by 12 millimeters, and weighing a mere 10 grams. It retails for around $240. It records the sound of the watch, computes beat, lift angle, rate, accuracy, and so on, and transmits the data onto a screen. Lepsi has also built another practical device: a demagnetizer, the Dock. It is affordable (about $260) and particularly user-friendly, in part because it

1

2

1 Watch analyzers by H2i, Witschi, and Lepsi (from left to right).

2 Lepsi's tiny watch analyzer tells all.

THE AFTERMARKET

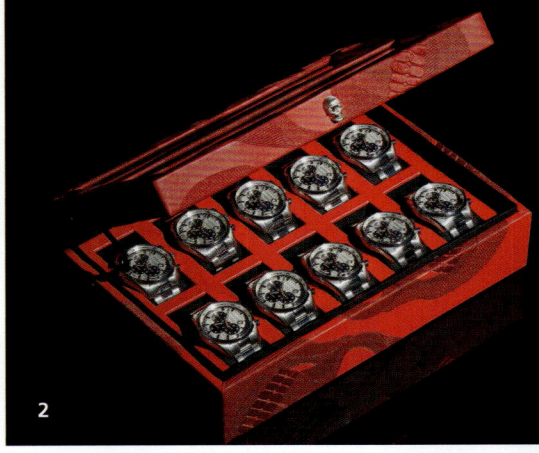

runs on four AAA batteries and uses very little power. When a watch is placed on it, a button will turn red if the watch is magnetized. Press the button, and it will turn green as soon as the watch has been demagnetized. The other convenience is the fact that the Dock also has space to integrate the Chrono, turning it into an all-in-one solution. The Watch Analyzer, the third product, is a kind of "seat" like the Witschi ChronoCube, which requires strapping in the watch and then connecting the device to a mobile phone or tablet.

User-friendliness and chic were the key qualities sought by **H2i**, a company founded in 2014 by two former members of the TAG Heuer team that produced the prizewinning Carrera Mikrogirder. Charles Rousset, a materials engineer, and Emmanuel Baudet, a research engineer at Lausanne's elite EPFL polytechnic, were intent on creating measurement tools for the watch industry that were not only functional but optimally designed as well. "Everything is sexy these days," says Rousset. "Vacuum cleaners are sexy, hairdryers are sexy. And that means excellent materials, and portability."

H2i has essentially three key products. A watch tester and demagnetizer for retailers has already found its way into a number of boutiques. Like the Lepsi products, they are easy to use, require little training for personnel, and act as teasers of sorts to satisfy a customer who has magnetized his or her watch, something that happens fairly frequently. Their analyzer is called the Oneof Accuracy2. It is a little box made of lightweight anodized aluminum with a soft covering and retails at $250. It fits easily in the hand or pocket. The kit comes with a standard USB cable for a mobile device. The company even got a special permission from Apple to use an original iPhone cable. You just place the test watch on the little box and within a few seconds, the app will show the three acoustic peaks of the ticktock and generate the information. H2i also offers a demagnetizer combined with analyzer for over $900.

A GOOD WIND

Coins, stamps, baseball cards, even Pokémon cards all have their own special albums and boxes to ease sorting, transportation, and storage. For watch collectors, the periphery is more substantial and at times important, since automatics with GMT calendars and moon phase, for example, should be kept wound to avoid complex resetting. Many companies make winders and, often, safes as well with winders and drawers for the precious chronometric cargo. These items can be quite expensive, but they are top-of-the-line, like a display case by Sattler with bulletproof glass doors (see *Wristwatch Annual 2019*).

Another very prolific company is Wolf 1834, a sort of one-stop shop for the watch and jewelry collector, and the traveler. Owner and CEO Simon Wolf is always ready to explore new markets, which accounts for the company's broad portfolio. At Baselworld 2019, he showed a set of company winders decorated with a small skull with LED lights in the eyes that change color. The "Memento Mori" series, he explained, was an attempt to break away from the very functional look of a winder and offer something a little more fashionable. The little skull turned out to be a hidden persuader, and the items became a hit with consumers along a broader front than expected.

What was surprising for Wolf was the fact that their original target group, the cool, the urban, the rapping crowd, were not the only ones buying the new winders. "We all love fashion, we've all drunk the Kool-Aid, we follow brands," he says with a smile. "Now we've bridged the gap between being a functional brand, so we need to cater to everybody, and that everybody is difficult to look after, because it can be a fifteen-year-old girl or a guy who is seventy-five!" So the brand

1 H2i's Accuracy2 is designed for look, feel, and quality.

2 A case for ten watches by Wolf 1834.

3 Wolf finds the trend: urban, savvy, sexy, skulls.

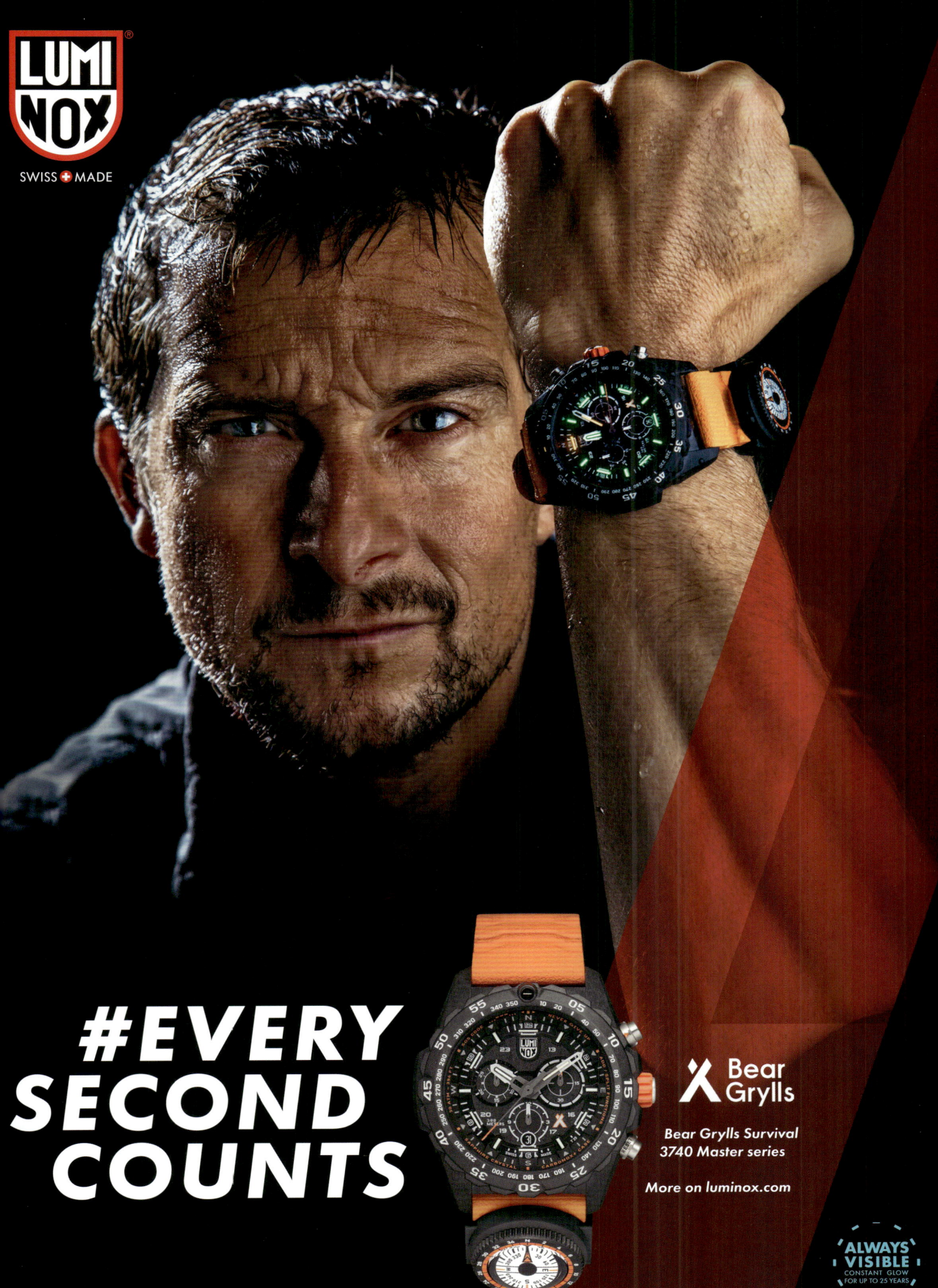

THE AFTERMARKET

1 Italian design, Swiss manufacturing from SwissKubik.

2 Hand-made cases: a tradition chez Vaudaux.

3 Vaudaux's gifted upholsterers cover everything and anything.

4 The payload of this talking piece: two loupes, 3× and 6×.

will be expanding this small but crucial idea—skulls, some with red and black glittering diamonds—to other products.

For other companies, understatement and some nobility remain the best strategy to attract the watch collector. SwissKubik began its rise producing Swiss-made cubic winder boxes that could be placed in safes. The focus of the brand is more on materials and winding technology, which has resulted in a number of collaborations with major watch brands. The latest product, the Travelbox, is an electric winder using a rechargeable battery or the power mains for energy, and expertly made to protect the precious cargo inside. SwissKubik has chosen a look that is modern, at times colorful—colorful, but understated as well. The technology inside is unimpeachable and remains the company's main selling point, it would seem. It's worth noting that SwissKubik recently bought up Scatola del Tempo, maker of august display cases for watches and a winder known as the Rotor One. The new owners updated some of the inner mechanics, but pretty much left the original design, a cylinder on a square base, which has lost none of its chic twenty years after its creation (1989).

THE WHOLE PACKAGE

There's no space to cover all the possibilities for storing our precious objects outside the few options mentioned above. Some will find blond wood better than burl, others will drop by IKEA, yet others will find their bliss in antique filing cabinets or Shaker furniture. In the case of high-end products like watches, jewelry, or any fine wares, it wouldn't do to use plain cardboard and brown wrapping paper. Indeed, a large industry works behind the scenes to design and manufacture boxes that are not only attractive and often clever, but also reflect something of the brand they will contain. The makers can be individuals, like the genial Stefan Berger of the "Atelier de Cuire" in the Jura, who hand-made leather sheaths for documentation of the highest-end Rudis Sylva watches. Or they can be a company like Vaudaux, with a long history of manufacturing *écrins* for many big brands.

Visiting Vaudaux is a fascinating experience. The company employs thirty-five people in Vernier on the outskirts of Geneva, and they work in various fields, from carpentry to leather and upholstery. They craft often intricate boxes for many big brands—the industry *omerta* prohibits me from saying which ones—producing boxes that must express something of the watch inside. It may be more than just luxurious materials. It might be a very clever way of opening the box, or of protecting the watch. These are signals often barely consciously registered by the buyer.

Watches are not the only containers they build or cover. Vaudaux makes presentation trays, suitcases, and trunks, and even carries its upholstery skills outside of its premises to things like banisters and elevators.

SPACE IS THE LIMIT

"We all think we're edgy, but we're all quite straightforward people," says Simon Wolf. "But we live through the things that we hold in our hands." It's an astute observation of why we are attracted to some objects and to certain coherent styles. So to close: For those who like playful things, and have enough cash on hand, there is always a toy to be had that will enliven a living room or a den, while also sparking conversations. It takes MB&F to come up with some madcap idea like the Project LpX, a collaboration with Loupe System, makers of magnifying glasses: a rocket ship of anodized aluminum with four polished and satin-finished stainless steel landing struts as a support. The rocket is just under a foot high, designed by former MB&F intern Maximilian Maertens (cf.: the T-Rex clock), and weighing 600 grams (21 ounces). It comes in four colors, each version limited to ninety-nine pieces. The motor section contains tritium gas tubes that will glow in the dark for quite a few years. As for the payload, it consists of two loupes, one 3×, the other 6× located in the fuselage. The rocket comes, dismantled, in a waterproof case that also contains a clip allowing the owner to attach a loupe to a mobile device for some very close-up images of his or her favorite watches. This is definitely a lifestyle-luxury-enhancing object, so let us avoid talking about the costs. Suffice to say, friends and family will raise an eyebrow, and as we know these days, any feedback is good feedback, apparently. Price? Better not ask.

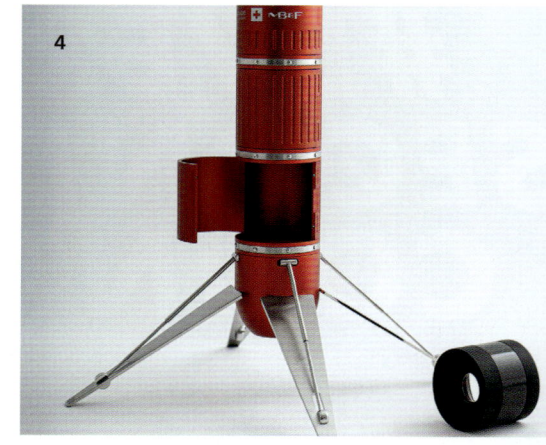

THE AFTERMARKET

THE CASE FOR THE CASE

You may never have heard of Xavier Dietlin, but you have surely seen his work. His father made metal doors and window frames. One day, one of his clients held a contest for a display case. He told his son to deal with it. "It was a catastrophe," says Xavier. "We probably came last. But the process was so fantastic, to put so much energy into creating a little bit of theater, it inspired me to get into the business." Today his client list reads like a *Who's Who* of *haute horlogerie*. A conversation with Xavier Dietlin.

Marton Radkai: *How did you acquire and refine your skills?*

Xavier Dietlin: I was trained as a designer, but I rely a lot on instinct. I do what I feel is right, and I've been lucky because till now, that has fit the market.

MR: *But you do have to look for inspiration, right?*

XD: Inspiration is available to anyone who is curious. I go to the theater, to museums, I listen to music. . . . And suddenly something touches you and you have to grab it. You might keep it for years, and then suddenly it will fit a display case or a product. A few years ago I saw a Mummenschanz play, and I came away with a notebook full of ideas, about lighting, poetry, and other things.

MR: *How can a display case exude emotion?*

XD: That's the magic. To make people dream, you have to tell them stories, And if you have a product you have to tell beautiful tales about it using images, or light. It's like a play on stage.

MR: *You even worked for MB&F. That must have been special.*

XD: Büsser has done a superb job playing with our dreams from childhood. He brings back all of those children's objects, spacecraft, Batmobiles, and things that are buried in our memory, so his products are full of great stories.

MR: *So there's a dialogue between the beholder and the object in the display case?*

XD: It was Voltaire who said: "If we are not sensitive we are never Sublime." And that is what we have to do, namely, wake up the sensitivity inside each of us, the thing that makes us vibrate.

MR: *We have to mention the "Raptor" for Hublot. How did that happen?*

XD: Jean-Claude Biver asked me to do something that no one else has, so I said you have to take off the glass case. Then, working with engineers, I found a way to make the presented watch disappear if someone tried to grab it.

MR: *Do you have a favorite display case?*

XD: The Raptor changed everything. But there's one that I did for Breguet, for the Pulsograph. A little tablet on the crown of the watch transmitted every vibration, every tick-tock from the watch to a resonating board made of wood from Risoux Forest next to l'Abbaye, where Breguets are made.

MR: *Thank you for the conversation.*

WATCH TECH

FOR BEAUTY'S SAKE

MARTON RADKAI

One of the most enigmatic complications on a wristwatch is no doubt the tourbillon. The term is usually translated as "whirlwind," but it actually refers to a swirling motion. And like the Mona Lisa's smile, what makes it so desirable, even controversial, is something of an enigma.

1 Art meets engineering in Thomas Prescher's Mysterious Double-Axis Tourbillon.

In an essay entitled "The Empire of Ugliness," Pierre Ryckmans (a.k.a. Simon Leys) decried a philistine world that aggressively and willfully hunts down beauty wherever it spots it, a beauty that is as much in the product as it is in the process that created the product. Newcomers to the watch-loving community, or those casually looking in, are also often amazed, even shocked, at the price of mechanical watches and, in particular, the magical effect a tourbillon will have on said price. Bulgari's elegant Octo Finissimo Automatic (see page 102), for instance, costs a proud $13,900 as a three-hand watch, almost 2D thin and supremely elegant in matte gray. But give it a tourbillon and some skeletonization, and the price inflates to nearly ten times that. It must be incredibly effective, right? Not so, says a colleague who would rather not be identified: "It's a Rube Goldberg machine." In

WATCH TECH

other words, it doesn't really serve any technical purpose, and thus needs to be dismissed.

There is some support for this view, even from the expert community. It all goes back to the now well-known origins of the complication. At the end of the eighteenth century, in his quest to make pocket watches more precise, Louis-Abraham Breguet realized that watch movements, hence precision, were being affected by gravity, because they usually hung in one position in a pocket. His solution was to place the whole regulatory unit (balance wheel and escapement) inside a rotating cage, which would then cancel out the effects of gravity.

The complication did not really catch on due, no doubt, to the sheer skills needed to actually build it. And then came the wristwatch, which, by its very nature, moves about and changes position, waiving any reason for the miniaturization of such a complicated mechanism. At least that's what logic would dictate. But watchmakers do not always follow the ratiocinations of the common man or woman. The word *complication* is not a hindrance for them, but rather an incentive. In the early 1920s, Alfred Helwig, a Glashütte watchmaker, even managed to build a tourbillon for a pocket watch that had no upper bridge holding it in place. This "flying tourbillon," which became a test for apprentices, already hinted at what the tourbillon would be used for: testing the skills of a watchmaker, and sheer esthetics, since now you could freely admire the mechanism.

Even if the tourbillon had lost some of its meaning in the age of the wristwatch, tiny steps in precision nevertheless mean something. Some early wristwatch tourbillons in Patek Philippe and Omega, for example, were invisible and purpose-made to win chronometry contests. "In general, technical advances in watchmaking have reduced the difference in precision between static escapements and caged ones," says Richard Habring, co-founder with his wife, Maria, of Habring². "Performance improvements are still possible with the latter, but they are really in the decimal points." Then came Audemars Piguet with a small, rectangular gold watch in 1986, with a tourbillon cutout on the dial.

While working at IWC, Habring introduced a tourbillon blueprint for the apprenticeship program, since building such a device was not for the weak-fingered. Later, when he launched his own brand, one of the first models he produced was a tourbillon, which was to fit into the space occupied by the base caliber's original escapement. "It was not a commercial success really, but it was mostly hand-made and was probably the cheapest tourbillon on the market at the time," Habring recalls.

1 The tourbillon of Breguet's Marine Equation Marchante.

2 Breguet, 1808: The tourbillon was hidden in back.

3 Alfred Helwig's flying tourbillon. ©Foundation German Watch Museum Glashütte/René Gaens

4 The 1986 tourbillon by Audemars Piguet, extra thin.

WATCH TECH

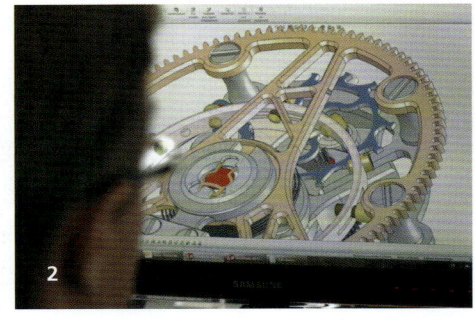

1 Pierre Favre, an expert in complications.

2 Computers assist construction, but the test is at the workbench.

3 Double-axis tourbillon in ArtyA's minute repeater.

4 A double-axis tourbillon.

5 One tourbillon, one watchmaker.

COMPLICATING MATTERS

Another watchmaker who sees the tourbillon as a way to achieve better chronometric values is Pierre Favre, owner of MHC in Geneva: "The moment your watch is in a vertical position," he explains, "the pins and the hairspring will be pulled downward by gravity, and that will affect precision." He also points out that watches are normally adjusted in six positions to get them as precise as possible, but being stationary, or even taking your watch off for several hours at night or while doing sports, could impact precision. So the simple tourbillon that revolves on one plane is not enough. What's needed is a second axis of rotation.

Favre is a specialist who works for a number of brands that outsource to him, usually with NDAs, the typical industry obsession with secrecy. One brand that does not mind being mentioned, though, is ArtyA, for whom Favre built a double-axis tourbillon in a remarkable timepiece with, in addition, a three-gong minute repeater. The double-axis tourbillon is a whole different dimension of difficult to manufacture. "It's like a gyroscope with the balance wheel oscillating inside," says Favre, "but you have to add a second axis, and now the system is carrying a lot more weight." Not only do all components need to be perfectly machined with extremely small tolerances, but weight must be very well balanced. "Imagine a chicken roasting on a spit, and the spit has not been centered properly," Favre explains. "If one side is heavier, the movement will struggle as it pulls the mechanism up, but then it will fall down the other side and increase amplitude of the hairspring."

Weighing components can be done on the computer, but as Favre points out, in the end, proof of the pudding will be at the workbench, when the mechanism has been assembled and tested. "The watchmaker will then have to take away a bit of material here and there, or reshape a part until perfect balance is achieved." So part of the exclusivity of a watch carrying such a device is the fact that one watchmaker will have worked on it over and over again.

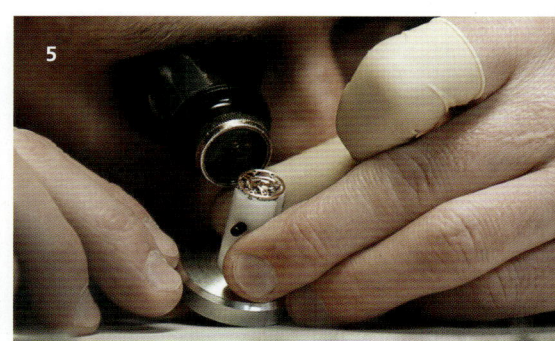

AVANTGARДE
EMOTION • INNOVATION • PROVOCATION

Babylonian Hand winding. Hand engraved movement. Three levels open dial with MOP ring. Blued hands. Stainless steel. 5 ATM. 500 pcs limited Edition.

LITTLE Treasury JEWELERS
2506 New Market Lane
Gambrills, MD 21054
410-721-7100

ALEXANDER SHOROKHOFF
UHRENMANUFAKTUR
GERMANY

WATCH TECH

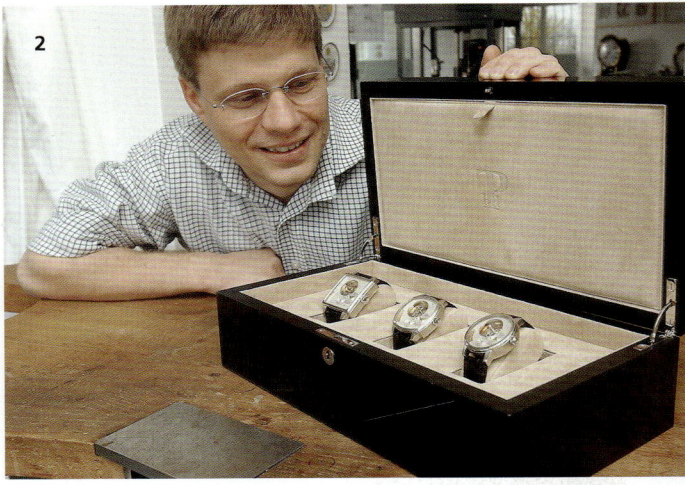

PER ASPERA AD ASTRA

For the figure skater, there is the quadruple axel, or the toe loop; for the mountain climber, it will be Annapurna, maybe, or the Matterhorn. For the watchmaker, it's the triple-axis tourbillon. Now comes, even more than with the double-axis tourbillon, the problem of space inside the case. The tourbillon is packed inside the watch and needs tolerances on all sides to turn properly, and no one wants to wear a small brick on their wrist. The parts, Favre points out on the computer image, are a mere 13/100th of a millimeter apart in some places, meaning that a shock to the watch can be a problem. "You do gain a few seconds' accuracy per day," says Favre, "but this is not the goal anymore."

And it isn't, not for Thomas Prescher, an independent watchmaker who lives and works near Biel/Bienne, a city of watchmaking. His biography through the ticktocking world of the Swiss watch industry remains to be told in full, as it reveals a man who has overcome many obstacles thanks to brittle energy and lots of conviction, all concealed in a boyish countenance, slightly unkempt hair, sparkling blue eyes, quick smile. In short, he is a romantic soul with the mind of a physicist or air traffic controller.

Thomas Prescher was one of the apprentices at IWC during Richard Habring's tenure, and he was immediately enthralled by the idea of building a tourbillon according to one of Habring's blueprints, even though yearling apprentices were not allowed to do so. He would finish his apprenticeship with a very nice half-flying pocket watch tourbillon.

At the time, he, like many other apostles of ultra-haute horlogerie, knew about the now famous Randall carriage clock, built in the 1970s, with a double-axis tourbillon. There was also a clock with a triple-axis tourbillon built by Richard Good and his son Timothy in

1 Thomas Prescher, engineer and romantic.

2 Three spectacular tourbillons put Prescher in the spotlight.

3 Thomas Prescher's unique Mysterious Automatic Double-Axis Tourbillon.

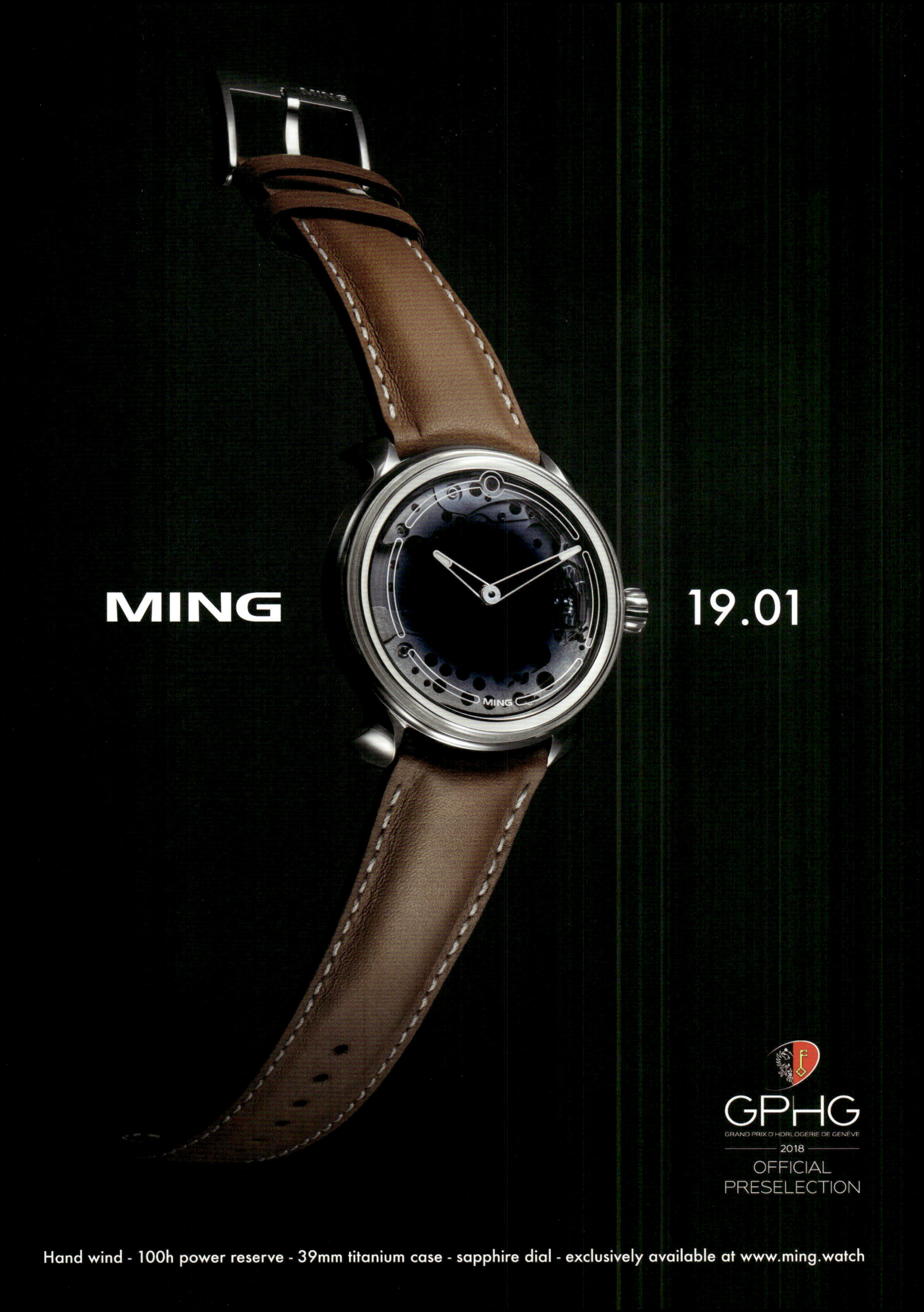

MING 19.01

Hand wind - 100h power reserve - 39mm titanium case - sapphire dial - exclusively available at www.ming.watch

WATCH TECH

1980. Habring had made a similar clock, and it was at IWC. Thomas Prescher saw it and fell head over heels in love with it: "The usefulness of a triple-axis tourbillon is zero in a clock, because it is always in the same position, but when I saw it, I was done for."

He spent the next years meandering from company to company refining his skills. In 2002, he opted for independence and began by making a double-axis tourbillon in a pocket watch, which afforded enough space. His ultimate goal was to put them in a wristwatch, and he was driven by a passion. Finally, he released a collection of three watches with a flying single-axis, a double-axis, and, for the first time in a wristwatch, a triple-axis tourbillon. That was in 2004. The watches were square, with a clock dial, subsidiary seconds, and a separate window with an incredible view of a gyrating tourbillon. The collections sold out.

I first met Prescher a few years later. He was at the AHCI stand with a watch that looked as if it had been built into a relic case. It had sapphire crystals front and back held together by a fairly thick frame. At the top were two barrels giving digital minutes and hours. Between them, a three-dimensional moon. On the lower edge were two half-cylinders with days left and months right indicated by a hand. These elements swung around and wound the automatic mechanism. In the middle of the "window," at the end of a cam that seemed hopelessly thin, was a double-axis tourbillon, whirling in all directions seemingly without any energy input. "Where is the movement?" I recall asking. "In the frame," he answered. That did it for me.

A DIFFERENT PARADIGM

The tourbillon is considered one of four "queens of complications"—next to the column wheel chronograph, the perpetual calendar, and the minute repeater. But of the four, it is the one that literally stands out, as it has, on the surface, no real purpose other than allegedly making a mechanical watch more precise. An honest watchmaker will tell you, if you need precision, any quartz watch will do, or a mobile phone.

This raises a more fundamental issue, namely of need or beauty. Should we stop playing chess because computers can do it so much better? Was South Korean Go master, Lee Se-dol right to quit playing, in November 2019, because he was beaten by a computer?

What the tourbillon offers, in Thomas Prescher's words, is the possibility of "function following form," which flies in the face of much of the current thought about efficiency and usefulness. Perhaps, though, this kind of thinking is simply too linear, too restricted by banal economic values, even too democratic, and leaves the artist no place to untether creative juices. The world is full of things that have only peripheral functionality and yet they do move us—not everyone, and not at the same time, or in the same way. But that ability to recognize something we call "beauty" and to feel a little emotional kick is the function of art, kinetic or static.

Architect and all-around creator Carlo Mollino produced furniture and other objects that were primarily form, it would seem. Even the Eiffel Tower, if you think of it, is in essence a concept piece for metal beams and bolts, and yet it has become a symbol of an entire nation. Its function, like that of so many useless pieces, is simply to be beautiful, exciting, fascinating, mysterious. The tourbillon, considered a waste of money and effort, has a message, especially in the hands of great masters, and that is that beauty itself is a function that cannot and should not be ignored.

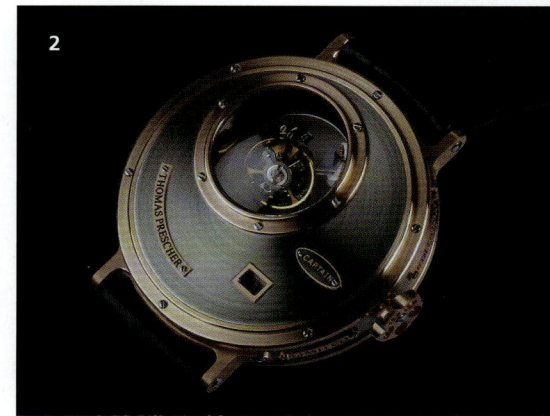

1 The triple-axis tourbillon for the wrist.

2 Prescher recalls his navy days: The Captain Nemo with the tourbillon in a porthole.

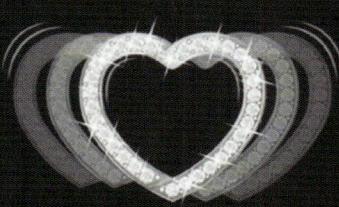

WATCH TECH

WHIRLWIND OVERVIEW

Ever since they resurfaced in wristwatches, tourbillons have become popular for those collecting *haute horlogerie* watches. Collectors are attracted to them for many reasons: the sheer fascination of the escapement spinning around, the exclusiveness of it all. Meanwhile, there are many tourbillons on the market that deserve mention, like the ones manufactured by Roger Dubuis, Jaeger-LeCoultre, Cartier, Glashütte Original, Blancpain, Harry Winston, and even Breguet. Independents are also doing striking work, like Beauregard and Louis Moinet. The list is long. Here is a small selection of the technical, the magic, and the fun.

Antoine Preziuso, an independent watchmaker near Geneva, and his son Florian worked for years to prove that tourbillons in a watch will synchronize through resonance. In the 47-millimeter TTR3 Blue Equalizer Frequencies, three one-minute tourbillons rotate around the dial on a plate once every ten minutes.

Greubel Forsey (page 162) never ceases to amaze with remarkable tourbillons. Their most intriguing timepiece may well be the Double Tourbillon 30°, which allows for a special view into the mechanism. The outer tourbillon turns in four minutes and the inner one in sixty seconds, and that's only a little bit of what the watch does.

There has been a bit of rivalry around who could make the biggest tourbillon. Apparently that honor goes to **Kerbedanz**, a small company from Neuchâtel that manufactures very high-end watches set with many jewels or decorated using other crafts. The Maximus Royal, startlingly set with rubies, boasts a 27-millimeter tourbillon placed in the middle of the dial.

Another clever positioning of a tourbillon was achieved by F.P.Journe (page 144) in the Tourbillon Souverain: It was placed vertically in the little 13.6-millimeter case.

Minimalist dials can enhance tourbillons, like that of Manufacture Royale's Titanium Duck Blue (see page 209). H. Moser & Cie's (page 164) Swiss Alp Watch Minute Repeater Concept Black goes further: The minute repeater is there so you can actually tell time . . .

WATCH TECH

MB&F's Flying T (page 213), with its high-domed sapphire and optional sea of diamonds reminds one of those snow globes, though it is up to the beholder to envision the figure dancing on the central flying tourbillon.

Paul Gerber (page 254) has fifty-plus years in the industry and nothing to prove. He has appeared twice in *Guinness World Records*. He has worked on his own brand, with all leading brands—always behind the scenes, and on one of the world's most complicated watches. On the side, he collects Oris alarm clocks. In one of those alarm clocks, he built a tourbillon. It's what great watchmakers do for fun.

Tourbillons are expensive, but they don't have to be. The TAG Heuer Carrera Chronograph Tourbillon Watch sells for around $15,000. But Michael Galarza, founded in New York, sells a tourbillon for under $2,000, throwing in GMT and a sun and moon indicator.

Animations tell stories, and stories create bonds, even if there is not a clearly delineated plot. Like Richard Mille's (page 268) RM 19-02, with its purple magnolia at 7 o'clock that unfolds its petals every five minutes or by means of a pusher to let a flying tourbillon rise up. The poetry is so fine, it makes one forget all the wizardry that makes it happen.

Any selection of tourbillons would be remiss without the spectacular work of Thomas Prescher, mentioned on page 42. He sets the mechanism onto a stage in the most prominent way possible. But there are those for whom the tourbillon can be a signature of sorts, a refinement that can elevate a watch or clock to a new height by appearing like a beauty mark or artistic graffiti. Imagine a Rolex Milgauss with a tourbillon. Rolex doesn't make tourbillons. But the company Label Noir does it as a customizing option. It's the place to go to turn your Rolex into a unique piece, or almost unique.

A. LANGE & SÖHNE

In summer 2015, A. Lange & Söhne inaugurated a new *manufacture* in Glashütte. It was a big enough event for German chancellor Angela Merkel to attend. It was a particularly nice capstone for the work of Walter Lange, who died in January 2017 after a life of outstanding entrepreneurship.

Lange, as the company is known for short, exemplifies the steady, careful, and effective way Germans do business. On December 7, 1990, on the exact day 145 years after the firm was founded by his great-grandfather Ferdinand Adolph Lange, Walter Lange re-registered the brand A. Lange & Söhne in its old hometown of Glashütte. Ferdinand Adolph had originally launched the company as a way to provide work to the local population. And shortly after German reunification in 1990, that is exactly what Glashütte needed as well.

Lange is known for its unique esthetic and mechanical codes. The three-quarter plate and all other structural components are made of German silver. The balance cock is always hand-engraved. The movements are all developed and manufactured by the company and are decorated and assembled by hand with the fine adjustment done in five positions. Patented innovations are always welcome, like the Lange large date, the SAX-O-MAT with an automatic "zero reset" for the second hand, or the patented constant force escapement (Lange 31, Lange Zeitwerk). Of the sixty-three newly developed calibers, fifty are currently in production and most are equipped with an in-house balance spring.

The entry-level family is the classic three-hand Saxonia, while the Lange 1, introduced in 1994, is considered the collection flagship. The anniversary year, 2019, was celebrated with a collection of various models in white gold dedicated to the milestones of that Lange family. The technical highlight of the year was the Zeitwerk Date, which was presented at the SIHH in January. This line of watches is celebrating ten years. It started with a digital display of jumping hours and minutes at 9 and 3, respectively.

Lange Uhren GmbH
Ferdinand-A.-Lange-Platz 1
D-01768 Glashütte
Germany

Tel.:
+49-35053-44-0

E-mail:
info@lange-soehne.com

Website:
www.lange-soehne.com

Founded:
1990

Number of employees:
750 employees, almost half of whom are watchmakers

U.S. distributor:
A. Lange & Söhne
645 Fifth Avenue
New York, NY 10022
800-408-8147

Most important collections/price range:
Lange 1 / $35,400 to $335,800; Saxonia / $15,500 to $62,100; 1815 / $24,800 to $236,900; Richard Lange / $33,900 to $231,500; Zeitwerk / $79,300 to $128,100

Lange 1 "25th Anniversary"
Reference number: 191.066
Movement: manually wound, Lange Caliber L121.1; ø 30.6 mm, height 5.7 mm; 43 jewels; 21,600 vph; swan-neck fine adjustment, hand-engraved balance cock, 8 screw-mounted gold chatons; 72-hour power reserve
Functions: hours, minutes, subsidiary seconds; power reserve indicator; large date
Case: white gold, ø 38.5 mm, height 10.7 mm; sapphire crystal; transparent case back; water-resistant to 3 atm; **Band:** reptile skin, buckle
Remarks: case back with hand-engraved hinged cover
Price: $47,900; limited to 250 pieces
Variations: normal version in yellow, white, or pink gold ($35,400)

Lange 1 Moon Phase
Reference number: 192.029
Movement: manually wound, Lange Caliber L121.3; ø 30.6 mm, height 5.7 mm; 47 jewels; 21,600 vph; 8 screw-mounted gold chatons, swan-neck fine adjustment, hand-engraved balance cock, hand-finished and -assembled parts; 72-hour power reserve
Functions: hours, minutes, subsidiary seconds; day/night indicator; power reserve indicator; large date, moon phase
Case: white gold, ø 38.5 mm, height 10.2 mm; sapphire crystal; transparent case back; water-resistant to 3 atm
Band: reptile skin, buckle
Price: $42,500; **Variations:** pink gold ($42,500); platinum ($54,700)

Grosse Lange 1 Moon Phase "25th Anniversary"
Reference number: 139.066
Movement: manually wound, Lange Caliber L095.3; ø 34.1 mm, height 4.7 mm; 45 jewels; 21,600 vph; 7 screw-mounted gold chatons, swan-neck fine adjustment, specially engraved balance cock; 72-hour power reserve
Functions: hours, minutes, subsidiary seconds; power reserve indicator; large date, moon phase
Case: white gold, ø 41 mm, height 9.4 mm; sapphire crystal; transparent case back; water-resistant to 3 atm
Band: reptile skin, buckle
Remarks: hand-engraved moon disk
Price: $51,500; limited to 25 pieces; **Variations:** normal version without engraving in pink gold ($49,200)

A. LANGE & SÖHNE

Lange 1 Time Zone
Reference number: 116.032
Movement: manually wound, Lange Caliber L031.1; ø 34.1 mm, height 6.7 mm; 54 jewels; 21,600 vph; 4 screw-mounted gold chatons; zone time (hours, minutes) with day/night indication and city ring, forward-switchable; 72-hour power reserve
Functions: hours, minutes, subsidiary seconds; 2nd time zone; large date; power reserve indicator; day/night indicator for both time zones
Case: pink gold, ø 41.9 mm, height 11 mm; sapphire crystal; transparent case back; water-resistant to 3 atm
Band: reptile skin, buckle
Price: $50,400
Variations: white gold with light dial ($50,400); platinum ($64,300)

Lange 1 Tourbillon Perpetual Calendar
Reference number: 720.038
Movement: automatic, Lange Caliber L082.1; ø 34.1 mm, height 7.8 mm; 76 jewels; 21,600 vph; 1-minute tourbillon with movement side stop function, off-center balance, 6 screw-mounted gold chatons; 50-hour power reserve
Functions: hours, minutes, subsidiary seconds; day/night indicator; perpetual calendar with large date, weekday, month, moon phase, leap year
Case: white gold, ø 41.9 mm, height 12.2 mm; sapphire crystal; transparent case back; water-resistant to 3 atm
Band: reptile skin, folding clasp
Price: $335,800; **Variations:** pink gold ($335,800)

Little Lange 1
Reference number: 181.038
Movement: manually wound, Lange Caliber L121.1; ø 30.6 mm, height 5.7 mm; 43 jewels; 21,600 vph; swan-neck fine adjustment, hand-engraved balance cock, 8 screw-mounted gold chatons, parts finished and assembled by hand; 72-hour power reserve
Functions: hours, minutes, subsidiary seconds; power reserve indicator; large date
Case: white gold, ø 36.8 mm, height 9.5 mm; sapphire crystal; transparent case back; water-resistant to 3 atm
Band: reptile skin, buckle
Remarks: guilloché light dial
Price: $35,100
Variations: pink gold with brown dial, white gold with purple dial ($35,100)

Odysseus
Reference number: 363.179
Movement: automatic, Lange Caliber L155.1; ø 32.9 mm, height 6.2 mm; 31 jewels; 28,800 vph; hand-engraved balance cock, screw balance, swan-neck fine adjustment; 50-hour power reserve
Functions: hours, minutes, subsidiary seconds; large date, weekday
Case: steel, ø 40.5 mm, height 11.1 mm; sapphire crystal; transparent case back; water-resistant to 3 atm
Band: stainless steel, folding clasp
Price: $28,800

Saxonia Moon Phase
Reference number: 384.031
Movement: automatic, Lange Caliber L086.5; ø 30.4 mm, height 5.2 mm; 40 jewels; 21,600 vph; hand-engraved balance cock, screw balance, swan-neck fine adjustment; 72-hour power reserve
Functions: hours, minutes, subsidiary seconds; large date, moon phase
Case: pink gold, ø 40 mm, height 9.8 mm; sapphire crystal; transparent case back; water-resistant to 3 atm
Band: reptile skin
Price: $30,900
Variations: white gold ($30,900)

Saxonia Thin
Reference number: 205.086
Movement: manually wound, Lange Caliber L093.1; ø 28 mm, height 2.9 mm; 21 jewels; 21,600 vph; screw balance, swan-neck fine adjustment, hand-engraved balance cock, 3 gold chatons; 72-hour power reserve
Functions: hours, minutes
Case: white gold, ø 39 mm, height 6.2 mm; sapphire crystal; transparent case back
Band: reptile skin, prong buckle in white gold
Remarks: solid silver dial faced with copper-blue gold flux
Price: $22,400
Variations: 37-mm case in white and pink gold, silver-colored dial ($15,900)

A. LANGE & SÖHNE

Datograph Auf/Ab "Lumen"
Reference number: 405.034
Movement: manually wound, Lange Caliber L951.7; ø 30.6 mm, height 8.1 mm; 46 jewels; 18,000 vph; 4 screw-mounted gold chatons, swan-neck fine adjustment, hand-engraved balance cock; 60-hour power reserve; **Functions:** hours, minutes, subsidiary seconds; power reserve indicator; flyback chronograph with precisely jumping minute counter; large date
Case: platinum, ø 41 mm, height 13.4 mm; sapphire crystal; transparent case back; water-resistant to 3 atm
Band: reptile skin, prong buckle in platinum
Remarks: semi-transparent dial with luminous displays
Price: $100,500; limited to 200 pieces
Variations: normal version in pink gold ($73,000); normal version in platinum ($94,400)

Datograph Perpetual Tourbillon
Reference number: 740.056
Movement: manually wound, Lange Caliber L952.2; ø 32.6 mm, height 9 mm; 59 jewels; 18,000 vph; 1-minute tourbillon; swan-neck fine adjustment, hand-engraved intermediate wheel and tourbillon cock; 50-hour power reserve; **Functions:** hours, minutes, subsidiary seconds; day/night indicator, power reserve indicator; flyback chronograph with precisely jumping minutes; perpetual calendar with large date, weekday, month, moon phase, leap year
Case: white gold, ø 41.5 mm, height 14.6 mm; sapphire crystal; transparent case back; water-resistant to 3 atm; **Band:** reptile skin, folding clasp
Price: $287,800; limited to 100 pieces
Variations: platinum, black dial ($299,800)

Triple Split
Reference number: 424.038
Movement: manually wound, Lange Caliber L132.1; ø 30.6 mm, height 9.4 mm; 46 jewels; 21,600 vph; off-center balance, in-house hairspring, column-wheel control or chronograph; 5 screw-mounted gold chatons; 55-hour power reserve
Functions: hours, minutes, subsidiary seconds; large date; power reserve indicator; flyback chronograph with triple flyback hand for reference measurements up to 12 hours, precisely jumping minute counter with double hand, continuous chrono hours
Case: white gold, ø 43.2 mm, height 15.6 mm; sapphire crystal; transparent case back; water-resistant to 3 atm; **Band:** reptile skin, folding clasp in white gold
Price: $146,300; limited to 100 pieces

Langematik Perpetual "Honeygold"
Reference number: 310.050
Movement: automatic, Lange Caliber L922.1 Sax-O-Mat; ø 30.4 mm, height 5.7 mm; 43 jewels; 21,600 vph; screw balance, swan-neck fine adjustment; bidirectional rotor with platinum, zero-reset time-setting mechanism, hand-engraved balance cock; 46-hour power reserve
Functions: hours, minutes, subsidiary seconds; day/night indicator; perpetual calendar with large date, weekday, month, moon phase, leap year
Case: "honeygold," ø 38.5 mm, height 10.2 mm; sapphire crystal; transparent case back; water-resistant to 3 atm; **Band:** reptile skin, buckle
Price: $85,000; limited to 100 pieces

Lange 31
Reference number: 130.039
Movement: manually wound, Lange Caliber L034.1; ø 37.3 mm, height 9.6 mm; 62 jewels; 21,600 vph; twin mainspring barrel, 3 screw-mounted gold chatons; constant force escapement (remontoir), stop-seconds mechanism, hand-engraved balance cock, parts finished and assembled by hand; 744-hour power reserve (31 days)
Functions: hours, minutes, subsidiary seconds; power reserve indicator; large date
Case: white gold, ø 45.9 mm, height 15.9 mm; sapphire crystal; transparent case back; water-resistant to 3 atm; **Band:** reptile skin, folding clasp
Remarks: comes with winding key
Price: $147,600; limited to 100 pieces

Zeitwerk
Reference number: 140.029
Movement: manually wound, Lange Caliber L043.1; ø 33.6 mm, height 9.3 mm; 68 jewels; 18,000 vph; 2 screw-mounted gold chatons, constant force escapement (remontoir), hand-engraved balance cock; 36-hour power reserve
Functions: hours, minutes (digital, jumping), subsidiary seconds; power reserve indicator
Case: white gold, ø 41.9 mm, height 12.6 mm; sapphire crystal; transparent case back; water-resistant to 3 atm
Band: reptile skin, buckle
Price: $79,300,
Variations: pink gold with silver-colored dial ($79,300)

A. LANGE & SÖHNE

Zeitwerk Date
Reference number: 148.038
Movement: manually wound, Lange Caliber L043.8; ø 37 mm, height 8.9 mm; 70 jewels; 18,000 vph; 2 screw-mounted gold chatons, constant force escapement (remontoir), hand-engraved balance cock; 72-hour power reserve
Functions: hours, minutes (digital, jumping), subsidiary seconds; power reserve indicator; date
Case: white gold, ø 44.2 mm, height 12.3 mm; sapphire crystal; transparent case back; water-resistant to 3 atm
Band: reptile skin, buckle
Price: $96,700

1815 Annual Calendar
Reference number: 238.032
Movement: manually wound, Lange Caliber L051.3; ø 30.6 mm, height 5.7 mm; 26 jewels; 21,600 vph; 3 screw-mounted gold chatons, hand-engraved balance cock, parts finished and assembled by hand; 72-hour power reserve
Functions: hours, minutes, subsidiary seconds; annual calendar with date, weekday, month, moon phase
Case: pink gold, ø 40 mm, height 10.1 mm; sapphire crystal; transparent case back; water-resistant to 3 atm
Band: reptile skin, buckle
Price: $41,200
Variations: white gold ($41,200)

1815 Chronograph
Reference number: 414.028
Movement: manually wound, Lange Caliber L951.5; ø 30.6 mm, height 6.1 mm; 34 jewels; 18,000 vph; 4 screw-mounted gold chatons, hand-engraved balance cock, parts finished and assembled by hand; 60-hour power reserve
Functions: hours, minutes, subsidiary seconds; flyback chronograph
Case: white gold, ø 39.5 mm, height 11 mm; sapphire crystal; transparent case back; water-resistant to 3 atm
Band: reptile skin, buckle
Price: $53,300
Variations: pink gold with silver-colored dial, white gold ($53,300)

1815 "Homage to Walter Lange"
Reference number: 297.026
Movement: manually wound, Lange Caliber L1924; ø 31.6 mm, height 6.1 mm; 36 jewels; 21,600 vph; 3 screw-mounted gold chatons, hand-engraved balance cock, parts finished and assembled by hand; 60-hour power reserve
Functions: hours, minutes, subsidiary seconds, jumping sweep seconds with start/stop function
Case: white gold, ø 40.5 mm, height 10.7 mm; sapphire crystal; transparent case back; water-resistant to 3 atm
Band: reptile skin, buckle
Price: $49,800; limited to 145 pieces
Variations: pink gold, limited to 90 pieces ($49,800); yellow gold, limited to 27 pieces ($49,800)

Richard Lange
Reference number: 232.032
Movement: manually wound, Lange Caliber L041.2; ø 30.6 mm, height 6 mm; 26 jewels; 21,600 vph; hand-engraved balance cock, 2 screw-mounted gold chatons, parts finished and assembled by hand, in-house balance spring with patent-pending anchoring clip; 38-hour power reserve
Functions: hours, minutes, sweep seconds
Case: pink gold, ø 40.5 mm, height 10.5 mm; sapphire crystal; transparent case back; water-resistant to 3 atm
Band: reptile skin, buckle
Price: $33,900
Variations: white gold ($33,900)

Richard Lange Jumping Seconds
Reference number: 252.029
Movement: manually wound, Lange Caliber L094.1; ø 33.6 mm, height 6 mm; 50 jewels; 21,600 vph; zero-reset mechanism, constant force escapement (remontoir); 42-hour power reserve
Functions: hours (off-center), minutes (off-center), large seconds (jumping); winding reminder
Case: white gold, ø 39.9 mm, height 10.6 mm; sapphire crystal; transparent case back; water-resistant to 3 atm
Band: reptile skin, buckle
Price: $75,100
Variations: pink gold with silver-colored dial, limited to 100 pieces ($78,600); platinum ($84,200)

A. LANGE & SÖHNE

Caliber L121.1
Manually wound; stop-seconds mechanism, 8 screw-mounted gold chatons, swan-neck fine adjustment; double spring barrel, 72-hour power reserve
Functions: hours, minutes, subsidiary seconds; power reserve indicator; large date
Diameter: 30.6 mm
Height: 5.7 mm
Jewels: 43
Balance: glucydur with eccentric adjustment cams
Frequency: 21,600 vph
Balance spring: made in-house
Shock protection: Kif
Remarks: plates and bridges of untreated German silver, decorated and assembled mostly by hand, hand-engraved balance cock

Caliber L095.3
Manually wound; 7 screw-mounted gold chatons, swan-neck fine adjustment, stop-seconds mechanism; single spring barrel, 72-hour power reserve
Functions: hours, minutes, subsidiary seconds; power reserve indicator; large date, moon phase
Diameter: 34.1 mm
Height: 4.7 mm
Jewels: 45
Balance: glucydur with eccentric adjustment cams
Frequency: 21,600 vph
Balance spring: made in-house
Shock protection: Kif
Remarks: plates of untreated German silver, decorated and assembled mostly by hand, hand-engraved balance cock

Caliber L082.1
Automatic 1-minute tourbillon with patented stop-seconds mechanism; one-way gold rotor with platinum mass; single barrel, 50-hour power reserve
Functions: hours, minutes, subsidiary seconds; day/night indicator; perpetual calendar with large date, weekday, month, moon phase, leap year
Diameter: 34.1 mm; **Height:** 7.8 mm
Jewels: 76, including 6 in screw-mounted gold chatons and 1 diamond capstone
Balance: glucydur with eccentric regulating cams
Frequency: 21,600 vph;
Balance spring: made in-house
Remarks: plates of untreated German silver, decorated and assembled mostly by hand, hand-engraved balance cock

Caliber L086.5
Automatic; single barrel, 72-hour power reserve
Functions: hours, minutes, subsidiary seconds; large date, moon phase
Diameter: 30.4 mm
Height: 5.2 mm
Jewels: 40
Balance: glucydur
Frequency: 21,600 vph
Balance spring: made in-house
Remarks: plates of untreated German silver, decorated and assembled mostly by hand, hand-engraved balance cock

Caliber L951.6
Manually wound; stop-seconds mechanism, jumping minute counter; single spring barrel, 60-hour power reserve
Functions: hours, minutes, subsidiary seconds; power reserve indicator; flyback chronograph; large date
Diameter: 30.6 mm
Height: 7.9 mm
Jewels: 46
Balance: glucydur with weighted screws
Frequency: 18,000 vph
Balance spring: made in-house
Shock protection: Incabloc
Remarks: plates of untreated German silver, decorated and assembled mostly by hand, hand-engraved balance cock

Caliber 952.2
Manually wound; 1-minute tourbillon; single spring barrel, 50-hour power reserve
Functions: hours, minutes, subsidiary seconds; day/night indicator, power reserve indicator; flyback chronograph, with precisely jumping minute counter; perpetual calendar with large date, weekday, month, moon phase, leap year
Diameter: 32.6 mm; **Height:** 9 mm
Jewels: 58, including 5 in screw-mounted gold chatons, 1 diamond capstone
Balance: glucydur with weighted screws; **Frequency:** 18,000 vph; **Balance spring:** made in-house
Remarks: plates and bridges of untreated German silver, decorated and assembled mostly by hand, hand-engraved intermediate wheel and tourbillon cock

A. LANGE & SÖHNE

Caliber L922.1 SAX-O-MAT
Automatic; bidirectional three-quarter rotor, zero-reset time-setting mechanism, stop-seconds mechanism; single spring barrel, 46-hour power reserve
Functions: hours, minutes, subsidiary seconds; additional 24-hour display, day/night indicator; perpetual calendar with large date, weekday, month, moon phase, leap year
Diameter: 30.4 mm; **Height:** 5.7 mm; **Jewels:** 43
Balance: glucydur with weighted screws
Frequency: 21,600 vph; **Balance spring:** Nivarox 1 with special end curve and swan-neck fine adjustment
Remarks: plates of untreated German silver, decorated and assembled mostly by hand, hand-engraved balance cock, calendar with 48-step program disk and precise moon phase differential

Caliber L132.1
Manually wound; column wheel control of chronograph functions; single spring barrel, 55-hour power reserve
Functions: hours, minutes, subsidiary seconds; power reserve indicator; flyback chronograph, with triple flyback for comparative time measurements of up to 12 hours, precisely jumping chrono and flyback minute counter, continuous chrono and split-second hour counter; **Diameter:** 30.6 mm; **Height:** 9.4 mm
Jewels: 46, including 5 in screw-mounted gold chatons
Balance: glucydur with eccentric adjustment cams
Frequency: 21,600 vph
Balance spring: made in-house
Remarks: plates of untreated German silver, decorated and assembled mostly by hand, hand-engraved balance cock

Caliber L034.1
Manually wound; key winding with torque brake; constant force mechanism (remontoir), stop-seconds mechanism; double mainsprings, each 185 cm long; 744-hour power reserve (31 days) with switch-off mechanism
Functions: hours, minutes, subsidiary seconds; power reserve indicator; large date
Diameter: 37.3 mm; **Height:** 9.6 mm; **Jewels:** 62
Balance: glucydur with weighted screws
Frequency: 21,600 vph; **Balance spring:** Nivarox 1 with special terminal curve and swan-neck fine adjustment; **Shock protection:** Kif
Remarks: plates of untreated German silver, decorated and assembled mostly by hand, hand-engraved balance cock

Caliber L043.8
Manually wound; jumping minute, constant force mechanism (remontoir), patented barrel spring mechanism, stop-seconds; single spring barrel, 72-hour power reserve
Functions: hours, minutes (digital, jumping), subsidiary seconds; power reserve indicator, acoustic signal every 10 minutes and on the hour (with switch-off mechanism); date
Diameter: 37 mm; **Height:** 8.9 mm
Jewels: 70
Balance: glucydur with eccentric adjustment cams
Frequency: 18,000 vph; **Balance spring:** made in-house, with hairspring clamp
Shock protection: Incabloc
Remarks: hand-engraved balance and anchor cock

Caliber L051.3
Manually wound; swan-neck fine adjustment, stop-seconds mechanism, German silver plates and bridges; single spring barrel, 72-hour power reserve
Functions: hours, minutes, subsidiary seconds; annual calendar with date, weekday, month, moon phase
Diameter: 30.6 mm
Height: 5.7 mm
Jewels: 26, including 3 in screw-mounted gold chatons
Balance: glucydur with weighted screws
Frequency: 21,600 vph
Balance spring: made in-house
Remarks: finished and assembled by hand, hand-engraved balance cock

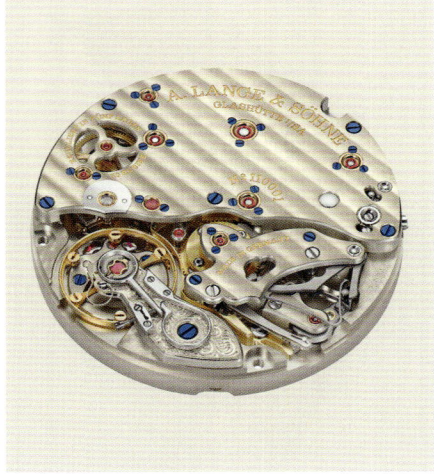

Caliber L094.1
Manually wound; constant force escapement (remontoir), swan-neck fine adjustment, stop-seconds mechanism; single spring barrel, 42-hour power reserve
Functions: hours (off-center), minutes (off-center), large second (jumping); rewind reminder
Diameter: 33.6 mm
Height: 6 mm
Jewels: 50, including 8 in screw-mounted gold chatons
Balance: glucydur with weighted screws
Frequency: 21,600 vph
Balance spring: made in-house
Remarks: untreated German silver plates and bridges, hand-engraved balance cock

ALEXANDER SHOROKHOFF

Alexander Shorokhoff Uhrenmanufaktur
Hanauer Strasse 25
63755 Alzenau
Germany

Tel.:
+49-6023-919-93

E-mail:
info@alexander-shorokhoff.de

Website:
www.alexander-shorokhoff.de

Founded:
2003

Number of employees:
15

Annual production:
approx. 900 watches

Distributor:
About Time Luxury Group
210 Bellevue Avenue
Newport, RI 02840
401-846-0598

Most important collections/price range
Heritage / starting at approx. $4,500;
Avantgarde / starting at approx. $1,500;
Vintage / starting at approx. $800

The ultimate goal for the watch connoisseur may be realizing one's own ideas for timepieces. In the first stages of his life, Alexander Shorokhoff, born in Moscow in 1960, was an engineer and then an architect with his own construction company. This turned out to be an excellent platform to begin expanding into the field of fine timepieces. In 1992, shortly after the demise of the Soviet Union, Shorokhoff founded a distribution company in Germany to market Russia's own Poljot watches. This gave him the insight and practice needed to launch phase two of his plan: establishing his own manufacturing facilities for an independent watch brand under his own name.

At Shorokhoff Watches, three main creative lines are bundled under the general concept "Art on the Wrist:" Heritage, Avantgarde, and Vintage. The three lines share a design with a distinctly artistic orientation. They all focus on technical quality, sophisticated hand-engraving, and the cultural backdrop. "We consider watches not only as timekeepers, but also as works of art," says Alexander Shorokhoff. It's a statement that can be seen in the watches. The brand is at home in the world of international and Russian art and culture. Each dial is designed down to the smallest detail. The engraving and finishing of the movements are unique as well.

All of them are taken apart in Alzenau, reworked, and then reassembled with great care, which is why the brand has stamped each watch with "Handmade in Germany." Some of the modules used in these timepieces were developed by the company itself. Before a watch leaves the *manufacture*, it is subjected to strict quality control. The timepiece's functionality must be given the cleanest bill of health before it can be sent out to jewelers around the world.

Avantgarde Levels
Reference number: AS.DT03-3
Movement: automatic, Caliber 2671.AS (base ETA 2671); ø 17.5 mm, height 4.8 mm; 25 jewels; 28,800 vph; 2 independent movements with hand-engraved oscillating masses; 42-hour power reserve
Functions: hours, minutes (double), sweep seconds; date
Case: stainless steel, ø 46.5 mm, height 12.5 mm; sapphire crystal; transparent case back; water-resistant to 5 atm
Band: ostrich leather, buckle
Price: $3,800; limited to 99 pieces

Avantgarde "Kandy 2"
Reference number: AS.KD-AVG02
Movement: automatic, ETA Caliber 2892-A2; ø 26.2 mm, height 3.6 mm; 21 jewels; 28,800 vph; hand-engraved oscillating mass; 47-hour power reserve
Functions: hours, minutes, sweep seconds; date
Case: stainless steel with black PVD coating, with yellow gold inserts, 41 mm × 41 mm, height 9 mm; sapphire crystal; water-resistant to 3 atm
Band: calfskin, buckle
Price: $3,500; limited to 100 pieces

Avantgarde "Kandy"
Reference number: AS.KD02-4G
Movement: automatic, ETA Caliber 2892-A2; ø 26.2 mm, height 3.6 mm; 21 jewels; 28,800 vph; hand-engraved oscillating mass; 47-hour power reserve
Functions: hours, minutes, sweep seconds; date
Case: stainless steel with black PVD coating, with red gold inserts, 41 × 41 mm, height 9 mm; sapphire crystal; water-resistant to 3 atm
Band: reptile skin, buckle
Price: $3,750
Variations: various dials

ALEXANDER SHOROKHOFF

Avantgarde "Los Craneos 2"
Reference number: AS.DT02-2
Movement: automatic, Caliber 2671.AS (base ETA 2671); ø 17.5 mm, height 4.8 mm; 25 jewels; 28,800 vph; 2 independent movements with hand-engraved oscillating masses; 42-hour power reserve
Functions: hours, minutes (double), sweep seconds; date
Case: stainless steel, ø 46.5 mm, height 12.5 mm; sapphire crystal; transparent case back; water-resistant to 5 atm
Band: ostrich leather, buckle
Price: $3,800; limited to 88 pieces

Avantgarde Revolution AVG
Reference number: AS.REV-AVG
Movement: automatic, Caliber 2671.AS (base ETA 2671); ø 17.5 mm, height 4.8 mm; 25 jewels; 28,800 vph; hand-engraved oscillating mass; 42-hour power reserve
Functions: hours, minutes, sweep seconds; date
Case: stainless steel, ø 43.5 mm, height 11.55 mm; sapphire crystal; transparent case back; water-resistant to 5 atm
Band: deerskin, buckle
Remarks: movement case is positioned off-center in case under single sapphire crystal
Price: $4,750; limited to 100 pieces

Avantgarde Tourbillon Tomorrow
Reference number: AS.TU55-1TM
Movement: manually wound, Concepto Caliber 8950; ø 30.4 mm, height 5.8 mm; 27 jewels; 28,800 vph; 1-minute tourbillon; hand-engraved and -embellished; 60-hour power reserve
Functions: hours, minutes, subsidiary seconds (on tourbillon cage)
Case: red gold, ø 43.5 mm, height 12.5 mm; sapphire crystal; water-resistant to 3 atm
Band: reptile skin, buckle
Remarks: various dials, limited to 5 pieces each
Price: on request

Avantgarde Initials
Reference number: AS.C01-IN
Movement: manually wound, Caliber 3133.AS; ø 31 mm; 23 jewels; 21,600 vph; fully skeletonized and chased movement; 36-hour power reserve
Functions: hours, minutes, subsidiary seconds; chronograph
Case: stainless steel, ø 43.5 mm, height 11.55 mm; sapphire crystal; transparent case back; water-resistant to 5 atm
Band: reptile skin, buckle
Remarks: remaining dial sections decorated with initials
Price: $11,000

Vintage "Lucky 8"
Reference number: AS.V3.02-R
Movement: manually wound, Poljot Caliber 2416; ø 24.6 mm, height 4.55 mm; 17 jewels; 18,000 vph; movement hand-engraved and -embellished; 42-hour power reserve
Functions: hours, minutes, sweep seconds; date
Case: stainless steel, ø 43.5 mm, height 11.5 mm; sapphire crystal; transparent case back; water-resistant to 5 atm
Band: ostrich leather, buckle
Remarks: various cases and dials, limited to 50 pieces each
Price: $1,800

Avantgarde Babylonian I
Reference number: AS.BYL01
Movement: manually wound, Caliber 2609.AS (base-Poljot 2609); ø 25.6 mm, height 4.05 mm; 17 jewels; 21,600 vph; rose gold–plated and finely finished movement; 42-hour power reserve
Functions: hours, minutes, sweep seconds
Case: stainless steel, ø 46.5 mm, height 11.5 mm; sapphire crystal; transparent case back; water-resistant to 5 atm
Band: ostrich leather, buckle
Price: $2,850; limited to 500 pieces

ALPINA

The brand Alpina essentially grew out of a confederation of watchmakers known as the Alpina Union Horlogère, founded by Gottlieb Hauser. The group expanded quickly to reach beyond Swiss borders into Germany, where it opened a factory in Glashütte. For a while in the 1930s it even merged with Gruen, one of the most important watch companies in the United States.

After World War II, the Allied Forces decreed that the name Alpina could no longer be used in Germany, and so that branch was renamed "Dugena" for Deutsche Uhrmacher-Genossenschaft Alpina, or the German Watchmaker Cooperative Alpina.

Today, Geneva-based Alpina is no longer associated with that watchmaker cooperative of yore. Now a sister brand of Frédérique Constant, it has a decidedly modern collection enhanced with a series of movements designed, built, and assembled in-house; the Tourbillon AL-980, the World Timer AL-718, the Automatic Regulator AL-950, the Small Date Automatic AL-710, and, more recently, the Flyback Chronograph Automatic AL-760, which features the patented Direct Flyback technology. Owners Peter and Aletta Stas have built up an outstanding business over the years, and in 2016 they sold it to Citizen Group, but continue managing the brands until 2020.

Alpina likes to call itself the inventor of the modern sports watch. Its iconic Block Uhr of 1933 and the Alpina 4 of 1938, with an in-house automatic movement, set the pace for all sports watches, with a waterproof stainless steel case, an amagnetic system, and shock absorbers. But beyond a target group engaged in water and air sports, the brand is now looking at the twenty-first-century hipsters, whose lives are electronic. The Horological Smartwatch, equipped with a quartz movement, connects with mobile phones and other electronic devices and can display the data on an analog dial. The idea of producing a watch for the active person with a liking for hip electronics and traditional mechanics has proven itself a good recipe for the brand.

Alpina Watch International SA
Route de la Galaise, 8
CH-1228 Plan-les-Ouates, Geneva
Switzerland

Tel.:
+41-0-22-860-87-40

E-mail:
info@alpina-watches.com

Website:
www.alpina-watches.com

Founded:
1883

Number of employees:
100

Annual production:
10,000 watches

U.S. distributor:
Alpina Frederique Constant USA
350 5th Avenue, 29th Floor
New York, NY 10118
646-438-8124
lmellor@usa.frederique-constant.com

Most important collections/price range:
AlpinerX / from approx. $995 to $1,295;
Seastrong Diver 300 GMT / from approx. $795 to 995; Startimer Pilot Automatic / from approx. $995 to 1,295

AlpinerX
Reference number: AL-283LBBW5AQ6
Movement: quartz, microchip
Functions: hours, minutes; altimeter, barometer, compass, GPS, UV indicator, temperature display, electronic motion and sleep monitoring, alarm, stopwatch, world time display; date
Case: stainless steel with titanium coating, fiberglass, ø 45 mm, height 14 mm; unidirectional 360-degree bezel; sapphire crystal; water-resistant to 10 atm
Band: calfskin, buckle
Price: $995

Seastrong Diver 300
Reference number: AL-525LGG4TV6
Movement: automatic, Caliber AL-525 (base Sellita SW200-1); ø 25.6 mm, height 4.6 mm; 26 jewels; 28,800 vph; 38-hour power reserve
Functions: hours, minutes, sweep seconds; date
Case: titanium with gray PVD coating, ø 44 mm, height 12 mm; unidirectional bezel, 0-60 scale; sapphire crystal; transparent case back; screw-in crown; water-resistant to 30 atm
Band: calfskin, buckle
Remarks: comes with additional rubber band
Price: $1,395

Startimer Pilot Heritage GMT
Reference number: AL-555LNS4H6B
Movement: automatic, Caliber AL-555 (base Sellita SW330-1); ø 25.6 mm, height 4.1 mm; 25 jewels; 28,800 vph; 38-hour power reserve
Functions: hours, minutes, sweep seconds; additional 24-hour display (2nd time zone), crown-activated inner scale; date
Case: stainless steel, 40.75 × 42 mm, height 12.65 mm; sapphire crystal; water-resistant to 10 atm
Band: stainless steel Milanese mesh, folding clasp
Price: $1,495

ANGELUS

Angelus
Manufacture La Joux-Perret SA
Boulevard des Eplatures 38
2300 La Chaux-de-Fonds
Switzerland

Tel:
+41-32-967-97-97

E-mail:
info@angelus-watches.com

Website:
www.angelus-watches.com

Founded:
1891; relaunched 2011

Number of employees:
about 100, including at the La Joux-Perret manufacture

Distributor:
Angelus USA
510 West 6th Street, Suite 309
Los Angeles, CA 90014
213-622-1133

Most important collections/price range
U50/U51 / $32,000; various tourbillons / $28,000 to $69,000

The watch landscape in Switzerland has always been rich in small, vital brands. Many are no longer active, but their names still make for weepy eyes with connoisseurs and collectors. And every now and then, an older company is revived with varying degrees of success. Angelus, founded by Gustave and Albert Stolz in Le Locle in 1891, quickly forged a reputation for complicated watches, notably repeaters and chronographs. The brothers, Catholics, named the brand after the first word of a standard Catholic prayer and the midday church bells.

One of the brand's claims to fame was a two-handed chronograph, which became a hit in the thirties, culminating in a contract with the Hungarian air force in 1940. The company then built a chronograph with a date, and later one of the first digital dates. Meanwhile, it was creating excellent movements, one of which drove Panerai's Mare Nostrum in the fifties. Among its most iconic models was the waterproof repeater/alarm called the Tinkler—a very limited series, hence extremely rare—and, in the seventies, a five-minute repeater, which never really got off the ground due to the quartz crisis, which brought Angelus to its knees . . .

Fast-forward to 2011. La Joux-Perret, a company known for movements and modules and behind Arnold & Son, relaunched the brand. Sébastien Chaulmontet designed the Tourbillon Lumière, which became the breakout watch in 2015, a modern, television-shaped behemoth recalling the travel clocks the company produced at one time. The tourbillon turns in one window, time appears in the other. It struck a chord: modern, slightly dissonant, but with gumption. In 2017, the model reappeared with a Mexican skull (Calavera) dial and accompanied by several other tourbillon models in more standard round watches. The year 2019 saw a diver tourbillon, a particularly fine way to explore the seabed. Angelus is making people talk, and that can easily mean success these days.

U10 Tourbillon Calavera
Reference number: 0LUAS.B01A.C001F
Movement: manually wound, Caliber A-100; ø 52.1 mm, height 30.4 mm; 38 jewels; 18,000 vph; 1-minute flying tourbillon with titanium bridge; rhodium-plated, satin-finished mainplate and bridges; double spring barrel, 90-hour power reserve
Functions: hours, minutes, dead-beat sweep seconds; power reserve indicator
Case: annealed stainless steel, ø 62.75 mm × 38 mm, height 15 mm; sapphire crystal; transparent case back; water-resistant to 3 atm
Band: reptile skin, buckle
Price: $120,000; unique piece

U50 Diver Tourbillon Black Edition
Reference number: 0TDAT.B01A.K008T
Movement: manually wound, Caliber A-300; ø 32.8 mm, height 4.3 mm; 23 jewels; 28,800 vph; 1-minute flying tourbillon; black DLC-coated, snailed and beveled mainplate and bridges, satin-finished blue skeletonized titanium bridges; 55-hour power reserve
Functions: hours, minutes, subsidiary seconds
Case: black DLC-coated titanium, ø 46 mm, height 12.47 mm; crown-adjustable unidirectional 60-minute timing bezel; sapphire crystal; transparent case back; water-resistant to 30 atm
Band: rubber, buckle
Remarks: 6-spoke design on wheels for rigidity
Price: $32,900; limited to 25 pieces

U20 Ultra-Skeleton Tourbillon
Reference number: 0TCAB.U01A.C004T
Movement: manually wound, Caliber A-250; ø 32.6 mm, height 5.78 mm; 18 jewels; 21,600 vph; 1-minute flying tourbillon; sapphire mainplate, satin-finished blue skeletonized titanium bridges; 90-hour power reserve
Functions: hours, minutes, subsidiary seconds
Case: titanium and NPT carbon fiber, ø 42 mm, height 10.3 mm; sapphire crystal; transparent case back; water-resistant to 3 atm
Band: reptile skin, buckle
Price: $69,900; limited to 18 pieces

ANONIMO

The brand Anonimo was launched in Florence, Italy. Watchmaking has a long history in Florence, going back to one Giovanni de Dondi (1318–1389), who built his first planetarium around 1368, or architect and goldsmith Lorenzo della Volpaia (1446–1512), who worked with calendars and astronomical instruments. And finally, there were the likes of the mathematician Galileo and the incomparable Leonardo da Vinci.

In more recent times, the Italian watch industry has been equipping submarine crews and frogmen with timepieces. The key technology comes from Switzerland, but the specialized know-how for making robust, water-resistant timepieces sprang from small enterprises with special competencies in building cases, notably of bronze. The founders of Anonimo understood this strength and decided to put it in the service of their "anonymous" brand—a name chosen to "hide" the fact that many small, discreet companies are involved in their superbly finished watches.

In 2013, Anonimo came out with three watch families running on Swiss technology: The mechanical movements are a combination of Dubois Dépraz modules and tried-and-true Sellita movements. On the whole, though, the collections reflect exquisite conception and manufacturing, and the quality of the materials is unimpeachable: corrosion-resistant stainless steel, fine bronze, and titanium. The design is definitely vintage, a bit 1960s with a hint of a cushion case, but use of only three numerals—4, 8, and 12, which sketch an A on the dial—is quite modern. On the military models, the crown has been placed in a protected area between the two upper lugs. Thanks to a clever hinge system, that crown can be pressed onto the case for an impermeable fit or released for time-setting. The Militare line is also home to a special-edition chronograph to celebrate Anonimo's status as official timer of the World Rally Championship, Italy section. Fans seeking a simpler dial have the Epurato line, including a number of different-colored dials, each with characteristic sunray effect. The Nautilo series was conceived for divers, chic and sportive and able to descend beyond 600 feet. The latest models look back to older Dino Zei Nautilos of the past, with hints of '60s-style cushion cases.

Anonimo SA
Chemin des Tourelles 4
CH-2400 Le Locle
Switzerland

Tel.:
+41-22-566-06-06

E-mail:
info@anonimo.com

Website:
www.anonimo.com

Founded:
1997; moved to Switzerland in 2013

Distributor:
Anonimo USA
1920 Dr. Martin Luther King Jr. Street North
Suite D
St. Petersburg, FL 33704
727-202-5946

Most important collections/price range:
Epurato, Militare, Nautilo / $2,300 to $5,700

Militare WRC Special Edition
Reference number: AM-1128.21.221.T64
Movement: automatic, Sellita Caliber SW300 with Dubois Dépraz model; ø 25.6 mm, height 5.6 mm; 31 jewels; 28,800 vph; oscillating mass with côtes de Genève; 42-hour power reserve
Functions: hours, minutes, subsidiary seconds; chronograph; date, tachymeter
Case: stainless steel with PVD, ø 43.4 mm, height 14.45 mm; sapphire crystal; bezel with tachymeter scale; transparent case back; water-resistant to 12 atm
Band: fireproofed textile with leather sections, buckle
Remarks: crown pressed into case between upper lugs for impermeable seal
Price: $5,680
Variations: as Militare

Epurato Verde Natura
Reference number: AM-4000.01.107.W66
Movement: automatic, Sellita Caliber SW200; ø 25.6 mm, height 4.6 mm; 25 jewels; 28,800 vph; 38-hour power reserve
Functions: hours, minutes, sweep seconds; date
Case: stainless steel, ø 42 mm, height 14 mm; sapphire crystal; water-resistant to 5 atm
Band: calfskin, buckle and interchangeable strap
Remarks: fir-tree green sunray dial
Price: $2,480
Variations: various dial colors and case materials (bronze, DLC)

Nautilo Vintage Blue
Reference number: AM-5019.06.103.I12
Movement: automatic, Sellita Caliber SW200-1; ø 25.6 mm, height 4.6 mm; 26 jewels; 28,800 vph; 38-hour power reserve
Functions: hours, minutes, sweep seconds; date
Case: stainless steel, ø 42 mm, height 11.8 mm; stainless steel bezel with blue ceramic inlay, unidirectional bezel with 0-60 scale; sapphire crystal; screw-in crown; water-resistant to 20 atm
Band: calfskin, buckle
Remarks: blue dial; interchangeable strap system
Price: $2,480
Variations: chocolate dial ($2,480); Nautilo as "Leopard" ($2,370; limited to 97 pieces), or Classic; on steel bracelet or rubber strap

Aristo Vollmer GmbH
Erbprinzenstr. 36
D-75175 Pforzheim
Germany

Tel.:
+49-7231-17031

E-mail:
info@aristo-vollmer.de

Website:
www.aristo-vollmer.de

Founded:
1907/1998

Number of employees:
16

Annual production:
9,000 watches and 9,000 bracelets

Distribution:
retail

U.S. distributor:
Long Island Watch, Marc Frankel
273 Walt Whitman Road, Suite 217
Huntington Station, NY 11746
631-470-0762
www.longislandwatch.com

Most important collections/price range:
Aristo watches starting at $400 up to Vollmer watches at $1,900; Erbprinz watches up to $1,600

ARISTO

"If you lie down with dogs . . ." goes the old saying. And if you work closely with watchmakers . . . you may catch their more beneficial bug and become one yourself. That, at any rate, is what happened to the watch case and metal bracelet manufacturer Vollmer, Ltd, established in Pforzheim, Germany, by Ernst Vollmer in 1922. Th rd-generation president Hansjörg Vollmer decided he was interested in producing watches as well.

Vollmer, who studied business in Stuttgart, had the experience, but also the connections with manufacturers in Switzerland. He speaks French fluently, another asset. He acquired Aristo and launched a series of pilot's watches in 1998 housed in sturdy titanium cases with bold onion crowns and secured with Vollmer's own light and comfortable titanium bracelets. Bit by bit, thanks to affordable prices and no-nonsense design—reviving some classic dials from World War II—Vollmer's watches caught hold. The collection grew with limited editions and a few chronometers.

In October 2005, Vollmer GmbH and Aristo Watches finally consolidated for a bigger impact. Besides their own lines, they produce quartz watches, automatics, and chronographs under the names Messerschmitt and Aristella. The Aristo brand has been trademarked worldwide and is sold mainly in Europe, North America, and Asia. The collection is divided up into Classic, Design, and Sports, with the mechanical segment further split based on elements Land, Water, and Air. The timepieces range from quality wristwatches with historical movements from older Swiss production to attractive ladies' watches and replicas of classic military watches, all assembled in Pforzheim. The company also has an established name as a manufacturer of classic pilot's watches. And it took another step toward the higher end of the market by launching the "Erbprinz" series, named after the street where the company also has a workshop for manufacturing metal bracelets.

Bauhaus Weimar
Reference number: 4H353M
Movement: automatic, Sellita Caliber SW200-1; ø 25.6 mm, height 4.6 mm; 26 jewels; 28,800 vph; 38-hour power reserve
Functions: hours, minutes, sweep seconds; date
Case: stainless steel, ø 40 mm, height 11.8 mm; mineral glass
Band: stainless steel Milanese mesh, folding clasp
Price: $605
Variations: silver-white dial; calfskin band

Unitas 6300
Reference number: 4H186
Movement: manually wound, Unitas Caliber 6300 (N); ø 29 mm, height 4.55 mm; 21 jewels; 18,000 vph; historically restored and finely finished; 36-hour power reserve
Functions: hours, minutes, sweep seconds
Case: stainless steel, ø 47 mm, height 13.5 mm; sapphire crystal; transparent case back; water-resistant to 5 atm
Band: calfskin, buckle
Price: $1,460; limited to 100 pieces
Variations: four different dials

Erbprinz Chronograph
Reference number: M8
Movement: automatic, ETA Caliber 7750; ø 30 mm, height 7.9 mm; 25 jewels; 28,800 vph; 42-hour power reserve
Functions: hours, minutes, subsidiary seconds; chronograph; date, weekday
Case: stainless steel, ø 44 mm, height 14.7 mm; sapphire crystal; transparent case back; water-resistant to 5 atm
Band: stainless steel Milanese mesh, folding clasp
Price: $1,500

ARMIN STROM

For more than thirty years, Armin Strom's name was associated mainly with the art of skeletonizing. But this "grandmaster of skeletonizers" then decided to entrust his life's work to the next generation, which turned out to be the Swiss industrialist and art patron Willy Michel.

Michel had the wherewithal to expand the one-man show into a full-blown *manufacture* able to conceive, design, and produce its own mechanical movements. The endeavor attracted Claude Geisler, a very skilled designer, and Michel's own son, Serge, who became business manager. When this triumvirate joined forces, it was able to come up with a technically fascinating movement at the quaint little *manufacture* in the Biel suburb of Bözingen within a brief period of time.

The new movement went on to grow into a family of ten, which forms the backbone of a new collection, including a tourbillon with microrotor—no mean feat for a small firm. The ARF15 caliber of the Mirrored Force Resonance, for example, features two balance wheels placed close enough to influence each other (resonance) and give the movement greater stability. The two oscillating systems are connected by a clutch spring. A similar movement is used in an exclusive, new, minute repeater.

This essential portfolio has given the *manufacture* the industrial autonomy to implement its projects quickly and independently. Armin Strom has additionally created an online configurator (on its homepage) giving fans and collectors the opportunity to personalize their watches. All components can be selected individually and combined, from the dial, hands, and finishing to the straps. The finished product can be picked up at a local dealership or at the manufacturer in Biel/Bienne, including a tour of the place.

Armin Strom AG
Bözingenstrasse 46
CH-2502 Biel/Bienne
Switzerland

Tel.:
+41-32-343-3344

E-mail:
info@arminstrom.com

Website:
www.arminstrom.com

Founded:
2006 (first company 1967)

Number of employees:
22

Annual production:
approx. 400 watches

U.S. representative:
Jean Marc Bories
Head of North America
929-353-5395
Jean-marc@arminstrom.com

Most important collections/price range:
Offers an online configurator for individual design using six in-house movements (manual, power reserve, automatic with or without date, tourbillon, resonance, and skeletons) / $9,900 to $100,000 plus

Dual Time Resonance Sapphire
Reference number: RGMT.11.AL.L.14.FC
Movement: manually wound, Caliber ARF17; 52.55 × 39.95 mm, height 11.67 mm; 70 jewels; 25,200 vph; 2 independent regulating systems connected by a resonance clutch spring; 4 spring barrels; hand-decorated mainplate and bridges; 110-hour power reserve; **Functions:** hours, minutes (double); additional 24-hour display (2nd time zone), power reserve indicator (double)
Case: sapphire crystal, 59 mm × 43.4 mm, height 13 mm; sapphire crystal; transparent case back; water-resistant to 5 atm
Band: reptile skin, double folding clasp
Price: $168,000; **Variations:** titanium ($169,000); rose gold ($185,000); white gold ($185,000)

Pure Resonance Water
Reference number: ST17-RW.05.AL.L.14
Movement: manually wound, Caliber ARF16; ø 34.4 mm, height 7.05 mm; 38 jewels; 25,200 vph; 2 independent regulating systems are connected by a resonance clutch spring and mutually stabilize each other; finely decorated mainplate and bridges; 48-hour power reserve
Functions: hours, minutes (off-center), subsidiary seconds
Case: stainless steel, ø 42 mm, height 12 mm; sapphire crystal; transparent case back; water-resistant to 5 atm
Band: reptile skin, buckle
Remarks: comes with extra rubber strap
Price: $49,000

Mirrored Force Resonance Fire
Reference number: RG15-RF.5N
Movement: manually wound, Caliber ARF15; ø 36.6 mm, height 7.7 mm; 43 jewels; 25,200 vph; 2 independent regulating systems are connected by a resonance clutch spring and mutually stabilize each other; movement finely finished; 48-hour power reserve
Functions: hours, minutes (off-center), double subsidiary seconds
Case: rose gold, ø 43.4 mm, height 13 mm; sapphire crystal; transparent case back; water-resistant to 5 atm
Band: reptile skin, buckle
Remarks: comes with extra rubber strap
Price: $67,000; limited to 50 pieces

Skeleton Pure Water
Reference number: ST15-PW.05
Movement: manually wound, Caliber ARM09-S; ø 36.6 mm, height 6.2 mm; 34 jewels; 18,000 vph; 2 spring barrels, screw balance with gold weight screws, Breguet hairspring, crown wheels visible on dial side; skeletonized, plate, gearwheels, and spring barrel bridges, mainplate with blue PVD coating; 168-hour power reserve
Functions: hours, minutes, subsidiary seconds; power reserve indicator
Case: stainless steel, ø 43.4 mm, height 13 mm; sapphire crystal; transparent case back; water-resistant to 5 atm; **Band:** reptile skin, buckle
Remarks: comes with extra rubber strap
Price: $32,400; limited to 100 pieces
Variations: Fire ($45,400); Air ($35,400)

Edge Double Barrel Rose Gold
Reference number: RG16-EB.5N
Movement: manually wound, Caliber ARM16; ø 36.6 mm, height 7.7 mm; 34 jewels; 18,000 vph; double spring barrel, winding wheels visible on dial side; 192-hour power reserve
Functions: hours, minutes, subsidiary seconds; power reserve indicator
Case: rose gold, ø 46.8 mm, height 13.2 mm; sapphire crystal; transparent case back; water-resistant to 5 atm
Band: reptile skin, buckle
Remarks: comes with extra rubber strap
Price: $39,900; limited to 100 pieces
Variations: stainless steel with black PVD coating ($26,900)

Tourbillon Skeleton Earth
Reference number: ST15-TE.90
Movement: manually wound, Caliber ATC11-S; ø 36.6 mm, height 6.2 mm; 24 jewels; 18,000 vph; 1-minute tourbillon, double spring barrel, skeletonized plates, wheels, and bridges, Breguet hairspring, screw balance with gold weight screws, crown wheels visible on dial side; 240-hour power reserve
Functions: hours, minutes, subsidiary seconds
Case: stainless steel with black PVD coating, ø 43.4 mm, height 13 mm; sapphire crystal; transparent case back; water-resistant to 5 atm
Band: reptile skin, double folding clasp
Price: $91,000
Variations: Air ($94,000); Fire ($101,000); Water ($91,000)

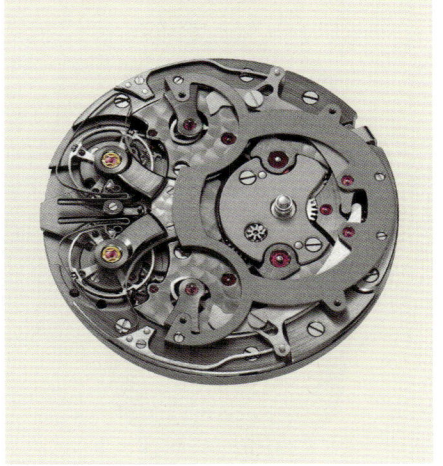

Minute Repeater Resonance
Reference number: TI19-RMR.SA.AL.M.43.FC
Movement: manually wound, Caliber ARR18; ø 39.4 mm, height 11.35 mm; 51 jewels; 25,200 vph; 2 independent mutually stabilizing regulating systems connected by a resonance clutch spring; finely decorated mainplate and bridges; 96-hour power reserve
Functions: hours, minutes (off-center), subsidiary seconds
Case: titanium, ø 47.7 mm, height 16.1 mm; sapphire crystal; transparent case back; water-resistant to 3 atm
Band: reptile skin, double folding clasp
Remarks: minute repeater visible on dial
Price: $350,000; limited to 10 pieces

Caliber ARF15
Manually wound, 25,200 vph; 2 separate regulating systems are connected by a resonance clutch spring and mutually stabilize each other; single spring barrel, 48-hour power reserve
Functions: hours, minutes (off-center), 2 independent symmetrically mirrored subsidiary seconds
Diameter: 36.6 mm
Height: 7.7 mm
Jewels: 43
Balance: 2 balance wheels oscillating in opposite directions on a single hairspring
Frequency: 25,200 vph
Remarks: 226 components; fine, hand-decorated movement

Caliber ARM16
Manually wound, gold escape wheel and pallet lever with hardened functional surfaces; double mainspring barrel, 192-hour power reserve
Functions: hours, minutes, subsidiary seconds; power reserve indicator
Diameter: 36.6 mm
Height: 7.7 mm
Jewels: 34
Balance: screw balance with variable inertia
Frequency: 18,000 vph
Balance spring: Breguet hairspring
Remarks: finely finished movement

ARNOLD & SON

John Arnold holds a special place among the British watchmakers of the eighteenth and nineteenth centuries because he was the first to organize the production of his chronometers along industrial lines. He developed his own standards and employed numerous watchmakers. During his lifetime, he is said to have manufactured around 5,000 marine chronometers, which he sold at reasonable prices to the Royal Navy and the West Indies merchant fleet. Arnold chronometers were packed in the trunks of some of the greatest explorers, from John Franklin and Ernest Shackleton to Captain Cook and Dr. Livingstone.

As Arnold & Son was once synonymous with precision timekeeping on the high seas, it stands to reason, then, that the modern brand should also focus its design policies on the interplay of time and geography as well as the basic functions of navigation. Independence from The British Masters Group has meant that the venerable English chronometer brand has been reorienting itself, setting its sights on classic, elegant watchmaking. With the expertise of watch manufacturer La Joux-Perret behind it (and the expertise housed in the building behind the complex on the main road between La Chaux-de-Fonds and Le Locle), it has been able to implement a number of new ideas.

There are two main lines: The Royal Collection celebrates John Arnold's art, with luxuriously designed models inspired from past creations with delicate complications, tourbillons or world-time displays, or unadorned manual windings featuring the new Caliber A&S 1001 by La Joux-Perret. The Instrument Collection is dedicated to exploring the seven seas and offers a sober look reflecting old-fashioned meters. Typically, these timepieces combine two displays on a single dial: a chronograph with jumping seconds, for example, between the off-center displays of time and the date hand or separate escapements driving a dual time display—left, the sidereal time; right, the solar time; and between the two, the difference. Perhaps the most remarkable timepiece in the collection is the skeletonized Time Pyramid, with a dual power reserve, a crown between the lugs, and an overall modern look.

Arnold & Son
38, boulevard des Eplatures
CH-2300 La Chaux-de-Fonds
Switzerland

Tel.:
+41-32-967-9797

E-mail:
info@arnoldandson.com

Website:
www.arnoldandson.com

Founded:
1995

Number of employees:
approx. 30

U.S. distributor:
Arnold & Son USA
510 West 6th Street, Suite 309
Los Angeles, CA 90014
213-622-1133

Most important collections/price range:
Globetrotter, Time Pyramid, Nebula, TB88, TBR, TE8 (Tourbillon), Time Pyramid, UTTE / from approx. $10,000 to $325,000

Time Pyramid Tourbillon
Reference number: 1TPBR.T01A
Movement: manually wound, Arnold & Son Caliber 8615; ø 37.60 mm, height 5.70 mm; 31 jewels; 21,600 vph; 1-minute tourbillon; finely finished parts, skeletonized movement; double spring barrel; 90-hour power reserve; **Functions:** hours, minutes, seconds on tourbillon; double power reserve indicator
Case: red gold, ø 44.6 mm, height 10.09 mm; sapphire crystal; transparent case back; water-resistant to 3 atm; **Band:** reptile skin, buckle
Remarks: pyramid-shaped movement inspired from table clocks by J. and R. Arnold; hours on sapphire disk, minutes on rhodium-plated ring
Price: $49,995; limited to 28 pieces
Variations: stainless steel ($39,995)

Time Pyramid Black
Reference number: 1TPBS.R01A
Movement: manually wound, Arnold & Son Caliber 1615; ø 37 mm, height 4.4 mm; 27 jewels; 21,600 vph; skeletonized movement; double spring barrel; 90-hour power reserve
Functions: hours, minutes, subsidiary seconds; double power reserve indicator
Case: stainless steel with black DLC coating, ø 44.6 mm, height 10 mm; sapphire crystal; transparent case back; water-resistant to 3 atm
Band: reptile skin, buckle
Remarks: pyramid-shaped movement inspired from table clocks by J. and R. Arnold
Price: $31,900; limited to 50 pieces
Variations: steel ($31,900); pink gold ($43,200)

Tourbillon Chronometer No. 36 Tribute Edition
Reference number: 1ETAS.B01A.C113S
Movement: manually wound, Arnold & Son Caliber 8600; ø 37.8 mm, height 5.9 mm; 33 jewels; 28,800 vph; 1-minute tourbillon; mainplate black DLC-coated, NAC-coated bridges and cocks, finely finished movement; 90-hour power reserve; COSC-certified chronometer
Functions: hours, minutes, subsidiary seconds
Case: stainless steel, ø 46 mm, height 12.66 mm; sapphire crystal; transparent case back; water-resistant to 3 atm
Band: reptile skin, buckle
Price: $37,400; limited to 28 pieces
Variations: pink gold ($55,400)

DBG Steel

Reference number: 1DGAS.S01AC121S
Movement: manually wound, Arnold & Son Caliber 1209; ø 35 mm, height 3.9 mm; 42 jewels; 21,600 vph; double spring barrel, 2 independent gearwheels and escapement systems; 40-hour power reserve
Functions: hours, minutes (double, 2 time zones), sweep seconds; day/night indicator (per time zone)
Case: stainless steel, ø 44 mm, height 9.89 mm; sapphire crystal; transparent case back; water-resistant to 3 atm
Band: reptile skin, buckle
Price: $27,900

Nebula Steel

Reference number: 1NEBR.A01A.C144A
Movement: manually wound, Arnold & Son Caliber 5101; ø 31.5 mm, height 4.04 mm; 24 jewels; 21,600 vph; skeletonized and finely finished movement with rhodium-plated chapter ring; 90-hour power reserve
Functions: hours, minutes, subsidiary seconds
Case: red gold, ø 38 mm, height 8.91 mm; sapphire crystal; transparent case back; water-resistant to 3 atm
Band: calfskin, buckle
Remarks: skeletonized dial
Price: $25,950; limited to 50 pieces
Variations: stainless steel with 41.5-mm case ($14,500)

DSTB

Reference number: 1ATAS.U01A.C121S
Movement: automatic, Arnold & Son Caliber 6003; ø 38 mm, height 7.39 mm; 32 jewels; 28,800 vph; true-beat escapement on dial, finely finished movement; 45-hour power reserve
Functions: hours, minutes (off-center), subsidiary seconds (jumping)
Case: stainless steel, ø 43.5 mm, height 13 mm; sapphire crystal; transparent case back; water-resistant to 3 atm
Band: reptile skin, buckle
Price: $30,750
Variations: black dial ($29,995); pink gold with anthracite dial ($48,550)

Eight-Day Royal Navy

Reference number: 1EDAS.U01A.D136A
Movement: manually wound, Arnold & Son Caliber 1016; ø 33 mm, height 4.7 mm; 33 jewels; 21,600 vph; 192-hour power reserve
Functions: hours, minutes, subsidiary seconds; power reserve indicator; date
Case: stainless steel, ø 43 mm, height 10.7 mm; sapphire crystal; transparent case back; water-resistant to 3 atm
Band: reptile skin, buckle
Price: $12,950
Variations: black and silver-white dial

HM Perpetual Moon Aventurine

Reference number: 1GLAR.I01A.C122A
Movement: manually wound, Arnold & Son Caliber 1512; ø 34 mm, height 5.35 mm; 27 jewels; 21,600 vph; astronomically precise 122-year moon phase; 90-hour power reserve
Functions: hours, minutes; moon phase
Case: pink gold, ø 42 mm, height 11.43 mm; sapphire crystal; transparent case back; water-resistant to 3 atm
Band: reptile skin, buckle
Remarks: blue aventurine dial, blue lacquered moon disk, hand-engraved sculptural red gold moon and stars
Price: $33,650
Variations: stainless steel with black or blue dial ($16,300 and $16,950)

Globetrotter

Reference number: 1WTAS.S01A.D137S
Movement: automatic, Arnold & Son Caliber 6022; ø 38 mm, height 6.55 mm (14 mm includes arched bridge and hemisphere); 29 jewels; 28,800 vph; 3D world time display in sculptural hemisphere design; 45-hour power reserve
Functions: hours, minutes; world time indicator (2nd time zone)
Case: stainless steel, ø 45 mm, height 17.2 mm; sapphire crystal; transparent case back; water-resistant to 3 atm
Band: calfskin, buckle
Price: $16,995

ARTYA

Shaking up the staid atmosphere of watchmaking can be achieved many ways. The conservative approach is to make some small engineering advance and then talk loudly of tradition and innovation. Yvan Arpa, founder of ArtyA watches, does it differently.

This refreshingly candid personality arrived at watchmaking because, after spending his *Wanderjahre* crossing Papua New Guinea on foot and practicing Thai boxing in its native land, any corporate mugginess back home did not quite cut it for him. Instead he turned the obscure brand Romain Jerome into the talk of the industry with novel material choices: "I looked for antimatter to gentrify common matter," he reflects, "like the rust: proof of the passage of time and the sworn enemy of watchmaking."

Leaving Romain Jerome liberated Arpa from brand constraints. He founded ArtyA, where he could get his "monster" off the slab as it were, with a divine spark. "I had worked with water, rust, dust, and other elements, and then I really caught fire," says Arpa. From cases hit with an electrical arc to cut-up Euro bills, Artya's watches hit nerves and drew a gamut of emotional responses. That's his aim, to surprise and amaze. His dials shake up the owner, and are often genuinely unique. They can include real butterfly wings and collages of earth, shells, pigments, or exquisite engravings by Bram Ramon, or mysterious mother-of-pearl crafting. One of Arpa's not-so-secret weapons in the fight for market share is his artist wife, Dominique Arpa-Cirpka. He never shuns a crazy idea, like the Son of Sound watches, with their guitar-shaped case and chrono pushers designed like guitar pegs. These pieces have landed in such divergent places as world-class museums and Alice Cooper's wrist.

Arpa wants us not only to wear a watch, but to reflect on aspects of our world and society, the meaning of money, bullets, skulls, our love-hate relationship with electronics, the passage of time, love and violence, the beauty of nature frozen in death, and the significance of music. His provocations, though, do not arise from a sophomoric need to be contrarian, but rather from his long and rich experience of an industry that tends to play it safe. No wonder Samsung recruited him to design their Gear 3 hybrid pocket watch . . .

Luxury Artpieces SA
Route de Thonon 146
CH-1222 Vésenaz
Switzerland

Tel.:
+41-22-752-4940

Website:
www.artya.com

Founded:
2010

Number of employees:
12

Annual production:
at least 365 (one a day)

U.S. distributor:
Contact headquarters for all enquiries.

Most important collections/price range:
Son of a Gun / $8,800 to $167,000; Son of Art / $3,800 to $21,000; Son of Earth / $4,300 to $183,000; Son of Love / $4,300 to $54,500; Son of Sound / $4,300 to $22,110; Son of Gears / $6,550 to $16,550

ArtyA Minute Repeater Platinum
Movement: manually wound, ArtyA; ø 30.6 mm, height 4.5 mm; 18,000 vph; 19 jewels; minute repeater; 41-hour power reserve
Functions: hours, minutes
Case: platinum, 40 mm, height 11.25 mm; transparent case back; water-resistant to 3 atm
Remarks: case completely engraved in neo-Renaissance style by Bram Ramon using bright-cut and regular engraving techniques
Band: reptile skin, buckle
Price: $300,000; unique piece

ArtyA 3 Gongs Minute Repeater, Regulator and Double Axis Tourbillon
Movement: manually wound, by MHC, design by ArtyA; ø 13.2 mm, height 6.6 mm; 21,600 vph; 46 jewels; double axis tourbillon, 30-second in one direction and 60-second in the other; minute repeater; 64-hour power reserve
Functions: hours (off-center), sweep minutes, seconds on tourbillon
Case: titanium and ArtyOr with PVD treatment, 64.6 mm × 47.3 mm, height 18.1 mm; sapphire crystal; transparent case back; water-resistant to 5 atm
Band: reptile skin, buckle
Remarks: special gongs, customizable
Price: $480,000; unique piece

ArtyA Son of the Alps
Movement: manually wound, ArtyA; ø 32.6 mm, height 5.7 mm; 19 jewels; 52-hour power reserve
Functions: hours, minutes
Case: stainless steel with black PVD treatment, 40.9 mm × 54.4 mm, height 10 mm; transparent case back; water-resistant to 3 atm
Remarks: dial skeletonized to form the Matterhorn as a tribute to Switzerland
Band: calfskin, buckle
Price: $6,900; unique piece

ARTYA

Son of Earth Gold Tobacco Engraved

Movement: automatic, ArtyA Aion; ø 26.20 mm, height 3.60 mm; 25 jewels; 28,800 vph; with côtes de Genève; rhodium-plated gold oscillator; COSC-certified; 52-hour power reserve
Functions: hours, minutes, sweep seconds
Case: black PVD, with pink gold bezel and lateral inserts, ø 44 mm, height 18 mm; engraved and screwed-down case back; water-resistant to 3 atm
Band: calfskin, buckle
Remarks: dial made of tobacco leaf the cigar-loving owner can select; case and bezel carved by Bram Ramon
Price: $35,000
Variations: stainless steel case ($5,900)

Son of Earth Cosmos

Movement: automatic, ArtyA Aion; ø 26.20 mm, height 3.60 mm; 25 jewels; 28,800 vph; with côtes de Genève; rhodium-plated gold oscillator; COSC-certified; 52-hour power reserve
Functions: hours, minutes, sweep seconds
Case: stainless steel, ø 44 mm, height 18 mm; engraved and screwed-open case back; water-resistant to 3 atm
Band: calfskin, buckle
Remarks: case and bezel seared by Tesla coil "lightning machine" dial decorated with pigments, diamonds by artist D. Arpa-Cirpka; bezel set with double row of diamonds
Price: $10,900
Variations: one of ten unique pieces

Son of Art Concrete

Movement: automatic, ArtyA Aion; ø 26.20 mm, height 3.60 mm; 25 jewels; 28,800 vph; with côtes de Genève; rhodium-plated gold oscillator; COSC-certified; 52-hour power reserve
Functions: hours, minutes, seconds
Case: stainless steel, ø 44 mm, height 18 mm; transparent case back; water-resistant to 3 atm
Band: calfskin, buckle
Remarks: concrete dial
Price: $8,900
Variations: one of nine unique pieces

Son of Sound Purple Rain

Movement: automatic ArtyA; ø 33 mm, height 12 mm; 19 jewels; 21,600 vph; 48-hour power reserve
Functions: sliding hours, minutes, subsidiary seconds; date; patented active "tuning pegs" system for chronograph functions/date setting; 30-minute counter
Case: stainless steel, 37 × 49 mm, height 15 mm; transparent engraved and screw-down case back; protected against humidity and dust but not water-resistant
Band: calfskin, buckle
Price: $20,100; unique piece

Son of a Gun No Refusal "Classic Edition"

Movement: automatic, A17 highly modified by ArtyA; ø 26.20 mm, height 3.60 mm; 25 jewels; 28,800 vph; 52-hour power reserve
Functions: hours, minutes, seconds
Case: stainless steel with PVD treatment, ø 44 mm, height 18 mm; transparent case back; water-resistant to 3 atm
Band: calfskin, buckle
Remarks: 11 Flobert 6-mm shot rounds under dial
Price: $14,900; limited to 99 pieces
Variations: with engraved target ($17,900; unique piece)

Son of Gears, Star Fluo

Movement: manually wound ArtyA movement; ø 33 mm, height 12 mm; 19 jewels; 21,600 vph; 52-hour power reserve
Functions: hours, minutes
Case: stainless steel with brushed lateral inserts, ø 44 mm, height 18 mm; engraved and screwed-down transparent case back; water-resistant to 3 atm
Band: calfskin, buckle
Remarks: skeletonized dial in shape of star over brightly colored three-quarter plate
Price: $7,900; unique 1/1
Variations: different case shapes and movement colors

AUDEMARS PIGUET

The history of Audemars Piguet is one of the most engaging stories of Swiss watchmaking folklore: Ever since their school days together in the Vallée de Joux, Jules-Louis Audemars (b. 1851) and Edward-Auguste Piguet (b. 1853) knew they would follow in the footsteps of their fathers and grandfathers and become watchmakers. They were members of the same sports association, sang in the same choir, attended the same vocational school—and both became outstandingly talented watchmakers. The *manufacture* founded over 140 years ago by these two is still in family hands, and it has become one of the leading names in the industry.

In the history of watchmaking, only a handful of watches really achieved cult status. One of them is the Royal Oak by Audemars Piguet. It was born as a radical answer to the global invasion of the quartz watch. Audemars Piguet contacted the designer Gérald Genta to create a watch for a new generation of customers, a sportive luxury timepiece with a modern look, which could be worn every day. The result was a luxurious watch of stainless steel. The octagonal bezel held down with boldly "industrial" hexagonal bolts onto a 39-millimeter case was almost provocative. The watch, big for its time, was nicknamed "Jumbo." It ran on the then thinnest automatic movement, a slice 3.05 millimeters high. The second key to the brand's enduring success was no doubt the acquisition of the atelier Renaud et Papi in 1992. APRP, as it is known, specializes in creating and executing complex complications, a skill it lets other brands share in as well.

The sporty Royal Oak collection allowed the company to expand its portfolio. In August 2009, it opened the Manufacture des Forges in Le Brassus.

At the SIHH, like clockwork, CEO François-Henry Bennahmias always presents a range of new models in the Royal Oak family with some remarkable complications. But in 2019 a surprise awaited, with the "Code 11.59" by Audemars Piguet, which suggests deep brand codes cloaked in modern garb. The new line of watches is composed of thirteen references, including five complications and six of the latest calibers. The cases are all forty-one millimeters and come in white or rose gold.

Manufacture d'Horlogerie Audemars Piguet
Route de France 16
CH-1348 Le Brassus
Switzerland

Tel.:
+41-21-642-3900

E-mail:
info@audemarspiguet.com

Website:
www.audemarspiguet.com

Founded:
1875

Number of employees:
approx. 1,300

Annual production:
40,000 watches

U.S. distributor:
Audemars Piguet (North America) Inc.
Service Center of the Americas
3040 Gulf to Bay Boulevard
Clearwater, FL 33759

Most important collections/price range:
CODE 11.59 / from approx. $26,000; Millenary / from approx. $28,400; Royal Oak / from approx. $17,800; special concept watches

CODE 11.59 Selfwinding

Reference number: 15210BC.OO.A321CR.01
Movement: automatic, AP Caliber 4302; ø 32 mm, height 4.8 mm; 32 jewels; 28,800 vph; gold rotor, finely finished movement; 70-hour power reserve
Functions: hours, minutes, sweep seconds; date
Case: white gold, ø 41 mm, height 10.7 mm; sapphire crystal; transparent case back; water-resistant to 3 atm
Band: reptile skin, buckle
Price: $26,800

CODE 11.59 Selfwinding

Reference number: 15210OR.OO.A099CR.01
Movement: automatic, AP Caliber 4302; ø 32 mm, height 4.8 mm; 32 jewels; 28,800 vph; gold rotor, finely finished movement; 70-hour power reserve
Functions: hours, minutes, sweep seconds; date
Case: rose gold, ø 41 mm, height 10.7 mm; sapphire crystal; transparent case back; water-resistant to 3 atm
Band: reptile skin, buckle
Price: $26,800
Variations: black dial ($26,800)

CODE 11.59 Chronograph

Reference number: 26393BC.OO.A321CR.01
Movement: automatic, AP Caliber 4401; ø 32 mm, height 6.8 mm; 40 jewels; 28,800 vph; skeletonized gold rotor, finely finished movement; 70-hour power reserve
Functions: hours, minutes, subsidiary seconds; flyback chronograph; date
Case: white gold, ø 41 mm, height 12.6 mm; sapphire crystal; transparent case back; water-resistant to 3 atm
Band: reptile skin, buckle
Price: $42,400
Variations: rose gold ($42,400)

AUDEMARS PIGUET

CODE 11.59 Chronograph
Reference number: 26393OR.OO.A002CR.01
Movement: automatic, AP Caliber 4401; ø 32 mm, height 6.8 mm; 40 jewels; 28,800 vph; skeletonized gold rotor, finely finished movement; 70-hour power reserve
Functions: hours, minutes, subsidiary seconds; flyback chronograph; date
Case: rose gold, ø 41 mm, height 12.6 mm; sapphire crystal; transparent case back; water-resistant to 3 atm
Band: reptile skin, buckle
Price: $42,400
Variations: white gold ($42,400)

CODE 11.59 Perpetual Calendar
Reference number: 26394OR.OO.D321CR.01
Movement: automatic, AP Caliber 5134; ø 29 mm, height 4.31 mm; 38 jewels; 19,800 vph; skeletonized gold rotor, finely finished movement; 40-hour power reserve
Functions: hours, minutes; perpetual calendar with date, weekday, calendar week, month, moon phase, leap year
Case: rose gold, ø 41 mm, height 10.9 mm; sapphire crystal; transparent case back
Band: reptile skin, folding clasp
Remarks: aventurine dial
Price: $74,500

CODE 11.59 Minute Repeater Supersonnerie
Reference number: 26395BC.OO.D321CR.01
Movement: manually wound, AP Caliber 2953; ø 30 mm, height 6 mm; 32 jewels; 21,600 vph; movement finely finished; 72-hour power reserve
Functions: hours, minutes, subsidiary seconds; minute repeater
Case: white gold, ø 41 mm, height 13.5 mm; sapphire crystal
Band: reptile skin, folding clasp
Remarks: volume amplifier for minute repeater using special resonance board; enamel dial
Price: on request

CODE 11.59 Flying Tourbillon
Reference number: 26396BC.OO.D321CR.01
Movement: automatic, AP Caliber 2950; ø 31.5 mm, height 6.24 mm; 27 jewels; 21,600 vph; flying 1-minute tourbillon; skeletonized gold rotor, finely finished movement; 65-hour power reserve
Functions: hours, minutes
Case: white gold, ø 41 mm, height 11.8 mm; sapphire crystal; transparent case back; water-resistant to 3 atm
Band: reptile skin, folding clasp
Price: on request

CODE 11.59 Tourbillon Openworked
Reference number: 26600OR.OO.D002CR.01
Movement: manually wound, AP Caliber 2948; ø 32.25 mm, height 4.97 mm; 19 jewels; 21,600 vph; flying 1-minute tourbillon; fully skeletonized movement; 80-hour power reserve
Functions: hours, minutes
Case: rose gold, ø 41 mm, height 10.7 mm; sapphire crystal; transparent case back; water-resistant to 3 atm
Band: reptile skin, folding clasp
Price: on request

Royal Oak Chronograph
Reference number: 26315OR.OO.1256OR.01
Movement: automatic, AP Caliber 2385; ø 26.2 mm, height 5.5 mm; 37 jewels; 21,600 vph; completely hand-decorated movement; 40-hour power reserve
Functions: hours, minutes, subsidiary seconds; chronograph; date
Case: rose gold, ø 38 mm, height 11 mm; bezel screwed to case back with 8 white gold screws; sapphire crystal; screw-in crown and pushers; water-resistant to 5 atm
Band: rose gold, folding clasp
Price: $52,700

AUDEMARS PIGUET

Royal Oak Chronograph
Reference number: 26315ST.OO.1256ST.01
Movement: automatic, AP Caliber 2385; ø 26.2 mm, height 5.5 mm; 37 jewels; 21,600 vph; hand-decorated movement; 40-hour power reserve
Functions: hours, minutes, subsidiary seconds; chronograph; date
Case: stainless steel, ø 38 mm, height 11 mm; bezel screwed to case back with 8 white gold screws; sapphire crystal; screw-in crown and pushers; water-resistant to 5 atm
Band: stainless steel, folding clasp
Price: $23,800

Royal Oak Chronograph
Reference number: 26315ST.OO.1256ST.02
Movement: automatic, AP Caliber 2385; ø 26.2 mm, height 5.5 mm; 37 jewels; 21,600 vph; hand-decorated movement; 40-hour power reserve
Functions: hours, minutes, subsidiary seconds; chronograph; date
Case: stainless steel, ø 38 mm, height 11 mm; bezel screwed to case back with 8 white gold screws; sapphire crystal; screw-in crown and pushers; water-resistant to 5 atm
Band: stainless steel, folding clasp
Price: $23,800

Royal Oak Chronograph
Reference number: 26331ST.OO.1220ST.01
Movement: automatic, AP Caliber 2385; ø 26.2 mm, height 5.5 mm; 37 jewels; 21,600 vph; hand-decorated movement; 40-hour power reserve
Functions: hours, minutes, subsidiary seconds; chronograph; date
Case: stainless steel, ø 41 mm, height 11 mm; bezel screwed to case back with 8 white gold screws; sapphire crystal; screw-in crown and pusher; water-resistant to 5 atm
Band: stainless steel, folding clasp
Price: $24,300

Royal Oak
Reference number: 15500ST.OO.1220ST.01
Movement: automatic, AP Caliber 4302; ø 32 mm, height 4.8 mm; 32 jewels; 28,800 vph; movement finely finished; 70-hour power reserve
Functions: hours, minutes, sweep seconds; date
Case: stainless steel, ø 41 mm, height 10.4 mm; bezel screwed to case back with 8 white gold screws; sapphire crystal; water-resistant to 5 atm
Band: stainless steel, folding clasp
Price: $19,200

Royal Oak
Reference number: 15500OR.OO.1220OR.01
Movement: automatic, AP Caliber 4302; ø 32 mm, height 4.8 mm; 32 jewels; 28,800 vph; movement finely finished; 70-hour power reserve
Functions: hours, minutes, sweep seconds; date
Case: rose gold, ø 41 mm, height 10.4 mm; bezel screwed to case back with 8 white gold screws; sapphire crystal; transparent case back; water-resistant to 5 atm
Band: rose gold, folding clasp
Price: $50,500

Royal Oak "Jumbo" Extra-Thin
Reference number: 15202BA.OO.1240BA.02
Movement: automatic, AP Caliber 2121; ø 28.4 mm, height 3.05 mm; 36 jewels; 19,800 vph; movement finely finished by hand; 40-hour power reserve
Functions: hours, minutes; date
Case: yellow gold, ø 39 mm, height 8.1 mm; bezel screwed to case back with 8 white gold screws; sapphire crystal; water-resistant to 5 atm
Band: yellow gold, folding clasp
Price: $55,400
Variations: stainless steel; white gold

AUDEMARS PIGUET

Royal Oak Offshore Chronograph

Reference number: 26401RO.OO.A087CA.01
Movement: automatic, AP Caliber 3126/3840; ø 29.92 mm, height 7.16 mm; 59 jewels; 21,600 vph; 50-hour power reserve
Functions: hours, minutes, subsidiary seconds; chronograph; date
Case: rose gold, ø 44 mm, height 14.4 mm; ceramic bezel screwed to case back with 8 white gold screws; sapphire crystal; transparent case back; ceramic crown and pusher, screw-in crown; water-resistant to 10 atm
Band: rubber, buckle
Price: $48,300
Variations: various bands, dials, and cases

Royal Oak Offshore Chronograph

Reference number: 26400SO.OO.A335CA.01
Movement: automatic, AP Caliber 3126/3840; ø 29.92 mm, height 7.16 mm; 59 jewels; 21,600 vph; 50-hour power reserve
Functions: hours, minutes, subsidiary seconds; chronograph; date
Case: stainless steel, ø 44 mm, height 14.4 mm; ceramic bezel screwed to case back with 8 white gold screws; sapphire crystal; transparent case back; ceramic crown and pusher, screw-in crown; water-resistant to 10 atm
Band: rubber, buckle
Price: $32,200
Variations: various bands, dials, and cases

Royal Oak Offshore Chronograph

Reference number: 26480TI.OO.A027CA.01
Movement: automatic, AP Caliber 2385; ø 26.2 mm, height 5.5 mm; 37 jewels; 21,600 vph; hand-decorated movement; 40-hour power reserve
Functions: hours, minutes, subsidiary seconds; chronograph; date
Case: titanium, ø 42 mm, height 12.8 mm; bezel screwed to case back with 8 white gold screws; sapphire crystal; water-resistant to 10 atm
Band: rubber, buckle
Remarks: comes with white rubber band
Price: $26,800

Royal Oak Concept Flying Tourbillon GMT

Reference number: 26589IO.OO.D002CA.01
Movement: manually wound, Audemars Piguet Caliber 2954; ø 35.6 mm, height 9.9 mm; 24 jewels; 21,600 vph; flying 1-minute tourbillon; movement finely finished by hand; 237-hour power reserve
Functions: hours, minutes; additional 24-hour display (2nd time zone), crown position indicator for function changes
Case: titanium, ø 44 mm, height 16.1 mm; ceramic bezel screwed to case back with 8 white gold screws; sapphire crystal; transparent case back; ceramic crown and pushers; water-resistant to 10 atm
Band: rubber, folding clasp
Price: on request

Millenary Frosted Gold Opal Dial

Reference number: 77244OR.GG.1272OR.01
Movement: manually wound, AP Caliber 5201; 32.74 × 28.59 mm, height 4.16 mm; 19 jewels; 21,600 vph; inverted movement design with balance and escapement on dial side; 49-hour power reserve
Functions: hours, minutes, subsidiary seconds
Case: rose gold, 39.5 × 35.4 mm; bezel and lugs of "frosted gold"; sapphire crystal; transparent case back
Band: rose gold "Polish" mesh bracelet, folding clasp
Remarks: mother-of-pearl dials
Price: $53,000

Ladies' Millenary

Reference number: 77247BC.ZZ.1272BC.01
Movement: manually wound, AP Caliber 5201; 32.74 × 28.59 mm, height 4.16 mm; 19 jewels; 21,600 vph; inverted movement design with balance and escapement on dial side; 49-hour power reserve
Functions: hours, minutes, subsidiary seconds
Case: white gold, 39.5 × 35.4 mm; bezel and lugs of "frosted gold"; sapphire crystal; transparent case back
Band: rose gold "Polish" mesh bracelet, folding clasp
Remarks: mother-of-pearl dials
Price: $53,000

AUDEMARS PIGUET

Caliber 4302

Automatic; bidirectionally winding gold rotor; single spring barrel, 70-hour power reserve
Functions: hours, minutes, sweep seconds; date
Diameter: 32 mm
Height: 4.8 mm
Jewels: 32
Balance: with variable inertia
Frequency: 28,800 vph
Remarks: beveled and polished steel parts, plate with perlage, bridges with côtes de Genève; 257 parts

Caliber 4401

Automatic; column wheel control of chronograph functions; skeletonized gold rotor; single spring barrel, 70-hour power reserve
Functions: hours, minutes, subsidiary seconds; flyback chronograph; date
Diameter: 32 mm
Height: 6.8 mm
Jewels: 40
Balance: with variable inertia
Frequency: 28,800 vph
Remarks: beveled and polished steel parts, plate with perlage, bridges with côtes de Genève; 367 parts

Caliber 2950

Automatic; flying 1-minute tourbillon; skeletonized rotor; single spring barrel, 65-hour power reserve
Functions: hours, minutes
Diameter: 31.5 mm
Height: 6.24 mm
Jewels: 27
Frequency: 21,600 vph
Remarks: 270 parts

Caliber 5134

Automatic; flying spring barrel; 40-hour power reserve
Functions: hours, minutes; perpetual calendar with date, weekday, calendar week, month, moon phase, leap year
Diameter: 29 mm
Height: 4.31 mm
Jewels: 38
Balance: with variable inertia
Frequency: 19,800 vph
Balance spring: flat hairspring
Remarks: hand-decorated movement; gold rotor; 374 parts

Caliber 2953

Manually wound; single spring barrel, 72-hour power reserve
Functions: hours, minutes, subsidiary seconds; minute repeater
Diameter: 30 mm
Height: 6 mm
Jewels: 32
Balance: with variable inertia
Frequency: 21,600 vph
Remarks: beveled and polished steel parts, plate with perlage, bridges with côtes de Genève; 362 parts

Caliber 2948

Manually wound; flying 1-minute tourbillon; skeletonized movement; single spring barrel, 80-hour power reserve
Functions: hours, minutes
Diameter: 32.25 mm
Height: 4.97 mm
Jewels: 19
Frequency: 21,600 vph
Remarks: black-coated structural parts; 196 parts

AVERITAS

AVeritas Watches
105 McLaughlin Road
Suite F
Rochester, NY 14615

Tel.:
585-662-8225

E-mail:
info@AVeritas.com

Website:
www.AVeritas.com

Founded:
2006

Number of employees:
3

Annual production:
150–200

Distribution:
direct to consumer

Most important collections/price range:
Primus / $1,489; Demetior / $3,950; Paerio / $7,995

J. Michael Brady's interest in watches was sparked by his grandfather's love of mechanical watches. His first career move, however, was engineering and the establishment of a manufacturing company specializing in optical components with micron tolerances. The watches came in 2006, when he created custom timepieces on commissions for close friends. These bespoke watches were powered by traditional mechanical movements supplied by various Swiss manufacturers.

Fast-forward a few years, and Brady decided to formally launch the AVeritas brand he had been considering for quite some time. In 2009, he started making his AVeritas cases using the machines he already owned, with the first fruits of his labors being the Aurora and Primus lines. These were powered by a traditionally finished manually wound Swiss movement placed inside a coin-edge case. These two original designs show just how different the same case can look when framing different dials.

Expanding beyond the original cast of two, Brady has since added another six variations of his original idea. These timepieces all combine traditional forms of watchmaking with bold avant-garde dial designs that appear inspired from nature itself. There are the "thunderbolts" on the Regulator that flash away from the center of the dial, and the swirling pattern on the Lunar Date, which contrasts with old-fashioned cathedral hands. The central dial of the Demetrior, on the other hand, is animated by a blend of two different patterns, one square and rational, like a parquet floor, the other more flowing. At any rate, each watch Brady produces is surprising in its own way. Not being bound to a specific DNA gives Brady a great deal of liberty to create. The watches are all powered by robust ETA movements.

Demetior
Movement: automatic, modified ETA/Valjoux 7750; ø 30 mm, height 9.2 mm; 25 jewels; 28,800 vph; finely finished with perlage, côtes de Genève, blued screws, custom rotor; 44-hour power reserve
Functions: hours, minutes, subsidiary seconds; 12-hour totalizer; analog date
Case: stainless steel case, crown, and pushers, ø 44 mm at bezel, height 15.1 mm; coin-edge bezel; sapphire crystal; transparent case back; water-resistant to 5 atm
Band: leather, buckle
Price: $3,950; limited to 90 pieces
Variations: various color options

Lunar Date
Movement: automatic, modified ETA Caliber 2892 base; ø 25.6 mm, height 4.1 mm; 26 jewels; 28,800 vph; 42-hour power reserve
Functions: hours, minutes, seconds; moon phase; analog date
Case: stainless steel, ø 42 mm at bezel, height 13 mm; coin-edge bezel; sapphire crystal; transparent case back; water-resistant to 5 atm
Band: leather, buckle
Price: $4,495; limited to 90 pieces

Regulator
Movement: manually wound, modified ETA Caliber 6498; ø 37.2 mm, height 4.5 mm; 17 jewels; 18,000 vph; finely finished movement with côtes de Genève and blued screws; 53-hour power reserve
Functions: hours, minutes, seconds in regulator format
Case: stainless steel, ø 44 mm, height 12.5 mm; sapphire crystal; transparent case back; water-resistant to 5 atm
Remarks: dial decorated with thunderbolt motif
Band: leather, buckle
Price: $4,479

AZIMUTH

Creativity can take on all forms and accept all forms as well. This appears to be the philosophy behind Azimuth, an independent watch brand that has sprouted an eclectic and surprising bouquet of watch designs. For the company, the path is by no means well-beaten: Azimuth always guarantees a raised eyebrow with avant-garde designs for luxury timepieces.

The company has produced several iconic models, like the Mr. Roboto, which looks, indeed, like a robot and is perfectly in tune with our times. Then there is the self-explanatory Spaceship series and the Automobile series, like the TT and GT, which all enjoy cult status. The Gran Turismo takes its cue from the racetracks of a generation ago.

For 2019, Azimuth once again started pushing the envelope, always a good idea for an unconventional company. It dipped into its Spaceship collection to create the Predator 2.0, which might have been the product of sci-fi writers and scientists dreaming of space travel. Cyber-robotics and interplanetary exploration are currently woven into the fabric of everyday life; the idea of centuries-old horological traditions being progressive and disruptive is now embraced by legions of watch lovers all over the world.

The Predator 2.0 is powered by a hand-wound caliber. The watch's bridges are crafted in aluminum, which makes the movement extra-light. "The Predator 2.0 is yet another expression of our desire to always be bold and adventurous in the field of mechanical watchmaking. The watch's inspiration, design and technical qualities are driven by our never-ending quest in the field of progressive horology," says Azimuth's CEO and technical director, Giuseppe Picchi.

Azimuth Watch Co. Sàrl
Rue des Draizes no. 5
CH-2000 Neuchâtel
Switzerland

Tel.:
+41-79-765-1466

E-mail:
gpi@azimuthwatch.com
sales@azimuthwatch.com

Website:
www.azimuthwatch.com

Founded:
2003

Number of employees:
6

U.S. distributor:
About Time Luxury Group
210 Bellevue Avenue
Newport, RI 02840
401-952-4684

Most important collection/price range:
SP-1 with a wide range of different models / from $4,850

SP-1 Gran Turismo
Reference number: SP.SS.GT.L003
Movement: automatic winding, ETA 2671; 28,800 vph; ø 17.2 mm, height 4.80 mm
Functions: hours, minutes, seconds
Case: stainless steel with black PVD treatment, 50 × 45 mm; water-resistant to 3 atm
Band: calfskin strap, folding clasp
Price: $4,850; limited to 100 pieces
Variations: top in high-gloss polished stainless steel, gold PVD coating or urban camouflage PVD coating

SP-1 Gran Turismo Pavé Diamonds
Reference number: SP.SS.GT.N006
Movement: automatic winding, ETA 2671; 28,800 vph; ø 17.2 mm, height 4.80 mm
Functions: hours, minutes, seconds
Case: stainless steel, 50 × 45 mm; bezel set with diamonds; water-resistant to 3 atm
Band: calfskin strap, folding clasp
Remarks: available in full pavé setting
Price: $26,000

SP-1 Twin Turbo
Reference number: SP.SS.TT.N002
Movement: manual winding, ETA 2512-1; 21,600 vph; ø 17.2 mm, height 2.85 mm
Functions: hours, minutes, 2 time zones
Case: stainless steel and aluminum, 51 × 50 mm; water-resistant to 3 atm
Band: calfskin strap, folding clasp
Remarks: 2 vintage movements
Price: $6,000; limited to 88 pieces
Variations: top hood in silver, yellow, red (red limited to 50 pieces)

AZIMUTH

SP-1 Predator 2.0
Reference number: SP.Ti.PR.N001
Movement: manual winding, AZM 769 modified and skeletonized, 21,600 vph; ø 36.6 mm, height 4.5 mm
Functions: jumping hours, minutes, seconds
Case: titanium and stainless steel, diameter 44 mm, domed sapphire crystal; water-resistant to 3 atm
Band: rubber, folding clasp
Remarks: 3D titanium minute hand
Price: $5,700
Variations: case in bronze

SP-1 King Casino
Reference number: SP.KC.SS.N001
Movement: automatic, in-house modified (base ETA), 21,600 vph; ø 25.6 mm, height 6.0 mm
Functions: casino game function via crown; hours, minutes, seconds
Case: stainless steel, 45 × 45 mm, domed sapphire crystal; water-resistant to 3 atm
Band: calfskin, folding clasp
Remarks: roulette and baccarat game functions
Price: $3,650
Variations: chocolate color–plated or yellow gold–plated

SP-1 Crazy Rider
Reference number: SP.SS.CR.N004
Movement: automatic, in-house modified, 28,800 vph; ø 47.7 mm, height 4.35 mm
Functions: 24-hour chain drive hour system, minutes
Case: stainless steel with PVD treatment, titanium bezel with black PVD treatment, 55 × 36 mm, sapphire crystal; water-resistant to 3 atm
Band: calfskin, folding clasp
Price: $5,250

SP-1 Mr. Roboto Bronzo
Reference number: SP.BR.MRB.L001
Movement: automatic, in-house modified, 28,800 vph; ø 32.5 mm, height 6.7 mm
Functions: regulator hours, retrograde minutes, GMT
Case: bronze, 43 mm × 50 mm, sapphire crystal; water-resistant to 3 atm
Band: calfskin, bronze tang buckle
Price: $7,000; limited to 100 pieces

SP-1 Mr. Roboto R2
Reference number: SP.SS.ROT.N001
Movement: automatic, in-house modified, sapphire rotor, 28,800 vph; ø 32.5 mm, height 6.7 mm
Functions: regulator hours, retrograde minutes, GMT
Case: stainless steel, 47 × 55 mm, sapphire crystal; water-resistant to 3 atm
Band: calfskin, folding clasp
Price: $6,000
Variations: mid-case in titanium with blue PVD treatment

SP-1 Twin Barrel Tourbillon
Reference number: SP.TB.TI.L001
Movement: manual winding tourbillon, in-house modified, 5-day power reserve, twin barrels, 28,800 vph; 36.3 × 32.0 mm, height 6.4 mm
Functions: jumping hours, minutes, specially modified twin-disk jumping hour system on 3D minute hand
Case: titanium with carbon fiber side inserts, 45 × 50 mm, height 18 mm; domed sapphire crystal; water-resistant to 5 atm
Band: calfskin, folding clasp
Price: $89,000; limited to 25 pieces

BALL WATCH CO.

Engineer, Fireman, Trainmaster, Conductor . . . these names for the Ball Watch Co. collections trace back to the company's origins and evoke the glorious age when trains puffing smoke and steam crisscrossed America. Back then, the pocket watch was a necessity to maintain precise rail schedules. By 1893, many companies had adopted the General Railroads Timepiece Standards, which included such norms as regulation in at least five positions, precision to within thirty seconds per week, Breguet balance springs, and so on. One of the chief players in developing the standards was Webster Clay Ball. This farmboy-turned-watchmaker from Fredericktown, Ohio, decided to leave the homestead for a more lucrative occupation. He apprenticed as a watchmaker, became a salesperson for Dueber watch cases, and finally opened the Webb C. Ball Company in Cleveland. In 1891, he added the position of chief inspector of the Lake Shore Lines to his CV. When a hogshead's watch stopped for a few minutes, resulting in a lethal crash near Kipton, Ohio, Ball decided to establish quality benchmarks for watch manufacturing that included amagnetic technology. He also set up an inspection system for the timepieces.

Today, Ball Watch Co. has maintained its lineage, although now producing in Switzerland. These rugged, durable watches aim to be "accurate in adverse conditions," so the company tagline says—and at a very good price. Functionality remains a top priority, so Ball will go to special lengths to work special technologies into its timepieces. Ball has developed special oils for cold temperatures, for instance. And it is one of few brands to use tritium gas tubes to light up dials, hands, and markers. For those who need to read the time accurately in dark places—divers, pilots, commandos, hunters, etc.—this is essential.

Ball Watch Company SA
Rue du Châtelot 21
CH-2300 La Chaux-de-Fonds
Switzerland

Tel.:
0041-32-724-53-00

E-mail:
info@ballwatch.ch

Website:
www.ballwatch.com
shop.ballwatch.ch

Founded:
1891

U.S. distributor:
Ball Watch USA:
888-660-0691

Most important collections/price range:
Engineer, Fireman, Trainmaster / $1,300 to $6,500

Engineer Hydrocarbon Original

Reference number: DM2118B-SCJ-BK
Movement: automatic, Ball Caliber RR1102-CSL; ø 25.6 mm, height 5.05 mm; 25 or 26 jewels; 28,800 vph; 38-hour power reserve; COSC-certified chronometer; SpringLOCK® antishock system
Functions: hours, minutes, sweep seconds; day, date
Case: stainless steel, ø 40 mm, height 14.55 mm; sapphire unidirectional bezel with micro gas tubes; sapphire crystal; crown protection system; water-resistant to 20 atm
Band: stainless steel, folding buckle and extension
Remarks: micro gas tube illumination; amagnetic
Price: $3,199

Engineer Hydrocarbon AeroGMT II

Reference number: DG2018C-S3C-BK
Movement: automatic, Ball Caliber RR1201-C; ø 25.6 mm, height 4.1 mm; 21 jewels; 28,800 vph; 42-hour power reserve; COSC-certified chronometer
Functions: hours, minutes, sweep seconds; date; 2nd time zone indication
Case: stainless steel, ø 42 mm, height 13.85 mm; sapphire bidirectional bezel with micro gas tube illumination; sapphire crystal; crown protection system; water-resistant to 10 atm
Band: stainless steel, folding buckle and extension
Remarks: shock-resistant; amagnetic
Price: $3,499
Variations: rubber strap

Engineer Hydrocarbon Submarine Warfare Chronograph

Reference number: DC2276A-SJ-BK
Movement: automatic, Ball Caliber RR1402; ø 30 mm, height 7.9 mm; 25 jewels; 28,800 vph; 48-hour power reserve
Functions: hours, minutes, subsidiary seconds; day, date; 12-hour chronograph
Case: titanium, ø 42 mm, height 17.9 mm; stainless steel unidirectional bezel; sapphire crystal; crown protection system; water-resistant to 30 atm
Band: tapered titanium and stainless steel, folding buckle and extension
Remarks: micro gas tube illumination; amagnetic
Price: $3,199; **Variations:** ceramic bezel; stainless steel case; stainless steel bracelet; rubber strap

BALL WATCH CO.

Engineer Hydrocarbon NEDU
Reference number: DC3026A-SC-BK
Movement: automatic, Ball Caliber RR1402-C; ø 30 mm, height 7.9 mm; 25 jewels; 28,800 vph; 48-hour power reserve; COSC-certified chronometer
Functions: hours, minutes, subsidiary seconds; day, date; 12-hour chronograph operable underwater
Case: stainless steel, ø 42 mm, height 17.30 mm; patented helium system; ceramic unidirectional bezel; sapphire crystal; crown protection system; water-resistant to 60 atm
Band: titanium/stainless steel, folding buckle and extension
Remarks: micro gas tube illumination; amagnetic
Price: $5,099
Variations: blue dial; rubber strap

Engineer Master II Diver
Reference number: DM3020A-SAJ-BK
Movement: automatic, Ball Caliber RR1102; ø 25.6 mm, height 5.05 mm; 25 or 26 jewels; 28,800 vph; 38-hour power reserve
Functions: hours, minutes, sweep seconds; day, date
Case: stainless steel, ø 42 mm, height 14.55 mm; inner bezel with micro gas tube illumination; sapphire crystal; screw-in crown; water-resistant to 30 atm
Band: stainless steel, folding buckle
Remarks: micro gas tube illumination; amagnetic
Price: $2,499
Variations: rubber strap

Engineer Master II Skindiver Heritage
Reference number: DM3208C-SC-BK
Movement: automatic, Ball Caliber RR1102-C; ø 25.6 mm, height 5.05 mm; 25 or 26 jewels; 28,800 vph; 38-hour power reserve; COSC-certified chronometer
Functions: hours, minutes, sweep seconds; date
Case: stainless steel, ø 41 mm, height 14.9 mm; unidirectional bezel; mu-metal shield; sapphire crystal; screw-in crown; water-resistant to 10 atm
Band: stainless steel, folding buckle
Remarks: micro gas tube illumination; amagnetic
Price: $2,799

Engineer Master II Aviator
Reference number: NM1080C-L14A-BK
Movement: automatic, Ball Caliber RR1102; ø 25.6 mm, height 5.05 mm; 25 or 26 jewels; 28,800 vph; 38-hour power reserve
Functions: hours, minutes, sweep seconds; day, date
Case: stainless steel, ø 46 mm, height 11.55 mm; mu-metal shield; antireflective convex sapphire crystal; screw-in crown; water-resistant to 10 atm
Band: calfskin, standard buckle
Remarks: micro gas tube illumination; amagnetic
Price: $1,999
Variations: stainless steel bracelet; rubber strap

Engineer II Moon Phase
Reference number: NM2282C-LLJ-BK
Movement: automatic, Ball Caliber RR1801; ø 25.6 mm, height 5.05 mm; 25 jewels; 28,800 vph; 42-hour power reserve
Functions: hours, minutes, sweep seconds; date, moon phase
Case: stainless steel, ø 41 mm; sapphire crystal; screw-in crown; water-resistant to 10 atm; Amortiser® antishock system
Band: reptile skin strap, standard buckle
Remarks: micro gas tube illumination; luminous moon phase indication; amagnetic
Price: $1,799
Variations: stainless steel bracelet; blue, gray dial

Engineer II Magneto S
Reference number: NM3022C-N1CJ-BK
Movement: automatic, Ball Caliber RR1103-CSL; ø 25.6 mm, height 4.6 mm; 25 or 26 jewels; 28,800 vph; 38-hour power reserve; COSC-certified chronometer; SpringLOCK® antishock system
Functions: hours, minutes, sweep seconds; date
Case: stainless steel, ø 42 mm, height 12.9 mm; A-PROOF® amagnetic system; sapphire crystal; screw-in crown; transparent case back; water-resistant to 10 atm
Band: cordura fabrics, standard buckle
Remarks: micro gas tube illumination
Price: $3,399

BALL WATCH CO.

Engineer III Carbolight
Reference number: NM3028C-P1CJ-BK
Movement: automatic, Ball Caliber RR1103-C; ø 25.6 mm, height 4.6 mm; 25 or 26 jewels; 28,800 vph; 38-hour power reserve; COSC-certified chronometer
Functions: hours, minutes, sweep seconds; magnified date
Case: Mu-metal and carbide composite, ø 43 mm, height 13 mm; sapphire crystal; screw-in crown; water-resistant to 10 atm
Band: rubber strap, standard buckle
Remarks: micro gas tube illumination; amagnetic
Price: $2,199
Variations: blue dial

Engineer III Pioneer
Reference number: NM2026C-S15CJ-BK
Movement: automatic, Ball Caliber RR1103-C; ø 25.6 mm, height 4.6 mm; 25 or 26 jewels; 28,800 vph; 38-hour power reserve; COSC-certified chronometer
Functions: hours, minutes, sweep seconds; magnified date
Case: 904L stainless steel, ø 40 mm, height 12.45 mm; sapphire crystal; screw-in crown; water-resistant to 10 atm
Band: 904L stainless steel, folding buckle
Remarks: micro gas tube illumination; amagnetic
Price: $1,899
Variations: blue dial

Trainmaster Eternity
Reference number: NM2080D-S1J-BE
Movement: automatic, Ball Caliber RR1102; ø 25.6 mm, height 5.05 mm; 25 or 26 jewels; 28,800 vph; 38-hour power reserve
Functions: hours, minutes, sweep seconds; day, date
Case: stainless steel, ø 39.5 mm, height 11.8 mm; sapphire crystal; screw-in crown; transparent case back; water-resistant to 3 atm
Band: stainless steel bracelet, folding buckle
Remarks: micro gas tube illumination
Price: $2,299
Variations: black dial; reptile skin strap

Trainmaster Endeavour Chronometer
Reference number: NM3288D-LL2CJ-WH
Movement: automatic, Ball Caliber RR1101-C; ø 25.6 mm, height 3.6 mm; 21 jewels; 28,800 vph; 42-hour power reserve; COSC-certified chronometer
Functions: hours, minutes, sweep seconds; date
Case: stainless steel, ø 40 mm, height 10.3 mm; sapphire crystal; water-resistant to 5 atm
Band: reptile skin strap, folding buckle
Remarks: micro gas tube illumination; amagnetic
Price: $2,149; limited to 250 pieces
Variations: stainless steel bracelet; calfskin strap

Trainmaster Manufacture 80 Hours
Reference number: NM3280D-S1CJ-BK
Movement: automatic, Ball Caliber RRM7309-C; ø 34.24 mm, height 5.16 mm; 25 jewels; 28,800 vph; 80-hour power reserve; COSC-certified chronometer
Functions: hours, minutes, sweep seconds; date
Case: stainless steel, ø 40 mm, height 12.25 mm; sapphire crystal; transparent case back; screw-in crown; water-resistant to 5 atm
Band: stainless steel bracelet, folding buckle
Remarks: micro gas tube illumination; amagnetic
Price: $2,799

Trainmaster Worldtime
Reference number: GM2020D-S1CJ-SL
Movement: automatic, Ball Caliber RR1501-C; ø 31.4 mm, height 6.95 mm; 25 jewels; 28,800 vph; 38-hour power reserve; COSC-certified chronometer
Functions: hours, minutes, sweep seconds; day, date; world time display
Case: stainless steel, ø 41 mm, height 12.5 mm; sapphire crystal; transparent case back; screw-in crown; water-resistant to 5 atm
Band: stainless steel bracelet, folding buckle
Remarks: micro gas tube illumination; amagnetic
Price: $2,699
Variations: black dial; reptile skin strap

BALL WATCH CO.

Trainmaster Worldtime Chronograph
Reference number: CM2052D-LL1J-SLBE
Movement: automatic, Ball Caliber RR1502; ø 30 mm, height 7.9 mm; 25 jewels; 28,800 vph; 48-hour power reserve
Functions: hours, minutes, subsidiary seconds; day, date; chronograph with accumulated measurement up to 12 hours; world time display
Case: stainless steel, ø 42 mm, height 13.7 mm; sapphire crystal; transparent case back; screw-in crown; water-resistant to 5 atm
Band: reptile skin strap, standard buckle
Remarks: micro gas tube illumination
Price: $4,399; **Variations:** black with red dial, silver with red dial; stainless steel bracelet

Fireman Enterprise
Reference number: NM2188C-S5J-BK
Movement: automatic, Ball Caliber RR1103; ø 25.6 mm, height 4.6 mm; 25 or 26 jewels; 28,800 vph; 38-hour power reserve
Functions: hours, minutes, sweep seconds; magnified date
Case: stainless steel, ø 40 mm, height 11.3 mm; sapphire crystal; screw-in crown; water-resistant to 10 atm
Band: stainless steel bracelet, folding buckle
Remarks: micro gas tube illumination
Price: $1,199
Variations: white dial; NATO strap

Fireman NECC
Reference number: DM3090A-P5J-BK
Movement: automatic, Ball Caliber RR1103; ø 25.6 mm, height 4.6 mm; 25 or 26 jewels; 28,800 vph; 38-hour power reserve
Functions: hours, minutes, sweep seconds; magnified date
Case: stainless steel with TiC titanium carbide coating, ø 42 mm, height 13.2 mm; stainless steel carbide rotating bezel; sapphire crystal; transparent case back; screw-in crown; water-resistant to 30 atm
Band: rubber strap, standard buckle
Remarks: micro gas tube illumination; amagnetic
Price: $1,599
Variations: white or blue dial; stainless steel case; stainless steel bracelet

Fireman Victory
Reference number: NM2098C-S5J-SL
Movement: automatic, Ball Caliber RR1103; ø 25.6 mm, height 4.6 mm; 25 or 26 jewels; 28,800 vph; 38-hour power reserve
Functions: hours, minutes, sweep seconds; date
Case: stainless steel, ø 40 mm, height 11.6 mm; sapphire crystal; screw-in crown; water-resistant to 10 atm
Band: stainless steel bracelet, folding buckle
Remarks: micro gas tube illumination
Price: $1,499
Variations: black or blue dial; calfskin

Engineer III Bronze
Reference number: NM2186C-L3J-BK
Movement: automatic, Ball Caliber RR1102-SL; ø 25.6 mm, height 5.05 mm; 25 or 26 jewels; 28,800 vph; 38-hour power reserve; SpringLOCK® antishock system
Functions: hours, minutes, sweep seconds; day, date
Case: bronze, ø 43 mm, height 13.45 mm; mu-metal shield; sapphire crystal; screw-in crown; water-resistant to 10 atm; Amortiser® antishock system
Band: calfskin, standard buckle
Remarks: micro gas tube illumination; amagnetic
Price: $2,300

Engineer M Marvelight
Reference number: NM2128C-S1C-BE
Movement: automatic, Ball Caliber RRM7309-C; ø 34.24 mm, height 5.16 mm; 25 jewels; 28,800 vph; 80-hour power reserve; COSC-certified chronometer
Functions: hours, minutes, sweep seconds; date
Case: stainless steel, ø 43 mm, height 12.85 mm; sapphire crystal; transparent case back; screw-in crown; water-resistant to 10 atm; Amortiser® antishock system
Band: stainless steel bracelet, folding buckle
Remarks: micro gas tube illumination; amagnetic
Price: $2,499
Variations: 40-mm case; black or gray dial; calfskin strap

BAUME & MERCIER

Baume & Mercier, a company founded in 1830, has staked a claim on the market by its ability to keep a finger on the pulse of stylish, urban fashionistas, who are looking for affordable yet remarkable timepieces. Since the early 2000s, it has managed to create a number of noteworthy—and often copied—classics, like the Riviera and the Catwalk. In recent years, the company has explored the men's market with the Classima Executives line and models like the Clifton Club Indian family, which not only appealed to the consumer's inner motorcyclist, but also harked back to the watchmaking glory of days gone by, when Baume & Mercier was celebrated as a chronograph specialist.

Being a part of the Richemont Group has boosted the brand's technical value. After four years of development in a close cooperation with ValFleurier, the Group's movement manufacturer, and the RIMS research and innovation team, Baume & Mercier released its first in-house *manufacture* movement, the Baumatic Caliber BM12-1975A. In 2019, the brand presented a new version of the caliber, numbered BM13-1975A. This one features a conventional hairspring that is protected from magnetic fields, since, for patent reasons, the company is not allowed to use silicon. It still boasts its five-day power reserve and accuracy of just –4/+6 seconds per day for the COSC-certified models. Also noteworthy is the fact that the movement only needs servicing every seven years, which compares favorably to the three to five years required by classic mechanical watches.

The Baume & Mercier BM13 caliber drives five of the new Clifton models, including one with a rose gold case and a white dial. The stainless steel models of the collection do not have COSC certification.

Baume & Mercier continues to produce models for women, of course, including eight new ones in stainless steel in the Classima Lady line. The range is wide, with new dials and case sizes and a choice of quartz or automatic movements. Each one delivers classic functions such as hours, minutes, and date. They come on a stainless steel bracelet and a triple folding clasp with safety pushers. Two of the high-end models come with a mother-of-pearl dial and a case set with diamonds.

Baume & Mercier
Rue André de Garrini 4
CH-1217 Meyrin
Switzerland

Tel.:
+41-22-580-2948

Website:
www.baume-et-mercier.com

Founded:
1830

Annual production:
100,000 (estimated)

U.S. distributor:
Baume & Mercier
Richemont North America
New York, NY 10022
800-637-2437

Most important collections/price range:
Clifton (men) / $2,200 to $24,500; Classima (men and women) / $990 to $5,950; Hampton (men and women) / $2,500 to $15,000; Linea (women) / $1,950 to $15,750; Promesse (women) / $2,100 to $4,850

Clifton Club
Reference number: 10486
Movement: automatic, ETA Caliber 2893-2; ø 25.6 mm, height 4.1 mm; 21 jewels; 28,800 vph; 42-hour power reserve
Functions: hours, minutes, sweep seconds; additional 24-hour display (2nd time zone); date
Case: stainless steel, ø 42 mm, height 10.6 mm; nonrotating bezel, with 0-24 scale; sapphire crystal; screw-in crown; water-resistant to 10 atm
Band: calfskin, triple folding clasp
Price: $2,200

Clifton Baumatic
Reference number: 10467
Movement: automatic, Caliber Baumatic BM13.1975A COSC; 21 jewels; 28,800 vph; silicon escapement; balance with variable inertia; 120-hour power reserve
Functions: hours, minutes, sweep seconds; date
Case: stainless steel, ø 40 mm, height 11.1 mm; sapphire crystal; transparent case back; water-resistant to 5 atm
Band: reptile skin, buckle
Price: $2,990

Clifton Club Automatic Bronze
Reference number: 10503
Movement: automatic, ETA Caliber 2892-A2; 21 jewels; 28,800 vph; 42-hour power reserve
Functions: hours, minutes, sweep seconds; date
Case: bronze, ø 42 mm, height 10.3 mm; unidirectional bezel, 0-60 scale; sapphire crystal; screw-in crown; water-resistant to 10 atm
Band: calfskin, buckle
Price: $2,790

BAUME & MERCIER

Classima Lady
Reference number: 10479
Movement: automatic, ETA Caliber 2892-A2; 21 jewels; 28,800 vph; 42-hour power reserve
Functions: hours, minutes, sweep seconds; date
Case: stainless steel, ø 31 mm, height 8.25 mm; bezel set with 60 diamonds; sapphire crystal; transparent case back; water-resistant to 5 atm
Band: stainless steel, triple folding clasp
Remarks: mother-of-pearl dial
Price: $4,150

Classima Automatic Dual Time
Reference number: 10483
Movement: automatic, ETA Caliber 2893-2; 21 jewels; 28,800 vph; 42-hour power reserve
Functions: hours, minutes, sweep seconds; additional 24-hour display (2nd time zone); date
Case: stainless steel, ø 42 mm, height 9.15 mm; sapphire crystal; transparent case back; water-resistant to 5 atm
Band: stainless steel, triple folding clasp
Price: $2,750

Classima Automatic
Reference number: 10453
Movement: automatic, Sellita Caliber SW200; 28,800 vph; 38-hour power reserve
Functions: hours, minutes, sweep seconds; date
Case: stainless steel, ø 42 mm, height 8.93 mm; sapphire crystal; water-resistant to 5 atm
Band: calfskin, buckle
Price: $1,650

Clifton Baumatic
Reference number: 10518
Movement: automatic, Caliber Baumatic BM13.1975A COSC; 21 jewels; 28,800 vph; silicon escapement; balance with variable inertia; 120-hour power reserve; COSC-certified chronometer
Functions: hours, minutes, sweep seconds; date
Case: stainless steel, ø 40 mm, height 11.1 mm; sapphire crystal; transparent case back; water-resistant to 5 atm
Band: reptile skin, buckle
Price: $2,990

Clifton Baumatic
Reference number: 10505
Movement: automatic, Caliber Baumatic BM13.1975A COSC; 21 jewels; 28,800 vph; silicon escapement; balance with variable inertia; 120-hour power reserve
Functions: hours, minutes, sweep seconds; date
Case: stainless steel, ø 40 mm, height 11.1 mm; sapphire crystal; transparent case back; water-resistant to 5 atm
Band: stainless steel, triple folding clasp
Price: $3,150

Clifton Baumatic
Reference number: 10469
Movement: automatic, Caliber Baumatic BM13.1975A COSC; height 4.2 mm; 21 jewels; 28,800 vph; silicon escapement; balance with variable inertia; 120-hour power reserve
Functions: hours, minutes, sweep seconds; date
Case: pink gold, ø 39 mm, height 10.74 mm; sapphire crystal; transparent case back; water-resistant to 5 atm
Band: reptile skin, buckle
Price: $7,200

BELL & ROSS

If there is such a class as "military chic," Bell & Ross is undoubtedly one of the leaders. The Paris-headquartered brand develops, manufactures, assembles, and regulates its timepieces in a modern factory in La Chaux-de-Fonds in the Jura mountains of Switzerland. The early models had a certain stringency that one might associate with soldierly life, but in the past years, working with outside specialists, the company has ventured into even more complicated watches such as tourbillons and wristwatches with uncommon shapes. This kind of ambitious innovation has only been possible since perfume and fashion specialist Chanel—which also maintains a successful watch line in its own right—became a significant Bell & Ross shareholder and brought the watchmaker access to the production facilities where designers Bruno Belamich and team can create more complicated, more interesting designs for their esthetically unusual "instrument" watches. And to prove perhaps that watchmakers are not riding the coattails (or fenders) of iconic cars, in 2016 Belamich and his team presented the AeroGT at the Geneva International Auto Show, a super–sports car that can stand on its own next to a series of same-class Italians.

Belamich continues to prove his skills where technical features and artful proportions are concerned, and what sets Bell & Ross timepieces apart from those of other, more traditional professional luxury makers is their special, roguish look—a delicate balance between striking, martial, and poetic. And it is this beauty for the eye to behold that makes the company's wares popular with style-conscious "civilians" as well as with the pilots, divers, astronauts, sappers, and other hard-riding professionals drawn to Bell & Ross timepieces for their superior functionality. And the brand is capable of producing more feminine timepieces as well, or at least objects that will stimulate the inner warrior that slumbers in everyone.

Bell & Ross Ltd.
8 rue Copernic
F-75116 Paris
France

Tel.:
+33-1-73-73-93-00

E-mail:
sav@bellross.com

Website:
www.bellross.com

Founded:
1992

U.S. distributor:
Bell & Ross, Inc.
605 Lincoln Road, Suite 300
Miami Beach, FL 33139
888-307-7887
information@bellross.com
www.bellross.com

Most important collections/price range:
Instrument BR-X1, BR 01, and BR 03 / approx. $3,100 to $200,000

BR03-92 Diver Green Bronze
Reference number: BR0392-D-G-BR/SCA
Movement: automatic, Caliber BR-CAL.302 (base ETA 2892-A2); ø 25.6 mm, height 3.6 mm; 21 jewels; 28,800 vph; 42-hour power reserve
Functions: hours, minutes, sweep seconds; date
Case: bronze, 42 × 42 mm, height 12.05 mm; unidirectional bezel screwed to monocoque case with 4 screws, with 0-60 scale; sapphire crystal; screw-in crown; water-resistant to 30 atm
Band: rubber buckle
Price: $3,990; limited to 999 pieces

BR03-92 Diver Black Matte
Reference number: BR0392-D-BL-CE/SRB
Movement: automatic, Caliber BR-CAL.302 (base ETA 2892-2); ø 25.6 mm, height 3.6 mm; 21 jewels; 28,800 vph; 42-hour power reserve
Functions: hours, minutes, sweep seconds; date
Case: ceramic, 42 × 42 mm, height 13.35 mm; unidirectional bezel screwed to monocoque case with 4 screws, with 0-60 scale; sapphire crystal; screw-in crown; water-resistant to 30 atm
Band: rubber buckle
Price: $3,990

BR03-94 Black Matte
Reference number: BR0394-BL-CE
Movement: automatic, Caliber BR-CAL.301 (base ETA 2894-2); ø 28.6 mm, height 6.1 mm; 37 jewels; 28,800 vph; 42-hour power reserve
Functions: hours, minutes, subsidiary seconds; chronograph; date
Case: ceramic, 42 × 42 mm, height 12.5 mm; bezel screwed to monocoque case with 4 screws; sapphire crystal; water-resistant to 10 atm
Band: rubber, buckle
Price: $5,400

BELL & ROSS

BRV2-92 Military Beige
Reference number: BRV292-BEI-ST/SF
Movement: automatic, Caliber BR-CAL.302 (base SW300-1 elaborate execution); ø 25.6 mm, height 3.6 mm; 25 jewels; 28,800 vph; 42-hour power reserve
Functions: hours, minutes, sweep seconds; date
Case: stainless steel, ø 41 mm, height 11.50 mm; bidirectional bezel, 0-60 scale; sapphire crystal; transparent case back; screw-in crown; water-resistant to 10 atm
Band: textile, folding clasp
Price: $2,900
Variations: stainless steel bracelet ($3,200)

BR03-92 MA-1
Reference number: BR0392-KAO-CE/SCA
Movement: automatic, Caliber BR-CAL.302 (base SW300-1 elaborate execution); ø 25.6 mm, height 3.6 mm; 25 jewels; 28,800 vph; 42-hour power reserve
Functions: hours, minutes, sweep seconds; date
Case: ceramic, 42 × 42 mm, height 10.4 mm; sapphire crystal; screw-in crown; water-resistant to 10 atm
Band: calfskin, buckle
Price: $3,900; limited to 999 pieces

BR03-92 Bi-Compass
Reference number: BR0392-IDC-CE/SRB
Movement: automatic, Caliber BR-CAL.302 (base SW300-1 elaborate execution); ø 25.6 mm, height 3.6 mm; 25 jewels; 28,800 vph; 42-hour power reserve
Functions: hours (disk display), minutes, sweep seconds; date
Case: ceramic, 42 × 42 mm, height 10.4 mm; bezel screwed to monocoque case with 4 screws; sapphire crystal; screw-in crown; water-resistant to 10 atm
Band: rubber, buckle
Price: $3,900; limited to 999 pieces

BR03-94 R.S.19
Reference number: BR0394-RS19/SRB
Movement: automatic, Caliber BR-CAL.301 (base ETA 2894-2 elaborate execution); ø 28.6 mm, height 6.1 mm; 37 jewels; 28,800 vph; 42-hour power reserve
Functions: hours, minutes, subsidiary seconds; chronograph; date
Case: titanium, 42 × 42 mm, height 12.4 mm; bezel screwed to monocoque case with 4 screws, with 0-60 scale; sapphire crystal; water-resistant to 10 atm
Band: rubber, buckle
Remarks: homage to Renault F1 Team
Price: $6,500; limited to 999 pieces

BRV3-94 R.S.19
Reference number: BRV394-RS19/SCA
Movement: automatic, Caliber BR-CAL.301 (base ETA 2894-2 elaborate execution); ø 28.6 mm, height 6.1 mm; 37 jewels; 28,800 vph; 42-hour power reserve
Functions: hours, minutes, subsidiary seconds; chronograph; date
Case: stainless steel, ø 43 mm, height 12.95 mm; bidirectional bezel, 0-60 scale; sapphire crystal; transparent case back; screw-in crown; water-resistant to 10 atm
Band: calfskin, folding clasp
Remarks: dedicated to Renault F1 Team
Price: $4,400; limited to 999 pieces

BRX1 Phantom
Reference number: BRX1-PHANTOM/SRB
Movement: automatic, Caliber BR-CAL.313 (base ETA 2892-2 with Dubois Dépraz model); ø 25.6 mm; 56 jewels; 28,800 vph; skeletonized movement; 42-hour power reserve
Functions: hours, minutes, subsidiary seconds; chronograph; date
Case: titanium with black PVD coating, 45 mm × 45 mm, height 14.8 mm; bezel screwed to monocoque case with 4 screws; sapphire crystal; water-resistant to 10 atm
Band: rubber, buckle
Price: $19,900; limited to 250 pieces

BLANCPAIN

In its advertising, the Blancpain watch brand has always proudly declared that, since 1735, the company has never made quartz watches and never will. Indeed, Blancpain is Switzerland's oldest watchmaker, and by sticking to its ideals, the company was put out of business by the "quartz boom" of the 1970s.

The Blancpain brand we know today came into being in the mid-eighties, when Jean-Claude Biver and Jacques Piguet purchased the venerable name. The company was subsequently moved to the Frédéric Piguet watch factory in Le Brassus, where it quickly became largely responsible for the renaissance of the mechanical wristwatch. This success caught the attention of the Swatch Group—known at that time as SMH. In 1992, it swooped in and purchased both companies to add to its portfolio. Movement fabrication and watch production were melded to form the Blancpain Manufacture in mid-2010.

But being quartzless does not mean being old-fashioned. Over the past several years, Blancpain president Marc A. Hayek has put a great deal of energy into developing the company's technical originality. He is frank about the fact that making new calibers did harness most of Blancpain's creative potential, leaving little to apply to its existing collection of watches. Still, in terms of complications, Blancpain watches have always been in a class of their own. Furthermore, the farsighted move now means that other brands in the family have outstanding movements at their disposal, notably the Z9 from Harry Winston.

The Blancpain portfolio has been growing and subtly modernizing with each new model. The watches feature the company's own basic movement and a choice of manual or automatic winding, like the new collection, the Fifty Fathoms Bathyscaphe, a modern interpretation of the classic diver's watch of 1953. The product families were all consolidated into four families: the Villeret, the legendary Fifty Fathoms diver's watches, a graceful series for women, and a collection of unique pieces that express the brand's artistic and watchmaking prowess.

Blancpain SA
Le Rocher 12
CH-1348 Le Brassus
Switzerland

Tel.:
+41-21-796-3636

Website:
www.blancpain.com

Founded:
1735

U.S. distributor:
Blancpain
The Swatch Group (U.S.), Inc.
1200 Harbor Boulevard
Weehawken, NJ 07086
201-271-4680

Most important collections/price range:
L'Evolution, Villeret, Fifty Fathoms, Le Brassus, Women / $9,800 to $400,000

Villeret Quantième Perpétuel

Reference number: 6659-3631-55B
Movement: automatic, Blancpain Caliber 5939A; ø 32 mm, height 7.25 mm; 42 jewels; 28,800 vph; 192-hour power reserve
Functions: hours, minutes, subsidiary seconds; perpetual calendar with date, weekday, month, moon phase, leap year
Case: pink gold, ø 42 mm, height 13.5 mm; sapphire crystal; transparent case back; water-resistant to 3 atm
Band: reptile skin, folding clasp
Remarks: enamel dial
Price: $58,900
Variations: pink gold Milanese mesh bracelet ($78,200)

Villeret Tourbillon Volant Heure Sautante Minute Rétrograde

Reference number: 66260-3633-55B
Movement: manually wound, Blancpain Caliber 260MR; ø 32 mm, height 5.85 mm; 39 jewels; 21,600 vph; flying 1-minute tourbillon; 144-hour power reserve
Functions: hours (digital, jumping), minutes (retrograde)
Case: pink gold, ø 42 mm, height 11 mm; sapphire crystal; transparent case back; water-resistant to 3 atm
Band: reptile skin, folding clasp
Remarks: enamel dial
Price: $148,800

Villeret Ultraplate

Reference number: 6605-1127-55B
Movement: manually wound, Blancpain Caliber 11A4B; ø 27.4 mm, height 2.8 mm; 21 jewels; 21,600 vph; 100-hour power reserve
Functions: hours, minutes; power reserve display (on rear)
Case: stainless steel, ø 40 mm, height 7.39 mm; sapphire crystal; transparent case back; water-resistant to 3 atm
Band: reptile skin, folding clasp
Price: $9,800

BLANCPAIN

Villeret Quantième Complet GMT
Reference number: 6676-1127-55B
Movement: automatic, Blancpain Caliber 67A5; ø 27 mm, height 6 mm; 28 jewels; 28,800 vph; double spring barrel, 72-hour power reserve
Functions: hours, minutes; additional 24-hour display (2nd time zone); full calendar with date, weekday, month, moon phase
Case: ø 40 mm, height 11.8 mm; sapphire crystal; transparent case back; water-resistant to 3 atm
Band: reptile skin, folding clasp
Price: $15,900

Villeret Grande Date Jour Rétrograde
Reference number: 6668-3642-55B
Movement: automatic, Blancpain Caliber 6950GJ; ø 32 mm, height 5.27 mm; 40 jewels; 28,800 vph; 72-hour power reserve
Functions: hours, minutes, sweep seconds; large date, weekday (retrograde)
Case: pink gold, ø 40 mm, height 11.1 mm; sapphire crystal; transparent case back; water-resistant to 3 atm
Band: reptile skin, folding clasp
Remarks: opaline dial
Price: $24,500

Fifty Fathoms Automatic
Reference number: 5015-12B30-B52A
Movement: automatic, Blancpain Caliber 1315; ø 30.6 mm, height 5.65 mm; 35 jewels; 28,800 vph; silicon hairspring; 120-hour power reserve
Functions: hours, minutes, sweep seconds; date
Case: ceramic, ø 43.6 mm, height 13.83 mm; unidirectional bezel with sapphire crystal inlay, with 0-60 scale; sapphire crystal; transparent case back; water-resistant to 30 atm
Band: textile, buckle
Price: $15,700
Variations: blue dial and bezel

Fifty Fathoms Barracuda
Reference number: 5008B-1130-B52A
Movement: automatic, Blancpain Caliber 1151; ø 27.4 mm, height 3.25 mm; 28 jewels; 28,800 vph; 100-hour power reserve
Functions: hours, minutes, sweep seconds; date
Case: stainless steel, ø 40.3 mm, height 13.23 mm; unidirectional bezel with sapphire crystal inlay, with 0-60 scale; sapphire crystal; transparent case back; screw-in crown; water-resistant to 30 atm
Band: rubber, folding clasp
Price: $14,100; limited to 500 pieces

Fifty Fathoms Automatic
Reference number: 5015-3603C-63B
Movement: automatic, Blancpain Caliber 1315; ø 30.6 mm, height 5.65 mm; 35 jewels; 28,800 vph; silicon hairspring; 120-hour power reserve
Functions: hours, minutes, sweep seconds; date
Case: red gold, ø 45 mm, height 15.4 mm; unidirectional bezel with sapphire crystal inlay, with 0-60 scale; sapphire crystal; transparent case back; water-resistant to 30 atm
Band: textile, buckle
Price: $35,800
Variations: titanium

Fifty Fathoms Bathyscaphe Quantième Complet
Reference number: 5054-1110-B52A
Movement: automatic, Blancpain Caliber 6654.P; ø 32 mm, height 5.48 mm; 28 jewels; 28,800 vph; 72-hour power reserve
Functions: hours, minutes, sweep seconds; full calendar with date, weekday, month, moon phase
Case: stainless steel, ø 43 mm, height 13.9 mm; unidirectional bezel with ceramic inlay, with 0-60 scale; sapphire crystal; transparent case back; screw-in crown; water-resistant to 30 atm
Band: textile, buckle
Price: $14,800

BLANCPAIN

X Fathoms
Reference number: 5018-1230-64A
Movement: automatic, Blancpain Caliber 9918B (base Blancpain 1315); ø 36 mm, height 13 mm; 48 jewels; 28,800 vph; 3 spring barrels, 120-hour power reserve
Functions: hours, minutes, sweep seconds; mechanical depth gauge (2-part scale) with maximum depth indicator, 5-minute short-time counter (countdown)
Case: titanium, ø 55.65 mm, height 24 mm; unidirectional bezel, with 0-60 scale; sapphire crystal; helium valve; water-resistant to 30 atm
Band: rubber, buckle
Price: $40,700

Fifty Fathoms Nageurs de Combat
Reference number: 5015E-1130-B52A
Movement: automatic, Blancpain Caliber 1315; ø 30.6 mm, height 5.65 mm; 35 jewels; 28,800 vph; silicon spring; 120-hour power reserve
Functions: hours, minutes, sweep seconds; date
Case: stainless steel, ø 45 mm, height 15.7 mm; unidirectional bezel with sapphire crystal insert, with 0-60 scale; sapphire crystal; transparent case back; screw-in crown; water-resistant to 30 atm
Band: textile, buckle
Price: $15,500; limited to 300 pieces

Air Command
Reference number: AC01-1130-63A
Movement: automatic, Blancpain Caliber F388B; ø 31.8 mm, height 6.65 mm; 35 jewels; 28,800 vph; 50-hour power reserve
Functions: hours, minutes; flyback chronograph
Case: stainless steel, ø 42.5 mm, height 13.77 mm; bidirectionally rotating bezel with ceramic inlay, with 0-60 scale; sapphire crystal; transparent case back; water-resistant to 3 atm
Band: calfskin, buckle
Price: $19,800; limited to 500 pieces

Villeret Women Ultraplate
Reference number: 6104-3642-55A
Movement: automatic, Blancpain Caliber 913; ø 21 mm, height 3.28 mm; 20 jewels; 28,800 vph; 40-hour power reserve
Functions: hours, minutes, sweep seconds
Case: pink gold, ø 29.2 mm, height 9.2 mm; sapphire crystal; transparent case back; water-resistant to 10 atm
Band: reptile skin, buckle
Price: $12,700

Villeret Women Date
Reference number: 6127-4628-95A
Movement: automatic, Blancpain Caliber 1151; ø 27.4 mm, height 3.25 mm; 28 jewels; 28,800 vph; 100-hour power reserve
Functions: hours, minutes, sweep seconds; date
Case: stainless steel, ø 33.2 mm, height 9.15 mm; bezel set with diamonds; sapphire crystal; transparent case back; water-resistant to 3 atm
Band: reptile skin, buckle
Price: $22,900

Villeret Women Quantième Moonphase
Reference number: 6126-2987-55B
Movement: automatic, Blancpain Caliber 913QL; ø 23.7 mm, height 4.5 mm; 20 jewels; 28,800 vph; 40-hour power reserve
Functions: hours, minutes, sweep seconds; date, moon phase
Case: red gold, ø 33.2 mm, height 10.2 mm; bezel set with diamonds; sapphire crystal; transparent case back; water-resistant to 3 atm
Band: reptile skin, folding clasp
Remarks: dial set with 8 diamonds
Price: $15,900

BLANCPAIN

Caliber F385
Automatic; column wheel control of chronograph functions; single spring barrel, 50-hour power reserve
Functions: hours, minutes, subsidiary seconds; flyback chronograph; date
Diameter: 31.8 mm
Height: 6.65 mm
Jewels: 37
Balance: silicon
Frequency: 36,000 vph
Balance spring: flat hairspring
Shock protection: Kif
Remarks: finely worked movement, bridges with côtes de Genève

Caliber 2358
Automatic; escapement with 1-minute carrousel; single spring barrel, 65-hour power reserve
Functions: hours, minutes; minute repeater with cathedral chimes; flyback chronograph, sweep 30-minute counter
Diameter: 32.8 mm
Height: 11.7 mm
Jewels: 59
Balance: glucydur with golden regulating screws
Frequency: 28,800 vph
Balance spring: flat hairspring
Shock protection: Kif
Remarks: hand-engraved bridges and rotor; 546 parts

Caliber 913
Automatic; single spring barrel, 40-hour power reserve
Functions: hours, minutes, sweep seconds
Diameter: 21 mm
Height: 3.28 mm
Jewels: 20
Balance: glucydur
Frequency: 28,800 vph
Remarks: 174 parts

Caliber 152B
Manually wound; inverted movement with time indication on movement side, bridges with black ceramic inlay; single spring barrel, 40-hour power reserve
Functions: hours, minutes
Diameter: 35.64 mm
Height: 2.95 mm
Jewels: 21
Balance: screw balance
Frequency: 21,600 vph
Balance spring: flat hairspring
Shock protection: Kif

Caliber 225L
Automatic; flying 1-minute carrousel, 2 separate gear works; single spring barrel, 120-hour power reserve
Functions: hours, minutes; date, moon phase
Diameter: 31.9 mm
Height: 6.86 mm
Jewels: 40
Balance: glucydur with screw balance
Frequency: 28,800 vph
Balance spring: silicon
Shock protection: Kif
Remarks: 281 parts

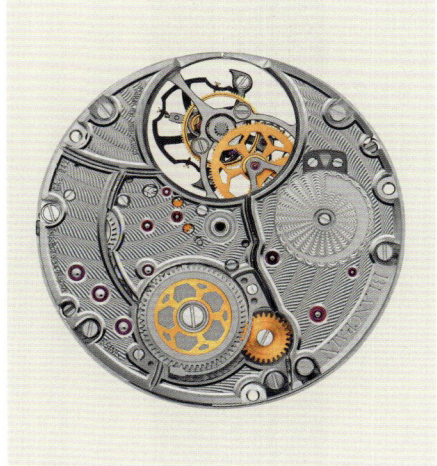

Caliber 242
Automatic; flying 1-minute tourbillon with silicon balance and pallet fork horns; peripheral rotor at edge of movement; quadruple spring barrel, 288-hour power reserve
Functions: hours, minutes; power reserve indicator (on rear)
Diameter: 30.6 mm
Height: 6.1 mm
Jewels: 43
Balance: silicon
Frequency: 21,600 vph
Remarks: finely finished movement, hand-guillochéed bridges; 243 parts

BORGWARD

It is not unusual for prospective watch brand founders to search for the name of a dormant or even defunct horological company to connect their business with a glorious past. Watchmaker Jürgen Betz looked elsewhere when he launched a series of watches under the name Borgward. This former automobile company had a reputation for outstanding quality, reliability, and durability. For connoisseurs and fans, Borgward meant technical prowess, perfect styling, and precision engineering.

Carl F. Borgward began his career as an automobile designer in 1924, when he built a small three-wheeled van. In the early 1930s, he took over the Hansa-Lloyd automobile factory and went on to conquer a global market with the Lloyd, Goliath, and Borgward brands. The real Borgward legend, however, began in the 1950s with the "Goddess," the famed Isabella Coupé, whose elegant lines and state-of-the-art technology heralded a new era in automotive design in Germany. In 1961, the company went bankrupt due to poor management. But the legend lives on and became the inspiration for Betz when building his Borgward watch B511. Support came from his friend Eric Borgward, grandson of Carl. Since then, Borgward Zeitmanufaktur has produced three collections: the B511 limited to 511 pieces, the P100 limited to 1,890 pieces, and the B2300 limited to 1,942 pieces. They are all "made in Germany" but based on Swiss technology. At the heart of each watch is either an ETA 2824 with three hands and calendar or the famous ETA 7750 Valjoux chronograph automatic.

In 2018, Betz came out with a special series, the 41, named for the aluminum-bodied Borgward that raced at Le Mans sixty-five years earlier, in 1953. That car, restored, was again at the Le Mans Classic race in 2018.

Borgward
Zeitmanufaktur GmbH & Co. KG
Markgrafenstrasse 16
D-79588 Efringen-Kirchen
Germany

Tel.:
+49-7628-805-7840

E-mail:
manufaktur@borgward.ag

Website:
www.borgward.ag

Founded:
2010

Number of employees:
3

Annual production:
approx. 180

Distribution:
Please contact Borgward directly for enquiries.

Most important collections:
P100, B2300, 1957, New Heritage Steam

FortyOne Deluxe
Reference number: FORTY.VK.01.V10
Movement: automatic, ETA Caliber 7751; ø 30 mm, height 7.9 mm; 25 jewels; 28,800 vph; finely finished with côtes de Genève; 42-hour power reserve
Functions: hours, minutes, subsidiary seconds; additional 24-hour display (2nd time zone); chronograph; full calendar with date, weekday, month
Case: stainless steel, ø 42.5 mm, height 14.5 mm; sapphire crystal; transparent case back; water-resistant to 5 atm
Band: calfskin, buckle
Remarks: recalling the Borgward Hansa RS 1500 number 41 that raced at Le Mans in 1953
Price: $6,500; limited to 41 pieces
Variations: stainless steel bracelet ($6,695)

FortyOne Chronograph Medium
Reference number: FORTY.CM.04
Movement: automatic, ETA Caliber 7753; ø 30 mm, height 7.9 mm; 25 jewels; 28,800 vph; finely finished with côtes de Genève; 42-hour power reserve
Functions: hours, minutes, subsidiary seconds; chronograph
Case: stainless steel, ø 36 mm, height 15.5 mm; sapphire crystal; transparent case back; water-resistant to 5 atm
Band: calfskin, buckle
Remarks: recalling the Borgward Hansa RS 1500 number 41 that raced at Le Mans in 1953
Price: $3,050; limited to 41 pieces; **Variations:** stainless steel bracelet ($3,245); leather strap and stainless steel bracelet ($3,400); diamonds ($5,800)

FortyOne Chronograph
Reference number: FORTY.CL.04.V70
Movement: automatic, ETA Caliber 7753; ø 30 mm, height 7.9 mm; 25 jewels; 28,800 vph; finely finished with côtes de Genève; 42-hour power reserve
Functions: hours, minutes, subsidiary seconds; chronograph
Case: stainless steel, ø 40 mm, height 16 mm; sapphire crystal; transparent case back; water-resistant to 5 atm
Band: calfskin, buckle
Remarks: recalling the Borgward Hansa RS 1500 number 41 that raced at Le Mans in 1953
Price: $3,050; limited to 41 pieces
Variations: stainless steel bracelet ($3,245)

Big FortyOne Chronograph
Reference number: BIGFORTY.CL.01.V10
Movement: automatic, ETA Caliber 7753; ø 30 mm, height 7.9 mm; 25 jewels; 28,800 vph; finely finished with côtes de Genève; 42-hour power reserve
Functions: hours, minutes, subsidiary seconds; chronograph
Case: stainless steel, ø 44 mm, height 15 mm; sapphire crystal; transparent case back; water-resistant to 5 atm
Band: calfskin, buckle
Remarks: recalling the Borgward Hansa RS 1500 number 41 that raced at Le Mans in 1953
Price: $3,160; limited to 41 pieces
Variations: stainless steel bracelet ($3,355)

FortyOne 24H
Reference number: FORTY24.HA.01.V10
Movement: manually wound, Borgward Caliber B24H (base ETA 6498-1); ø 36.6 mm, height 4.5 mm; 17 jewels; 18,000 vph; finely finished with côtes de Genève; 46-hour power reserve
Functions: 24 hours, minutes, subsidiary seconds
Case: stainless steel, ø 44 mm, height 12.5 mm; sapphire crystal; transparent case back; water-resistant to 5 atm
Band: calfskin, buckle
Remarks: recalling the Borgward Hansa RS 1500 number 41 that raced at Le Mans in 1953
Price: $2,090; limited to 41 pieces
Variations: stainless steel bracelet ($2,250)

New Heritage Steam Chronograph
Reference number: NHS.CL.01
Movement: automatic, ETA Caliber 7750-2; ø 30 mm, height 7.9 mm; 25 jewels; 28,800 vph; blackened oscillating mass; movement decorated with perlage and côtes de Genève; 42-hour power reserve
Functions: hours, minutes, subsidiary seconds; chronograph
Case: stainless steel, ø 44 mm, height 15 mm; bezel in bronze; sapphire crystal; transparent case back; water-resistant to 5 atm
Band: calfskin, buckle
Price: $2,995; limited to 98 pieces
Variations: stainless steel bracelet ($3,190)

Fiftyseven
Reference number: B57.CL.06.MIL
Movement: automatic, ETA Caliber 7750; ø 30 mm, height 7.9 mm; 25 jewels; 28,800 vph; blackened oscillating mass; movement decorated with perlage and côtes de Genève; 42-hour power reserve
Functions: hours, minutes; chronograph; date, weekday
Case: stainless steel, ø 40 mm, height 15.9 mm; sapphire crystal; transparent case back; water-resistant to 5 atm
Band: stainless steel Milanese mesh, folding clasp
Price: $3,140
Variations: calfskin strap ($2,940); various dial colors

Deluxe
Reference number: DELUXE.CL.09
Movement: automatic, ETA Caliber 7751; ø 30 mm, height 7.9 mm; 25 jewels; 28,800 vph; personalized oscillating mass, movement decorated with perlage and côtes de Genève; 46-hour power reserve
Functions: hours, minutes, subsidiary seconds; additional 24-hour display; chronograph; date, weekday, month, moon phase
Case: stainless steel, ø 42.5 mm, height 14.5 mm; sapphire crystal; transparent case back; water-resistant to 10 atm
Band: calfskin, buckle
Price: $7,830
Variations: stainless steel Milanese mesh bracelet ($8,030); various personalization options

P100 Retrospective
Reference number: P100R.AL.02
Movement: automatic, ETA Caliber 2824-2; ø 25.6 mm, height 4.6 mm; 25 jewels; 28,800 vph; blackened oscillating mass; movement decorated with perlage and côtes de Genève; 42-hour power reserve
Functions: hours, minutes, sweep seconds; date
Case: stainless steel, ø 40 mm, height 12 mm; sapphire crystal; transparent case back; water-resistant to 5 atm
Band: calfskin, buckle
Price: $1,590; limited to 1,890 pieces
Variations: stainless steel Milanese mesh ($1,760); white or brown dial

BOVET

If any brand can claim real connections to China, it is Bovet, founded by Swiss businessman Edouard Bovet. Bovet emigrated to Canton, China, in 1818 and sold four watches of his own design there. On his return to Switzerland in 1822, he set up a company for shipping his Fleurier-made watches to China. The company name, pronounced "Bo Wei" in Mandarin, became a synonym for "watch" in Asia and at one point had offices in Canton. For more than eighty years, Bovet and his successors supplied the Chinese ruling class with valuable timepieces.

In 2001, the brand was bought by entrepreneur Pascal Raffy. He ensured the company's industrial independence by acquiring several other companies as well, notably the high-end watchmaker Swiss Time Technology (STT) in Tramelan, which he renamed Dimier 1738. In addition to creating its own line of watches, this *manufacture* produces complex technical components such as tourbillons for Bovet watches. Assembly of Bovet creations takes place at the headquarters in the thirteenth-century Castle of Môtiers in Val-de-Travers not far from Fleurier.

Bovet is an equal opportunity manufacturer of fine watches for men and women. These high-end timekeepers do have several distinctive features. The first is intricate dial work, featuring not only complex architecture in the men's series, but also intricate guilloché patterns and very fine enameling techniques, as in the Poppies, where 138 diamonds meet bold red grand-feu poppies, a work by artist and jewelry designer Ilgiz Fazulzyanov. The latest development is a case shaped like a slant-top desk, which makes for easy reading of time.

The second special feature is placement of the lugs and crown at 12 o'clock, recalling Bovet's tasteful pocket watches of the nineteenth century. On some models, the wristbands are made to be easily removed so the watch can be worn on a chain or cord. Other watches convert to table clocks, and the Amadeo Fleurier Miss Audrey series can even be worn as a necklace.

Bovet Fleurier S.A.
109 Pont-du-Centenaire
CP109
CH-1228 Plan-les-Ouates
Switzerland

Tel.:
+41-22-731-4638

E-mail:
info@bovet.com

Website:
www.bovet.com

Founded:
1822

Annual production:
around 2,000 timepieces

U.S. distributor:
Bovet LLC U.S.A.
888-909-1822

Most important collections/price range:
Amadeo Fleurier, Dimier, Pininfarina, Sportster / $18,500 to $1,000,000

Récital 26 Brainstorm Chapter One
Reference number: R260004
Movement: manually wound, Bovet Caliber 17DM04-SMP; ø 38.5 mm, height 15.70 mm; 18,000 vph; 1-minute double-sided flying tourbillon; spherical winding system; 10-day power reserve
Functions: hours, minutes, seconds on tourbillon; date; hemispherical moon phase; power reserve indicator
Case: ø 46.30 mm, height 15.95 mm; sapphire crystal; transparent case back; water-resistant to 3 atm
Band: reptile skin, buckle
Remarks: "slant-top desk" case; convex quartz dial
Price: $360,000; unique piece; **Variations:** blue or green quartz dial, black or red propeller-shaped dial ($318.000); limited to 60 movements

Récital 27—Limited Edition Mexico
Reference number: R270005-G1-01
Movement: manually wound, Bovet Caliber 17DM04-3FPL; ø 30.45 mm, with 36.09-mm module, height 15.70 mm; 21,600 vph; 1-minute, double-sided flying tourbillon; 7-day power reserve
Functions: 3 time zones with hours, minutes; subsidiary seconds on rear; 24 city references, day/night indicator for 2 time zones, double hemisphere moon phase; power reserve indicator
Case: red gold, ø 46.30 mm, height 15.95 mm; sapphire crystal; transparent case back; water-resistant to 3 atm; **Band:** reptile skin, buckle
Remarks: "slant-top desk" case
Price: $82,100

Récital 22 Grand Récital
Reference number: R220001-USA
Movement: manually wound, Bovet Caliber 17DM03-TEL; ø 38 mm, height 15.70 mm; 18,000 vph; 1-minute, double-sided flying tourbillon; 9-day power reserve
Functions: hours (24), minutes (retrograde), seconds (on double-sided tourbillon), double-sided date, moon phase; power reserve indicator, perpetual calendar (retrograde);
Case: platinum, ø 46.30 mm, height 19.60 mm; sapphire crystal; transparent case back; water-resistant to 3 atm
Band: reptile skin, buckle
Price: $502,000; limited to 60 movements
Variations: red gold ($470,000).

BOVET

Amadeo Fleurier 36 Miss Audrey
Reference number: AS36007-SD12
Movement: automatic, Bovet Caliber 11BA13; ø 26.20 mm, height 5.09 mm; 28,800 vph; 42-hour power reserve
Functions: hours, minutes
Case: stainless steel, ø 36 mm, height 11.25 mm; sapphire crystal; bezel set with 60 round diamonds; water-resistant to 3 atm
Band: synthetic satin with calfskin lining, buckle
Remarks: 4 diamond indices; necklace bow set with diamonds
Price: $19,500
Variations: turquoise guilloché dial

Amadeo Fleurier 39—"Poppies"
Reference number: AF39809-SD123
Movement: automatic, Bovet Caliber 11BA13; ø 26.20 mm, height 5.07 mm; 28,800 vph; 72-hour power reserve
Functions: hours, minutes
Case: white gold, ø 39 mm, height 5.07 mm; convertible case; attachment ring, bezel, and hasps set with 94 diamonds; crown and lugs set with 5 cabochon diamonds; sapphire crystal; water-resistant to 3 atm
Band: reptile skin, buckle
Remarks: grand-feu enamel miniature painting of poppies on dial, set with 161 diamonds
Price: $142,000; unique piece

Amadeo Fleurier 43
Reference number: AF43604
Movement: automatic, Bovet Caliber 11BA12; ø 26.20 mm, height 5.07 mm; 28,800 vph; 72-hour power reserve
Functions: hours, minutes
Case: red gold, ø 39 mm, height 5.07 mm; sapphire crystal; water-resistant to 3 atm
Band: reptile skin, buckle
Remarks: enamel miniature painting of red dragon on mother-of-pearl
Price: $76,000; unique piece
Variations: with gold dragon motif on dial

19Thirty Fleurier
Reference number: NTR0023
Movement: manually wound, Bovet Caliber 11BM04; ø 35.5 mm, height 3.80 mm; 21,600 vph; 7-day power reserve
Functions: hours, minutes, subsidiary seconds; power reserve indicator
Case: red gold, ø 42 mm, height 9.05 mm; sapphire crystal; transparent case back; water-resistant to 3 atm
Band: reptile skin, buckle
Price: $29,500
Variations: blue or black dial; with Arabic, Roman, or Chinese numerals

Virtuoso IX
Reference number: AIVIX001
Movement: manually wound, Bovet Caliber 17BM04-DFR; ø 36.09 mm; 18,000 vph; 1-minute flying tourbillon; spherical winding system; blued bridges on back; 10-day power reserve
Functions: hours (off-center), minutes, seconds (on tourbillon cage); big date; power reserve indicator; additional 24-hour hand (2nd time zone); 24 city references; reversed hand-fitting
Case: red gold, ø 46.3 mm, height 16 mm; sapphire crystal; transparent case back; water-resistant to 3 atm
Band: reptile skin, buckle
Remarks: flexible lugs to turn watch into table watch or pocket watch; blue flinqué dial
Price: $280,000; limited edition of 39 pieces
Variations: platinum ($326,000; limited to 39 pieces)

Amadeo Fleurier Virtuoso V
Reference number: ACHS016
Movement: manually wound, Bovet Caliber 13BM11AIHSMR; ø 31.00 mm, height 5.09 mm; 21,600 vph; 5-day power reserve
Functions: jumping hours, minutes (retrograde); hours, minutes, seconds on rear
Case: red gold, ø 43.5 mm, height 15.70 mm; sapphire crystal; transparent case back; water-resistant to 3 atm
Band: reptile skin, buckle
Remarks: reversed hand-fitting
Price: $70,000

BREGUET

We never quite lose that attachment to the era in which we were born and grew up, nor do some brands. Abraham-Louis Breguet (1747–1823), who hailed from Switzerland, brought his craft to Paris in the *Sturm und Drang* atmosphere of the late eighteenth century. It was fertile ground for one of the most inventive watchmakers in the history of horology, and his products soon found favor with the highest levels of society.

Little has changed two centuries later. After a few years of drifting, in 1999 the brand carrying this illustrious name became the prize possession of the Swatch Group and came under the personal management of Nicolas G. Hayek, CEO. Hayek worked assiduously to restore the brand's roots, going as far as rebuilding the legendary Marie Antoinette pocket watch and contributing to the restoration of the Petit Trianon at Versailles.

Breguet is a full-fledged *manufacture*, and this has allowed it to forge ahead uncompromisingly with upscale watches and even jewelry. In modern facilities on the shores of Lake Joux, traditional craftsmanship still plays a significant role in the production of its fine watches, but at the same time, Breguet is one of the few brands to work with modern materials for its movements. This is not just a PR trick, but rather a sincere attempt to improve quality and rate precision. Many innovations have debuted at Breguet, for instance pallet levers and balance wheels made of silicon, the first Breguet hairspring with the arched terminal curve made of this glassy material, or even a mechanical high-frequency balance beating at 72,000 vph. Other innovations include the electromagnetic regulation of a minute repeater or the use of two micromagnets to achieve contactless anchoring of a balance-wheel staff.

Breguet, now under the auspices of Nicolas G. Hayek's grandson, Marc A. Hayek, continues to explore the edges of the technologically possible in watchmaking, while maintaining the brand's particular connection to traditional processes and esthetic codes. Be it a tourbillon or a sports watch, like the Type XXI models, Breguet always gives off a scent of luxury.

Montres Breguet SA
CH-1344 L'Abbaye
Switzerland

Tel.:
+41-21-841-9090

Website:
www.breguet.com

Founded:
1775 (Swatch Group since 1999)

U.S. distributor:
Breguet
The Swatch Group (U.S.), Inc.
1200 Harbor Boulevard, 7th Floor
Weehawken, NJ 07087
201-271-1400

Most important collections:
Classique, Tradition, Héritage, Marine, Reine de Naples, Type XX, Type XXI, Type XXII

Classique 5177

Reference number: 5177 BB 2Y 9V6
Movement: automatic, Breguet Caliber 777Q; ø 27.1 mm; 26 jewels; 28,800 vph; silicon hairspring, pallet lever, and escape wheel; 55-hour power reserve
Functions: hours, minutes, sweep seconds; date
Case: white gold, ø 38 mm, height 8.8 mm; sapphire crystal; transparent case back; water-resistant to 3 atm
Band: reptile skin, buckle
Remarks: enamel dial
Price: $23,700

Classique Phase de Lune Dame

Reference number: 9088BB 29 964 DD0D
Movement: automatic, Breguet Caliber 537L; ø 20 mm; 26 jewels; 25,200 vph; silicon hairspring and escapement; 45-hour power reserve
Functions: hours, minutes, subsidiary seconds; moon phase
Case: white gold, ø 30 mm, height 9.8 mm; bezel and lugs set with 66 diamonds; sapphire crystal; transparent case back; water-resistant to 3 atm
Band: reptile skin, buckle
Remarks: enamel dial
Price: $28,700
Variations: without diamonds ($24,200); mother-of-pearl dial ($29,200); rose gold ($28,200)

Classique Extra-Plat

Reference number: 5157 BR 11 9V6
Movement: automatic, Breguet Caliber 502.3; ø 27.1 mm, height 2.4 mm; 35 jewels; 21,600 vph; silicon pallet fork horns and hairspring; 45-hour power reserve
Functions: hours, minutes
Case: rose gold, ø 38 mm, height 5.4 mm; sapphire crystal; transparent case back; water-resistant to 3 atm
Band: reptile skin, buckle
Price: $18,800
Variations: white gold ($18,800)

BREGUET

Classique Extra-Thin Tourbillon
Reference number: 5367 BR 299WU
Movement: automatic, Breguet Caliber 581; ø 36 mm, height 3 mm; 33 jewels; 28,800 vph; 1-minute tourbillon, silicon pallet lever and hairspring; hubless peripheral rotor for winding; 80-hour power reserve
Functions: hours, minutes, subsidiary seconds (on tourbillon cage)
Case: platinum, ø 42 mm, height 7.45 mm; sapphire crystal; transparent case back; water-resistant to 3 atm
Band: reptile skin, folding clasp
Remarks: enamel dial
Price: $147,500
Variations: rose gold ($161,800)

Classique Hora Mundi
Reference number: 5717BR EU 9ZU
Movement: automatic, Breguet Caliber 77F0; ø 27.1 mm, height 6.15 mm; 43 jewels; 28,800 vph; silicon pallet lever, escape wheel, and hairspring; 55-hour power reserve
Functions: hours, minutes, sweep seconds; world time display, day/night indicator (2nd time zone); date
Case: rose gold, ø 43 mm, height 13.55 mm; sapphire crystal; transparent case back; screw-in crown; water-resistant to 3 atm
Band: reptile skin, folding clasp
Price: $78,900
Variations: platinum ($94,200)

Classique "La Musicale"
Reference number: 7800BR AA 9YV02
Movement: automatic, Breguet Caliber 901; ø 38.9 mm, height 8.7 mm; 59 jewels; 28,800 vph; silicon anchor/anchor escape wheel, Breguet balance with regulating screws; music box with peg disk/gong strips, hand-guillochéed sonorous "liquid metal" membrane, magnetic striking regulator; 45-hour power reserve; **Functions:** hours, minutes, sweep seconds; power reserve display; alarm clock with music mechanism and function display
Case: rose gold, ø 48 mm, height 16.6 mm; sapphire crystal; water-resistant to 3 atm; **Band:** reptile skin, folding clasp; **Remarks:** hand-guilloché, platinum-plated gold dial, revolves when melody is played
Price: $89,600; **Variations:** white gold ($90,100)

Tradition Dame
Reference number: 7038BR 18 9V6 D00D
Movement: automatic, Breguet Caliber 505 SR; ø 33 mm; 38 jewels; 21,600 vph; silicon Breguet hairspring and lever pallets; 50-hour power reserve
Functions: hours, minutes (off-center), subsidiary seconds (retrograde)
Case: rose gold, ø 37 mm, height 11.85 mm; bezel set with 68 diamonds; sapphire crystal; transparent case back; crown with ruby cabochon; water-resistant to 3 atm
Band: reptile skin, buckle set with 19 diamonds
Price: $38,100
Variations: white gold ($38,900)

Tradition Seconde Rétrograde
Reference number: 7097BB G1 9WU
Movement: automatic, Breguet Caliber 505 SR1; ø 33 mm; 38 jewels; 21,600 vph; silicon Breguet hairspring and lever pallets; 50-hour power reserve
Functions: hours, minutes (off-center), subsidiary seconds (retrograde)
Case: white gold, ø 40 mm, height 11.65 mm; sapphire crystal; transparent case back; water-resistant to 3 atm
Band: reptile skin, folding clasp
Price: $33,500
Variations: rose gold ($32,700)

Tradition
Reference number: 7057BR R9 9W6
Movement: manually wound, Breguet Caliber 507DR1; ø 33 mm; 34 jewels; 21,600 vph; silicon Breguet hairspring and lever pallets; 50-hour power reserve
Functions: hours, minutes (off-center), subsidiary seconds (retrograde)
Case: rose gold, ø 40 mm, height 11.65 mm; sapphire crystal; transparent case back; water-resistant to 3 atm
Band: reptile skin, buckle
Price: $27,600

BREGUET

Marine Date
Reference number: 5517TI G2 5ZU
Movement: automatic, Breguet Caliber 777A; ø 33.8 mm; 26 jewels; 28,800 vph; silicon pallets and hairspring; 55-hour power reserve
Functions: hours, minutes, sweep seconds; date
Case: titanium, ø 40 mm, height 11.5 mm; sapphire crystal; transparent case back
Band: rubber, folding clasp
Price: $17,300
Variations: reptile skin band ($17,300); rose gold ($28,600); white gold ($28,600); titanium bracelet ($19,900)

Marine Chronograph
Reference number: 5527BB Y2 9WV
Movement: automatic, Breguet Caliber 582QA; ø 32.7 mm; 28 jewels; 28,800 vph; silicon pallets and hairspring; 48-hour power reserve
Functions: hours, minutes, subsidiary seconds; chronograph; date
Case: white gold, ø 42.3 mm, height 13.85 mm; sapphire crystal; transparent case back; screw-in crown; water-resistant to 10 atm
Band: reptile skin, folding clasp
Price: $33,800
Variations: rubber strap ($33,800); rose gold ($33,800); titanium ($22,600); titanium bracelet ($24,100)

Marine Alarme Musicale
Reference number: 5547BR 12 9ZU
Movement: automatic, Breguet Caliber 518F/1; ø 27.1 mm; 36 jewels; 28,800 vph; silicon pallets and hairspring; 45-hour power reserve
Functions: hours, minutes, sweep seconds; additional 24-hour display (2nd time zone), power reserve indicator for chimes; alarm (adjustable to the minute); date
Case: rose gold, ø 40 mm, height 13.05 mm; sapphire crystal; transparent case back; water-resistant to 5 atm
Band: reptile skin, folding clasp
Price: $39,900
Variations: rubber strap ($39,900); white gold ($39,900); titanium ($28,600); titanium bracelet ($31,200)

Marine Équation Marchante
Reference number: 5887BR 12 9WV
Movement: automatic, Breguet Caliber 581DPE; ø 37.2 mm; 57 jewels; 28,800 vph; 1-minute tourbillon; silicon anchor, escape wheel, and hairspring; 80-hour power reserve
Functions: hours, minutes, subsidiary seconds (on tourbillon cage); running equation of time; perpetual calendar with date (retrograde), weekday, month
Case: rose gold, ø 43.9 mm, height 11.75 mm; sapphire crystal; transparent case back; water-resistant to 10 atm
Band: reptile skin, folding clasp
Price: $215,000
Variations: platinum ($230,400)

Héritage Tourbillon
Reference number: 5497BR 12 9V6
Movement: manually wound, Breguet Caliber 187H; ø 26 mm; 21 jewels; 18,000 vph; 1-minute tourbillon; 50-hour power reserve
Functions: hours, minutes (off-center), subsidiary seconds (on tourbillon cage)
Case: rose gold, 35 mm × 42 mm; sapphire crystal; water-resistant to 3 atm
Band: reptile skin, folding clasp
Price: $127,900
Variations: platinum ($142,900)

Héritage
Reference number: 5410BR 12 9VV
Movement: automatic, Breguet Caliber 516GG; ø 25.6 mm; 30 jewels; 28,800 vph; silicon hairspring; 65-hour power reserve
Functions: hours, minutes, subsidiary seconds; large date
Case: rose gold, 35 mm × 42 mm, height 12.9 mm; sapphire crystal; water-resistant to 3 atm
Band: reptile skin, buckle
Price: $27,700
Variations: white gold ($28,700)

BREGUET

Type XXI Chronograph
Reference number: 3810BR 92 9ZU
Movement: automatic, Breguet Caliber 584 Q; ø 30 mm; 25 jewels; 28,800 vph; silicon hairspring and escapement, central minute totalizer; 45-hour power reserve
Functions: hours, minutes, subsidiary seconds; additional 24-hour display (2nd time zone); flyback chronograph; date
Case: rose gold, ø 42 mm, height 15.2 mm; unidirectional bezel, 0-60 scale; sapphire crystal; transparent case back; water-resistant to 10 atm
Band: calfskin, folding clasp
Price: $20,900

Type XXI Chrono Cadran Vintage
Reference number: 3817ST X2 3ZU
Movement: automatic, Breguet Caliber 584 Q/2; ø 30 mm; 26 jewels; 28,800 vph; silicon hairspring and escapement, central minute totalizer; 48-hour power reserve
Functions: hours, minutes, subsidiary seconds; additional 24-hour display (2nd time zone); flyback chronograph; date
Case: stainless steel, ø 42 mm, height 15.2 mm; unidirectional bezel, 0-60 scale; sapphire crystal; transparent case back; water-resistant to 10 atm
Band: calfskin
Price: $13,900

Type XXI Chronograph
Reference number: 3810TI H2 TZ9
Movement: automatic, Breguet Caliber 584 Q/2; ø 30 mm; 26 jewels; 28,800 vph; silicon hairspring and escapement, central minute totalizer; 45-hour power reserve
Functions: hours, minutes, subsidiary seconds; additional 24-hour display (2nd time zone); flyback chronograph; date
Case: titanium, ø 42 mm, height 15.2 mm; unidirectional bezel, 0-60 scale; sapphire crystal; transparent case back; water-resistant to 10 atm
Band: titanium, folding clasp
Price: $15,400
Variations: reptile skin band ($12,800)

Reine de Naples
Reference number: 8908BB 52 964 D00D
Movement: automatic, Breguet Caliber 537 DRL2; ø 19.7 mm; 45 jewels; 25,200 vph; silicon Breguet balance wheel, escapement, and hairspring; 45-hour power reserve
Functions: hours, minutes, subsidiary seconds; power reserve indicator; moon phase
Case: white gold, 28.45 × 36.5 mm, height 10.05 mm; bezel and dial set with 128 diamonds; sapphire crystal; transparent case back; crown with sapphire cabochon
Band: reptile skin, folding clasp set with diamonds
Price: $36,100
Variations: rose gold ($36,100)

Reine de Naples
Reference number: 8918BR 5T 964 D00D
Movement: automatic, Breguet Caliber 537/1; ø 19.7 mm; 20 jewels; 21,600 vph; 40-hour power reserve
Functions: hours, minutes
Case: rose gold, 24.95 × 33 mm, height 13.05 mm; bezel and flange set with 117 diamonds; sapphire crystal; transparent case back; crown with ruby cabochon; water-resistant to 3 atm
Band: reptile skin, folding clasp set with 26 diamonds
Remarks: mother-of-pearl dial with drop-shaped diamonds
Price: $35,100
Variations: white gold ($36,100)

Reine de Naples "Jour Nuit"
Reference number: 8998BB 11 974 DD0D
Movement: automatic, Breguet Caliber 78CS; ø 19.7 mm; 45 jewels; 25,200 vph; silicon hairspring; 57-hour power reserve
Functions: hours, minutes; titanium disk for rotating day/night indicator
Case: white gold, 34 × 42.5 mm, height 10.8 mm; bezel and dial set with 73 diamonds; sapphire crystal; transparent case back; crown with diamond cabochon
Band: reptile skin, folding clasp
Remarks: handmade guilloché on gold dial
Price: $123,900
Variations: rose gold ($122,900)

BREITLING

In 1884, Léon Breitling opened his workshop in St. Imier in the Jura Mountains and immediately began specializing in integrated chronographs. His business strategy was to focus consistently on instrument watches with a distinctive design. High quality standards and the rise of aviation completed the picture.

Today, Breitling's relationship with air sports and commercial and military aviation is clear from its brand identity. The watch company hosts a series of aviation days, owns an aerobatics team, and sponsors several aviation associations.

The unveiling of its own, modern chronograph movement at Basel in 2009 was a major milestone in the company's history and also a return to its roots. The new design was to be "100 percent Breitling" and industrially produced in large numbers at a reasonable cost. Although Breitling's operations in Grenchen and in La Chaux-de-Fonds both boast state-of-the-art equipment, the contract for the new chronograph was awarded to a small team in Geneva. By 2006, the brand-new Caliber B01 had made the COSC grade with flying colors, and it has enjoyed great popularity ever since. For the team of designers, the innovative centering system on the reset mechanism that requires no manual adjustment was one of the great achievements. Since then, the in-house caliber has evolved, but the cost for the company was immense. Ultimately, owner Théodore Schneider, in the second generation, decided to put management in the hands of Georges Kern of IWC fame. Together with the new owners, the investment company CVC Capital Partners, Kern decided to expand the brand beyond the pilot watch niche and look to the untapped markets in the Far East. The new collections were streamlined and given more defined profiles, a recipe he brought in from his IWC days. The winged logo was replaced mostly with a coquettish "B." Prices range from around $3,500 to the $10,000 region, and that includes ladies' watches. No more quartz, only mechanical. The company will also be making its own chronographs using the B1 movement and movements from outside vendors.

Breitling
Schlachthausstrasse 2
CH-2540 Grenchen
Switzerland

Tel.:
+41-32-654-5454

E-mail:
sales@breitlingusa.com

Website:
www.breitling.com

Founded:
1884

Annual production:
700,000 (estimated)

U.S. distributor:
Breitling U.S.A. Inc.
206 Danbury Road
Wilton, CT 06897
203-762-1180
www.breitling.com

Most important collections:
Navitimer 1, Navitimer 8, Avenger, Premier, Chronomat, Superocean Heritage, Superocean, Professional

Aviator 8 B01 Chronograph 43
Reference number: AB0119131B1P1
Movement: automatic, Breitling Caliber B01; ø 30 mm, height 7.2 mm; 47 jewels; 28,800 vph; column wheel control of chronograph functions; COSC-certified chronometer; 70-hour power reserve
Functions: hours, minutes, subsidiary seconds; chronograph; date
Case: stainless steel, ø 43 mm, height 13.97 mm; bidirectional bezel, with reference marks; sapphire crystal; screw-in crown; water-resistant to 10 atm
Band: reptile skin, folding clasp
Price: $7,710

Aviator 8 B01 Chronograph 43
Reference number: AB0119131C1A1
Movement: automatic, Breitling Caliber B01; ø 30 mm, height 7.2 mm; 47 jewels; 28,800 vph; column wheel control of chronograph functions; COSC-certified chronometer; 70-hour power reserve
Functions: hours, minutes, subsidiary seconds; chronograph; date
Case: stainless steel, ø 43 mm, height 13.97 mm; bidirectional bezel reference mark; sapphire crystal; screw-in crown; water-resistant to 10 atm
Band: stainless steel, folding clasp
Price: $8,080

Aviator 8 Chronograph 43
Reference number: A13316101B1A1
Movement: automatic, Breitling Caliber 13 (base ETA 7750); ø 30 mm, height 7.9 mm; 25 jewels; 28,800 vph; COSC-certified chronometer; 42-hour power reserve
Functions: hours, minutes, subsidiary seconds; chronograph; date, weekday
Case: stainless steel, ø 43 mm, height 14.17 mm; bidirectional bezel, with reference mark; sapphire crystal; screw-in crown; water-resistant to 10 atm
Band: stainless steel, folding clasp
Price: $5,930

Navitimer 1 B01 Chronograph 46
Reference number: AB0127211B1A1
Movement: automatic, Breitling Caliber B01; ø 30 mm, height 7.2 mm; 47 jewels; 28,800 vph; column wheel control of chronograph functions; COSC-certified chronometer; 70-hour power reserve
Functions: hours, minutes, subsidiary seconds; chronograph; date
Case: stainless steel, ø 46 mm, height 14.51 mm; bidirectional bezel with integrated slide rule and tachymeter scale; sapphire crystal; transparent case back; water-resistant to 3 atm
Band: stainless steel, folding clasp
Price: $9,250

Navitimer 1 B01 Chronograph 43
Reference number: AB0121211B1X1
Movement: automatic, Breitling Caliber B01; ø 30 mm, height 7.2 mm; 47 jewels; 28,800 vph; column wheel control of chronograph functions; COSC-certified chronometer; 70-hour power reserve
Functions: hours, minutes, subsidiary seconds; chronograph; date
Case: stainless steel, ø 43 mm, height 14.22 mm; bidirectional bezel with integrated slide rule and tachymeter scale; sapphire crystal; water-resistant to 3 atm
Band: calfskin, buckle
Price: $8,305
Variations: stainless steel bracelet ($9,250)

Superocean Héritage II B20 Automatic 46
Reference number: AB2020121B1S1
Movement: automatic, Breitling Caliber B20 (base Tudor MT 5612); ø 31.8 mm, height 6.5 mm; 28 jewels; 28,800 vph; COSC-certified chronometer; 70-hour power reserve
Functions: hours, minutes, sweep seconds; date
Case: stainless steel, ø 46 mm, height 15 mm; unidirectional bezel with ceramic insert; sapphire crystal; screw-in crown; water-resistant to 20 atm
Band: rubber, folding clasp
Price: $4,660
Variations: stainless steel Milanese mesh band ($4,985)

Superocean Héritage II B20 Automatic 46
Reference number: AB2020121B1A1
Movement: automatic, Breitling Caliber B20 (base Tudor MT 5612); ø 31.8 mm, height 6.5 mm; 28 jewels; 28,800 vph; COSC-certified chronometer; 70-hour power reserve
Functions: hours, minutes, sweep seconds; date
Case: stainless steel, ø 46 mm, height 15 mm; unidirectional bezel with ceramic insert; sapphire crystal; screw-in crown; water-resistant to 20 atm
Band: stainless steel Milanese mesh, folding clasp
Price: $4,985
Variations: rubber band ($4,660)

Superocean Héritage II B20 Automatic 42
Reference number: AB2010161C1S1
Movement: automatic, Breitling Caliber B20 (base Tudor MT 5612); ø 31.8 mm, height 6.5 mm; 28 jewels; 28,800 vph; COSC-certified chronometer; 70-hour power reserve
Functions: hours, minutes, sweep seconds; date
Case: stainless steel, ø 42 mm, height 14.35 mm; unidirectional bezel with ceramic insert; sapphire crystal; screw-in crown; water-resistant to 20 atm
Band: rubber, folding clasp
Price: $4,660
Variations: black band and dial; stainless steel Milanese mesh band ($4,985)

Super Avenger II
Reference number: A13371111B2A1
Movement: automatic, Breitling Caliber 13 (base ETA 7750); ø 30 mm, height 7.9 mm; 25 jewels; 28,800 vph; COSC-certified chronometer; 42-hour power reserve
Functions: hours, minutes, subsidiary seconds; chronograph; date
Case: stainless steel, ø 48 mm, height 17.75 mm; unidirectional bezel, 0-60 scale; sapphire crystal; screw-in crown; water-resistant to 30 atm
Band: stainless steel, folding clasp
Price: $5,835
Variations: rubber band ($5,635)

BREITLING

Colt Automatic 44
Reference number: A17388101B1A1
Movement: automatic, Breitling Caliber 17 (base ETA 2824-2); ø 25.6 mm, height 4.6 mm; 25 jewels; 28,800 vph; COSC-certified chronometer; 38-hour power reserve
Functions: hours, minutes, sweep seconds; date
Case: stainless steel, ø 44 mm, height 11.25 mm; unidirectional bezel, 0-60 scale; sapphire crystal; water-resistant to 20 atm
Band: stainless steel, folding clasp
Price: $3,620
Variations: blue dial

Navitimer Ref. 806 1959 Re-Edition
Reference number: AB0910371B1X1
Movement: manually wound, Breitling Caliber B09; ø 30 mm, height 6.7 mm; 39 jewels; 28,800 vph; column wheel control of chronograph functions; COSC-certified chronometer; 70-hour power reserve
Functions: hours, minutes, subsidiary seconds; chronograph
Case: stainless steel, ø 40.9 mm, height 12.86 mm; bidirectional white gold bezel with integrated slide rule and tachymeter scale; sapphire crystal; transparent case back; water-resistant to 3 atm
Band: calfskin, buckle
Price: $8,600

Superocean Héritage II Chronograph 44 Outerknown
Reference number: M133132A1C1W1
Movement: automatic, Breitling Caliber 13 (base ETA 7750); ø 30 mm, height 7.9 mm; 25 jewels; 28,800 vph; COSC-certified chronometer; 42-hour power reserve
Functions: hours, minutes, subsidiary seconds; chronograph; date, weekday
Case: stainless steel with black DLC coating, ø 44 mm, height 15.65 mm; unidirectional bezel with ceramic insert, 0-60 scale; sapphire crystal; screw-in crown; water-resistant to 20 atm
Band: textile, folding clasp
Price: $7,100

Chronomat B01 Chronograph 44
Reference number: AB0115101F1A1
Movement: automatic, Breitling Caliber B01; ø 30 mm, height 7.2 mm; 47 jewels; 28,800 vph; column wheel control of chronograph functions; COSC-certified chronometer; 70-hour power reserve
Functions: hours, minutes, subsidiary seconds; chronograph; date
Case: stainless steel, ø 44 mm, height 16.95 mm; unidirectional bezel, 0-60 scale; sapphire crystal; screw-in pushers and crown; water-resistant to 50 atm
Band: stainless steel, folding clasp
Price: $8,720
Variations: reptile skin band and buckle ($8,150)

Superocean Héritage II B01 Chronograph 44
Reference number: AB0162121B1S1
Movement: automatic, Breitling Caliber B01; ø 30 mm, height 7.2 mm; 47 jewels; 28,800 vph; COSC-certified chronometer; 70-hour power reserve
Functions: hours, minutes, subsidiary seconds; chronograph; date
Case: stainless steel, ø 44 mm, height 15.5 mm; unidirectional bezel with ceramic insert; sapphire crystal; screw-in crown; water-resistant to 20 atm
Band: rubber, folding clasp
Price: $7,665
Variations: stainless steel bracelet ($7,990)

Navitimer 1 B01 Airline Edition "PanAm"
Reference number: AB01212B1C1A2
Movement: automatic, Breitling Caliber B01; ø 30 mm, height 7.2 mm; 47 jewels; 28,800 vph; COSC-certified chronometer; 70-hour power reserve
Functions: hours, minutes, subsidiary seconds; chronograph; date
Case: stainless steel, ø 43 mm, height 14.25 mm; bezel with integrated slide rule; sapphire crystal; transparent case back; water-resistant to 3 atm
Band: stainless steel, folding clasp
Remarks: limited Navitimer series with various models in airline color codes from the 1960s
Price: $9,225

BREITLING

Navitimer 1 Automatic 38
Reference number: A17325211C1P1
Movement: automatic, Breitling Caliber 17 (base ETA 2824-2); ø 25.6 mm, height 4.6 mm; 25 jewels; 28,800 vph; COSC-certified chronometer; 40-hour power reserve
Functions: hours, minutes, sweep seconds; date
Case: stainless steel, ø 38 mm, height 10.1 mm; bidirectional bezel with integrated slide rule and tachymeter scale; sapphire crystal; water-resistant to 3 atm
Band: reptile skin, buckle
Price: $4,310

Superocean II Automatic 46 Blacksteel
Reference number: M17368B71B1S1
Movement: automatic, Breitling Caliber 17 (base ETA 2824-2); ø 25.6 mm, height 4.6 mm; 25 jewels; 28,800 vph; COSC-certified chronometer; 40-hour power reserve
Functions: hours, minutes, sweep seconds; date
Case: stainless steel with black DLC coating, ø 46 mm, height 16.85 mm; unidirectional bezel, 0-60 scale; sapphire crystal; screw-in crown; helium valve; water-resistant to 200 atm
Band: rubber, buckle
Price: $4,850

Superocean II 42
Reference number: A17365D11C1A1
Movement: automatic, Breitling Caliber 17 (base ETA 2824-2); ø 25.6 mm, height 4.6 mm; 25 jewels; 28,800 vph; COSC-certified chronometer; 40-hour power reserve
Functions: hours, minutes, sweep seconds; date
Case: stainless steel, ø 42 mm, height 13.3 mm; unidirectional bezel, 0-60 scale; sapphire crystal; screw-in crown; helium valve; water-resistant to 50 atm
Band: stainless steel, folding clasp
Price: $3,950
Variations: rubber band and buckle

Caliber B01
Automatic; column wheel control of chronograph functions; vertical clutch; single spring barrel; COSC-certified chronometer; 70-hour power reserve
Functions: hours, minutes, subsidiary seconds; chronograph; date
Diameter: 30 mm
Height: 7.2 mm
Jewels: 47
Balance: glucydur
Frequency: 28,800 vph

Caliber B04
Automatic; column wheel control of chronograph functions; vertical clutch; single spring barrel; COSC-certified chronometer; 70-hour power reserve
Functions: hours, minutes, subsidiary seconds; additional 24-hour display (2nd time zone); chronograph; date
Diameter: 30 mm
Height: 7.4 mm
Jewels: 47
Balance: glucydur
Frequency: 28,800 vph

Caliber B05
Automatic; column wheel control of chronograph functions; vertical clutch; time zone disk connected to hand mechanism by planetary transmission; single spring barrel; COSC-certified chronometer; 70-hour power reserve
Functions: hours, minutes, subsidiary seconds; world time display (crown-set 2nd time zone); chronograph; date
Diameter: 30 mm
Height: 8.1 mm
Jewels: 56
Balance: glucydur
Frequency: 28,800 vph

BREMONT

At the 2012 Olympic Games in London, stuntman Gary Connery parachuted into the stadium wearing an outfit that made him look suspiciously like the Queen. He was also the first to jet suit out of a helicopter. On both occasions he was wearing a Bremont. And so do many other adventurous types, like polar explorer Ben Saunders or Levison Wood, who was the first person to walk the length of the Nile.

Bremonts are the brainchild of brothers Nick and Giles English, themselves dyed-in-the-wool pilots and restorers of vintage airplanes. The brand name has a story: To avoid a storm, the brothers were forced to land their vintage biplane in a field in southern France. The farmer, a former World War II pilot, was more than happy to put them up for the night. His name: Antoine Bremont.

These British-made timepieces hit the market in 2007 and have climbed in the eyes of consumers. They use sturdy, COSC-certified automatic movements from Switzerland, hardened steel, a patented shock-absorbing system, and a rotor whose design recalls a flight of planes. The brand has sought its inspiration from such British icons as the Spitfire, Bletchley Park (where the German codes were broken during World War II), or Jaguar sports cars and, most recently, Norton motorcycles. It also partnered with Boeing to produce an elegant range of watches on an organic polymer strap. Water sport is another area Bremont has explored, with models inspired by the legendary J-Class yachts, like the ladies' model AC I 32, and a special set devoted to the America's Cup.

In 2010, the watches started being manufactured in Henley-on-Thames, where, in 2017, Bremont became the first official timekeeper for the Henley Royal Regatta, one of Great Britain's top rowing events. Another state-of-the-art factory for making cases and some movement components was recently moved to the Henley facility.

Bremont Watch Company
P.O. Box 4741
Henley-on-Thames
RG9 9BZ
Oxfordshire
United Kingdom

Tel.:
+44-800-817-4281

E-mail:
info@bremont.com

Website:
www.bremont.com

Founded:
2002

Number of employees:
100+

Annual production:
several thousand watches

U.S. distributor:
Michael Pearson
Michael.Pearson@bremont.com
Anthony Kozlowsky
Anthony.kozlowsky@bremont.com
Bremont Inc.
501 Madison Avenue
New York, NY 10022
855-273-6668

Most important collections/price range:
ALT1, Armed Forces collection, Bremont Boeing, Bremont Jaguar, MB, SOLO, Supermarine, U-2, and limited editions / $3,600 to $42,500

Jaguar D-Type
Reference number: BJ-D-LE/R
Movement: automatic, Bremont BE50AE (base ETA 7750); ø 30 mm, height 7.9; 28 jewels; 28,800 vph; ISO 3159-certified chronometer; 42-hour power reserve
Functions: hours, minutes, subsidiary seconds; chronograph; date
Case: satin-brushed and hardened stainless steel, ø 43 mm, height 16 mm; bezel with integrated tachymeter scale; transparent case back; sapphire crystal; water-resistant to 10 atm
Band: calfskin, buckle
Remarks: miniaturized Jaguar D-Type steering wheel rotor
Price: $7,295

Jaguar MKI
Movement: automatic, Bremont BWC/01-10; ø 33.4 mm; 25 jewels; 28,800 vph; 50-hour power reserve
Functions: hours, minutes, subsidiary seconds; date
Case: stainless steel, ø 43 mm, height 16 mm; transparent case back; sapphire crystal; water-resistant to 10 atm
Band: calfskin, buckle
Remarks: miniaturized Jaguar E-Type steering wheel rotor with Growler emblem
Price: $11,395

Broadsword
Reference number: HMAF-Broadsword-S
Movement: automatic, modified Caliber BE-95AE; ø 25.6 mm, height 5.6 mm; 31 jewels; 28,800 vph; Bremont molded and decorated skeletonized rotor; ISO 3159-certified chronometer; 38-hour power reserve
Functions: hours, minutes, subsidiary seconds; date
Case: stainless steel, ø 40 mm, height 12.69 mm; case back engraved with Her Majesty's Armed Forces heraldic badges; sapphire crystal; water-resistant to 10 atm
Band: sailcloth, buckle
Price: $3,445

BREMONT

ALT1-P2/CR
Reference number: ALT1-P2/CR/R
Movement: automatic, modified Caliber BE-53AE; ø 30 mm, height 7.9 mm; 27 jewels; 28,800 vph; Bremont molded and decorated skeletonized rotor; ISO 3159-certified chronometer; 42-hour power reserve
Functions: hours, minutes, subsidiary seconds; chronograph; date
Case: stainless steel, DLC-treated case barrel, ø 43 mm, height 16 mm; exhibition case back; sapphire crystal; water-resistant to 10 atm
Band: leather, folding clasp with security clasp
Price: $4,995

ALT1-C
Reference number: ALT1-C/WH-BK
Movement: automatic, Caliber BE-50AE (base ETA "Valjoux" 7750-SO BI AC); ø 30 mm, height 7.9 mm; 25 jewels; 28,800 vph; ISO 3159-certified chronometer; 42-hour power reserve
Functions: hours, minutes, subsidiary seconds; chronograph; date
Case: stainless steel, barrel with black DLC treatment, ø 43 mm, height 16 mm; sapphire crystal; transparent case back; water-resistant to 10 atm
Band: calfskin, buckle
Price: $6,495
Variations: stainless steel bracelet

Martin-Baker MBIII
Reference number: MBIII-10th-Anniversary-S
Movement: automatic, Caliber BE-93-2AE (base Sellita SW330); ø 25.6 mm, height 4.1 mm; 25 jewels; 28,800 vph; soft iron cage for amagnetic protection; ISO 3159-certified chronometer; 38-hour power reserve
Functions: hours, minutes, sweep seconds; sweep 24-hour display; date
Case: stainless steel, titanium case barrel, ø 43 mm, height 12 mm; inner crown-operated bidirectional bezel; sapphire crystal; screw-down case back with engraving of Martin-Baker MK16 ejector seat; water-resistant to 10 atm
Band: calfskin, buckle
Price: $5,595
Variations: stainless steel bracelet

Solo 34
Reference number: SOLO-34-AJ-MP-S
Movement: automatic, modified Caliber BE-92AV; ø 3.6 mm; 25 jewels; 28,800 vph; Bremont molded and skeletonized rotor; ISO 3159-certified chronometer; 42-hour power reserve
Functions: hours, minutes, sweep seconds; date
Case: stainless steel, ø 34 mm, height 10.7 mm; transparent screw-down case back; sapphire crystal; water-resistant to 10 atm
Band: leather, buckle
Remarks: mother-of-pearl dial
Price: $4,395
Variations: various straps

S300 White
Reference number: S300-WH-R
Movement: automatic, Caliber, BE-92AE (base ETA 2892-2); ø 25.6 mm, height 4.6 mm; 25 jewels; 28,800 vph; ISO 3159-certified chronometer; 38-hour power reserve
Functions: hours, minutes, seconds; date
Case: hardened stainless steel, DLC-treated case barrel; ø 43 mm, height 13 mm; bidirectional bezel; screw-down case back with decoration; sapphire crystal; water-resistant to 30 atm
Band: stainless steel buckle
Remarks: comes with rubber strap
Price: $4,095

Solo 37 Black
Reference number: SOLO-37/BK-SI/R
Movement: automatic, customized Caliber BE-36AE; ø 28 mm, height 5.05 mm; 26 jewels; 28,800 vph; molded and skeletonized rotor; ISO 3159-certified chronometer; 38-hour power reserve
Functions: hours, minutes, sweep seconds; date
Case: hardened stainless steel, ø 43 mm, height 16 mm; bidirectional bezel; DLC-treated case barrel; transparent case back; sapphire crystal; water-resistant to 10 atm
Band: rubber, titanium buckle
Remarks: gold indices
Price: $3,995

BRM

For Bernard Richards, the true sign of luxury lies in "technical skills and perfection in all stages of manufacture." The exterior of the product is of course crucial, but all of BRM's major operations for making a wristwatch—such as encasing, assembling, setting, and polishing—are performed by hand in his little garage-like factory located outside Paris in Magny-sur-Vexin.

BRM is devoted to the ultra-mechanical look with the *haute-horlogerie* feel of high-end materials. His inspiration at the start came from the 1940s, the age of axle grease, pinups, real pilots, and a can-do attitude. The design: three dimensions visible to the naked eye, big mechanical landscapes. The inside: custom-designed components, fitting perfectly into Richards's automotive ideal. Gradually, though, Richards has been modernizing.

BRM's unusual timepieces have mainly been based on the tried and trusted ETA movements. The new GTM, featuring a printed and UV-treated world on the dial, runs on one, for example. But Richards has set lofty goals for himself and his young venture, for he intends to set up a true *manufacture* in his French factory. His BiRotor model is thus outfitted with the Precitime, an autonomous caliber conceived and manufactured on French soil. The movement features BRM's shock absorbers mounted on the conical springs of its so-called Isolastic system. Plates and bridges are crafted in ARCAP, rotors are made of Fortale and tantalum. The twin rotors, found at 12 and 6 o'clock, are mounted on double rows of ceramic bearings that require no lubrication.

When not building eccentric timepieces, Richards lets BRM aficionados do their own thing: When visiting the BRM website, they can construct a V12-44-BRM model on their own.

BRM
(Bernard Richards Manufacture)
2 Impasse de L'Aubette
ZA des Aulnaies
F-95420 Magny en Vexin
France

Tel.:
+33-1-61-02-00-25

Website:
www.brm-manufacture.com

Founded:
2003

Number of employees:
20

Annual production:
approx. 2,000 pieces

U.S. distributor:
BRM Manufacture North America
25 Highland Park Village, Suite 100-777
Dallas, TX 75205
214-231-0144
usa@brm-manufacture.com

Price range:
$3,000 to $150,000

GMT6
Movement: automatic, ETA Caliber 2824/2 modified in-house; ø 25.6 mm, height 4.6 mm; 25 jewels; 28,800 vph; skeletonized dial; 38-hour power reserve
Functions: hours, minutes, seconds; 24-hour time zone (numbers printed on bezel rim); date
Case: titanium with black PVD, ø 46 mm, height 10 mm; 24 reference flags printed on bezel, user rotates home flag to hour hand to compute time in other zones; steel crown and lugs; crystal sapphire; transparent case back; screw-in crown; water-resistant to 5 atm
Remarks: UV-treated white world map printed on dial
Band: leather, buckle
Price: $6,950

TR1 Tourbillon
Movement: automatic, Precitime Caliber; ø 30 mm, height 7.9 mm; 26 jewels; 28,800 vph; 46-hour power reserve; 105-second tourbillon in ARCAP with reversed cage for visible escapement and suspended by 2 micro springs; patented Isolastic system with 4 shock absorbers; automatic assembly with ceramic ball bearings
Functions: hours, minutes, sweep seconds
Case: titanium, ø 52 mm; sapphire crystal; antireflective on both sides; transparent case back; water-resistant to 10 atm
Band: leather, buckle
Price: $145,350
Variations: 48-mm case ($136,150)

BiRotor
Movement: automatic, Precitime Caliber BiRotor; 24 × 32 mm; 35 jewels; 28,800 vph; 45-hour power reserve; Fortale HR and tantalum double rotors on ceramic ball bearings; patented Isolastic system with 4 shock absorbers, ARCAP plates, bridges
Functions: hours, minutes, subsidiary seconds
Case: titanium with rose gold crown and strap lugs, 40 × 48 mm, height 9.9 mm; domed sapphire crystal; antireflective on both sides; domed sapphire crystal transparent case back; water-resistant to 30 m
Band: Nomex, buckle
Price: $68,500

R46
Movement: automatic, heavily modified ETA Caliber 2161; ø 38 mm; 35 jewels; 28,800 vph; 48-hour power reserve; patented Isolastic system with 3 shock absorbers; Fortale HR, tantalum and aluminum rotor; hand-painted Gulf colors
Functions: hours, minutes, sweep seconds; power reserve indication
Case: Makrolon with rose gold crown and strap lugs, ø 46 mm, height 10 mm; sapphire crystal; antireflective on both sides; exhibition case back; water-resistant to 3 atm
Band: leather, buckle
Price: $24,750; limited to 30 pieces

R12-46
Movement: automatic, ETA Valjoux Caliber 7753 modified in-house; ø 30 mm, height 7.90 mm; 27 jewels; 28,800 vph; skeletonized dial; shock absorbers connected to block; 42-hour power reserve
Functions: hours, minutes, subsidiary seconds; chronograph; date
Case: bronze, ø 46 mm, height 14 mm; stainless steel lugs and crown with black PVD; crystal sapphire; transparent case back; water-resistant to 10 atm
Band: leather, bronze buckle
Price: $13,550

MK 44 Green
Movement: automatic, ETA Valjoux Caliber 7753; ø 30 mm, height 7.90 mm; 27 jewels; 28,800 vph; 42-hour power reserve
Functions: hours, minutes, subsidiary seconds; date; chronograph
Case: Makrolon (polycarbonate), ø 45 mm; pushers, lugs, crown from single titanium block; sapphire crystal; exhibition case back; water-resistant to 10 atm
Band: technical fabrics for extra lightness
Remarks: lightest automatic chronograph ever made; skeleton dial with blue hands
Price: $13,450
Variations: many options with configurator

DDF12-44-AR
Movement: automatic, ETA Valjoux Caliber 7753 modified in-house; ø 30 mm, height 7.90 mm; 27 jewels; 28,800 vph; skeletonized dial; shock absorbers connected to block; 42-hour power reserve
Functions: hours, minutes, subsidiary seconds; chronograph; date
Case: titanium with black PVD coating, ø 44 mm; stainless steel lugs and pushers; sapphire crystal; transparent case back; water-resistant to 10 atm
Band: leather, buckle
Remarks: skeletonized dial with red hands
Price: $12,750

V12-46-TSAABL
Movement: automatic, ETA Valjoux Caliber 7753 modified in-house; ø 30 mm, height 7.90 mm; 27 jewels; 28,800 vph; skeletonized dial; shock absorbers connected to movement, 3 vertical, 3 horizontal; 42-hour power reserve
Functions: hours, minutes, subsidiary seconds; chronograph; date with 10-hour corrector
Case: titanium with rose gold crown and strap lugs, ø 46 mm, height 12 mm; sapphire crystal; antireflective on both sides; transparent case back; screw-in crown; water-resistant to 10 atm
Band: calfskin, folding clasp
Price: $16,700
Variations: hands and springs in different colors on request

R50 MK
Movement: automatic, heavily modified ETA Caliber 2161; ø 38 mm; 35 jewels; 28,800 vph; 48-hour power reserve; patented Isolastic system with 3 shock absorbers; Fortale HR, tantalum, and aluminum rotor; hand-painted Gulf colors
Functions: hours, minutes, sweep seconds; power reserve indication
Case: Makrolon with rose gold crown and strap lugs, ø 50 mm, height 13.2 mm; sapphire crystal; antireflective on both sides; exhibition case back; water-resistant to 3 atm
Band: leather, buckle
Price: $28,550; limited to 30 pieces
Variations: rose gold ($65,000)

BULGARI

Although Bulgari is one of the largest jewelry manufacturers in the world, watches have always played an important role for the brand. The purchase of Daniel Roth and Gérald Genta in the Vallée de Joux opened new perspectives for its timepieces, thanks to specialized production facilities and the watchmaking talent in the Vallée de Joux—especially where complicated timepieces are concerned. In March 2011, luxury goods giant Louis Vuitton Moët Hennessy (LVMH) secured all the Bulgari family shares in exchange for 16.5 million LVMH shares and a say in the group's future. The financial backing of the megagroup boosted the company's strategy to become fully independent.

In mid-2013, Jean-Christophe Babin, the man who turned TAG Heuer into a leading player in sports watches, was chosen to head the venerable brand. He pushed for integration, meaning the company now builds complete watches, including its own cases and dials, and a number of outstanding calibers, like the 168 automatic based on a design by the great nineteenth-century watchmaker Jean Frédéric Leschot.

Under the bold leadership of Guido Terrini, the watch division has also been pushing the envelope with a series of increasingly thin and complicated automatics. After the tourbillon in 2014 came a minute repeater in 2016, which is 3.12 millimeters high and whose dial features slotted indices for better sound transmission. The 5.15-millimeter-high Octo Finissimo Automatic, with the Caliber BVL 138, was the talk of Baselworld in 2017. And in 2019 appeared a chronograph GMT that is 6.9 millimeters high, wound with a hubless peripheral rotor and featuring an hour hand that can be quickly clicked through the time zones.

Bulgari Horlogerie SA
rue de Monruz 34
CH-2000 Neuchâtel
Switzerland

Tel.:
+41-32-722-7878

E-mail:
info@bulgari.com

Website:
www.bulgari.com

Founded:
1884 (Bulgari Horlogerie was founded in the early 1980s as Bulgari Time)

U.S. distributor:
Bulgari Corporation of America
555 Madison Avenue
New York, NY 10022
212-315-9700

Most important collections/price range:
Bulgari-Bulgari / from approx. $4,700 to $30,300; Diagono / from approx. $3,200; Octo / from approx. $9,500 to $690,000 and above; Daniel Roth and Gérald Genta collections

Octo Finissimo Chronograph

Reference number: BGO42C14TTXTCHGMT
Movement: automatic, Bulgari Caliber BVL 318 Finissimo; ø 36 mm, height 3.3 mm; 37 jewels; 21,600 vph; hubless peripheral rotor with platinum oscillating mass; column wheel control of chronograph functions; finely finished with côtes de Genève; 60-hour power reserve; **Functions:** hours, minutes, subsidiary seconds; additional 24-hour display (2nd time zone); chronograph
Case: titanium, ø 42 mm, height 6.9 mm; sapphire crystal; transparent case back; water-resistant to 3 atm
Band: titanium, folding clasp
Remarks: currently the thinnest automatic chronograph movement
Price: $17,600; **Variations:** reptile skin band

Octo Finissimo Automatic

Movement: automatic, Bulgari Caliber BVL 138 Finissimo; ø 36 mm, height 2.23 mm; 23 jewels; 21,600 vph; platinum microrotor; finely finished with côtes de Genève; 60-hour power reserve
Functions: hours, minutes, subsidiary seconds
Case: titanium, ø 40 mm, height 5.15 mm; sapphire crystal; transparent case back
Band: reptile skin, buckle
Price: $12,800
Variations: titanium bracelet ($13,900)

Octo Finissimo Automatic

Reference number: BGOPGCTAUTO
Movement: automatic, Bulgari Caliber BVL 138 Finissimo; ø 36 mm, height 2.23 mm; 23 jewels; 21,600 vph; platinum microrotor; finely finished with côtes de Genève; 60-hour power reserve
Functions: hours, minutes, subsidiary seconds
Case: rose gold, ø 40 mm, height 5.15 mm; sapphire crystal; transparent case back
Band: rose gold, folding clasp
Price: $43,400

BULGARI

Octo Finissimo Skeleton
Reference number: BGO40CCXTSK
Movement: manually wound, Bulgari Caliber BVL 128SK; ø 36 mm, height 2.35 mm; 28,800 vph; skeletonized bridges and plates; 65-hour power reserve
Functions: hours, minutes, subsidiary seconds; power reserve indicator
Case: ceramic, ø 40 mm, height 5.37 mm; sapphire crystal; transparent case back; screw-in crown; water-resistant to 3 atm
Band: ceramic, folding clasp
Price: $24,700

Octo Finissimo Tourbillon Skeleton
Reference number: BGO40PLC3TBXTSK
Movement: manually wound, Bulgari Caliber BVL 268 Finissimo Squelette; ø 32.6 mm, height 1.95 mm; 26 jewels; 21,600 vph; flying 1-minute tourbillon; skeletonized and finely finished movement; 62-hour power reserve
Functions: hours, minutes
Case: platinum, ø 40 mm, height 5 mm; sapphire crystal; transparent case back; water-resistant to 3 atm
Band: reptile skin, buckle
Price: $132,000

Octo Finissimo Tourbillon Skeleton
Reference number: BGO40PLC3TBXTSK
Movement: manually wound, Bulgari Caliber BVL 268 Finissimo Squelette; ø 32.6 mm, height 1.95 mm; 26 jewels; 21,600 vph; flying 1-minute tourbillon; skeletonized and finely finished movement; 62-hour power reserve
Functions: hours, minutes
Case: platinum, ø 40 mm, height 5 mm; sapphire crystal; transparent case back; water-resistant to 3 atm
Band: reptile skin, buckle
Price: $132,000

Octo Finissimo Tourbillon Automatic
Reference number: BGO42C14TTBXTSKAUTO
Movement: automatic, Bulgari Caliber BVL 288; ø 36 mm, height 1.95 mm; 24 jewels; 21,600 vph; flying 1-minute tourbillon; hubless peripheral rotor; 55-hour power reserve
Functions: hours, minutes
Case: titanium, ø 42 mm, height 3.95 mm; sapphire crystal; transparent case back; water-resistant to 3 atm
Band: titanium, double folding clasp
Remarks: currently the thinnest wristwatch with automatic movement and tourbillon
Price: $118,000

Octo Finissimo Tourbillon Automatic
Reference number: BGO42CCXTSKAUTO
Movement: automatic, Bulgari Caliber BVL 288; ø 36 mm, height 1.95 mm; 24 jewels; 21,600 vph; flying 1-minute tourbillon; hubless peripheral rotor; 55-hour power reserve
Functions: hours, minutes
Case: carbon composite, ø 42 mm, height 3.95 mm; sapphire crystal; transparent case back; water-resistant to 3 atm
Band: carbon composite, double folding clasp
Remarks: currently the thinnest mechanical automatic watch with tourbillon
Price: $130,000

Octo Finissimo Tourbillon Ultranero
Reference number: BGO40BTLTBXT
Movement: manually wound, Bulgari Caliber BVL 268 Finissimo Tourbillon; ø 32.6 mm, height 1.95 mm; 26 jewels; 21,600 vph; flying 1-minute tourbillon; finely finished movement; 52-hour power reserve
Functions: hours, minutes
Case: titanium with black DLC coating, ø 40 mm, height 5 mm; sapphire crystal; transparent case back; rose gold screw-in crown; water-resistant to 3 atm
Band: reptile skin, buckle
Price: $99,000

BULGARI

Octo L'Originale Velocissimo Chronograph
Reference number: BGO41C14TVDCH
Movement: automatic, Bulgari Caliber BVL 328 Velocissimo (base Zenith "El Primero"); ø 30 mm, height 6.62 mm; 31 jewels; 36,000 vph; column wheel controller of chronograph functions, silicon escapement; 50-hour power reserve
Functions: hours, minutes, subsidiary seconds; chronograph; date
Case: titanium, ø 41 mm, height 13.07 mm; sapphire crystal; transparent case back; water-resistant to 10 atm
Band: rubber, folding clasp
Price: $10,200

Octo L'Originale
Reference number: BGO41PBBSGVD
Movement: automatic, Bulgari Caliber BVL 191; ø 26.2 mm, height 3.8 mm; 26 jewels; 28,800 vph; finely finished with côtes de Genève; 42-hour power reserve
Functions: hours, minutes, sweep seconds; date
Case: stainless steel with black DLC coating, ø 41.5 mm, height 10.5 mm; red gold lower bezel and crown; sapphire crystal; transparent case back; water-resistant to 10 atm
Band: rubber, folding clasp
Price: $8,650

Octo L'Originale Velocissimo Chronograph
Reference number: BGO41PBBSGVDCH
Movement: automatic, Bulgari Caliber BVL 328 Velocissimo (base Zenith "El Primero"); ø 30 mm, height 6.62 mm; 31 jewels; 36,000 vph; column wheel control of chronograph functions, silicon escapement; 50-hour power reserve
Functions: hours, minutes, subsidiary seconds; chronograph; date
Case: stainless steel with black DLC coating, ø 41.5 mm, height 13.07 mm; red gold lower bezel and crown; sapphire crystal; transparent case back; water-resistant to 10 atm
Band: rubber, folding clasp
Price: $11,800

Octo Finissimo Automatic Ceramica
Reference number: BGO40BCCXTAUTO
Movement: automatic, Bulgari Caliber BVL 138 Finissimo; ø 36 mm, height 2.23 mm; 23 jewels; 21,600 vph; platinum microrotor; finely finished with côtes de Genève; 60-hour power reserve
Functions: hours, minutes, subsidiary seconds
Case: ceramic, ø 40 mm, height 5.15 mm; sapphire crystal; transparent case back
Band: ceramic, folding clasp
Price: $15,600

Octo Roma
Reference number: OC41C5SPGLD
Movement: automatic, Bulgari Caliber BVL 191; ø 26.2 mm, height 3.8 mm; 26 jewels; 28,800 vph; finely finished with côtes de Genève; 42-hour power reserve
Functions: hours, minutes, sweep seconds; date
Case: stainless steel, ø 41 mm, height 10.5 mm; rose gold lower bezel and crown; sapphire crystal; transparent case back; water-resistant to 10 atm
Band: stainless steel, folding clasp
Price: $7,800
Variations: comes with different cases, straps, and dials

Octo Roma Tourbillon Sapphire
Reference number: BGO44PGLTBSK/BLUE
Movement: manually wound, Bulgari Caliber BVL 206; ø 34 mm, height 5 mm; 21,600 vph; flying 1-minute tourbillon; skeletonized movement, bridges with blue DLC coating; 64-hour power reserve
Functions: hours, minutes
Case: rose gold, ø 44 mm, height 12.45 mm; sapphire crystal; transparent case back; water-resistant to 5 atm
Band: reptile skin, folding clasp
Price: $89,000

BULGARI

Octo Grande Sonnerie
Reference number: OC44CPGLTBGSQP
Movement: automatic, Bulgari Caliber BVL 5307; 82 jewels; 1-minute tourbillon; 48-hour power reserve
Functions: hours, minutes; minute repeater; dual power reserve indicator; perpetual calendar with date, weekday, month, moon phase, leap year
Case: carbon, ø 44 mm; sapphire crystal; rose gold crown and pushers
Band: reptile skin, folding clasp
Price: $833,000; limited to 3 pieces

Bulgari Bulgari
Reference number: BB41C3BSD/MB
Movement: automatic, Bulgari Caliber BVL 191; ø 26.2 mm, height 3.8 mm; 26 jewels; 28,800 vph; finished with côtes de Genève; 42-hour power reserve
Functions: hours, minutes, sweep seconds; date
Case: bronze, ø 41 mm, height 8.7 mm; sapphire crystal; water-resistant to 5 atm
Band: rubber, folding clasp
Price: $5,600

Bulgari Bulgari
Reference number: BB41C3BSD/MB
Movement: automatic, Bulgari Caliber BVL 191; ø 26.2 mm, height 3.8 mm; 26 jewels; 28,800 vph; finished with côtes de Genève; 42-hour power reserve
Functions: hours, minutes, sweep seconds; date
Case: stainless steel with black DLC coating, ø 41 mm, height 8.7 mm; sapphire crystal; water-resistant to 5 atm
Band: rubber, folding clasp
Price: $4,100

Caliber BVL 138 Finissimo
Automatic; flying platinum microrotor; flying single spring barrel, 60-hour power reserve
Functions: hours, minutes, subsidiary seconds; date
Diameter: 36 mm
Height: 2.23 mm
Jewels: 23
Balance: glucydur
Frequency: 21,600 vph
Balance spring: flat hairspring index for fine adjustment
Shock protection: Incabloc
Remarks: finely finished with côtes de Genève

Caliber BVL 318 Finissimo
Automatic; hubless peripheral rotor with platinum oscillating mass; column wheel control of chronograph functions; flying spring barrel; 60-hour power reserve
Functions: hours, minutes, subsidiary seconds; additional 24-hour display (2nd time zone); chronograph
Diameter: 36 mm; **Height:** 3.3 mm
Jewels: 37
Balance: glucydur
Frequency: 21,600 vph
Balance spring: flat hairspring index for fine adjustment
Shock protection: Incabloc
Remarks: finely finished with côtes de Genève; currently the thinnest chronograph movement

Caliber BVL 288
Automatic; flying 1-minute tourbillon; hubless peripheral rotor; single spring barrel, 55-hour power reserve
Functions: hours, minutes
Diameter: 36 mm
Height: 1.95 mm
Jewels: 24
Frequency: 21,600 vph
Remarks: engine of the thinnest automatic wristwatch—including a tourbillon

CARL F. BUCHERER

While luxury watch brand Carl F. Bucherer is still rather young, the Lucerne-based Bucherer jewelry dynasty behind it draws its vast know-how from more than ninety years of experience in the conception and design of fine wristwatches.

In 2005, Bucherer joined its Sainte-Croix-headquartered partner, Techniques Horlogères Appliquées SA (THA), to manufacture its own movement. THA was integrated into the Bucherer Group and the watch company renamed Carl F. Bucherer Technologies SA (CFBT). The Sainte-Croix operation is led by technical director Dr. Albrecht Haake, who oversees a staff of about twenty. Dr. Haake is currently focusing much of his energy on furthering the capacities at the workshop. "Industrialization is not a question of cost, but rather a question of quality," says Haake.

The Swiss company also expanded its Lengnau location to create a competence center that can focus on manufacturing its own movements as well as in-house watches. The famed automatic caliber with the peripheral rotor went through a thorough revamping process with the idea of industrializing it. For its 130th birthday, in 2018, the company decided to create a special "floating" tourbillon for its Manero collection. Not only does it feature a hubless peripheral rotor but the power transmission to the tourbillon is done from the side, making it invisible to the observer. And in 2019, Bucherer launched the appropriately named Heritage collection. It is composed of timepieces like the Heritage BiCompax Annual Chronograph and the Heritage Tourbillon Double Peripheral that draw inspiration from the brand's historical models and give them a modern look.

Bucherer AG
Carl F. Bucherer
Langensandstrasse 27
CH-6002 Lucerne
Switzerland

Tel.:
+41-41-369-7070

E-mail:
info@carl-f-bucherer.com

Website:
www.carl-f-bucherer.com

Founded:
1919, repositioned under the name Carl F. Bucherer in 2001

Number of employees:
approx. 200

Annual production:
approx. 30,000 watches

U.S. distributor:
Carl F. Bucherer North America
1805 South Metro Parkway
Dayton, OH 45459
937-291-4366
info@cfbna.com; www.carl-f-bucherer.com

Most important collections/price range:
Patravi, Manero, Alacria, and Pathos / core price segment $5,000 to $30,000

Heritage Tourbillon Double Peripheral
Reference number: 00.10802.03.13.01
Movement: automatic, Caliber CFB T3000; ø 36.5 mm, height 4.6 mm; 32 jewels; 21,600 vph; silicon escapement; flying 1-minute tourbillon with invisible peripheral drive, hubless peripheral rotor with rose gold oscillating mass; hand-engraved white gold bridge; COSC-certified chronometer; 65-hour power reserve
Functions: hours, minutes, subsidiary seconds (on tourbillon cage)
Case: rose gold, ø 42.5 mm, height 11.9 mm; sapphire crystal; transparent case back; water-resistant to 3 atm
Band: reptile skin, folding clasp
Price: $88,888

Heritage BiCompax Annual Chronograph
Reference number: 00.10803.07.42.01
Movement: automatic, Caliber CFB 1972; ø 30 mm, height 7.3 mm; 47 jewels; 28,800 vph; 42-hour power reserve
Functions: hours, minutes, subsidiary seconds; chronograph; annual calendar with large date, month
Case: stainless steel, ø 41 mm, height 14.05 mm; rose gold bezel, crown, and pushers; sapphire crystal; transparent case back; water-resistant to 3 atm
Band: calfskin, folding clasp
Price: $10,500

Heritage BiCompax Annual Chronograph
Reference number: 00.10803.08.12.01
Movement: automatic, Caliber CFB 1972; ø 30 mm, height 7.3 mm; 47 jewels; 28,800 vph; 42-hour power reserve
Functions: hours, minutes, subsidiary seconds; chronograph; annual calendar with large date, month
Case: stainless steel, ø 41 mm, height 14.05 mm; sapphire crystal; transparent case back; water-resistant to 3 atm
Band: rubber, folding clasp
Price: $7,200

CARL F. BUCHERER

Patravi ScubaTec "Black Manta"
Reference number: 00.10632.28.33.99
Movement: automatic, Caliber CFB 1950.1; ø 26.2 mm, height 4.6 mm; 25 jewels; 28,800 vph; COSC-certified chronometer; 38-hour power reserve
Functions: hours, minutes, sweep seconds; date
Case: titanium with black DLC coating, ø 44.6 mm, height 13.45 mm; unidirectional bezel with ceramic insert, 0-60 scale; sapphire crystal; screw-in crown; helium valve; water-resistant to 50 atm
Band: rubber with recycled textile insert, folding clasp with extension link
Price: $7,200
Variations: stainless steel with stainless steel bracelet ($6,700); stainless steel with rubber band ($6,200)

Manero Flyback
Reference number: 00.10919.03.33.02
Movement: automatic, Caliber CFB 1970; ø 30.4 mm, height 7.9 mm; 25 jewels; 28,800 vph; 42-hour power reserve
Functions: hours, minutes, subsidiary seconds; flyback chronograph; date
Case: rose gold, ø 43 mm, height 14.45 mm; sapphire crystal; transparent case back; water-resistant to 3 atm
Band: antelope leather, buckle
Price: $16,900

Manero Flyback
Reference number: 00.10919.03.33.01
Movement: automatic, Caliber CFB 1970; ø 30.4 mm, height 7.9 mm; 25 jewels; 28,800 vph; 42-hour power reserve
Functions: hours, minutes, subsidiary seconds; flyback chronograph; date
Case: rose gold, ø 43 mm, height 14.45 mm; sapphire crystal; transparent case back; water-resistant to 3 atm
Band: reptile skin, buckle
Price: $16,900

Manero Flyback
Reference number: 00.10919.08.33.01
Movement: automatic, Caliber CFB 1970; ø 30.4 mm, height 7.9 mm; 25 jewels; 28,800 vph; 42-hour power reserve
Functions: hours, minutes, subsidiary seconds; flyback chronograph; date
Case: stainless steel, ø 43 mm, height 14.45 mm; sapphire crystal; transparent case back; water-resistant to 3 atm
Band: reptile skin, buckle
Price: $6,200

Manero Peripheral 43mm
Reference number: 00.10921.08.33.01
Movement: automatic, Caliber CFB A2050; ø 30.6 mm, height 5.28 mm; 33 jewels; 28,800 vph; hubless peripheral rotor with tungsten oscillating mass; COSC-certified chronometer; 55-hour power reserve
Functions: hours, minutes, subsidiary seconds; date
Case: stainless steel, ø 43.1 mm, height 11.2 mm; sapphire crystal; transparent case back; water-resistant to 3 atm
Band: reptile skin, buckle
Price: $6,800
Variations: white dial ($6,800); red gold ($17,600)

Manero Peripheral 43mm
Reference number: 00.10921.08.23.21
Movement: automatic, Caliber CFB A2050; ø 30.6 mm, height 5.28 mm; 33 jewels; 28,800 vph; hubless peripheral rotor with tungsten oscillating mass; COSC-certified chronometer; 55-hour power reserve
Functions: hours, minutes, subsidiary seconds; date
Case: stainless steel, ø 43.1 mm, height 11.2 mm; sapphire crystal; transparent case back; water-resistant to 3 atm
Band: stainless steel, folding clasp
Price: $7,200
Variations: reptile skin band ($6,800)

CARL F. BUCHERER

Manero Tourbillon Double Peripheral
Reference number: 00.10920.03.13.01
Movement: automatic, Caliber CFB T3000; ø 36.5 mm, height 4.6 mm; 32 jewels; 21,600 vph; silicon escapement; flying 1-minute tourbillon with invisible peripheral drive, hubless peripheral rotor with tungsten oscillating mass; COSC-certified chronometer; 65-hour power reserve
Functions: hours, minutes, subsidiary seconds (on tourbillon cage)
Case: rose gold, ø 43.1 mm, height 11.57 mm; sapphire crystal; transparent case back; water-resistant to 3 atm
Band: reptile skin, folding clasp
Price: $68,000

Patravi ScubaTec
Reference number: 00.10632.22.53.01
Movement: automatic, Caliber CFB 1950.1; ø 26.2 mm, height 4.6 mm; 25 jewels; 28,800 vph; COSC-certified chronometer; 38-hour power reserve
Functions: hours, minutes, sweep seconds; date
Case: red gold, ø 44.6 mm, height 13.45 mm; unidirectional bezel with ceramic insert, 0-60 scale; sapphire crystal; screw-in crown; helium valve and crown protection in blackened titanium; water-resistant to 50 atm
Band: rubber, folding clasp with extension link
Price: $23,600
Variations: stainless steel with stainless steel bracelet ($6,700); stainless steel with rubber band ($6,200); rose gold and stainless steel with rubber band ($9,600)

Patravi TravelTec
Reference number: 00.10620.08.33.02
Movement: automatic, Caliber CFB 1901.1; ø 28.6 mm, height 7.3 mm; 39 jewels; 28,800 vph; COSC-certified chronometer; 42-hour power reserve
Functions: hours, minutes, subsidiary seconds; 3 time zone display; chronograph; date
Case: stainless steel, ø 46.6 mm, height 15.5 mm; pusher-activated, bidirectional inner bezel with 24-hour division for a 3rd time zone; sapphire crystal; screw-in crown; water-resistant to 5 atm
Band: rubber, folding clasp
Price: $10,900

CFB T3000
Automatic; floating 1-minute tourbillon; silicon escapement, bidirectional peripheral tungsten rotor turning on edge of movement, on spring-based bearings; precision adjustment mechanism; single spring barrel; COSC-certified chronometer; 65-hour power reserve
Functions: hours, minutes, subsidiary seconds; date
Diameter: 36.5 mm
Height: 4.6 mm
Jewels: 32
Balance: glucydur
Frequency: 21,600 vph
Balance spring: flat hairspring
Shock protection: Incabloc

CFB A2050
Automatic; bidirectional peripheral tungsten rotor turning on edge of movement, on spring-based bearings; precision adjustment mechanism; single spring barrel, 55-hour power reserve
Base caliber: CFB A2000
Functions: hours, minutes, subsidiary seconds; date
Diameter: 30.6 mm
Height: 5.28 mm
Jewels: 33
Balance: glucydur
Frequency: 28,800 vph
Balance spring: flat hairspring
Shock protection: Incabloc

CFB A1000
Automatic; bidirectional peripheral tungsten rotor turning on edge of movement, on spring-based bearings; precision adjustment mechanism; single spring barrel, 55-hour power reserve
Functions: hours, minutes, subsidiary seconds, large date
Diameter: 32 mm
Height: 6.3 mm
Jewels: 33
Balance: glucydur
Frequency: 21,600 vph
Balance spring: flat hairspring
Shock protection: Incabloc
Related calibers: CFB A1002 (with large date, weekday, and power reserve indicator), CFB A1003 (with large date and weekday)

CARTIER

Since the Richemont Group's founding, Cartier has played an important role in the luxury concern as its premier brand and instigator of turnover. Although it took a while for Cartier to find its footing and convince the male market of its masculinity, any concerns about Cartier's seriousness and potential are being dispelled by facts. "We aimed to become a key player in *haute horlogerie*, and we succeeded," said CEO Bernard Fornas at a July 2012 press conference at the company's main manufacturing site in La Chaux-de-Fonds. The company is growing by leaps and bounds—a components manufacturing site employing 400 people is being built at the growing Richemont campus in Meyrin (Geneva).

It was Richemont Group's purchase of the Roger Dubuis *manufacture* in Geneva a few years ago that paved the way to the brand's independence and vertical integration. Under its brilliant head of fine watchmaking, Carole Forestier-Kasapi, Cartier has become a serious producer of movements, among them the 1904, which made its debut in the Calibre model. With a diameter of 42 mm, this strikingly designed men's watch is also well positioned in the segment. The designation 1904 MC is a reference to the year in which Louis Cartier developed the first wristwatch made for men—a pilot's watch custom designed for his friend and early pioneer of aviation, Alberto Santos-Dumont.

The automatic movement is a largely unadorned yet efficient machine, powered by twin barrels. The central rotor sits on ceramic ball bearings, and the adjustment of the conventional escapement is by an excenter screw. It is available for chronographs or diver's watches. But mainly, it has positioned Cartier as one of the most serious and effective makers of high-end watches in a very competitive industry.

Cartier
1201 Genève
Switzerland

E-mail:
contact.na@cartier.com

Website:
www.cartier.com

Founded:
1847

Number of employees:
approx. 1,300 (watch manufacturing)

U.S. distributor:
Cartier North America
645 Fifth Avenue
New York, NY 10022
1-800-CARTIER
www.cartier.us

Most important collections:
Santos de Cartier, Panthère de Cartier, Baignoire, Tank, Ballon Bleu de Cartier, Drive de Cartier, Calibre de Cartier, Clé de Cartier, Ronde de Cartier

Santos de Cartier Skeleton
Reference number: WHSA0007
Movement: manually wound, Cartier Caliber 9611 MC; 28.6 × 28.6 mm, height 3.97 mm; 20 jewels; 21,600 vph; skeleton movement integrating Roman hour numeral; 2 spring barrels, 72-hour power reserve
Functions: hours, minutes
Case: stainless steel, ø 39.8 mm, height 9.08 mm; bezel screwed to case back with 8 screws; sapphire crystal; transparent case back; crown with sapphire cabochon; water-resistant to 10 atm
Band: stainless steel, double folding clasp
Remarks: comes with additional reptile skin strap with QuickSwitch changing system
Price: $26,800
Variations: rose gold ($63,500)

Santos de Cartier Skeleton
Reference number: WHSA0009
Movement: manually wound, Cartier Caliber 9612 MC; 28.6 × 28.6 mm, height 3.97 mm; 20 jewels; 28,800 vph; skeleton movement integrating Roman hour numeral; 2 spring barrels, 72-hour power reserve
Functions: hours, minutes
Case: stainless steel with black ADLC case, ø 39.8 mm, height 9.08 mm; bezel screwed to case back with 8 screws; sapphire crystal; transparent case back; crown with sapphire cabochon; water-resistant to 10 atm
Band: reptile skin, double folding clasp
Remarks: comes with additional reptile skin strap with QuickSwitch changing system
Price: $26,800

Santos de Cartier
Reference number: WGSA0011
Movement: automatic, Cartier Caliber 1847 MC; ø 25.6 mm; 23 jewels; 28,800 vph; 40-hour power reserve
Functions: hours, minutes, sweep seconds; date
Case: rose gold, ø 39.8 mm, height 9.08 mm; sapphire crystal; crown with spinel cabochon; water-resistant to 10 atm
Band: calfskin, double folding clasp
Remarks: comes with additional reptile skin strap with QuickSwitch changing system
Price: $17,800
Variations: 35-mm case ($15,400)

Santos de Cartier
Reference number: WSSA0013
Movement: automatic, Cartier Caliber 1847 MC; ø 25.6 mm; 23 jewels; 28,800 vph; 40-hour power reserve
Functions: hours, minutes, sweep seconds; date
Case: stainless steel, ø 39.8 mm, height 9.08 mm; sapphire crystal; crown with spinel cabochon; water-resistant to 10 atm
Band: stainless steel, double folding clasp
Remarks: comes with additional reptile skin strap with QuickSwitch changing system
Price: $6,850

Santos de Cartier
Reference number: WSSA0009
Movement: automatic, Cartier Caliber 1847 MC; ø 25.6 mm; 23 jewels; 28,800 vph; 40-hour power reserve
Functions: hours, minutes, sweep seconds; date
Case: stainless steel, ø 39.8 mm, height 9.08 mm; sapphire crystal; crown with spinel cabochon; water-resistant to 10 atm
Band: stainless steel, double folding clasp
Remarks: comes with additional reptile skin strap with QuickSwitch changing system
Price: $6,850
Variations: 35-mm case ($6,250)

Santos de Cartier Chronograph
Reference number: WSSA0017
Movement: automatic, Cartier Caliber 1904-CH MC; ø 25.6 mm, height 5.72 mm; 35 jewels; 28,800 vph; 2 spring barrels, 48-hour power reserve
Functions: hours, minutes, subsidiary seconds; chronograph; date
Case: stainless steel, ø 43.3 mm, height 12.5 mm; bezel with ADLC coating; sapphire crystal; water-resistant to 10 atm
Band: rubber, double folding clasp
Remarks: comes with additional reptile skin strap with QuickSwitch changing system
Price: $8,950
Variations: rose gold ($24,700)

Santos de Cartier Chronograph
Reference number: WGSA0017
Movement: automatic, Cartier Caliber 1904-CH MC; ø 25.6 mm, height 5.72 mm; 35 jewels; 28,800 vph; 2 spring barrels, 48-hour power reserve
Functions: hours, minutes, subsidiary seconds; chronograph; date
Case: rose gold, ø 43.3 mm, height 12.5 mm; sapphire crystal; water-resistant to 10 atm
Band: reptile skin, double folding clasp
Remarks: comes with additional rubber strap with QuickSwitch changing system
Price: $24,700
Variations: stainless steel ($8,950)

Tonneau Dual Time Zone Skeleton
Reference number: WHTN0006
Movement: manually wound, Cartier Caliber 9919; 24 × 37.8 mm, height 7.9 mm; 35 jewels; 28,800 vph; skeletonized movement; 2 spring barrels, 60-hour power reserve
Functions: hours, minutes; additional 12-hour display (2nd time zone)
Case: platinum, 29.8 × 52.4 mm, height 11.9 mm; sapphire crystal; transparent case back; crown with sapphire cabochon
Band: reptile skin, double folding clasp
Remarks: comes with reptile skin strap
Price: $78,500; limited to 100 pieces
Variations: rose gold; limited to 100 pieces

Tonneau
Reference number: WGTN0005
Movement: manually wound, Cartier Caliber 1917 MC; 12.9 × 16 mm, height 2.9 mm; 19 jewels; 21,600 vph; 38-hour power reserve
Functions: hours, minutes
Case: platinum, 23 × 46.3 mm, height 7.2 mm; sapphire crystal; crown with ruby cabochon
Band: reptile skin, double folding clasp
Price: $26,200; limited to 100 pieces

CARTIER

Drive de Cartier
Reference number: WSNM0004
Movement: automatic, Cartier Caliber 1904-PS MC; ø 24.9 mm, height 4.5 mm; 27 jewels; 28,800 vph; 48-hour power reserve
Functions: hours, minutes, subsidiary seconds; date
Case: stainless steel, 40 × 41 mm, height 11.3 mm; sapphire crystal; water-resistant to 3 atm
Band: reptile skin, double folding clasp
Price: $6,250
Variations: black dial; pink gold, price on request

Drive de Cartier
Reference number: WGNM0003
Movement: automatic, Cartier Caliber 1904-PS MC; ø 24.9 mm, height 4.5 mm; 27 jewels; 28,800 vph; 48-hour power reserve
Functions: hours, minutes, subsidiary seconds; date
Case: rose gold, 40 × 41 mm, height 11.3 mm; sapphire crystal; water-resistant to 3 atm
Band: reptile skin, double folding clasp
Price: $16,600
Variations: stainless steel ($6,250)

Drive de Cartier Extra-Flat
Reference number: WSNM0011
Movement: manually wound, Cartier Caliber 430 MC; ø 20 mm, height 2.15 mm; 18 jewels; 21,600 vph; 43-hour power reserve
Functions: hours, minutes
Case: stainless steel, 38 × 39 mm, height 6.6 mm; sapphire crystal; water-resistant to 3 atm
Band: reptile skin, buckle
Price: $5,600
Variations: yellow gold ($14,200)

Drive de Cartier Moon Phase
Reference number: WSNM0008
Movement: automatic, Cartier Caliber 1904-LU MC; ø 25 mm, height 5.2 mm; 25 jewels; 28,800 vph; 48-hour power reserve
Functions: hours, minutes; moon phase
Case: stainless steel, 40 × 41 mm, height 12 mm; sapphire crystal
Band: reptile skin, double folding clasp
Price: $7,850
Variations: red gold ($21,000)

Drive de Cartier Second Time Zone
Reference number: WSNM0005
Movement: automatic, Cartier Caliber 1904-FU MC; ø 25 mm, height 5.2 mm; 28 jewels; 28,800 vph; finely finished with côtes de Genève; 48-hour power reserve
Functions: hours, minutes, subsidiary seconds; additional 12-hour display (2nd time zone, retrograde); day/night indicator; large date
Case: stainless steel, 40 × 41 mm, height 12.63 mm; sapphire crystal; water-resistant to 3 atm
Band: reptile skin, double folding clasp
Price: $8,750
Variations: rose gold ($19,600)

Calibre de Cartier Diver Blue
Reference number: WSCA0010
Movement: automatic, Cartier Caliber 1904 MC; ø 25.6 mm, height 4 mm; 27 jewels; 28,800 vph; 2 spring barrels, 47-hour power reserve
Functions: hours, minutes, subsidiary seconds; date
Case: stainless steel, ø 42 mm, height 11 mm; bezel with blue DLC coating, unidirectional bezel with 0-60 scale; sapphire crystal; screw-in crown; water-resistant to 30 atm
Band: calfskin with rubber overlay, buckle
Price: $7,900

Calibre de Cartier Diver
Reference number: W7100056
Movement: automatic, Cartier Caliber 1904 MC; ø 25.6 mm, height 4 mm; 27 jewels; 28,800 vph; 2 spring barrels, 47-hour power reserve
Functions: hours, minutes, subsidiary seconds; date
Case: stainless steel, ø 42 mm, height 11 mm; unidirectional bezel set with black DLC coating, 0-60 scale; sapphire crystal; screw-in crown; water-resistant to 30 atm
Band: rubber, buckle
Price: $7,900
Variations: black DLC coating ($8,950)

Calibre de Cartier Diver
Reference number: W7100052
Movement: automatic, Cartier Caliber 1904-PS MC; ø 25.6 mm, height 4 mm; 27 jewels; 28,800 vph; 2 spring barrels, 47-hour power reserve
Functions: hours, minutes, subsidiary seconds; date
Case: red gold, ø 42 mm, height 11 mm; unidirectional bezel with ceramic insert, 0-60 scale; sapphire crystal; screw-in crown; water-resistant to 30 atm
Band: rubber, buckle
Price: $23,600

Calibre de Cartier Diver Blue
Reference number: WGCA0009
Movement: automatic, Cartier Caliber 1904-PS MC; ø 25.6 mm, height 4 mm; 27 jewels; 28,800 vph; 2 spring barrels, 47-hour power reserve
Functions: hours, minutes, subsidiary seconds; date
Case: red gold, ø 42 mm, height 11 mm; unidirectional bezel with ceramic insert, 0-60 scale; sapphire crystal; screw-in crown; water-resistant to 30 atm
Band: calfskin with rubber overlay, buckle
Price: $23.600
Variations: stainless steel ($7,900)

Tank MC
Reference number: W5330C03
Movement: automatic, Cartier Caliber 1904-PS MC; ø 25.6 mm, height 4 mm; 27 jewels; 28,800 vph; 2 spring barrels, 48-hour power reserve
Functions: hours, minutes, subsidiary seconds; date
Case: stainless steel, 34.3 × 44 mm, height 9.5 mm; sapphire crystal; transparent case back; water-resistant to 3 atm
Band: reptile skin, folding clasp
Price: $6,750
Variations: rose gold ($17,800)

Tank MC
Reference number: W5330001
Movement: automatic, Cartier Caliber 1904-PS MC; ø 25.6 mm, height 4 mm; 27 jewels; 28,800 vph; 2 spring barrels, 48-hour power reserve
Functions: hours, minutes, subsidiary seconds; date
Case: rose gold, 34.3 × 44 mm, height 9.5 mm; sapphire crystal; transparent case back; water-resistant to 3 atm
Band: reptile skin, folding clasp
Price: $17,800
Variations: stainless steel ($6,750)

Tank MC
Reference number: WSTA0010
Movement: automatic, Cartier Caliber 1904-PS MC; ø 25.6 mm, height 4 mm; 27 jewels; 28,800 vph; 2 spring barrels, 48-hour power reserve
Functions: hours, minutes, subsidiary seconds; date
Case: stainless steel, 34.3 × 44 mm, height 9.5 mm; sapphire crystal; transparent case back; water-resistant to 3 atm
Remarks: blue flinqué dial
Band: reptile skin, folding clasp
Price: $7,000
Variations: white dial ($6,750)

CASIO

Well before the electronic wrist-borne airplane dashboards that thrill the neophiles of today, there was Casio. Many who came of age in the 1970s might remember watches with alarms, or calculators, that were very affordable. While you couldn't do too much with them, they did put the fun in function and made you feel like Dick Tracy, or even Mr. Spock. But as an electronics company, while certainly not hurting, Casio was not creating a buzz. Until 1983. And the impetus came from a young man.

Kikuo Ibe, a young man and Casio employee, dropped and shattered his own watch and decided it was time to set a standard. He was determined to build a watch that could withstand a fall from a three-story building as well as survive submersion, dust, dirt, and general abuse that would put G-Shock on top of the tough timepiece pyramid.

Launched in 1983, Casio's G-Shock has become quite a sensation the world 'round. Built to withstand shocks that would destroy lesser watches, this remarkable timepiece—essentially, the ultimate tool watch—had another major advantage: It was democratically priced.

Since its inception, G-Shock has gone through hundreds and even thousands of variations in size, style, and functionality while retaining the common core value of creating the world's toughest, most resilient timepieces possible. During G-Shock's evolution, Casio brought forth a multitude of functions and connectivity to the wristwatch and effectively pre-dated the modern tech-wear trend.

Having developed its massive audience over the last three decades, G-Shock has recently begun adding higher-end designs. These new models retain the robust nature that makes a G-Shock what it is, while incorporating new materials as well as Japanese-inspired decorations like the "hammered" bezel in limited edition releases. These new variations place the popular watch squarely into collector-level price points with special editions from lines like the MTG, MRG, and Master of G watches.

Casio
6-2, Hon-machi 1-chome
Shibuya-ku
Tokyo 151-8543
Japan

Tel.:
973-361-5400

E-mail:
info@casio.com

Website:
www.casio.com

Founded:
1957

Number of employees:
12,298

U.S. distributor:
Casio America
570 Mt. Pleasant Ave.
Dover, NJ 07801

Most important collections/price range:
MR-G / $2,800 to $7,400; Baby-G, G-Shock, Edifice, Oceanus, Wave Ceptor / $100 to $5,000

Rangeman
Reference number: GPR B1000
Movement: quartz
Functions: digital hours, minutes, seconds; GPS with backtrack, waypoint memory; digital compass, barometer, altimeter, thermometer, depth gauge; chronograph, countdown; date with sunrise/sunset, tides, moon phase, world time
Case: resin with carbon fiber inserts, 57.7 mm × 20.2 mm, sapphire crystal; water-resistant to 20 atm
Band: rubber, folding clasp
Remarks: multifunctional digital display with solar and magnetic induction charging; Bluetooth connectivity
Price: $800
Variations: different colors

MT-G
Reference number: MTG B100-1A
Movement: quartz, solar power multifunctional analog display
Functions: analog hours, minutes; chronograph, countdown timer; date with calendar, world time, alarm, GPS
Case: stainless steel, 51.7 mm × 14.4 mm, sapphire crystal; water-resistant to 20 atm
Band: stainless steel, folding clasp
Remarks: radio frequency atomic time control, phone finder, Bluetooth connectivity
Price: $800
Variations: different colors

MR-G
Reference number: MRGG2000HB-1A
Movement: quartz regulated analog display, power reserve up to 23 months from full solar charge on low power mode
Functions: analog hours, minutes; chronograph, countdown timer; date, day, world time alarm, perpetual calendar, LED light
Case: stainless steel with hand-decorated bezel in Japanese tsuiki hammered style, 49.8 mm × 14.9 mm; water-resistant to 20 atm
Band: titanium with DLC treatment, folding safety clasp
Remarks: solar powered, GPS hybrid radio-controlled time synchronization; Bluetooth connectivity
Price: $5,000; **Variations:** Cobarion alloy bezel ($3,700), titanium case with black DLC bezel ($2,800)

Chanel
135, avenue Charles de Gaulle
F-92521 Neuilly-sur-Seine Cedex
France

Tel.:
+33-1-41-92-08-33

Website:
www.chanel.com

Founded:
1914

Distribution:
retail and 200 Chanel boutiques worldwide

U.S. distributor:
Chanel Fine Jewelry and Watches
600 Madison Avenue, 19th Floor
New York, NY 10022
212-715-4741
www.chanel.com

Most important collections:
J12, Première, Boy.Friend, Monsieur de Chanel

CHANEL

After putting the occasional jewelry watch onto the market earlier, the family-owned Chanel opened its own horology division in 1987, a move that gave the brand instant access to the world of watchmaking art. While the brand's first collections were directed exclusively at its female clientele, it was actually with the rather simple and masculine J12 that Chanel finally achieved a breakthrough. That was in 1999, twenty years ago. The designer was Jacques Helleu. The J12 collection showpiece, the Rétrograde Mystérieuse, was a stroke of genius—courtesy of the innovative think tank Renaud et Papi. Its sleek ceramic case and complex mechanics instantly propelled Chanel into the world of *haute horlogerie*.

It was designer Arnaud Chastaingt who created the new J12.1. It still comes in brilliant white ceramic, but a black limited edition has been added as well. Inside is a new movement built by Kenissi, a joint venture Chanel shares with Tudor and Breitling. It no longer has a silicon hairspring, and it has returned to the soft iron cage to protect from magnetic fields.

Chanel has started steering toward a younger, dynamic crowd with two collections that suggest a rapprochement between the sexes: The "Vendôme" rectangular Boy.Friend marries a feeling of subdued luxury and asceticism, and is as such so fascinating that its diamond-studded version won the Ladies' Prize at the 2018 edition of the GPHG. The Monsieur de Chanel is a purist, 40-millimeter watch with jumping hour and retrograde minutes driven by the Caliber 1. As for the Première Camélia, with the Caliber 2 inside, it continues in this vein, with a movement skeletonized to form a camellia. The watch comes in three versions bearing various amounts of diamonds.

Boy.Friend Skeleton Edition Noire
Reference number: H5944
Movement: manually wound, Chanel Caliber 3; 19.7 × 23.2 mm, height 3.9 mm; 21 jewels; 28,800 vph; skeletonized movement, bridges and cock coated in black ADLC; 55-hour power reserve
Functions: hours, minutes, subsidiary seconds
Case: stainless steel and black ceramic, 28.6 × 37 mm, height 8.4 mm; ceramic bezel; sapphire crystal; transparent case back; water-resistant to 3 atm
Band: reptile skin, buckle
Price: $34,150; limited to 55 pieces

Monsieur Edition Noire
Reference number: H5486
Movement: manually wound, Chanel Caliber I; ø 32 mm, height 5.5 mm; 30 jewels; 28,800 vph; blackened mainplate and bridges; 2 spring barrels; 72-hour power reserve
Functions: hours (digital, jumping), minutes (retrograde), subsidiary seconds
Case: stainless steel and black ceramic, ø 42 mm, height 10.4 mm; sapphire crystal; transparent case back; water-resistant to 3 atm
Band: reptile skin, buckle
Price: $27,500; limited to 55 pieces

J12 Automatic
Reference number: H5697
Movement: automatic, Chanel Caliber 12.1; ø 26 mm, height 4.99 mm; 28 jewels; 28,800 vph; 70-hour power reserve; COSC-certified chronometer
Functions: hours, minutes, sweep seconds; date
Case: stainless steel and black ceramic, ø 38 mm, height 12 mm; unidirectional bezel with ceramic insert, 0-60 scale; sapphire crystal; screw-in crown, with ceramic cabochon; water-resistant to 20 atm
Band: ceramic, double folding clasp
Price: $5,700
Variations: white ceramic ($4,850 H6345); as Edition Noire, limited to 55 pieces ($4,800 H6346)

CHOPARD

The Chopard *manufacture* was founded by Louis-Ulysse Chopard in 1860 in the tiny village of Sonvillier in the Jura mountains of Switzerland. In 1963, it was purchased by Karl Scheufele, a goldsmith from Pforzheim, Germany, and revived as a producer of fine watches and jewelry.

The past seventeen years have seen a breathtaking development, when Karl Scheufele's son, Karl-Friedrich, and his sister, Caroline, decided to create watches with in-house movements, thus restoring the old business launched by Louis-Ulysse back in the nineteenth century.

In the 1990s, literally out of nowhere, Chopard opened up its watchmaking *manufacture* in the sleepy town of Fleurier in the Val-de-Travers, which had not yet experienced the revival of the mechanical watch. Karl-Friedrich Scheufele was convinced that the future of the industry lay in producing high-end timepieces, in spite of what many competitors were saying. The success of the L.U.C models with their own calibers silenced the doubters, even more so when ETA began restricting its sales of base calibers to the industry. Over twenty years later, Chopard's own Fleurier Ebauches SA has restored Fleurier's tradition as a hub of *ébauche* (movement kits) production. Chopard now has a line-up of eleven calibers, ranging from simple three-hander automatics to a tourbillon, a perpetual calendar, chronographs, an ultra-high-frequency chronometer, and a minute repeater.

The company also continues to support the Geneva Watchmaking School with special *ébauches* for the students, a demonstration of its commitment to the industry. With its wide range of *manufacture* watch models and over 160 boutiques worldwide, the brand enjoys firm footing in the rarefied air of *haute horlogerie*.

Chopard & Cie. SA
8, rue de Veyrot
CH-1217 Meyrin (Geneva)
Switzerland

Tel.:
+41-22-719-3131

E-mail:
info@chopard.ch

Website:
www.chopard.ch

Founded:
1860

Distribution:
160 boutiques

U.S. distributor:
Chopard USA
75 Valencia Ave, Suite 1200
Coral Gables, FL 33134
1-800-CHOPARD
www.us.chopard.com

Most important collections/price range:
Superfast / $9,860 to $32,900; L.U.C / from $8,190; Imperiale / from $5,310; Classic Racing / $5,040 to $41,900; Happy Sport / from $5,300

L.U.C Flying T Twin
Reference number: 161978-5001
Movement: automatic, L.U.C Caliber 96.24-L; ø 27.4 mm, height 3.3 mm; 25 jewels; 25,200 vph; flying 1-minute tourbillon, microrotor; 2 spring barrels, 65-hour power reserve; Geneva Seal, COSC-certified chronometer
Functions: hours, minutes, subsidiary seconds (on tourbillon cage)
Case: rose gold, ø 40 mm, height 7.2 mm; sapphire crystal; transparent case back; water-resistant to 3 atm
Band: reptile skin, buckle
Remarks: case made of certified fair-traded gold, limited to 250 pieces; rose gold dial with hand-guilloché, limited to 50 pieces
Price: on request

L.U.C Grand Complication Full Strike
Reference number: 161947-1001
Movement: manually wound, L.U.C Caliber 08.01-L; ø 37.2 mm, height 7.97 mm; 63 jewels; 28,800 vph; sapphire crystal resonating body; 60-hour power reserve; Geneva Seal, COSC-certified chronometer
Functions: hours, minutes, subsidiary seconds; power reserve indicator, minute repeater
Case: white gold, ø 42.5 mm, height 11.55 mm; sapphire crystal; transparent case back
Band: reptile skin, folding clasp
Remarks: case made of certified fair-traded gold; limited to 20 pieces
Price: on request
Variations: rose gold

L.U.C Grand Complication Perpetual Chrono
Reference number: 161973-9001
Movement: manually wound, L.U.C Caliber 03.10-L; ø 33 mm, height 8.32 mm; 42 jewels; 28,800 vph; German silver mainplate and balance cock; 60-hour power reserve; Geneva Seal, COSC-certified chronometer
Functions: hours, minutes, sweep seconds; day/night indicator; flyback chronograph; perpetual calendar with large date, weekday, month, moon phase, leap year
Case: platinum, ø 45 mm, height 15.06 mm; sapphire crystal; transparent case back; water-resistant to 3 atm
Band: reptile skin, folding clasp
Price: on request; limited to 20 pieces
Variations: diamond bezel; white or rose gold

CHOPARD

L.U.C Quattro

Reference number: 161926-1002
Movement: manually wound, L.U.C Caliber 98.01-L; ø 28.6 mm, height 3.7 mm; 39 jewels; 28,800 vph; 4 spring barrels, swan-neck fine adjustment, gold rotor; 216-hour power reserve; Geneva Seal, COSC-certified chronometer
Functions: hours, minutes, subsidiary seconds; power reserve indicator; date
Case: white gold, ø 43 mm, height 8.84 mm; sapphire crystal; transparent case back; water-resistant to 5 atm
Band: reptile skin, buckle
Price: $25,800; limited to 50 pieces
Variations: rose gold; platinum

L.U.C All in One

Reference number: 161925-9003
Movement: manually wound, L.U.C Caliber 05.01-L; ø 33 mm, height 11.75 mm; 42 jewels; 28,800 vph; 1-minute tourbillon; 170-hour power reserve; Geneva Seal, COSC-certified chronometer
Functions: hours, minutes, subsidiary seconds; day/night indicator, power reserve indicator, time equation, sunrise/sunset (on movement side); perpetual calendar with large date, weekday, month, orbital astronomical moon phase, leap year
Case: white gold, ø 46 mm, height 18.5 mm; sapphire crystal; transparent case back; water-resistant to 3 atm
Band: reptile skin, buckle
Price: on request; limited to 10 pieces

Mille Miglia GTS 2019 Race Edition

Reference number: 168571-3004
Movement: automatic, ETA Caliber 7750; ø 30.4 mm, height 7.9 mm; 25 jewels; 28,800 vph; 48-hour power reserve; COSC-certified chronometer
Functions: hours, minutes, subsidiary seconds; chronograph; date
Case: stainless steel, ø 44 mm, height 13.79 mm; sapphire crystal; screw-in crown; water-resistant to 10 atm
Band: calfskin, folding clasp
Price: $7,390; limited to 1,000 pieces
Variations: stainless steel with rose gold elements

Mille Miglia GTS 2019 Race Edition

Reference number: 168571-6002
Movement: automatic, ETA Caliber 7750; ø 30.4 mm, height 7.9 mm; 25 jewels; 28,800 vph; 48-hour power reserve; COSC-certified chronometer
Functions: hours, minutes, subsidiary seconds; chronograph; date
Case: stainless steel, ø 44 mm, height 13.79 mm; bezel, crown, and pushers in rose gold; sapphire crystal; water-resistant to 10 atm
Band: calfskin, folding clasp
Price: $10,900; limited to 250 pieces
Variations: stainless steel

Mille Miglia GTS Power Control

Reference number: 168566-3011
Movement: automatic, Chopard Manufacture Caliber 01.08-C; ø 28.8 mm, height 4.95 mm; 40 jewels; 28,800 vph; 60-hour power reserve; COSC-certified chronometer
Functions: hours, minutes, sweep seconds; power reserve indicator; date
Case: stainless steel, ø 43 mm, height 11.43 mm; sapphire crystal; transparent case back; screw-in crown; water-resistant to 10 atm
Band: calfskin, folding clasp
Price: $6,800; limited to 500 pieces

Mille Miglia Classic Chronograph

Reference number: 168589-3002
Movement: automatic, ETA Caliber 2894-2; ø 28.6 mm, height 6.1 mm; 37 jewels; 28,800 vph; 42-hour power reserve; COSC-certified chronometer
Functions: hours, minutes, subsidiary seconds; chronograph; date
Case: stainless steel, ø 42 mm, height 12.67 mm; sapphire crystal; transparent case back; screw-in crown; water-resistant to 5 atm
Band: rubber, buckle
Price: $5,260

CHOPARD

L.U.C Time Traveler One
Reference number: 161942-9001
Movement: automatic, L.U.C Caliber 01.05-L; ø 35.3 mm, height 6.52 mm; 39 jewels; 28,800 vph; 60-hour power reserve; COSC-certified chronometer
Functions: hours, minutes, sweep seconds; world time display (2nd time zone); date
Case: platinum, ø 42 mm, height 12.09 mm; crown-activated scale ring, with reference city names; sapphire crystal; transparent case back; water-resistant to 5 atm
Band: reptile skin, buckle
Price: $37,900
Variations: stainless steel; rose gold

L.U.C Time Traveler One
Reference number: 168574-3001
Movement: automatic, L.U.C Caliber 01.05-L; ø 35.3 mm, height 6.52 mm; 39 jewels; 28,800 vph; 60-hour power reserve; COSC-certified chronometer
Functions: hours, minutes, sweep seconds; world time display (2nd time zone); date
Case: stainless steel, ø 42 mm, height 12.09 mm; crown-activated scale ring, with reference city names; sapphire crystal; transparent case back; water-resistant to 5 atm
Band: reptile skin, buckle
Price: $13,700
Variations: rose gold; platinum

L.U.C Chrono One Flyback
Reference number: 168596-3001
Movement: automatic, L.U.C Caliber 03.03-L; ø 28.8 mm, height 7.6 mm; 45 jewels; 28,800 vph; gold rotor; 60-hour power reserve; COSC-certified chronometer
Functions: hours, minutes, subsidiary seconds; flyback chronograph; date
Case: stainless steel, ø 42 mm, height 13.42 mm; sapphire crystal; transparent case back; water-resistant to 10 atm
Band: reptile skin, buckle
Price: $26,900; limited to 250 pieces

L.U.C GMT One
Reference number: 168579-3001
Movement: automatic, L.U.C Caliber 01.10-L; ø 31.9 mm, height 5.95 mm; 31 jewels; 28,800 vph; bridges with côtes de Genève; 60-hour power reserve; COSC-certified chronometer
Functions: hours, minutes, sweep seconds; additional 24-hour display (2nd time zone); date
Case: stainless steel, ø 42 mm, height 11.71 mm; sapphire crystal; transparent case back; water-resistant to 5 atm
Band: reptile skin, buckle
Price: $10,200
Variations: rose gold ($20,600)

L.U.C Perpetual Twin
Reference number: 168561-3001
Movement: automatic, L.U.C Caliber 96.22-L; ø 33 mm, height 6 mm; 29 jewels; 28,800 vph; 2 spring barrels, microrotor in gold with heavy-metal oscillating mass; with côtes de Genève; 65-hour power reserve; COSC-certified chronometer
Functions: hours, minutes, subsidiary seconds; perpetual calendar with large date, weekday, month, leap year
Case: stainless steel, ø 43 mm, height 11.47 mm; sapphire crystal; transparent case back; water-resistant to 3 atm
Band: reptile skin, buckle
Price: $24,700

L.U.C Regulator
Reference number: 161971-5001
Movement: manually wound, L.U.C Caliber 98.02-L; ø 30.4 mm, height 4.9 mm; 39 jewels; 28,800 vph; 4 spring barrels; bridges with côtes de Genève; 216-hour power reserve; Geneva Seal, COSC-certified chronometer
Functions: hours (off-center), minutes, subsidiary seconds; additional 24-hour display (2nd time zone), power reserve indicator; date
Case: rose gold, ø 43 mm, height 9.78 mm; sapphire crystal; transparent case back; water-resistant to 3 atm
Band: reptile skin, buckle
Price: $32,000

L.U.C Lunar One
Reference number: 161927-5001
Movement: automatic, L.U.C Caliber 96.13-L; ø 33 mm, height 6 mm; 32 jewels; 28,800 vph; 65-hour power reserve; Geneva Seal, COSC-certified chronometer
Functions: hours, minutes, subsidiary seconds; additional 24-hour display (2nd time zone); perpetual calendar with large date, weekday, month, orbital moon phase display, leap year
Case: rose gold, ø 43 mm, height 11.47 mm; sapphire crystal; transparent case back; water-resistant to 5 atm
Band: reptile skin, folding clasp
Price: $60,600
Variations: platinum; white gold

L.U.C Lunar Big Date
Reference number: 161969-1001
Movement: automatic, L.U.C Caliber 96.20-L; ø 33 mm, height 5.25 mm; 33 jewels; 28,800 vph; with côtes de Genève; 65-hour power reserve; COSC-certified chronometer
Functions: hours, minutes, subsidiary seconds; large date, orbital moon phase display
Case: white gold, ø 42 mm, height 11.04 mm; sapphire crystal; transparent case back; water-resistant to 5 atm
Band: reptile skin, buckle
Price: $30,300
Variations: rose gold ($30,300)

L.U.C XPS Twist QF
Reference number: 161945-1001
Movement: automatic, L.U.C Caliber 96-26-L; ø 27.4 mm, height 3.3 mm; 29 jewels; 28,800 vph; microrotor in gold; 2 spring barrels; 65-hour power reserve; COSC-certified chronometer, Qualité Fleurier
Functions: hours, minutes, subsidiary seconds; date
Case: white gold, ø 40 mm, height 7.2 mm; sapphire crystal; transparent case back; screw-in crown; water-resistant to 3 atm
Band: reptile skin, buckle
Remarks: case made of gold with Fairmined certification
Price: $20,400; limited to 250 pieces
Variations: yellow gold

L.U.C XP
Reference number: 168592-3002
Movement: automatic, L.U.C Caliber 96.53-L; ø 27.4 mm, height 3.3 mm; 27 jewels; 28,800 vph; heavy-metal rotor, bridges with côtes de Genève; 58-hour power reserve
Functions: hours, minutes
Case: stainless steel, ø 40 mm, height 7.2 mm; sapphire crystal; transparent case back; water-resistant to 3 atm
Band: leather and merino wool, buckle
Price: $8,810
Variations: white or rose gold

L.U.C XPS
Reference number: 161948-5002
Movement: automatic, L.U.C Caliber 96.12-L; ø 27.4 mm, height 3.3 mm; 29 jewels; 28,800 vph; gold rotor, bridges with côtes de Genève; 65-hour power reserve; COSC-certified chronometer
Functions: hours, minutes, subsidiary seconds
Case: rose gold, ø 40 mm, height 7.2 mm; sapphire crystal; transparent case back; water-resistant to 3 atm
Band: reptile skin, buckle
Remarks: case made of gold with Fairmined certification
Price: $18,000; limited to 100 pieces

L.U.C XPS 1860 Edition
Reference number: 161946-5001
Movement: automatic, L.U.C Caliber 96.01-L; ø 27.4 mm, height 3.3 mm; 29 jewels; 28,800 vph; gold rotor; 2 spring barrels; 65-hour power reserve; Geneva Seal, COSC-certified chronometer
Functions: hours, minutes, subsidiary seconds; date
Case: rose gold, ø 40 mm, height 7.2 mm; sapphire crystal; transparent case back; water-resistant to 3 atm
Band: reptile skin, buckle
Price: $21,700; limited to 250 pieces
Variations: white gold

CHOPARD

Caliber L.U.C 96.24-L
Automatic; flying 1-minute tourbillon; gold microrotor; double spring barrel, 65-hour power reserve; Geneva Seal, COSC-certified chronometer
Functions: hours, minutes
Diameter: 27.4 mm
Height: 3.3 mm
Jewels: 25
Balance: glucydur
Frequency: 25,200 vph
Balance spring: flat hairspring, Nivarox 1
Remarks: 190 parts

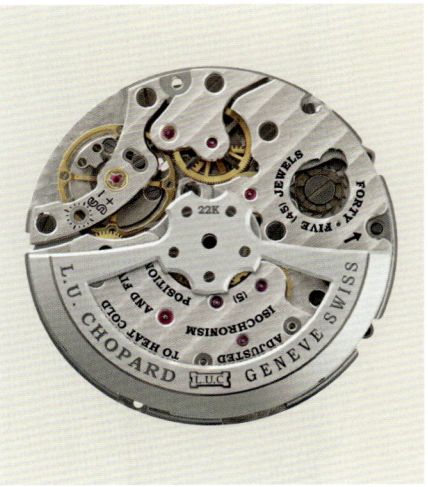

Caliber L.U.C 03.03-L
Automatic; column wheel control of chronograph functions, vertical chronograph clutch, stop-seconds mechanism with automatic zero-reset; skeletonized gold rotor; single spring barrel, 60-hour power reserve; COSC-certified chronometer
Functions: hours, minutes, subsidiary seconds; flyback chronograph; date
Diameter: 28.8 mm
Height: 7.6 mm
Jewels: 45
Balance: Variner with 4 weighted screws
Frequency: 28,800 vph
Balance spring: flat hairspring
Remarks: perlage on mainplate, beveled bridges with côtes de Genève; 359 parts

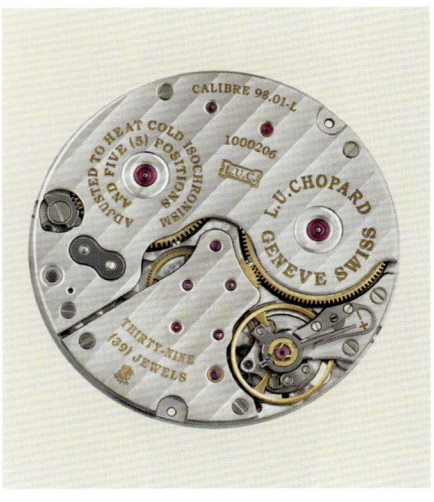

Caliber L.U.C 98.01-L
Manually wound; swan-neck fine regulation; quadruple spring barrel running in twin series barrel springs, 216-hour power reserve; Geneva Seal, COSC-certified chronometer
Functions: hours, minutes, subsidiary seconds; power reserve indicator; date
Diameter: 28.6 mm
Height: 3.7 mm
Jewels: 39
Frequency: 28,800 vph
Balance spring: Breguet hairspring
Remarks: 223 parts

Caliber L.U.C 96.53-L
Automatic; microrotor; double spring barrel, 58-hour power reserve; COSC-certified chronometer
Functions: hours, minutes
Diameter: 27.4 mm
Height: 3.3 mm
Jewels: 27
Balance: glucydur
Frequency: 28,800 vph
Balance spring: flat hairspring, Nivarox 1
Remarks: bridges with côtes de Genève; 172 parts

Caliber L.U.C 03.10-L
Manually wound; German silver mainplate and balance cock; single spring barrel, 60-hour power reserve; Geneva Seal, COSC-certified chronometer
Functions: hours, minutes, sweep seconds; day/night indicator; flyback chronograph; perpetual calendar with large date, weekday, month, moon phase, leap year
Diameter: 33 mm
Height: 8.32 mm
Jewels: 42
Balance: Variner with 4 weighted screws
Frequency: 28,800 vph
Balance spring: flat hairspring

Caliber L.U.C 08.01-L
Manually wound; sapphire crystal resonance body for repeater mechanism; single spring barrel, 60-hour power reserve; Geneva Seal, COSC-certified chronometer
Functions: hours, minutes, subsidiary seconds; power reserve indicator, minute repeater
Diameter: 37.2 mm
Height: 7.97 mm
Jewels: 63
Frequency: 28,800 vph
Balance spring: hairspring with Phillips end curve
Remarks: German silver plate and balance cock; 533 parts

Christophe Claret SA
Route du Soleil d'Or 2
CH-2400 Le Locle
Switzerland

Tel.:
+41-32-933-0000

E-mail:
info@christopheclaret.com

Website:
www.christopheclaret.com

Founded:
manufacture 1989, brand 2009

Number of employees:
70

Distribution:
Contact the manufacture directly.

Most important collections:
Traditional complications (Maestro/Mecca/Allegro/Aventicum/Maestoso/Kantharos/Soprano), Extreme line (X-TREM-1), gaming watches (Poker/Baccara/Blackjack), and ladies' complications line (Margot, Layla, Marguerite)

CHRISTOPHE CLARET

Individuals like Christophe Claret eat, drink, and breathe watchmaking and have developed careers based on pushing the envelope to the very edge of what's possible.

By the age of twenty-three, the Lyon-born Claret was in Basel, where he was spotted by the late Rolf Schnyder of Ulysse Nardin and commissioned to make a minute repeater with jacquemarts. In 1989, he opened his *manufacture*, a nineteenth-century mansion extended with a state-of-the-art machining area. Indeed, Claret embraces wholeheartedly the potential in modern tools to create the precise pieces needed to give physical expression to exceedingly complex ideas.

Over the years, Claret created complications and movements for many major brands, like Ulysse Nardin and Harry Winston.

Twenty years after establishing his business, Claret finally launched his own complex watches: models like the DualTow, with its hours and minutes on two tracks, minute repeater, and complete view of the great ballet of arms and levers inside. Then came the Adagio, again a minute repeater, with a clear dial that manages a second time zone and large date. In 2011, Claret wowed the watch world with a humorous, on-the-wrist gambling machine telling time and playing blackjack, craps, or roulette. It was followed by the stunning X-TREM-1, a turbocharged DualTow with two spheres controlled by magnets hovering along the numeral tracks to tell the time plus a tourbillon.

The list goes on and on. Whatever Claret produces—the Margot, for women, the art-laden Aventicum, or the Angelico, a complex tourbillon with a fusée and carbon nanofiber cable escapement—his signature is always present: a total dedication to power mechanics and an infallible sense of style. The winding rotor of the Marguerite, a high-end mechanical ladies' watch, features rubies that will point to "He loves me" or "He loves me not" engraved on the case back and separated by a little heart.

Angelico
Reference number: MTR.DTC08.000-010
Movement: manually wound, Christophe Claret Caliber DTC08; ø 41.1 mm, height 14.2 mm; 62 jewels; 18,000 vph; 1-minute tourbillon with chronometer escapement, power regulation with carbon nanofiber cable and fusée; 2 serially ordered spring barrels, 72-hour power reserve
Functions: hours (digital, jumping), minutes (index tip); additional 24-hour display (2nd time zone), day/night indicator
Case: titanium, red gold, ø 45.5 mm, height 17.45 mm; sapphire crystal; transparent case back; water-resistant to 3 atm; **Band:** reptile skin, folding clasp
Price: CHF 238,000; limited to 10 pieces; **Variations:** titanium, limited to 10 pieces (CHF 218,000)

Maestro Mamba
Reference number: MTR.DMC16.230-258 MAMBA
Movement: manually wound, Christophe Claret Caliber DMC16; ø 36.25 mm, height 10.5 mm; 33 jewels; 21,600 vph; inverted movement construction with balance on dial; 168-hour power reserve
Functions: hours, minutes, manually activated memo display; large date (double digit) on pyramid base
Case: black PVD-coated titanium, ø 42 mm, height 16 mm; sapphire crystal; transparent case back
Band: reptile skin, folding clasp
Remarks: comes with extra python leather strap; limited to 28 pieces
Price: CHF 96,000

Margot Velours
Reference number: MTR.EMT18.000-020
Movement: automatic, Christophe Claret Caliber EMT17; ø 38.4 mm, height 9.76 mm; 95 jewels; 28,800 vph; 2 spring barrels, 72-hour power reserve
Functions: hours, minutes; pusher produces acoustic signal and lets petals vanish, text appears randomly in window
Case: white gold and titanium with blue PVD, ø 42.5 mm, height 14.5 mm; bezel and lugs set with 64 diamonds; sapphire crystal; transparent case back
Band: reptile skin, folding clasp
Remarks: the watch has the answer: "He loves me, he loves me not . . ."
Price: CHF 198,000; limited to 20 pieces

CHRONOSWISS

Chronoswiss has been assembling its signature watches—which boast such features as coin edge bezels and onion crowns—since 1983. Founder Gerd-Rüdiger Lang loved to joke about having "the only Swiss watch factory in Germany," as the brand used Swiss technology with concepts and designs "made in Germany," in Karlsfeld, near Munich, to be precise.

Lang also created regulator watches in the 1980s, a pioneering idea that found many fans of new ways to tell the time. Whether in a rectangular or round case, with a tourbillon or without, the off-center dial became the absolute identity of Chronoswiss watches and remains so to this day. It was a remarkable bit of inspiration and somewhat anachronistic back then.

Chronoswiss has always been a little on the edge of the industry in terms of style and technical developments. It created the enduring *manufacture* caliber C.122—based on an old Enicar automatic movement with a patented rattrapante mechanism—and its Chronoscope chronograph has earned a solid reputation for technical prowess. The Pacific and Sirius models, additions to the classic collection, point the company in a new stylistic direction designed to help win new buyers and the attention of the international market.

In March 2012, a Swiss couple, Oliver and Eva Ebstein, purchased Chronoswiss and moved the company headquarters to Lucerne, Switzerland, but without changing the essential codes of the brand. Recent models reveal the brand to be faithful to its regulator and coin edges, and the large crown, though the dial has acquired a three-dimensional design. The Flying Regulator and the Regulator Jumping Hour find the minute hand hovering freely over the dial, with the hours and seconds on bridges. The name "Atelier Lucerne" appears on the dial, a hint of the new premises, but the trusty C.122 beats inside many of these new models.

Chronoswiss AG
Löwenstrasse 16b
CH-6004 Lucerne
Switzerland

Tel.:
+41-41-552-2100

E-mail:
shopmanager@chronoswiss.com

Website:
www.chronoswiss.com

Founded:
1983

Number of employees:
approx. 30

Annual production:
up to 4,000 wristwatches

U.S. distributor:
BeauGeste Inc.
132 East 43rd Street
#341 The Chrysler Building
New York, NY 10017
212-847-1371
Chronoswiss US Service Office
Shami Fine Watchmaking
155 Willowbrook Blvd.
Suite 320
Wayne, NJ 07470
973-785-0004

Most important collections/price range:
Approx. 30 models including Regulator, Flying Regulator, Sirius Chronograph Moon Phase, Sirius Chronograph Skeleton, Sirius Artist, Timemaster Big Date, Timemaster Chronograph GMT / approx. $4,650 to $47,000

Flying Grand Regulator Open Gear ReSec
Reference number: CH-6926-BLBL
Movement: automatic, Chronoswiss Caliber C.301; ø 36.5 mm; 28,800 vph; dial-side hand gear train (transmission wheel); finely finished movement; 42-hour power reserve
Functions: hours (off-center), minutes, subsidiary seconds (retrograde)
Case: stainless steel with blue DLC coating, ø 44 mm, height 13.35 mm; sapphire crystal; transparent case back; water-resistant to 10 atm
Band: reptile skin, folding clasp
Remarks: hand-guillochéed dial
Price: $9,900; limited to 50 pieces

Flying Grand Regulator Open Gear ReSec
Reference number: CH-6921R-GRSI
Movement: automatic, Chronoswiss Caliber C.301; ø 36.5 mm; 28,800 vph; dial-side hand gear train (transmission wheel); finely finished movement; 42-hour power reserve
Functions: hours (off-center), minutes, subsidiary seconds (retrograde)
Case: red gold, ø 44 mm, height 13.35 mm; sapphire crystal; transparent case back; water-resistant to 10 atm
Band: reptile skin, folding clasp
Remarks: hand-guillochéed dial
Price: $19,950; limited to 50 pieces

Regulator Classic
Reference number: CH-8773-GRBK
Movement: automatic, Chronoswiss Caliber C.295; ø 25.6 mm, height 4.35 mm; 27 jewels; 28,800 vph; 42-hour power reserve
Functions: hours (off-center), minutes, subsidiary seconds
Case: stainless steel, ø 41 mm, height 12.7 mm; sapphire crystal; transparent case back; water-resistant to 10 atm
Band: stainless steel, folding clasp
Price: $4,750
Variations: 37-mm case; galvanic blue and silver colored dial

CHRONOSWISS

Regulator Classic
Reference number: CH-4023-BL
Movement: automatic, Chronoswiss Caliber C.295; ø 25.6 mm, height 4.35 mm; 27 jewels; 28,800 vph; 42-hour power reserve
Functions: hours (off-center), minutes, subsidiary seconds
Case: stainless steel, ø 37 mm, height 10.54 mm; sapphire crystal; transparent case back; water-resistant to 10 atm
Band: stainless steel, folding clasp
Price: $4,750
Variations: 41-mm case; galvanic silver or beige dial

Flying Regulator Open Gear Anniversary Edition
Reference number: CH-8753-BKOR
Movement: automatic, Chronoswiss Caliber C.299; ø 35.2 mm, height 6.11 mm; 31 jewels; 28,800 vph; dial-side hand gear train (transmission wheel); finely finished movement; 42-hour power reserve
Functions: hours (off-center), minutes, subsidiary seconds
Case: stainless steel, ø 41 mm, height 13.85 mm; sapphire crystal; transparent case back; water-resistant to 10 atm
Band: reptile skin, folding clasp
Remarks: special edition for 35th anniversary of brand with hand-guillochéed dials, 35 pieces each
Price: $8,300

Flying Regulator Open Gear
Reference number: CH-8753-SISI
Movement: automatic, Chronoswiss Caliber C.299; ø 35.2 mm, height 6.11 mm; 31 jewels; 28,800 vph; hand mechanism (transmission wheel) relocated to dial side; finely finished movement; 42-hour power reserve
Functions: hours (off-center), minutes, subsidiary seconds
Case: stainless steel, ø 41 mm, height 13.85 mm; sapphire crystal; transparent case back; water-resistant to 10 atm
Band: reptile skin, folding clasp
Price: $6,680
Variations: pink gold ($16,300)

Flying Regulator Night and Day Limited Edition
Reference number: CH-8763-3LSI
Movement: automatic, Chronoswiss Caliber C.296; ø 25.2 mm, height 4.35 mm; 27 jewels; 28,800 vph; skeletonized rotor; finely finished movement; 42-hour power reserve
Functions: hours (off-center), minutes, subsidiary seconds; day/night indicator; date
Case: stainless steel, ø 41 mm, height 13.85 mm; sapphire crystal; transparent case back; water-resistant to 10 atm
Band: reptile skin, folding clasp
Remarks: hand-guillochéed dial
Price: $8,650; limited to 50 pieces

Flying Regulator Night and Day
Reference number: CH-8763-BLBL
Movement: automatic, Chronoswiss Caliber C.296; ø 25.2 mm, height 4.35 mm; 27 jewels; 28,800 vph; skeletonized rotor; finely finished movement; 42-hour power reserve
Functions: hours (off-center), minutes, subsidiary seconds; day/night indicator; date
Case: stainless steel, ø 41 mm, height 13.85 mm; sapphire crystal; transparent case back; water-resistant to 10 atm
Band: reptile skin, folding clasp
Remarks: winner of 2019 Red Dot Design Award
Price: $6,950

Flying Grand Regulator Skeleton
Reference number: CH-6725S-REBK
Movement: manually wound, Chronoswiss Caliber C.677S; ø 37.2 mm, height 4.5 mm; 17 jewels; 18,000 vph; screw balance, swan-neck fine adjustment; skeletonized mainplate, bridges, and gearwheels; finely finished movement; 46-hour power reserve
Functions: hours (off-center), minutes, subsidiary seconds
Case: stainless steel with black DLC coating, ø 44 mm, height 12.48 mm; sapphire crystal; transparent case back; water-resistant to 3 atm
Band: reptile skin, folding clasp
Price: $10,300; limited to 30 pieces

CHRONOSWISS

Flying Grand Regulator
Reference number: CH-6725-YEBK
Movement: manually wound, Chronoswiss Caliber C.678; ø 37.2 mm, height 4.5 mm; 17 jewels; 18,000 vph; screw balance, swan-neck fine adjustment; finely finished movement; 46-hour power reserve
Functions: hours (off-center), minutes, subsidiary seconds
Case: stainless steel with black DLC coating, ø 44 mm, height 12.48 mm; sapphire crystal; transparent case back; water-resistant to 3 atm
Band: reptile skin, folding clasp
Price: $9,900; limited to 30 pieces

Flying Regulator Manufacture
Reference number: CH-1243.3-BLBL
Movement: automatic, Chronoswiss Caliber C.122; ø 26.8 mm, height 5.3 mm; 30 jewels; 21,600 vph; skeletonized rotor; finely finished movement; 40-hour power reserve
Functions: hours (off-center), minutes, subsidiary seconds
Case: stainless steel, ø 40 mm, height 12 mm; sapphire crystal; transparent case back; water-resistant to 3 atm
Band: reptile skin, buckle
Remarks: winner of 2019 Red Dot Design Award
Price: $7,200
Variations: black DLC treatment ($7,750); pink gold ($16,950)

Flying Regulator Jumping Hour
Reference number: CH-8321R-BKBK
Movement: automatic, Chronoswiss Caliber C.283; ø 30 mm, height 5.35 mm; 27 jewels; 28,800 vph; skeletonized rotor; finely finished movement; 42-hour power reserve
Functions: hours (digital, jumping), minutes (off-center), subsidiary seconds
Case: pink gold, ø 40 mm, height 12 mm; sapphire crystal; transparent case back; water-resistant to 3 atm
Band: reptile skin, buckle
Price: $17,450
Variations: stainless steel ($7,900); stainless steel with black DLC coating ($8,250)

Artist Regulator Jumping Hour
Reference number: CH-8323E-BL
Movement: automatic, Chronoswiss Caliber C.283; ø 29.4 mm, height 5.35 mm; 27 jewels; 28,800 vph; skeletonized, hand-guilloché on rotor; finely finished movement, partially guillochéed by hand; 42-hour power reserve
Functions: hours (digital, jumping), minutes (off-center), subsidiary seconds
Case: stainless steel, ø 40 mm, height 9.75 mm; sapphire crystal; transparent case back; water-resistant to 3 atm
Band: reptile skin, buckle
Remarks: dial with hand-guilloché and enamel
Price: $10,300

Sirius Chronograph Moon Phase
Reference number: CH-7541LR
Movement: automatic, Chronoswiss Caliber C.755 (base ETA 7750); ø 30 mm, height 7.9 mm; 25 jewels; 28,800 vph; perlage on movement, côtes de Genève, skeletonized rotor; finely finished movement; 46-hour power reserve
Functions: hours, minutes, subsidiary seconds; chronograph; date, moon phase
Case: pink gold, ø 41 mm, height 15.45 mm; sapphire crystal; transparent case back; water-resistant to 3 atm
Band: reptile skin, buckle
Price: $19,150
Variations: stainless steel ($7,950)

Sirius Chronograph Skeleton
Reference number: CH-7543S
Movement: automatic, Chronoswiss Caliber C.741 S (base ETA 7750); ø 30 mm, height 7.9 mm; 25 jewels; 28,800 vph; entirely skeletonized movement with ribbing; 46-hour power reserve
Functions: hours, minutes, subsidiary seconds; chronograph; date
Case: stainless steel, ø 41 mm, height 15.45 mm; sapphire crystal; transparent case back; water-resistant to 3 atm
Band: reptile skin, buckle
Remarks: skeletonized dial
Price: $10,400
Variations: pink gold ($22,950)

Claude Meylan
Route de l'Hôtel de Ville 2
CH-1344 L'Abbaye
Switzerland

Tel.:
+41-21 841 14 57

E-mail:
info@claudemeylan.ch

Website:
www.claudemeylan.ch

Founded:
originally mid-18th century; revived in mid-20th century and purchased in 2011

Number of employees:
7

Annual production:
approx. 1,000 pieces

Most important collections/price range:
Tortue, Ligne Lac / $4,500 to $6,850; Légendes series / up to $33,000

CLAUDE MEYLAN

In the quest for recognition, many companies, especially the smaller ones, look for a niche in which they can excel. The Swiss brand Claude Meylan, located in L'Abbaye near Joux Lake in the heart of watch country, specializes in skeletonization, which is the art of removing as much material as possible from bridges, plates, the dial, even the hands. The exercise is not just for fun. First, it transforms a watch, making it transparent and allowing a view of the mechanical innards. Second, it allows for imaginative designs using what's left of the material, notably the bridges. These can be either abstract or representative.

Skeletonization has become fairly popular in recent years, but it's not as simple as it might sound. As the various metal components are hollowed out and properly finished with chamfering and sanding, the tensions within the material change. This can then have a deleterious effect on the functioning of the mechanism, since the bridges and plates are in fact used to hold and stabilize the movement.

In 1988, Claude Meylan founded his company. It was taken over soon after by another watchmaker, Henri Berney, who kept up the old tradition. In 2011, the next CEO took charge, Philippe Belais, who also heads Vaudaux, a maker of high-end boxes and cases in Geneva.

The company has five main collections, all relating in some way to the region: Lac, for Joux Lake; l'Abbaye; Légendes (exploring local tales); Lionne, the river that flows by the workshops; and, finally, Tortue, whose tonneau case is reminiscent of a turtle. The brand's tagline, "sculptors of time," does live up to its products, which show many different aspects of the art of skeletonization. The Tortue line, for example, features delicate vine-like elements spreading across the movement, while one skeleton in the Lionne collection looks like a snowflake. Motorities is a paean to vintage race cars, whose finely tuned engines are often compared with watch movements. More abstract—and very clever—is the "Fenêtre sur temps," whose hour hand is carved into the revolving dial to reveal the movement as time goes by.

Lac Motorities
Reference number: 6049 M
Movement: automatic, ETA Caliber 2512; ø 17.2 mm, height 3 mm; 17 jewels; 21,600 vph; 38-hour power reserve
Functions: hours, minutes, sweep seconds
Case: stainless steel, ø 35 mm, height 10.9 mm; sapphire crystal; transparent case back; water-resistant to 3 atm
Remarks: cut-out and colored dial with vintage car racing motifs seen front and back
Band: calfskin, buckle
Price: $4,100
Variations: various vintage car motifs

Lac "Fenêtre sur temps"
Reference number: 6046-E
Movement: manually wound, Unitas Caliber 6497; ø 36.6 mm, height 4.5 mm; 17 jewels; 18,000 vph; openworked rotating dial; rhodium-plated bridges; 46-hour power reserve
Functions: hours (hand-cut into rotating dial), minutes
Case: stainless steel, ø 42 mm, height 11 mm; sapphire crystal; transparent case back; water-resistant to 3 atm
Band: leather, buckle
Price: $3,750
Variations: blue or brown dials

Skeleton Tortue
Reference number: 6047
Movement: manually wound, Claude Meylan Caliber 165CM16; ø 40 mm, height 4.5 mm; 17 jewels; 18,000 vph; openworked dial, bi-colored black/rose gold movement; 38-hour power reserve
Functions: hours, minutes, subsidiary seconds
Case: stainless steel, ø 40 × 43 mm, height 12 mm; sapphire crystal; transparent case back; water-resistant to 3 atm
Band: leather, buckle
Price: $4,500
Variations: comes in a variety of color schemes

CORUM

Founded in 1955, Switzerland's youngest luxury watch brand, Corum, celebrated sixty years of unusual—and sometimes outlandish—case and dial designs in 2015. The brand has had quite a busy history, but still by and large remains true to the collections launched by founders Gaston Ries and his nephew René Bannwart: the Admiral's Cup, Bridges, and Heritage. Among Corum's most iconic pieces is the legendary Golden Bridge baguette movement, which has received a complete makeover in recent years with the use of modern materials and complicated mechanisms. The development of these extraordinary movements required great watchmaking craftsmanship and expansion and modernization of the product development department.

The Bridges collection has always been an eye-catcher with its unusual movement, originally the brainchild of the great watchmaker Vincent Calabrese. Its introduction was a milestone in watchmaking history. And the Golden Bridge recently acquired a new highlight: in the Golden Bridge Tourbillon Panoramique with all components appearing to float in thin air.

To secure its financial future, Corum was sold to China Haidian Group (now Citychamp Watch & Jewellery Group) in April 2013. The move gave the brand financial independence and access to the crucial Chinese market. The group also took over Eterna and Rotary to establish a strong manufacturing base in Switzerland.

Today, the sporty Admiral's Cup collection is divided into two families: the classical Legend and the more athletic AC-One 45. The colorful nautical number flags have returned to the Admiral's Cup dials. For the brand's sixtieth birthday, in 2015, it produced a Legend with a flying tourbillon and revived the remarkable Bubble in a limited series. It earned its moniker from the domed shape of the crystal. Corum's vision is expressed in its logo: a key facing the sky, which symbolizes both the mysteries to be discovered as well as openness to the new.

Montres Corum Sàrl
Rue du Petit-Château 1
Case postale 374
CH-2301 La Chaux-de-Fonds
Switzerland

Tel.:
+41-32-967-0670

E-mail:
info@corum.ch

Website:
www.corum.ch

Founded:
1955

Number of employees:
160 worldwide

Annual production:
16,000 watches

U.S. distributor:
Montres Corum USA
CWJ Brands
1551 Sawgrass Corporate Parkway
Suite 109
Sunrise, FL 33323
954-279-1220
www.corum.ch

Most important collections/price range:
Admiral's Cup, Golden Bridge, Bubble, and Heritage, Romvlvs and Artisan, 150 models in total /approx. $1,500 to over $1,000,000

Golden Bridge Stream
Reference number: B313/03371
Movement: automatic, Caliber CO 313; 11.25 × 33.18 mm; 26 jewels; 28,800 vph; variable inertia balance, baguette movement with gold bridges and plates, linear winding with sliding platinum weight; 40-hour power reserve
Functions: hours, minutes
Case: red gold, 31 × 42.2 mm, height 14.7 mm; sapphire crystal; transparent case back; water-resistant to 3 atm
Band: reptile skin, triple folding clasp
Remarks: baguette movement with linear winding with sliding platinum weight flanked by 3D microstructures reminiscent of Golden Gate Bridge
Price: $68,100; limited to 88 pieces

Golden Bridge Round
Reference number: B113/03010
Movement: manually wound, Caliber CO 113; 4.9 × 34 mm, height 3 mm; 19 jewels; 28,800 vph; baguette movement, hand-engraved bridges and gold mainplate
Functions: hours, minutes
Case: red gold, ø 43 mm, height 8.8 mm; sapphire crystal; transparent case back; water-resistant to 3 atm
Band: reptile skin, triple folding clasp
Remarks: baguette movement flanked by 3D microstructures
Price: $47,300
Variations: diamond bezel ($55,300)

Golden Bridge Round
Reference number: B113/03831
Movement: manually wound, Caliber CO 113; 4.9 × 34 mm, height 3 mm; 19 jewels; 28,800 vph; hand-engraved baguette movement, bridges, and mainplate
Functions: hours, minutes
Case: titanium with black DLC coating, ø 43 mm, height 8.8 mm; sapphire crystal; transparent case back; rose gold crown; water-resistant to 3 atm
Band: rubber, triple folding clasp
Remarks: baguette movement flanked by 3D microstructures
Price: $25,000; limited to 68 pieces

CORUM

Admiral Legend 42
Reference number: A395/04015
Movement: automatic, Caliber CO 395 (base ETA 2892-A2); ø 25.9 mm; 27 jewels; 28,800 vph; 42-hour power reserve
Functions: hours, minutes, subsidiary seconds; date
Case: stainless steel with black PVD coating, ø 42 mm, height 9.5 mm; bezel set with blue rubber coating; sapphire crystal; transparent case back; water-resistant to 5 atm
Band: rubber, triple folding clasp
Price: $5,200; limited to 100 pieces

Admiral Legend 42
Reference number: A395/03857
Movement: automatic, Caliber CO 395 (base ETA 2892-A2); ø 25.9 mm; 27 jewels; 28,800 vph; 42-hour power reserve
Functions: hours, minutes, subsidiary seconds; date
Case: stainless steel, ø 42 mm, height 9.5 mm; sapphire crystal; transparent case back; water-resistant to 5 atm
Band: rubber, triple folding clasp
Price: $4,500

Admiral Legend 42 Chronograph
Reference number: A984/03797
Movement: automatic, Caliber CO 984 (base ETA 2894-2); ø 32 mm, height 6.1 mm; 37 jewels; 28,800 vph; 42-hour power reserve
Functions: hours, minutes, subsidiary seconds; chronograph; date
Case: stainless steel with blue PVD coating, ø 42 mm, height 12.3 mm; sapphire crystal; transparent case back; water-resistant to 3 atm
Band: stainless steel with blue PVD coating, triple folding clasp
Price: on request

Admiral AC-One 45 Chronograph
Reference number: A132/03876
Movement: automatic, Caliber CO 132; ø 25.6 mm, height 6.1 mm; 39 jewels; 28,800 vph; rotor with black PVD coating; 42-hour power reserve
Functions: hours, minutes, subsidiary seconds; chronograph; date
Case: titanium, ø 45 mm, height 14.3 mm; sapphire crystal; transparent case back; water-resistant to 10 atm
Band: rubber, triple folding clasp
Price: $9,900

Admiral AC-One 45 Openworked Automatic
Reference number: A297/03897
Movement: automatic, Caliber CO 297; ø 25.6 mm; 39 jewels; 28,800 vph; skeletonized movement; 42-hour power reserve
Functions: hours, minutes, subsidiary seconds; power reserve indicator; chronograph with 3-minute counter
Case: titanium, ø 45 mm, height 14.3 mm; sapphire crystal; transparent case back; water-resistant to 10 atm
Band: rubber with textile layer, triple folding clasp
Remarks: skeletonized dial
Price: $25,700

Admiral AC-One 45 Openworked Tourbillon
Reference number: A298/03901
Movement: automatic, Caliber CO 298; ø 25.6 mm; 39 jewels; 28,800 vph; 1-minute tourbillon; skeletonized movement; 42-hour power reserve
Functions: hours, minutes, subsidiary seconds; power reserve indicator; chronograph with 3-minute counter
Case: red gold, ø 45 mm, height 14.3 mm; bezel with black DLC coating; sapphire crystal; transparent case back; water-resistant to 10 atm
Band: rubber with textile layer, triple folding clasp
Remarks: skeletonized dial
Price: $65,800

CORUM

$20 Coin
Reference number: C082/03167
Movement: automatic, Caliber CO 082; ø 25.6 mm; 21 jewels; 28,800 vph; 42-hour power reserve
Functions: hours, minutes
Case: yellow gold, ø 43 mm, height 7.6 mm; sapphire crystal
Band: reptile skin, buckle
Remarks: dial and case back manufactured of "Double Eagle" gold dollar coin
Price: $26,200

Heritage LAB 01
Reference number: Z410/03861
Movement: automatic, Caliber CO 410; 30 × 32 mm; 27 jewels; 28,800 vph; microrotor; partially skeletonized movement; 50-hour power reserve
Functions: hours, minutes
Case: titanium with black DLC coating, rubber inlay on flanks, 39.89 × 55 mm, height 11.75 mm; sapphire crystal; transparent case back; water-resistant to 5 atm
Band: rubber, triple folding clasp
Remarks: skeletonized dial
Price: $13,800; limited to 99 pieces

Heritage LAB 01
Reference number: Z410/03860
Movement: automatic, Caliber CO 410; 30 × 32 mm; 27 jewels; 28,800 vph; microrotor; partially skeletonized movement; 50-hour power reserve
Functions: hours, minutes
Case: titanium with black DLC coating, rubber inlay on flanks, 39.89 × 55 mm, height 11.75 mm; sapphire crystal; transparent case back; water-resistant to 5 atm
Band: rubber, triple folding clasp
Remarks: skeletonized dial
Price: $13,800; limited to 99 pieces

Bubble 47 Chronograph
Reference number: L771/03542
Movement: automatic, Caliber CO 771; ø 29.9 mm; 28 jewels; 28,800 vph; 55-hour power reserve
Functions: hours, minutes, subsidiary seconds; chronograph; date
Case: titanium with black PVD coating, ø 47 mm, height 20.8 mm; sapphire crystal; transparent case back; water-resistant to 10 atm
Band: rubber, buckle
Remarks: domed sapphire crystal
Price: $7,300; limited to 88 pieces

Bubble 47
Reference number: L407/03573
Movement: automatic, Caliber CO 407; ø 29.9 mm; 33 jewels; 28,800 vph; 42-hour power reserve
Functions: hours, minutes, sweep seconds
Case: titanium, ø 47 mm, height 20.05 mm; sapphire crystal; transparent case back; water-resistant to 10 atm
Band: rubber with textile overlay, buckle
Remarks: domed sapphire crystal
Price: $10,700

Bubble 47 Central Tourbillon
Reference number: L406/03664
Movement: automatic, Caliber CO 406; ø 29.9 mm; 38 jewels; 28,800 vph; central, flying 1-minute tourbillon; 65-hour power reserve
Functions: hours, minutes (mysterious time display without visible hands)
Case: titanium, ø 47 mm, height 19.6 mm; sapphire crystal; transparent case back; water-resistant to 10 atm
Band: rubber with textile overlay, buckle
Remarks: domed sapphire crystal
Price: $80,400

CUERVO Y SOBRINOS

Cuba means a lot of things to different people. Today it seems to be the last bastion of genuine retro in an age of frenzied technology. However, turn the clock back to the early twentieth century and you find that Ramón Rio y Cuervo and his sister's sons (his nephews, the "sobrinos" of the brand name) kept a watchmaking workshop and an elegant store on Quinta Avenida, where they sold fine Swiss pocket watches—and more modest American models as well. With the advent of tourism from the coast of Florida, their business developed with wristwatches, whose dials Don Ramón soon had printed with *Cuervo y Sobrinos*—"Cuervo and Nephews."

An Italian watch enthusiast, Marzio Villa, resuscitated Cuervo y Sobrinos in 2002 and started manufacturing in the Italian-speaking region of Switzerland and in cooperation with various Swiss watchmakers. The tagline "Latin heritage, Swiss manufacture" says it all. These timepieces epitomize—or even romanticize—the island's heyday. The lines are at times elegant and sober, or blatantly vintage with fissured dial effect, like the Robusto line, or radiate the ease of those who still have time on their hands, like the Prominente. Colors hint at cigar leaves and sepia photos in frames of old gold. The Esplendidos even includes a special series dedicated to the Cigar Smoking World Championship (CSWC). Playfulness is also a Cuervo y Sobrinos quality: The Piratas have buttons shaped like the muzzle of a blunderbuss, a cannonball crown, and a porthole flange.

CyS SA
Rue du Doubs, 6
CH-2340
Switzerland

Tel.:
+41 21-552-18-82

E-mail:
contact@cuervoysobrinos.com

Website:
www.cuervoysobrinos.com

Founded:
1882

Annual production:
3,500 watches

Distributor:
Provenance Gems LLC
ines@provenancegems.com
800-305-3869

Most important collections/price range:
Historiador, Prominente, Torpedo, Robusto / $2,000 to $20,000; higher for perpetual calendars and tourbillon models

Day Date Churchill
Reference number: 2810.1CGT
Movement: automatic, CYS 5204 (base SW 240); ø 29 mm, height 5.5 mm; 26 jewels; 28,800 vph; 38-hour power reserve; rotor with fan decoration and CyS engraving
Functions: hours, minutes, sweep seconds; date at 3 o'clock
Case: stainless steel, 43 mm, height 12.45 mm; sapphire crystal; patented screw-in crown system; transparent case back; water-resistant to 3 atm
Remarks: dial with structured gray to look like an old fissured (*craquelé*) dial
Band: reptile skin, folding clasp
Price: $3,900; limited to 200 pieces

Esplendido CSWC Series
Reference number: 2414.1TC
Movement: automatic, CYS 5103 (base Soprod M100); ø 25.6 mm, height 3.6 mm; 25 jewels; 28,800 vph; 42-hour power reserve; rotor with fan decoration and CyS engraving
Functions: hours, minutes, sweep seconds; date at 6 o'clock
Case: stainless steel, ø 42 × 32 mm, height 8.3 mm; sapphire crystal; screw-down transparent case back; water-resistant to 3 atm
Band: reptile skin, buckle
Remarks: replica of 1950s watch
Price: $2,750

Prominente Caramelo
Reference number: 1015.1YE
Movement: automatic, ETA Caliber 2893-1; ø 25.60 mm, height 4.10 mm; 21 jewels; 28,800 vph; 42-hour power reserve
Functions: hours, minutes, sweep seconds; GMT (on dial); date
Case: stainless steel, ø 40 mm, height 9.9 mm; sapphire crystal; integrated and protected key winding crown; water-resistant to 3 atm
Band: reptile skin, folding clasp
Remarks: vintage look inspired by 1950s Cuervo y Sobrinos timepieces
Price: $3,200

Czapek & Cie
18 Rue de la Corraterie
CH-1204 Geneva
Switzerland

Tel.:
–41 22 557 41 41

E-mail:
info@czapek.com

Website:
www.czapek.com

Founded:
2012

U.S. distributor:
Horology Works
11 Flagg Road
West Hartford, CT 06117
860-986-9676
info@horologyworks.com

Most important collections/price range:
Quai des Bergues men's and ladies' watches / from $12,000 to $45,800; Place Vendôme / up to $226,000; Faubourg de Cracovie / up to $26,800

CZAPEK & CIE.

Until recently, the name Czapek was literally unknown. Born in Bohemia (Czech Republic today) in 1811, Frantiszek Czapek fought in the failed Polish insurrection of 1832 against Russia and then fled to Geneva. In 1839, he joined fellow Pole Jean de Patek. When the contract expired in 1845, Patek decided on a partnership with Mr. Philippe, inventor of the keyless watch. Czapek went on to become purveyor of watches to Emperor Napoleon III and author of a book on watches. Then he vanished without a trace sometime in the late 1860s.

Entrepreneur, art specialist, and occasional watch collector Harry Guhl bought the name and brought together a management team. They chose Czapek's model No. 3430 as a model upon which to build up a new brand. It's an intriguing piece with elongated Roman numerals and superbly cut fleur-de-lys hands. The piece also has two oddly placed subdials at 7:30 and 4:30, one for small seconds, the other featuring a clever double hand for the seven-day power reserve and days of the week. It would serve as a model for the new brand's portfolio.

The team sought out some of the best suppliers in Switzerland, including Jean-François Mojon for the in-house calibers (double barrel spring, open ratchets), Donzé for the grand-feu dials with the secret signature, and Aurélien Bouchet for the fine fleur-de-lys hands. Funding came from subscribers over the crowd equity sites Raizers and Crowd for Angels.

The first collection, the Quai des Bergues, came out in November 2015 and won the Public Prize of the Grand Prix d'Horlogerie de Genève a year later. Next came the Place Vendôme in homage to the great square in Paris where Czapek actually had a boutique. The Faubourg de Cracovie, 2018, is a classic chronograph, but with a grand-feu dial and, once again, the fine hands that reach all the back to Czapek's day. Lately, the company has been expanding on its existing collections by adding new colors (blue and salmon, for instance) and creating a special guilloché called "resonance," which resembles the rippling pattern made by raindrops falling on a still body of water.

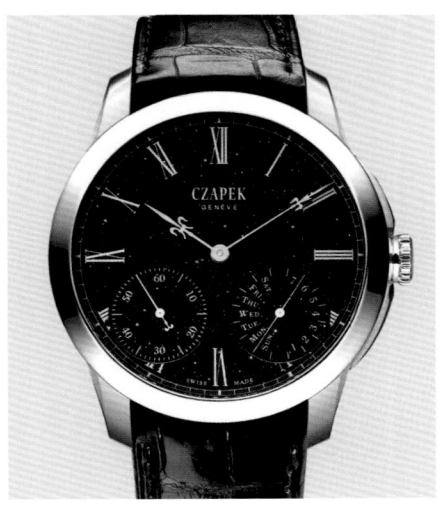

Quai des Bergues "Midnight in Geneva"

Movement: manually wound, Czapek Caliber SXH1; ø 32 mm, height 4.75 mm; 21,600 vph; 2 barrel springs, double open ratchets; 168-hour power reserve
Functions: hours, minutes, subsidiary seconds; power reserve indicator; weekdays
Case: XO steel, ø 42.5 mm, height 11.9 mm; sapphire crystal; crown protectors integrated into case barrel; transparent case back; night blue aventurine dial; water-resistant to 5 atm
Band: reptile skin, buckle
Price: $18,900; limited to 15 pieces per year
Variations: various case materials and dial colors

Faubourg de Cracovie "Sockeye"

Movement: automatic, Czapek Caliber SXH3; ø 30 mm, height 6.95 mm; 36,000 vph, vertical clutch; linear hammer, 65-hour power reserve; diamond blasted bridges, snailed "trottoirs"
Functions: hours, minutes, subsidiary seconds; chronograph, date
Case: stainless steel, ø 41.5 mm, height 10.8 mm; sapphire crystal; transparent case back; water-resistant to 10 atm
Band: reptile skin, folding clasp
Remarks: blued-steel arrow hands; special alloy dial in salmon color with "résonance" guilloché pattern
Price: $25,300
Variations: various color combinations on dial

Place Vendôme "Ombres"

Movement: manually wound, Czapek Caliber SXH2; ø 34.8 mm, height 9.8 mm; 21,600 vph; 1-minute tourbillon (off-center); open ratchet; finely decorated bridges and mainplate; 60-hour power reserve
Functions: hours, minutes, subsidiary seconds (on tourbillon cage); 2nd time zone; day/night indicator; power reserve indicator
Case: titanium, ø 43.5 mm, height 14.6 mm; sand-blasted case barrel; sapphire crystal; transparent case back; grand-feu black enamel dial; water-resistant to 3 atm
Band: reptile skin, titanium buckle
Remarks: white gold arrow-shaped hands
Price: $93,000; limited to 25 pieces
Variations: platinum ($121,000)

DAVOSA

One of the more important brands occupying the lower segment of the market is Davosa, which manufactures a range of pilot watches, quality divers (with helium valve), dress watches, and ladies' watches, all at very affordable prices. The brand has even come out with an apnea training watch that cleverly comes out of its case. The company uses solid Swiss movements, which it occasionally modifies for its own designs, or it experiments with special coatings like the "gun" PVD coating on the latest Argonautics, which is dark green. The most recent series is dedicated to Isaac Newton. Among these dressy in a sporty sort of way timepieces, one finds a limited edition automatic chronograph with a moon phase, at under $2,400.

To create a broad portfolio requires experience, and that is something Davosa has in spades. The company was founded in 1891. Back then, farmer Abel Frédéric Hasler spent the long winter months in Tramelan, in Switzerland's Jura mountains, making silver pocket watch cases. Later, two of his brothers ventured out to the city of Geneva and opened a watch factory. The third brother also opted to engage with the watch industry and moved to Biel. The entire next generation of Haslers went into watchmaking as well.

The name Hasler & Co. appeared on the occasional package mailed in Switzerland or overseas. Playing the role of unassuming private-label watchmakers, the Haslers remained in the background and let their customers in Europe and the United States run away with the show. It wasn't until after World War II that brothers Paul and David Hasler dared produce their own timepieces.

The long experience with watchmaking and watches culminated in 1987 with the brothers developing their own line of watches under the brand name Davosa. The Haslers then signed a partnership with the German distributor Bohle. In Germany, mechanical watches were experiencing a boom, so the brand was able to evolve quickly. In 2000, Corinna Bohle took over as manager of strategic development. Davosa now reaches well beyond Switzerland's borders and has become an integral part of the world of mechanical watches.

Hasler & Co. SA
CH-2543 Lengnau
Switzerland

E-mail:
info@davosa.com

Website:
www.davosa.com

Founded:
1881

U.S. distributor:
Davosa U.S.A
11256 Brandywine Lake Way,
Boynton Beach, FL 33473
877-DAVOSA1
info@davosa-usa.com
www.davosa-usa.com

Most important collections/price range:
Apnea Diver, Argonautic, Classic, Gentleman, Military, Newton, Pilot, Ternos, Titanium / $600 to $2,400

Newton Pilot Moonphase Chronograph Limited Edition
Reference number: 161.586.55
Movement: automatic, ETA Caliber 7751; ø 30 mm, height 7.9 mm; 25 jewels; 28,800 vph; 42-hour power reserve
Functions: hours, minutes, subsidiary seconds; additional 24-hour display; chronograph; full calendar with date, weekday, month, moon phase
Case: stainless steel, ø 44 mm, height 14 mm; sapphire crystal; transparent case back; water-resistant to 5 atm
Band: calfskin, buckle
Price: $2,398

Newton Pilot Day-Date
Reference number: 161.585.45
Movement: automatic, ETA Caliber 2834-2; ø 29.4 mm, height 5.05 mm; 25 jewels; 28,800 vph; 38-hour power reserve
Functions: hours, minutes, sweep seconds; date, weekday
Case: stainless steel, ø 44 mm, height 11 mm; sapphire crystal; transparent case back; water-resistant to 5 atm
Band: calfskin, buckle
Price: $898

Evo 1908 Automatic
Reference number: 161.575.14
Movement: automatic, Sellita Caliber SW260; ø 25.6 mm, height 5.6 mm; 31 jewels; 28,800 vph; 38-hour power reserve
Functions: hours, minutes, subsidiary seconds; date
Case: stainless steel, 36 × 39.5 mm, height 12 mm; sapphire crystal; transparent case back; water-resistant to 5 atm
Band: calfskin, buckle
Price: $998
Variations: various straps and dials

DAVOSA

Argonautic BG
Reference number: 161.522.02
Movement: automatic, Sellita Caliber SW200-1; ø 25.6 mm, height 4.6 mm; 26 jewels; 28,800 vph; 38-hour power reserve
Functions: hours, minutes, sweep seconds; date
Case: stainless steel, ø 42.5 mm, height 13.5 mm; unidirectional bezel with ceramic insert, 0-60 scale; sapphire crystal; screw-in crown; helium valve; water-resistant to 30 atm
Band: stainless steel, folding clasp, with safety lock and extension link
Price: $798
Variations: various colors

Apnea Diver Automatic
Reference number: 161.570.55
Movement: automatic, Sellita Caliber SW200-1; ø 25.6 mm, height 4.6 mm; 25 jewels; 28,800 vph; 38-hour power reserve
Functions: hours, minutes, sweep seconds
Case: stainless steel with black PVD coating, ø 46 mm, height 12.5 mm; unidirectional bezel with ceramic insert, 0-60 scale; sapphire crystal; screw-in crown; water-resistant to 20 atm
Band: rubber, buckle
Remarks: case can be removed and set upright for breathing training
Price: $1,098
Variations: bicolor with partial PVD coating ($1,098); without PVD coating ($998)

Argonautic Lumis T25
Reference number: 161.580.40
Movement: automatic, Sellita Caliber SW200-1; ø 25.6 mm, height 4.6 mm; 26 jewels; 28,800 vph; 38-hour power reserve
Functions: hours, minutes, sweep seconds; date
Case: stainless steel, ø 43 mm, height 13.8 mm; unidirectional bezel with ceramic insert, 0-60 scale; sapphire crystal; screw-in crown; helium valve; water-resistant to 30 atm
Band: stainless steel Milanese mesh, folding clasp with safety lock
Remarks: hands and indices with colored tritium gas tubes
Price: $868
Variations: various bands and colors

Ternos Professional GMT Black&White Limited Edition
Reference number: 161.571.15
Movement: automatic, Sellita Caliber SW330-1; ø 25.6 mm, height 4.1 mm; 25 jewels; 28,800 vph; 42-hour power reserve
Functions: hours, minutes, sweep seconds; additional 24-hour display (2nd time zone); date
Case: stainless steel, ø 42 mm, height 15.5 mm; unidirectional bezel with ceramic insert, with 0-24 scale; sapphire crystal; screw-in crown; water-resistant to 20 atm
Band: stainless steel, folding clasp, with safety lock and extension link
Remarks: comes with additional nylon band
Price: $1,348

Ternos Professional
Reference number: 161.559.45
Movement: automatic, Sellita Caliber SW200-1; ø 25.6 mm, height 4.6 mm; 25 jewels; 28,800 vph; 38-hour power reserve
Functions: hours, minutes, sweep seconds; date
Case: stainless steel, ø 42 mm, height 15.5 mm; unidirectional bezel with ceramic insert, 0-60 scale; sapphire crystal; screw-in crown; helium valve; water-resistant to 50 atm
Band: stainless steel, folding clasp, with safety lock and extension link
Price: $878
Variations: various colors

Ternos Pro 500 Black Suit Limited Edition
Reference number: 161.583.50
Movement: automatic, Sellita Caliber SW200-1; ø 25.6 mm, height 4.6 mm; 25 jewels; 28,800 vph; 38-hour power reserve
Functions: hours, minutes, sweep seconds; date
Case: stainless steel with black DLC coating, ø 42 mm, height 15.5 mm; unidirectional bezel with ceramic insert, 0-60 scale; sapphire crystal; screw-in crown; water-resistant to 50 atm
Band: stainless steel, folding clasp, with safety lock and extension link
Price: $949

DEEP BLUE

As far as anyone can tell, the fish do not care what you are wearing on your wrist. For the diver, it has to be accurate, genuinely water-resistant, and readable in less-than-ideal conditions. Those are the basics—or should be—of any real diver's watch. The rest is in the eye of the beholder. And it seems that New York–based Deep Blue does not wander too far off home plate, as it were. Founder Stan Betesh launched his company with the idea of providing divers with an array of tough watches that do the job and have the look and feel of a professional-quality diver's watch at a fraction of what you might expect to pay.

Little did he know in 2007—that is, more than a decade ago—that his watches would achieve cult status among divers. Deep Blue watches are accurate, robust, and ready for life in the open and underwater. There's no need to hide them in a safe, and getting banged up a little does them no harm—it's called patina, and it gives these timepieces the look and feel of a real tool watch . . . which is what they are.

The collection includes all sorts of models for every type of diving. The power is supplied by Miyota or ETA calibers, occasionally quartz movements. Some have special features like ceramic bezels; some are water-resistant to as much as 3,000 meters, like the Depthmaster, whose dimensions (ø 49 mm, height 19.5) and weight (300 g) will certainly contribute to the speed of the diver's descent.

For its tenth anniversary, the brand launched the Master 2000 Diver, which offers the buyer a variety of dial colors, from black to bright orange. Lots of care is given to lighting the dial, with generous application of Superluminova and the occasional use of autoluminescent tritium tubes, which may well attract some interesting fish. The second commemorative watch features this special technology: the Daynight Recon T-100 Tritium Diver 1 in a 45-mm stainless steel case with a ceramic 120-click unidirectional rotating bezel.

Deep Blue Watches
1716 Coney Island Avenue
Suite 3r
Brooklyn, NY 11230

Tel.:
718-484-7717

Website:
www.deepbluewatches.com

E-mail:
info@deepbluewatches.com

Founded:
2007

Number of employees:
70

Annual output:
n/a

Distribution:
Retail

Most important collections/price range:
Master 1000, Diver 1000, Defender / $300 to $500; Pro Sea Diver / $500 to $900; Daynight / $600 to $1,000; Alpha, Marine, Ocean / $700 to $1,500; Blue Water / $600 to $1,400

Daynight Recon Tritium T-100 GMT Swiss Automatic

Reference number: DNRECONGMTT100
Movement: automatic, ETA Caliber 2893-2; ø 25.6 mm, height 4.6 mm; 25 jewels; 28,800 vph
Functions: hours, minutes, sweep seconds; date, 2nd time zone
Case: stainless steel, ø 45 mm, height 16.5 mm; unidirectional bezel with 0-120 scale; transparent case back; sapphire crystal; water-resistant to 50 atm
Band: stainless steel bracelet with wetsuit extension
Remarks: blue wave dial with tritium gas–filled tube illumination on hands and hour markers
Price: $1,449
Variations: black dial

Daynight Recon Tritium Valjoux T100

Reference number: DNT100DVR7750
Movement: automatic, ETA Valjoux 7750; ø 30 mm, height 7.9 mm; 25 jewels; 28,800 vph
Functions: hours, minutes, subsidiary seconds; chronograph; weekday, date
Case: stainless steel, ø 45 mm, height 16.5 mm; screw-down case back; screw-in crown; unidirectional bezel with 0-120 scale; sapphire crystal; water-resistant to 50 atm
Band: stainless steel bracelet
Remarks: tritium gas–filled tube illumination on hands and hour markers
Price: $1,999
Variations: blue or white dial

Daynight Rescue Tritium T-100

Reference number: DNRESCURGMTT100
Movement: automatic, ETA Caliber 2893-2; ø 25.6 mm, height 4.6 mm; 25 jewels; 28,800 vph
Functions: hours, minutes, sweep seconds; 2nd time zone; date
Case: stainless steel, ø 45 mm, height 16.5 mm; unidirectional bezel with 0-120 scale; transparent case back; sapphire crystal; water-resistant to 50 atm
Band: stainless steel bracelet with wetsuit extension
Remarks: tritium gas–filled tube illumination on hands and hour markers
Price: $1,449
Variations: black dial

Detroit Watch Company, LLC
P.O. Box 60
Birmingham, MI 48012

Tel:
248-321-5601

E-mail:
info@detroitwatchco.com

Founded:
2013

Number of employees:
3

Annual production:
500 watches

Distribution:
direct sales only

Most important collections/price range:
M1 Woodward Moonphase, 1701 Pontchartrain GMT, 1701 L'Horloge; B24 Liberator / $998 to $2,650

DETROIT WATCH COMPANY

Founders Patrick Ayoub and Amy Ayoub launched Detroit Watch Company in 2013 with the first and only mechanical timepieces designed and assembled in Detroit, Michigan. Patrick, a car designer, and Amy, an interior designer, share a passion for original design and timepieces and have worked hard to develop their brand, which draws inspiration from, and celebrates, the city of "Détroit."

Detroit means a lot of things to different people, and because the history of the people and places have shaped the city, Detroit's stories are also part of the Detroit Watch Company's collective story, which deserves to be told. Their introductory timepiece, the 1701, for instance, commemorates Antoine de la Mothe Cadillac, Knight of St. Louis, who, with his company of colonists, arrived at Détroit on July 24, 1701. On that day, under the patronage of Louis XIV and protected by the flag of France, the city of Détroit, then called Fort Pontchartrain, was founded.

People phoning Detroit will understand why the company came out with a watch named 313—it's the area code of the city that brought cars and Motown (*motor + town*) music to the world. Needless to say, the dial looks like an old-fashioned phone dial. Now the company has decided to include a few more of the U.S. area codes for good measure. And where did those cars ride and race informally? On Woodward Avenue, the first mile of concrete highway in the USA, where carriages once rolled. It's the name for a collection of sporty chronographs.

The Detroit Watch Company timepieces are beautifully designed and hand-assembled in-house, and may be purchased directly through the Detroit Watch Company website.

M1 Woodward Moonphase

Reference number: DWC M1W-Moonphase
Movement: automatic, ETA Caliber 7751; ø 30 mm, height 7.9 mm; 25 jewels; 28,800 vph; 48-hour power reserve
Functions: hours, minutes, subsidiary seconds; chronograph; date, day, month, moon phase
Case: stainless steel, ø 42 mm, height 14.5 mm; sapphire crystal with antireflective coating, screw-down exhibition case back with engraving; water-resistant to 5 atm
Band: calfskin, folding clasp
Price: $2,550

City Collection 313

Reference number: DWC-CITY-313
Movement: automatic, ETA Caliber 2824-2; ø 26.6 mm, height 4.6 mm; 26 jewels; 28,800 vph; 38-hour power reserve
Functions: hours, minutes, subsidiary seconds
Case: stainless steel, ø 42 mm, height 9.4 mm; sapphire crystal with antireflective coating, screw-down case back with engraving; water-resistant to 5 atm
Band: calfskin, buckle
Price: $998
Variations: black on black dial, transparent case back (starting at $998)
Also available in area codes: 202, 212, 305, 312, 415, 416, 504, 512, 713, 818, 310

1701 Pontchartrain GMT Great Lakes Edition

Reference number: DWC-1701GMTGLE-S1
Movement: automatic, ETA Caliber 2893-2; ø 26.6 mm, height 4.1 mm; 21 jewels; 28,800 vph; 42-hour power reserve
Functions: hours, minutes, subsidiary seconds; 2nd time zone, date
Case: stainless steel, ø 42 mm, height 13 mm; sapphire crystal with antireflective coating, unidirectional bezel, screw-down crown; water-resistant to 300 atm; helium release crown
Band: calfskin, buckle
Price: $1,495
Variations: 1701 Pontchartrain ($1,395)

DOXA

Watch aficionados who have visited the world-famous museum in Le Locle will know that the little castle in which it is housed once belonged to Georges Ducommun, the founder of Doxa. The *manufacture* was launched as a backyard operation in 1889 and originally produced pocket watches. Quality products and good salesmanship quickly put Doxa on the map, but the company's real game-changer came in 1967 with the uncompromising SUB 300, a heavy, bold diver's watch. It featured a unidirectional bezel with the official U.S. dive table engraved on it. The bright orange dial might seem quite ostentatious, but, in fact, it offers the best legibility under water. It also marked the beginning of a trend for colorful dials.

Doxa made a number of attractive, sportive watches, like the Ultraspeed and the Régulateur, but its claim to fame these days rests on its wide range of diver's watches. Their popularity was boosted early on by the commercialization of diving in the 1970s. Thriller writer Clive Cussler, chairman and founder of the National Underwater and Marine Agency (NUMA), even chose a Doxa as gear for his action hero Dirk Pitt.

Many of the brand's watches are revivals of iconic designs from the late sixties, but with improved technology, enabling divers to go down to 1,500 meters and still read the time. For the brand's 130th anniversary, though, it issued a limited edition piece in gold, with a gold bracelet as an option for those who need a full-fledged luxury feel.

Montres DOXA SA
Rue de Zurich 23A
P.O. Box 6031
2500 Bienne 6, Switzerland

Tel.:
+41-32-44-42-72

E-mail:
contact@doxa-watches.com

Website:
www.doxa.ch

Founded:
1889

Number of employees:
35

Distribution:
Retail and direct sales
For the USA:
877-255-5017

Most important collections/price range:
Doxa Sub dive watch collection / $990 to $4,900

SUB 200 T.GRAPH
50th Anniversary Edition

Reference number: 805.40.351LE.13
Movement: manually wound, Valjoux 7734; ø 31 mm, height 6.65 mm; 17 jewels; 18,000 vph; 45-hour power reserve
Functions: hours, minutes, subsidiary seconds; chronograph; date
Case: yellow gold, ø 43 mm, height 15 mm; unidirectional bezel with engraved decompression scale; sapphire crystal; screw-in crown; screw-down case back with sailboat engraving; water-resistant to 30 atm
Band: rubber, folding clasp
Price: $43,800; limited to 13 pieces
Variations: comes with yellow gold bracelet ($69,800)

SUB 200

Reference number: 799.10.101LE.10
Movement: automatic, ETA Caliber 2824-2; ø 25.6 mm, height 4.6 mm; 25 jewels; 28,800 vph
Functions: hours, minutes, sweep seconds; date
Case: stainless steel, ø 42 mm, height 14 mm; unidirectional bezel with 0-60 scale; sapphire crystal; case back with special anniversary engraving; screw-in crown; water-resistant to 20 atm
Band: stainless steel, folding clasp with safety lock
Price: $990; limited to 130 pieces

SUB 1200T Professional

Reference number: 872.10.351.10
Movement: automatic, ETA Caliber 2824-2; ø 25.6 mm, height 4.6 mm; 25 jewels; 28,800 vph
Functions: hours, minutes, sweep seconds; date
Case: stainless steel, ø 42.5 mm, height 13.4 mm; helium valve release, unidirectional no-decompression dive table bezel; sapphire crystal; screw-in crown; water-resistant to 120 atm
Band: stainless steel, folding clasp with extension link
Price: $1,890
Variations: Sharkhunter (black dial), Caribbean (blue dial)

Montres duManège Sàrl
Rue du manège 16
CH-2300 La Chaux-de-Fonds
Switzerland

Tel.:
+41-32-913-32-33

E-mail:
info@dumanege.com

Website:
www.dumanege.com

Founded:
2011

Number of employees:
4

Annual production:
approx. 300 watches

U.S. distributors:
Brands Consulting, LLC
Thierry Chaunu
Wells Fargo Bank, N.A
420 Montgomery
San Francisco, CA 94104
646-732-1822
thierrychaunu@gmail.com

Most important collections/price range:
DM Exploration / $7,500 to $18,900; Heritage / $3,175 to $10,000; Heritage Art / $12,500 and higher

DUMANÈGE

Strictly speaking, the term "Swiss-made" is something of a misnomer when applied to watches. With a few exceptions, the horological hotbed of the country is, in fact, the narrow French-speaking region in the west of the country. Geneva is only one of the hubs here, of course, the real forge for Swiss watches being located in the stark Jura mountains, especially La-Chaux-de-Fonds and neighboring Le Locle, joint members of the UNESCO World Heritage club.

But the names of these towns never appear on a watch, oddly. Until 2014, when a young *chaudefonnier*, Julien Fleury, decided to put the name of his native city on a dial. As a graphic designer with training in jewelry, he had a clear idea of what his watches were meant to look like. And he had a vision for developing his brand.

He called upon family and friends, pulled out all stops with contacts, and managed to get onto the market a collection of large, sportive watches, which he sold by subscription. He called it DM Exploration, the initials standing for his brand's name, duManège, a reference to the magnificent nineteenth-century riding school in La-Chaux-de-Fonds that was later used for low-cost cooperative living.

Inside the watch, a trusty Technotime movement. Today, the Exploration comes as a monopusher chronograph with a Valjoux engine. On the dial, "La-Chaux-de-Fonds."

Would he make it? Fleury is a marathon runner. He paced himself and looked to the future. After Exploration came the Heritage line, a three-hander with date exuding the charm of a classic Swiss watch. Its main line features an ivory-white dial. The Heritage's sparsely populated dial allowed Fleury not only to exercise his talents as a jeweler, but also to explore a number of decorative crafts, from miniature painting (for bespoke pieces) to grand-feu enameling, notably, a watch featuring stylized fir trees (*sapins*) as a tribute to the main element of Art Nouveau in the Jura mountains of Switzerland.

Exploration

Reference number: DM.E.CMP-A.TI.45.100-1
Movement: automatic, Valjoux 7750; ø 30 mm, height 7.9 mm; 29 jewels; 28,800 vph; special black duManège treatment on bridges; 48-hour power reserve
Functions: hours, minutes, subsidiary seconds; monopusher chronograph
Case: titanium, ø 45.5 mm, height 14 mm; sapphire crystal; bezel with black DLC treatment; transparent case back; water-resistant to 5 atm
Remarks: black opaline, with blue touches
Band: rubber, buckle
Price: $5,650
Variations: steel ($5,200); titanium with black DLC ($6,850); pink gold ($14,700)

Heritage

Reference number: DM.H.Q-A.WG.42.132-1
Movement: manually wound, ETA Caliber 2892-2; ø 25.6 mm, height 3.6 mm; 21 jewels; 28,800 vph; 42-hour power reserve
Functions: hours, minutes, sweep seconds
Case: white gold, ø 42 mm, height 9.5 mm; sapphire crystal; water-resistant to 3 atm
Band: reptile skin, folding clasp
Remarks: blue aventurine dial
Price: $10,350; limited edition of 26 pieces
Variations: red gold ($10,350); stainless steel ($2,950)

Heritage Sapin

Reference number: DM.H.Q-A.WG-S.42.152-1
Movement: manually wound, ETA Caliber 2892-2; ø 25.6 mm, height 3.6 mm; 21 jewels; 28,800 vph; 42-hour power reserve
Functions: hours, minutes, sweep seconds
Case: "extra" white gold, ø 42 mm, height 9.5 mm; bezel set with 70 diamonds; sapphire crystal; water-resistant to 3 atm
Band: reptile skin, folding clasp
Remarks: champlevé enamel dial depicting fir trees
Price: $21,050
Variations: dials using different crafts

EBERHARD & CO.

Eberhard & Co.
73, Ave. Léopold-Robert
CH-2300 La Chaux-de-Fonds
Switzerland

Tel.:
+41-32-342-5141

E-mail:
info@eberhard1887.com

Website:
www.eberhard1887.com

Founded:
1887

Distribution:
Contact main office for information on U.S. distribution.

Most important collections:
Chrono 4; 8 Jours, Tazio Nuvolari; Extra-fort; Gilda; Scafograf

Chronographs weren't always the main focus of the Eberhard & Co. brand. In 1887, Georges-Emile Eberhard rented a workshop in La Chaux-de-Fonds to produce a small series of pocket watches, but it was the unstoppable advancement of the automotive industry that gave the young company its inevitable direction. By the 1920s, Eberhard was producing timekeepers for the first auto races. In Italy, Eberhard & Co. functioned well into the 1930s as the official timekeeper for all important events relating to motor sports. And the Italian air force later commissioned some split-second chronographs from the company, one of which went for 56,000 euros at auction.

Eberhard & Co. is still doing well, thanks to the late Massimo Monti. In the 1990s, he associated the brand with legendary racer Tazio Nuvolari. The company dedicated a chronograph collection to Nuvolari and sponsored the annual Gran Premio Nuvolari vintage car rally in his hometown of Mantua.

With the launch of its four-counter chronograph, this most Italian of Swiss watchmakers underscored its expertise and ambitions where short time/sports time measurement is concerned. Indeed, Eberhard & Co.'s Chrono 4 chronograph, featuring four little counters all in a row, has brought new life to the chronograph in general. CEO Mario Peserico has continued to develop it, putting out versions with new colors and slightly altered looks.

The brand is pure vintage, so it will come as no surprise that it regularly reissues and updates some of its older, popular models, like the two-totalizer Contograph chrono from the 1960s, which originally allowed the user to calculate phone units exactly (*conto* = bill). In 2016, it relaunched the venerable 1950s Scafograph. The latest resurrection: the Caliber EB 140, a beautifully simple, 28,800-vph movement that can be admired through the case back of its 1887 Hand-Wound model.

Quadrifoglio Verde

Reference number: 31070
Movement: automatic, ETA Caliber 7750; ø 30 mm, height 7.9 mm; 25 jewels; 28,800 vph; 42-hour power reserve
Functions: hours, minutes; chronograph
Case: stainless steel, ø 43 mm, height 13.5 mm; sapphire crystal; case back affixed with 8 screws; water-resistant to 3 atm
Band: textile with calfskin overlay, buckle
Price: $5,900

Scafograf GMT

Reference number: 41038
Movement: automatic, ETA Caliber 2893-2; ø 25.6 mm, height 4.1 mm; 21 jewels; 28,800 vph; 42-hour power reserve
Functions: hours, minutes, sweep seconds; additional 24-hour display (2nd time zone); date
Case: stainless steel, ø 43 mm, height 11.8 mm; bidirectional bezel with ceramic insert, with 0-24 scale; sapphire crystal; screw-in crown; water-resistant to 10 atm
Band: stainless steel, folding clasp
Price: $4,700
Variations: blue dial; rubber strap ($3,880)

Chrono 4 130

Reference number: 31129
Movement: automatic, Eberhard Caliber EB 251-12 ½; ø 33 mm, height 7.5 mm; 53 jewels; 28,800 vph; 4 counters in a row
Functions: hours, minutes, subsidiary seconds; additional 24-hour display; chronograph; date
Case: stainless steel, ø 42 mm, height 13.3 mm; sapphire crystal; screw-in crown; water-resistant to 50 m
Band: calfskin, buckle
Price: $6,480
Variations: various dials, with steel bracelet

EBERHARD & CO.

8 Jours Grande Taille
Reference number: 21027
Movement: manually wound, Eberhard Caliber EB 896 (base ETA 7001); ø 34 mm, height 5 mm; 25 jewels; 21,600 vph; 2 spring barrels, 8-day power reserve
Functions: hours, minutes, subsidiary seconds; power reserve indicator
Case: stainless steel, ø 41 mm, height 10.85 mm; sapphire crystal; transparent case back; water-resistant to 3 atm
Band: reptile skin, buckle
Price: $5,350
Variations: black dial

Scafograf 300
Reference number: 41034
Movement: automatic, ETA Caliber 2824-2; ø 25.6 mm, height 4.6 mm; 25 jewels; 28,800 vph; 42-hour power reserve
Functions: hours, minutes, sweep seconds; date
Case: stainless steel, ø 43 mm, height 12.6 mm; unidirectional bezel with ceramic insert, 0-60 scale; sapphire crystal; screw-in crown; helium valve; water-resistant to 30 atm
Band: rubber, buckle
Price: $3,260
Variations: blue indices; stainless steel bracelet ($4,070)

Scafograf GMT "The Black Sheep" Limited Edition
Reference number: 41040
Movement: automatic, ETA Caliber 2893-2; ø 25.6 mm, height 4.1 mm; 21 jewels; 28,800 vph; 42-hour power reserve
Functions: hours, minutes, sweep seconds; additional 24-hour display (2nd time zone); date
Case: stainless steel with black DLC coating, ø 43 mm, height 11.8 mm; bidirectional bezel with ceramic insert, with 0-24 scale; sapphire crystal; screw-in crown; water-resistant to 10 atm
Band: rubber, buckle
Price: $5,130; limited to 500 pieces

Extra-Fort Automatic
Reference number: 41029
Movement: automatic, Caliber SW200-1; ø 35.6 mm, height 4.6 mm; 26 jewels; 28,800 vph; 42-hour power reserve
Functions: hours, minutes, sweep seconds; date
Case: stainless steel, ø 40 mm, height 10.07 mm; sapphire crystal; screw-in crown; water-resistant to 5 atm
Band: reptile skin, buckle
Price: $3,300
Variations: silver white or black dial, steel bracelet

Nuvolari Legend
Reference number: 31138
Movement: automatic, ETA Caliber 7750; ø 30 mm, height 7.9 mm; 25 jewels; 28,800 vph; 42-hour power reserve
Functions: hours, minutes; chronograph
Case: stainless steel, ø 43 mm, height 13.5 mm; sapphire crystal; transparent case back; screw-in crown; water-resistant to 3 atm
Band: calfskin, buckle
Remarks: stylized gold Alfa Romeo on rotor
Price: $5,790

1887 Hand-Wound
Reference number: 21028
Movement: automatic, Eberhard EB 140 Caliber; ø 31 mm, height 3.43 mm; 18 jewels; 28,800 vph; finely decorated movement with gold engravings, sunburst patterns and blued screws, 40-hour power reserve
Functions: hours, minutes, sweep seconds; date
Case: stainless steel, ø 41.8 mm, height 9.6 mm; sapphire crystal; transparent case back; screw-in crown; water-resistant to 3 atm
Band: calfskin, buckle
Remarks: clous de Paris finishing on dial
Price: $4,450

ETERNA

Eterna is a milestone in watchmaking. Founded in 1856 in what was then a village, Grenchen, the company, named Dr. Girard & Schild, became a *manufacture*, producing pocket watches under Urs Schild in 1870. Among its earliest claims to fame was the first wristwatch with an alarm, released in 1908, by which time the company had taken on the name Eterna. Forty years later came the legendary Eterna-matic, featuring five micro ball bearings for an automatic winding rotor. At the slightest movement of the watch, the rotor began to turn and set in motion what was another newly developed system of two ratchet wheels, which, independent of the rotational direction, lifted the mainspring over the automatic gears. Today, the five micro ball bearings used to cushion that rotor are the inspiration for Eterna's stylized pentagon-shaped logo.

In 2007, the company launched its Caliber 39, an automatic chronograph with three totalizers. This led to an entire family of eighty-eight versions. Modules for additional indicators or functions could be affixed with just a few screws or connected by way of a bridge. Thanks to the famous ball bearing–mounted Spherodrive winding mechanism, the movement has a power reserve of sixty-eight hours.

So, ironically perhaps, Eterna, whose original movement division became a separate company called ETA (now with the Swatch Group), has returned to building its own movements. It was acquired by F.A. Porsche Beteiligungen GmbH and started manufacturing for Porsche Design. But in 2011, International Volant Ltd., a wholly owned subsidiary of Citychamp, bought up the Porsche-owned shares in Eterna, opening many opportunities in Asia through its chain of retailers. In March 2014, Eterna and Porsche finally separated, freeing up Eterna's technical and financial resources to focus on growth. The company released new iterations of older models, notably the Super KonTiki Chronograph, a flyback equipped with the 31916A in-house caliber, and a new interpretation of the original Super KonTiki (no chronograph) that accompanied Thor Heyerdahl on his legendary expedition. But if the production of wristwatches has slowed a bit, the company is drawing the attention of other, smaller brands seeking a flexible movement for their production.

Eterna SA
Schützenstrasse 40
CH-2540 Grenchen
Switzerland

Tel.:
+41-32-654-7211

Website:
www.eterna.com

Founded:
1856

Number of employees:
approx. 80

U.S. distributor:
CWJ Brands
1551 Sawgrass Blvd., Unit 109
Sunrise, FL 33323
954-279-1220

Most important collections:
KonTiki, Eternity, 1948

Adventic Date 41 mm
Reference number: 29.70.43.42.1353
Movement: automatic, base Sellita Caliber SW200-1; ø 25.6 mm, height 4.6 mm; 26 jewels; 28,800 vph; 38-hour power reserve
Functions: hours, minutes, sweep seconds; date
Case: stainless steel with black PVD coating, ø 41 mm, height 10.85 mm; screw-down case back; sapphire crystal; water-resistant to 20 atm
Band: calfskin, folding clasp
Price: $2,600

1940 Telemeter Chronograph Flyback Bronze Manufacture
Reference number: 7950.78.54.1416
Movement: automatic, Eterna Caliber 3916A; ø 30.4 mm, height 7.9 mm; 35 jewels; 28,800 vph; 60-hour power reserve
Functions: hours, minutes, subsidiary seconds; flyback chronograph; date
Case: bronze, ø 42 mm, height 14.1 mm; sapphire crystal; transparent case back; water-resistant to 5 atm
Band: calfskin, buckle
Price: $5,100; limited to 100 pieces

1948 For Him Automatic 40 mm
Reference number: 2955.41.13.1387
Movement: automatic, base Sellita Caliber SW300-1; ø 25.6 mm, height 3.6 mm; 25 jewels; 28,800 vph; 42-hour power reserve
Functions: hours, minutes, sweep seconds; date
Case: stainless steel with black PVD coating, ø 40 mm, height 10.21 mm; screw-down case back; sapphire crystal; water-resistant to 20 atm
Band: reptile skin, folding clasp
Price: $2,200
Variations: white eggshell dial ($2,250)

KonTiki Bronze Manufacture
Reference number: 1291.78.49.1422
Movement: automatic, Eterna Caliber 3902A; ø 30.4 mm, height 5.6 mm; 30 jewels; 28,800 vph; 65-hour power reserve
Functions: hours, minutes, sweep seconds
Case: bronze, ø 44 mm, height 14.05 mm; unidirectional bezel with ceramic insert, with 0-60 scale; sapphire crystal; transparent case back; water-resistant to 20 atm
Band: calfskin, buckle
Price: $2,950; limited to 300 pieces

KonTiki Diver Gent
Reference number: 1290.41.89.1418
Movement: automatic, Sellita Caliber SW200-1; ø 25.6 mm, height 4.6 mm; 26 jewels; 28,800 vph; 38-hour power reserve
Functions: hours, minutes, sweep seconds; date
Case: stainless steel, ø 44 mm, height 12.2 mm; unidirectional bezel with ceramic insert, 0-60 scale; sapphire crystal; water-resistant to 20 atm
Band: rubber, folding clasp
Price: $1,800

Kontiki Automatic Four-Hands 42 mm
Reference number: 1598.33.41.1722
Movement: automatic, base Sellita Caliber SW200-1; ø 25.6 mm, height 4.6 mm; 26 jewels; 28,800 vph; 38-hour power reserve
Functions: hours, minutes, sweep seconds; date
Case: stainless steel with anthracite PVD coating, ø 42 mm, height 13.2 mm; screw-in crown; screw-down case back; sapphire crystal; water-resistant to 20 atm
Band: stainless steel with anthracite PVD, folding clasp
Price: $2,870
Variations: different cases and straps

 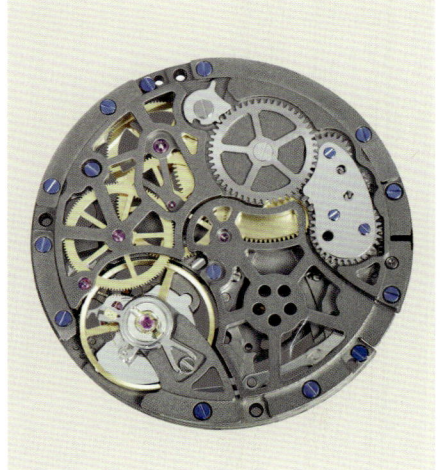 

Caliber 3916A
Automatic; rotor on ball bearings; single spring barrel, 65-hour power reserve
Functions: hours, minutes, subsidiary seconds, flyback chronograph, date
Diameter: 30.4 mm
Height: 7.9 mm
Jewels: 35
Balance: glucydur
Frequency: 28,800 vph
Balance spring: flat hairspring
Shock protection: Incabloc

Caliber 3902M
Manually wound; completely skeletonized with matte finish; single spring barrel, 65-hour power reserve
Functions: hours, minutes, sweep seconds
Diameter: 30.4 mm
Height: 4.95 mm
Jewels: 20
Balance: glucydur
Frequency: 28,800 vph
Balance spring: flat hairspring
Shock protection: Incabloc

Caliber 3902A
Automatic; rotor on ball bearings; single spring barrel, 65-hour power reserve
Functions: hours, minutes sweep seconds
Diameter: 30.4 mm
Height: 5.6 mm
Jewels: 30
Balance: glucydur
Frequency: 28,800 vph
Balance spring: flat hairspring
Shock protection: Incabloc

FABERGÉ

Peter Carl Fabergé (1846–1920), son of a St. Petersburg jeweler of French Protestant stock and supplier to the Romanovs, is a legend. In 1885, he was commissioned by Tsar Alexander III to produce a special Easter egg for the tsarina. He did so, employing the best craftspeople of the time, and in the process catapulted himself into the good graces of the Romanovs. This also meant exile when the Bolsheviks took over in 1918. His sons set up a jewelry and restoration business in Paris.

After being sold several times during the twentieth century, the name Fabergé finally ended up being owned by Pallinghurst, a holding company with investments in mining that include the famous Gemfields, a specialist in colored stones.

In 2013, Fabergé decided to launch a new portfolio of watches. Utilizing colored stones and platinum was a foregone conclusion. Victor Mayer, a former licensee, took on the enamel guilloché dials of the Fabergé Flirt core collection, which received a Vaucher movement. For the men's watch, Renaud & Papi produced a subtly modern flying tourbillon with a geometrically openworked dial. But the pièce de résistance, the Lady Compliquée, was assigned to Jean-Marc Wiederrecht of Agenhor, who created a movement driving a retrograde peacock's tail (Peacock) or a wave of frost (Winter) to display the minutes, while the hours circle the dial in the opposite direction. It won a prize at the prestigious Grand Prix d'Horlogerie de Genève.

Sourcing quality continues to pay up for Fabergé with a new crop of outstanding watches, like the iteration of the Visionnaire DTZ, which features an almost invisible rotor oscillating just on the edge of the dial and a second time zone under a magnifying glass in the middle. The Visionnaire Chronograph has the three chrono hands stacked atop each other in the middle of the dial and required an entirely new module from Agenhor. The new model, Dynamique, has been primped with restive orange touches. Meanwhile, the Lady Libertine collection continues to grow, with fascinating gem layouts. As for the Flirt line, it offers all sorts of bright or staid colors, with or without diamonds, depending on how much the wearer wants to attract attention . . .

Fabergé
1 Cathedral Piazza
London, SW1E 5BP
United Kingdom

Tel.:
+44-20-7518-7297

E-mail:
information@faberge.com

Website:
www.faberge.com

Founded:
1842, current watch department relaunched 2013

Annual production:
approx. 350 watches

U.S. distributor:
Contact: sales@faberge.com

Most important collections:
Flirt; Summer in Provence; Compliquée; Visionnaire (DTZ & Chronograph); Altruist; Dalliance

Compliquée Peacock Ruby

Movement: manually wound, Caliber AGH6901 exclusive for Fabergé; ø 32.7 mm, height 3.58 mm; 38 jewels; 21,600 vph; 50-hour power reserve
Functions: hours (on disk at crown), minutes (retrograde)
Case: platinum, 38 mm, height 12.90 mm; 54 diamonds on bezel; transparent back; sapphire crystal; water-resistant to 3 atm
Band: reptile skin, platinum buckle
Remarks: after the 1908 Fabergé Peacock Egg; dial set with rubies and diamonds, hand-engraved peacock on dial
Price: $89,000
Variations: Lady Compliquée Peacock Emerald, Lady Compliquée Peacock Black Sapphire

Compliquée Peacock

Movement: manually wound, Caliber AGH6901 exclusive for Fabergé; ø 32.7 mm, height 3.58 mm; 38 jewels; 21,600 vph; 50-hour power reserve
Functions: hours (on disk at crown), minutes (retrograde)
Case: platinum, 38 mm, height 12.90 mm; 54 diamonds on bezel; transparent back; sapphire crystal; water-resistant to 3 atm
Band: reptile skin, platinum buckle
Remarks: after the 1908 Fabergé Peacock Egg; dial set with diamonds, tourmalines, and tsavorites, hand-engraved peacock on dial
Price: $89,000
Variations: Compliquée Peacock Ruby, Compliquée Peacock Black Sapphire

Peacock Black

Movement: manually wound, Caliber AGH 6901 exclusive for Fabergé; ø 32.7 mm, height 3.58 mm; 38 jewels; 21,600 vph; 50-hour power reserve
Functions: hours (on disk at crown), minutes (retrograde)
Case: white gold, 38 mm; transparent back; sapphire crystal; water-resistant to 3 atm
Band: reptile skin, white gold buckle
Remarks: black lacquer dial, black painted mother-of-pearl hour ring
Price: $34,500

FABERGÉ

Visionnaire DTZ

Movement: automatic, Caliber AGH 6924 exclusive for Fabergé; ø 34.8, height 8.3 mm; 30 jewels; 21,600 vph; 50-hour power reserve; mainplate, bridges with côtes de Genève
Functions: hours, minutes, central dual time zone (24-hour indication)
Case: rose gold and titanium, ø 43 mm; sapphire crystal; transparent case back; water-resistant to 5 atm
Remarks: mysterious rotor with blue coloring on dial side and TC3 luminescent coating
Band: reptile skin, rose gold and titanium folding clasp
Price: $29,500
Variations: white gold and titanium ($29,500)

Visionnaire Chronograph Ceramic

Movement: automatic, Caliber AGH 6361; ø 34.40, height 7.17 mm; 67 jewels; 21,600 vph; 60-hour power reserve; mainplate, bridges with côtes de Genève
Functions: hours, minutes; central chronograph
Case: black ceramic and dark gray DLC treated titanium, ø 43 mm, height 14.34 mm; sapphire crystal; transparent case back; water-resistant to 5 atm
Remarks: black dial with mysterious rotor on dial side; TC1 luminescent coating
Band: reptile skin, folding clasp
Price: $34,500
Variations: rose gold and titanium with opaline dial ($39,500); ceramic ($40,000)

Visionnaire Chronograph Rose Gold

Movement: automatic, Caliber AGH 6361; ø 34.40, height 7.17 mm; 67 jewels; 21,600 vph; 60-hour power reserve; mainplate, bridges with côtes de Genève
Functions: hours, minutes; central chronograph
Case: rose gold and titanium, ø 43 mm, height 14.34 mm; sapphire crystal; transparent case back; water-resistant to 5 atm
Remarks: black dial with mysterious rotor on dial side; TC1 luminescent coating
Band: reptile skin, folding clasp
Price: $45,000
Variations: rose gold and titanium with opaline dial ($39,500)

Fabergé Lady Libertine I

Movement: manually wound, Caliber AGH 6911 exclusive for Fabergé; ø 30 mm, height 3.2 mm; 15 jewels; 21,600 vph; 50-hour power reserve; bridges with côtes de Genève
Functions: hours, minutes
Case: rose gold, 36 mm; sapphire crystal; transparent case back; bezel set with diamonds; water-resistant to 1 atm
Remarks: circular central space with representation of terrain in Zambia where emeralds for dial are mined; stylized arrowheads to point to hours and minutes
Band: reptile skin, rose gold buckle
Price: on request

Flirt

Movement: automatic, Vaucher Caliber 3000; ø 23.3 mm, height 3.9 mm; 28 jewels; 28,800 vph; white gold rotor; 50-hour power reserve
Functions: hours, minutes
Case: white gold, ø 36 mm; transparent case back; sapphire crystal; water resistant to 3 atm
Remarks: yellow lacquered middle ring
Band: reptile skin, buckle
Price: $14,000
Variations: various dial colors, set with diamonds

Fabergé Lady Libertine II

Movement: manually wound, Caliber AGH 6911 exclusive for Fabergé; ø 30 mm, height 3.2 mm; 15 jewels; 21,600 vph; 50-hour power reserve; bridges with côtes de Genève
Functions: hours, minutes
Case: white gold, ø 36 mm; sapphire crystal; transparent case back; bezel set with diamonds; water-resistant to 1 atm
Remarks: circular central space with representation of terrain in Zambia where emeralds for dial are mined; stylized arrowheads to point to hours and minutes
Band: reptile skin, white gold buckle
Price: on request

F.P. JOURNE

Born in Marseilles in 1957, François-Paul Journe might have become something else had he concentrated in school. He was kicked out and went to Paris, where he completed watchmaking school before going to work for his watchmaking uncle. And he has never looked back. By the age of twenty he had made his first tourbillon and soon was producing watches for connoisseurs.

He then moved to Switzerland, where he started out with handmade creations for a limited clientele and developed the most creative and complicated timekeepers for other brands before taking the plunge and founding his own in the heart of Geneva. The timepieces he basically single-handedly and certainly single-mindedly—hence his tagline *invenit et fecit*—conceives and produces are of such extreme complexity that it is no wonder that they leave his workshop in relatively small quantities. Journe has won numerous top awards, some several times over. He particularly values the Prix de la Fondation de la Vocation Bleustein-Blanchet, since it came from his peers.

The family of Journe watches is divided into four collections: the automatic Octa collection, with classic complications; the lineSport, focusing on contemporary sportive esthetics; and the Elégante collection, an electromechanical watch providing 8 to 18 years of autonomy, depending on whether it is in daily use or in sleeping mode. The fourth is the Souveraine, featuring a minute repeater, a constant force tourbillon with dead-beat seconds, and a unique Chronomètre à Résonance with two escapements beating in resonance and providing chronometer precise timekeeping.

François-Paul Journe continues to develop new and fascinating ideas for his watches. Their fascination, though, lies in the combination of modernity, complexity, and order.

Montres Journe SA
17 rue de l'Arquebuse
CH-1204 Geneva
Switzerland

Tel.:
+41-22-322-09-09

E-mail:
info@fpjourne.com

Website:
www.fpjourne.com

Founded:
1999

Number of employees:
135

Annual production:
850–900 watches

U.S. distributor:
Montres Journe America
Epic Hotel
270 Biscayne Boulevard Way
Miami, FL 33131
305-572-9802
america@fpjourne.com

Most important collections:
Souveraine, Octa, lineSport, Élégante
(Prices are in Swiss francs. Use daily exchange rate for calculations.)

Répétition Souveraine

Movement: manually wound, F.P. Journe Caliber 1408; ø 32.20 mm, height 4.04 mm; 33 jewels; 21,600 vph; minute repeater chimes hours, quarters, and minutes; 312 components; rose gold plate and bridges
Functions: central hours and minutes, subsidiary seconds; chime indicator with hammers visible on dial; power reserve indicator
Case: stainless steel, ø 40 mm, height 8.65 mm; sapphire crystal; screw-in crown and pusher; transparent case back
Band: reptile skin, steel folding clasp
Price: CHF 204,100

Chronomètre Optimum

Movement: manually wound, F.P. Journe Caliber 1501 in rose gold; ø 34.4 mm, height 3.75 mm; 44 jewels; 21,600 vph; rose gold plate and bridges; double spring barrel, constant force remontoir, EPHB biaxial escapement, balance spiral with Phillips curve, dead-beat seconds on back; rose gold plate and bridges
Functions: hours, minutes, subsidiary seconds; power reserve indicator
Case: platinum, ø 40 mm, height 10.1 mm; sapphire crystal; transparent case back
Band: alligator skin, buckle
Price: CHF 91,800
Variations: 6N gold, 40- or 42-mm (CHF 87,900)

Tourbillon Souverain

Movement: manually wound, F.P. Journe Caliber 1519 in rose gold; ø 34.6 mm, height 10.86 mm; 32 jewels; 21,600 vph; vertical tourbillon with constant force; balance with variable inertia; 80-hour power reserve; rose gold plate and bridges
Functions: hours, minutes, subsidiary dead-beat seconds; power reserve indicator
Case: platinum, ø 42 mm, height 13.6 mm; sapphire crystal; transparent case back;
Remarks: 6N gold guilloché dial made from gold bridges
Band: calfskin, folding clasp
Price: CHF 247,800
Variations: 6N gold (CHF 243,900)

Chronomètre à Résonance

Movement: manually wound, F.P. Journe Caliber 1499.3 in rose gold; ø 32.6 mm, height 4.2 mm; 40 jewels; 21,600 vph; unique concept of 2 escapements mutually influencing and stabilizing each other through acoustic resonance; rose gold plate and bridges
Functions: hours, minutes, subsidiary seconds; 2nd time zone; power reserve indicator
Case: platinum, ø 40 mm, height 9.1 mm; sapphire crystal; transparent case back
Band: alligator skin, platinum buckle
Price: CHF 84,100
Variations: 6N gold (CHF 80,200)

Octa Divine

Movement: automatic, F.P. Journe Caliber 1300.3 in rose gold; ø 30.8 mm, height 5.7 mm; 39 jewels; 21,600 vph; 160-hour chronometric hour power reserve; 6N gold rotor with guilloché, rose gold plate and bridges
Functions: hours, minutes, subsidiary seconds; large date; moon phase; power reserve indicator
Case: platinum, ø 40 mm, height 10.6 mm; sapphire crystal; transparent case back
Band: alligator skin, buckle
Remarks: white gold dial and silver hour circle with screwed steel circle
Price: CHF 49,800
Variations: 6N gold, 40- or 42-mm case (CHF 45,900)

Automatique Réserve (lineSport)

Movement: automatic, F.P. Journe Caliber 1300.3 in aluminum alloy; ø 34.6 mm, height 6.15 mm; 37 jewels; 21,600 vph; 80-hour power reserve (without chronograph)
Functions: hours, minutes; 1-second, 20-second, and 10-minute chronograph subdials at 10, 2, and 6 o'clock
Case: titanium, ø 44 mm, height 11 mm; sapphire crystal; transparent case back
Band: titanium bracelet and folding clasp
Price: CHF 38,800
Variations: 6N gold (CHF 60,400) or platinum (CHF 90,500)

Centigraphe (lineSport)

Movement: manually wound, F.P. Journe Caliber 1506; ø 34.4 mm, height 5.6 mm; 26 jewels; 21,600 vph; 80-hour power reserve (without chronograph); rose gold plate and bridges
Functions: hours, minutes; 1-second, 20-second, and 10-minute chronograph subdials at 10, 2, and 6 o'clock; rattrapante and seconds register 60 seconds at 9 o'clock, register 30 jumping minutes at 3 o'clock, large date at 6 o'clock
Case: platinum, ø 44 mm, height 11.6 mm; sapphire crystal; transparent case back
Band: platinum, folding clasp
Variations: titanium (CHF 60,400) or 6N gold (CHF 81,900)
Price: CHF 112,100

Elégante 48 mm

Movement: electromechanical, F.P. Journe Caliber 1210; 28.5 × 28.3 mm, height 3.13 mm; 18 jewels; quartz frequency 32,768 Hz; autonomy: daily use up to 10 years, 18 years in standby mode
Functions: hours, minutes, subsidiary seconds; motion detector with inertia weight at 4:30
Case: Titalyt, 48 × 40 mm, height 7.95 mm; sapphire crystal; transparent case back
Band: dark gray rubber, titalyt and steel folding clasp
Remarks: goes into standby mode after 35 minutes without motion, microprocessor keeps time, restarts automatically, sets time when watch put back on; luminescent dial
Price: CHF 11,500
Variations: in 48 mm: titanium or Titalyt set with diamonds (CHF 24,400); various strap colors

Elégante 40 mm Jewelry

Movement: electromechanical, F.P. Journe Caliber 1210; 28.5 × 28.3 mm, height 3.13 mm; 18 jewels; quartz frequency 32,768 Hz; autonomy: daily use up to 10 years, 18 years in standby mode
Functions: hours, minutes, subsidiary seconds; motion detector with inertia weight at 4:30
Case: platinum, 40 × 35 mm, height 7.35 mm; set with diamonds and sapphires; sapphire crystal; transparent case back; **Band:** blue satin strap, 3 other colors available, platinum folding clasp
Remarks: goes into standby mode after 35 minutes without motion, microprocessor keeps time, restarts automatically, sets time when watch put back on
Price: CHF 46,100; **Variations:** titanium or Titalyt with rubber strap (CHF 11,300); with 2 rows of diamonds (CHF 13,400)

FRANCK MULLER

Francesco "Franck" Muller has been considered one of the great creative minds in the industry ever since he designed and built his first tourbillon watch back in 1986. In fact, he never ceased amazing his colleagues and competition ever since, with his astounding timepieces that combined complications in a new and imaginative manner.

But a while ago the "master of complications" stepped away from the daily business of the brand, leaving space for the person who had paved young Muller's way to fame, Vartan Sirmakes. It was Sirmakes, previously a specialist in watch cases, who had contributed to the development of the double-domed, tonneau-shaped Cintrée Curvex case, with its elegant, 1920s retro look. The complications never stop, either. Franck Muller created the Gigatourbillons, which are 20 millimeters across, and the Revolution series has a tourbillon that rises toward the crystal.

Even a brand that prides itself on a traditional look must make some concessions to modern esthetics. The more recent Vanguards and pieces like the Skafander reveal an edginess that generates attractive tensions in that traditional Art-Deco tonneau-shaped case that is so typical of the brand.

Muller and Sirmakes founded the Franck Muller Group Watchland in 1997. The Group now holds the majority interest in thirteen other companies, eight of which are watch brands. During the 2009 economic crisis, the company downsized somewhat, but it was only a glitch in an otherwise well-planned-out strategy to focus on developing complicated watches, like the Vanguard series, which has gone through numerous iterations, including being skeletonized. The far-reaching synergies within the Group mean that the success of the leader is indeed trickling laterally to the other participants, like Barthelay, Backes & Strauss, ECW, Martin Braun, Pierre Kunz, Rodolphe, Smalto Timepieces, and Roberto Cavalli by Franck Muller.

Groupe Franck Muller Watchland SA
22, route de Malagny
CH-1294 Genthod
Switzerland

Tel.:
+41-22-959-88-88

E-mail:
contact@franckmuller.ch

Website:
www.franckmuller.com

Founded:
1991

Number of employees:
approx. 500 (estimated)

U.S. distributor:
Franck Muller USA, Inc.
207 W. 25th Street, 8th Floor
New York, NY 10001
212-463-8898
www.franckmuller.com

Most important collections:
Giga Tourbillon, Aeternitas, Revolution, Evolution 3-1, Vanguard, Cintrée Curvex

Vanguard Gravity Yachting Skeleton
Reference number: V 45 T GRAVITY CS YACHT SQT
Movement: manually wound, FM Caliber CS-03; 38.4 × 39.6 mm, height 9.1 mm; 24 jewels; 18,000 vph; 1-minute tourbillon, skeletonized movement; 120-hour power reserve
Functions: hours, minutes
Case: rose gold, 44 × 53.7 mm, height 12.65 mm; sapphire crystal; transparent case back; water-resistant to 3 atm
Band: rubber with textile overlay, buckle
Price: $141,600
Variations: stainless steel ($131,600); white gold ($141,600)

Vanguard Yachting Anchor Skeleton
Reference number: V 45 S6 SQT ANCRE FM YACHT (BL)
Movement: manually wound, FM Caliber 1740-VS; 37.05 × 40.2 mm, height 6 mm; 21 jewels; 18,000 vph; inverted skeletonized movement; 168-hour power reserve
Functions: hours, minutes, subsidiary seconds; power reserve indicator, fine adjustment
Case: stainless steel, 44 × 53.7 mm, height 12.65 mm; sapphire crystal; transparent case back; yellow gold crown; water-resistant to 3 atm
Band: textile, buckle
Price: $37,400
Variations: rose, white, or yellow gold ($45,400)

Vanguard World Timer GMT
Reference number: V 45 HU AC BR 5N (5N)
Movement: automatic, FM Caliber 2802-GMT24HM; 26 × 31 mm, height 6 mm; 23 jewels; 28,800 vph; 42-hour power reserve
Functions: hours, minutes, sweep seconds; world time display (2nd time zone)
Case: stainless steel, 44 × 53.7 mm, height 14.5 mm; rose gold bezel; sapphire crystal; rose gold crown; water-resistant to 3 atm
Band: rubber with reptile skin overlay, folding clasp
Price: $25,700

FRANCK MULLER

Skafander
Reference number: SKF 46 DV SC DT AC BR (AC)
Movement: automatic, FM Caliber 2800-SK; ø 31.5 mm, height 5.47 mm; 24 jewels; 28,800 vph; 42-hour power reserve
Functions: hours, minutes, sweep seconds
Case: stainless steel, 46 × 57 mm, height 15.6 mm; crown-activated scale ring, 0-60 scale, pushers with locking system to avoid accidental activation; sapphire crystal; screw-in crown; water-resistant to 10 atm
Band: rubber, buckle
Price: $14,800

Skafander Chronograph
Reference number: SKF 46 DV CC DT
Movement: automatic, FM Caliber 2800-SK-CC; ø 31.5 mm, height 5.44 mm; 37 jewels; 28,800 vph; 42-hour power reserve
Functions: hours, minutes, subsidiary seconds; chronograph; date
Case: titanium with black PVD coating, 46 × 57 mm, height 15.6 mm; crown-activated scale ring, 0-60 scale, pushers with locking system to avoid accidental activation; sapphire crystal; screw-in crown; water-resistant to 10 atm
Band: rubber, buckle
Price: $22,800
Variations: stainless steel ($22,800); rose gold ($33,800)

Vanguard Racing
Reference number: V 45 SC DT RACING (NR)
Movement: automatic, FM Caliber 2800-DT; ø 25.6 mm, height 3.6 mm; 21 jewels; 28,800 vph; 42-hour power reserve
Functions: hours, minutes, sweep seconds; date
Case: rose gold, 44 × 53.7 mm, height 12.7 mm; sapphire crystal; transparent case back; water-resistant to 3 atm
Band: calfskin, buckle
Price: $18,800
Variations: stainless steel ($9,200)

Vanguard Crazy Hours
Reference number: V 45 CH BR (BL)
Movement: automatic, FM Caliber 2800 CH; ø 25.6 mm, height 5.6 mm; 27 jewels; 28,800 vph; jumping hour mechanism with "crazy" hour; 42-hour power reserve
Functions: hours (jumping), minutes, sweep seconds
Case: stainless steel, 44 × 53.7 mm, height 13.7 mm; sapphire crystal; transparent case back; water-resistant to 3 atm
Band: reptile skin, buckle
Price: $16,200

Remember
Reference number: 2850 SC REM
Movement: automatic, FM Caliber 2800 INV; ø 26.2 mm, height 3.6 mm; 25 jewels; 28,800 vph; inverted movement, hands move anticlockwise; 42-hour power reserve
Functions: hours, minutes, sweep seconds
Case: rose gold, 31 × 43 mm, height 7.3 mm; sapphire crystal; transparent case back; water-resistant to 3 atm
Band: reptile skin, buckle
Price: $18,000
Variations: stainless steel ($11,000); white gold ($18,000); platinum ($28,000)

Vanguard Lady Skeleton
Reference number: V 32 S6 SQT
Movement: manually wound, FM Caliber 1540 VS5; 26.75 × 32 mm, height 5.9 mm; 21 jewels; 18,000 vph; skeletonized movement with rose gold–coated bridges; 96-hour power reserve
Functions: hours, minutes, subsidiary seconds
Case: rose gold, 32 × 42.3 mm, height 9.9 mm; sapphire crystal; transparent case back; water-resistant to 3 atm
Band: reptile skin, buckle
Price: $26,800
Variations: stainless steel ($20,800)

FRÉDÉRIQUE CONSTANT

Peter and Aletta Stas, the Dutch couple who founded Frédérique Constant, have always sought to make high-end watches for consumers without deep pockets. So high-end, in fact, that in 2004 they went public with the brand's first movement produced entirely in-house and equipped with innovative silicon components. The move was in line with the other strategy of staying independent, and it was crowned a success. The Heart Beat calibers proved to be reliable, popular, and affordable.

Since 1991, the Dutch couple have genuinely lived up to the tagline they use for their Swiss brand: "live your passion." The watch brand, named for Aletta's great-grandmother Frédérique Schreiner and Peter's great-grandfather Constant Stas, was conceived in the late 1980s. The new company had its work cut out for it: Frédérique Constant had to compete in a watch market truly saturated with brands.

The Stases parlayed affordable watches into a modern four-floor factory in Geneva's industrial Plan-les-Ouates, with ample room for manufacturing, administrative offices, conference rooms, a fitness area, and a cafeteria. Being in touch with the zeitgeist remained a key strategy, which generated the Horological Smartwatch, for example, equipped with a quartz movement and a mobile phone connection.

In 2016, Frédérique Constant and sister brand Alpina were sold to the Japanese brand Citizen. The move will increase the brand's presence on the market, with capacity scheduled to increase to 250,000 timepieces in the coming years. In the future, visitors will be able to visit Frédérique Constant's "Manufacture Experience," which will be set up on the ground floor of the Genevan facility. It will have exhibitions about the brand's history, the design process, and the making and assembling of the movements.

Frédérique Constant SA
Chemin du Champ des Filles 32
CH-1228 Plan-les-Ouates (Geneva)
Switzerland

Tel.:
+41-22-860-0440

E-mail:
info@frederique-constant.com

Website:
www.frederique-constant.com

Founded:
1988

Number of employees:
100

Annual production:
approx. 146,000 watches

U.S. distributor:
Alpina Frederique Constant USA
350 5th Avenue, 29th Floor
New York, NY 10118
646-438-8124
lmellor@usa.frederique-constant.com

Most important collections/price range:
Tourbillon Perpetual Calendar Manufacture / from approx. $21,995 to $32,995; Hybrid Manufacture / from approx. $3,695 to $3,895; Worldtimer Manufacture / from approx. $4,195 to 4,395; Vintage Rally Healey Chronograph / from approx. $2,795 to $3,095; Ladies' Automatic Double Heart Beat / from approx. $1,995

Classic Hybrid Manufacture
Reference number: FC-750N4H4
Movement: automatic, Caliber FC-750; ø 30 mm, height 6.28 mm; 33 jewels; 28,800 vph; additional quartz movement for smart functions; 42-hour power reserve
Functions: hours, minutes, sweep seconds; additional 24-hour display (2nd time zone); smart functions such as activity and sleep, alarm function, rate analysis of mechanical movement; date
Case: stainless steel with rose gold PVD coating, ø 42 mm, height 12.84 mm; sapphire crystal; transparent case back; water-resistant to 5 atm
Band: reptile skin, folding clasp
Price: $3,895

Slimline Perpetual Calendar Manufacture
Reference number: FC-775G4S6
Movement: automatic, Caliber FC-775; ø 30 mm, height 6.2 mm; 26 jewels; 28,800 vph; 38-hour power reserve
Functions: hours, minutes; perpetual calendar with date, weekday, month, moon phase, leap year
Case: stainless steel, ø 42 mm, height 12 mm; sapphire crystal; transparent case back; water-resistant to 3 atm
Band: reptile skin, folding clasp
Price: $8,795

Slimline Power Reserve Manufacture
Reference number: FC-723WR3S4
Movement: automatic, Caliber FC-723; ø 30.5 mm, height 6.2 mm; 28 jewels; 28,800 vph; 50-hour power reserve
Functions: hours, minutes; power reserve indicator; date
Case: stainless steel with rose gold PVD, ø 40 mm, height 11.2 mm; sapphire crystal; transparent case back; water-resistant to 3 atm
Band: reptile skin, folding clasp
Price: $3,495

FRÉDÉRIQUE CONSTANT

Moonphase Manufacture
Reference number: FC-712MN4H6
Movement: automatic, Caliber FC-712; ø 30 mm, height 7.1 mm; 28 jewels; 28,800 vph; 38-hour power reserve
Functions: hours, minutes, sweep seconds; date, moon phase
Case: stainless steel, ø 42 mm, height 11.6 mm; sapphire crystal; transparent case back; water-resistant to 5 atm
Band: calfskin, buckle
Price: $2,595

Yacht Timer Regatta Countdown
Reference number: FC-380VT4H2B
Movement: automatic, Caliber FC-380; ø 30 mm, height 6.2 mm; 26 jewels; 28,800 vph; 46-hour power reserve
Functions: hours, minutes; regatta countdown (5-minute counter)
Case: stainless steel, ø 42 mm, height 14.1 mm; bezel, crown, and pushers coated with rose gold PVD; sapphire crystal; transparent case back; water-resistant to 10 atm
Band: stainless steel, folding clasp
Price: $3,395

Ladies' Automatic Double Heart Beat
Reference number: FC-310LGDHB3B2B
Movement: automatic, Caliber FC-310 (base Sellita SW200-1); ø 25.6 mm, height 4.6 mm; 26 jewels; 28,800 vph; partially skeletonized mainplate under escapement; 38-hour power reserve
Functions: hours, minutes, sweep seconds
Case: stainless steel, ø 36 mm, height 9.85 mm; sapphire crystal; transparent case back; water-resistant to 5 atm
Band: stainless steel, folding clasp
Remarks: dial is opened and set with 6 diamonds
Price: $1,995

Horological Smartwatch Gents Classics
Reference number: FC-285LGS5B6
Movement: quartz, microchip
Functions: hours, minutes; alarm and measurement of activities and sleep, SMS alerts; date
Case: stainless steel, ø 42 mm, height 13.35 mm; sapphire crystal
Band: calfskin, buckle
Price: $995

Caliber FC-975
Automatic; 1-minute tourbillon; single spring barrel, 38-hour power reserve
Functions: hours, minutes, subsidiary seconds; perpetual calendar with date, weekday, month, leap year
Diameter: 30 mm
Height: 6.67 mm
Jewels: 33
Balance: silicon
Frequency: 28,800 vph
Balance spring: flat hairspring
Shock protection: Incabloc
Remarks: 250 parts

Caliber FC-750
Automatic; mechanical and electronic movement hybrid; single spring barrel, 42-hour power reserve
Functions: hours, minutes, sweep seconds; smart functions such as activity and sleep, alarm, rate analysis of mechanical movement; date
Diameter: 30 mm
Height: 6.28 mm
Jewels: 33
Frequency: 28,800 vph
Balance spring: flat hairspring
Shock protection: Incabloc
Remarks: 180 parts

GIRARD-PERREGAUX

When Girard-Perregaux CEO Luigi ("Gino") Macaluso died in 2010, the former minority partner of Sowind Group, PPR (Pinault, Printemps, Redoute), increased its equity stake to 51 percent. Under the leadership of Michele Sofisti since 2011, the brand has been charting a rather bold course that includes some technically sharp developments with the support of a strong development team and an excellently equipped production department. Under his guidance, the company has reduced its multitude of references but continues treading the fine line between fashionable watches and technical miracles. The various combinations of tourbillons and the gold bridges remain the company specialty. The most dazzling talking piece lately has undoubtedly been the Constant Escapement, a new concept that stores energy by buckling an ultrathin silicon blade and then releasing it to the balance wheel. Like many sophisticated systems, it was born of the banal: Inventor Nicolas Déhon was absentmindedly bending a train ticket one day when he was suddenly struck by the simple thought. As the ticket bent, it collected energy that was released in even bursts when it straightened out.

In 2015, Antonio Calce (of Eterna and Corum fame) became the company CEO and launched a freshening-up program, which included its marketing strategies. The Vintage 1945 and the elegant GP 1966 are still the mainstays of the brand, together with the Competizione chronographs. But Calce has also decided to put the ladies' Cat's Eye collection in the limelight and given a serious facelift to the Three Bridges tourbillon.

Like many brands in the Era of Vintage, Girard-Perregaux has been revisiting its past milestones. The company turned the much coveted Laureato from 1975 into a flagship of sorts. Something in the octagonal bezel on the round base epitomizes our contemporary sportive-elegant style. The collection now boasts a skeleton version, a chronograph, and even a flying tourbillon model.

Girard-Perregaux
1, Place Girardet
CH-2300 La Chaux-de-Fonds
Switzerland

Tel.:
+41-32-911-3333

Website:
www.girard-perregaux.com

Founded:
1791

Number of employees:
280

Annual production:
approx. 12,000 watches

U.S. distributor:
Girard-Perregaux
Tradema of America, Inc.
7900 Glades Road, Suite 200
Boca Raton, FL 33434
833-GPWATCH
www.girard-perregaux.com

Most important collections/price range:
Laureato / Vintage 1945 / approx. $7,500 to $625,000; ww.tc / $12,300 to $23,800; GP 1966 / $7,500 to $291,000

Laureato 42mm Automatic

Reference number: 81010-11-431-11A
Movement: automatic, GP Caliber 01800-0013; ø 30 mm, height 3.97 mm; 28 jewels; 28,800 vph; 54-hour power reserve
Functions: hours, minutes, sweep seconds; date
Case: stainless steel, ø 42 mm, height 10.88 mm; sapphire crystal; transparent case back; water-resistant to 10 atm
Band: stainless steel, triple folding clasp
Price: $11,600
Variations: silver or gray dial; reptile skin strap ($10,800); titanium/rose gold with reptile skin strap ($16,000)

Laureato 42mm Automatic

Reference number: 81010-11-634-11A
Movement: automatic, GP Caliber 01800-0013; ø 30 mm, height 3.97 mm; 28 jewels; 28,800 vph; 54-hour power reserve
Functions: hours, minutes, sweep seconds; date
Case: stainless steel, ø 42 mm, height 10.88 mm; sapphire crystal; transparent case back; water-resistant to 10 atm
Band: stainless steel, triple folding clasp
Price: $11,600
Variations: silver or blue dial; reptile skin strap ($10,800); titanium/rose gold with reptile skin strap ($16,000)

Laureato Absolute Automatic 44mm

Reference number: 81070-21-491-FH6A
Movement: automatic, GP Caliber 03300-1060; ø 25.95 mm, height 3.36 mm; 27 jewels; 28,800 vph; 46-hour power reserve
Functions: hours, minutes, sweep seconds; date
Case: titanium with black PVD coating, ø 44 mm, height 14.65 mm; sapphire crystal; transparent case back; water-resistant to 30 atm
Band: rubber, triple folding clasp
Price: $9,900

GIRARD-PERREGAUX

Laureato Absolute Chronograph 44mm
Reference number: 81060-21-491-FH6A
Movement: automatic, GP Caliber 03300-1058; ø 25.95 mm, height 6.5 mm; 63 jewels; 28,800 vph; 46-hour power reserve
Functions: hours, minutes, subsidiary seconds; chronograph; date
Case: titanium with black PVD coating, ø 44 mm, height 14.65 mm; sapphire crystal; transparent case back; water-resistant to 30 atm
Band: rubber, triple folding clasp
Price: $12,900

Laureato Chronograph 42mm
Reference number: 81020-11-131-11A
Movement: automatic, GP Caliber 03300-0137/0138/0141; ø 25.95 mm, height 6.5 mm; 63 jewels; 28,800 vph; 46-hour power reserve
Functions: hours, minutes, subsidiary seconds; chronograph; date
Case: stainless steel, ø 42 mm, height 12.01 mm; sapphire crystal; water-resistant to 10 atm
Band: stainless steel, triple folding clasp
Price: $15,000
Variations: reptile skin strap ($14,200)

Laureato Chronograph 42mm
Reference number: 81020-11-431-11A
Movement: automatic, GP Caliber 03300-0137/0138/0141; ø 25.95 mm, height 6.5 mm; 63 jewels; 28,800 vph; 46-hour power reserve
Functions: hours, minutes, subsidiary seconds; chronograph; date
Case: stainless steel, ø 42 mm, height 11.9 mm; sapphire crystal; water-resistant to 10 atm
Band: stainless steel, triple folding clasp
Price: $15,000
Variations: reptile skin strap ($14,200)

Laureato Skeleton 42mm "Earth-to-Sky" Edition
Reference number: 81015-32-432-32A
Movement: automatic, GP Caliber 01800-1041; ø 29.9 mm, height 4.16 mm; 25 jewels; 28,800 vph; skeletonized movement with blue coating; 54-hour power reserve
Functions: hours, minutes, subsidiary seconds
Case: ceramic, ø 42 mm, height 10.93 mm; sapphire crystal; transparent case back; water-resistant to 10 atm
Band: ceramic, triple folding clasp made of titanium
Price: $38,400

Laureato Flying Tourbillon Skeleton
Reference number: 99110-52-000-52A
Movement: automatic, GP Caliber 09520-0001; ø 32.5 mm, height 6.2 mm; 28 jewels; 21,600 vph; flying 1-minute tourbillon; gold microrotor; skeletonized movement; 50-hour power reserve
Functions: hours, minutes
Case: rose gold, ø 42 mm, height 10.76 mm; sapphire crystal; transparent case back; crown in rose gold; water-resistant to 3 atm
Band: rose gold, double folding clasp
Price: $129,000
Variations: white gold ($136,000)

Quasar
Reference number: 99295-43-000-BA6A
Movement: automatic, GP Caliber 09400-01035; ø 36 mm, height 9.54 mm; 27 jewels; 21,600 vph; 1-minute tourbillon under 3 bridges, skeletonized movement, titanium bridges with PVD coating; white gold microrotor; 60-hour power reserve
Functions: hours, minutes
Case: sapphire crystal, ø 46 mm, height 15.25 mm; sapphire crystal; transparent case back; water-resistant to 3 atm
Band: reptile skin, triple folding clasp
Price: $194,000

GIRARD-PERREGAUX

Neo Bridges 45mm "Earth-to-Sky" Edition
Reference number: 84000-21-632-BH6A
Movement: automatic, GP Caliber 08400-0002; ø 32 mm, height 5.45 mm; 29 jewels; 21,600 vph; symmetrical skeleton construction; NAC-coated mainplate, PVD-coated bridges; microrotor; 54-hour power reserve
Functions: hours, minutes
Case: titanium with black DLC coating, ø 45 mm, height 12.18 mm; sapphire crystal; transparent case back; water-resistant to 3 atm
Band: reptile skin with rubber overlay, triple folding clasp
Price: $26,800

La Esmeralda Tourbillon
Reference number: 99275-53-000-BA6E
Movement: automatic, GP Caliber 09400-0016; ø 36.6 mm, height 8.41 mm; 27 jewels; 21,600 vph; 1-minute tourbillon under 3 bridges; platinum microrotor; balance with variable inertia and golden adjustment screws, hairspring with Phillips end curve; 60-hour power reserve
Functions: hours, minutes
Case: white gold, ø 44 mm, height 14.55 mm; sapphire crystal; transparent case back; water-resistant to 3 atm
Band: reptile skin, folding clasp
Price: $212,000

Cosmos
Reference number: 99292-21-651-BA6F
Movement: manually wound, GP Caliber 09320-1098; ø 37.85 mm, height 13.1 mm; 52 jewels; 21,600 vph; 1-minute tourbillon; 2 fully sculptural representations of globes and the cosmos; 60-hour power reserve
Functions: hours, minutes (off-center); additional 24-hour display (2nd time zone), day/night indicator; sky map (display of zodiac signs)
Case: titanium, ø 47 mm, height 22.32 mm; sapphire crystal; transparent case back; water-resistant to 3 atm
Band: reptile skin, triple folding clasp
Price: $294,000

GP 1966 40mm
Reference number: 49555-11-131-BB60
Movement: automatic, GP Caliber 03300-0130; ø 25.6 mm, height 3.36 mm; 27 jewels; 28,800 vph; 46-hour power reserve
Functions: hours, minutes, sweep seconds; date
Case: stainless steel, ø 40 mm, height 8.9 mm; sapphire crystal; transparent case back; water-resistant to 3 atm
Band: reptile skin, buckle
Price: $7,900
Variations: various dials

GP 1966 ww.tc 40mm
Reference number: 49557-11-132-BB6C
Movement: automatic, GP Caliber 03300-0022; ø 25.6 mm, height 5.71 mm; 32 jewels; 28,800 vph; 46-hour power reserve
Functions: hours, minutes, subsidiary seconds; world time display, day/night indicator (2nd time zone)
Case: stainless steel, ø 40 mm, height 12 mm; crown-activated scale ring with reference cities; sapphire crystal; transparent case back; water-resistant to 3 atm
Band: reptile skin, folding clasp
Price: $12,900
Variations: stainless steel bracelet ($13,700)

GP 1966 38mm
Reference number: 49525-52-131-BK6A
Movement: automatic, GP Caliber 03300-00030; ø 25.6 mm, height 3.36 mm; 27 jewels; 28,800 vph; 46-hour power reserve
Functions: hours, minutes, sweep seconds; date
Case: rose gold, ø 38 mm, height 8.62 mm; sapphire crystal; transparent case back; water-resistant to 3 atm
Band: reptile skin, buckle
Price: $16,900

GIRARD-PERREGAUX

Caliber GP01800-0008

Automatic; single spring barrel, 54-hour power reserve
Functions: hours, minutes, sweep seconds; date
Diameter: 30 mm
Height: 3.97 mm
Jewels: 28
Frequency: 28,800 vph

Caliber GP3300

Automatic; rotor with ceramic ball bearings, stop-seconds mechanism; single spring barrel, 46-hour power reserve
Functions: hours, minutes, sweep seconds or subsidiary seconds at 9 o'clock; date
Diameter: 25.6 mm
Height: 3.2 mm
Jewels: 27
Balance: glucydur
Frequency: 28,800 vph
Balance spring: flat hairspring, fine adjustment
Shock protection: Kif
Remarks: 185 parts

Caliber GP09400-01035

Automatic; 1-minute tourbillon, bidirectional winding rotor; symmetrical skeleton construction with 3 bridges made of PVD-coated titanium; single spring barrel, 60-hour power reserve
Functions: hours, minutes
Diameter: 36 mm
Height: 9.54 mm
Jewels: 27
Balance: screw balance
Frequency: 21,600 vph
Remarks: modern version of a tourbillon under 3 gold bridges; 260 parts

Caliber GP09400-0016

Automatic; 1-minute tourbillon, bidirectional winding rotor; symmetrical movement with 3 white gold bridges; single spring barrel, 60-hour power reserve
Functions: hours, minutes
Diameter: 36.6 mm
Height: 8.41 mm
Jewels: 27
Balance: screw balance
Frequency: 21,600 vph
Remarks: 310 parts

Caliber GP09320-1098

Manually wound; 1-minute tourbillon; symmetrical skeleton construction with 2 bridges; single spring barrel, 60-hour power reserve
Functions: hours, minutes (off-center); sky map (with zodiac display) and 24-hour display (2nd time zone) as a sculptural globe
Diameter: 37.85 mm
Height: 13.1 mm
Jewels: 52
Balance: screw balance
Frequency: 21,600 vph
Remarks: 362 parts

Caliber GP08400-0002

Automatic; symmetrical skeleton construction with 2 bridges; microrotor; single spring barrel, 54-hour power reserve
Functions: hours, minutes
Diameter: 32 mm
Height: 5.45 mm
Jewels: 29
Frequency: 21,600 vph
Remarks: NAC-coated platinum, titanium bridges with black PVD coating; 208 parts

GLASHÜTTE ORIGINAL

Is there a little nostalgia creeping into the designers at Glashütte Original? Or is it just understated ecstasy for older looks? The retro touches that started appearing again a few years ago with the Sixties Square Tourbillon are still in vogue as the company delves into its own past for inspiration, such as the use of a special silver treatment on dials.

Glashütte Original *manufacture* roots go back to the mid-nineteenth century, though the name itself came later. The company, which had a sterling reputation for precision watches, became subsumed in the VEB Glashütter Uhrenbetriebe, a group of Glashütte watchmakers and suppliers who were collectivized as part of the former East German system. After reunification, the company took up its old moniker of Glashütte Original, and in 1995, the *manufacture* released an entirely new collection. Later, it purchased Union Glashütte. In 2000, the Swiss Swatch Group acquired the whole company and invested in expanding the production space at Glashütte Original headquarters.

Manufacturing depth has reached 95 percent. All movements are designed by a team of experienced in-house engineers, while the components they comprise, such as plates, screws, pinions, wheels, levers, spring barrels, balance wheels, and tourbillon cages, are manufactured in the upgraded production areas. These parts are lavishly finished by hand before assembly by a group of talented watchmakers. Even dials are in-house. Among the highlights of its catalog are the Senator Chronometer, which boasts second and minute hands that automatically jump to zero when the crown is pulled, allowing for extremely accurate time setting; and the Spezialist, a diver's watch that is modeled on a design from 1969, which was developed especially for frogmen and sports divers and is not only precise but very resistant to shocks.

Glashütter Uhrenbetrieb GmbH
Altenberger Strasse 1
D-01768 Glashütte
Germany

Tel.:
+49-350-53-46-0

E-mail:
info@glashuette-original.com

Website:
www.glashuette-original.com

Founded:
1990 registration of the Glashütter Uhrenbetrieb GmbH; Glashütte Original brand name registered in 1994

U.S. distributor:
Glashütte Original
The Swatch Group (U.S.), Inc.
1200 Harbor Boulevard
Weehawken, NJ 07087
201-271-1400

Most important collections/price range:
Senator, Pano, Spezialist, Vintage, Ladies / $4,900 to $152,300

Senator Chronometer Tourbillon—Limited Edition

Reference number: 1-58-05-01-03-30
Movement: manually wound, Glashütte Original Caliber 58-05; ø 36.6 mm, height 8.48 mm; 85 jewels; 21,600 vph; flying 1-minute tourbillon, silicon hairspring, screw balance with 18 weighted screws, swan-neck fine adjustment; hand-engraved balance cock, finely finished movement; 70-hour power reserve; DIN-certified chronometer
Functions: hours, minutes (off-center), subsidiary seconds (on tourbillon cage); power reserve indicator
Case: platinum, ø 42 mm, height 12 mm; sapphire crystal; transparent case back; water-resistant to 5 atm
Band: reptile skin, folding clasp
Price: $152,300; limited to 25 pieces

PanoLunar Tourbillon

Reference number: 1-93-02-05-05-05
Movement: automatic, Glashütte Original Caliber 93-02; ø 32.2 mm, height 7.65 mm; 48 jewels; 21,600 vph; flying 1-minute tourbillon, screw balance with 18 weighted screws, 2 diamond endstones, blued screws, skeletonized rotor with gold oscillating mass; 48-hour power reserve
Functions: hours, minutes (off-center), subsidiary seconds (on tourbillon cage); panorama date, moon phase
Case: pink gold, ø 40 mm, height 13.1 mm; sapphire crystal; transparent case back; water-resistant to 5 atm
Band: reptile skin, folding clasp
Price: $100,400
Variations: buckle ($98,600)

Senator Cosmopolite

Reference number: 1-89-02-03-02-30
Movement: automatic, Glashütte Original Caliber 89-02; ø 39.2 mm, height 8 mm; 63 jewels; 28,800 vph; swan-neck spring to regulate rate symmetry; 72-hour power reserve
Functions: hours, minutes, subsidiary seconds; additional 12-hour display (2nd time zone), world time indicator with 35 time zones, day/night indicator, power reserve indicator; panorama date
Case: stainless steel, ø 44 mm, height 14 mm; sapphire crystal; transparent case back; water-resistant to 5 atm
Band: reptile skin, folding clasp
Price: $21,500
Variations: pink gold ($37,100); white gold ($38,600)

GLASHÜTTE ORIGINAL

Senator Chronometer
Reference number: 1-58-01-02-05-30
Movement: manually wound, Glashütte Original Caliber 58-01; ø 35 mm, height 6.47 mm; 58 jewels; 28,800 vph; Glashütte three-quarter plate, second reset when crown is pulled allowing precise setting of minutes hand; DIN certified chronometer
Functions: hours, minutes, subsidiary seconds; day/night indicator, power reserve indicator; panorama date
Case: red gold, ø 42 mm, height 12.47 mm; sapphire crystal; transparent case back; water-resistant to 5 atm
Band: reptile skin, folding clasp
Price: $26,100
Variations: buckle ($24,300); white gold with blue dial ($27,600)

Senator Excellence Perpetual Calendar
Reference number: 1-36-02-02-05-30
Movement: automatic, GO Cal. 36-02; ø 32.2 mm, height 7.35 mm; 49 jewels; 28,800 vph; silicon hairspring, screw balance, swan-neck fine adjustment, skeletonized rotor with gold oscillating mass, finely finished movement; 100-hour power reserve
Functions: hours, minutes, sweep seconds; perpetual calendar with panorama date, weekday, month, moon phase, leap year
Case: red gold, ø 42 mm, height 12.8 mm; sapphire crystal; transparent case back; water-resistant to 5 atm
Band: reptile skin, folding clasp
Price: $32,800; **Variations:** buckle ($31,000); stainless steel ($20,100)

Senator Excellence Panorama Date Moonphase
Reference number: 1-36-04-04-02-30
Movement: automatic, Glashütte Original Caliber 36-04; ø 32.2 mm, height 6.7 mm; 43 jewels; 28,800 vph; silicon hairspring, screw balance with 4 regulator screws, swan-neck fine adjustment, skeletonized rotor with gold oscillating mass, finely finished movement; 100-hour power reserve
Functions: hours, minutes, sweep seconds; panorama date, moon phase
Case: stainless steel, ø 42 mm, height 12.2 mm; sapphire crystal; transparent case back; water-resistant to 5 atm; **Band:** reptile skin, folding clasp
Price: $10,700; **Variations:** buckle ($10,400); silver gray or blue dial ($10,700)

Senator Excellence Panorama Date
Reference number: 1-36-03-03-02-31
Movement: automatic, Glashütte Original Caliber 36-03; ø 32.2 mm, height 6.7 mm; 41 jewels; 28,800 vph; silicon hairspring, screw balance with 4 regulator screws, swan-neck fine adjustment, skeletonized rotor with gold oscillating mass; 100-hour power reserve
Functions: hours, minutes, sweep seconds; panorama date
Case: stainless steel, ø 42 mm, height 12.2 mm; sapphire crystal; transparent case back; water-resistant to 5 atm; **Band:** reptile skin, folding clasp
Price: $9,700; **Variations:** buckle ($9,400); blue or white dial ($9,700)

PanoMaticLunar
Reference number: 1-90-02-11-35-30
Movement: automatic, Glashütte Original Caliber 90-02; ø 32.6 mm, height 7 mm; 47 jewels; 28,800 vph; screw balance with 18 weighted screws, duplex swan-neck fine adjustment, skeletonized rotor with gold oscillating mass, finely finished movement; 42-hour power reserve
Functions: hours, minutes (off-center), subsidiary seconds; panorama date, moon phase
Case: red gold, ø 40 mm, height 12.7 mm; sapphire crystal; transparent case back; water-resistant to 5 atm
Band: reptile skin, folding clasp
Price: $20,500
Variations: buckle ($18,700); silver or black dial ($20,500); stainless steel ($9,900)

PanoInverse—Limited Edition
Reference number: 1-66-08-01-03-30
Movement: manually wound, Glashütte Original Caliber 66-08; ø 38.3 mm, height 5.95 mm; 31 jewels; 28,800 vph; Glashütte three-quarter plate, screw balance with 18 weighted screws, duplex swan-neck fine adjustment; inverted movement construction, hand-engraved structural parts; 41-hour power reserve
Functions: hours, minutes (off-center), subsidiary seconds; power reserve indicator
Case: platinum, ø 42 mm, height 12 mm; sapphire crystal; transparent case back; water-resistant to 5 atm
Band: reptile skin, folding clasp
Price: $45,700; limited to 25 pieces

GLASHÜTTE ORIGINAL

SeaQ 1969
Reference number: 1-39-11-01-80-33
Movement: automatic, Glashütte Original Caliber 39-11; ø 26 mm, height 4.3 mm; 25 jewels; 28,800 vph; swan-neck fine adjustment, skeletonized rotor with heavy metal oscillating mass, finely finished movement; 40-hour power reserve
Functions: hours, minutes, sweep seconds; date
Case: stainless steel, ø 39.5 mm, height 12.15 mm; unidirectional bezel, 0-60 scale; sapphire crystal; transparent case back; screw-in crown; water-resistant to 20 atm
Band: rubber, folding clasp
Price: $9,000; limited to 69 pieces
Variations: textile strap ($9,000); buckle ($8,700); as unlimited version ($9,000)

SeaQ Panorama Date
Reference number: 1-36-13-01-80-70
Movement: automatic, Glashütte Original Caliber 36-13; ø 32.2 mm, height 6.7 mm; 41 jewels; 28,800 vph; silicon hairspring, screw balance with 4 regulator screws, swan-neck spring to regulate rate symmetry, skeletonized rotor with gold oscillating mass; 100-hour power reserve
Functions: hours, minutes, sweep seconds; panorama date
Case: stainless steel, ø 43.2 mm, height 15.65 mm; unidirectional bezel, 0-60 scale; sapphire crystal; transparent case back; screw-in crown; water-resistant to 30 atm; **Band:** stainless steel, folding clasp
Price: $12,400
Variations: rubber or textile strap ($11,500)

Seventies Panorama Date
Reference number: 2-39-47-13-12-04
Movement: automatic, Glashütte Original Caliber 39-47; ø 30.95 mm, height 5.9 mm; 39 jewels; 28,800 vph; swan-neck fine adjustment, Glashütte three-quarter plate with traditional stripe finish, skeletonized rotor with gold oscillating mass, finely finished movement; 40-hour power reserve
Functions: hours, minutes, sweep seconds; panorama date
Case: stainless steel, 40 × 40 mm, height 11.5 mm; sapphire crystal; transparent case back; screw-in crown; water-resistant to 10 atm
Band: reptile skin, folding clasp
Price: $8,700; **Variations:** gray or silver dial ($8,700); rubber strap ($8,700); stainless steel bracelet ($9,900)

Sixties Panorama Date
Movement: automatic, Glashütte Original Caliber 39-47; ø 30.95 mm, height 5.9 mm; 39 jewels; 28,800 vph; swan-neck fine adjustment, Glashütte three-quarter plate with traditional stripe finish, skeletonized rotor with gold oscillating mass; finely finished movement; 40-hour power reserve
Functions: hours, minutes, sweep seconds; panorama date
Case: stainless steel, ø 42 mm, height 12.4 mm; sapphire crystal; transparent case back; water-resistant to 3 atm
Band: calfskin, buckle
Price: $8,000
Variations: silver, black, or blue dial ($8,000)

Sixties
Reference number: 1-39-52-01-01-04
Movement: automatic, Glashütte Original Caliber 39-52; ø 26 mm, height 4.3 mm; 25 jewels; 28,800 vph; swan-neck fine adjustment, Glashütte three-quarter plate with traditional stripe finish, skeletonized rotor with gold oscillating mass, finely finished movement; 40-hour power reserve
Functions: hours, minutes, sweep seconds
Case: rose gold, ø 39 mm, height 9.4 mm; sapphire crystal; transparent case back; water-resistant to 3 atm
Band: reptile skin, buckle
Price: $12,800
Variations: black dial ($12,800); stainless steel ($6,400)

PanoMatic Luna
Reference number: 1-90-12-03-12-02
Movement: automatic, Glashütte Original Caliber 90-12; ø 32.6 mm, height 7 mm; 47 jewels; 28,800 vph; duplex swan-neck fine adjustment, hand-engraved balance cock; 42-hour power reserve
Functions: hours, minutes, subsidiary seconds; panorama date, moon phase
Case: stainless steel, ø 39.4 mm, height 12 mm; bezel with 64 diamonds; sapphire crystal; transparent case back; crown with diamond; water-resistant to 3 atm
Band: reptile skin, buckle
Remarks: mother-of-pearl dial
Price: $17,500
Variations: white or dark mother-of-pearl dial ($17,500)

GLASHÜTTE ORIGINAL

Caliber 36
Automatic; single spring barrel, 100-hour power reserve
Functions: hours, minutes, sweep seconds
Diameter: 32.2 mm; **Height:** 4.45 mm
Jewels: 27
Balance: screw balance with 4 regulating screws
Frequency: 28,800 vph
Balance spring: silicon, swan-neck spring to regulate rate symmetry
Shock protection: Incabloc
Remarks: very finely finished movement, three-quarter plate with Glashütte stripe finish, skeletonized rotor with gold oscillating mass; **Related caliber:** 36-02 (perpetual calendar), 36-03 (panorama date), 36-04 (panorama date and moon phase)

Caliber 37
Automatic; single spring barrel, 70-hour power reserve
Functions: hours, minutes, subsidiary seconds; power reserve indicator; flyback chronograph; panorama date
Diameter: 31.6 mm
Height: 8 mm
Jewels: 65
Balance: screw balance with 4 gold regulating screws
Frequency: 28,800 vph
Balance spring: flat hairspring, swan-neck spring to regulate rate symmetry
Remarks: finely finished movement, beveled edges, polished steel parts, blued screws, three-quarter plate with Glashütte stripe finish, skeletonized rotor with 21-kt gold oscillating mass

Caliber 39
Automatic; single spring barrel, 40-hour power reserve
Functions: hours, minutes, sweep seconds (base caliber)
Diameter: 26.2 mm; **Height:** 4.3 mm
Jewels: 25
Balance: glucydur
Frequency: 28,800 vph
Balance spring: flat hairspring, swan-neck fine adjustment
Shock protection: Incabloc
Related Caliber: 39-55 (GMT, 40 jewels), 38-52 (automatic, 25 jewels), 39-50 (perpetual calendar, 48 jewels), 38-41/39-42 (panorama date, 44 jewels), 39-31 (chronograph, 51 jewels), 39-21/39-22 (date, 25 jewels)

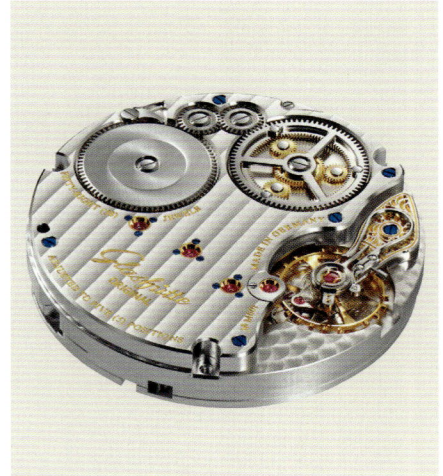

Caliber 58-01
Manually wound; 2nd reset when crown is pulled allowing precise setting of minutes hand; single spring barrel, 44-hour power reserve
Functions: hours, minutes, subsidiary seconds; day/night indicator, power reserve indicator with planetary drive; panorama date
Diameter: 35 mm
Height: 6.5 mm
Jewels: 58
Balance: screw balance with 18 weighted screws
Frequency: 28,800 vph
Balance spring: flat hairspring, swan-neck fine adjustment
Remarks: three-quarter plate with Glashütte stripe finish, hand-engraved balance cock

Caliber 58-05
Manually wound; flying 1-minute tourbillon; single spring barrel, 70-hour power reserve
Functions: hours, minutes (off-center), subsidiary seconds (on tourbillon cage); power reserve indicator
Diameter: 36.6 mm
Height: 8.48 mm
Jewels: 85
Balance: screw balance with 18 weighted screws
Frequency: 21,600 vph
Balance spring: silicon
Remarks: finely finished movement, beveled edges, polished steel parts, three-quarter plate with Glashütte stripe finish, blued screws, ratchet wheel with double sunburst brushing, hand-polished structural parts

Caliber 61
Manually wound; single spring barrel, 42-hour power reserve
Functions: hours, minutes (off-center), subsidiary seconds; flyback chronograph; panorama date
Diameter: 32.2 mm
Height: 7.2 mm
Jewels: 41
Balance: screw balance with 18 weighted screws
Frequency: 28,800 vph
Balance spring: flat hairspring, swan-neck fine adjustment
Remarks: finely finished movement, beveled edges, polished steel parts, screw-mounted gold chatons, blued screws, bridges and balance cock with Glashütte stripe finish, hand-engraved balance cock

GLASHÜTTE ORIGINAL

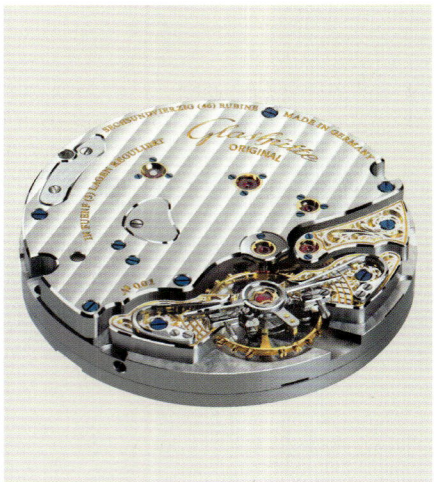

Caliber 65
Manually wound; single spring barrel, 42-hour power reserve
Functions: hours, minutes (off-center), subsidiary seconds; power reserve indicator; panorama date
Diameter: 32.2 mm
Height: 6.1 mm
Jewels: 48
Balance: screw balance with 18 weighted screws
Frequency: 28,800 vph
Balance spring: flat hairspring, duplex swan-neck fine adjustment for rate symmetry
Shock protection: Incabloc
Remarks: finely finished movement, three-quarter plate with Glashütte stripe finish, hand-engraved balance bridge

Caliber 89-02
Automatic; single spring barrel, 72-hour power reserve
Functions: hours, minutes, subsidiary seconds; 2nd time zone, world time with 37 time zones, day/night indicator, power reserve indicator; panorama date
Diameter: 39.2 mm
Height: 8 mm
Jewels: 63
Balance: screw balance with 4 gold regulating screws
Frequency: 28,800 vph
Balance spring: flat hairspring, duplex swan-neck fine adjustment for rate symmetry
Shock protection: Incabloc
Remarks: winding gears with double sun brushing, three-quarter plate with Glashütte stripe finish, hand-engraved balance bridge

Caliber 90
Automatic; single spring barrel, 42-hour power reserve
Functions: hours, minutes (off-center), subsidiary seconds; panorama date, moon phase
Diameter: 32.6 mm
Height: 5.4 mm
Jewels: 28
Balance: screw balance with 18 weighted screws
Frequency: 28,800 vph
Balance spring: flat hairspring, duplex swan-neck fine adjustment for rate symmetry
Shock protection: Incabloc
Remarks: eccentric, skeletonized, 21-kt gold oscillating weight, hand-engraved balance bridge

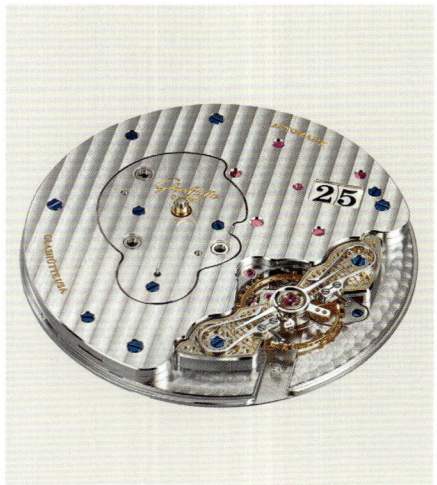

Caliber 91-02
Automatic; inverted movement with rate regulator on dial side; single spring barrel, 42-hour power reserve
Functions: hours, minutes (off-center), subsidiary seconds; panorama date
Diameter: 38.2 mm
Height: 7.1 mm
Jewels: 49
Balance: screw balance with 18 weighted screws
Frequency: 28,800 vph
Balance spring: flat hairspring, duplex swan-neck fine adjustment for rate symmetry
Shock protection: Incabloc
Remarks: finely finished movement, three-quarter plate with Glashütte stripe finish

Caliber 93-02
Automatic; flying tourbillon, single spring barrel, 48-hour power reserve
Functions: hours, minutes (off-center), subsidiary seconds (on tourbillon cage); panorama date, moon phase
Diameter: 32.2 mm
Height: 7.65 mm
Jewels: 48, plus 2 diamond endstones
Balance: screw balance with 18 weighted screws in rotating frame
Frequency: 21,600 vph
Balance spring: flat hairspring
Remarks: finely finished movement, off-center skeletonized rotor, with 21-kt gold oscillating mass

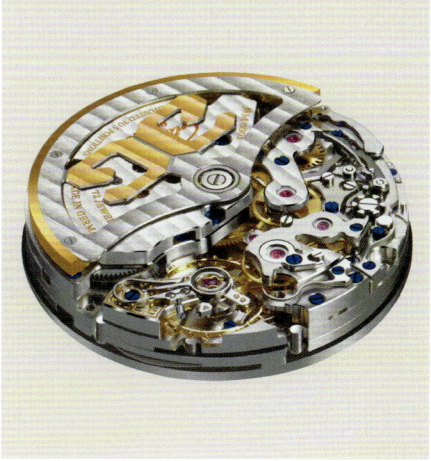

Caliber 96-01
Automatic; twin spring barrel, bidirectional winding in 2 speeds via stepped reduction gear; 42-hour power reserve
Functions: hours, minutes (off-center), subsidiary seconds; 2-digit counter (pusher-controlled, forward and backward); flyback chronograph; panorama date
Diameter: 32.2 mm
Height: 8.9 mm
Jewels: 72
Balance: screw balance with 18 weighted screws
Frequency: 28,800 vph
Balance spring: flat hairspring, swan-neck fine adjustment
Remarks: separate wheel bridges for winding and chronograph, finely finished movement

GRAHAM

Graham
Boulevard des Eplatures 38
CH-2300 La Chaux-de-Fonds
Switzerland

Tel.:
+41-32-910-9888

E-mail:
info@graham1695.com

Website:
www.graham1695.com

Founded:
1995

Number of employees:
approx. 30

Annual production:
5,000–7,000 watches

U.S. distributor:
Graham Watchmakers
169 East Flagler Street, Suite 932
Miami, FL 33131
305-890-6409
m.leemon@graham1695.com

Most important collections:
Geo.Graham, Chronofighter, Silverstone, Swordfish

In the mid-1990s, unusual creations gave an old English name in watchmaking a brand-new life. In the eighteenth century, George Graham perfected the cylinder escapement and the dead-beat escapement as well as inventing the chronograph. For these contributions and more, Graham certainly earned the right to be considered one of the big wheels in watchmaking history.

Despite his merits in the development of precision timekeeping, it was the mechanism he invented to measure short times—the chronograph—that became the trademark of his wristwatch company. To this day, the fundamental principle of the chronograph hasn't changed at all: A second set of hands can be engaged to or disengaged from the constant flow of energy of the movement. Given the British Masters' aim to honor this English inventor, it is certainly no surprise that the Graham collection includes quite a number of fascinating chronograph variations.

In 2000, the company released the Chronofighter, with its striking thumb-controlled lever mechanism—a modern twist on a function designed for World War II British fighter pilots, who couldn't activate the crown button of their flight chronographs with their thick gloves on. To enhance the retro look and feel, the brand decided to release several models bearing famous World War II pinups. The company has also started a special series to "give back," as it were. Made of a special carbon, this U.S. Navy Seal Chronofighter also features a special camo look designed to help hide soldiers from satellite cameras. A part of the sales of these watches will go to the nonprofit Navy Seal Foundation.

The attraction of the brand remains in the muscle watch-sportive look, which it seems to have relinquished in part for a sober-sportive look in the Swordfish line. In recent years, Graham has also added comparatively conventionally designed watches to its collection. For lovers of special pieces, there are the models of the Geo.Graham series. It was the name used by the brilliant watchmaker-inventor.

Swordfish Bronze
Reference number: 2SXAK.G01A
Movement: automatic, Graham Caliber G1710; ø 30 mm; 34 jewels; 28,800 vph; 48-hour power reserve
Functions: hours, minutes, subsidiary seconds; chronograph
Case: bronze, ø 46 mm; sapphire crystal; transparent case back; water-resistant to 10 atm
Band: rubber with mesh structure, bronze buckle
Price: $8,950

Chronofighter Superlight Carbon Tourbillograph
Reference number: 2CCBK.B35A
Movement: automatic, Graham Caliber G1780; ø 30 mm; 34 jewels; 28,800 vph; 1-minute tourbillon with gold bridges; column wheel control of chronograph functions; 48-hour power reserve
Functions: hours, minutes, subsidiary seconds (on tourbillon cage); chronograph
Case: carbon fiber "Superlight," ø 47 mm, height 15 mm; sapphire crystal; transparent case back; crown and pusher with finger lever on left side; water-resistant to 10 atm
Band: rubber, carbon fiber buckle
Remarks: carbon dial
Price: $29,950; limited to 100 pieces

Chronofighter Grand Vintage Arabic Numerals
Reference number: 2CVDS.B29A
Movement: automatic, Graham Caliber G1747; ø 30 mm; 25 jewels; 28,800 vph; 48-hour power reserve
Functions: hours, minutes, subsidiary seconds; chronograph; date
Case: stainless steel, ø 47 mm, height 15 mm; sapphire crystal; transparent case back; crown and pusher with finger lever on left side; water-resistant to 10 atm
Band: calfskin, buckle
Price: $6,450
Variations: various straps and dials

GRAND SEIKO

In 2017, Shinji Hattori, president of the Seiko Watch Company, announced that the Grand Seiko line had become a separate *manufacture* brand. In the years since, these watches have developed their own identity.

One must say, however, that this separate path had been taking shape for a while already. The Grand Seiko watches always existed in a segment of their own and had become something of a focus for collectors. For the brand's fiftieth anniversary in 2010, the Grand Seiko collection was given a host of new models and started being sold in the European market.

What makes the Grand Seiko collection special is the "Spring Drive" technology, a technology invented by a Seiko engineer that took twenty-eight years to perfect and, according to the company, six hundred prototypes. Essentially, it consists of a complex combination of mostly mechanical parts with a small but crucial electronic regulating element to tame the energy from the mainspring. These watches also boast some classical mechanical hijinks, such as the "High-Beat" balance with 36,000 vibrations per hour. The basic platform for all movements is the 9S mechanical caliber, introduced in 1998. It has been continuously improved over time, notably with the use of a special alloy called SPRON, used for the mainspring and the hairspring. Grand Seiko also draws on micromechanical systems (MEMS) technology to make parts boasting tolerances of a thousandth of a millimeter. It's no surprise that classic watch fans have welcomed the Grand Seikos into their midst. The range of models has been widened with a number of sportive divers' watches that are giving established Swiss brands some stiff competition when it comes to price and amenities.

Seiko Holdings
Ginza, Chuo, Tokyo
Japan

Website:
www.grand-seiko.com

Founded:
1881

Number of employees:
90,000 (for the entire holding)

U.S. distributor:
Grand Seiko Corporation of America
1111 MacArthur Boulevard
Mahwah, NJ 07430
201-529-5730
info@grand-seiko.us.com
www.grand-seiko.us.com

Most important collections/price range:
Elegance, Sport, Heritage / approx. $5,000 to $59,000

Elegance Mechanical Hand-Wound
Reference number: SBGK005
Movement: manually wound, Seiko Caliber 9S63; ø 28.4 mm, height 4.9 mm; 33 jewels; 28,800 vph; amagnetic protection to 4,800 A/m; 72-hour power reserve
Functions: hours, minutes, subsidiary seconds; power reserve indicator
Case: stainless steel, ø 39 mm, height 11.6 mm; sapphire crystal; transparent case back; water-resistant to 3 atm
Band: reptile skin, folding clasp
Price: $7,400; limited to 1,500 pieces

Elegance Ladies' Automatic
Reference number: STGK007
Movement: automatic, Seiko Caliber 9S27; ø 19.4 mm, height 4.5 mm; 35 jewels; 28,800 vph; amagnetic protection to 4,800 A/m; 50-hour power reserve
Functions: hours, minutes, sweep seconds; date
Case: stainless steel, ø 27.8 mm, height 11.2 mm; sapphire crystal; transparent case back; water-resistant to 10 atm
Band: stainless steel, folding clasp
Remarks: dial with 11 diamonds
Price: $5,500

Elegance Spring Drive
Reference number: SBGA407
Movement: automatic, Seiko Caliber 9R65; ø 30 mm, height 5.1 mm; 30 jewels; electromagnetic Tri-Synchro Regulator escapement system with sliding wheel; amagnetic protection to 4,800 A/m; 72-hour power reserve
Functions: hours, minutes, sweep seconds; power reserve indicator; date
Case: stainless steel, ø 40.2 mm, height 12.8 mm; sapphire crystal; transparent case back; screw-in crown; water-resistant to 10 atm
Band: reptile skin, folding clasp
Price: $5,800

GRAND SEIKO

Sport Spring Drive Limited Edition
Reference number: SBGA403
Movement: automatic, Seiko Caliber 9R15; ø 30 mm, height 5.8 mm; 30 jewels; electromagnetic Tri-Synchro Regulator escapement system with sliding wheel; amagnetic protection to 4,800 A/m; 72-hour power reserve
Functions: hours, minutes, sweep seconds; power reserve indicator; date
Case: titanium (with hard coating), ø 44.5 mm, height 14.3 mm; sapphire crystal; transparent case back; screw-in crown; water-resistant to 20 atm
Band: titanium, folding clasp
Price: $10,600; limited to 500 pieces

Sport Spring Drive Chronograph
Reference number: SBGC201
Movement: automatic, Seiko Caliber 9R86; ø 30 mm, height 7.6 mm; 50 jewels; electromagnetic Tri-Synchro Regulator escapement system with sliding wheel; amagnetic protection to 4,800 A/m; 72-hour power reserve
Functions: hours, minutes, subsidiary seconds; additional 24-hour display (2nd time zone), power reserve indicator; chronograph; date
Case: stainless steel, ø 43.5 mm, height 16 mm; sapphire crystal; transparent case back; screw-in crown and pushers; water-resistant to 10 atm
Band: stainless steel, folding clasp
Price: $8,200

Sport Spring Drive Diver's
Reference number: SBGA229
Movement: automatic, Seiko Caliber 9R65; ø 30 mm, height 5.1 mm; 30 jewels; electromagnetic Tri-Synchro Regulator escapement system with sliding wheel; amagnetic protection to 4,800 A/m; 72-hour power reserve
Functions: hours, minutes, sweep seconds; power reserve indicator; date
Case: stainless steel, ø 44 mm, height 14.5 mm; unidirectional bezel, 0-60 scale; sapphire crystal; transparent case back; screw-in crown; water-resistant to 20 atm
Band: stainless steel, folding clasp with safety lock and extension link
Price: $6,000

Heritage High-Precision Quartz
Reference number: SBGV225
Movement: quartz, Seiko Caliber 9F82; twin pulse control motor, amagnetic up to 4,800 A/m
Functions: hours, minutes, sweep seconds; date
Case: stainless steel, ø 40 mm, height 10 mm; sapphire crystal; water-resistant to 10 atm
Band: stainless steel, folding clasp
Price: $2,500

Heritage High-Beat 36,000 GMT
Reference number: SBGJ201
Movement: automatic, Seiko Caliber 9S86; ø 28.4 mm, height 6.6 mm; 37 jewels; 36,000 vph; amagnetic protection to 4,800 A/m; 55-hour power reserve
Functions: hours, minutes, sweep seconds; additional 24-hour display (2nd time zone); date
Case: stainless steel, ø 40 mm, height 14 mm; sapphire crystal; transparent case back; screw-in crown; water-resistant to 10 atm
Band: stainless steel, folding clasp
Price: $6,300

Heritage Spring Drive
Reference number: SBGA211
Movement: automatic, Seiko Caliber 9R65; ø 30 mm, height 5.1 mm; 30 jewels; electromagnetic Tri-Synchro Regulator escapement system with sliding wheel; amagnetic protection to 4,800 A/m; 72-hour power reserve
Functions: hours, minutes, sweep seconds; power reserve indicator; date
Case: titanium (with hard coating), ø 41 mm, height 12.5 mm; sapphire crystal; transparent case back; screw-in crown; water-resistant to 10 atm
Band: titanium, folding clasp
Price: $5,800

GREUBEL FORSEY

In 2004, when Alsatian Robert Greubel and Englishman Stephen Forsey presented a new movement at Baselworld, eyes snapped open: Their watch featured not one, but *two* tourbillon carriages working at a 30° incline. In their design, Forsey and Greubel not only took up the basic Abraham-Louis Breguet idea of canceling out the deviations of the balance by the continuous rotation of the tourbillon cage, but they went further, creating a quadruple tourbillon.

In 2010, Greubel Forsey moved into new facilities at a renovated farmhouse between Le Locle and La Chaux-de-Fonds and a brand-new modern building. After capturing an Aiguille D'Or for the magical Double Tourbillon 30° and the Grand Prix d'Horlogerie in Geneva, these two wizards of technically extreme watchmaking snatched up the top prize at the International Chronometry Competition in Le Locle for the Double Tourbillon 30°.

Greubel and Forsey continue to stun the watch community with some spectacular pieces, like the Quadruple Tourbillon Secret, which shows the complex play of the tourbillons through the case back, and the Greubel Forsey GMT with the names of world cities and a huge floating globe. Their first Art Piece came out in 2013, a most natural collaboration with British miniaturist Willard Wigan, who can sculpt the head of a pin. In 2019, their Art Piece pays homage to their own 30° tourbillon.

Meanwhile, Greubel and Forsey continue to push for tiny increments in chronometric precision. This involves building works of engineering art with, for instance, two inclined oscillators "linked by a spherical differential that averages rating differences and ensures an optimal performance at all times whether in stabilised (horizontal or vertical) positions or dynamically (on the wrist)," to quote their website. Can one go further? Can one get an even more precise rate? Apparently, yes, with four tourbillons connected to a spherical differential, each trying to cancel gravity.

Greubel Forsey SA
Eplatures-Grise 16
CH-2301 La Chaux-de-Fonds
Switzerland

Tel.:
+41-32-925-4545

E-mail:
info@greubelforsey.com
press@greubelforsey.com

Website:
www.greubelforsey.com

Founded:
2004

Number of employees:
approx. 100

Annual production:
approx. 100 watches

U.S. distributor:
Time Art Distribution
550 Fifth Avenue
New York, NY 10036
212-221-8041
info@timeartdistribution.com

Remarks:
Prices given only in Swiss francs (before taxes). Use daily exchange rate for conversion.

GMT Quadruple Tourbillon
Reference number: P300
Movement: manually wound, GF Caliber; ø 39.5 mm, height 13 mm; 84 jewels; 21,600 vph; two 4-minute outer tourbillons, within each a 1-minute tourbillon inclined at 30°, coupled by a spherical differential gear; 3 spring barrels; 72-hour power reserve
Functions: hours, minutes, subsidiary seconds; spherical world time display (2nd time zone), day/night indicator, power reserve indicator, additional 24-hour display on movement side
Case: white gold, ø 46.5 mm, height 17.45 mm; sapphire crystal; transparent case back; water-resistant to 3 atm
Band: reptile skin, folding clasp
Price: CHF 760,000; limited to 11 pieces

Art Piece Edition Historique
Reference number: P381
Movement: manually wound, GF Caliber; ø 36.4 mm, height 12.37 mm; 50 jewels; 21,600 vph; 4-minute outer tourbillon, 1-minute inner tourbillon inclined at 30°, balance with variable inertia, Phillips end curve, 2 spring barrels, finely finished movement decorated with microengraved writing; 72-hour power reserve
Functions: hours, minutes (off-center, disk display and indices), subsidiary seconds; power reserve indicator
Case: platinum, ø 44 mm, height 15.95 mm; sapphire crystal; transparent case back; water-resistant to 3 atm
Band: reptile skin, folding clasp
Remarks: third "Art Piece" as homage to the double 30° tourbillon
Price: CHF 550,000; limited to 11 pieces

Balancier Contemporain
Reference number: P180
Movement: manually wound, GF Caliber; ø 32.4 mm, height 9.2 mm; 33 jewels; 21,600 vph; balance with variable inertia, Phillips end curve, 2 spring barrels, finely finished movement with microengraving; 72-hour power reserve
Functions: hours, minutes (off-center), subsidiary seconds; power reserve indicator
Case: white gold, ø 39.6 mm, height 12.21 mm; sapphire crystal; transparent case back; water-resistant to 3 atm
Band: reptile skin, buckle
Price: CHF 195,000; limited to 33 pieces

OLD NORTHEAST JEWELERS

Old Northeast Jewelers – St. Petersburg & Tampa, FL

Buying, Selling, Repairing Fine Watches nationally since 1979. We Love Trades! 727-898-4377.

Nationally buying expensive pocket and wrist watches including Patek Philippe, Cartier, Longines, Breitling, Omega and Tag Heuer.

AWCI Certified Watchmakers, Graduate Gemologists, and Jeweler on-site every day.

H. MOSER & CIE.

H. Moser & Cie has been making a name for itself in the industry as a serious watchmaker, though not averse to flashes of humor, like the Swiss Mad (sic) Watch made of Vacherin Mont d'Or cheese it presented at the SIHH 2017 (the cheese for the case is mixed with a hardening resin). And there's the Swiss Alp watch, made to look like an Apple Watch, but with all the essential Moser codes.

The company was originally founded by one Heinrich Moser (1805–1874) from Schaffhausen, where he served as "city watchmaker." He moved to Le Locle and, in 1825, founded his company at age twenty-one. Soon after, he moved to Saint Petersburg, Russia, where ambitious watchmakers were enjoying a good market. In 1828, H. Moser & Cie. was brought to life—a brand resuscitated in modern times by a group of investors and watch experts together with Moser's great-grandson, Roger Nicholas Balsiger.

With the support of a host of Swiss and German specialists, the company returned to quality fundamentals. Its claim to fame is movements that contain a separate, removable escapement module supporting the pallet lever, escape wheel, and balance. The latter is fitted with the Straumann spring, made by Precision Engineering, another one of the Moser Group companies.

This small company has considerable technical know-how, which is probably what attracted MELB Holding, owners of Hautlence, and now majority owners of H. Moser shares. Under a new CEO, the brand redefined its style: understatement, soft tones, and subtle technicity. The three core collections, Endeavour, Venturer, and Pioneer, feature "clean" dials in solid colors, including the blackest black, called Vantablack. The month hand on the Endeavour is a mere arrowhead in the center of the dial that points to the hours, which double as the months. At the SIHH 2019, the company even presented the ultimate in pure: a minute repeater with no hands at all, just the activating pushers to help the owner tell the time.

H. Moser & Cie.
Rundbuckstrasse 10
CH-8212 Neuhausen am Rheinfall
Switzerland

Tel.:
+41-52-674-0050

E-mail:
info@h-moser.com

Website:
www.h-moser.com

Founded:
1828

Number of employees:
60

Annual production:
approx. 1,500 watches

U.S. distributor:
Horology Works LLC
11 Flagg Road
West Hartford, CT 06117
860-986-9676
mmargolis@horologyworks.com
Westime
254 North Rodeo Drive
Beverly Hills, CA 90210
310-271-0000
info@westime.com

Most important collections/price range:
Endeavour / approx. $17,200 to $110,000;
Pioneer / approx. $11,900 to $49,900; Swiss Alp Watch / approx. $21,900 to $650,000;
Venturer / approx. $19,500 to $100,000

Endeavour Concept Tourbillon Minute Repeater

Reference number: 1903-0200
Movement: manually wound, Caliber HMC 903; ø 33 mm, height 9.62 mm; 34 jewels; 21,600 vph; escapement with flying 1-minute tourbillon, skeletonized tourbillon bridge, finely hand-finished movement; 90-hour power reserve
Functions: hours, minutes; minute repeater
Case: white gold, ø 43 mm, height 14 mm; sapphire crystal; transparent case back
Band: reptile skin, buckle
Price: $320,000; limited to 10 pieces

Swiss Alp Watch Minute Repeater Tourbillon

Reference number: 5901-0200
Movement: manually wound, Caliber HMC 901; 30 × 35 mm, height 6.25 mm; 29 jewels; 21,600 vph; escapement with flying minutes tourbillon, skeletonized bridges; 90-hour power reserve
Functions: hours, minutes; minute repeater
Case: white gold, 39.8 × 45.8 mm, height 11 mm; sapphire crystal; transparent case back
Band: reptile skin, buckle
Price: $292,000

Endeavour Tourbillon Concept

Reference number: 1804-0200
Movement: automatic, Moser Caliber HMC 804; ø 32 mm, height 5.5 mm; 21,600 vph; interchangeable escapement with flying 1-minute tourbillon, Straumann double hairspring, skeletonized bridges, oscillating mass in pink gold; 72-hour power reserve
Functions: hours, minutes
Case: white gold, ø 42 mm, height 11.6 mm; sapphire crystal; transparent case back
Band: antelope leather, folding clasp
Price: $69,000; limited to 20 pieces
Variations: smoky dial

H. MOSER & CIE.

Endeavour Flying Hours Cosmic Green
Reference number: 1806-0201
Movement: automatic, Moser Caliber HMC 806; ø 32 mm, height 6.5 mm; 35 jewels; 21,600 vph; Straumann double hairspring; 72-hour power reserve
Functions: hours (3 jumping and rotating disks), minutes (on disk segment)
Case: white gold, ø 42 mm, height 12.3 mm; sapphire crystal; transparent case back
Band: reptile skin, buckle
Price: $35,000; limited to 100 pieces

Endeavour Flying Hours Superluminova Blue
Reference number: 1806-0202
Movement: automatic, Moser Caliber HMC 806; ø 32 mm, height 6.5 mm; 35 jewels; 21,600 vph; Straumann double hairspring; 72-hour power reserve
Functions: hours (3 jumping and rotating disks), minutes (on disk segment)
Case: white gold, ø 42 mm, height 12.3 mm; sapphire crystal; transparent case back
Band: reptile skin, buckle
Price: $35,000; limited to 100 pieces

Venturer Concept Vantablack
Reference number: 2327-0410
Movement: manually wound, Moser Caliber HMC 327; ø 32 mm, height 4.5 mm; 29 jewels; 18,000 vph; interchangeable escapement with Straumann hairspring; 72-hour power reserve
Functions: hours, minutes; power reserve indicator (on movement side)
Case: rose gold, ø 39 mm, height 11.9 mm; sapphire crystal; transparent case back
Remarks: dial in Vantablack, one of the darkest substances known
Band: reptile skin, buckle
Price: $25,000

Caliber HMC 341
Manually wound; exchangeable escapement with beveled wheels, hardened gold pallet fork and escapement wheel; screw-mounted gold chatons; double spring barrel, 168-hour power reserve
Functions: hours, minutes, subsidiary seconds; power reserve indicator; perpetual calendar with large date and small sweep month hand, leap year (dial side)
Diameter: 34 mm; **Height:** 5.8 mm
Jewels: 28
Balance: glucydur with white gold screws
Frequency: 18,000 vph
Balance spring: Straumann with Breguet end curve
Shock protection: Incabloc
Remarks: double-pull crown mechanism for easy switching of crown position

Caliber HMC 802
Automatic; exchangeable 1-minute tourbillon, double hairspring; single spring barrel, 72-hour power reserve
Functions: hours, minutes; additional 12-hour display (2nd time zone, display on request)
Diameter: 34 mm
Height: 6.5 mm
Jewels: 33
Balance: glucydur with white gold screws
Frequency: 21,600 vph
Balance spring: Straumann double hairspring
Shock protection: Incabloc
Remarks: rotor with gold oscillating mass

Caliber HMC 100
Manually wound; exchangeable escapement, gold pallet fork and escapement wheel; double mainspring barrel, 168-hour power reserve
Functions: hours, minutes, subsidiary seconds; power reserve indicator (on movement side); large date
Diameter: 34 mm
Height: 6.3 mm
Jewels: 31
Balance: glucydur with white gold screws
Frequency: 18,000 vph
Balance spring: Straumann with Breguet end curve
Shock protection: Incabloc
Remarks: double-pull crown mechanism for easy switching of crown position

HABRING²

Fine mechanical works of art are created with smaller and larger complications in a small workshop in Austria's Völkermarkt, where the name Habring² stands for Maria Kristina Habring and her husband, Richard. "You get two for one," he jokes. The couple's first watch labeled with their own name came out in 2004: a simple three-handed watch based on a refined and unostentatiously decorated ETA pocket watch movement, the Unitas 6498-1. In connoisseur circles the news spread like wildfire that exceptional quality down to the smallest detail was hidden behind its inconspicuous specifications.

Since then, they have put their efforts into a wide range of products, notably their movements, like the Caliber A09, which is available in both a manual and a bidirectionally wound automatic version. All the little details that differentiate this caliber are either especially commissioned or are made in-house. Its sporty version drives a pilot's watch. Also more or less in-house are the components of Habring²'s Seconde Foudroyante, with the foudroyante mechanism fed by a separate spring barrel.

For the twentieth anniversary of the IWC double chronograph, Habring² built a limited, improved edition. The movement, based on the ETA 7750 "Valjoux," was conceived in 1991/1992 with an additional module between the chronograph and automatic winder. Suffice to say, the five-member team's technical sophistication is remarkable. They do not shy away from modern materials like silicon, or technologies, or ion etching. But they also keep their feet on the ground, using classic materials like steel. And whatever they can't do in-house, they will purchase to ensure quality, like the perpetual calendar module that goes into the brand's flagship model, the Perpetual Doppel.

Habring Uhrentechnik OG
Hauptplatz 16
A-9100 Völkermarkt
Austria

Tel.:
+43-4232-51-300

E-mail:
info@habring.com

Website:
www.habring2.com

Founded:
1997

Number of employees:
3

Annual production:
200 watches

U.S. retailers:
Martin Pulli (USA-East)
215-508-4610
www.martinpulli.com
Passion Fine Jewelry (USA-West)
858-794-8000
www.passionfinejewelry.com

Most important collections/price range:
Felix / from $5,200; Jumping Second / from $6,400; Doppel 3 / from $8,750; Chrono COS / from $8,100

Perpetual Doppel
Reference number: Perpetual Doppel
Movement: manually wound, Habring Caliber A11P; ø 30 mm, height 8.7 mm; 27 jewels; 28,800 vph; tangential screw fine adjustment, amagnetic escapement with Carl Haas hairspring, monopusher for chronograph functions, finely finished movement; 48-hour power reserve
Functions: hours, minutes, subsidiary seconds; split-second chronograph; perpetual calendar with date, weekday, month, moon phase, leap year
Case: stainless steel, ø 43 mm, height 12 mm; sapphire crystal; transparent case back; water-resistant to 3 atm
Band: calfskin, buckle
Price: $24,300

Doppel Felix
Reference number: Doppel Felix
Movement: manually wound, Habring Caliber A11R; ø 30 mm, height 8.4 mm; 27 jewels; 28,800 vph; Triovis fine adjustment; 48-hour power reserve
Functions: hours, minutes, subsidiary seconds; flyback chronograph
Case: stainless steel, ø 42 mm, height 13 mm; sapphire crystal; transparent case back; water-resistant to 5 atm
Band: calfskin, buckle
Price: $8,750
Variations: various dials; with date function ($9,300)

COS Felix
Reference number: COS Felix
Movement: automatic, Habring Caliber A11COS; ø 30 mm, height 7.9 mm; 25 jewels; 28,800 vph; Triovis fine adjustment, chronograph functions activated by turning crown (Crown Operation System)
Functions: hours, minutes, subsidiary seconds; chronograph
Case: stainless steel, ø 42 mm, height 13 mm; sapphire crystal; transparent case back; water-resistant to 5 atm
Band: calfskin, buckle
Price: $8,100
Variations: titanium ($9,200); manually wound ($8,100); various dials; with date function ($8,650)

HABRING²

Felix
Reference number: Felix
Movement: manually wound, Habring Caliber A11B; ø 30 mm, height 4.2 mm; 18 jewels; 28,800 vph; Triovis fine adjustment, finely finished movement; 48-hour power reserve
Functions: hours, minutes, subsidiary seconds
Case: stainless steel, ø 38.5 mm, height 7 mm; sapphire crystal; transparent case back; water-resistant to 3 atm
Band: calfskin, buckle
Price: $5,200

Felix
Reference number: Felix
Movement: manually wound, Habring Caliber A11B; ø 30 mm, height 4.2 mm; 18 jewels; 28,800 vph; Triovis fine adjustment, finely finished movement; 48-hour power reserve
Functions: hours, minutes, subsidiary seconds
Case: stainless steel, ø 38.5 mm, height 7 mm; sapphire crystal; transparent case back; water-resistant to 3 atm
Band: calfskin, buckle
Price: $5,200
Variations: various dials

Erwin
Reference number: Erwin
Movement: manually wound, Habring Caliber A11MS; ø 30 mm, height 5.3 mm; 21 jewels; 28,800 vph; Triovis fine adjustment, finely finished movement; 48-hour power reserve
Functions: hours, minutes, sweep seconds (jumping)
Case: stainless steel, ø 38.5 mm, height 9 mm; sapphire crystal; transparent case back; water-resistant to 3 atm
Band: calfskin, buckle
Price: $6,400
Variations: various dials

Jumping Second Pilot Date
Reference number: Jumping Second Pilot Date
Movement: automatic, Habring Caliber A11SD; ø 36.6 mm, height 7.9 mm; 24 jewels; 28,800 vph; Triovis fine adjustment; 48-hour power reserve
Functions: hours, minutes, sweep seconds, (jumping); date
Case: stainless steel, ø 42 mm, height 13 mm; sapphire crystal; transparent case back
Band: calfskin, buckle
Price: $7,150
Variations: manually wound version ($6,700)

Foudroyante Felix
Reference number: Foudroyante Felix
Movement: manually wound, Habring Caliber A11FD; ø 30 mm, height 7.9 mm; 23 jewels; 28,800 vph; tangential screw for fine adjustment, escapement with Carl Haas hairspring, finely finished movement; 48-hour power reserve
Functions: hours, minutes, sweep seconds (jumping); foudroyante display of eighth of a second ("seconde foudroyante"); date
Case: stainless steel, ø 42 mm, height 13 mm; sapphire crystal; transparent case back; water-resistant to 5 atm
Band: calfskin, buckle
Price: $7,950
Variations: automatic winding ($8,300)

Repetition
Reference number: Repetition
Movement: manually wound, Habring Caliber 11B (base with Dubois Dépraz D90 module); ø 36 mm, height 7.85 mm; 18 jewels; 28,800 vph; Triovis fine adjustment, finely finished movement; 48-hour power reserve
Functions: hours, minutes, subsidiary seconds; 5-minute repetition
Case: titanium, ø 42 mm, height 13.5 mm; sapphire crystal; transparent case back
Band: calfskin, buckle
Price: $20,900

HAGER

Keeping it simple and smart is a Hager specialty. The company, owned and operated by American service veteran Pierre "Pete" Brown is named after the town where the company was started in 2009. The business model was equally streamlined: create high-quality and affordable automatic watches accessible to those who have never experienced the joy of owning a mechanical watch. The look: rugged and refined, for individuals with a bit of adventure in their bones.

The timepieces are designed by Brown and his small team in Hagerstown. All the cues are there for the watch connoisseur, the brushed and polished cases with beveled edges, two-tiered stadium dial, with brass markers and hands outlined in black and coated with Superluminova, domed sapphire crystal, 120-click ceramic bezels and 24-click GMT ceramic bezels also enhanced with Superluminova. The cases are rated a sportive 20 atm, meaning they are good for more than just washing the dishes. Inside them beats one of a variety of automatic winding Swiss and Japanese mechanical movements that are both installed and regulated in the USA. The latest is the Atelier 1, a Swiss-American collaboration, which fits into the Commando 10th Anniversary watch, a tough diver with a straightforward, practical look. At any rate, the spirit of elegant adventure is in each of the collections. Even the BroadArrow, with its uncluttered dial, has a dynamic look and feel.

Brown is well aware of the foibles of the watch industry, one major complaint being customer service. His personal boast since launching the company is that Hager Watch has never charged a customer for a repair yet, even when it's clear that the customer is at fault. "We aren't just selling watches," says Brown, "we are selling the experience of owning a luxury timepiece. That's not to say that at some point we will have to reverse this because of overall costs, but it's been a hallmark of our brand and it builds brand loyalty."

Hager Watches
36 South Potomac Street
Suite 204
Hagerstown, MD 21740

Tel.:
240-232-2172

E-mail:
info@hagerwatches.com

Website:
www.hagerwatches.com

Founded:
2009

Number of employees:
2

Annual production:
1,000–1,500 watches

Most important collections/price range:
Commando, GMT Aquamariner, U2 / $550 to $1,050

Commando 10th Anniversary
Reference number: 25517
Movement: automatic, Atelier Caliber 1; ø 25.6 mm, height 4.6 mm; 22 jewels; 28,800 vph; 44-hour power reserve
Functions: hours, minutes, sweep seconds; date
Case: stainless steel, ø 40 mm, height 13 mm; screw-in crown; unidirectional bezel with black ceramic insert; sapphire crystal; screw-down sapphire case back with logo; water-resistant to 30 atm
Band: stainless steel with 2-button clasp and 2-button slidelock extension system
Price: $950
Variations: stainless steel with black or ceramic insert ($950)

GMT Traveler Red/Blue Insert
Reference number: 16738
Movement: automatic, Soprod C125; ø 25.6 mm, height 5.67 mm; 25 jewels; 28,800 vph; 40-hour power reserve
Functions: hours, minutes, sweep seconds; date; 2nd time zone
Case: stainless steel, ø 40 mm, height 13 mm; screw-in crown; unidirectional bezel with black ceramic insert; sapphire crystal; screw-down sapphire case back with logo; water-resistant to 30 atm
Band: stainless steel with 2-button clasp and 2-button slidelock extension system
Price: $1,050
Variations: stainless steel with black or blue or black and blue ceramic insert ($1,050)

BroadArrow
Reference number: D0529G
Movement: automatic, Soprod C125; ø 25.6 mm, height 5.67 mm; 25 jewels; 28,800 vph; 40-hour power reserve
Functions: hours, minutes, seconds; sweep 2nd time zone
Case: stainless steel, ø 42 mm, height 10.5 mm; sapphire crystal; screw-down case back; water-resistant to 20 atm
Band: stainless steel, stitching, folding clasp with slidelock extension
Price: $1,050
Variations: stainless steel with seconds at 6 o'clock ($800) and 3-hand ($950)

Hamilton International Ltd.
Mattenstrasse 149
CH-2503 Biel/Bienne
Switzerland

Tel.:
+41-32-343-4004

E-mail:
info@hamiltonwatch.com

Website:
www.hamiltonwatch.com
shop.hamiltonwatch.com

Founded:
1892

U.S. distributor:
Hamilton
Swatch Group (US), Inc.
703 Waterford Way, Suite 450
Miami, FL 33126
800-234-8463
Hamilton.US@swatchgroup.com

Price range:
between approx. $500 and $2,500

HAMILTON

The Hamilton Watch Co. was founded in 1892 in Lancaster, Pennsylvania, and, within a very brief period, grew into one of the world's largest *manufactures*. Around the turn of the twentieth century, every second railway employee in the United States was carrying a Hamilton watch in his pocket, not only to make sure the trains were running punctually, but also to assist in coordinating them and organizing schedules. And during World War II, the American army officers' kits included a service Hamilton.

Hamilton is the sole survivor of the large U.S. watchmakers—if only as a brand within the Swiss Swatch Group. At one time, Hamilton had itself owned a piece of the Swiss watchmaking industry in the form of the Büren brand in the 1960s and 1970s. As part of a joint venture with Heuer-Leonidas, Breitling, and Dubois Dépraz, Hamilton-Büren also made a significant contribution to the development of the automatic chronograph. Just prior in its history, the tuning fork watch pioneer was all the rage when it took the new movement technology and housed it in a modern case created by renowned industrial designer Richard Arbib. The triangular Ventura hit the watch-world ground running in 1957, in what was truly a frenzy of innovation that benefited the brand especially in the U.S. market. The American spirit of freedom and belief in progress this model embodies, something evoked in Hamilton's current marketing, are taken quite seriously by its designers—even those working in Biel, Switzerland. Today's collections are more inspired from adventure and aviator watches. The brand also continues to focus on revamped remakes of its classics, and prices have come down a bit as a reaction to the unstable markets.

Khaki X-Wind Day Date
Reference number: H77765541
Movement: automatic, Hamilton Caliber H-30 (base ETA 2834-2); ø 25.6 mm, height 5.05 mm; 25 jewels; 21,600 vph; 80-hour power reserve
Functions: hours, minutes, sweep seconds; date, weekday
Case: stainless steel, ø 45 mm, height 12.8 mm; crown-activated scale ring with slide rule to calculate drift angle with side winds; sapphire crystal; transparent case back; water-resistant to 10 atm
Band: calfskin, buckle
Price: $1,095

Khaki Field Murph Auto
Reference number: H70605731
Movement: automatic, Hamilton Caliber H-10 (base ETA 2824-2); ø 25.6 mm, height 4.6 mm; 25 jewels; 21,600 vph; 80-hour power reserve
Functions: hours, minutes, sweep seconds
Case: stainless steel, ø 42 mm, height 11 mm; sapphire crystal; water-resistant to 10 atm
Band: calfskin, buckle
Price: $995

Khaki Field Mechanical
Reference number: H69449861
Movement: manually wound, Hamilton Caliber H-50 (base ETA 2801-2); ø 25.6 mm, height 3.35 mm; 17 jewels; 21,600 vph; 80-hour power reserve
Functions: hours, minutes, sweep seconds
Case: stainless steel with green PVD coating, ø 38 mm, height 9.5 mm; sapphire crystal; water-resistant to 5 atm
Band: calfskin, buckle
Price: $575

HAMILTON

Jazzmaster Auto Chrono
Reference number: H32586881
Movement: automatic, Hamilton Caliber H-21 (base ETA 7750); ø 30 mm, height 7.9 mm; 25 jewels; 28,800 vph; 60-hour power reserve
Functions: hours, minutes, subsidiary seconds; chronograph; date
Case: stainless steel, ø 42 mm, height 15.23 mm; sapphire crystal; transparent case back; water-resistant to 10 atm
Band: calfskin, buckle
Price: $1,745

Intra-Matic Auto Chrono
Reference number: H38416541
Movement: automatic, Hamilton Caliber H-31 (base ETA 7753); ø 30 mm, height 7.9 mm; 27 jewels; 21,600 vph; 60-hour power reserve
Functions: hours, minutes, subsidiary seconds; chronograph; date
Case: stainless steel, ø 40 mm, height 14.45 mm; sapphire crystal; water-resistant to 10 atm
Band: calfskin, buckle
Price: $2,195

Ventura Skeleton
Reference number: H24595331
Movement: automatic, Hamilton Caliber H-10-S (base ETA 2824-2); ø 25.6 mm, height 4.6 mm; 25 jewels; 21,600 vph; skeletonized movement; 80-hour power reserve
Functions: hours, minutes, sweep seconds
Case: stainless steel with black PVD coating, 42.5 × 44.6 mm, height 11.38 mm; sapphire crystal; transparent case back; water-resistant to 5 atm
Band: rubber, buckle
Remarks: skeletonized dial
Price: $1,995; limited to 999 pieces

Khaki X-Wind Auto Chrono
Reference number: H77616533
Movement: automatic, Hamilton Caliber H-21 (base ETA 7750); ø 30 mm, height 7.9 mm; 25 jewels; 28,800 vph; 60-hour power reserve; COSC-certified chronometer
Functions: hours, minutes, subsidiary seconds; chronograph; date, weekday
Case: stainless steel, ø 45 mm, height 15.55 mm; crown-activated scale ring with slide rule to calculate drift angle with side winds; sapphire crystal; transparent case back; screw-in crown; water-resistant to 10 atm
Band: calfskin, buckle
Price: $1,595

Jazzmaster Open Heart Auto
Reference number: H32565135
Movement: automatic, ETA Caliber 2824-2; ø 25.6 mm, height 4.6 mm; 25 jewels; 28,800 vph; 38-hour power reserve
Functions: hours, minutes, sweep seconds
Case: stainless steel, ø 40 mm, height 10.8 mm; sapphire crystal; transparent case back; water-resistant to 10 atm
Band: stainless steel, folding clasp
Remarks: partially skeletonized dial
Price: $975

Khaki Field Mechanical
Reference number: H69439931
Movement: manually wound, Hamilton Caliber H-50 (base ETA 2801-2); ø 25.6 mm, height 3.35 mm; 17 jewels; 28,800 vph; 42-hour power reserve
Functions: hours, minutes, sweep seconds
Case: stainless steel, ø 38 mm, height 9.5 mm; sapphire crystal; water-resistant to 5 atm
Band: textile, buckle
Price: $495

HANHART

Hanhart 1882 GmbH
Hauptstrasse 33
D-78148 Gütenbach
Germany

Tel.:
+49-7723-93-44-0

E-mail:
info@hanhart.com

Website:
www.hanhart.com

Founded:
1882 in Diessenhofen, Switzerland;
in Germany since 1902

Number of employees:
22

Annual production:
approx. 1,000 chronographs and 30,000 stopwatches

U.S. distributor:
BluePointe, LLC
207 W. Millbrook Rd.
Raleigh, NC 27609
888-333-4895

Most important collections/price range:
Mechanical stopwatches / from approx. $600;
Pioneer / from approx. $1,070; Primus / from approx. $2,300

The reputation of this rather special company really goes back to the twenties and thirties. At the time, the brand manufactured affordable and robust stopwatches, pocket watches, and chronograph wristwatches. These core timepieces were what the fans of instrument watches wanted, and so they were thrilled as the company slowly abandoned its quartz dabbling of the eighties and reset its sights on the brand's rich and honorable tradition. A new collection was in the wings, raising expectations of great things to come. Support by the shareholding Gaydoul Group provided the financial backbone to get things moving.

Hanhart managed to rebuild a name for itself with a foot in Switzerland and the other in Germany, but it began to drift after the 2009 recession. Following bankruptcy, the company reorganized under the name Hanhart 1822 GmbH and moved everything to its German hometown. It has also returned to its stylistic roots: The characteristic red start/stop pusher graces the new collections, even on the bi-compax chronos of the Racemasters, which come with a smooth bezel. Pilots' chronographs have never lost any of their charm, either, and Hanhart was already making them in the 1930s, notably the Caliber 41 and the Tachy Tele, with asymmetrical pushers and the typical red pusher. These timepieces have to survive extreme conditions, like shocks and severe temperature fluctuations. Hanhart's long tradition and expertise with flyers' chronographs struck a chord with the Austrian Army. It ordered a special edition of the Primus series decorated with the coat of arms of the Austrian Air Force on the dial and certified by the military.

Pioneer One Blue Dial
Reference number: 762.270
Movement: automatic, Sellita Caliber SW200-1; ø 25.6 mm, height 4.6 mm; 26 jewels; 28,800 vph; 38-hour power reserve
Functions: hours, minutes, sweep seconds; date
Case: stainless steel, ø 42 mm, height 12 mm; bidirectional bezel with reference markings; sapphire crystal; water-resistant to 10 atm
Band: calfskin, buckle
Price: $1,070

Pioneer One Gray Dial
Reference number: 762.240
Movement: automatic, Sellita Caliber SW200-1; ø 25.6 mm, height 4.6 mm; 26 jewels; 28,800 vph; 38-hour power reserve
Functions: hours, minutes, sweep seconds; date
Case: stainless steel, ø 42 mm, height 12 mm; bidirectional bezel with reference markings; sapphire crystal; water-resistant to 10 atm
Band: calfskin, buckle
Price: $1,070

Primus Carrier Pilot
Reference number: 740.271
Movement: automatic, Caliber HAN3809 (base ETA 7750); ø 30 mm, height 10.4 mm; 28 jewels; 28,800 vph; 42-hour power reserve
Functions: hours, minutes, subsidiary seconds; chronograph; date
Case: stainless steel, ø 44 mm, height 15 mm; sapphire crystal; transparent case back; screw-in crown; water-resistant to 10 atm
Band: textile, folding clasp
Remarks: mobile lugs
Price: $2,970

HARRY WINSTON

Harry Winston
701 Fifth Avenue
New York, NY 10022

Tel.:
212-399-1000

Website:
www.harrywinston.com

Founded:
1932

Most important collections:
Avenue, Emerald, Midnight, Premier, Ocean, Opus, Project Z, Histoire de Tourbillon

Swatch Group's purchase of the luxury brand Harry Winston in early 2013 for $1 billion came as something of a surprise. But considering the upward flow of money worldwide, banking on a proven high-end luxury brand would seem obvious. On his many travels, founder Harry Winston (1896–1978) bought, recut, and set some of the twentieth century's greatest gems. He was succeeded by his son Ronald, a gifted craftsman himself with several patents in precious metals processing.

It was Ronald Winston who added watches to the company's portfolio, inaugurating two lines: one showcasing the finest precious gems to dovetail with the company's overall focus, and the other containing clever, complicated timepieces. The latter generated the thirteen models of the Opus line, each of which was developed in conjunction with one exceptional independent watchmaker per year in very small series and containing an exclusive *manufacture* movement. The roster of artist-engineers included such names as François-Paul Journe, Vianney Halter, Felix Baumgartner, and Greubel Forsey all the way to Denis Giguet and Emmanuel Bouchet.

With Nayla Hayek, daughter of Swatch founder Nicolas Hayek, as CEO, the brand has been benefiting from synergies with other Swatch brands, notably Blancpain. But change is in the air, as the company puts forth its crafts powers in the Premier family, which has seen the use of feathers, butterfly wings, and now micromosaics of glass. The frankly Art Deco Avenue line is a reference to Fifth Avenue in New York, where Harry Winston opened shop originally. It is celebrating its twentieth anniversary in 2019 with a special moon phase. Meanwhile, the Opus line has become dormant and the ultra-technical Histoire du Tourbillon has reached its final installment with number 10. The Z line continues, however, with fine watches in cases made of a zirconium alloy, Zalium.

Avenue Classic 20th Anniversary Moon Phase

Reference number: AVEQMP21WW003
Movement: quartz, Harry Winston Caliber HW5203; 13 mm × 21.3 mm, height 3.1 mm
Functions: hours, minutes, subsidiary seconds; moon phase
Case: white gold, 21.4 mm × 36.1 mm, height 7.47 mm; bezel set with 43 brilliant-cut diamonds, sapphire crystal; diamond on crown; water-resistant to 3 atm; **Band:** white gold, with brilliant-cut diamonds and sapphires, buckle
Remarks: beaded mother-of-pearl dial on gold base, emerald applique, 52 brilliant-cut diamonds
Price: $106,500; limited edition of 20 pieces
Variations: rose gold; various bands and dials

Avenue Classic Sweet Valentine

Reference number: AVEQHM21WW295
Movement: quartz, Harry Winston Caliber HW1044; 13 mm × 15.55 mm, height 2.20 mm
Functions: hours, minutes
Case: white gold, 21.4 mm × 36.1 mm, height 7.47 mm; case set with 48 brilliant-cut diamonds, 1 ruby and 1 heart-cut ruby; sapphire crystal; diamond on crown; water-resistant to 3 atm
Band: reptile skin, buckle set with 6 brilliant-cut diamonds
Remarks: mother-of-pearl dial on gold base, emerald applique, 3D red mother-of-pearl hearts
Price: $49,700; limited edition of 14 pieces

Avenue Classic Moon Phase

Reference number: AVEQMP21RR001
Movement: quartz, Harry Winston Caliber HW5203; 13 mm × 21.3 mm, height 3.1 mm
Functions: hours, minutes, subsidiary seconds; moon phase
Case: white gold, 21.4 mm × 36.1 mm, height 7.47 mm; case set with 29 brilliant-cut diamonds, sapphire crystal; diamond on crown; water-resistant to 3 atm
Band: white gold, buckle
Remarks: beaded, Havana-brown mother-of-pearl dial on gold base, emerald applique; set with 84 brilliant-cut diamonds (including bracelet)
Price: $37,400; limited edition of 20 pieces
Variations: blue-beaded mother-of-pearl dial

Histoire de Tourbillon 10
Reference number: HCOMQT53WW001
Movement: manually wound, Harry Winston Caliber HW4702; ø 45 mm × 32 mm, height 12.85 mm (on tourbillon bridge); 95 jewels; 21,600 vph; variable inertia with gold screws; four 36-second counterclockwise tourbillons, 2 groups of 2 serially coupled spring barrels with rapid rotation; titanium bridges; 55-hour power reserve
Functions: hours, minutes; power reserve indicator
Case: white gold; ø 53.3 mm × 39.1 mm × 17.60 mm; transparent case back; water-resistant to 3 atm
Band: reptile skin, white gold buckle
Price: on request; limited to 10 pieces
Variations: rose gold or Winstonium alloy

Project Z13
Reference number: OCEAMP42ZZ001
Movement: automatic, Harry Winston Caliber HW3202; ø 26.2 mm, height 5.37 mm; 28 jewels; 28,800 vph; flat silicon hairspring, rotor in white gold, fine finishing with radial côtes de Genève; 68-hour power reserve
Functions: hours, retrograde minutes; date
Case: Zalium, ø 42.2 mm, height 11.27 mm; sapphire crystal; transparent case back; water-resistant to 10 atm
Band: calfskin with denim effect, buckle
Price: $24,300; limited to 300 pieces

Harry Winston Avenue Dual Time Automatic
Reference number: AVEATZ37RR001
Movement: automatic, Caliber HW3502; ø 32 mm, height 5.2 mm; 32 jewels; 28,800 vph; flat silicon spring, white gold rotor, with côtes de Genève; circular grain, beveled bridges; **Functions:** hours, minutes; 2nd time zone (retrograde): day/night indicator; date
Case: Sedna gold, 53.8 × 35.8 mm, height 10.7 mm; sapphire crystal; transparent case back; water-resistant to 3 atm
Band: reptile skin, Sedna gold buckle
Remarks: smoky white sapphire crystal dial, emerald appliques
Price: $38,300; **Variations:** Zalium, with Zalium buckle ($22,200)

Premier Precious Micromosaic 36 mm
Reference number: PRNAHM36WW024
Movement: automatic, Harry Winston Caliber HW2008; ø 26.2 mm, height 3.37 mm; 28 jewels; 28,800 vph; balance spring, skeletonized rotor in white gold, fine finishing with circular côtes de Genève, rhodium plating; 72-hour power reserve
Functions: hours, minutes
Case: white gold, ø 36 mm, height 8.48 mm; case set with 57 brilliant-cut diamonds, sapphire crystal; diamond on crown; water-resistant to 3 atm; **Band:** reptile skin, white gold buckle set with 17 diamonds
Remarks: dial handmade micromosaic glass
Price: $43,300; **Variations:** dial in various colors, brown, red, and turquoise

Premier Precious Peacock 36 mm
Reference number: PRNAHM36WW026
Movement: automatic, Harry Winston Caliber HW2008; ø 26.2 mm, height 3.37 mm; 28 jewels; 28,800 vph; balance spring, skeletonized rotor in white gold, fine finishing with circular côtes de Genève, rhodium plating; 72-hour power reserve
Functions: hours, minutes
Case: white gold, ø 36 mm, height 8.48 mm; case set with 57 brilliant-cut diamonds, sapphire crystal; diamond on crown; water-resistant to 3 atm
Band: reptile skin, buckle set with 17 diamonds
Remarks: dial handmade micromosaic glass with 152 diamonds and 8 sapphires with peacock design
Price: $51,800; limited to 30 pieces
Variations: dial in blue, green, and turquoise

Ocean Retrograde 42 mm
Reference number: OCEAHR42RR001
Movement: automatic, Harry Winston Caliber HW3306; ø 34 mm, height 5.37 mm; 35 jewels, 28,800 vph; silicon hairspring, skeletonized rotor in white gold, fine finishing with circular côtes de Genève
Functions: jumping retrograde hours, minutes off-center, retrograde seconds; retrograde date
Case: rose gold, ø 42.2 mm, height 11.27 mm; sapphire crystal; diamond on crown; water-resistant to 10 atm
Band: reptile skin, buckle
Price: $42,100; **Variations:** set with baguette-cut diamonds ($110,100), white gold set with baguette-cut diamonds ($111,200)

HAUTLENCE

Time can be read in so many ways. Back in 2004, after spending years in the Swiss watch industry, Guillaume Tetu and Renaud de Retz decided that their idea for tracking it was new and unique. They were not watchmakers, but they knew whom to bring on board for the genesis of Hautlence, an anagram of Neuchâtel, the town where their small company is located. And soon, the first HL model was produced: a fairly large, rectangular timepiece with the ratios of a television set and a lively and visible mechanical life. All good things in watchmaking being small, the big innovation was a "connecting rod," as Tetu calls it, to propel the hour disk. When the retrograde minute hand reaches the end of its arc, it triggers the rod, which advances the hour.

Having survived the Great Recession, Hautlence persisted, thinned down and without de Retz. The watches evolved, developing shape and character. For the HLq, the movement was reengineered for a round case. Instead of a tourbillon, Hautlence has found a way to have the whole escapement rotate four times a day.

In 2012, Hautlence became the first member of the brand-new MELB Holding, headed by Georges-Henri Meylan (formerly of Audemars Piguet) and former Breguet CFO Bill Muirhead. The experience and contacts of these two horological powerhouses have energized the brand. The Atelier and Signature series were streamlined and given a little more structure. The stark industrial look is now tempered with daubs of color, but prices have been lowered by the use of trusty Soprod engines in some models. Then, in 2014, the brand acquired former French soccer star Eric Canton, an art collector as well and an edgy personality, as an ambassador, which goes along well with the chic-steampunkish look and the brand's will to be different, come what may. Under a new CEO, Sandro Reginelli, Hautlence found its deeply technical roots again, bringing out the incredible Sphere in 2019, as well as the boldly punk Punk.

Hautlence
Rue Numa-Droz 150
CH-2300 La Chaux-de-Fonds
Switzerland

Tel.:
+41-32-924-00-60

E-mail:
info@hautlence.com

Website:
www.hautlence.com

Founded:
2004

Number of employees:
10

Annual production:
150 watches

U.S. distributor:
Westime
8569 Westime Sunset Boulevard
West Hollywood, CA 90069
310-289-0808
info@westime.com
www.westime.com

Most important collections:
Concepts d'Exception, Atelier, Signature

HL2.3 Punk
Movement: automatic, in-house caliber HL2.0 mobile bridge-type caliber; 37.8 × 33.2 mm, height 12.35 mm; 18,000 vph; 92 jewels; côtes de Genève, components decorated and finished by hand; 45-hour power reserve
Functions: hours, retrograde minutes; power reserve indicator
Case: titanium with black PVD, 50 × 42 × 17.8 mm; 84 steel studs (1.75–5.75 mm); rose gold crown and case back screws; 3D beveled sapphire crystals; water-resistant to 3 atm
Band: reptile skin, folding clasp
Price: $220,000; limited to 28 pieces

HL Vagabonde Tourbillon 01
Movement: automatic HTL 405-1 based on H. Moser & Cie HMC 804 automatic caliber; ø 32.00 mm; 21,600 vph; 35 jewels; 1-minute tourbillon; bidirectional rotor; côtes de Genève, decorated and finished by hand, stain-brushed bridges with blue PVD; 72-hour power reserve
Functions: skeleton hours split over two levels
Case: pink gold, ø 46 × 39 mm, height 12 mm; beveled sapphire crystal; transparent case back; water-resistant to 3 atm
Band: rubber-lined reptile skin, folding clasp
Price: $79,000

HL Sphere
Movement: manually wound, HTL 501-1; ø 32.00 mm, height 5.5 mm; 38 jewels; 21,600 vph; components decorated and finished by hand; 72-hour power reserve
Functions: hour, retrograde minutes
Case: satin-finished and polished white gold, 46 × 39 mm, height 12 mm, with 3.75-mm dome; polished white gold crown; transparent case back; water-resistant to 3 atm
Band: reptile skin, folding clasp
Remarks: spherical hour, with braked retrograde minute system
Price: $99,000

MK II CRUXIBLE
HELLION™

Life, Liberty and the Pursuit

In 1944, the Hellion was the name of one of many experimental weapons systems designed to clear beaches at arm's length ahead of the amphibious landings. In the end, the weapons systems proved ineffective, but the name Hellion came to describe the spirit of the pilots who flew missions over the Pacific and the people that built the foundation of the UDT/SEALs. Pilots such as John Glenn of the VMF-218 "Hellions". The kind of people who threw themselves at a heavily defended beach dressed as if on a snorkeling holiday with the subtle addition of towing 40 lbs of explosives. The kind of person that hands a hotel manager today's equivalent of $50,000 in back pay towards a V-J Day party for his teammates and asks only to be notified once the tab ran out; ending the party...12 days later it turns out.

It's from this tradition we drew the name for the second variant of the Mk II Cruxible, the Cruxible-Hellion. Starting with the specifications laid out by the US Navy air arm and combat swimmers, the Mk II Cruxible-Hellion would have exceeded either set of requirements.

Life, Liberty, and the Pursuit.

For additional information and to order direct visit: www.mkiiwatches.com

HERMÈS

Thierry Hermès's timing was just right. When he founded his saddlery in Paris in 1837, France's middle class was booming and spending money on beautiful things and activities like horseback riding. Hermès became a household name and a symbol of good taste—not too flashy, not trendy, useful. The advent of the automobile gave rise to luggage, bags, headgear, and soon Hermès, still in family hands today, diversified its range of products—foulards, fashion, porcelain, glass, perfume, and gold jewelry are active parts of its portfolio.

Watches were a natural, especially with the advent of the wristwatch in the years prior to World War I. Hermès even had a timepiece that could be worn on a belt. But some time passed before the company engaged in "real" watchmaking. In 1978, La Montre Hermès opened its watch manufactory in Biel.

Rather than just produce fluffy lifestyle timepieces, Hermès has gone to the trouble to get an in-depth grip on the business. "Our philosophy is all about the quality of time," says Laurent Dordet, who took over as CEO from Luc Perramond in March 2015. "It's about imagination; we want people to dream." "Poetic complications" is what allowed the company to navigate between classy but plain watches and muscular tool timepieces bristling with complications. On the one hand there was the esthetics: the lively leaning numerals of the Arceau series or the bridoon recalling the company's equine roots at 12 o'clock for holding the strap. As for in-house complications, they are produced in collaboration with external designers, notably Jean-Marc Wiederrecht and his company, Agenhor. In the Slim line, one finds a thin perpetual calendar with modern numerals that raise it above the standard retro watch. The clever "Temps Suspendu" lets the wearer stop time for a moment. There are also fascinating moon phase displays, or charming countdowns that will add a little romantic pizzazz to the last hour before a rendezvous.

La Montre Hermès
Erlenstrasse 31A
CH-2555 Brügg
Switzerland

Tel.:
+41-32-366-7100

E-mail:
info@montre-hermes.ch

Website:
www.hermes.ch

Founded:
1978

Number of employees:
150

Annual production:
not specified

U.S. distributor:
Hermès of Paris, Inc.
55 East 59th Street
New York, NY 10022
800-441-4488
www.hermes.com

Most important collections/price range:
Arceau, Cape Cod, Clipper, Dressage, Faubourg, Heure H, Klikti, Kelly, Medor, Slim / $2,400 to $500,000

Arceau L'Heure de la Lune

Reference number: AR1.890.740/MM88
Movement: automatic, Hermès Caliber H1837 with "L'heure de la lune" module; ø 38 mm, height 7.9 mm; 42 jewels; 28,800 vph; finely finished movement; 42-hour power reserve
Functions: hours, minutes (off-center); date, double phase (for northern and southern hemispheres)
Case: white gold, ø 43 mm; sapphire crystal; transparent case back; water-resistant to 3 atm
Band: reptile skin, folding clasp
Remarks: meteorite dial with photorealistic moon disks; rotating disks act as moon phase displays
Price: $25,500
Variations: aventurine dial ($25,500)

Arceau Le Temps Suspendu

Reference number: AR8.97A.222/MM41
Movement: automatic, ETA Caliber 2892 (modified); ø 26 mm, height 5.6 mm; 28,800 vph; hands can be parked at 12:30, then started again at current time with pusher; double spring barrel; 42-hour power reserve
Functions: hours, minutes; date (retrograde)
Case: stainless steel, ø 43 mm; sapphire crystal; transparent case back; water-resistant to 3 atm
Band: reptile skin, folding clasp
Price: $22,400

Slim d'Hermès L'Heure Impatiente

Reference number: CA4.870.220/MM7K
Movement: automatic, Hermès Caliber H1912 (base with "L'heure impatiente" module); ø 31.96 mm, height 5.9 mm; 36 jewels; 28,800 vph; mainplate and bridges with snail and côtes de Genève decoration; 50-hour power reserve
Functions: hours, minutes; "Heure impatiente" alarm with 60-minute countdown
Case: rose gold, ø 40.5 mm, height 10.67 mm; sapphire crystal; transparent case back; water-resistant to 3 atm
Band: reptile skin, buckle
Price: $39,900

Slim d'Hermès Titanium

Reference number: CA2.841.330/MM88
Movement: automatic, Hermès Caliber H1950; ø 30 mm, height 2.6 mm; 29 jewels; 21,600 vph; microrotor; 42-hour power reserve
Functions: hours, minutes, subsidiary seconds
Case: titanium, ø 39.5 mm, height 8.11 mm; sapphire crystal; transparent case back; water-resistant to 3 atm
Band: reptile skin, buckle
Price: $8,050
Variations: rose gold ($19,050); stainless steel ($7,650)

Carré H

Reference number: T12.710.230/VB343
Movement: automatic, Hermès Caliber H1912; ø 23.3 mm, height 3.7 mm; 28 jewels; 28,800 vph; 50-hour power reserve
Functions: hours, minutes, sweep seconds
Case: stainless steel, 38 × 38 mm, height 10.8 mm; sapphire crystal; transparent case back; water-resistant to 3 atm
Band: calfskin, buckle
Price: $7,350

Cape Cod Milanaise

Reference number: CC2.710.226/4708
Movement: quartz
Functions: hours, minutes
Case: stainless steel, 29 × 29 mm, height 7.8 mm; sapphire crystal; water-resistant to 3 atm
Band: stainless steel Milanese mesh, folding clasp
Price: $3,725

Galop d'Hermès

Reference number: GA1.270.221/ZZ95
Movement: quartz
Functions: hours, minutes
Case: red gold, 26 × 40.8 mm; sapphire crystal; water-resistant to 3 atm
Band: reptile skin, buckle
Price: $9,500
Variations: set with diamonds ($15,400)

Heure H Double Jeu

Reference number: HH1.231.337/VB89
Movement: quartz
Functions: hours, minutes
Case: stainless steel, with 122 diamonds, 21 × 21 mm; sapphire crystal; water-resistant to 3 atm
Band: calfskin, buckle
Price: $6,700
Variations: white dial

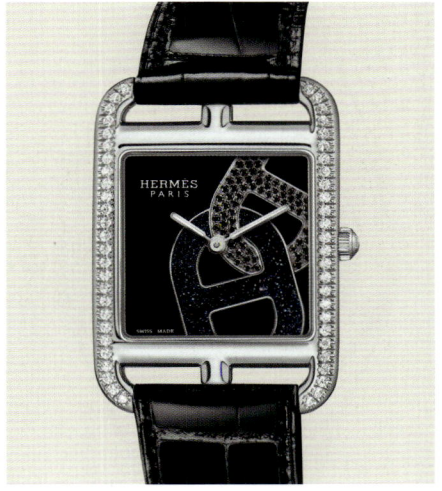

Cape Cod Chaîne d'Ancre

Reference number: CC3.730.334/ZZ89-I
Movement: quartz
Functions: hours, minutes
Case: stainless steel, set with 42 diamonds, 29 × 29 mm; sapphire crystal; water-resistant to 3 atm
Band: reptile skin, buckle
Remarks: diamond set with 71 black spinels
Price: $10,550
Variations: white dial with diamonds ($10,550)

HUBLOT

Ever since Hublot moved into a new, modern, spacious factory building in Nyon, near Geneva—in the midst of a recession, no less—the brand has evolved with stunning speed. The growth has been such that Hublot has even built a second factory, which is even bigger than the first. The ground-breaking ceremony took place on March 3, 2014, and the man holding the spade was Hublot chairman Jean-Claude Biver, who is also head of LVMH's Watch Division.

Hublot grew and continues to grow thanks to a combination of innovative watchmaking and extremely vigorous communication. It was together with current CEO Ricardo Guadalupe that Biver developed the idea of fusing different and at times incompatible materials in a watch: carbon composite and gold, ceramic and steel, denim and diamonds. In 2011, the brand introduced the first scratchproof precious metal, an alloy of gold and ceramic named "Magic Gold." In 2014, Hublot came out with a watch whose dial is made of osmium, one of the world's rarest metals. Using a new patented process, Hublot has also implemented a unique concept of cutting wafer-thin bits of glass that are set in the open spaces of a skeletonized movement plate.

The "art of fusion" tagline drove the brand into all sorts of technical and scientific partnerships and created a buzz that is ongoing, apparently, regardless of the economic environment. Even fashion house Sartoria Rubinacci was picked up by the Hublot radar for a Classic Fusion Chronograph with hound's-tooth pattern. And during the past decade, Hublot also managed to verticalize. Most of the brand's models are now run on in-house Unico, Meca-10, or Tourbillon movements.

Hublot's concept is based on the idea of "being the first, different and unique." To achieve that goal, it has associated its name with major sports events and brands (FIFA Football World Cup, the UEFA Champions' League, UEFA EURO, and Ferrari) and has attracted highly visible brand ambassadors, like soccer stars Kylian Mbappé and Pelé, and sprinter extraordinaire Usain Bolt.

Hublot SA
Chemin de la Vuarpillière 33
CH-1260 Nyon
Switzerland

Tel.:
+41-22-990-9000

E-mail:
info@hublot.ch

Website:
www.hublot.com

Founded:
1980

Number of employees:
approx. 700

Annual production
approx. 50,000 watches

U.S. distributor:
Hublot of America, Inc.
100 N. Biscayne Blvd., Suite 1900
Miami, FL 33132
786-405-8677

Most important collections/price range:
Big Bang / $11,000 to $1,053,000; Classic Fusion / $5,200 to $474,000; Manufacture Piece (MP) / $82,000 to $579,000

Classic Fusion Orlinski Titanium

Reference number: 550.NS.1800.RX.ORL19
Movement: automatic, Caliber HUB 1100 (base Sellita SW300); ø 25.6 mm, height 3.6 mm; 25 jewels; 28,800 vph; personalized Hublot rotor; 42-hour power reserve
Functions: hours, minutes, sweep seconds
Case: titanium, ø 40 mm, height 11.1 mm; bezel screwed to case with 6 titanium screws; sapphire crystal; transparent case back; water-resistant to 5 atm
Band: rubber, folding clasp
Price: $11,500
Variations: rose gold ($22,500)

Classic Fusion Aerofusion Chronograph Orlinski Red Ceramic

Reference number: 525.CF.0130.RX.ORL19
Movement: automatic, Caliber HUB 1155; ø 30 mm, height 7.1 mm; 60 jewels; 28,800 vph; skeletonized movement; 42-hour power reserve
Functions: hours, minutes, subsidiary seconds; chronograph
Case: red ceramic, ø 45 mm, height 13.45 mm; bezel screwed to case with 6 black-plated titanium screws; sapphire crystal; transparent case back; water-resistant to 5 atm
Band: rubber, folding clasp
Price: $24,100; limited to 200 pieces; **Variations:** black ceramic ($18,800); green ceramic ($19,300)

Classic Fusion Ferrari GT 3D Carbon

Reference number: 526.QB.0124.VR
Movement: automatic, Caliber HUB 1281 "Unico"; ø 30 mm, height 6.75 mm; 43 jewels; 28,800 vph; mainplate and bridges with gray coating; 72-hour power reserve
Functions: hours, minutes, subsidiary seconds; flyback chronograph; date
Case: carbon 3D fiber, ø 45 mm, height 13.15 mm; bezel screwed to case with 4 titanium screws; sapphire crystal; microblasted titanium case back; water-resistant to 10 atm; **Band:** calfskin folding clasp
Price: $27,300; limited to 500 pieces
Variations: titanium (limited to 1,000 pieces, $22,000); rose gold (limited to 500 pieces, $38,800)

HUBLOT

Big Bang Tourbillon Red Sapphire
Reference number: 405.JR.0120.RT
Movement: manually wound, Caliber HUB 6016; ø 34 mm, height 5.7 mm; 25 jewels; 21,600 vph; 1-minute tourbillon; skeletonized movement; 115-hour power reserve
Functions: hours, minutes; power reserve indicator
Case: red sapphire crystal, ø 45 mm, height 14.25 mm; bezel screwed to case with 6 titanium screws; sapphire crystal; red sapphire crystal case back; water-resistant to 3 atm
Band: rubber, titanium folding clasp
Price: $164,000
Variations: blue sapphire ($174,000)

Big Bang MP-11 King Gold 3D Carbon
Reference number: 911.OQ.0118.RX
Movement: manually wound, Caliber HUB 9011; ø 34 mm, height 10.95 mm; 39 jewels; 28,800 vph; 7 spring barrels stacked perpendicularly to movement axes, force transmission via oblique spur gears; 336-hour power reserve; **Functions:** hours, minutes (off-center); power reserve indicator
Case: rose gold satin-finished and polished gold, ø 45 mm, height 14.4 mm; 3D carbon fiber bezel screwed to case with 6 titanium screws; sapphire crystal; transparent case back; water-resistant to 3 atm
Band: rubber, folding clasp
Price: $89,500; limited to 100 pieces;
Variations: set with diamonds ($148,000)

Big Bang Meca-10 Nicky Jam Ceramic "X" Setting
Reference number: 414.CI.4010.LR.4096.N JA19
Movement: manually wound, Caliber HUB 1201; ø 34.8 mm, height 6.8 mm; 24 jewels; 21,600 vph; 240-hour power reserve
Functions: hours, minutes, subsidiary seconds; power reserve indicator
Case: ceramic, ø 45 mm, height 15.95 mm; bezel set with sapphires and tsavorites, screwed to case with 6 titanium screws; sapphire crystal; microblasted black ceramic and sapphire crystal case back with printed "Nicky Jam" signature; water-resistant to 10 atm
Band: rubber with reptile skin overlay, folding clasp
Price: $53,600; limited to 50 pieces

Big Bang Unico Blue Magic
Reference number: 411.ES.5119.RX
Movement: automatic, Caliber HUB 1242 "Unico"; ø 30 mm, height 8.05 mm; 38 jewels; 28,800 vph; mainplate and bridges coated black; 72-hour power reserve
Functions: hours, minutes, subsidiary seconds; flyback chronograph; date
Case: blue ceramic, ø 45 mm, height 15.45 mm; bezel screwed to case with 6 titanium screws; sapphire crystal; transparent case back; water-resistant to 10 atm
Band: rubber, folding clasp
Price: $20,900; limited to 500 pieces
Variations: red ceramic ($26,200)

Big Bang Unico Italia Independent Titanium Teak
Reference number: 411.NQ.5129.NR.ITI19
Movement: automatic, Caliber HUB 1242 "Unico"; ø 30 mm, height 8.05 mm; 38 jewels; 28,800 vph; anthracite-coated mainplate and bridges; 72-hour power reserve
Functions: hours, minutes, subsidiary seconds; flyback chronograph; date
Case: titanium, ø 45 mm, height 15.45 mm; carbon bezel with teak inlay screwed to case with 6 titanium screws; sapphire crystal; transparent case back; water-resistant to 10 atm
Band: rubber with sailcloth overlay, folding clasp
Remarks: comes with sunglasses
Price: $24,100; limited to 100 pieces

Big Bang Unico King Gold Rainbow
Reference number: 411.OX.9910.LR.0999
Movement: automatic, Caliber HUB 1242 "Unico"; ø 30 mm, height 8.05 mm; 38 jewels; 28,800 vph; black-coated mainplate and bridges; 72-hour power reserve
Functions: hours, minutes, subsidiary seconds; flyback chronograph; date
Case: rose gold set with 176 precious stones, ø 45 mm, height 15.45 mm; bezel set with 48 precious stones and screwed to case with 6 titanium screws; sapphire crystal; transparent case back; water-resistant to 10 atm
Band: rubber with reptile skin overlay, folding clasp
Price: $91,600

HUBLOT

Big Bang Unico Sang Bleu Blue Ceramic

Reference number: 415.EX.7179.VR.MXM19
Movement: automatic, Caliber HUB 1213 "Unico"; ø 30 mm, height 8.05 mm; 28 jewels; 28,800 vph; 72-hour power reserve
Functions: hours, minutes, sweep seconds (disk display with vertex indices)
Case: ceramic, ø 45 mm, height 15.55 mm; bezel screwed to case with 6 titanium screws; sapphire crystal; transparent case back; water-resistant to 10 atm
Band: calfskin, folding clasp
Price: $20,900; limited to 200 pieces
Variations: white ceramic (limited to 200 pieces, $20,900)

Big Bang Unico Sang Bleu II King Gold

Reference number: 418.OX.1108.RX.MXM19
Movement: automatic, Caliber HUB 1240.MXM "Unico"; ø 30 mm, height 8.05 mm; 38 jewels; 28,800 vph; 72-hour power reserve
Functions: hours, minutes, subsidiary seconds (disk display with vertex indices); chronograph (disk display with vertex indices); date
Case: rose gold, ø 45 mm, height 16.5 mm; titanium bezel screwed to case with 6 titanium screws; sapphire crystal; transparent case back; water-resistant to 10 atm
Band: rubber, folding clasp
Price: $47,300; limited to 100 pieces
Variations: titanium (limited to 200 pieces, $25,200)

Spirit of Big Bang Tourbillon Carbon Blue

Reference number: 645.QL.7117.RX
Movement: manually wound, Caliber HUB 6020; ø 31.65 mm, height 5.7 mm; 25 jewels; 21,600 vph; 1-minute tourbillon; skeletonized movement; 115-hour power reserve
Functions: hours, minutes (off-center); power reserve indicator
Case: carbon fiber, 42 × 51 mm, height 13.25 mm; bezel screwed to case with 6 titanium screws; sapphire crystal; transparent case back; water-resistant to 3 atm
Band: rubber, folding clasp
Price: $94,700; limited to 100 pieces
Variations: black carbon fiber (limited to 100 pieces, $94,700)

Spirit of Big Bang Yellow Sapphire

Reference number: 641.JY.0190.RT
Movement: automatic, Caliber HUB 4700 (base Zenith El Primero); ø 30 mm, height 6 mm; 31 jewels; 36,000 vph; 50-hour power reserve
Functions: hours, minutes, subsidiary seconds; chronograph; date
Case: yellow sapphire crystal, 42 × 51 mm, height 15.2 mm; bezel screwed to case with 6 titanium screws; sapphire crystal; transparent case back; water-resistant to 5 atm
Band: transparent yellow rubber, folding clasp
Price: $106,000; limited to 100 pieces
Variations: blue sapphire (limited to 100 pieces, $106,000)

Caliber HUB 1201

Manually wound skeletonized movement; silicon pallet lever and escape wheel; double mainspring barrel, 240-hour power reserve
Functions: hours, minutes, subsidiary seconds; power reserve indicator; date
Diameter: 34.80 mm
Height: 6.8 mm
Jewels: 24
Balance: CuBe
Frequency: 21,600 vph
Balance spring: flat hairspring with fine adjustment
Shock protection: Incabloc
Remarks: 223 parts

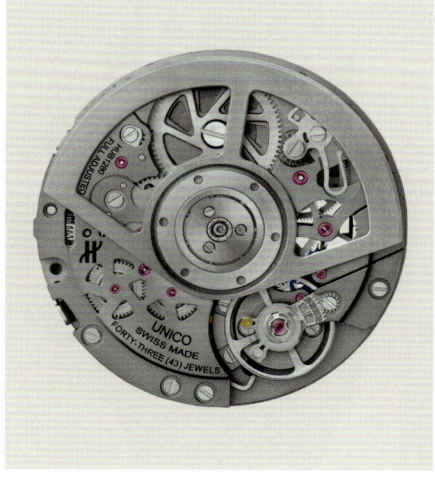

Caliber HUB 1280

Automatic; column wheel control of chronograph functions; silicon pallet lever and escapement, removable escapement; double-pawl automatic winding (Pellaton system), winding rotor with ceramic ball bearing; single spring barrel, 72-hour power reserve
Functions: hours, minutes, subsidiary seconds; flyback chronograph; date
Diameter: 30 mm
Height: 6.75 mm
Jewels: 43
Balance: glucydur
Frequency: 28,800 vph
Balance spring: flat hairspring with fine adjustment
Shock protection: Incabloc
Remarks: 354 parts

HYT SA
Rue de Prébarreau 17
CH-2000 Neuchâtel
Switzerland

Tel.:
+41 32-323-2770

E-mail:
contact@hytwatches.com

Website:
www.hytwatches.com

Founded:
2012

Number of employees:
45 (including the sister company Preciflex)

Annual production:
approx. 350 wristwatches

U.S. retailers:
Contact main office in Neuchâtel for information on U.S. retailers.

Most important collections/price range:
Various models with a liquid time display / $39,000 to $320,000

HYT

The earliest timekeepers were water clocks, known as clepsydras. The ancient Greeks had already devised a system by which water was guided from one vessel into another through an orifice of a predetermined diameter. Time was read on a calibrated scale on the second vessel. The three founders of HYT loved this idea of displaying the passage of time with moving fluids, and so they set out to solve the many problems generated if one were to introduce a liquid into a watch.

They developed a closed system made up of a capillary tube that would serve as a time track. It had a special pump-tank at either end that could either receive or pump out liquid. The two tanks had their dedicated space at 6 o'clock. After much research, they realized that the tube needed to be filled with two liquids, not one. Their different physical properties means they don't mix and thus create a sharp line at the point where they meet, which could serve as a pointer.

The pump-tanks were based on sensors used by NASA, a piston-driven bellows made of ultrathin but robust material that bends easily, but offers a stable surface. This allows very exact amounts of liquid to be pumped from one tank into the other. The system is driven by an in-house mechanical movement and cams. But it requires a clever thermal compensation system for the fluid in the tube. HYT became an instant sensation when it came out with its first watch in 2012.

Most important, perhaps, the concept leaves lots of opportunities for designs and new technological gimmicks, be that a miniature hand-wound generator, or luminescent liquids. The recent Soonow takes the vanitas idea of the skull to new heights. There is no minute indication, but the right eye blinks "soon" and "now."

Soonow
Reference number: H02237
Movement: manually wound, HYT Caliber 101; ø 37.8 mm, height 10.1 mm; 35 jewels; 28,800 vph; module with 2 bellows and a capillary tube containing 2 immiscible fluids, the meeting between the 2 liquids is the hour pointer; thermal compensator; 65-hour power reserve; **Functions:** hours (capillary display, retrograde), subsidiary seconds (in left eye); power reserve indicator (in right eye)
Case: stainless steel with black DLC coating, ø 48.8 mm, height 20 mm; sapphire crystal; screw-in crown; water-resistant to 5 atm; **Band:** rubber, folding clasp
Remarks: skull silhouette shows the hours, right eye blinks "soon" and "now" every second
Price: $75,000; limited to 25 pieces

H1.0
Reference number: H02095-A
Movement: manually wound, HYT Caliber 101; ø 37.8 mm, height 10.1 mm; 35 jewels; 28,800 vph; module with 2 bellows and a capillary tube containing 2 immiscible fluids, the meeting between the 2 liquids is the hour pointer; thermal compensator; 65-hour power reserve
Functions: minutes (off-center), hours (capillary display, retrograde), subsidiary seconds; power reserve indicator
Case: stainless steel with anthracite PVD coating, ø 48.8 mm, height 20 mm; sapphire crystal; screw-in crown; water-resistant to 5 atm
Band: rubber, folding clasp
Price: $49,000

H0
Reference number: H02138
Movement: manually wound, HYT Caliber 101; ø 37.8 mm, height 10.1 mm; 35 jewels; 28,800 vph; module with 2 bellows and a capillary tube containing 2 immiscible fluids, the meeting between the 2 liquids is the hour pointer; thermal compensator; 65-hour power reserve
Functions: minutes (off-center), hours (capillary display, retrograde), subsidiary seconds; power reserve indicator
Case: stainless steel with anthracite DLC coating, ø 48.8 mm, height 18.7 mm; sapphire crystal; water-resistant to 3 atm; **Band:** rubber, folding clasp
Price: $39,000; limited to 25 pieces
Variations: black display fluid

ITAY NOY

Our relationship to precious objects is complex and ultimately reveals as much about ourselves as about the object. Furthermore, the relationship we build up with precious objects is special. Itay Noy's watches, each unique in its look and feel, seem made to foster this conversation and, in many ways, keep it going. It began with the City Squares model, which shows time on the backdrop of a map of the owner's favorite or native city. In 2013, Noy showcased a square watch run on a Technotime automatic movement with a face-like dial that changes with the movement of the hands, a tongue-in-cheek reminder of our daily communication with our phones and the meaning of the frame.

Exploring this intimacy between the watch and the owner is an endless source of inspiration for Noy, a jeweler by trade who, with time, as it were, has begun reaching into the engineer's magic box—including working on a bespoke movement with a Swiss firm. In 2016, he created the Chrono Gears, which essentially runs on a large invisible circular gear that drives a.m. and p.m. indicators and more. A year later, Time Tone, another "dynamic dial," to use his term, gave the owner the choice of a colored hour disk that only he or she will know, while the minute hand does its work in the center of the dial. The Full Month shows the date or the moon appearing through a circle of digits carved into the dial. The 2019 object is a subtle reminder that hours are almost irrelevant, but every minute counts: ReOrder has the hours digitally flashing on a sandwich dial, haphazardly it would seem . . .

It's no wonder that Noy's collections find their way into museums and special exhibitions. They are works of kinetic art.

Itay Noy
P.O. Box 16661
Tel Aviv 6116601
Israel

Tel.:
+972-352-47-380

E-mail:
studio@itay-noy.com

Website:
www.itay-noy.com

Founded:
2000

Number of employees:
4

Annual production:
150–200 pieces

U.S. distributor:
Please contact Studio Itay Noy for information.
www.itay-noy.com

Most important collections/price range:
Time Tone, ReOrder, Full Month, Chrono Gears, Part Time / $2,400 to $9,800

ReOrder
Reference number: REORDER.BL
Movement: manually wound IN.IP13; ø 36.6 mm, height 5.5 mm; 20 jewels; 21,600 vph; 42-hour power reserve
Functions: dynamic dial with 12 digit-shaped windows indicating the hours, minutes, and central seconds
Case: stainless steel, ø 44 mm, height 12 mm; sapphire crystal dome; transparent case back; water-resistant to 5 atm
Band: handmade leather band, double folding clasp
Price: $6,800; limited and numbered edition of 24 pieces
Variations: gold plated

Full Month
Reference number: FM-NUM.WT
Movements: automatic, Caliber IN.VMF5400; 30 mm, height 3 mm; 29 jewels; 21,600 vph; extra-thin microrotor; 48-hour power reserve
Functions: hours, minutes, sweep seconds; full date window
Case: stainless steel, 40 mm × 44 mm, height 7.44 mm; sapphire crystal; transparent case back; water-resistant to 5 atm
Band: leather, double folding clasp
Remarks: date projected through digit-shaped slits in dial
Price: $9,800; limited and numbered edition of 18 pieces

Full Month—Moon
Reference number: FM-MOON
Movements: automatic, Caliber IN.VMF5400; 30 mm, height 3 mm; 29 jewels; 21,600 vph; extra-thin microrotor; 48-hour power reserve
Functions: hours, minutes, sweep seconds; full date window
Case: stainless steel, 40 mm × 44 mm, height 7.44 mm; sapphire crystal; transparent case back; water-resistant to 5 atm
Band: leather, double folding clasp
Remarks: date projected through digit-shaped slits in dial
Price: $11,800; limited and numbered edition of 18 pieces

Time Tone
Reference number: TT.BK
Movement: manually wound IN.IP13; ø 36.6 mm, height 5.5 mm; 20 jewels; 21,600 vph; 42-hour power reserve
Functions: hours with special disk display; minutes, seconds
Case: stainless steel, ø 44 mm, height 12 mm; sapphire crystal; transparent case back; water-resistant to 5 atm
Band: handmade leather band, double folding clasp
Remarks: dynamic dial with colored disks owner can choose as "secret" hour hand
Price: $5,800; limited and numbered edition of 24 pieces
Variations: blue dial

Celestial Time
Reference number: CT.W
Movement: manually wound IN.IP13; ø 36.6 mm, height 5.5 mm; 20 jewels; 21,600 vph; 42-hour power reserve
Functions: hours displayed as astrological sign, minutes, seconds
Case: stainless steel, ø 44 mm, height 12 mm; sapphire crystal dome; transparent case back; water-resistant to 5 atm
Band: leather, double folding clasp
Remarks: dynamic dial with zodiac signs owner can choose as "secret" hour hand
Price: $5,800; limited and numbered edition of 24 pieces
Variations: Western or Chinese zodiac signs

Chrono Gears
Reference number: CG.BK
Movement: manually wound IN.IP13; ø 36.6 mm, height 5.5 mm; 20 jewels; 21,600 vph; 42-hour power reserve
Functions: chronogear hand indicator for a.m./p.m., chronogear hand indicator for 8 time situations, central hours, minutes, seconds
Case: stainless steel, ø 44 mm, height 12 mm; sapphire crystal; transparent case back; water-resistant to 5 atm
Band: leather, double folding clasp
Price: $6,800; limited and numbered edition of 24 pieces
Variations: blue dial

Open Mind
Reference number: OM-S
Movement: manually wound, 6497-1; ø 36.6 mm, height 4.5 mm; 17 jewels; 21,600 vph; open-worked dial reveals escapement; 38-hour power reserve
Functions: hours, minutes, subsidiary seconds
Case: stainless steel, ø 44 mm, height 12 mm; sapphire crystal; transparent case back; water-resistant to 5 atm
Band: leather, double folding clasp
Price: $4,400; limited and numbered edition of 99 pieces
Variations: blue dial

ID-Hebrew
Reference number: ID-HEB.BL
Movement: automatic, Miyota caliber 90S5; ø 25.6 mm, height 3.9 mm; 24 jewels; 28,800 vph; 42-hour power reserve
Functions: hours, minutes, sweep seconds
Case: stainless steel, ø 42.4 mm, height 10 mm; sapphire crystal; screw-down case back; water-resistant to 5 atm
Band: leather band
Price: $2,800; limited and numbered edition of 99 pieces
Variations: black leather strap

X-Ray
Reference number: XRAY6498
Movement: manually wound, ETA Caliber 6498-1; ø 36.6 mm, height 4.5 mm; 17 jewels; 21,600 vph; 38-hour power reserve
Functions: hours, minutes, subsidiary seconds
Case: stainless steel, ø 41.6 mm, height 10 mm; sapphire crystal; screw-down case back; water-resistant to 5 atm
Band: leather, double folding clasp
Price: $3,640; limited and numbered edition of 99 pieces
Variations: gold-plated dial ($3,900); brown leather strap

IWC

It was an American who laid the cornerstone for an industrial watch factory in Schaffhausen—now environmentally state-of-the-art facilities. In 1868, Florentine Ariosto Jones, watchmaker and engineer from Boston, crossed the Atlantic to the then low-wage venue of Switzerland to open the International Watch Company Schaffhausen.

Jones was a talented designer as well, who had a significant influence on the development of watch movements. Soon, he gave IWC its own seal of approval, the *Ingenieursmarke* (Engineer's Brand), a standard it still maintains today. The company has never deviated from that course, in spite of many different owners. In 2000, it joined Richemont Group.

CEO George Kern (at Breitling since 2017) introduced a bit of flashiness. He pushed in-house movements, such as those found in the Da Vinci and Ingenieur models, and of course the Portuguese, which is still going strong more than seventy-five years after it was first released.

The firm's 150th anniversary was celebrated in 2018 under a new CEO (Christoph Grainger-Herr). A total of twenty-seven limited edition special models were shown at the beginning of the year, each with "150 Years" stamped on the back. The range covers robust pilot's watches, refined Da Vincis, elegant Portofinos, and complicated Portuguese. And then there is the unabashedly retro Pallweber series, which borrows from a pocket watch from the 1880s showing digital time.

IWC movements include the Jones caliber, named for the IWC founder, and the pocket watch caliber 89, introduced in 1946 as the creation of then technical director Albert Pellaton. Four years later, Pellaton created the first IWC automatic movement and, with it, a company monument. In 2019, the company reworked its iconic pilot's watches, whose design recalls iconic navigation watches like the Mark 11 that IWC supplied the RAF with. These large watches are not just replicas. They contain modern elements that ensure their timelessness. The careful balance between tapping into past glories to keep fans happy and bringing newcomers to the brand continues to boost IWC.

International Watch Co.
Baumgartenstrasse 15
CH-8201 Schaffhausen
Switzerland

Tel.:
+41-52-635-6565

E-mail:
info@iwc.com

Website:
www.iwc.com

Founded:
1868

Number of employees:
approx. 750

U.S. distributor:
IWC North America
645 Fifth Avenue, 5th Floor
New York, NY 10022
800-432-9330

Most important collections/price range:
Da Vinci, Pilot's, Portuguese, Ingenieur, Aquatimer, Pallweber / approx. $4,000 to $260,000

Pilot's Watch Timezoner Spitfire Edition "The Longest Flight"

Reference number: IW395501
Movement: automatic, IWC Caliber 82760; ø 30 mm; 25 jewels; 28,800 vph; Pellaton winding system; 60-hour power reserve
Functions: hours, minutes, sweep seconds; additional 24-hour display; date
Case: stainless steel, ø 46 mm, height 15.2 mm; bidirectional bezel for rapid setting of local time, with city references; sapphire crystal; screw-in crown; water-resistant to 6 atm
Band: textile, buckle
Remarks: limited to 250 pieces for the round-the-world flight of the Silver Spitfire
Price: $12,400

Big Pilot's Watch Perpetual Calendar Spitfire

Reference number: IW503601
Movement: automatic, IWC Caliber 52615; ø 37.8 mm, height 9 mm; 54 jewels; 28,800 vph; Pellaton winding system; 168-hour power reserve
Functions: hours, minutes, subsidiary seconds; power reserve indicator; perpetual calendar with date, weekday, month, moon phase, 4-digit year display
Case: bronze, ø 46.2 mm, height 15.4 mm; sapphire crystal; transparent case back; screw-in crown; water-resistant to 6 atm
Band: calfskin, buckle
Price: $28,200; limited to 250 pieces

Pilot's Watch UTC Spitfire Edition "MJ271"

Reference number: IW327101
Movement: automatic, IWC Caliber 82710; ø 30 mm, 22 jewels; 28,800 vph; Pellaton winding system, amagnetic soft iron core; 60-hour power reserve
Functions: hours, minutes, sweep seconds; additional 24-hour display (2nd time zone); date
Case: bronze, ø 41 mm, height 14.2 mm; sapphire crystal; water-resistant to 6 atm
Band: calfskin, buckle
Remarks: limited to 271 pieces for the planned round-the-world flight of the Silver Spitfire (marked MJ271)
Price: $8,950

Pilot's Watch Chronograph Spitfire

Reference number: IW387901
Movement: automatic, IWC Caliber 69380 (base ETA 7750); ø 30 mm, height 7.9 mm; 33 jewels; 28,800 vph; amagnetic soft iron core; 46-hour power reserve
Functions: hours, minutes, subsidiary seconds; chronograph; date, weekday
Case: stainless steel, ø 41 mm, height 15.3 mm; sapphire crystal; screw-in crown; water-resistant to 6 atm
Band: textile, buckle
Price: $5,700

Pilot's Watch Automatic Spitfire

Reference number: IW326802
Movement: automatic, IWC Caliber 32110; ø 28.2 mm, height 4.2 mm; 21 jewels; 28,800 vph; amagnetic soft iron core; 72-hour power reserve
Functions: hours, minutes, sweep seconds; date
Case: bronze, ø 39 mm, height 10.6 mm; sapphire crystal; screw-in crown; water-resistant to 6 atm
Band: calfskin, buckle
Price: $4,900

Pilot's Watch Automatic 36

Reference number: IW324010
Movement: automatic, IWC Caliber 35111 (base Sellita SW300-1); ø 25.6 mm, height 3.6 mm; 25 jewels; 28,800 vph; amagnetic soft iron core; 42-hour power reserve
Functions: hours, minutes, sweep seconds; date
Case: stainless steel, ø 36 mm, height 10.7 mm; sapphire crystal; screw-in crown; water-resistant to 6 atm
Band: stainless steel, folding clasp
Price: $5,150

Pilot's Watch Chronograph Top Gun

Reference number: IW389101
Movement: automatic, IWC Caliber 69380 (base ETA 7750); ø 30 mm, height 7.9 mm; 33 jewels; 28,800 vph; amagnetic soft iron core; 46-hour power reserve
Functions: automatic, minutes, subsidiary seconds; chronograph; date, weekday
Case: ceramic, ø 44.5 mm, height 15.7 mm; sapphire crystal; screw-in crown; water-resistant to 6 atm
Band: textile, buckle
Price: $7,550

Pilot's Watch Double Chronograph Top Gun Ceratanium

Reference number: IW371815
Movement: automatic, IWC Caliber 79420 (base ETA 7750); ø 30 mm, height 7.9 mm; 29 jewels; 28,800 vph; amagnetic soft iron core; 44-hour power reserve
Functions: hours, minutes, subsidiary seconds; split-second chronograph; date, weekday
Case: special ceramic-titanium alloy (ceratanium), ø 44 mm, height 16.8 mm; sapphire crystal; screw-in crown; water-resistant to 6 atm
Band: textile, buckle
Price: $14,600

Pilot's Watch Perpetual Calendar Chronograph "Le Petit Prince"

Reference number: IW392202
Movement: automatic, IWC Caliber 89630; ø 30 mm, height 9 mm; 51 jewels; 28,800 vph; 68-hour power reserve
Functions: hours, minutes, subsidiary seconds; flyback chronograph; perpetual calendar with date, weekday, month, moon phase, 4-digit year display
Case: red gold, ø 43 mm, height 15.9 mm; sapphire crystal; transparent case back; screw-in crown; water-resistant to 6 atm
Band: calfskin, folding clasp
Price: $38,300; limited to 250 pieces

IWC

Aquatimer Chronograph Edition "Laureus Sport for Good"
Reference number: IW379507
Movement: automatic, IWC Caliber 89365; ø 30 mm, height 7.5 mm; 35 jewels; 28,800 vph; 68-hour power reserve
Functions: hours, minutes, subsidiary seconds; chronograph; date
Case: stainless steel with black rubber coating, ø 45 mm, height 16.9 mm; crown-activated scale ring, 0-60 scale; sapphire crystal; screw-in crown; water-resistant to 30 atm
Band: rubber, buckle
Price: $11,700; limited to 1,000 pieces

Portuguese Yacht Club Chronograph
Reference number: IW390507
Movement: automatic, IWC Caliber 89361; ø 30 mm, height 7.5 mm; 38 jewels; 28,800 vph; Pellaton winding system, column wheel control of chronograph functions; 68-hour power reserve
Functions: hours, minutes, subsidiary seconds; flyback chronograph; date
Case: stainless steel, ø 43.5 mm, height 14.2 mm; sapphire crystal; transparent case back; screw-in crown; water-resistant to 6 atm
Band: rubber, folding clasp
Price: $12,100

Portuguese Automatic
Reference number: IW500712
Movement: automatic, IWC Caliber 52010; ø 37.8 mm, height 7.5 mm; 31 jewels; 28,800 vph; 168-hour power reserve
Functions: hours, minutes, subsidiary seconds; power reserve indicator; date
Case: stainless steel, ø 42.3 mm, height 14.2 mm; sapphire crystal; transparent case back; water-resistant to 3 atm
Band: reptile skin, buckle
Price: $12,700

Portofino Hand-Wound Eight Days
Reference number: IW510115
Movement: manually wound, IWC Caliber 59210; ø 37.8 mm, height 5.8 mm; 30 jewels; 28,800 vph; Breguet hairspring; 192-hour power reserve
Functions: hours, minutes, subsidiary seconds; power reserve indicator; date
Case: stainless steel, ø 45 mm, height 11.7 mm; sapphire crystal; transparent case back; water-resistant to 3 atm
Band: suede, buckle
Price: $9,700

Da Vinci Automatic Moon Phase 36
Reference number: IW459306
Movement: automatic, IWC Caliber 35800; ø 25.6 mm, height 5.35 mm; 25 jewels; 28,800 vph; 42-hour power reserve
Functions: hours, minutes, sweep seconds; moon phase
Case: stainless steel, ø 36 mm, height 11.7 mm; sapphire crystal; water-resistant to 3 atm
Band: reptile skin, buckle
Price: $8,500
Variations: red gold

Tribute to Pallweber Edition "150 Years" Pocket Watch
Reference number: IW505101
Movement: manually wound, IWC Caliber 94200; ø 37.8 mm, height 7.3 mm; 54 jewels; 28,800 vph; Breguet hairspring; 60-hour power reserve
Functions: hours, minutes (digital), subsidiary seconds
Case: red gold, ø 52 mm, height 14.2 mm; sapphire crystal
Band: red gold, chain
Price: $66,500; limited to 50 pieces

IWC

Caliber 32110

Automatic; silicon anchor and escape wheel; stop-seconds mechanism; double-pawl winding (Pellaton system); single spring barrel, 72-hour power reserve
Functions: hours, minutes, sweep seconds; date
Diameter: 28.2 mm
Height: 4.2 mm
Jewels: 21
Frequency: 28,800 vph

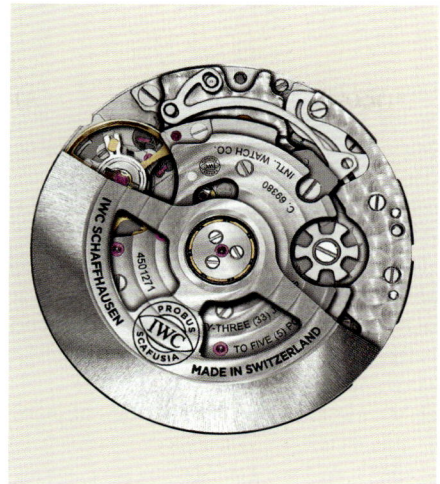

Caliber 69380

Automatic; column wheel control of chronograph functions; single spring barrel, 46-hour power reserve
Functions: hours, minutes, subsidiary seconds; chronograph; date, weekday
Diameter: 30 mm
Height: 7.9 mm
Jewels: 33
Balance: glucydur
Frequency: 28,800 vph

Caliber 52615

Automatic; double-pawl winding (Pellaton system) with ceramic wheels; double spring barrel, 168-hour power reserve
Functions: hours, minutes, subsidiary seconds; power reserve indicator; perpetual calendar with month, weekday, date, double moon phase display (for northern and southern hemispheres), 4-digit year display
Diameter: 37.8 mm
Height: 9 mm
Jewels: 54
Balance: with variable inertia
Frequency: 28,800 vph
Balance spring: Breguet
Shock protection: Incabloc

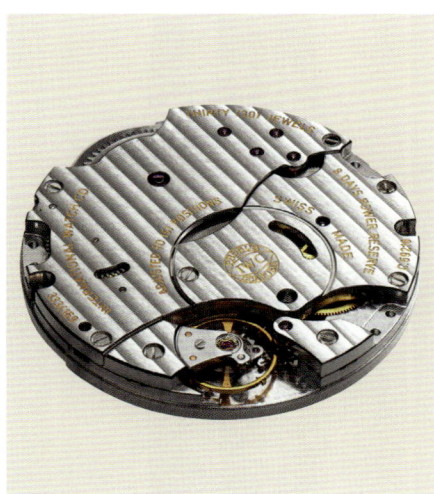

Caliber 59210

Manually wound; single spring barrel, 192-hour power reserve
Functions: hours, minutes, subsidiary seconds; power reserve indicator; date
Diameter: 37.8 mm
Height: 5.8 mm
Jewels: 30
Balance: glucydur with variable inertia
Frequency: 28,800 vph
Balance spring: Breguet
Shock protection: Incabloc

Caliber 89361

Automatic; double-pawl winding (Pellaton system); column wheel control of chronograph functions; single spring barrel, 68-hour power reserve
Base caliber: 89000
Functions: hours, minutes, subsidiary seconds; flyback chronograph; date
Diameter: 30 mm
Height: 7.46 mm
Jewels: 38
Balance: glucydur with variable inertia
Frequency: 28,800 vph
Balance spring: flat hairspring
Shock protection: Incabloc
Remarks: concentric chronograph counter for minutes and hours

Caliber 98295 "Jones"

Manually wound; single spring barrel, 46-hour power reserve
Base caliber: 98000
Functions: hours, minutes, subsidiary seconds
Diameter: 38.2 mm
Height: 5.3 mm
Jewels: 18
Balance: screw balance with fine adjustment cams
Frequency: 18,000 vph
Balance spring: Breguet
Shock protection: Incabloc
Remarks: exceptionally long regulator index; three-quarter plate of German silver, hand-engraved balance cock

JAEGER-LECOULTRE

The Jaeger-LeCoultre *manufacture* has had a long and tumultuous history. In 1833, Antoine LeCoultre opened his own workshop for the production of gearwheels. Having made his fortune, he then did what many other artisans did: In 1866, he had a large house built and brought together all the craftspeople needed to produce timepieces, from the watchmakers to the turners and polishers. He outfitted the workshop with the most modern machinery of the day, all powered by a steam engine. "La Grande Maison" was the first watch *manufacture* in the Vallée de Joux.

At the start of the twentieth century, the grandson of the company founder, Jacques-David LeCoultre, built slender, complicated watches for the Paris manufacturer Edmond Jaeger. The Frenchman was so impressed with these that, after a few years of fruitful cooperation, he engineered a merger of the two companies.

In the 1970s, the German VDO Group (later Mannesmann) took over the company and helped it weather the quartz crisis.

In 2000, Mannesmann's watch division (JLC, IWC, A. Lange & Söhne) sold Jaeger-LeCoultre to the Richemont Group. Given the group's strength, Jaeger-LeCoultre continued to grow. A vast array of calibers (around 1,250, in fact), including minute repeaters, tourbillons, and other *grandes complications,* a lubricant-free movement, and more than 400 patents, tell their own story. Today, it is the largest employer in the Vallée de Joux—just as it was back in the 1860s. The most enduring collection produced by the brand is probably the Reverso, which can swivel around to show a second watch face on the back. Jaeger-LeCoultre boasts other iconic collections, like the Master, the Polaris, the Rendez-Vous, and the Atmos.

The brand has always managed to unify technical wizardry with a very fine sense of esthetics. The largest employer in the Vallée de Joux excels in what is known as *métiers rares,* rare handcrafts, and in a rather fascinating ability to create extraordinary timepieces, like the Millionomètre and the famous Gyrotourbillon.

Manufacture Jaeger-LeCoultre
Rue de la Golisse, 8
CH-1347 Le Sentier
Switzerland

Tel.:
+41-21-852-0202

E-mail:
info@jaeger-lecoultre.com

Website:
www.jaeger-lecoultre.com

Founded:
1833

Number of employees:
over 1,000

Annual production:
approx. 50,000 watches

U.S. distributor:
Jaeger-LeCoultre
645 Fifth Avenue
New York, NY 10022
800-JLC-TIME
www.jaeger-lecoultre.com

Most important collections/price range:
Atmos / starting at $6,600; Duomètre / starting at $39,100; Geophysic / starting at $9,100; Master / starting at $5,700; Polaris / starting at $6,600; Rendez-Vous / starting at $8,700; Reverso / starting at $4,150

Polaris Chronograph
Reference number: 902 81 80
Movement: automatic, JLC Caliber 751H; ø 25.6 mm, height 5.7 mm; 37 jewels; 28,800 vph; skeletonized rotor; 65-hour power reserve
Functions: hours, minutes; chronograph
Case: stainless steel, ø 42 mm, height 11.9 mm; sapphire crystal; transparent case back; water-resistant to 10 atm
Band: stainless steel, double folding clasp
Price: $10,700
Variations: calfskin strap ($9,850)

Polaris Chronograph
Reference number: 902 84 71
Movement: automatic, JLC Caliber 751H; ø 25.6 mm, height 5.7 mm; 37 jewels; 28,800 vph; skeletonized rotor; 65-hour power reserve
Functions: hours, minutes; chronograph
Case: stainless steel, ø 42 mm, height 11.9 mm; sapphire crystal; transparent case back; water-resistant to 10 atm
Band: calfskin, double folding clasp
Price: $9,750
Variations: stainless steel bracelet ($10,800)

Polaris Chronograph
Reference number: 902 24 50
Movement: automatic, JLC Caliber 751H; ø 25.6 mm, height 5.7 mm; 37 jewels; 28,800 vph; skeletonized rotor; 65-hour power reserve
Functions: hours, minutes; chronograph
Case: pink gold, ø 42 mm, height 11.9 mm; sapphire crystal; transparent case back; water-resistant to 10 atm
Band: reptile skin, double folding clasp
Price: $23,900

JAEGER-LECOULTRE

Polaris Automatic
Reference number: 900 84 80
Movement: automatic, JLC Caliber 898E/1; ø 26 mm, height 3.3 mm; 30 jewels; 28,800 vph; 40-hour power reserve
Functions: hours, minutes, sweep seconds
Case: stainless steel, ø 41 mm, height 11.2 mm; crown-activated scale ring, with 0-60 scale; sapphire crystal; transparent case back; water-resistant to 10 atm
Band: calfskin, double folding clasp
Price: $6,600
Variations: stainless steel bracelet ($7,600)

Polaris Automatic
Reference number: 900 81 70
Movement: automatic, JLC Caliber 898E/1; ø 26 mm, height 3.3 mm; 30 jewels; 28,800 vph; 40-hour power reserve
Functions: hours, minutes, sweep seconds
Case: stainless steel, ø 41 mm, height 11.2 mm; crown-activated scale ring, with 0-60 scale; sapphire crystal; transparent case back; water-resistant to 10 atm
Band: stainless steel, double folding clasp
Price: $7,450
Variations: calfskin strap ($6,700)

Polaris Date
Reference number: 906 86 70
Movement: automatic, JLC Caliber 899A/1; ø 26 mm, height 4.6 mm; 32 jewels; 28,800 vph; 38-hour power reserve
Functions: hours, minutes, sweep seconds; date
Case: stainless steel, ø 42 mm, height 13.1 mm; crown-activated scale ring, with 0-60 scale; sapphire crystal; transparent case back; water-resistant to 20 atm
Band: rubber, double folding clasp
Price: $7,600

Polaris Memovox
Reference number: 903 86 70
Movement: automatic, JLC Caliber 956; ø 28 mm, height 7.45 mm; 23 jewels; 28,800 vph; 45-hour power reserve
Functions: hours, minutes, sweep seconds; alarm; date
Case: stainless steel, ø 42 mm, height 15.9 mm; crown-activated scale ring, with 0-60 scale; sapphire crystal; water-resistant to 20 atm
Band: rubber, double folding clasp
Price: $12,600

Polaris Chronograph WT
Reference number: 905 T4 80
Movement: automatic, JLC Caliber 752A; ø 28 mm, height 5.7 mm; 37 jewels; 28,800 vph; 2 spring barrels, 65-hour power reserve
Functions: hours, minutes; world time indicator (2nd time zone); chronograph
Case: titanium, ø 44 mm, height 12.5 mm; sapphire crystal; transparent case back; water-resistant to 10 atm
Band: calfskin, double folding clasp
Price: $14,100

Polaris Chronograph WT
Reference number: 905 T4 70
Movement: automatic, JLC Caliber 752A; ø 28 mm, height 5.7 mm; 37 jewels; 28,800 vph; 2 spring barrels, 65-hour power reserve
Functions: hours, minutes; world time indicator (2nd time zone); chronograph
Case: titanium, ø 44 mm, height 12.5 mm; sapphire crystal; transparent case back; water-resistant to 10 atm
Band: reptile skin, double folding clasp
Price: $14,100
Variations: calfskin strap ($14,300)

JAEGER-LECOULTRE

Reverso Classic Medium Small Seconds
Reference number: 243 85 22
Movement: manually wound, JLC Caliber 822/2; 17.2 × 22 mm, height 2.94 mm; 19 jewels; 21,600 vph; 42-hour power reserve
Functions: hours, minutes, subsidiary seconds
Case: stainless steel, 25.5 × 42.9 mm, height 7.5 mm; sapphire crystal; water-resistant to 3 atm
Band: calfskin, buckle
Remarks: case can be turned and rotated 180°
Price: $6,100

Reverso Tribute Moon
Reference number: 395 84 20
Movement: manually wound, JLC Caliber 853A; 17.2 × 22 mm, height 5.15 mm; 19 jewels; 21,600 vph; 42-hour power reserve
Functions: hours, minutes; additional 12-hour display (2nd time zone), day/night indicator (on rear); date, moon phase
Case: stainless steel, 29.9 × 49.4 mm, height 10.9 mm; sapphire crystal; water-resistant to 3 atm
Remarks: case can be turned and rotated 180°
Band: reptile skin, double folding clasp
Price: $13,400

Reverso Tribute Gyrotourbillon
Reference number: 394 64 20
Movement: manually wound, JLC Caliber 179; 26.2 × 41 mm, height 5.97 mm; 52 jewels; 21,600 vph; double-axis spherical tourbillon with different rotation times (60 and 12.6 seconds), Gyrolab balance with hemispheric hairspring; certified chronometer according to German Industrial Norm (DIN)
Functions: hours, minutes, subsidiary seconds (on tourbillon cage); additional 12-hour display (2nd time zone, on movement side), day/night indicator
Case: platinum, 31 × 51.1 mm, height 12.4 mm; sapphire crystal; water-resistant to 3 atm
Band: reptile skin, double folding clasp
Remarks: case can be turned and rotated 180°
Price: $314,000; limited to 75 pieces

Reverso Tribute Duoface
Reference number: 390 24 20
Movement: manually wound, JLC Caliber 854A/2; 17.2 × 22 mm, height 3.8 mm; 19 jewels; 21,600 vph; 42-hour power reserve
Functions: hours, minutes, subsidiary seconds; additional 24-hour display (2nd time zone) on rear
Case: red gold, 25.5 × 42.9 mm, height 9.2 mm; sapphire crystal; water-resistant to 3 atm
Band: reptile skin, folding clasp
Remarks: case can be turned and rotated 180°
Price: $10,400

Reverso Classic Large Duoface Small Seconds
Reference number: 384 25 20
Movement: manually wound, JLC Caliber 854A/2; 17.2 × 22 mm, height 3.8 mm; 19 jewels; 21,600 vph; 42-hour power reserve
Functions: hours, minutes, subsidiary seconds; additional 24-hour display (2nd time zone, on movement side)
Case: red gold, 28.3 × 47 mm, height 10.3 mm; sapphire crystal; water-resistant to 3 atm
Band: reptile skin, buckle
Remarks: case can be turned and rotated 180°
Price: $20,100
Variations: stainless steel ($8,700)

Reverso Tribute Duoface
Reference number: 398 84 82
Movement: manually wound, JLC Caliber 854A/2; 17.2 × 22 mm, height 3.8 mm; 19 jewels; 21,600 vph; 42-hour power reserve
Functions: hours, minutes, subsidiary seconds; additional 24-hour display (2nd time zone) on rear
Case: stainless steel, 28.3 × 47 mm, height 10.3 mm; sapphire crystal; water-resistant to 3 atm
Band: calfskin, double folding clasp
Remarks: case can be turned and rotated 180°
Price: $10,400

JAEGER-LECOULTRE

Master Ultra-Thin Perpetual
Reference number: 130 84 70
Movement: automatic, JLC Caliber 868/1; ø 27.8 mm, height 4.72 mm; 46 jewels; 38-hour power reserve
Functions: hours, minutes, sweep seconds; perpetual calendar with date, weekday, month, moon phase, 4-digit year display
Case: stainless steel, ø 39 mm, height 9.2 mm; sapphire crystal; transparent case back; water-resistant to 5 atm
Band: reptile skin, double folding clasp
Price: $19,000

Master Ultra-Thin Moon Enamel
Reference number: 136 35 E1
Movement: automatic, JLC Caliber 925/2; ø 26 mm, height 4.9 mm; 30 jewels; 28,800 vph; 70-hour power reserve
Functions: hours, minutes, sweep seconds; date, moon phase
Case: white gold, ø 39 mm, height 10.04 mm; sapphire crystal; transparent case back; water-resistant to 5 atm
Band: reptile skin, buckle
Remarks: enamel dial
Price: $35,800; limited to 100 pieces

Master Ultra-Thin Tourbillon Enamel
Reference number: 132 34 E1
Movement: automatic, JLC Caliber 978F; ø 30 mm, height 7.2 mm; 35 jewels; 28,800 vph; 1-minute tourbillon; 45-hour power reserve
Functions: hours, minutes, subsidiary seconds (on tourbillon cage); date
Case: white gold, ø 40 mm, height 12.13 mm; sapphire crystal; transparent case back; water-resistant to 5 atm
Band: reptile skin, double folding clasp
Remarks: enamel dial
Price: $88,500; limited to 50 pieces

Master Ultra-Thin Perpetual Enamel
Reference number: 130 35 E1
Movement: automatic, JLC Caliber 868A/2; ø 26 mm, height 4.72 mm; 46 jewels; 28,800 vph; 70-hour power reserve
Functions: hours, minutes, sweep seconds; perpetual calendar with date, weekday, month, moon phase, 4-digit year display
Case: white gold, ø 39 mm, height 10.44 mm; sapphire crystal; transparent case back; water-resistant to 5 atm
Band: reptile skin, buckle
Remarks: enamel dial
Price: $55,000; limited to 50 pieces

Master Ultra-Thin Tourbillon
Reference number: 168 24 10
Movement: automatic, JLC Caliber 978G; ø 30 mm, height 6.5 mm; 33 jewels; 28,800 vph; 1-minute tourbillon; 45-hour power reserve
Functions: hours, minutes, subsidiary seconds (on tourbillon cage)
Case: red gold, ø 40 mm, height 10.77 mm; sapphire crystal; transparent case back; water-resistant to 5 atm
Band: reptile skin, double folding clasp
Price: $70,500

Master Ultra-Thin Date
Reference number: 123 84 20
Movement: automatic, JLC Caliber 899/1; ø 26 mm, height 3.3 mm; 32 jewels; 28,800 vph; 38-hour power reserve
Functions: hours, minutes, sweep seconds; date
Case: stainless steel, ø 39 mm, height 7.8 mm; sapphire crystal; transparent case back; water-resistant to 5 atm
Band: reptile skin, double folding clasp
Price: $7,500

JAEGER-LECOULTRE

Caliber 179
Manually wound; double-axis spherical tourbillon with different rotation times (60 and 12.6 seconds); double spring barrel, 40-hour power reserve
Functions: hours, minutes, subsidiary seconds (on tourbillon cage); additional 12-hour display (2nd time zone) and day/night indicator (on rear)
Measurements: 26.2 × 41 mm
Height: 6.85 mm
Jewels: 52
Balance: Gyrolab with hemispheric hairspring
Remarks: 385 parts

Caliber 751H
Automatic; column wheel control of chronograph functions; double spring barrel, 65-hour power reserve
Functions: hours, minutes, subsidiary seconds; chronograph
Diameter: 26.2 mm
Height: 5.7 mm
Jewels: 37
Balance: screw balance with 4 weights
Frequency: 28,800 vph
Balance spring: flat hairspring
Shock protection: Kif

Caliber 752A
Automatic; column wheel control of chronograph functions; double spring barrel, 65-hour power reserve
Functions: hours, minutes, subsidiary seconds; chronograph; date; world time indicator
Diameter: 26.2 mm
Height: 5.7 mm
Jewels: 37
Balance: screw balance with 4 weights
Frequency: 28,800 vph
Balance spring: flat hairspring
Shock protection: Kif
Remarks: plate with perlage, bridges with côtes de Genève

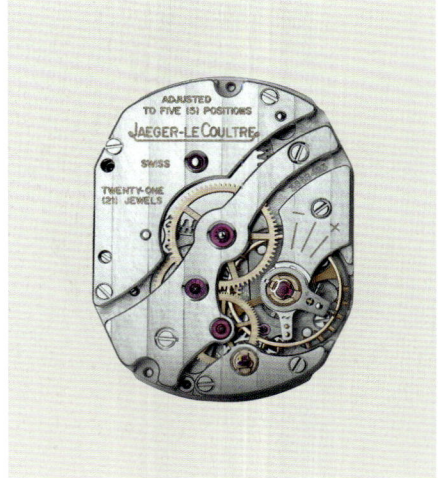

Caliber 822/2
Manually wound; single spring barrel, 42-hour power reserve
Functions: hours, minutes, subsidiary seconds
Measurements: 17.2 × 22 mm
Height: 2.94 mm
Jewels: 19
Balance: screw balance
Frequency: 21,600 vph
Balance spring: flat hairspring

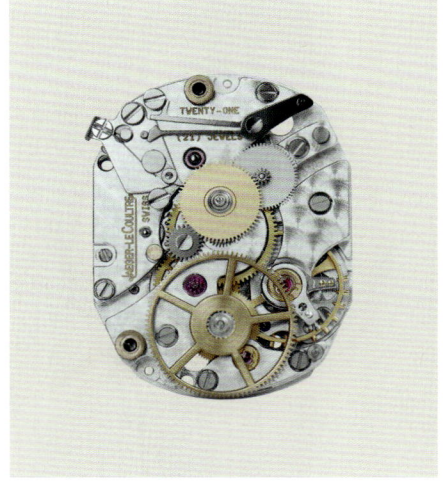

Caliber 854A/2
Manually wound; single spring barrel, 42-hour power reserve
Functions: hours, minutes, subsidiary seconds; additional 24-hour display (2nd time zone) on movement side
Measurements: 13 × 15.2 mm
Height: 3.8 mm
Jewels: 19
Balance: glucydur
Frequency: 21,600 vph
Balance spring: flat hairspring
Shock protection: Kif
Remarks: 160 parts

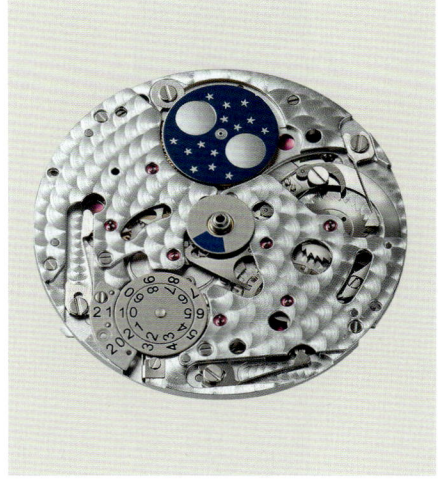

Caliber 868/1
Automatic; single spring barrel, 38-hour power reserve
Functions: hours, minutes, sweep seconds; perpetual calendar with date, weekday, month, moon phase, 4-digit year display
Diameter: 27.8 mm
Height: 4.72 mm
Jewels: 46
Balance: glucydur
Frequency: 28,800 vph
Remarks: 336 parts

JAEGER-LECOULTRE

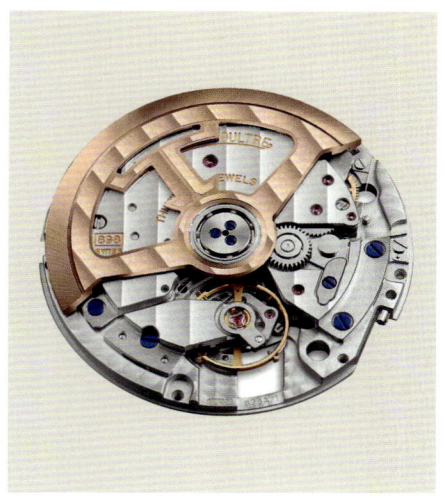

Caliber 898E/1

Automatic; single spring barrel, 40-hour power reserve
Functions: hours, minutes, sweep seconds
Diameter: 26 mm
Height: 3.3 mm
Jewels: 30
Balance: glucydur, 4 regulating screws
Frequency: 28,800 vph
Balance spring: flat hairspring
Shock protection: Kif

Caliber 925/2

Automatic; single spring barrel, 70-hour power reserve
Functions: hours, minutes, sweep seconds; date, moon phase
Diameter: 26 mm
Height: 4.9 mm
Jewels: 30
Frequency: 28,800 vph
Remarks: 245 parts

Caliber 868/A2

Automatic; single spring barrel, 70-hour power reserve
Functions: hours, minutes, sweep seconds; perpetual calendar with date, weekday, month, moon phase, 4-digit year display
Diameter: 26 mm
Height: 4.72 mm
Jewels: 46
Balance: glucydur
Frequency: 28,800 vph
Remarks: 332 parts

Caliber 956

Automatic; automatic winding for the time and alarm mechanisms; single spring barrel, 45-hour power reserve
Functions: hours, minutes, sweep seconds; date; alarm
Diameter: 28 mm
Height: 7.45 mm
Jewels: 23
Balance: glucydur
Frequency: 28,800 vph
Balance spring: flat hairspring
Remarks: perlage on mainplate, bridges with côtes de Genève, element for sounding board

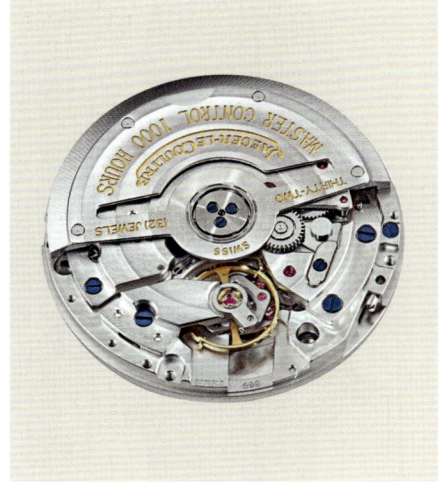

Caliber 899/1

Automatic; single spring barrel, 38-hour power reserve
Functions: hours, minutes, sweep seconds; date
Diameter: 26 mm
Height: 3.3 mm
Jewels: 32
Frequency: 28,800 vph
Remarks: 219 parts

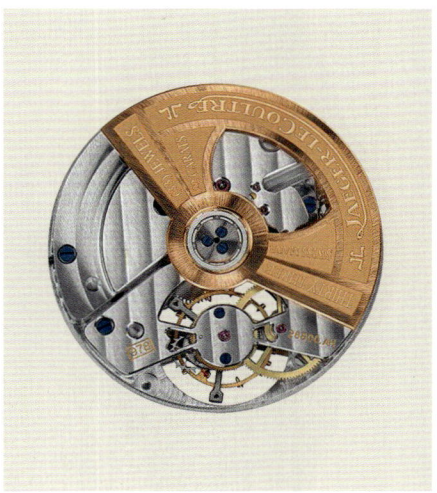

Caliber 978F

Automatic; 1-minute tourbillon, gold rotor; single spring barrel, 45-hour power reserve
Functions: hours, minutes, subsidiary seconds (on tourbillon cage); subsidiary dial for date, with jumping hand between the 15th and 16th
Diameter: 30 mm
Height: 7.2 mm
Jewels: 35
Balance: glucydur with weighted screws
Frequency: 28,800 vph
Balance spring: Breguet hairspring
Shock protection: Kif
Remarks: mainplate with perlage, bridges with côtes de Genève; 302 parts

JAQUET DROZ

Though this watch brand first gained real notice when it was bought by the Swatch Group in 2001, Jaquet Droz looks back on a long tradition. Pierre Jaquet-Droz (1721–1790) was actually supposed to be a pastor, but instead followed the call to become a mechanic and a watchmaker. In the mid-eighteenth century, he began to push the limits of micromechanics, and his enthusiasm for it quickly led him to work on watch mechanisms and more complicated movements, which he attempted to operate through purely mechanical means.

Jaquet-Droz became famous in Europe for his automatons. More than once, he had to answer to religious institutions, whose guardians of public morals suspected there might be some devil's work and witchcraft behind his mechanical children, scribes, and organists. He even designed prostheses. A small enterprise in La Chaux-de-Fonds still produces items of this applied art, proof that the name Jaquet-Droz is still alive and well in the Jura mountains, and its watches combined with automatons continue to thrill collectors and enthusiasts alike.

The Swatch Group has developed an esthetically and technically sophisticated collection based on outstanding wristwatch movements from Le Brassus (the former Frédéric Piguet movement factory, now serving as the exclusive extended workbench for the top-of-the-line brands in the Swatch Group portfolio). In recent years, the classically beautiful watch dials have taken on a slightly modern look without losing any of their identity. The brand has also amazed the watch world with a number of beautiful and clever automatons for the wrist.

Montres Jaquet Droz SA
CH-2300 La Chaux-de-Fonds
Switzerland

Tel.:
+41-32-924-2888

E-mail:
info@jaquet-droz.com

Website:
www.jaquet-droz.com

Founded:
1738

U.S. Distribution:
The Swatch Group (U.S.), Inc.
1200 Harbor Boulevard
Weehawken, NJ 07086
201-271-1400
www.swatchgroup.com

Most important collections:
Les Ateliers d'Art, Grande Seconde, Grande Seconde SW, Astrale Collection, Petite Heure Minute, Lady 8

Grande Seconde Skelet-One
Reference number: J003525541
Movement: automatic, Jaquet Droz Caliber 2663 SQ; ø 26.2 mm, height 3.8 mm; 30 jewels; 28,800 vph; double spring barrel, silicon pallet fork horns and hairspring; skeletonized movement, oscillating mass in white gold; 68-hour power reserve
Functions: hours, minutes (off-center), subsidiary seconds
Case: ceramic, ø 41.5 mm, height 12.48 mm; sapphire crystal; transparent case back; water-resistant to 3 atm
Band: textile, folding clasp
Remarks: sapphire crystal dial
Price: $23,600

Grande Seconde Off-Centered Chronograph Blue
Reference number: J007830241
Movement: automatic, Jaquet Droz Caliber 26M5R; 34 jewels; 21,600 vph; silicon hairspring and anchor horns; column wheel control of chronograph functions using a single pusher; oscillating mass in red gold; 40-hour power reserve
Functions: hours, minutes (off-center); chronograph; date
Case: stainless steel, ø 43 mm, height 14.83 mm; sapphire crystal; water-resistant to 3 atm
Band: reptile skin, folding clasp
Price: $19,400

Petite Heure Minute Smalta Clara Tiger
Reference number: J005504500
Movement: automatic, Jaquet Droz Caliber 6150; ø 17.5 mm; 29 jewels; 21,600 vph; 38-hour power reserve
Functions: hours, minutes (off-center)
Case: white gold, ø 35 mm, height 10.85 mm; bezel and lugs set with 100 diamonds; sapphire crystal; water-resistant to 3 atm
Band: satin, buckle
Remarks: dial encasement of translucent enamel, mother-of-pearl dial
Price: $54,600; limited to 28 pieces

Jörg Schauer
c/o Stowa GmbH & Co. KG
Gewerbepark 16
D-75331 Engelsbrand
Germany

Tel.:
+49-7082-942630

E-mail:
info@stowa.com

Website:
www.stowa.com

Founded:
1990

Number of employees:
25

Annual production:
approx. 500 watches

Distribution:
direct sales; online shop; please contact the address in Germany

JÖRG SCHAUER

Jörg Schauer's watches are first and foremost cool. The cases have been carefully worked; the look is planned to draw the eye. After all, he is a perfectionist and leaves nothing to chance. He works on every single case himself, polishing and performing his own brand of magic for as long as it takes to display his personal touch. This time-consuming process is one that Schauer believes is absolutely necessary. "I do this because I place a great deal of value on the fact that my cases are absolutely perfect," he explains. "I can do it better than anyone, and I would never let anyone else do it for me."

Schauer, a goldsmith by training, has been making watches since 1990. He began by doing one-off pieces in precious metals for collectors and then opened his business and simultaneously moved to stainless steel. His style is to produce functional, angular cases with visibly screwed-down bezels and straightforward dials in plain black or white. Forget finding any watch close to current trends in his collection; Schauer only builds timepieces that he genuinely likes.

Purchasing a Schauer is not that easy. He has chosen a strategy of genuine quality over quantity and produces only about 500 watches annually. This includes special watches like the One-Hand Durowe, running on a modified Unitas made by the movement manufacturer Durowe, which Schauer acquired in 2002. It has been revived as the One-Hand 44. His production structure is a vital part of his success and includes prototyping, movement modification, finishing, case production, dial painting, and printing—all done in Schauer's own workshop in Engelsbrand. Any support he needs from the outside he prefers to find among regional specialists.

One-Hand 44 Limited

Reference number: Einzeiger44limitiert
Movement: manually wound, modified ETA Caliber 6498; ø 36.6 mm, height 4.5 mm; 17 jewels; 18,000 vph; handmade gearwheel bridge; finely finished movement; 38-hour power reserve
Functions: hours (interim lines)
Case: stainless steel, ø 44 mm, height 10.6 mm; bezel fixed with 12 screws; sapphire crystal; transparent case back; water-resistant to 5 atm
Band: rubber, double folding clasp
Price: $2,646; limited to 100 pieces

Edition 10

Reference number: Ed10
Movement: automatic, ETA Caliber 7753; ø 30 mm, height 7.9 mm; 27 jewels; 28,800 vph; finished with ornamental stripes and blued screws, exclusive engraved "Schauer" rotor; 48-hour power reserve
Functions: hours, minutes, subsidiary seconds; chronograph
Case: stainless steel, ø 42 mm, height 15 mm; bezel fixed with 12 screws; sapphire crystal; transparent case back; water-resistant to 5 atm
Band: calfskin, double folding clasp
Price: $3,820
Variations: stainless steel bracelet ($4,110); reptile skin strap ($3,775); manually wound movement ($4,200)

Edition 12

Reference number: Ed12
Movement: automatic, ETA Caliber 7753; ø 30 mm, height 7.9 mm; 27 jewels; 28,800 vph; finished with ornamental stripes and blued screws, exclusive engraved "Schauer" rotor; 48-hour power reserve
Functions: hours, minutes, subsidiary seconds; chronograph
Case: stainless steel, ø 41 mm, height 15 mm; bezel fixed with 12 screws; sapphire crystal; transparent case back; water-resistant to 5 atm
Band: calfskin, double folding clasp
Price: $4,325
Variations: stainless steel bracelet ($4,725); reptile skin strap ($4,325); manually wound movement ($4,675)

JS WATCH CO.

When they weren't pillaging Europe and terrorizing populations from the British Isles to Russia, the Vikings were in fact a very hardworking and talented bunch, and when not roaming about, they tended their fields, their herds, their houses, and, as a number of exhibitions in the past twenty years have shown, made jewelry. Their work in this field is remarkable and fed their commercial supply chains, to use a modern term.

Iceland is where many descendants of the Norsemen live—a rugged and stark landscape, with over three hundred volcanoes and long winter nights. The ability to design and create fine jewelry lives on, and since 2003, the tiny country with a population of 330,000 has been producing watches as well, thanks to three friends, designer Grimkell Sigurþórsson, watchmaker Sigurður Gilbertsson, and Júlíus Heiðarsson.

Their first launch in 2005 of one hundred watches sold out within half a year, and so they persisted, using Swiss or German parts and movements (ETA, Sellita), but creating watches with some unique features paying tribute to their small but very creative country. The timepieces are inspired and named after an event, place, or year in Iceland or Icelandic history. "We made the Sif N.A.R.T., which was named for the first helicopter of Iceland's Coast Guard rescue teams and the North Atlantic Rescue Timer," says Sigurþórsson, now the Director of Design & Marketing of the tiny company. In 2018, when Iceland qualified for the Football World Cup, JS Watch Co. was ready with a limited series.

Other ways of tying their product to their country are the use of volcanic ash from the Eyjafjallajökull on the dial, or carving head letters (Höfðaletur) or Viking motifs into the case, as with the Frisland Goð Special Edition. The watches are otherwise very sober in style, classical and well balanced. They are worn by ordinary people, as well as some international stars who seem to appreciate the understatement radiated by this self-effacing brand

JS Watch Co.
Hverfisgata 82B
101 Reykjavik
Iceland

Tel.:
+354-551-05-00

E-mail:
info@jswatch.com

Website:
www.jswatch.com

Founded:
2003

Number of employees:
5

Annual production:
500 pieces

Distribution:
Retail and direct sales
info@jswatch.com
+354-551-41-00

Most important collections/price range:
Collection 101, Frisland, Islandus, Sif N.A.R.T. / $1,650 to $11,860

Collection 101 10 Year Edition
Reference number: 101-10-1
Movement: automatic, Soprod Caliber M100; ø 25.60 mm, height 3.60 mm; 25 jewels; 28,800 vph; 42-hour power reserve
Functions: central hours, minutes, subsidiary seconds; date
Case: stainless steel, ø 38.5 mm, height 10.3 mm; sapphire crystal; transparent case back; water-resistant to 5 atm
Band: ostrich skin, buckle
Price: $1,650
Variations: steel Milanese mesh bracelet ($1,885); in 32-mm with white and black dials

Islandus 1919 44 mm
Reference number: 191-44-3
Movement: automatic, Soprod Caliber M100; ø 25.60 mm, height 3.60 mm; 25 jewels; 28,800 vph; 42-hour power reserve
Functions: central hours, minutes, subsidiary seconds; date
Case: stainless steel, ø 44 mm, height 11.5 mm; sapphire crystal; transparent case back; water-resistant to 5 atm
Band: reptile skin, buckle
Price: $2,280
Variations: black dial

Sif N. A. R. T.
Reference number: Sif-40-4
Movement: automatic, ETA Caliber 2892A-2; ø 25.60 mm, height 3.60 mm; 25 jewels; 28,800 vph; 42-hour power reserve
Functions: central hours, minutes, subsidiary seconds; date
Case: brushed stainless steel black PVD, ø 40 mm, height 13.5 mm; extra-thick 4-mm sapphire crystal; screw-down crown; transparent case back; water-resistant to 100 atm
Band: calfskin, buckle
Remarks: official watch of the Icelandic Coast Guard
Price: $2,280
Variations: various straps, folding clasp; Volcano Edition with black and red dial ($7,248)

Uhrenfabrik Junghans GmbH & Co. KG
Geisshaldenstrasse 49
D-78713 Schramberg

Tel.:
+49-742-218-0

E-mail:
info@junghans.de

Website:
www.junghans.de

Founded:
1861

Number of employees:
127

Annual production:
approx. 60,000 watches

U.S. distributor:
DKSH Luxury & Lifestyle North America Inc.
9-D Princess Road
Lawrenceville, NJ 08648
609-750-8800

Most important collections/price range:
Meister; Max Bill by Junghans; MEGA; Form / from approx. $395 to $2,500; special pieces up to $10,000

JUNGHANS

Germany has another horological success story besides Glashütte. Schramberg, a recondite town in the Black Forest, is where Erhard Junghans founded a watchmaking factory in 1861. His son Arthur then developed it into a large-scale production site built on American models. And so Schramberg became the hub of the watchmaking world. Nearly three thousand men and women worked at that factory and made nine thousand wall clocks and alarm clocks daily.

In the boom years after World War II, the company, with its logo featuring a star, manufactured wristwatches. It went on to ring in modern times with its own solar and radio-controlled watches. Junghans was twice the official timekeeper at the Olympic Games, and for a long time it remained the largest chronometer maker in the world.

Mechanical watches made their comeback in the 1990s, which is when many people remembered the precision timekeepers from the Black Forest. Among them was Dr. Hans-Jochem Steim, a successful entrepreneur from Schramberg, who decided to boost the rebirth of the Schramberg brand. Steim and his son purchased the company and decided to take on the financing of the necessary structural measures themselves. Just in time for the company's 150th anniversary (2011), Junghans devised a new production and distribution schedule. Today, the brand is proud of its extensive collection of high-quality wristwatches, ranging from genuine icons of design to major classics, all the way to sporty chronographs. The Junghans success is also driving the growth of a number of suppliers. Schramberg is once again a big name in the region, and its fame has even spread throughout Germany and beyond. In 2018, the company opened a watch- and clockmaking museum in the restored Terrassenbau, a century-old terraced construction that allowed Junghans employees to work with outstanding natural lighting. Seven of the building's nine floors are devoted to company history and the history of the watch industry in the Black Forest. In the same year, Junghans came out with a brand-new radio-controlled movement, the Caliber J101, designed to mix high-tech with a classic look.

Meister Chronoscope Terrassenbau
Reference number: 027/4729.00
Movement: automatic, Caliber J880.1 (base ETA 7750); ø 30 mm, height 7.9 mm; 25 jewels; 28,800 vph; rhodium-plated movement, blued screws, rotor with côtes de Genève; 48-hour power reserve
Functions: hours, minutes, subsidiary seconds; chronograph; date, weekday; **Case:** stainless steel, ø 40.7 mm, height 13.9 mm; Plexiglas; water-resistant to 3 atm; **Band:** reptile skin, buckle
Remarks: hardened Plexiglas, antiscratch coating; anniversary model for 100th anniversary of Junghans's terraced industrial building
Price: $2,195; limited to 1,000 pieces
Variations: rose gold (limited to 100 pieces, $9,995)

Meister Chronoscope
Reference number: 027/7924.00
Movement: automatic, Caliber J880.1 (base ETA 7750 or Sellita SW500); ø 30 mm, height 7.9 mm; 25 jewels; 28,800 vph; rhodium-plated movement, blued screws, rotor with côtes de Genève; 48-hour power reserve; **Functions:** hours, minutes, subsidiary seconds; chronograph; date, weekday
Case: stainless steel with rose gold PVD coating, ø 40.7 mm, height 13.9 mm; Plexiglas; transparent case back; water-resistant to 3 atm
Band: reptile skin, buckle
Remarks: hardened Plexiglas with scratch-resistant coating
Price: $2,095; **Variations:** gray dial and horse leather strap ($2,095); without PVD, on link bracelet ($1,895)

Meister Telemeter
Reference number: 027/3380.44
Movement: automatic, Caliber J880.3 (base ETA 2892-2 with Dubois Dépraz module); ø 30 mm, height 6.5 mm; 45 jewels; 28,800 vph; rhodium-plated movement, blued screws, rotor with côtes de Genève; 42-hour power reserve
Functions: hours, minutes, subsidiary seconds; chronograph
Case: stainless steel, ø 40.8 mm, height 12.6 mm; Plexiglas; transparent case back; water-resistant to 3 atm
Band: stainless steel, folding clasp
Remarks: hardened Plexiglas with scratch-resistant coating
Price: $2,395; **Variations:** calfskin strap ($2,295)

JUNGHANS

Meister Pilot
Reference number: 027/3591.00
Movement: automatic, Caliber J880.4 (base ETA 2824-2 with Dubois Dépraz module); ø 30 mm, height 7.6 mm; 49 jewels; 28,800 vph; rhodium-plated movement, rotor with côtes de Genève; 38-hour power reserve
Functions: hours, minutes, subsidiary seconds; chronograph
Case: stainless steel, ø 43.3 mm, height 14.4 mm; sapphire crystal; water-resistant to 10 atm
Band: calfskin, buckle
Price: $2,495
Variations: black leather strap and green luminescent mass; with DLC coating ($2,695)

Meister Calendar
Reference number: 027/4906.00
Movement: automatic, Caliber J800.3 (base ETA 2824-2 or Sellita SW200-1 with Dubois Dépraz module); ø 25.6 mm, height 6.2 mm; 25 or 26 jewels; 28,800 vph; rhodium-plated movement, blued screws, rotor with côtes de Genève; 42-hour power reserve
Functions: hours, minutes, sweep seconds; full calendar with date, weekday, month, moon phase
Case: stainless steel, ø 40.4 mm, height 12 mm; Plexiglas; transparent case back; water-resistant to 3 atm; **Band:** horse leather, buckle
Remarks: hardened Plexiglas with scratch-resistant coating
Price: $2,095
Variations: rose gold PVD coating ($2,295)

Meister MEGA
Reference number: 058/4803.44
Movement: quartz, multifrequency radio-controlled movement J101.66; radio-controlled time zone recognition and setting accurate to the second, app-based time-setting; "eternal" date (in quartz mode also)
Functions: hours, minutes, sweep seconds; date
Case: stainless steel, ø 38.4 mm, height 9.6 mm; sapphire crystal; transparent case back; water-resistant to 5 atm
Band: stainless steel, folding clasp
Price: $1,290

Max Bill Chronoscope 100 Years Bauhaus
Reference number: 027/9900.02
Movement: automatic, Caliber J880.2 (base ETA 7750 or Sellita SW500); ø 30 mm, height 7.9 mm; 25 jewels; 28,800 vph; 48-hour power reserve
Functions: hours, minutes; chronograph; date
Case: white gold, ø 40 mm, height 14.4 mm; sapphire crystal; transparent case back
Band: calfskin, buckle
Price: $8,995; limited to 100 pieces

Max Bill Automatic 100 Years Bauhaus
Reference number: 027/4901.02
Movement: automatic, Caliber J800.1 (base ETA 2824-2 or Sellita SW200-1); ø 25.6 mm, height 4.6 mm; 25 or 26 jewels; 28,800 vph; 38-hour power reserve
Functions: hours, minutes, sweep seconds; date
Case: stainless steel with anthracite PVD coating, ø 38 mm, height 10 mm; sapphire crystal; transparent case back; water-resistant to 3 atm
Band: calfskin, buckle
Price: $1,395; limited to 1,000 pieces

Form A 100 Years Bauhaus
Reference number: 027/4937.44
Movement: automatic, Caliber J800.2 (base ETA 2824-2 or Sellita SW200-1); ø 25.6 mm, height 4.6 mm; 25 or 26 jewels; 28,800 vph; 38-hour power reserve
Functions: hours, minutes, sweep seconds; date
Case: stainless steel, ø 39.3 mm, height 9.5 mm; sapphire crystal; transparent case back; water-resistant to 5 atm
Band: stainless steel Milanese mesh, folding clasp
Price: $1,095

KOBOLD

Kobold Watch Company, LLC
1801 Parkway View Drive
Pittsburgh, PA 15205

Tel.:
724-533-3000

E-mail:
info@koboldwatch.com

Website:
www.koboldwatch.com

Founded:
1998

Number of employees:
8

Annual production:
maximum 2,500 watches

Distribution:
factory-direct, select retailers

Most important collection/price range:
Soarway / $2,150 to $35,000

Like many others in the field, Michael Kobold had already developed an interest in the watch industry in childhood. As a young man, he found a mentor in Chronoswiss founder Gerd-Rüdiger Lang, who encouraged him to start his own brand. This he did in 1998—at the age of nineteen, while he was still a student at Carnegie Mellon University.

Today, Kobold Watch Company is headquartered in a big red barn on a farm in Amish country, Pennsylvania. There it manufactures cases, movement components, dials, hands, and even straps. The brand's centerpiece is the Soarway collection and the fabled Soarway case, which was originally created in 1999 by explorer Ranulph Fiennes, master watchmaker and Chronoswiss founder Lang, as well as company founder Kobold, himself an avid mountain climber. And "adventure" also means muscle and tool watches, like the Phantom Black Ops chronograph or the Richard Byrd Tactical, watches that can stay on the wrist even when the wearer is diving.

Kobold's love of the Himalayas has driven his commitment to the people of Nepal. He produces leather accessories and straps there and uses the operation to offer women vocational training. In 2015, he launched the Soarway Foundation to help Nepal in the event of earthquakes. Coincidentally, a few weeks later the first of two struck, devastating the country and the subsidiary. To help in such emergencies and others, he has started an initiative to get fire trucks to the country, hence the making of fire truck–themed watches. Kobold Nepal also works with Maiti Nepal to reintegrate trafficked women into society. Kobold has contributed to the renaissance of American watchmaking and originally set its sights even higher, namely, on an in-house U.S.-made movement. Things have changed, though. "We make tough, rugged watches and so the case plays a more important role than the movement," says Kobold. "So for now, we're concentrating on making the toughest cases possible. One day, we'll tackle making in-house movements." The Soarway collection includes several novelties, such as the Soarway Transglobe, a watch with a second time zone that displays minutes as well as hours.

Seal

Reference number: KD 842121
Movement: automatic, ETA 2892-A2; ø 36 mm, height 3.6 mm; 21 jewels; 28,800 vph; 46-hour power reserve
Functions: hours, minutes, sweep seconds
Case: stainless steel, ø 44 mm, height 17.0 mm; unidirectional rotating bezel; sapphire crystal; screw-down case back; water-resistant to 100 atm
Band: canvas, signed buckle
Price: $4,250

Seal GMT U.S. Submarine Service

Reference number: KD 892121
Movement: automatic, ETA 2893-A2; ø 36 mm, height 3.6 mm; 25 jewels; 28,800 vph; 46-hour power reserve
Functions: hours, minutes, sweep seconds; date; 2nd time zone
Case: stainless steel, ø 44 mm, height 17.0 mm; unidirectional rotating bezel; sapphire crystal; screw-down case back; water-resistant to 100 atm
Band: canvas, signed buckle
Price: $4,750

Polar Surveyor

Reference number: KD 9265842
Movement: automatic, Caliber K.751 (base ETA 7754); ø 30 mm, height 8.3 mm; 28 jewels; 28,800 vph; 42-hour power reserve
Functions: hours, minutes, subsidiary seconds; date; chronograph
Case: stainless steel, ø 41 mm, height 15.3 mm; sapphire crystal; screw-down case back; screw-in crown; water-resistant to 30 atm
Band: canvas, signed buckle
Price: $5,750

KUDOKE

Stefan Kudoke, a watchmaker from Frankfurt/Oder, has made a name for himself as an extremely skilled and imaginative creator of timepieces. He apprenticed with two experienced watchmakers and graduated as the number one trainee in the state of Brandenburg. This earned him a stipend from a federal program promoting gifted individuals. He then moved on to one of the large *manufactures* in Glashütte, where he refined his skills in its workshop for complications and prototyping. At the age of twenty-two, with a master's diploma in his pocket, he decided to get an MBA and then devote himself to building his own company.

His guiding principle is individuality, and that is not possible to find in a serial product. So Kudoke began building unique pieces. By realizing the special wishes of customers, he manages to reflect each person's uniqueness in each watch. And he has produced some out-of-the-ordinary pieces, like the ExCentro 1 and 2, or more recently a watch with an octopus that seems to be climbing out of the case. Even his more minimalistic pieces, like the Kudoke 1 and 2 are deeply thought out. Their strength also lies in the subtle interplay of forms and colors, which won Kudoke the "Petite Aiguille" prize at the coveted Grand Prix d'Horlogerie Genève in November 2019 for the Kudoke 2.

His specialties include engraving and goldsmithing. Within his creations bridges may in fact be graceful bodies, or the fine skeletonizing of a plate fragment, a world of figures and garlands. His recent creations include a skull watch, done with characteristic care, and the minimalistic Kurt.

Kudoke Uhren
Tannenweg 5
D-15236 Frankfurt (Oder)
Germany

Tel.:
+49-335-280-0409

E-mail:
info@kudoke.eu

Website:
www.kudoke.eu

Founded:
2007

Number of employees:
1

Annual production:
30–50 watches

Distribution:
Contact the brand directly for information.

Price range:
approx. $4,500 to $11,500

Kudoke 1
Movement: manually wound, Kudoke Caliber 1; ø 30 mm, height 4.3 mm; 18 jewels; 28,800 vph; hand-engraved and finished movement; 46-hour power reserve
Functions: hours, minutes, subsidiary seconds
Case: stainless steel, ø 39 mm, height 9.5 mm; sapphire crystal; transparent case back
Band: reptile skin, buckle
Price: $9,270

Kudoke 2
Movement: manually wound, Kudoke Caliber 1-Version 24h; ø 30 mm, height 5.05 mm; 18 jewels; 28,800 vph; hand-engraved and finished movement; 46-hour power reserve
Functions: hours, minutes; additional 24-hour display
Case: stainless steel, ø 39 mm, height 10.7 mm; sapphire crystal; transparent case back
Band: reptile skin, buckle
Remarks: hand-engraved celestial disk with 3-color galvanic treatment
Price: $8,870

KudOktopus
Movement: manually wound, modified ETA Caliber 6498; ø 36.6 mm, height 4.5 mm; 17 jewels; 18,000 vph; screw balance, polished anchor and escape wheel, hand-skeletonized movement, sculptural rendering of octopus in 3 galvanic colors; 46-hour power reserve
Functions: hours, minutes
Case: stainless steel, ø 42 mm, height 10.7 mm; sapphire crystal; transparent case back
Band: reptile skin, buckle
Price: $9,170

Laurent Ferrier
Route de Saint Julien 150
CH-1228 Plan-les-Ouates
Switzerland

Tel.:
+41-22-716-3388

E-mail:
info@laurentferrier.ch

Website:
www.laurentferrier.ch

Founded:
2010

Number of employees:
12

Annual production:
135

U.S. distributor:
Totally Worth It, LLC
76 Division Avenue
Summit, NJ 07901-2309
201-894-4710
724-263-2286
info@totallyworthit.com

Most important collections/price range:
Variations of the Galet / from $40,000 to $345,000

LAURENT FERRIER

A rock rolling along a riverbed or being buffeted by coastal surf will, over time, achieve a kind of perfect shape, streamlined, flowing, smooth. It will usually become a comfortable touchstone for the human hand, a beautiful pebble, or *galet* in French. And that is the name given to the watches made by Laurent Ferrier in Geneva, Switzerland. The name refers to the special look and feel of the cases, which are just one hallmark of this very unusual, yet classical, watch brand.

The metaphor of the rock in water optimizing its form in a slow but consistent process could apply to Laurent Ferrier himself. He is a real person, the offspring of a watchmaking family from the Canton of Neuchâtel, and a trained watchmaker. As a young man he had a passion for cars, too, and even raced seven times at the 24 Hours of Le Mans. In 2009, after thirty-five years of employment at Patek Philippe working on new movements, Ferrier decided he had been shaped enough by his industry. He gathered up his deep experience and founded his own enterprise. He was joined by his son, Christian Ferrier, a watchmaker in his own right, and fellow former race driver François Sérvanin.

One of the first watches was a tourbillon using a natural escapement with a double hairspring, ensuring greater accuracy (a technical idea going back to Breguet). It has returned now a decade later to celebrate the fiftieth anniversary of Ferrier's race. The tourbillon is once again concealed on the movement side (as it used to be)—very intriguing and effective—keeping the dial free of clutter. Purists always praise the brand's minimal dials, the spear hands, and the drop markers. The case, smooth and sporty, is a redux of 1970s design.

The flagship Galet keeps evolving. The annual calendar still manages to appear understated, and at the 2019 SIHH, Ferrier proudly presented a form watch inspired by a bridge construction, a timepiece that almost magically fits any wrist.

Galet Annual Calendar School Piece
Reference number: LCF025
Movement: manually wound, Laurent Ferrier Caliber LF126.01; ø 31.6 mm, height 5.80 mm; 21,600 vph; 23 jewels; Swiss lever escapement, finely decorated bridges and mainplate; semi-instantaneous calendar with correction forward or backward; 80-hour power reserve
Functions: hours, minutes, subsidiary seconds; day, date; power reserve indicator on rear
Case: stainless steel, ø 40 mm, height 10.10 mm; ball-shaped crown; sapphire crystal front, transparent case back; water-resistant to 3 atm
Band: reptile skin, buckle or folding clasp
Price: $58,000; **Variations:** red gold ($63,000)

Bridge One
Reference number: LCF 032.AC.E01
Movement: manually wound, Laurent Ferrier Caliber LF707.01; ø 22.20 mm × 30 mm, height 4.35 mm; 21,600 vph; 21 jewels; Swiss lever escapement, finely decorated bridges and mainplate; 80-hour power reserve
Functions: hours, minutes, subsidiary seconds
Case: stainless steel, ø 44 mm × 30 mm, height 10.70 mm; domed and tinted sapphire crystal; transparent case back; ball-shaped crown; water-resistant to 3 atm
Remarks: case inspired from a bridge: grand-feu white enamel dial
Band: reptile skin, buckle or folding clasp
Price: $42,000; **Variations:** slate-gray dial ($37,000)

Tourbillon Grand Sport
Reference number: LCF041.AC.G1G0
Movement: manually wound, Laurent Ferrier Caliber LF707.01; ø 31.60 mm, height 5.57 mm; 21,600 vph; 23 jewels; Swiss lever escapement, finely decorated bridges and mainplate; 1-minute tourbillon on rear; 80-hour power reserve
Functions: hours, minutes, subsidiary seconds
Case: stainless steel, ø 44 mm, height 10.40 mm; ball-shaped crown; sapphire crystal front, transparent case back; water-resistant to 10 atm
Band: rubber, folding clasp
Price: $185,000; limited to 12 pieces

LONGINES

The Longines winged hourglass logo is the world's oldest trademark, according to the World Intellectual Property Organization (WIPO). Since its founding in 1832, the brand has manufactured somewhere in the region of 35 million watches, making it one of the genuine heavyweights of the Swiss watch world. In 1983, Nicolas G. Hayek merged the two major Swiss watch manufacturing groups ASUAG and SIHH into what would later become the Swatch Group. Longines, the leading ASUAG brand, barely missed capturing the same position in the new concern; that honor went to Omega, the SIHH frontrunner. However, from a historical and technical point of view, this brand has what it takes to be at the helm of any group. Was it not Longines that equipped polar explorer Roald Amundsen and air pioneer Charles Lindbergh with their watches? It has also been the timekeeper at many Olympic Games and, since 2007, the official timekeeper for the French Open at Roland Garros. In fact, this brand is a major sponsor at many sports events, from riding to archery.

It is not surprising then to find that this venerable Jura company also has an impressive portfolio of in-house calibers in stock, from simple manual winders to complicated chronographs. This broad technological base has benefited the company. As a genuine "one-stop shop," the brand can supply the Swatch Group with anything from cheap, thin quartz watches to heavy gold chronographs and calendars with quadruple retrograde displays. Longines does have one particular specialty, besides elegant ladies' watches and modern sports watches, in that it often has the luxury of rebuilding the classics from its own long history.

Longines Watch Co.
Rue des Noyettes 8
CH-2610 St.-Imier
Switzerland

Tel.:
+41-32-942-5425

E-mail:
info@longines.com

Website:
www.longines.com

Founded:
1832

Number of employees:
worldwide approx. 2,000

U.S. distributor:
Longines
The Swatch Group (U.S.), Inc.
Longines Division
703 Waterford Way, Ste. 450
Miami, FL 33126
800-897-9477
www.longines.com

Most important collections/price range:
The Longines Master Collection, Longines DolceVita, Conquest V.H.P., HydroConquest, Heritage Collection / from approx. $1,000 to $6,500

HydroConquest
Reference number: L3.784.4.56.9
Movement: automatic, Longines Caliber L888 (base ETA A31.L01); ø 25.6 mm, height 3.85 mm; 21 jewels; 25,200 vph; 64-hour power reserve
Functions: hours, minutes, sweep seconds; date
Case: ceramic, ø 43 mm; unidirectional bezel with ceramic insert, 0-60 scale; sapphire crystal; screw-in crown; water-resistant to 30 atm
Band: rubber, double folding clasp with safety lock and fine adjustment
Price: $3,725

HydroConquest
Reference number: L3.781.4.96.6
Movement: automatic, Longines Caliber L888.2 (base ETA A31.L01); ø 25.6 mm, height 3.85 mm; 21 jewels; 25,200 vph; 64-hour power reserve
Functions: hours, minutes, sweep seconds; date
Case: stainless steel, ø 41 mm, height 11.9 mm; unidirectional bezel with ceramic insert, 0-60 scale; sapphire crystal; screw-in crown; water-resistant to 30 atm
Band: stainless steel, double folding clasp, with safety lock and extension link
Price: $1,600
Variations: various straps and dials

HydroConquest Chronograph
Reference number: L3.883.4.76.9
Movement: automatic, Longines Caliber L688 (base ETA A08.L01); ø 30 mm, height 7.9 mm; 27 jewels; 28,800 vph; 54-hour power reserve
Functions: hours, minutes, subsidiary seconds; chronograph; date
Case: stainless steel, ø 43 mm, height 15.6 mm; unidirectional bezel with ceramic insert, 0-60 scale; sapphire crystal; screw-in crown; water-resistant to 30 atm
Band: rubber, double folding clasp, with safety lock
Price: $2,450

LONGINES

Master Collection Annual Calendar
Reference number: L2.920.4.92.6
Movement: automatic, Longines Caliber L897 (base ETA A31.L81); ø 25.6 mm, height 5.2 mm; 21 jewels; 25,200 vph; 64-hour power reserve
Functions: hours, minutes, sweep seconds; annual calendar with date, month
Case: stainless steel, ø 42 mm; sapphire crystal; transparent case back; water-resistant to 3 atm
Band: stainless steel, triple folding clasp
Price: $2,450
Variations: reptile skin ($2,450)

Master Collection Moonphase
Reference number: L2.673.4.78.3
Movement: automatic, Longines Caliber L687 (base ETA A08.L91); ø 30 mm, height 7.9 mm; 25 jewels; 28,800 vph; 54-hour power reserve
Functions: hours, minutes, subsidiary seconds; additional 24-hour display; chronograph; full calendar with date, weekday, month, moon phase
Case: stainless steel, ø 40 mm, height 14.3 mm; sapphire crystal; transparent case back; water-resistant to 3 atm
Band: reptile skin, triple folding clasp
Price: $3,325
Variations: stainless steel bracelet ($3,325)

Master Collection Moonphase
Reference number: L2.673.4.92.0
Movement: automatic, Longines Caliber L687 (base ETA A08.L91); ø 30 mm, height 7.9 mm; 25 jewels; 28,800 vph; 54-hour power reserve
Functions: hours, minutes, subsidiary seconds; additional 24-hour display; chronograph; full calendar with date, weekday, month, moon phase
Case: stainless steel, ø 40 mm, height 14.3 mm; sapphire crystal; transparent case back; water-resistant to 3 atm
Band: reptile skin, triple folding clasp
Price: $3,325
Variations: stainless steel bracelet ($3,325)

Master Collection Automatic
Reference number: L2.793.8.78.3
Movement: automatic, Longines Caliber L888 (base ETA A31.L01); ø 25.6 mm, height 3.85 mm; 21 jewels; 25,200 vph; 64-hour power reserve
Functions: hours, minutes, sweep seconds; date
Case: rose gold, ø 40 mm; sapphire crystal; transparent case back; water-resistant to 3 atm
Band: reptile skin, triple folding clasp
Price: $5,900

Conquest Classic
Reference number: L2.386.4.88.6
Movement: quartz
Functions: hours, minutes, sweep seconds; date
Case: stainless steel, ø 34 mm; sapphire crystal; water-resistant to 5 atm
Band: stainless steel, triple folding clasp
Remarks: mother-of-pearl dial with 11 diamonds
Price: $1,350

Conquest Classic
Reference number: L2.386.4.72.6
Movement: quartz
Functions: hours, minutes, sweep seconds; date
Case: stainless steel, ø 34 mm; sapphire crystal; water-resistant to 5 atm
Band: stainless steel, triple folding clasp
Price: $950

LONGINES

Conquest Moonphase
Reference number: L3.381.4.97.6
Movement: quartz
Functions: hours, minutes, sweep seconds; date, moon phase
Case: stainless steel, ø 34 mm; sapphire crystal; screw-in crown; water-resistant to 30 atm
Band: stainless steel, triple folding clasp
Remarks: dial set with 11 diamonds
Price: $1,275

Elegant Collection
Reference number: L4.910.4.92.2
Movement: automatic, Longines Caliber L888 (base ETA A31.L01); ø 25.6 mm, height 3.85 mm; 21 jewels; 25,200 vph; 64-hour power reserve
Functions: hours, minutes, sweep seconds; date
Case: stainless steel, ø 39 mm, height 8.6 mm; sapphire crystal; transparent case back; water-resistant to 3 atm
Band: reptile skin, buckle
Price: $1,900

Record Collection
Reference number: L2.821.4.72.6
Movement: automatic, Longines Caliber L888.4 (base ETA A31.L11); ø 25.6 mm, height 3.85 mm; 21 jewels; 25,200 vph; 64-hour power reserve; COSC-certified chronometer
Functions: hours, minutes, sweep seconds; date
Case: stainless steel, ø 40 mm, height 10.8 mm; sapphire crystal; transparent case back; water-resistant to 3 atm
Band: stainless steel, triple folding clasp
Price: $2,025

Legend Diver Watch
Reference number: L3.774.2.50.9
Movement: automatic, Longines Caliber L888 (base ETA A31.L01); ø 25.6 mm, height 3.85 mm; 21 jewels; 25,200 vph; 64-hour power reserve
Functions: hours, minutes, sweep seconds; date
Case: stainless steel with black PVD coating, ø 42 mm, height 12.7 mm; crown-activated scale ring with 0-60 scale; sapphire crystal; screw-in crown; water-resistant to 30 atm
Band: rubber, double folding clasp with extension link
Price: $2,700
Variations: stainless steel bracelet, calfskin strap, rubber strap with deployment buckle (starting at $2,300)

Skin Diver Watch
Reference number: L2.822.4.56.2
Movement: automatic, Longines Caliber L888 (base ETA A31.L01); ø 25.6 mm, height 3.85 mm; 21 jewels; 25,200 vph; 64-hour power reserve
Functions: hours, minutes, sweep seconds
Case: stainless steel, ø 42 mm; unidirectional aluminum bezel, 0-60 scale; sapphire crystal; screw-in crown; water-resistant to 30 atm
Band: calfskin, buckle
Price: $2,600
Variations: rubber strap, stainless steel bracelet

The Lindbergh Hour Angle Watch
Reference number: L2.678.4.11.0
Movement: automatic, Longines Caliber L699 (base ETA A07.L01); ø 36.6 mm, height 7.9 mm; 24 jewels; 28,800 vph; 46-hour power reserve
Functions: hours, minutes, sweep seconds, rotatable inner dial to synchronize second hand with radio time signals
Case: stainless steel, ø 47.5 mm, height 16.3 mm; bidirectional bezel with scale for time synchronization; sapphire crystal; water-resistant to 3 atm
Remarks: case back with hinged cover
Band: reptile skin, buckle
Price: $5,000

Les Ateliers Louis Moinet SA
Rue du Temple 1
CH-2072 Saint-Blaise
Switzerland

Tel.:
+41-32-753-6814

E-mail:
info@louismoinet.com

Website:
www.louismoinet.com

Founded:
2005

U.S. distributor:
Fitzhenry Consulting
1029 Peachtree Parkway, #346
Peachtree City, GA 30269
561-212-6812
Don@fitzhenry.com

Most important collections:
Memoris, Sideralis, Tempograph Chrome, Spacewalker, Ultravox; numerous unique pieces

LOUIS MOINET

In the race to be the first to invent something new, Louis Moinet (1768–1853) emerged as a notable winner: In 2013, a *Compteur de tierces* from 1816 was shown to the public, a chronograph that counts one-sixtieth of a second with a frequency of 216,000 vph. It was proudly signed by Moinet. This professor at the Academy of Fine Arts in Paris and president of the Société Chronométrique was in fact one of the most inventive, multitalented men of his time. He worked with such eminent watchmakers as Breguet, Berthoud, Winnerl, Janvier, and Perrelet. Among his accomplishments is an extensive two-volume treatise on horology.

Following in such footsteps is hardly an easy task, but Jean-Marie Schaller and Micaela Bertolucci decided that their idiosyncratic creations were indeed imbued with the spirit of the great Frenchman. They work with a team of independent designers, watchmakers, movement specialists, and suppliers to produce the most unusual wristwatches filled with clever functions and surprising details. The Jules Verne chronographs have hinged levers, for example, and the second hand on the Tempograph changes direction every ten seconds.

Increasingly, this independent-minded brand is exploring the space-time continuum. The dial of the chronograph-watch Memoris, for the centenary of the invention of the chronograph by Louis Moinet, is dotted with stars. The Sideralis, presented in 2016, features fragments of the famous Rosetta stone and dust from Mars and the moon, and the Metropolis Mexico has a bit of the Allende meteorite showing through the dial. And space is honored by a watch made in collaboration with Alexey Leonov, who died in October 2019: He was the first person to leave an orbiting capsule to take a little spacewalk . . .

SpaceWalker
Reference number: LM-62.50G.25
Movement: manually wound, Louis Moinet Caliber LM 48; ø 37.65 mm, height 10.33 mm; 20 jewels; 21,600 vph; 72-hour power reserve; "satellite" 13.59-mm tourbillon balanced by a diamond on the cage; rhodium-plated, satin-brushed mainplate, bridges with côtes de Genève; **Functions:** hours, minutes
Case: rose gold with engravings, ø 47.4 mm, height 16.9 mm; sapphire crystal; transparent case back; water-resistant to 5 atm
Remarks: tourbillon and rotating diamond represent spaceship of 1965 Voskhod-2 mission, when Alexey Leonov walked in space
Band: reptile skin, double folding clasp
Price: $229,000; limited to 12 pieces
Variations: without engravings ($199,000)

Metropolis Mexico
Reference number: LM-45.10.ME
Movement: automatic, Louis Moinet Caliber LM45; ø 30.4 mm, height 6.7 mm; 22 jewels; 28,800 vph; 48-hour power reserve; côtes de Genève, circular-grained wheels, clous de Paris on rotor
Functions: hours, minutes, subsidiary seconds
Case: stainless steel, ø 43.2 mm, height 14.8 mm; sapphire crystal; screw-in transparent back; water-resistant to 5 atm
Band: reptile skin, folding clasp
Remarks: skeletonized dial and hour markers; Allende meteorite fragment in window at 3 o'clock
Price: $19,500; limited to 12 pieces

Ultravox
Reference number: LM-56.50.50
Movement: automatic, Louis Moinet Caliber LM 56; ø 38.40 mm, height 8.38 mm; 52 jewels; 21,600 vph; sunburst côtes de Genève on rhodium-plated bridges; 38-hour power reserve
Functions: hours, minutes; hour repeater
Case: rose gold, ø 46.5 mm, height 14.5 mm; sapphire crystal; transparent case back; water-resistant to 5 atm
Remarks: dial-side repeating mechanism
Band: reptile skin, folding clasp
Price: $149,500; limited to 28 pieces

LOUIS VUITTON

The philosophy of this over-150-year-old brand states that any product bearing the name Louis Vuitton must be manufactured in the company's own facilities. That is why Louis Vuitton has allowed itself the luxury of building its own workshop in Switzerland, specifically in La Chaux-de-Fonds, at the technology center of LVMH (Louis Vuitton, Moët & Hennessy).

Designing is carried out in Paris at the company headquarters, and it is obvious that it would not suit an upscale watch to simply cobble together various parts supplied by outside workshops. The cases and dials with all the details and the hands are all exclusive Louis Vuitton designs, as are other components, such as the pushers and the band clasps, in other words, all that is needed to ensure a unique look. In 2011, Louis Vuitton purchased the dial maker Léman Cadran and the movement specialist Fabrique du Temps (both in Geneva), giving the company a great deal of independence vis-à-vis other brands in the group. And helping it clinch a Geneva Seal for its brand-new tourbillon, whose transparency almost makes it "mysterious." A year after came the Tambour Moon Mystérieuse Flying Tourbillon driven by a minimalist movement that floats between sapphire crystals without any visible contact to the crown or the case.

For a small *manufacture*, Louis Vuitton has been brave. It has produced the LV Fifty Five collection, the Tambour, and the unconventional Escale world-time watch featuring hand-painted scale fields in the style of the monograms that Louis Vuitton uses to mark its bags. The new Tambour Moons bring together high fashion and "quartz" watchmaking. And for the incurably connected, the brand has developed the Tambour Horizon with a variety of colorful dials.

Louis Vuitton Malletier
2, rue du Pont Neuf
75001
France

Tel.:
+33-1-55-80-41-40

Website:
www.vuitton.com

Founded:
1854

U.S. distributor:
Louis Vuitton
1-866-VUITTON
www.louisvuitton.com

Most important collections/price range:
Tambour / Voyage / LV Fifty Five / Escale / from $3,250

Tambour All Black Chronograph
Reference number: Q1A62Z
Movement: automatic, ETA Caliber 2894-2; ø 28.6 mm, height 6.3 mm; 28 jewels; 28,800 vph; 42-hour power reserve
Functions: hours, minutes, subsidiary seconds; chronograph; date
Case: stainless steel with black PVD coating, ø 46 mm; sapphire crystal; water-resistant to 10 atm
Band: reptile skin, buckle
Price: $7,550

Tambour All Black Petite Seconde
Reference number: Q1D22Z
Movement: automatic, ETA Caliber 2895-2; ø 25.6 mm, height 4.35 mm; 27 jewels; 28,800 vph; 42-hour power reserve
Functions: hours, minutes, subsidiary seconds; date
Case: stainless steel with black PVD coating, ø 41.5 mm; sapphire crystal; transparent case back; water-resistant to 10 atm
Band: reptile skin, buckle
Price: $5,300

Tambour All Black and Gold Chronograph
Movement: automatic, ETA Caliber 2894-2; ø 28.6 mm, height 6.3 mm; 28 jewels; 28,800 vph; 42-hour power reserve
Functions: hours, minutes, subsidiary seconds; chronograph; date
Case: stainless steel with black PVD coating, red gold lugs and pushers, ø 46 mm; sapphire crystal; water-resistant to 10 atm
Band: reptile skin, double folding clasp
Price: $11,000

LOUIS VUITTON

Tambour Spin Time Air
Reference number: Q1EG60
Movement: automatic, LV Caliber 88; ø 35.2 mm; height 7.2 mm; 26 jewels; 28,800 vph; 35-hour power reserve
Functions: hours (jumping), minutes
Case: white gold, ø 42.5 mm; sapphire crystal; transparent case back; water-resistant to 5 atm
Band: reptile skin, double folding clasp
Price: $57,000

Tambour Moon Mystérieuse Flying Tourbillon
Movement: manually wound, LV Caliber 110; 13 × 34 mm; 17 jewels; 21,600 vph; flying 1-minute tourbillon without visible drive under sapphire bridges; 80-hour power reserve; Geneva Seal, Qualité Fleurier
Functions: hours, minutes
Case: platinum, ø 45 mm, height 10.6 mm; sapphire crystal; transparent case back; water-resistant to 50 atm
Band: reptile skin, double folding clasp
Price: $242,000

Voyager Tourbillon Volant
Reference number: Q7EB50
Movement: automatic, LV Caliber 81; 28 jewels; 28,800 vph; flying 1-minute tourbillon; 40-hour power reserve
Functions: hours, minutes
Case: white gold, ø 41 mm; sapphire crystal; water-resistant to 5 atm
Band: reptile skin, double folding clasp
Remarks: case and dial set with 189 diamonds
Price: $139,000

Tambour Horizon Monogram Eclipse
Movement: quartz, Smartwatch with Android and iOS compatibility
Functions: hours, minutes; world time display (2nd time zone), customized dials, flight data service, special app for guided city tours, weather and temperature indication, step counter; perpetual calendar with date, weekday, month
Case: stainless steel, ø 42 mm, height 12.6 mm; sapphire crystal; transparent case back; water-resistant to 3 atm
Band: calfskin, double folding clasp
Price: $2,750

Escale Worldtime Blue
Reference number: Q5EK50
Movement: automatic, LV Caliber 106; ø 37 mm, height 6.65 mm; 26 jewels; 28,800 vph; 38-hour power reserve
Functions: hours, minutes; world time display (2nd time zone) for 24 time zones using hand-painted rotating disk
Case: titanium, ø 41 mm, height 9.75 mm; white gold bezel, lugs, and crown; sapphire crystal; water-resistant to 3 atm
Band: reptile skin, folding clasp
Price: $52,000

Tambour Damier Graphite
Movement: quartz
Functions: hours, minutes, sweep seconds
Case: stainless steel, ø 41.5 mm; sapphire crystal; water-resistant to 10 atm
Band: textile, double folding clasp
Price: $3,500

LUMINOX

Watches, as the old industry axiom goes, are jewelry for men. And some men do like watches that express masculinity in no uncertain terms, or that feel like real tools, or that recall the cockpits of fast-moving vehicles. So when Barry Cohen came across the tiny tritium gas–filled luminescent tubes made by the Swiss company mb-microtech, he spotted an opportunity. Here was a way to give sports watches the kind of illumination that would make them dependable and practical time-givers at night. The radioactive tritium, which has a half-life of 12.32 years, makes a coating on the inside of the tubes glow for up to 25 years.

Cohen and his business partner Richard Timbo called their brand Luminox, derived from the Latin "light" and "night." They created a collection of rugged-looking sports timepieces that soon found a loyal following. In 1992 came the first big breakthrough, when a Luminox watch prevailed in a tough competition to become a mission watch for Navy SEALs. The brand now established a reputation, and soon other law enforcement agencies and organizations began ordering watches, notably F-117 Nighthawk and Stealth pilots.

As the brand grew and expanded beyond American borders, it continued developing its product. A new lightweight carbon compound case with a matte finish was developed that is insensitive to outside temperatures. The latest versions of this case can withstand dives of up to 300 meters. A special mineral crystal was also developed that is highly scratch resistant.

Luminox also partnered with the Swiss company Mondaine, famous for its Railroad Watch and the Helvetica, to manufacture watches in their premises in Switzerland. A new company, called Lumondi Inc., was founded to oversee the two brands after Mondaine purchased the 50 percent of remaining shares from Barry Cohen in November 2016.

Luminox watches are unabashedly muscular and outdoorsy. Wherever extreme sports or activities are being performed, that is where Luminox finds its fans. The Scott Cassell Deep Dive Automatic, for example, was made for explorer and deep-seas diver Scott Cassell as part of his "essential gear." The watches are run either on Swiss quartz or on mechanical movements.

Lumondi Inc. (Luminox Watches)
27 W. 24th Street, Suite 804
New York, NY 10010

Tel.:
917-522-3600

E-mail:
info@luminoxusa.com

Website:
www.luminox.com
shop.luminox.com

Founded:
1989

Most important collections:
Navy SEAL 3500, Leatherback Sea, Turtle Giant, XCOR Aerospace

Scott Cassell Deep Dive Automatic
Reference number: 1523
Movement: automatic, ETA Caliber 2826-2; ø 25.6 mm, height 6.2 mm; 25 jewels; 28,800 vph; 38-hour power reserve
Functions: hours, minutes, sweep seconds; large date
Case: stainless steel, ø 44 mm, height 17 mm; unidirectional bezel with blue aluminum ring, bezel locker at 3 o'clock; sapphire crystal with antireflective coating; helium release valve; stainless steel screw-in case back; water-resistant to 50 atm
Band: rubber strap, stainless steel buckle
Remarks: constant glow for up to 25 years in any light condition
Price: $2,000
Variations: black/yellow dial with black rubber strap

XCOR Aerospace Automatic Valjoux Chronograph
Reference number: 5261
Movement: automatic, ETA Caliber 7750 Valjoux; ø 30 mm, height 7.9; 25 jewels; 28,800 vph; 42-hour power reserve
Functions: hours, minutes, chronograph; date
Case: titanium and black PVD, ø 45.5 mm, height 18 mm; sapphire crystal; titanium screw-down case back; water-resistant to 20 atm
Band: calfskin, titanium buckle
Remarks: constant glow for up to 25 years in any light condition
Price: $3,000

F-117 Nighthawk
Reference number: 6422
Movement: quartz, Ronda Caliber 515; ø 26.2 mm, height 3 mm
Functions: hours, minutes; date; 2nd time zone
Case: stainless steel IP gun metal, ø 44 mm, height 12.6 mm; bidirectional bezel; sapphire crystal; water-resistant to 20 atm
Band: stainless steel and buckle with black PVD
Remark: constant glow for up to 25 years in any light condition
Price: $1,400
Variations: Kevlar strap with black stitching, black leather lining, and black PVD buckle

MANUFACTURE ROYALE

Manufacture Royale SA
ZI Le Day
CH-1337 Vallorbe
Switzerland

Tel.:
+41-21-843-01-01

E-mail:
info@manufacture-royale.com

Website:
www.manufacture-royale.com

Founded:
by Voltaire in 1770, revived in 2010

Number of employees:
5

Annual production:
150 watches

Distribution:
Retail and online

Most important collections/price range:
ADN Spirit / from $26,800; Androgyne / from $52,500; 1770 / from $30,500; Opera / $367,500

Originally, Manufacture Royale was the short-lived watch factory belonging to a genuinely interesting personality of the eighteenth century: François-Marie Arouet (1694–1778), or Voltaire, a brilliant playwright, historian, freewheeling philosopher, historian, and all-around thinker. He opposed slavery and the death penalty, for instance, and, thanks to his stunning wealth, could fire satirical barbs at the powers-that-be, from iniquitous aristocrats and crowned heads to a budding, conservative middle class. In Geneva, where he often found refuge from the French king, he went further: The local established bourgeoisie steadfastly refused to give political and economic rights to a class of craftsmen known as the *natifs*, whose origins were not local and who made up nearly half the population. In 1770, at his estate in neighboring Ferney-Voltaire (France), Voltaire opened a number of workshops for these discriminated people, including the "Manufacture Royale," which produced very respectable watches.

In 2010, four highly experienced and related watch executives, Gérard, David, and Alexis Gouten, and Marc Guten, decided to revive the brand. Their basic idea: high-end complications, affordable prices, *manufacture* movements assembled in-house.

The brand has gained lots of experience since its foundation and the self-confidence to sally into more experimental realms, but without ever disturbing the fundamental classicism of the timepieces. The 1770 Haute Voltige series is definitely twenty-first century, with its second time zone cowering under the mysterious bridges that rise from the dial to hold the balance wheel over the dial. Strong colors and a bold design, with just hands and two tourbillons whirling at different speeds, give the Micromégas family a very noticeable look. As for the ADN, it cuts to the chase, literally, with extreme skeletonization, but inside a redesigned, somewhat softer Androgyne case.

ADN Spirit Steel & Forged Carbon Bronze
Reference number: ADN46.04CS04.MC
Movement: manually wound, Caliber MR10; ø 32.6 mm, height 7.40 mm; 21 jewels, 48-hour power reserve, 28,800 vph; CVD-coated plates and bridges
Functions: hours, minutes, small seconds
Case: DLC-coated stainless steel and forged carbon, ø 46 mm, height 12.35 mm; sapphire crystal, screw-down transparent sapphire case back; water-resistant to 3 atm
Band: Nebur Tec strap, triple folding clasp
Price: $31,400; limited edition of 28 pieces per model
Variations: stainless steel ($26,800)

Micromegas Titanium Bespoke
Reference number: 1770MM45.08.D.K
Movement: automatic, MR04 Caliber; ø 36 mm, height 8.7 mm; 26 jewels; 1-minute flying tourbillon (28,800 vph) and 6-second tourbillon (21,600 vph), both with silicon escapement wheel and levers; 40-hour power reserve
Functions: hours (off-center), minutes
Case: titanium, ø 45 mm, height 11.8 mm; transparent case back; water resistant to 3 atm
Band: reptile skin, titanium buckle
Price: $189,000
Variations: different color patterns

Androgyne Rose Gold Bespoke
Reference number: AN43.08P08.LB
Movement: manually wound, MR02 Caliber; 17 jewels; ø 30.9 mm, height 6.26 mm; 21,600 vph; 1-minute tourbillon; 108-hour power reserve
Functions: hours, minutes
Case: rose gold, ø 43 mm, height 10.20 mm, sapphire crystal; water resistant to 3 atm
Remarks: skeletonized bridges in different colors
Band: reptile skin, buckle
Price: $72,500

MAURICE LACROIX

Maurice Lacroix watches are found in sixty countries. The heart of the company, however, remains the production facilities in the highlands of the Jura, in Saignelégier and Montfaucon, where the brand built La Manufacture des Franches-Montagnes SA (MFM) outfitted with state-of-the-art CNC technology for the production of very specific individual parts and movement components.

The watchmaker can thank the clever interpretations of "classic" pocket watch characteristics for its steep ascent in the 1990s. Since then, the *manufacture* has redesigned the complete collection, banning every lick of Breguet-like bliss from its watch designs. In the upper segment, *manufacture* models such as the chronograph and the retrograde variations on Unitas calibers set the tone. In the lower segment, modern "little" complications outfitted with module movements based on ETA and Sellita are the kings. The brand is mainly associated with the hypnotically turning square wheel, the "roue carrée." The idea was used for the latest ladies' watch, the Power of Love, which has three turning hearts forming the word "love" at regular intervals.

Maurice Lacroix's drive to freshen up its look has earned the brand a great deal of recognition in past years, notably eleven Red Dot awards.

In 2011, DKSH (Diethelm Keller & SiberHegner) became the majority shareholder of the Maurice Lacroix Group. This Swiss holding company, which specializes in international market expansions, now has 1,800 points of sale in thirty-five countries the world round. This has ensured Maurice Lacroix a strong position in all major markets, with flagship stores and its own boutiques.

Maurice Lacroix SA
Rüschlistrasse 6
CH-2502 Biel/Bienne
Switzerland

Tel.:
+41-44-209-1111

E-mail:
info@mauricelacroix.com

Website:
www.mauricelacroix.com

Founded:
1975

Number of employees:
about 250 worldwide

Annual production:
approx. 90,000 watches

U.S. distributor:
DKSH Luxury & Lifestyle North America Inc.
9-D Princess Road
Lawrenceville, NJ 08648
609-750-8800

Most important collections/price range:
Aikon / $890 to $2,900; Les Classiques / $950 to $4,300; Eliros / $690 to $1,390; Fiaba (ladies') / $980 to $2,900; Pontos / $1,750 to $7,900; Masterpiece *manufacture* models / $6,800 to $14,900

Masterpiece Square Wheel Retrograde

Reference number: MP6058-SS001-310-1
Movement: automatic, Caliber ML 258 (base Sellita SW200 with ML module); ø 34 mm, height 8.6 mm; 37 jewels; 28,800 vph; 36-hour power reserve
Functions: hours, minutes, subsidiary seconds; date (retrograde)
Case: stainless steel, ø 43 mm, height 15 mm; sapphire crystal; transparent case back; water-resistant to 10 atm
Band: reptile skin, folding clasp
Price: $7,490
Variations: silver dial

Masterpiece Calendar Retrograde

Reference number: MP6568-SS001-132-1
Movement: automatic, Caliber ML 190; ø 36.6 mm, height 9.9 mm; 50 jewels; 18,000 vph; 52-hour power reserve
Functions: hours, minutes, subsidiary seconds; power reserve indicator; date (retrograde)
Case: stainless steel, ø 43 mm, height 15 mm; sapphire crystal; transparent case back; water-resistant to 5 atm
Band: reptile skin, folding clasp
Price: $4,500

Masterpiece Gravity

Reference number: MP6118-SS001-434-1
Movement: automatic, Caliber ML 230; ø 37.2 mm, height 9.05 mm; 35 jewels; 18,000 vph; inverted movement construction with escapement on dial; silicon pallet lever and pallet fork; 48-hour power reserve
Functions: hours, minutes (off-center), subsidiary seconds
Case: stainless steel, ø 43 mm, height 16.2 mm; sapphire crystal; transparent case back; water-resistant to 5 atm
Band: reptile skin, folding clasp
Price: $13,900
Variations: various cases and dials

MAURICE LACROIX

Aikon Mercury
Reference number: AI6088-SS002-030-1
Movement: automatic, Caliber ML 225; ø 36.6 mm, height 8.9 mm; 54 jewels; 28,800 vph; skeletonized and finely finished movement; bridges with black PVD coating; 38-hour power reserve
Functions: hours, minutes, subsidiary seconds
Case: stainless steel, ø 44 mm, height 14 mm; sapphire crystal; water-resistant to 10 atm
Band: stainless steel, double folding clasp
Remarks: when changing position, the 2 hands shift to the "12" position, when the watch is horizontal, they tell time again
Price: $7,690

Aikon Skeleton Manufacture
Reference number: AI6028-PVB01-030-1
Movement: automatic, Caliber ML 234; ø 36.6 mm, height 8.7 mm; 34 jewels; 18,000 vph; completely skeletonized movement; 52-hour power reserve
Functions: hours, minutes, subsidiary seconds
Case: stainless steel with black PVD coating, ø 45 mm, height 13 mm; sapphire crystal; transparent case back; screw-in crown; water-resistant to 10 atm
Band: calfskin, double folding clasp
Price: $6,190

Aikon Skeleton Manufacture
Reference number: AI6028-SS001-030-1
Movement: automatic, Caliber ML 234; ø 36.6 mm, height 8.7 mm; 34 jewels; 18,000 vph; completely skeletonized movement; 52-hour power reserve
Functions: hours, minutes, subsidiary seconds
Case: stainless steel, ø 45 mm, height 13 mm; sapphire crystal; transparent case back; screw-in crown; water-resistant to 10 atm
Band: reptile skin, double folding clasp
Price: $5,890

Aikon Venturer
Reference number: AI6058-SS002-430-1
Movement: automatic, Sellita Caliber SW200-1; ø 25.6 mm, height 4.6 mm; 26 jewels; 28,800 vph; 38-hour power reserve
Functions: hours, minutes, sweep seconds; date
Case: stainless steel, ø 43 mm, height 11.6 mm; unidirectional bezel with ceramic insert, 0-60 scale; sapphire crystal; screw-in crown; water-resistant to 30 atm
Band: stainless steel, folding clasp
Price: $1,990

Aikon Venturer
Reference number: AI6058-SS001-330-1
Movement: automatic, Sellita Caliber SW200-1; ø 25.6 mm, height 4.6 mm; 26 jewels; 28,800 vph; 38-hour power reserve
Functions: hours, minutes, sweep seconds; date
Case: stainless steel, ø 43 mm, height 11.6 mm; unidirectional bezel with ceramic insert, 0-60 scale; sapphire crystal; screw-in crown; water-resistant to 30 atm
Band: rubber, folding clasp
Price: $1,890

Aikon Automatic Chronograph
Reference number: AI6038-SS001-133-1
Movement: automatic, Caliber ML 112 (base ETA 7750); ø 30 mm, height 7.9 mm; 25 jewels; 28,800 vph; 48-hour power reserve
Functions: hours, minutes, subsidiary seconds; chronograph; date, weekday
Case: stainless steel, ø 44 mm, height 15 mm; sapphire crystal; transparent case back; screw-in crown; water-resistant to 20 atm
Band: calfskin, double folding clasp
Price: $2,990; limited to 500 pieces

MAURICE LACROIX

Aikon Automatic Chronograph
Reference number: AI6038-SS001-132-1
Movement: automatic, Caliber ML 112 (base ETA 7750); ø 30 mm, height 7.9 mm; 25 jewels; 28,800 vph; 48-hour power reserve
Functions: hours, minutes, subsidiary seconds; chronograph; date, weekday
Case: stainless steel, ø 44 mm, height 15 mm; sapphire crystal; transparent case back; screw-in crown; water-resistant to 20 atm
Band: calfskin, double folding clasp
Price: $2,890

Aikon Automatic Date Black
Reference number: AI6008-PVB01-330-1
Movement: automatic, Caliber ML 115 (base Sellita SW200-1); ø 25.6 mm, height 4.6 mm; 26 jewels; 28,800 vph; 38-hour power reserve
Functions: hours, minutes, sweep seconds; date
Case: stainless steel with black PVD coating, ø 42 mm, height 11 mm; sapphire crystal; transparent case back; screw-in crown; water-resistant to 20 atm
Band: calfskin, double folding clasp
Price: $1,990

Aikon Automatic Date
Reference number: AI6008-SS002-331-1
Movement: automatic, Caliber ML 115 (base Sellita SW200-1); ø 25.6 mm, height 4.6 mm; 26 jewels; 28,800 vph; 38-hour power reserve
Functions: hours, minutes, sweep seconds; date
Case: stainless steel, ø 42 mm, height 11 mm; sapphire crystal; transparent case back; screw-in crown; water-resistant to 20 atm
Band: stainless steel, double folding clasp
Price: $1,990

Aikon Automatic Date
Reference number: AI6008-SS001-430-1
Movement: automatic, Caliber ML 115 (base Sellita SW200-1); ø 25.6 mm, height 4.6 mm; 26 jewels; 28,800 vph; 38-hour power reserve
Functions: hours, minutes, sweep seconds; date
Case: stainless steel, ø 42 mm, height 11 mm; sapphire crystal; transparent case back; screw-in crown; water-resistant to 20 atm
Band: calfskin, double folding clasp
Price: $1,890

Eliros Chronograph Black
Reference number: EL1098-PVB01-310-1
Movement: quartz
Functions: hours, minutes, subsidiary seconds; chronograph; date
Case: stainless steel with black PVD coating, ø 40 mm, height 10 mm; sapphire crystal; water-resistant to 5 atm
Band: calfskin, buckle
Price: $990

Eliros Chronograph
Reference number: EL1098-PVP01-210-1
Movement: quartz
Functions: hours, minutes, subsidiary seconds; chronograph; date
Case: stainless steel with rose gold PVD coating, ø 40 mm, height 10 mm; sapphire crystal; water-resistant to 5 atm
Band: calfskin, buckle
Price: $940

MB&F

MB&F
Boulevard Helvétique 22
Case postale 3466
CH-1211 Geneva 3
Switzerland

Tel.:
+41-22-786-3618

E-mail:
info@mbandf.com

Website:
www.mbandf.com

Founded:
2005

Number of employees:
26

Annual production:
approx. 220 watches

U.S. distributors:
Westime Los Angeles and Miami
310-470-1388 (Los Angeles)
786-347-5353 (Miami)
info@westime.com
Provident Jewelry, Florida
561-747-4449; nick@providentjewelry.com
Stephen Silver, Redwood City (California)
650-325-9500; www.shsilver.com
Cellini, New York
212-888-0505; contact@cellinijewelers.com

Most important collections/price range:
Horological Machines / from $63,000; Legacy Machines / from $64,000

Maximilian Büsser & Friends goes beyond the standard idea of a brand. Perhaps calling it a tribe would be better: one aiming to create unique works of horology. MB&F is doing something unconventional in an industry that usually takes its innovation in small doses.

After seeing the Opus projects to fruition at Harry Winston, Büsser decided it was time to set the creators free. At MB&F he acts as initiator and coordinator. His Horological Machines are developed and realized in cooperation with highly specialized watchmakers, inventors, and designers in an "idea collective" creating unheard-of mechanical timepieces of great inventiveness, complication, and exclusivity. The composition of this collective varies as much as each machine. Number 5 ("On the Road Again") is an homage to the 1970s, when streamlining rather than brawn represented true strength. The display in the lateral window is reflected by a prism. The "top" of the watch opens to let in light to charge the Superluminova numerals on the disks. As for the Space Pirate, Number 6, it is a talking piece that makes a genial nod to sci-fi moviemakers, and all the talk was real: The model won a coveted Red Dot "Best of the Best" award in 2015. Contrasting sharply with the modern productions are the Legacy Machines, which reach into horological history and reinterpret past mechanical feats.

The spirit of Büsser is always present in each new watch. Perhaps the most intimate Legacy Machine, though, is the Flying T, dedicated to the women in his life (notably his late mother, who never saw it finished): a central tourbillon, an inclined lateral dial only the wearer can see, all under a vaulted sapphire crystal, and available, too, on a sea of diamonds. It is vented freely in the M.A.D. Gallery in Geneva, where "mechanical art objects" on display are beautiful, intriguing, technically impeccable, and sometimes perfectly useless. They have their own muse and serve as worthy companions to the sci-fi-inspired table clocks that MB&F produces with L'épée 1938. One is shaped like a spaceship. The other is a huge spider.

Legacy Machine FlyingT
Reference number: 05.WSL.B
Movement: automatic, MB&F Caliber LM FlyingT; 30 jewels; central, flying 1-minute tourbillon; double spring barrel; dial inclined at 50 degrees; 100-hour power reserve
Functions: hours, minutes
Case: white gold, with diamonds, 38 × 20 mm; sapphire crystal; transparent case back; separate winding crowns for winding and time setting; water-resistant to 3 atm
Band: reptile skin, buckle
Price: $115,000

Legacy Machine Perpetual
Reference number: 03.TL.G
Movement: manually wound, MB&F Caliber LM3; ø 36.6 mm, height 12.6 mm; 41 jewels; 18,000 vph; double spring barrel, inverted movement design with 1 balance floating over dial; finely finished with côtes de Genève; 72-hour power reserve
Functions: hours, minutes (off-center); power reserve indicator; perpetual calendar with date, weekday, month, leap year (backward counting)
Case: titanium, ø 44 mm, height 17.5 mm; sapphire crystal; transparent case back; water-resistant to 3 atm
Band: reptile skin, folding clasp
Price: $157,000; limited to 50 pieces

HM7 Aquapod
Reference number: 70.TGL.B
Movement: automatic, MB&F Caliber HM7; ø 31.4 mm, height 17.45 mm; 35 jewels; 18,000 vph; flying 1-minute tourbillon, 3D vertical architecture, titanium and platinum rotor; 72-hour power reserve
Functions: hours, minutes (on spherical titanium-aluminum disk)
Case: titanium, ø 53.8 mm, height 21.3 mm; unidirectional bezel in sapphire crystal, with 0-60 scale; sapphire crystal; transparent case back; screw-in crowns for winding and time setting; water-resistant to 5 atm
Band: rubber, folding clasp
Price: $115,000; limited to 50 pieces

MEISTERSINGER

In 2014, MeisterSinger completed a long process of reorientation, setting the German brand in redux mode. At Baselworld 2014, it presented a portfolio of exclusively one-hand watches, the actual core of the brand. These watches express a relaxed and self-determined approach to the perception of time apparent in the special diurnal rituals that everyone knows, young, old, in private, or at work. These rituals actually divide up and define certain moments. And it is the reiteration of these moments which leads to order, or at least avoiding chaos.

Founder Martin Brassler launched his little collection of stylistically neat one-hand dials at the beginning of the new millennium. Looking at these ultimately simplified dials does tempt one to classify the one-hand watch as an archetype. The single hand simply cannot be reduced any further, and the 144 minutes for 12 hours around the dial do have a normative function of sorts. In a frenetic era when free time has become so rare, these watches slow things down a little. The most recent one-hander does provide the hour, jumping very precisely in a window under 12 o'clock—hence its Italian name *Salthora*, or "jumping hour."

Minimalism, however, does not mean less dynamism. Brassler always has some exciting idea, like the fun Metris, or the rigorously elegant Lunascope moon phase. The Vintago is vintage lookalike, with a disk display of the date at 3 o'clock. The Black Line, for its part, pays homage to the color black and its potential depths.

Design, product planning, service, and management all happen in Münster, Germany. The watches, however, are Swiss made, with ETA and Sellita movements. The Circularis is the brand's first model with an in-house movement, a manually wound caliber with two barrel springs developed in collaboration with the Swiss firm Synergies Horlogères.

MeisterSinger GmbH & Co. KG
Hafenweg 46
D-48155 Münster
Germany

Tel.:
+49-251-133-4860

E-mail:
info@meistersinger.de

Website:
www.meistersinger.de

Founded:
2001

Number of employees:
13

Annual production:
approx. 10,000 watches

U.S. distributor:
Duber Time
1920 Dr. MLK Jr. Street North
Suite #D
St. Petersburg, FL 33704
727-202-3262
damir@meistersingertime.com

Most important collections/price range:
from approx. $1,200 to $7,000

N° 03 Bronze
Reference number: AM917BR
Movement: automatic, ETA Caliber 2824-2 or Sellita SW200-1; ø 25.6 mm, height 4.6 mm; 25 or 26 jewels; 28,800 vph; with côtes de Genève; 38-hour power reserve
Functions: hours (each scale line indicates 5 minutes); date
Case: bronze, ø 43 mm, height 11.5 mm; sapphire crystal; transparent case back; water-resistant to 5 atm
Band: calfskin, buckle
Price: $2,395

Perigraph Bronze
Reference number: AM1017BR
Movement: automatic, ETA Caliber 2824-2 or Sellita SW200-1; ø 25.6 mm, height 4.6 mm; 25 or 26 jewels; 28,800 vph; with côtes de Genève; 38-hour power reserve
Functions: hours (each scale line indicates 5 minutes); date
Case: bronze, ø 43 mm, height 11.5 mm; sapphire crystal; transparent case back; water-resistant to 5 atm
Band: calfskin, buckle
Price: $2,495
Variations: stainless steel with ivory, gray, or blue dial ($1,995); stainless steel with black PVD coating ($2,395)

Metris Bronze
Reference number: ME917BR
Movement: automatic, ETA Caliber 2824-2 or Sellita SW200-1; ø 25.6 mm, height 4.6 mm; 25 or 26 jewels; 28,800 vph; 38-hour power reserve
Functions: hours (each scale line indicates 5 minutes); date
Case: bronze, ø 38 mm, height 11.1 mm; sapphire crystal; transparent case back; water-resistant to 20 atm
Band: calfskin, buckle
Price: $2,295

MEISTERSINGER

Vintago
Reference number: VT903
Movement: automatic, Sellita Caliber SW200-1; ø 25.6 mm, height 4.6 mm; 26 jewels; 28,800 vph; 38-hour power reserve
Functions: hours (each scale line indicates minutes); date
Case: stainless steel, ø 38 mm, height 10.15 mm; sapphire crystal; transparent case back; water-resistant to 5 atm
Band: calfskin, buckle
Price: $1,895
Variations: various dial colors

Urban Day Date
Reference number: URDD902
Movement: automatic, Miyota Caliber 8285; ø 29.2 mm, height 5.94 mm; 21 jewels; 21,600 vph; 42-hour power reserve
Functions: hours (each scale line indicates 5 minutes); date, weekday
Case: stainless steel, ø 40 mm, height 13.25 mm; sapphire crystal; transparent case back; water-resistant to 5 atm
Band: textile, buckle
Remarks: comes with additional calfskin strap
Price: $1,195
Variations: various dial colors

Pangaea Date
Reference number: PM903
Movement: automatic, Sellita Caliber SW200-1; ø 25.6 mm, height 4.6 mm; 26 jewels; 28,800 vph; 38-hour power reserve
Functions: hours (each scale line indicates 5 minutes); date
Case: stainless steel, ø 40 mm, height 11.25 mm; sapphire crystal; transparent case back; water-resistant to 5 atm
Band: calfskin, buckle
Price: $2,145

Lunascope
Reference number: LS901
Movement: automatic, ETA Caliber 2836-2 with MeisterSinger module; ø 25.6 mm, height 5.05 mm; 25 jewels; 28,800 vph; 38-hour power reserve
Functions: hours (each scale line indicates 5 minutes); date, moon phase
Case: stainless steel, ø 40 mm, height 12 mm; sapphire crystal; transparent case back; water-resistant to 5 atm
Band: calfskin, buckle
Price: $3,845

Salthora Meta X
Reference number: SAMX902
Movement: automatic, ETA Caliber 2824-2 or Sellita SW200-1 with in-house module for jumping hours display; ø 25.6 mm, height 6.9 mm; 25 or 26 jewels; 28,800 vph; with côtes de Genève; 38-hour power reserve
Functions: hours (digital, jumping), minutes
Case: stainless steel, ø 43 mm, height 14.2 mm; unidirectional ceramic bezel, with 0-60 scale; sapphire crystal; screw-in crown; water-resistant to 20 atm
Band: stainless steel Milanese bracelet, folding clasp
Price: $3,820
Variations: green indices; blue dial and bezel; calfskin strap with rubber coating ($3,495)

N° 01 40 mm
Reference number: DM317
Movement: manually wound, Sellita Caliber SW210; ø 25.6 mm, height 3.4 mm; 19 jewels; 28,800 vph; 42-hour power reserve
Functions: hours (each scale line indicates 5 minutes)
Case: stainless steel, ø 40 mm, height 11.5 mm; sapphire crystal; transparent case back; water-resistant to 5 atm
Band: calfskin, buckle
Price: $1,695
Variations: various dial colors

MIDO

Among the legacies of World War I was the popularization of the wristwatch, which had freed up soldiers' and aviators' hands to fight and steer, respectively, and permitted artillery officers to coordinate barrages. And, not surprisingly, this led to a kind of re-industrialization of the watch industry. Among the earliest companies to appear on the scene was Mido, which was founded on November 11, 1918—Armistice Day—by Georges Schaeren in Solothurn, Switzerland. The name means "I measure" in Spanish.

At first, the brand produced colorful and imaginative watches that were well suited to the Roaring Twenties. But in the 1930s Mido began making more serious, robust, sportive timepieces better suited for everyday use. For the watch fan of today, water resistance and self-winding are normal. Mido, however, was already offering this functionality in the 1930s with the introduction of the Multifort, which really put the company on the map. This Swiss manufacturer was equally innovative with its movements. It developed a number of very practical novelties like the Radiotime model (1939) and the Multicenterchrono (1941), which today have become genuine collectors' items.

In 1971 the Schaeren family sold the company to the General Watch Co. Ltd., a holding company belonging to ASUAG, which, in turn became the SMH and, ultimately, Swatch Group. Mido continues to produce mostly mechanical watches with about one-quarter of its production devoted to quartz movements. In 1998, Mido decided to revive some of its older watchmaking values. The Multifort, Commander, Battalion, and Baroncelli collections are each in their own way expressions of that mission. Nothing in-your-face, just affordable timepieces with the basic hallmarks of a good Swiss watch, like côtes de Genève on the rotors and, in some cases, even COSC certification. In the meantime, the brand has extended its sales potential to about 2,700 retailers in seventy countries.

Mido SA
Chemin des Tourelles 17
CH-2400 Le Locle
Switzerland

Tel.:
+41 32 933 35 11

Website:
www.mido.ch

Founded:
1918

Number of employees:
50 (estimated)

Annual production:
over 100,000

U.S. Distributor:
Mido, division of The Swatch Group (U.S.) Inc.
703 Waterford Way, Suite 450
Miami, FL 33126
www.midowatches.com

Most important collections/price range:
Baroncelli, Commander, Commander II, Multifort; Ocean Star / $800 to $2,300

Baroncelli Chronometer

Reference number: M027.408.16.061.00
Movement: automatic, Mido Caliber 80.821 (base ETA C07.821); ø 25.6 mm, height 5.22 mm; 25 jewels; 21,600 vph; silicon hairspring; rotor with côtes de Genève; 80-hour power reserve; COSC-certified chronometer
Functions: hours, minutes, sweep seconds; date
Case: stainless steel, ø 40 mm, height 9.43 mm; sapphire crystal; transparent case back; water-resistant to 3 atm
Band: calfskin, folding clasp
Price: $1,130

Baroncelli II

Reference number: M8600.4.15.1
Movement: automatic, Mido Caliber 80.611 (base ETA C07.811); ø 25.6 mm, height 4.74 mm; 25 jewels; 21,600 vph; rotor with côtes de Genève; 80-hour power reserve; COSC-certified chronometer
Functions: hours, minutes, sweep seconds; date
Case: stainless steel, ø 38 mm, height 9.1 mm; sapphire crystal; transparent case back; water-resistant to 5 atm
Band: stainless steel, folding clasp
Price: $870

Commander Shade

Reference number: M8429.3.23.11
Movement: automatic, ETA Caliber 2836-2; ø 25.6 mm, height 5.05 mm; 25 jewels; 28,800 vph; rotor with côtes de Genève; 38-hour power reserve
Functions: hours, minutes, sweep seconds; date, weekday
Case: stainless steel with rose gold PVD coating, ø 37 mm, height 10.45 mm; sapphire crystal; water-resistant to 5 atm
Band: stainless steel Milanese mesh with rose gold PVD coating, folding clasp
Price: $1,070

MIDO

Commander Shade
Reference number: M8429.4.27.11
Movement: automatic, ETA Caliber 2836-2; ø 25.6 mm, height 5.05 mm; 25 jewels; 28,800 vph; rotor with côtes de Genève; 38-hour power reserve
Functions: hours, minutes, sweep seconds; date, weekday
Case: stainless steel, ø 37 mm, height 10.45 mm; sapphire crystal; water-resistant to 5 atm
Band: stainless steel Milanese mesh, folding clasp
Price: $870

Ocean Star
Reference number: M026.430.36.091.00
Movement: automatic, Mido Caliber 80.621 (base ETA C07.621); ø 25.6 mm, height 5.22 mm; 25 jewels; 21,600 vph; rotor with côtes de Genève; 80-hour power reserve
Functions: hours, minutes, sweep seconds; date, weekday
Case: stainless steel with rose gold PVD coating, ø 42.5 mm, height 11.75 mm; unidirectional bezel, 0-60 scale; sapphire crystal; screw-in crown; water-resistant to 20 atm
Band: calfskin, buckle
Price: $970

Ocean Star
Reference number: M026.430.36.041.00
Movement: automatic, Mido Caliber 80.621 (base ETA C07.621); ø 25.6 mm, height 5.22 mm; 25 jewels; 21,600 vph; rotor with côtes de Genève; 80-hour power reserve
Functions: hours, minutes, sweep seconds; date, weekday
Case: stainless steel with rose gold PVD coating, ø 42.5 mm, height 11.75 mm; unidirectional bezel, 0-60 scale; sapphire crystal; screw-in crown; water-resistant to 20 atm
Band: textile, buckle
Remarks: additional calfskin strap
Price: $970

Ocean Star Diver 600
Reference number: M026.608.11.041.00
Movement: automatic, Mido Caliber 80.821 (base ETA C07.821); ø 25.6 mm, height 5.22 mm; 25 jewels; 21,600 vph; silicon hairspring; rotor with côtes de Genève; 80-hour power reserve; COSC-certified chronometer
Functions: hours, minutes, sweep seconds; date
Case: stainless steel, ø 43.5 mm, height 14.05 mm; unidirectional bezel, 0-60 scale; sapphire crystal; screw-in crown; helium valve; water-resistant to 60 atm
Band: stainless steel, folding clasp with extension link
Remarks: certified according to European diving equipment standards
Price: $1,700

Ocean Star Diver 600
Reference number: M026.608.37.051.00
Movement: automatic, Mido Caliber 80.821 (base ETA C07.821); ø 25.6 mm, height 5.22 mm; 25 jewels; 21,600 vph; silicon hairspring; rotor with côtes de Genève; 80-hour power reserve; COSC-certified chronometer
Functions: hours, minutes, sweep seconds; date
Case: stainless steel with black DLC coating, ø 43.5 mm, height 14.05 mm; unidirectional bezel, 0-60 scale; sapphire crystal; screw-in crown; helium valve; water-resistant to 60 atm
Band: rubber, buckle
Remarks: certified according to European diving equipment standards
Price: $1,070

Baroncelli Wild Stone
Reference number: M035.207.37.491.00
Movement: automatic, Mido Caliber 80.611 (base ETA C07.611); ø 25.6 mm, height 4.74 mm; 25 jewels; 21,600 vph; rotor with côtes de Genève; 80-hour power reserve
Functions: hours, minutes, sweep seconds; date
Case: stainless steel with rose gold PVD coating, ø 33 mm, height 9.75 mm; sapphire crystal; transparent case back; water-resistant to 5 atm
Band: textile, folding clasp
Remarks: dial with blue aventurine
Price: $1,090

MING

It takes a certain courage to launch a new watch brand in a crowded market that is subject to emotional swings. Ming, however, is no ordinary brand. It is a cooperative enterprise made up of six watchmaking enthusiasts from around the world. Leading the team is Ming Thein, a well-known photographer, designer, corporate strategist, and watch fan. He hails from Malaysia. Added up, the Ming team boasts a total of eighty solid years' experience collecting watches of all sorts, from vintage pieces to avant-garde works of kinetic art, from robust ground-level timepieces to custom-made products in the six-figure range.

Each of their purchases always gave them a genuine feeling of value and happiness. The mission of the six brand founders was therefore to reconnect with that feeling of emotional excitement that comes from discovering an authentic diamond in the rough. Their strategy was to create a series of watches that are conscientiously finished and stand out thanks to some subtle details. They also wanted their timepieces to be accessible to a large circle of collectors—in other words, affordable. The company is clear about one thing: They are not a classical *manufacture*. Rather, they cooperate with partners that are compatible with the brand's esthetic goals and price points. Most of these partners work with major established Swiss brands. All Ming watches are assembled, adjusted, and tested in Switzerland. The final quality control is then done in Kuala Lumpur by Ming Thein in person. "Ming is our way to share our cooperative's experience with other fans," he says, "people who would like to discover real horology above and beyond well-known labels and logos, and regardless whether they are experienced collectors or have just discovered their passion for watches."

Horologer Ming Sdn Bhd
B-3A-3, Sunway Palazzio
1 Jalan Sri Hartamas 3
50480 Kuala Lumpur
Malaysia

E-mail:
hello@ming.watch

Website:
www.ming.watch

Founded:
2017

Number of employees:
5

Annual production:
500–1,000 watches

Distribution:
online, direct sales

Most important collections:
19.01, 19.02, 17.06.
Note: All dollar prices are indicative, since the watches are priced in Swiss francs.

19.01
Reference number: 19.01
Movement: manually wound, Ming Caliber MSE100.1 (Schwarz Etienne base); ø 30.4 mm, height 5.35 mm; 25 jewels; 21,600 vph; partially skeletonized, sandblasted bridges; 2 spring barrels, 100-hour power reserve
Functions: hours, minutes
Case: titanium, ø 39 mm, height 10.9 mm; sapphire crystal; transparent case back; water-resistant to 5 atm
Band: calfskin, buckle
Remarks: dyed sapphire crystal dial, front sapphire crystal with engraved markings
Price: starting at $7,600

19.02 Worldtimer
Reference number: 19.02
Movement: automatic, Ming Caliber ASE220.1 (Schwarz Etienne base); ø 30.4 mm, height 5.55 mm; 34 jewels; 21,600 vph; microrotor; partially skeletonized movement, galvanized movement bridges; 70-hour power reserve
Functions: hours, minutes; world time display (2nd time zone)
Case: titanium, ø 39 mm, height 11.2 mm; sapphire crystal; transparent case back; water-resistant to 5 atm
Band: calfskin, buckle
Remarks: dyed central sapphire crystal, front sapphire crystal with engraved markings
Price: starting at $11,000

17.06 Copper
Reference number: 17.06
Movement: automatic, modified ETA Caliber 2824-2; ø 25.6 mm, height 4.6 mm; 25 jewels; 28,800 vph; 42-hour power reserve
Functions: hours, minutes
Case: stainless steel, ø 38 mm, height 10 mm; sapphire crystal; transparent case back; water-resistant to 10 atm
Band: calfskin, buckle
Remarks: metal dial with copper-colored paint, floating sapphire crystal ring with luminous indices
Price: $1,300
Variations: "Monolith" version with matte DLC-coated stainless steel case and black dial ($1,550)

Mk II Corporation
303 W. Lancaster Avenue, #283
Wayne, PA 19087

E-mail:
info@mkiiwatches.com

Website:
www.mkiiwatches.com

Founded:
2002

Number of employees:
3

Annual production:
800 watches

Distribution:
direct sales and select retail

Most important collections/price range:
Ready-to-Wear Collection / $500 to $995;
Bencrafted™ Collection / $1,000 to $2,000

If vintage and unserviceable watches had their say, they would probably be naturally attracted to Mk II for the name alone, which is a military designation for the second generation of equipment. The company, which was founded by watch enthusiast and maker Bill Yao in 2002, not only puts retired designs back into service, but also modernizes and customizes them. Before the screwed-down crown, diving watches were not nearly as reliably sealed, for example. And some beautiful old pieces were made with plated brass cases or featured Bakelite components, which are either easily damaged or have aged poorly. The company substitutes not only proven modern materials, but also modern manufacturing methods and techniques to ensure a better outcome.

These are material issues that the team at Mk II handles with great care. They will not, metaphorically speaking, airbrush a Model-T. As genuine watch lovers themselves, they make sure that the final design is in the spirit of the watch itself, which still leaves a great deal of leeway for many iterations, given a sufficient number of parts. In the company's output, vintage style and modern functionality are key. The watches are assembled by hand at the company's workshop in Pennsylvania—and subjected to a rigorous regime of testing. The components are individually inspected, the cases tested at least three times for water resistance, and at the end the whole watch is regulated in six positions. Looking to the future, Mk II aspires to carry its clean vintage style into the development of what it hopes will be future classics of its own.

Paradive
Reference number: CD04.1-1002N
Movement: automatic (hack setting), Seiko Caliber SII NE15; ø 27.40 mm, height 5.32 mm; 24 jewels; 21,600 vph; 50-hour power reserve; rotor decorated with côtes de Genève
Functions: hours, minutes, sweep seconds, date
Case: stainless steel, ø 41.2 mm, height 15.50 mm; 120-click unidirectional bezel; high domed sapphire crystal with antireflective coating; screw-down case back; screw-in crown; water-resistant to 20 atm
Band: nylon
Price: $895
Variations: without date, dive bezel

Hawkinge AGL
Reference Number: CG05-3001N
Movement: automatic (hack setting), Seiko Caliber SII NE15 (made in Japan); ø 27.40 mm, height 5.32 mm; 24 jewels; 21,600 vph; 50-hour power reserve; rotor decorated with côtes de Genève
Functions: hours, minutes, sweep seconds
Case: stainless steel; ø 37.80 mm, height 12.75 mm; domed sapphire crystal with antireflective coating; screw-down case back; screw-in crown; water-resistant to 10 atm
Band: nylon
Price: $595
Variations: leather strap

Cruxible
Reference Number: CG06-2001N
Movement: automatic (hack setting), Seiko Caliber SII NE15 (made in Japan); ø 27.40 mm, height 5.32 mm; 24 jewels; 21,600 vph; 50-hour power reserve; rotor decorated with côtes de Genève
Functions: hours, minutes, sweep seconds
Case: stainless steel, ø 39 mm, height 13.55 mm; domed sapphire crystal with antireflective coating; screw-down case back; screw-in crown; water-resistant to 10 atm
Band: nylon
Price: $649
Variations: with date, leather strap

MONDAINE

On February 23, 1983, Switzerland's Migros supermarket chain presented its annual report to the business press. In addition to the reams of paper, each reporter present received a watch. The day after, all the papers in Switzerland were talking not about groceries but rather about the birth of the M-Watch, the *Volksuhr,* the "people's watch." It was a week before the coming-out of Swatch . . .

Few have ever realized that the "M" stood not for Migros but for Mondaine Watch, a company founded in the early fifties by Erwin Bernheim, who parlayed a side job dealing in watches into a sizable company carrying several brands. The Migros cooperation was a major coup. But then Bernheim, now joined by his sons Ronnie and André, decided to make something quintessentially Swiss. After some intense brainstorming, they locked onto the Swiss Railways (SBB) clock, originally designed by the Bauhaus engineer Hans Hilfiker (1901–1993).

Like its model, which hangs in every Swiss railway station, this watch features a simple dial with the characteristic red second hand with its round end, recalling the stationmaster's signaling pan and making for greater legibility at a distance. It became a sensation and has appeared in dozens of iterations, with black dials, eco-friendly straps, dash clocks, kitchen clocks, and so forth. A special series was even made that replicates the characteristic 58.5-second journey of the second hand that travelers always see. Before hitting the 12, the second hand pauses to let all clocks in Swiss railway stations be synchronized.

In 2014, the two brothers, co-CEOs since their father's death, came out with a new Swiss icon: the Helvetica, the first watch to pay tribute to a font. It is in some ways a contradiction, a watch that attracts attention by being as unobtrusive as possible. Helvetica's only character with a serif is the number 1. It was cleverly worked into the lugs.

Mondaine Watch Ltd.
Etzelstrasse 27
CH-8808 Pfäffikon SZ
Switzerland

Tel.:
+41-58 666 88 00

E-mail:
info@mondaine.com

Website:
www.mondaine.com

Founded:
1951

Number of employees
120

Distributor:
Mondaine USA
Lumondi Inc.
27 W. 24th St., Suite 700B
New York, NY 10010
www.mondaine-usa.com
917-522-3421

Most important collections/price range:
Swiss Railways Watch and Helvetica / $195 to $395

Official Swiss Railways Watch Evo Big Automatic
Reference number: A132.30348.11SBB
Movement: automatic, Sellita Caliber SW2120-1; ø 25.6 mm, height 5.6 mm; 25 jewels; 28,800 vph; 38-hour power reserve
Functions: hours, minutes, sweep seconds; day, date
Case: stainless steel, ø 40 mm, height 10 mm; hardened mineral glass; transparent case back; water-resistant to 10 atm
Band: leather, buckle
Price: $650
Variations: different diameters and dials; quartz

Official Swiss Railways Watch Evo Big
Reference number: MSE.40111.LG
Movement: quartz, Ronda 513; ø 25.6 mm, height 3 mm; 1 jewel
Functions: hours, minutes, sweep seconds
Case: gold-plated stainless steel, ø 40 mm, height 12 mm; sapphire crystal; water-resistant to 5 atm
Band: leather, buckle
Price: $295
Variations: various case diameters

Helvetica Hand Winder
Reference number: MH1.R3610.LG
Movement: manually wound, Sellita Caliber SW210-1; ø 25.6 mm, height 3.35 mm; 19 jewels; 28,800 vph; 50-hour power reserve
Functions: hours, minutes, sweep seconds; date
Case: stainless steel, ø 40 mm, height 8 mm; sapphire crystal; water-resistant to 3 atm
Band: leather, buckle
Price: $1,150

Montblanc Montre SA
10, chemin des Tourelles
CH-2400 Le Locle
Switzerland

Tel.:
+41-32-933-8888

E-mail:
service@montblanc.com

Website:
www.montblanc.com

Founded:
1997 (1906 in Hamburg)

Number of employees:
worldwide approx. 3,000

U.S. distributor:
Montblanc North America
645 Fifth Avenue, 7th Floor
New York, NY 10022
800-995-4810
www.montblanc.com

Most important collections:
Heritage Chronométrie, Heritage Spirit, Meisterstück, Star, Nicolas Rieussec, 4810, TimeWalker, Collection Villeret, 1858 Collection

MONTBLANC

It was with great skill and cleverness that Nicolas Rieussec (1781–1866) used the invention of a special chronograph—the "Time Writer," a device that released droplets of ink onto a rotating sheet of paper—to make a name for himself. Montblanc, once famous only for its exclusive writing implements, borrowed that name on its way to becoming a distinguished watch brand. Within a few years, it had created an impressive range of chronographs driven by in-house calibers: from simple automatic stopwatches to flagship pieces with two independent spring barrels for time and "time-writing."

The Richemont Group, owner of Montblanc, has placed great trust in its "daughter" company, having put the little *manufacture* Minerva, which it purchased at the beginning of 2007, at the disposal of Montblanc. Minerva, which was founded in Villeret in 1858, was already building keyless pocket watches in the 1880s, and by the early twentieth century was producing monopusher chronographs with a reputation for precision. Today, the Minerva Institute serves as a kind of think tank for the future, a place where young watchmakers can absorb the old traditions and skills, as well as the wealth of experience and mind-set of the masters.

Montblanc is continuing the Minerva tradition today with four leading collections: the 1858, the Heritage, the Star Legacy, and the TimeWalker line, as well as a ladies' line, the Bohème.

1858 Geosphere

Reference number: 119286
Movement: automatic, Montblanc Caliber MB 29.25; 26 jewels; 28,800 vph; 42-hour power reserve
Functions: hours, minutes; additional 12-hour display (2nd time zone), synchronously counter-rotating world time indicators for northern and southern hemispheres; date
Case: stainless steel, ø 42 mm, height 12.8 mm; bezel with ceramic inlay; sapphire crystal; transparent case back; water-resistant to 10 atm
Band: calfskin, folding clasp
Price: $5,600

1858 Geosphere Bronze

Reference number: 119909
Movement: automatic, Montblanc Caliber MB 29.25; 26 jewels; 28,800 vph; 42-hour power reserve
Functions: hours, minutes; additional 12-hour display (2nd time zone), synchronously counter-rotating world time indicators for northern and southern hemispheres; date
Case: bronze, ø 42 mm, height 12.8 mm; bezel with ceramic insert; sapphire crystal; water-resistant to 10 atm
Band: textile, buckle
Price: $6,300; limited to 1858 pieces

1858 Automatic Chronograph

Reference number: 119908
Movement: automatic, Montblanc Caliber MB 25.11; ø 30 mm, height 7.9 mm; 27 jewels; 28,800 vph; 48-hour power reserve
Functions: hours, minutes, subsidiary seconds; chronograph
Case: bronze, ø 42 mm, height 14.55 mm; sapphire crystal; water-resistant to 10 atm
Band: textile, buckle
Price: $5,000; limited to 1858 pieces

MONTBLANC

1858 Split Second Chronograph
Reference number: 119910
Movement: manually wound, Montblanc Caliber MB M16.31; ø 38.4 mm, height 8.13 mm; 22 jewels; 18,000 vph; column wheel control of chronograph functions using a single pusher; 50-hour power reserve
Functions: hours, minutes, subsidiary seconds; split-second chronograph
Case: bronze, ø 44 mm, height 14.55 mm; sapphire crystal; transparent case back
Band: reptile skin, buckle
Price: $31,000; limited to 100 pieces

Heritage Pulsograph
Reference number: 119914
Movement: manually wound, Montblanc Caliber MB M13.21; ø 29.5 mm, height 6.4 mm; 22 jewels; 18,000 vph; screw balance, column wheel control of chronograph functions using single pushers; 55-hour power reserve
Functions: hours, minutes, subsidiary seconds; chronograph
Case: stainless steel, ø 40 mm, height 12.65 mm; sapphire crystal; transparent case back; water-resistant to 10 atm
Band: reptile skin, buckle
Price: $30,000; limited to 100 pieces

Heritage Perpetual Calendar
Reference number: 119926
Movement: automatic, Montblanc Caliber MB 29.22; ø 28.2 mm, height 4.95 mm; 77 jewels; 28,800 vph; 48-hour power reserve
Functions: hours, minutes; additional 12-hour display (2nd time zone); perpetual calendar with date, weekday, month, moon phase, leap year
Case: red gold, ø 40 mm, height 12.3 mm; sapphire crystal; transparent case back; water-resistant to 5 atm
Band: reptile skin, buckle
Price: $26,240; limited to 100 pieces

Heritage Monopusher Chronograph
Reference number: 119952
Movement: automatic, Montblanc Caliber MB 25.12; ø 30 mm, height 7.9 mm; 27 jewels; 28,800 vph; monopusher for column wheel control of chronograph functions; 48-hour power reserve
Functions: hours, minutes, subsidiary seconds; chronograph
Case: stainless steel, ø 42 mm, height 14.65 mm; sapphire crystal; water-resistant to 10 atm
Band: stainless steel Milanese mesh, folding clasp
Price: $5,160

Heritage Automatic
Reference number: 119943
Movement: automatic, Montblanc Caliber MB 24.26 (base Sellita SW200-1); ø 25.6 mm, height 4.6 mm; 26 jewels; 28,800 vph; 38-hour power reserve
Functions: hours, minutes, sweep seconds
Case: stainless steel, ø 40 mm, height 11.65 mm; sapphire crystal; water-resistant to 5 atm
Band: reptile skin, buckle
Price: $2,270

Star Legacy Nicolas Rieussec Chronograph
Reference number: 119954
Movement: automatic, Montblanc Caliber MB R200; ø 31 mm, height 8.46 mm; 40 jewels; 28,800 vph; 2 barrel springs; monopusher for column wheel control of chronograph functions; 72-hour power reserve
Functions: hours, minutes, subsidiary seconds; additional 12-hour display (2nd time zone), day/night indicator; chronograph; date
Case: stainless steel, ø 44.8 mm, height 15.02 mm; sapphire crystal; transparent case back; water-resistant to 3 atm
Band: reptile skin, double folding clasp
Price: $8,000

Star Legacy Automatic Date
Reference number: 119956
Movement: automatic, Montblanc Caliber MB 24.01 (base ETA 2892-A2); ø 25.6 mm, height 3.6 mm; 21 jewels; 28,800 vph; 42-hour power reserve
Functions: hours, minutes, sweep seconds; date
Case: stainless steel, ø 42 mm, height 9.58 mm; sapphire crystal; transparent case back; water-resistant to 3 atm
Band: reptile skin, buckle
Price: $2,990

TimeWalker Manufacture Chronograph
Reference number: 119942
Movement: automatic, Montblanc Caliber MB 25.10; ø 30.15 mm, height 7.9 mm; 33 jewels; 28,800 vph; column wheel control of chronograph functions, screw balance; 46-hour power reserve
Functions: hours, minutes, subsidiary seconds; chronograph; date
Case: stainless steel, ø 43 mm, height 15.2 mm; ceramic bezel; sapphire crystal; transparent case back; water-resistant to 10 atm
Band: calfskin, triple folding clasp
Price: $5,400

TimeWalker Automatic Chronograph
Reference number: 119940
Movement: automatic, Montblanc Caliber MB 25.07 (base ETA 7750); ø 30 mm, height 7.9 mm; 25 jewels; 28,800 vph; 46-hour power reserve
Functions: hours, minutes, subsidiary seconds; chronograph; date
Case: stainless steel, ø 41 mm, height 14.54 mm; ceramic bezel; sapphire crystal; transparent case back; water-resistant to 10 atm
Band: rubber, buckle
Price: $3,370

Bohème Date Automatic
Reference number: 119920
Movement: automatic, Montblanc Caliber MB 24.17 (base ETA 2824-2); ø 25.6 mm, height 4.6 mm; 25 jewels; 28,800 vph; 38-hour power reserve
Functions: hours, minutes, sweep seconds; date
Case: stainless steel, ø 34 mm, height 9.32 mm; sapphire crystal; 8 diamond indices; water-resistant to 3 atm
Band: stainless steel, folding clasp
Price: $3,305

Bohème Day & Night
Reference number: 119932
Movement: automatic, Montblanc Caliber MB 24.10 (base ETA 2893-2); ø 25.6 mm, height 4.1 mm; 21 jewels; 28,800 vph; 42-hour power reserve
Functions: hours, minutes, sweep seconds; day/night indicator; date
Case: stainless steel, ø 30 mm, height 9.41 mm; sapphire crystal; water-resistant to 3 atm
Band: calfskin, buckle
Remarks: dial with 8 diamonds
Price: $3,140

Bohème Perpetual Calendar
Reference number: 123866
Movement: automatic, Montblanc Caliber MB 29.22; ø 28.2 mm, height 4.95 mm; 77 jewels; 28,800 vph; 45-hour power reserve
Functions: hours, minutes; additional 12-hour display (2nd time zone); perpetual calendar with date, weekday, month, moon phase, leap year
Case: stainless steel, ø 38 mm, height 11.85 mm; bezel set with 60 diamonds; sapphire crystal; transparent case back; water-resistant to 3 atm
Band: reptile skin, buckle
Price: $17,500

MONTBLANC

Caliber MB R200
Automatic; monopusher column wheel control, vertical chronograph clutch, stop-seconds mechanism; double spring barrel, 72-hour power reserve
Functions: hours, minutes, subsidiary seconds; additional 12-hour display (2nd time zone), chronograph; date
Diameter: 31 mm
Height: 8.46 mm
Jewels: 40
Balance: screw balance
Frequency: 28,800 vph
Balance spring: flat hairspring
Remarks: rhodium-plated mainplate with perlage, bridges with côtes de Genève

Caliber MB 25.10
Automatic; monopusher for column wheel control of chronograph functions, horizontal chronograph clutch, stop-seconds mechanism; single spring barrel, 46-hour power reserve
Functions: hours, minutes, subsidiary seconds; chronograph
Diameter: 30.15 mm
Height: 7.9 mm
Jewels: 33
Balance: screw balance
Frequency: 28,800 vph
Balance spring: flat hairspring
Remarks: 232 parts; rhodium-plated mainplate with perlage, bridges with côtes de Genève

Caliber MB M13.21
Manually wound; column wheel control of chronograph functions; single spring barrel, 60-hour power reserve
Functions: hours, minutes, subsidiary seconds; chronograph
Diameter: 29.5 mm
Height: 6.4 mm
Jewels: 22
Balance: screw balance with weights
Frequency: 18,000 vph
Balance spring: with Phillips end curve
Shock protection: Incabloc
Remarks: plates and German silver bridges, rhodium-plated, partially with perlage, hand-beveled

Caliber MB 29.22
Automatic; single spring barrel, 48-hour power reserve
Base caliber: Cartier 1904-PS MC
Functions: hours, minutes, sweep seconds; additional 12-hour display (2nd time zone); perpetual calendar with date, weekday, month, moon phase, leap year
Diameter: 28.2 mm
Height: 4.95 mm
Jewels: 77
Frequency: 28,800 vph
Balance spring: flat hairspring
Remarks: 378 parts

Caliber MB M16.68
Manually wound; exo-tourbillon with external balance spring; mainplate of German silver; single spring barrel, 50-hour power reserve
Functions: hours, minutes (off-center), subsidiary seconds (on tourbillon cage)
Diameter: 38.3 mm
Height: 10.6 mm
Jewels: 19
Balance: screw balance
Frequency: 18,000 vph
Balance spring: flat hairspring with Phillips end curve
Remarks: 218 parts, finely finished with côtes de Genève

Caliber MB M16.31
Manually wound; monopusher for column wheel control of chronograph functions, swan-neck fine adjustment; single spring barrel, 50-hour power reserve
Functions: hours, minutes, subsidiary seconds; split-second chronograph
Diameter: 38.4 mm
Height: 8.13 mm
Jewels: 22
Balance: screw balance with Breguet hairspring
Frequency: 18,000 vph
Balance spring: with Phillips end curve
Remarks: rhodium-plated mainplate with perlage, bridges with côtes de Genève, gold-plated wheelworks; 262 parts

Mühle Glashütte GmbH
Nautische Instrumente und Feinmechanik
Altenberger Strasse 35
D-01768 Glashütte
Germany

Tel.:
+49-35053-3203-0

E-mail:
info@muehle-glashuette.de

Website:
www.muehle-glashuette.de

Founded:
first founding 1869; second founding 1993

Number of employees:
47

U.S. distributor:
Mühle Glashütte
Old Northeast Jewelers
1131 4th Street North
St. Petersburg, FL 33701
800-922-4377
www.muehle-glashuette.com

Most important collections/price range:
mechanical wristwatches / approx. $1,399 to $5,400

MÜHLE GLASHÜTTE

The year 2019 brought two anniversaries for the firm Rob. Mühle & Sohn. The big one is the 150 years the company has produced precision measuring instruments and survived the ups and downs of German history. Originally, this was for the local watch industry and the German School of Watchmaking. By the early 1920s, the firm was supplying the automobile industry, making speedometers, automobile clocks, tachometers, and other measurement instruments.

As a supplier for the Wehrmacht, it drew Soviet bombing during World War II, and was then nationalized. After the fall of the Iron Curtain, Hans-Jürgen Mühle took the helm, followed, in 2007, by his son, Thilo Mühle.

The second, small, anniversary of 2019 is the quarter-century Mühle has been making wristwatches, a sideline of sorts that now overshadows the nautical instruments for which Mühle was famous. Its collection comprises mechanical wristwatches at entry- and mid-level prices. For these, the company uses Swiss base movements that are equipped with such in-house developments as a patented woodpecker-neck regulation and the Mühle rotor. The modifications are so extensive that they have led to the calibers having their own names. The traditional line named "R. Mühle & Sohn," introduced in 2014, is equipped with the RMK 1 and RMK 2 calibers. And there are other, somewhat less nautically inspired timepieces, like the Lunova series or the 29ers, which are simply elegant in an unspectacular way.

Panova Grün
Reference number: M1-40-76-NB
Movement: automatic, Sellita Caliber SW200-1; ø 25.6 mm, height 4.6 mm; 26 jewels; 28,800 vph; woodpecker-neck regulator, Mühle rotor, carefully reworked with special Mühle finish; 38-hour power reserve
Functions: hours, minutes, sweep seconds
Case: stainless steel, ø 40 mm, height 10.4 mm; sapphire crystal; screw-in crown; water-resistant to 10 atm
Band: textile, buckle
Price: $1,000
Variations: calfskin band ($1,000)

Teutonia IV Moon Phase
Reference number: M1-44-05-LB
Movement: automatic, Sellita Caliber SW280-1; ø 25.6 mm, height 5.4 mm; 26 jewels; 28,800 vph; woodpecker-neck regulator, Mühle rotor, carefully reworked with special Mühle finish; 38-hour power reserve
Functions: hours, minutes, sweep seconds; date, moon phase
Case: stainless steel, ø 41 mm, height 12.6 mm; sapphire crystal; transparent case back; water-resistant to 10 atm
Band: calfskin, double folding clasp
Price: $2,699
Variations: stainless steel bracelet ($2,799)

Sea-Timer BlackMotion
Reference number: M1-41-83-NB
Movement: automatic, Sellita Caliber SW200-1; ø 25.6 mm, height 4.6 mm; 26 jewels; 28,800 vph; woodpecker-neck regulator, Mühle rotor, carefully reworked with special Mühle finish; 38-hour power reserve
Functions: hours, minutes, sweep seconds; date
Case: stainless steel with black titanium carbide coating, ø 44 mm, height 12.5 mm; bidirectional bezel, 0-60 scale; sapphire crystal; transparent case back; water-resistant to 30 atm
Band: textile, buckle
Price: $2,599

MÜHLE GLASHÜTTE

ProMare Go
Reference number: M1-42-32-NB
Movement: automatic, Sellita Caliber SW200-1; ø 25.6 mm, height 4.6 mm; 26 jewels; 28,800 vph; woodpecker-neck regulator, Mühle rotor, carefully reworked with special Mühle finish; 38-hour power reserve
Functions: hours, minutes, sweep seconds; date
Case: stainless steel, ø 42 mm, height 12.2 mm; bidirectional bezel, 0-60 scale; sapphire crystal; transparent case back; screw-in crown; water-resistant to 30 atm
Band: rubber with leather overlay, buckle
Price: $2,100

Teutonia Sport I
Reference number: M1-29-65-LB
Movement: automatic, Mühle Caliber MU 9419 (base Sellita SW510-1); ø 30 mm, height 7.9 mm; 25 jewels; 28,800 vph; woodpecker-neck regulator, Mühle rotor, carefully reworked with special Mühle finish; 48-hour power reserve
Functions: hours, minutes, subsidiary seconds; chronograph; date
Case: stainless steel, ø 42.6 mm, height 15.5 mm; bidirectional bezel, 0-60 scale; sapphire crystal; transparent case back; screw-in crown; water-resistant to 10 atm
Band: calfskin, buckle
Price: $3,899

29er Big
Reference number: M1-25-33-MB
Movement: automatic, Sellita Caliber SW200-1, Mühle version; ø 25.6 mm, height 4.6 mm; 26 jewels; 28,800 vph; woodpecker-neck regulator, Mühle rotor, carefully reworked with special Mühle finish; 38-hour power reserve
Functions: hours, minutes, sweep seconds; date
Case: stainless steel, ø 42.4 mm, height 11.3 mm; sapphire crystal; transparent case back; screw-in crown; water-resistant to 10 atm
Band: stainless steel, folding clasp
Price: $2,199
Variations: calfskin strap ($2,099); rubber strap ($2,099)

29er Zeigerdatum
Reference number: M1-25-32-NB
Movement: automatic, Sellita Caliber SW221-1; ø 25.6 mm, height 5.05 mm; 26 jewels; 28,800 vph; woodpecker-neck regulator, Mühle rotor, carefully reworked with special Mühle finish; 38-hour power reserve
Functions: hours, minutes, sweep seconds; date
Case: stainless steel, ø 42.4 mm, height 12.2 mm; sapphire crystal; transparent case back; water-resistant to 10 atm
Band: textile, buckle
Price: $1,399
Variations: stainless steel bracelet ($1,630)

Robert Mühle Moon Phase
Reference number: M1-11-53-LB
Movement: manually wound, Robert Mühle Caliber RMK 04; ø 36.6 mm, height 8.35 mm; 36 jewels; 21,600 vph; engraved balance cock, with woodpecker-neck regulator, three-fifth plate with Glashütte long-slot click; 3 screw-mounted gold chatons; 56-hour power reserve
Functions: hours, minutes, subsidiary seconds; power reserve indicator; date, moon phase
Case: stainless steel, ø 42 mm, height 12.7 mm; sapphire crystal; transparent case back; water-resistant to 10 atm
Band: reptile skin, buckle
Price: $9,450; limited to 100 pieces

RMK 03
Manually wound; woodpecker-neck regulator; single spring barrel, 56-hour power reserve
Functions: hours, minutes, subsidiary seconds; power reserve indicator; date
Diameter: 36.6 mm
Height: 8.35 mm
Jewels: 33, including 3 in screw-mounted gold chatons
Balance: glucydur
Frequency: 21,600 vph
Balance spring: Nivarox
Remarks: three-fifth plate, Glashütter stopwork, hand-engraved balance cock

Nivrel Uhren
Gerd Hofer GmbH
Kossmannstrasse 3
D-66119 Saarbrücken
Germany

Tel.:
+49-681-584-6576

E-mail:
info@nivrel.com

Website:
www.nivrel.com

Founded:
1978

Number of employees:
10, plus external staff members

Distribution:
Please contact headquarters for enquiries.

Most important collections/price range:
mechanical watches, most with complications / approx. $600 to $45,000

NIVREL

In 1891, master goldsmith Friedrich Jacob Kraemer founded a jewelry and watch shop in Saarbrücken that proved to be the place to go for fine craftsmanship. Gerd Hofer joined the family business in 1956, carrying it on into the fourth generation. However, his true passion was for watchmaking. In 1993, he and his wife, Gitta, bought the rights to use the Swiss name Nivrel, a brand that had been established in 1936, and integrated production of these watches into their German-based operations.

Today, Nivrel is led by the Hofers' daughter Anja, who is keeping both lineages alive. Mechanical complications with Swiss movements of the finest technical level and finishing as well as gold watches in the high-end design segment of the industry are manufactured with close attention to detail and an advanced level of craftsmanship. In addition to classic automatic watches, the brand has introduced everything from complicated chronographs and skeletonized watches to perpetual calendars and tourbillons. The movements and all the "habillage" of the watches—case, dial, crystal, crown, etc.—are made in Switzerland. Watch design, assembly, and finishing are done in Saarbrücken.

Nivrel watches are a perfect example of how quickly a watch brand incorporating a characteristic style and immaculate quality can make a respected place for itself in the industry. Affordable prices also play a significant role in this brand's success, but they do not keep the brand from innovating. Nivrel has teamed up with the Department of Metallic Materials of Saarland University to develop a special alloy for repeater springs that is softer and does not need as much energy to press.

Héritage Automatique
Reference number: N 121.001 AAAB
Movement: automatic, ETA Caliber 2824-2; ø 25.6 mm, height 4.6 mm; 25 jewels; 28,800 vph; 38-hour power reserve
Functions: hours, minutes, sweep seconds; date
Case: stainless steel, ø 40 mm, height 10 mm; sapphire crystal; transparent case back
Band: calfskin, buckle
Price: $895

Replique Aviateur II
Reference number: N 121.001 AASDS
Movement: automatic, ETA Caliber 2824-2; ø 25.6 mm, height 4.6 mm; 25 jewels; 28,800 vph; 38-hour power reserve
Functions: hours, minutes, sweep seconds
Case: stainless steel, ø 40 mm, height 10 mm; sapphire crystal; transparent case back
Band: calfskin, buckle
Price: $670

Red Voyager
Reference number: N 148.001 AASDS
Movement: automatic, ETA Caliber 2824-2; ø 25.6 mm, height 4.6 mm; 25 jewels; 28,800 vph; 42-hour power reserve
Functions: hours, minutes, sweep seconds; date
Case: stainless steel, ø 43 mm, height 14.5 mm; unidirectional bezel, 0-60 scale; sapphire crystal; screw-in crown; water-resistant to 20 atm
Band: calfskin, buckle
Remarks: additional silicon strap
Price: $799; limited to 100 pieces

NOMOS

Still waters run deep, and discreet business practices at times travel far. Nomos, founded in 1990, has suddenly become a full-fledged *manufacture* with brand-new facilities and a smart policy of only so much growth as the small team gathered around the founder, Roland Schwertner, and his associate Uwe Ahrendt can easily absorb.

The collection has grown to thirteen model families in a short period of time, with around one hundred variations. The number of calibers available is growing at an impressive rate, including two luxury manually wound movements with fine finishings. The first one was the manually wound Alpha, but the one that made a splash was undoubtedly the DUW 4401 (Deutsche Uhrenwerke Nomos Glashütte), equipped with an in-house escapement with a spring "made in Germany." It will gradually be used in all the movements, including the new, automatic, ultrathin DUW 3001. The DUW 6101 features a safe and easy date correction, and it is a mere 3.6 millimeters high including the date, which fits well in the company's design efforts.

Speaking of design, the three hundred people working at Nomos include about forty design and communication staff at the Berlinblau in-house design studio and in the United States, where Nomos has offices (in New York) and about fifty points of sale. The key strategy: outstanding watches at an affordable price, a simple look full of subtle details, and marketing that is bold and humorous. Nomos, visibly, is a member of the *deutscher Werkbund*, precursor to the Bauhaus school, meaning pared-down industrial design, with a touch of Berlin's biting humor. This esthetic scrim, as it were, has produced the swimmer's watch Ahoi (as in "ship ahoy!"), with an optional synthetic strap like those that carry locker keys at Germany's public swimming pools, or the related, colorful Aqua series. Nomos has also been addressing the young and chic with the highly affordable Campus models. In 2018 came the Autobahn, designed in collaboration with Werner Aisslinger. And, yes, it definitely reminds one of a speedometer, with a fun open circle of luminescent segments.

Nomos Glashütte/SA
Roland Schwertner KG
Ferdinand-Adolph-Lange-Platz 2
01768 Glashütte
Germany

Tel.:
+49-35053-404-0

E-mail:
nomos@glashuette.com

Website:
nomos-glashuette.com

Founded:
1990

Number of employees:
approx. 300

U.S. distributor:
For the U.S. market, please contact:
NOMOS Glashuette USA Inc.
347 W. 36th St., Suite 600
New York, NY 10018
212-929-2575
contact@nomos-watches.com

Collections/price range:
Ahoi / $4,020 to $4,660; Autobahn / $4,800; Club / $1,500 to $4,060; Lambda / $17,000 to $20,000; Ludwig / $1,380 to $4,000; Lux / $19,500 to $21,500; Metro / $2,860 to $9,700; Orion / $1,600 to $4,350; Tangente / $1,440 to $4,980; Tangomat / $3,280 to $4,920; Tetra / $1,660 to $3,980; Zürich / $4,480 to $6,100

Tangente Sport Neomatik 42 Date Marine Black

Reference number: 581
Movement: automatic, Nomos caliber DUW 6101; ø 35.2 mm, height 3.6 mm; 27 jewels; 21,600 vph; three-quarter plate, finely finished movement; 42-hour power reserve
Functions: hours, minutes, subsidiary seconds; date
Case: stainless steel, ø 42 mm, height 10.9 mm; sapphire crystal; transparent case back; screw-down crown; water-resistant to 30 atm
Band: stainless steel, folding clasp
Price: $4,980

Tangente Sport Neomatik 42 Date

Reference number: 580
Movement: automatic, Nomos caliber DUW 6101; ø 35.2 mm, height 3.6 mm; 27 jewels; 21,600 vph; three-quarter plate, finely finished movement; 42-hour power reserve
Functions: hours, minutes, subsidiary seconds; date
Case: stainless steel, ø 42 mm, height 10.9 mm; sapphire crystal; transparent case back; screw-down crown; water-resistant to 30 atm
Band: stainless steel, folding clasp
Price: $4,980

Club Sport Neomatik 42 Date Black

Reference number: 781
Movement: automatic, Nomos caliber DUW 6101; ø 35.2 mm, height 3.6 mm; 27 jewels; 21,600 vph; three-quarter plate, finely finished movement; 42-hour power reserve
Functions: hours, minutes, subsidiary seconds; date
Case: stainless steel, ø 42 mm, height 10.2 mm; sapphire crystal; transparent case back; screw-down crown; water-resistant to 30 atm
Band: stainless steel, folding clasp
Price: $4,060

NOMOS

Tangente Neomatik 41 Update Ruthenium
Reference number: 181
Movement: automatic, Nomos caliber DUW 6101; ø 35.2 mm, height 3.6 mm; 27 jewels; 21,600 vph; three-quarter plate, finely finished movement; 42-hour power reserve
Functions: hours, minutes, subsidiary seconds; date
Case: stainless steel, ø 40.5 mm, height 7.9 mm; sapphire crystal; transparent case back; water-resistant to 5 atm
Band: horse leather, buckle
Price: $4,100

Tangente Neomatik 41 Update
Reference number: 180
Movement: automatic, Nomos caliber DUW 6101; ø 35.2 mm, height 3.6 mm; 27 jewels; 21,600 vph; three-quarter plate, finely finished movement; 42-hour power reserve
Functions: hours, minutes, subsidiary seconds; date
Case: stainless steel, ø 40.5 mm, height 7.9 mm; sapphire crystal; transparent case back; water-resistant to 5 atm
Band: horse leather, buckle
Price: $4,100

Orion Neomatik 41 Date Midnight Blue
Reference number: 363
Movement: automatic, Nomos caliber DUW 6101; ø 35.2 mm, height 3.6 mm; 27 jewels; 21,600 vph; three-quarter plate, finely finished movement; 42-hour power reserve
Functions: hours, minutes, subsidiary seconds; date
Case: stainless steel, ø 40.5 mm, height 9.4 mm; sapphire crystal; transparent case back; water-resistant to 5 atm
Band: horse leather, buckle
Price: $4,350

Tangente
Reference number: 139
Movement: manually wound, Nomos caliber Alpha; ø 23.3 mm, height 2.6 mm; 17 jewels; 21,600 vph; three-quarter plate, finely finished movement; 43-hour power reserve
Functions: hours, minutes, subsidiary seconds
Case: stainless steel, ø 35 mm, height 6.6 mm; sapphire crystal; transparent case back; water-resistant to 3 atm
Band: horse leather, buckle
Price: $2,180

Metro Date Power Reserve
Reference number: 1101
Movement: manually wound, Nomos caliber DUW 4401; ø 32.1 mm, height 2.8 mm; 23 jewels; 21,600 vph; three-quarter plate, finely finished movement; 42-hour power reserve
Functions: hours, minutes, subsidiary seconds; power reserve indicator; date
Case: stainless steel, ø 37 mm, height 7.7 mm; sapphire crystal; transparent case back; water-resistant to 3 atm
Band: horse leather, buckle
Price: $3,780

Metro Rose Gold 33
Reference number: 1170
Movement: automatic, Nomos caliber Alpha; ø 23.3 mm, height 2.6 mm; 17 jewels; 21,600 vph; three-quarter plate, finely finished movement; 43-hour power reserve
Functions: hours, minutes, subsidiary seconds
Case: rose gold, ø 33 mm, height 7.7 mm; sapphire crystal; transparent case back; water-resistant to 3 atm
Band: suede, buckle
Price: $7,200

NOMOS

Autobahn Neomatik 41 Date Sports Gray
Reference number: 1303
Movement: automatic, Nomos caliber DUW 6101; ø 35.2 mm, height 3.6 mm; 27 jewels; 21,600 vph; three-quarter plate, finely finished movement; 42-hour power reserve
Functions: hours, minutes, subsidiary seconds; date
Case: stainless steel, ø 41 mm, height 10.5 mm; sapphire crystal; transparent case back; water-resistant to 10 atm
Band: textile, buckle
Price: $4,800

Zürich World Time Midnight Blue
Reference number: 807
Movement: automatic, Nomos caliber DUW 5201; ø 31 mm, height 5.7 mm; 26 jewels; 21,600 vph; three-quarter plate, finely finished movement; 42-hour power reserve
Functions: hours, minutes, subsidiary seconds; world time
Case: stainless steel, ø 39.9 mm, height 10.9 mm; sapphire crystal; transparent case back; water-resistant to 3 atm
Band: textile, buckle
Price: $6,100

Ahoi
Reference number: 550
Movement: automatic, Nomos caliber DUW 5001; ø 31 mm, height 4.3 mm; 26 jewels; 21,600 vph; three-quarter plate, finely finished movement; 43-hour power reserve
Functions: hours, minutes, subsidiary seconds
Case: stainless steel, ø 40.3 mm, height 10.6 mm; sapphire crystal; transparent case back; screw-down crown; water-resistant to 20 atm
Band: textile, buckle
Price: $4,060

Club Campus 38
Reference number: 735
Movement: manually wound, Nomos caliber Alpha; ø 23.3 mm, height 2.6 mm; 17 jewels; 21,600 vph; three-quarter plate, finely finished movement; 43-hour power reserve
Functions: hours, minutes, subsidiary seconds
Case: stainless steel, ø 38.5 mm, height 8.5 mm; sapphire crystal; water-resistant to 10 atm
Band: suede, buckle
Price: $1,650

Club Campus Neomatik 39 Midnight Blue
Reference number: 767
Movement: automatic, Nomos caliber DUW 3001; ø 28.8 mm, height 3.2 mm; 27 jewels; 21,600 vph; three-quarter plate, finely finished movement; 43-hour power reserve
Functions: hours, minutes, subsidiary seconds
Case: stainless steel, ø 39.5 mm, height 8.4 mm; sapphire crystal; water-resistant to 20 atm
Band: textile, buckle
Price: $2,980

Club Campus Neomatik
Reference number: 748
Movement: automatic, Nomos caliber DUW 3001; ø 28.8 mm, height 3.2 mm; 27 jewels; 21,600 vph; three-quarter plate, finely finished movement; 43-hour power reserve
Functions: hours, minutes, subsidiary seconds
Case: stainless steel, ø 37 mm, height 8.4 mm; sapphire crystal; water-resistant to 20 atm
Band: stainless steel, folding clasp
Price: $2,780

Tangente 33 Duo
Reference number: 120
Movement: manually wound, Nomos caliber Alpha.2; ø 23.3 mm, height 2.6 mm; 17 jewels; 21,600 vph; three-quarter plate, finely finished movement; 43-hour power reserve
Functions: hours, minutes
Case: stainless steel, ø 32.8 mm, height 6.5 mm; sapphire crystal; water-resistant to 3 atm
Band: suede, buckle
Price: $1,440

Tetra 27 Duo
Reference number: 405
Movement: manually wound, Nomos caliber Alpha.2; ø 23.3 mm, height 2.6 mm; 17 jewels; 21,600 vph; three-quarter plate, finely finished movement; 43-hour power reserve
Functions: hours, minutes
Case: stainless steel, 27.5 × 27.5 mm, height 6.1 mm; sapphire crystal; water-resistant to 3 atm
Band: suede, buckle
Price: $1,660

Ludwig 33 Duo
Reference number: 240
Movement: manually wound, Nomos caliber Alpha.2; ø 23.3 mm, height 2.6 mm; 17 jewels; 21,600 vph; three-quarter plate, finely finished movement; 43-hour power reserve
Functions: hours, minutes
Case: stainless steel, ø 32.8 mm, height 6.5 mm; sapphire crystal; water-resistant to 3 atm
Band: suede, buckle
Price: $1,380

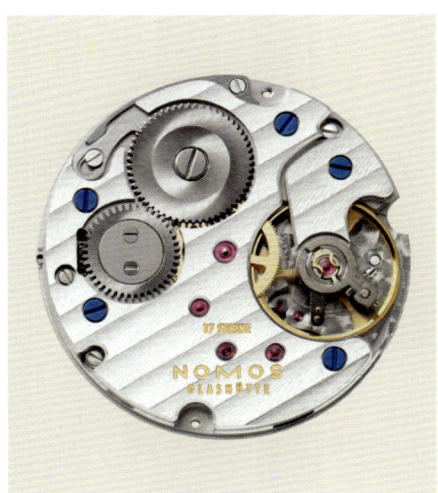

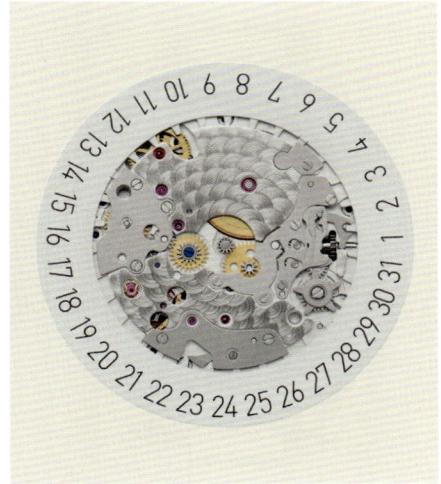

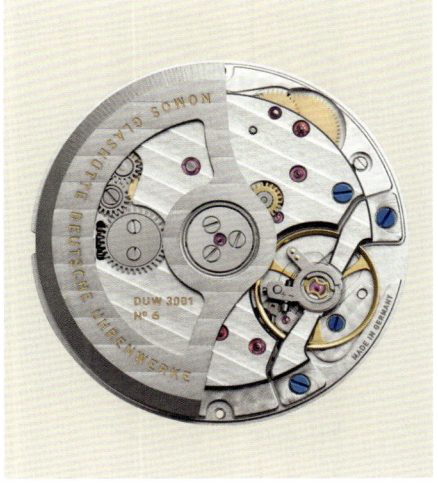

Caliber Alpha
Manually wound; 43-hour power reserve
Functions: hours, minutes, subsidiary seconds
Diameter: 23.3 mm
Height: 2.6 mm
Jewels: 17
Balance: made in-house
Frequency: 21,600 vph
Balance spring: Nivarox 1A
Shock protection: Incabloc
Remarks: three-quarter plate, rhodium-plated movement with Glashütte ribbing and Nomos perlage

Caliber DUW 6101
Automatic; single spring barrel, 43-hour power reserve
Functions: hours, minutes, subsidiary seconds; date
Diameter: 35.2 mm
Height: 3.6 mm
Jewels: 27
Balance: made in-house
Frequency: 21,600 vph
Balance spring: made in-house, tempered-blue
Shock protection: Incabloc
Remarks: three-quarter plate, rhodium-plated movement with Glashütte ribbing and Nomos perlage, gold-plated embossing

Caliber DUW 3001
Automatic; single spring barrel, 43-hour power reserve
Functions: hours, minutes, subsidiary seconds
Diameter: 28.8 mm
Height: 3.2 mm
Jewels: 27
Balance: made in-house
Frequency: 21,600 vph
Balance spring: made in-house, tempered-blue
Shock protection: Incabloc
Remarks: three-quarter plate, rhodium-plated movement with Glashütte ribbing and Nomos perlage

OMEGA

Omega is without a doubt the Swatch Group's brand with the greatest reach. An Omega has also been strapped to the arm of James Bond, no less, and it was the official timekeeper at the 2010 Winter Olympics in Vancouver. But even more famously, perhaps, it was a Speedmaster that made it to the moon in 1969, fastened to the arms of Neil Armstrong and Buzz Aldrin with long Velcro straps. Not surprisingly, Omega celebrated the fiftieth anniversary of this technological and public relations coup with an upgraded version of the manually wound Caliber 3861 chronograph and the Caliber 321, which will be reserved for exclusive models in the future. The latter looks almost identical to the moon caliber, but there are some details that have been improved.

Technology and design are very much responsible for Omega's success. The innovative coaxial escapement is used in almost all models by now. The new 15,000-gauss amagnetic movement introduced a few years ago has also been taking over the products. And there is a plethora of new "Master Chronometer" movements, which not only meet the stringent requirements set out by the COSC but also have to pass the tests developed by Switzerland's Federal Institute of Metrology (METAS). The testing and certification process is performed in the new production building at the entirely renovated Swatch Group premises in Bienne/Biel. After promulgating the benefits of decentralization for years, Omega appears to be returning to the good old *manufacture* system of all crafts under a single roof. Swatch Group subsidiary Nivarox-FAR has finally mastered the production of the difficult, oil-free parts of the system designed by Englishman George Daniels, although the escapement continues to include lubrication, as the long-term results of "dry" coaxial movements are less than satisfactory. Thus, the most important plus for this escapement design remains high rate stability after careful regulation. Omega has even revived the Ladymatic, adding a silicon spring and the trademark coaxial escapement.

Omega SA
Jakob-Stämpfli-Strasse 96
CH-2502 Biel/Bienne
Switzerland

Tel.:
+41-32-343-9211

E-mail:
info@omegawatches.com

Website:
www.omegawatches.com

Founded:
1848

U.S. distributor:
Omega
703 Waterford Way, Suite 920
Miami, FL 33126
800-766-6342
www.omegawatches.com

Speedmaster Apollo 11 50th Anniversary Limited Edition

Reference number: 310.60.42.50.99.001
Movement: manually wound, Omega Caliber 3861; ø 27 mm, height 6.9 mm, 26 jewels; 21,600 vph; coaxial escapement, silicon escapement and hairspring; amagnetic to 15,000 gauss; METAS-certified chronometer; 50-hour power reserve
Functions: hours, minutes, subsidiary seconds; chronograph
Case: yellow gold, ø 42 mm, height 13.8 mm; ceramic bezel; sapphire crystal; water-resistant to 5 atm
Band: yellow gold, folding clasp
Price: $34,600; limited to 1,014 pieces

Seamaster Aqua Terra Master Chronometer

Reference number: 220.10.41.21.01.001
Movement: automatic, Omega Caliber 8900; ø 29 mm, height 5.5 mm; 39 jewels; 25,200 vph; 2 spring barrels, coaxial escapement, silicon balance and hairspring, amagnetic to 15,000 gauss; METAS-certified chronometer; 60-hour power reserve
Functions: hours, minutes, sweep seconds; date
Case: stainless steel, ø 41 mm, height 13.2 mm; sapphire crystal; transparent case back; screw-in crown; water-resistant to 15 atm
Band: stainless steel, folding clasp
Price: $5,500
Variations: various dial colors; calfskin, reptile skin, or rubber strap

Seamaster Diver 300M

Reference number: 210.32.42.20.06.001
Movement: automatic, Omega Caliber 8800; ø 26 mm, height 4.6 mm; 35 jewels; 25,200 vph; 2 spring barrels, coaxial escapement, silicon balance and hairspring, amagnetic to 15,000 gauss; METAS-certified chronometer; 55-hour power reserve
Functions: hours, minutes, sweep seconds; date
Case: stainless steel, ø 42 mm, height 13.56 mm; unidirectional bezel with ceramic insert, 0-60 scale; sapphire crystal; transparent case back; screw-in crown; helium valve; water-resistant to 30 atm
Band: rubber, folding clasp
Price: $4,750

OMEGA

Seamaster Diver Ceramic Titanium

Reference number: 210.92.44.20.01.001
Movement: automatic, Omega Caliber 8806; ø 26 mm, height 4.6 mm; 35 jewels; 25,200 vph; coaxial escapement, silicon balance and hairspring; amagnetic to 15,000 gauss; METAS-certified chronometer; 55-hour power reserve
Functions: hours, minutes, sweep seconds
Case: ceramic, ø 43.5 mm, height 14.17 mm; unidirectional titanium bezel with ceramic insert, 0-60 scale; sapphire crystal; screw-in crown; helium valve; water-resistant to 30 atm
Band: rubber, buckle
Price: $8,100

Seamaster Diver 300M Chronograph

Reference number: 210.30.44.51.03.001
Movement: automatic, Omega Caliber 9900; ø 32.5 mm, height 7.6 mm; 54 jewels; 28,800 vph; 2 spring barrels, coaxial escapement, silicon balance and hairspring; amagnetic to 15,000 gauss; METAS-certified chronometer; 60-hour power reserve
Functions: hours, minutes, subsidiary seconds; chronograph; date
Case: stainless steel, ø 44 mm, height 17.2 mm; unidirectional bezel with ceramic insert, 0-60 scale; sapphire crystal; screw-in crown and ceramic pushers; helium valve; water-resistant to 30 atm
Band: stainless steel, folding clasp
Price: $7,450

Seamaster Aqua Terra Worldtimer

Reference number: 220.12.43.22.03.001
Movement: automatic, Omega Caliber 8938; ø 29 mm, height 6.5 mm; 39 jewels; 25,200 vph; coaxial escapement, silicon escapement and hairspring; amagnetic to 15,000 gauss; METAS-certified chronometer; 60-hour power reserve; COSC-certified chronometer
Functions: hours, minutes, sweep seconds; world time display (2nd time zone); date
Case: stainless steel, ø 43 mm, height 14.3 mm; sapphire crystal; transparent case back; screw-in crown; water-resistant to 15 atm
Band: rubber, buckle
Price: $8,900
Variations: stainless steel bracelet

Seamaster Planet Ocean Master Chronometer

Reference number: 215.30.44.21.04.001
Movement: automatic, Omega Caliber 8900; ø 29 mm, height 5.5 mm; 39 jewels; 25,200 vph; 2 spring barrels, coaxial escapement, silicon balance and hairspring; amagnetic to 15,000 gauss; METAS-certified chronometer; 60-hour power reserve
Functions: hours, minutes, sweep seconds; date
Case: stainless steel, ø 43.5 mm, height 16.04 mm; unidirectional bezel with ceramic insert, 0-60 scale; sapphire crystal; transparent case back; screw-in crown; helium valve; water-resistant to 60 atm
Band: stainless steel, folding clasp
Price: $6,500
Variations: black dial

Seamaster Planet Ocean Deep Black Master Chronometer

Reference number: 215.92.46.22.01.001
Movement: automatic, Omega Caliber 8906; ø 29 mm, height 6 mm; 38 jewels; 25,200 vph; 2 spring barrels, coaxial escapement, silicon balance and hairspring; amagnetic to 15,000 gauss; METAS-certified chronometer; 60-hour power reserve
Functions: hours, minutes, sweep seconds; additional 24-hour display (2nd time zone); date
Case: ceramic, ø 43.5 mm, height 17.04 mm; unidirectional bezel, 0-60 scale; sapphire crystal; screw-in crown; helium valve; water-resistant to 60 atm
Band: rubber with textile overlay, folding clasp
Price: $11,700

Seamaster Aqua Terra Railmaster

Reference number: 220.10.40.20.01.001
Movement: automatic, Omega Caliber 8806; ø 26 mm, height 4.6 mm; 35 jewels; 25,200 vph; coaxial escapement, silicon balance and hairspring, amagnetic to 15,000 gauss; METAS-certified chronometer; 55-hour power reserve
Functions: hours, minutes, sweep seconds
Case: stainless steel, ø 40 mm, height 12.65 mm; sapphire crystal; water-resistant to 15 atm
Band: stainless steel, folding clasp
Price: $5,000
Variations: various dials; calfskin strap; textile strap

OMEGA

Constellation Manhattan
Reference number: 131.15.29.20.55.001
Movement: automatic, Omega Caliber 8700; ø 20 mm, height 5.3 mm; 28 jewels; 25,200 vph; coaxial escapement, silicon balance and hairspring; amagnetic to 15,000 gauss; METAS-certified chronometer; 50-hour power reserve
Functions: hours, minutes, sweep seconds; date
Case: stainless steel, ø 27 mm, height 12.25 mm; bezel set with diamonds; sapphire crystal; water-resistant to 10 atm
Band: stainless steel, folding clasp
Remarks: dial set with 11 diamonds
Price: $10,100
Variations: various cases, dials, and straps

Globemaster Master Chronometer
Reference number: 130.33.39.21.03.001
Movement: automatic, Omega Caliber 8900; ø 29 mm, height 5.5 mm; 39 jewels; 25,200 vph; coaxial escapement, silicon balance and hairspring, amagnetic to 15,000 gauss; METAS-certified chronometer; 60-hour power reserve
Functions: hours, minutes, sweep seconds; date
Case: stainless steel, ø 39 mm, height 12.53 mm; sapphire crystal; water-resistant to 10 atm
Band: reptile skin, folding clasp
Price: $6,900
Variations: various dials; stainless steel bracelet; pink gold bezel; in pink gold

Speedmaster Dark Side of the Moon "Apollo 8"
Reference number: 311.92.44.30.01.001
Movement: manually wound, Omega Caliber 1869; ø 27 mm, height 6.87 mm; 19 jewels; 21,600 vph; 48-hour power reserve
Functions: hours, minutes, subsidiary seconds; chronograph
Case: ceramic, ø 44.25 mm, height 13.8 mm; sapphire crystal; transparent case back; water-resistant to 5 atm
Band: calfskin, buckle
Remarks: mainplate and bridges with carefully replicated moon surface
Price: $12,000

Speedmaster Ladies' Co-Axial Chronometer
Reference number: 324.30.38.50.06.001
Movement: automatic, Omega Caliber 3330; ø 30 mm, height 7.9 mm; 31 jewels; 28,800 vph; coaxial escapement, silicon balance and hairspring; COSC-certified chronometer; 52-hour power reserve
Functions: hours, minutes, subsidiary seconds; chronograph; date
Case: stainless steel, ø 38 mm, height 14.7 mm; bezel with ceramic inlay; sapphire crystal; water-resistant to 10 atm
Band: stainless steel, folding clasp
Price: $4,900

Speedmaster Moonphase
Reference number: 304.33.44.52.03.001
Movement: automatic, Omega Caliber 9904; ø 32.5 mm, height 8.35 mm; 54 jewels; 28,800 vph; 2 spring barrels, coaxial escapement, silicon balance and hairspring, amagnetic to 15,000 gauss; METAS-certified chronometer; 60-hour power reserve
Functions: hours, minutes, subsidiary seconds; chronograph; date, moon phase
Case: stainless steel, ø 44.25 mm, height 16.85 mm; bezel with ceramic inlay; sapphire crystal; water-resistant to 10 atm
Band: reptile skin, folding clasp
Price: $10,600

Speedmaster Apollo 11 50th Anniversary Limited Edition
Reference number: 310.20.42.50.01.001
Movement: manually wound, Omega Caliber 3861; ø 27 mm, height 6.9 mm; 26 jewels; 21,600 vph; coaxial escapement, silicon balance and hairspring; amagnetic to 15,000 gauss; METAS-certified chronometer; 50-hour power reserve
Functions: hours, minutes, subsidiary seconds; chronograph
Case: stainless steel, ø 42 mm, height 14 mm; ceramic bezel; sapphire crystal; water-resistant to 5 atm
Band: stainless steel, folding clasp
Price: $9,650; limited to 6,969 pieces

OMEGA

Caliber 8800
Automatic; coaxial escapement; amagnetic up to 15,000 gauss; METAS-certified chronometer; single spring barrel, 55-hour power reserve
Functions: hours, minutes, sweep seconds; date
Diameter: 26 mm
Height: 4.6 mm
Jewels: 35
Balance: silicon, without regulator
Frequency: 25,200 vph
Balance spring: silicon
Shock protection: Nivachoc
Remarks: blackened screws

Caliber 8807
Automatic; coaxial escapement; amagnetic up to 15,000 gauss; METAS-certified chronometer; single spring barrel, 55-hour power reserve
Functions: hours, minutes, sweep seconds
Diameter: 26 mm
Height: 4.6 mm
Jewels: 35
Balance: silicon, without regulator
Frequency: 25,200 vph
Balance spring: silicon
Shock protection: Nivachoc
Remarks: gold rotor, gold balance-wheel bridge, blackened screws

Caliber 8900
Automatic; coaxial escapement; amagnetic up to 15,000 gauss; METAS-certified chronometer; double spring barrel, 60-hour power reserve
Functions: hours, minutes, sweep seconds; date
Diameter: 29 mm
Height: 5.5 mm
Jewels: 39
Balance: silicon, without regulator
Frequency: 25,200 vph
Balance spring: silicon
Shock protection: Nivachoc
Remarks: mainplate, bridges and rotor with "arabesque" côtes de Genève, rhodium-plated, spring barrels, blackened balance wheel and screws

Caliber 9900
Automatic; coaxial escapement; column wheel control of chronograph functions; amagnetic up to 15,000 gauss; METAS-certified chronometer; double spring barrel, 60-hour power reserve
Functions: hours, minutes, subsidiary seconds; chronograph; date
Diameter: 32.5 mm
Height: 7.6 mm
Jewels: 5.4
Balance: silicon, without regulator
Frequency: 28,800 vph
Balance spring: silicon
Shock protection: Nivachoc
Remarks: mainplate, bridges and rotor with "arabesque" côtes de Genève

Caliber 1861
Manually wound; single spring barrel, 48-hour power reserve
Base caliber: Lémania 1873
Functions: hours, minutes, subsidiary seconds; chronograph
Diameter: 27 mm
Height: 6.87 mm
Jewels: 18
Frequency: 21,600 vph
Balance spring: flat hairspring
Remarks: rhodium-plated, gold-plated engravings; 234 parts

Caliber 3861
Manually wound; coaxial escapement, amagnetic protection to 15,000 gauss; METAS-certified chronometer; single spring barrel, 50-hour power reserve
Functions: hours, minutes, subsidiary seconds; chronograph
Diameter: 27 mm
Height: 6.87 mm
Jewels: 26
Frequency: 21,600 vph
Balance spring: silicon
Remarks: gold-plated movement ("Moonshine Gold"); 240 parts

ORIS

Oris has been producing mechanical watches in Hölstein, near Basel, Switzerland, since 1904. The brand's strategy has always been to keep prices low and quality high, so Oris has managed to expand in a segment relinquished by other big-name competitors as they sought their fortune in the higher-end markets. The result has been growing international success for Oris, whose portfolio is divided up into four "product worlds," each with its own distinct identity: aviation, motor sports, diving, and culture. In utilizing specific materials—a tungsten bezel for the divers, for example—and functions based on these types, Oris makes certain that each will fit perfectly into the world for which it was designed. Yet the heart of every watch houses a small, high-quality "high-mech" movement identifiable by the brand's standard red rotor.

The brand surprised everyone for its 110th birthday by signing off on the in-house Caliber 110, a plain, but technically efficient, manually wound movement. It was made together with the engineers from the Technical College of Le Locle, and features a massive barrel spring with a 6-foot (1.8-m) spring. It was followed by the Caliber 111 with an optimized spring that could provide ten days of power of even torque. The power reserve indicator on the right of the dial does not move evenly, however, due to the transmission ratio. Toward the end, the markers are somewhat longer to give a more accurate idea of the remaining power in the spring. Ever since, the company has come out with one caliber a year. The 112 has GMT function and day/night indication. The fourth in-house caliber, 113, was equipped with a clever sweep hand indication of calendar weeks that also shows the month. Add to that the apertures for date and day of the week, and you have a complete calendar for businesspeople and others who need to stay dialed into the date. And in 2018 came the 114, which is used in the ProPilot X, the first skeleton version of the watch, which suggests where the brand is going esthetically as well.

Oris SA
Ribigasse 1
CH-4434 Hölstein
Switzerland

Tel.:
+41-61-956-1111

E-mail:
MyOris@oris.ch

Website:
www.oris.ch

Founded:
1904

Number of employees:
90

U.S. distributor:
Oris Watches USA
50 Washington Street, Suite 302
Norwalk, CT 06854
203-857-4769

Most important collections/price range:
Divers Sixty-Five, Big Crown, Artelier, Aquis, ProPilot / approx. $1,100 to $5,500

Divers Sixty-Five

Reference number: 01 733 7707 4357
Movement: automatic, Oris Caliber 733 (base Sellita SW200-1); ø 25.6 mm, height 4.6 mm; 26 jewels; 28,800 vph; 38-hour power reserve
Functions: hours, minutes, sweep seconds; date
Case: stainless steel, ø 40 mm, height 12.8 mm; unidirectional bronze bezel, 0-60 scale; sapphire crystal; screw-in crown; water-resistant to 10 atm
Band: calfskin, buckle
Price: $2,000
Variations: stainless steel bracelet ($2,200)

Divers Sixty-Five Chronograph

Reference number: 01 771 7744 4354
Movement: automatic, Oris Caliber 771 (base Sellita SW510-1); ø 30 mm, height 7.9 mm; 27 jewels; 28,800 vph; 48-hour power reserve
Functions: hours, minutes, subsidiary seconds; chronograph
Case: stainless steel, ø 43 mm, height 16.2 mm; bronze bezel; sapphire crystal; water-resistant to 10 atm
Band: calfskin
Price: $4,000
Variations: stainless steel bracelet ($4,250)

Divers Sixty-Five Bicolor

Reference number: 01 733 7707 4355
Movement: automatic, Oris Caliber 733 (base Sellita SW200-1); ø 25.6 mm, height 4.6 mm; 26 jewels; 28,800 vph; 38-hour power reserve
Functions: hours, minutes, sweep seconds; date
Case: stainless steel, ø 40 mm, height 12.8 mm; unidirectional bronze bezel, 0-60 scale; sapphire crystal; screw-in crown; water-resistant to 10 atm
Band: stainless steel with bronze elements, folding clasp
Price: $2,350
Variations: calfskin band ($2,100)

Aquis Regulateur "Master Diver"
Reference number: 01 749 7734 7154
Movement: automatic, Oris Caliber 749 (base Sellita SW220-1); ø 25.6 mm, height 5.05 mm; 28 jewels; 28,800 vph; 38-hour power reserve
Functions: hours (off-center), minutes, subsidiary seconds; date
Case: titanium, ø 43.5 mm, height 12.65 mm; unidirectional bezel with ceramic insert, 0-60 scale; sapphire crystal; screw-in crown; helium valve; water-resistant to 30 atm
Band: titanium, folding clasp
Remarks: comes with additional rubber strap
Price: $3,350

Aquis Clean Ocean Limited Edition
Reference number: 01 733 7732 4185
Movement: automatic, Oris Caliber 733 (base Sellita SW200-1); ø 25.6 mm, height 4.6 mm; 26 jewels; 28,800 vph; 38-hour power reserve
Functions: hours, minutes, sweep seconds; date
Case: stainless steel, ø 39.5 mm, height 12.6 mm; unidirectional bezel with ceramic insert, 0-60 scale; sapphire crystal; screw-in crown; water-resistant to 30 atm
Band: stainless steel, folding clasp
Price: $2,300; limited to 2,000 pieces

ProDiver Dive Control Limited Edition
Reference number: 01 774 7727 7784
Movement: automatic, Oris Caliber 774 (base Sellita SW500); ø 30 mm, height 7.9 mm; 25 jewels; 28,800 vph; 48-hour power reserve
Functions: hours, minutes, subsidiary seconds; chronograph; date
Case: titanium with black DLC coating, ø 51 mm, height 19.5 mm; unidirectional bezel, 0-60 scale, with "Dive Control" locking system; sapphire crystal; screw-in crown and pushers
Band: rubber, folding clasp
Remarks: comes with rubber strap
Price: $4,950; limited to 500 pieces

Aquis Great Barrier Reef Limited Edition III
Reference number: 01 743 7734 4185
Movement: automatic, Oris Caliber 743 (base Sellita SW220-1); ø 25.6 mm, height 5.05 mm; 28 jewels; 28,800 vph; 38-hour power reserve
Functions: hours, minutes, subsidiary seconds; date
Case: stainless steel, ø 43.5 mm, height 12.9 mm; unidirectional bezel with ceramic insert, 0-60 scale; sapphire crystal; screw-in crown; water-resistant to 30 atm
Band: stainless steel, folding clasp
Price: $2,550; limited to 2,000 pieces

Aquis Date
Reference number: 01 733 7730 4135
Movement: automatic, Oris Caliber 733 (base Sellita SW200-1); ø 25.6 mm, height 4.6 mm; 26 jewels; 28,800 vph; 38-hour power reserve
Functions: hours, minutes, sweep seconds; date
Case: stainless steel, ø 43.5 mm, height 12.7 mm; unidirectional bezel with ceramic insert, 0-60 scale; sapphire crystal; transparent case back; screw-in crown; water-resistant to 30 atm
Band: stainless steel, folding clasp
Price: $2,100
Variations: calfskin band ($1,950); rubber strap ($1,900)

Aquis GMT Date
Reference number: 01 798 7754 4135
Movement: automatic, Oris Caliber 798 (base Sellita SW330-1); ø 25.6 mm, height 4.1 mm; 25 jewels; 28,800 vph; 42-hour power reserve
Functions: hours, minutes, sweep seconds; additional 24-hour display (2nd time zone); date
Case: stainless steel, ø 43.5 mm, height 12.8 mm; bidirectional bezel with ceramic insert, with 0-24 scale; sapphire crystal; screw-in crown; water-resistant to 30 atm
Band: stainless steel, folding clasp
Price: $2,700
Variations: calfskin strap ($2,550); rubber band ($2,500)

ORIS

Aquis Date Relief
Reference number: 01 733 7730 4153
Movement: automatic, Oris Caliber 733 (base Sellita SW200-1); ø 25.6 mm, height 4.6 mm; 26 jewels; 28,800 vph; 38-hour power reserve
Functions: hours, minutes, sweep seconds; date
Case: stainless steel, ø 43.5 mm, height 12.7 mm; unidirectional bezel, 0-60 scale; sapphire crystal; transparent case back; screw-in crown; water-resistant to 30 atm
Band: rubber, folding clasp with extension link
Price: $1,800
Variations: stainless steel bracelet ($2,000)

Aquis Big Day Date
Reference number: 01 752 7733 4135-07 4 24 64EB
Movement: automatic, Oris Caliber 752 (base Sellita SW220-1); ø 25.6 mm, height 5.05 mm; 26 jewels; 28,800 vph; 38-hour power reserve
Functions: hours, minutes, sweep seconds; date, weekday
Case: stainless steel, ø 45.5 mm, height 15.3 mm; unidirectional bezel with ceramic insert, 0-60 scale; sapphire crystal; screw-in crown; water-resistant to 50 atm
Band: rubber, folding clasp
Price: $2,200

Chronoris Date
Reference number: 01 733 7737 4054
Movement: automatic, Oris Caliber 733 (base Sellita SW200-1); ø 25.6 mm, height 4.6 mm; 26 jewels; 28,800 vph; 38-hour power reserve
Functions: hours, minutes, sweep seconds; date
Case: stainless steel, ø 39 mm, height 12.4 mm; crown-activated ring with 0-60 scale; sapphire crystal; water-resistant to 10 atm
Band: calfskin, buckle
Price: $1,750
Variations: stainless steel bracelet ($1,950); textile or rubber strap ($1,750)

Big Crown ProPilot Caliber 114
Movement: manually wound, Oris Caliber 114; ø 34 mm, height 6 mm; 40 jewels; 21,600 vph; 240-hour power reserve
Functions: hours, minutes, subsidiary seconds; additional 24-hour display (2nd time zone), power reserve indicator; date
Case: stainless steel, ø 44 mm, height 14 mm; sapphire crystal; transparent case back; screw-in crown; water-resistant to 10 atm
Band: reptile skin, folding clasp
Price: $6,100
Variations: textile strap ($5,800); stainless steel bracelet ($5,900)

Big Crown ProPilot Timer GMT
Reference number: 01 748 7756 4064
Movement: automatic, Oris Caliber 748 (base Sellita SW500-1); ø 32.2 mm, height 5.5 mm; 28 jewels; 28,800 vph; 38-hour power reserve
Functions: hours, minutes, subsidiary seconds; additional 24-hour display (2nd time zone); date
Case: stainless steel, ø 44 mm, height 12.8 mm; bidirectional bezel, 0-60 scale; sapphire crystal; transparent case back; screw-in crown; water-resistant to 10 atm
Band: textile, folding clasp
Price: $2,600
Variations: stainless steel bracelet ($2,800); calfskin band ($2,600)

Big Crown Pointer Date 80th Anniversary Edition
Reference number: 01 754 7741 3167
Movement: automatic, Oris Caliber 754 (base Sellita SW200-1); ø 25.6 mm, height 4.6 mm; 26 jewels; 28,800 vph; 38-hour power reserve
Functions: hours, minutes, sweep seconds; date
Case: bronze, ø 40 mm, height 11.8 mm; sapphire crystal; transparent case back; water-resistant to 5 atm
Band: calfskin, buckle
Price: $2,000

Officine Panerai
Viale Monza, 259
I-20126 Milan
Italy

Tel.:
+39-02-363-138

Website:
www.panerai.com

Founded:
1860 in Florence, Italy

Number of employees:
approx. 250

U.S. distributor:
Panerai
645 Fifth Avenue
New York, NY 10022
877-PANERAI
concierge.usa@panerai.com; www.panerai.com

Most important collections/price range:
Luminor / $5,000 to $25,000; Luminor 1950 / $8,000 to $30,000; Radiomir / $7,000 to $25,000; Radiomir 1940 / $8,000 to $133,000; special editions / $10,000 to $125,000; clocks and instruments / $20,000 to $250,000

PANERAI

Officine Panerai (in English: Panerai Workshops) joined the Richemont Group in 1997. Since then, it has made an unprecedented rise from an insider niche brand to a lifestyle phenomenon. The company, founded in 1860 by Giovanni Panerai, supplied the Italian navy with precision instruments. In the 1930s, the Florentine engineers developed a series of waterproof wristwatches that could be used by commandos under especially extreme and risky conditions. After 1997, under the leadership of Angelo Bonati, the company came out with a collection of oversize wristwatches, both stylistically and technically based on these historical models.

In 2002, Panerai opened a *manufacture* in Neuchâtel, and by 2005 it was already producing its own movements (caliber family P.2000). In 2009, the new "little" Panerai *manufacture* movements (caliber family P.9000) were released. From the start, the idea behind them was to provide a competitive alternative to the base movements available until a couple of years ago. In 2014, a new *manufacture* was inaugurated in Neuchâtel to handle development, manufacturing, assembly, and quality control under one roof.

Parallel to consolidating, the brand has been steadily expanding its portfolio of new calibers. Fairly early on, it came out with an automatic chronograph with a flyback function, the P.9100. This was followed by a string of new calibers, almost one per year, to gradually replace "foreign" movements. Notorious is the P.4000, with an off-center winding rotor. At 3.95 millimeters, it is very thin for Panerai, but then again, it was developed for a new set of models.

The three-day automatic movement P.9010 was released in 2016 and has served the brand well. In 2018, it got a companion, the Caliber OP XXXIV, which was purchased as an affordable alternative from Richemont Group.

Luminor Tourbillon GMT Lo Scienziato
Reference number: PAM00768
Movement: manually wound, Panerai Caliber P.2005/T; ø 36.6 mm, height 10.05 mm; 31 jewels; 28,800 vph; 3 spring barrels, 1-minute tourbillon; skeletonized movement; 144-hour power reserve
Functions: hours, minutes, subsidiary seconds; additional 12-hour display (2nd time zone), day/night indicator, power reserve indicator (on movement side)
Case: titanium, ø 47 mm, height 17.66 mm; carbon bezel; sapphire crystal; transparent case back; crown protector with hinged lever; water-resistant to 10 atm
Band: reptile skin, buckle
Price: $149,000

Luna Rossa Challenger Submersible
Reference number: PAM1039
Movement: automatic, Panerai Caliber P.9010/GMT; ø 31 mm, height 6 mm; 31 jewels; 28,800 vph; 2 spring barrels, 72-hour power reserve
Functions: hours, minutes, subsidiary seconds; additional 12-hour display (2nd time zone); date
Case: carbon fiber ("carbotech"), ø 47 mm; unidirectional bezel, 0-60 scale; sapphire crystal; crown protector with hinged lever; water-resistant to 30 atm
Band: rubber, buckle
Remarks: dial made of sailcloth from the Luna Rossa
Price: $21,600

Luminor Submersible Carbotech
Reference number: PAM01616
Movement: automatic, Panerai Caliber P.9010; ø 31 mm, height 6 mm; 31 jewels; 28,800 vph; 2 spring barrels, 72-hour power reserve
Functions: hours, minutes, subsidiary seconds; date
Case: carbon fiber ("carbotech"), ø 47 mm; unidirectional bezel, 0-60 scale; sapphire crystal; crown protector with hinged lever; water-resistant to 30 atm
Band: rubber, buckle
Price: $17,900

PANERAI

Luminor Marina
Reference number: PAM00977
Movement: automatic, Panerai Caliber P.9010; ø 31 mm, height 6 mm; 31 jewels; 28,800 vph; 2 spring barrels, 72-hour power reserve
Functions: hours, minutes, subsidiary seconds; date
Case: stainless steel, ø 42 mm; sapphire crystal; crown protector with hinged lever; water-resistant to 10 atm
Band: stainless steel, folding clasp
Price: $8,400

Luminor Yachts Challenge
Reference number: PAM01020
Movement: automatic, Panerai Caliber P.9100; ø 31 mm, height 8.15 mm; 37 jewels; 28,800 vph; 2 spring barrels, 72-hour power reserve
Functions: hours, minutes, subsidiary seconds; flyback chronograph
Case: rose gold, ø 44 mm; sapphire crystal; transparent case back; crown protector with hinged lever; water-resistant to 5 atm
Band: reptile skin, buckle
Remarks: main sponsor of Panerai Classic Yachts Challenge
Price: $28,300

Luminor Yachts Challenge
Reference number: PAM00764
Movement: automatic, Panerai Caliber P.9100; ø 31 mm, height 8.15 mm; 37 jewels; 28,800 vph; 2 spring barrels, 72-hour power reserve
Functions: hours, minutes, subsidiary seconds; flyback chronograph
Case: titanium, ø 44 mm; sapphire crystal; transparent case back; crown protector with hinged lever; water-resistant to 10 atm
Band: rubber, buckle
Remarks: main sponsor of Panerai Classic Yachts Challenge
Price: $13,300
Variations: black ceramic ($15,900)

Luminor Due
Reference number: PAM00926
Movement: automatic, Panerai Caliber P.900; ø 28.19 mm, height 4.2 mm; 23 jewels; 28,800 vph; 72-hour power reserve
Functions: hours, minutes, subsidiary seconds; date
Case: titanium, ø 38 mm; sapphire crystal; crown protector with hinged lever; water-resistant to 3 atm
Band: reptile skin, buckle
Remarks: sandwich dial with luminous mass on lower dial
Price: $6,900

Luminor Due
Reference number: PAM00903
Movement: automatic, Panerai Caliber OP XXXIV; ø 28.19 mm, height 4.2 mm; 22 jewels; 28,800 vph; 72-hour power reserve
Functions: hours, minutes, subsidiary seconds; date
Case: stainless steel, ø 38 mm, height 11.2 mm; sapphire crystal; crown protector with hinged lever; water-resistant to 3 atm
Band: calfskin, buckle
Price: $6,000
Variations: rose gold 1029 ($15,300)

Luminor Submersible
Reference number: PAM00683
Movement: automatic, Panerai Caliber OP XXXIV; ø 28.19 mm, height 4.2 mm; 23 jewels; 28,800 vph; 72-hour power reserve
Functions: hours, minutes, subsidiary seconds; date
Case: stainless steel, ø 42 mm; unidirectional bezel with ceramic insert, 0-60 scale; sapphire crystal; crown protector with hinged lever; water-resistant to 30 atm
Band: rubber, buckle
Price: $9,800

PANERAI

Luminor Submersible 1950 BMG-Tech

Reference number: PAM00799
Movement: automatic, Panerai Caliber P.9010; ø 31 mm, height 6 mm; 31 jewels; 28,800 vph; 2 spring barrels, 72-hour power reserve
Functions: hours, minutes, subsidiary seconds; date
Case: composite material, BMG tech (alloy of zirconium, copper, aluminum, titanium, nickel), ø 47 mm; unidirectional carbon composite bezel, 0-60 scale; sapphire crystal; crown protector with hinged lever; water-resistant to 30 atm
Band: rubber, buckle
Price: $15,300

Luminor Submersible Chrono Guillaume Néry Edition

Reference number: PAM00982
Movement: automatic, Panerai Caliber P.9100; ø 31 mm, height 8.15 mm; 37 jewels; 28,800 vph; 2 spring barrels, 72-hour power reserve
Functions: hours, minutes, subsidiary seconds; flyback chronograph
Case: titanium, ø 47 mm; unidirectional bezel with ceramic insert, 0-60 scale; sapphire crystal; crown protector with hinged lever; water-resistant to 30 atm
Band: rubber, buckle
Price: $19,400

Luminor Submersible Mike Horn Edition

Reference number: PAM00984
Movement: automatic, Panerai Caliber P.9010; ø 31 mm, height 6 mm; 31 jewels; 28,800 vph; 2 spring barrels, 72-hour power reserve
Functions: hours, minutes, subsidiary seconds; date
Case: titanium, ø 47 mm; unidirectional bezel, 0-60 scale; sapphire crystal; crown protector with hinged lever; water-resistant to 30 atm
Band: textile (recycled), buckle
Remarks: case of recycled titanium; sandwich dial with luminous mass on lower dial
Price: $20,500

Caliber P.2005/S

Manually wound; 30-second tourbillon, rotation along long axis, skeletonized mainplate and bridges; triple serial spring barrel, 144-hour power reserve
Functions: hours, minutes, subsidiary seconds; additional 24-hour display (2nd time zone), power reserve indicator (on rear)
Diameter: 36.6 mm
Height: 10.05 mm
Jewels: 31
Balance: glucydur
Frequency: 28,800 vph
Shock protection: Kif
Remarks: 277 parts

Caliber P.4002

Automatic; microrotor; double serial spring barrel, 72-hour power reserve
Functions: hours, minutes, subsidiary seconds; additional 12-hour display (2nd time zone); date
Diameter: 30 mm
Height: 4.8 mm
Jewels: 31
Balance: glucydur
Frequency: 28,800 vph
Balance spring: flat hairspring
Shock protection: Kif
Remarks: 288 parts

Caliber P.9010

Automatic; double serial spring barrel, 72-hour power reserve
Functions: hours, minutes, subsidiary seconds; date
Diameter: 31 mm
Height: 6 mm
Jewels: 31
Balance: glucydur
Frequency: 28,800 vph
Remarks: 200 parts

PARMIGIANI

What began as the undertaking of a single man—a gifted watchmaker and reputable restorer of complicated vintage timepieces—in the small town of Fleurier in Switzerland's Val de Travers has now grown into an empire of sorts comprising several factories and more than 400 employees.

Michel Parmigiani is in fact just doing what he has done since 1976 when he began restoring vintage works. An exceptional talent, his output soon attracted the attention of the Sandoz Family Foundation, an organization established by a member of one of Switzerland's most famous families in 1964. The foundation bought 51 percent of Parmigiani Mesure et Art du Temps SA in 1996, turning what was practically a one-man show into a full-fledged and fully financed watch *manufacture*.

After the merger, Swiss suppliers were acquired by the partners, furthering the quest for horological autonomy. Atokalpa SA in Alle (Canton of Jura) manufactures parts such as pinions, wheels, and micro components. Bruno Affolter SA in La Chaux-de-Fonds produces precious metal cases, dials, and other specialty parts. Les Artisans Boitiers (LAB) and Quadrance et Habillage (Q&H) in La Chaux-de-Fonds manufacture cases out of precious metals and dials as well. Elwin SA in Moutier specializes in turned parts. In 2003, the movement development and production department officially separated from the rest as Vaucher Manufacture, now an autonomous entity. Parmigiani has enjoyed great independence and was growing strongly for a while, notably in the United States. The recent instabilities in the industry as a whole have led to some shifts in strategies, as CEO Davide Traxler has stated in interviews. The old relationship with Bugatti was terminated, for example. (We are presenting a Parmigiani Bugatti watch here for the last time.) While China remains an attractive market, India, with its emerging middle class, is showing great potential.

Parmigiani Fleurier SA
Rue du Temple 11
CH-2114 Fleurier
Switzerland

Tel.:
+41-32-862-6630

E-mail:
info@parmigiani.ch

Website:
www.parmigiani.ch

Founded:
1996

Number of employees:
425

Annual production:
approx. 6,000 watches

U.S. distributor:
Parmigiani Fleurier Distribution Americas LLC
2655 S. Le Jeune Road
Penthouse 1G
Coral Gables, FL 33134
305-260-7770; 305-269-7770
americas@parmigiani.com

Most important collections/price range:
Kalpa, Tonda, Toric / approx. $7,800 to $700,000 for *haute horlogerie* watches; no limit for unique models

Tonda 1950
Reference number: PFC288-0000601-XA3142
Movement: automatic, Parmigiani Caliber PF702; ø 30 mm, height 2.6 mm; 21,600 vph; 48-hour power reserve
Functions: hours, minutes, subsidiary seconds
Case: stainless steel, ø 40 mm, height 8.2 mm; sapphire crystal; water-resistant to 3 atm
Band: reptile skin, folding clasp
Price: $11,900

Tonda 1950
Reference number: PFC288-1002401-HA1242
Movement: automatic, Parmigiani Caliber PF702; ø 30 mm, height 2.6 mm; 21,600 vph; 48-hour power reserve
Functions: hours, minutes, subsidiary seconds
Case: rose gold, ø 39 mm, height 8 mm; sapphire crystal; water-resistant to 3 atm
Band: reptile skin, folding clasp
Price: $18,100

Tonda Métrographe
Reference number: PFC274-0002500-XC1442
Movement: automatic, Parmigiani Caliber PF315; ø 28 mm, height 6 mm; 46 jewels; 28,800 vph; double spring barrel; finely finished with côtes de Genève; 42-hour power reserve
Functions: hours, minutes, subsidiary seconds; chronograph; date
Case: stainless steel, ø 40 mm, height 11.7 mm; sapphire crystal; transparent case back; water-resistant to 3 atm
Band: calfskin, folding clasp
Price: $11,900

PARMIGIANI

Toric Hémisphères Rétrograde
Reference number: PFC493-1000200-HA1242
Movement: automatic, Parmigiani Caliber PF317; ø 35.6 mm, height 5.45 mm; 28 jewels; 28,800 vph; double spring barrel, 50-hour power reserve
Functions: hours, minutes, subsidiary seconds; additional 12-hour display (2nd time zone) with day/night indicator; date (retrograde)
Case: rose gold, ø 42.8 mm, height 11.9 mm; sapphire crystal; water-resistant to 3 atm
Band: reptile skin, folding clasp
Price: $29,700

Toric Quantième Perpétuel Rétrograde
Reference number: PFH427-1602400-HA1241
Movement: automatic, Parmigiani Caliber PF333; ø 27 mm, height 5.5 mm; 32 jewels; 28,800 vph; 50-hour power reserve
Functions: hours, minutes, sweep seconds; perpetual calendar with date (retrograde), weekday, month, moon phase (double), leap year
Case: red gold, ø 42.5 mm, height 12.1 mm; sapphire crystal; water-resistant to 3 atm
Band: reptile skin, folding clasp
Price: $63,100

Toric Chronomètre
Reference number: PFC423-1600201-HA1241
Movement: automatic, Parmigiani Caliber PF441; ø 25.6 mm, height 3.7 mm; 29 jewels; 28,800 vph; double spring barrel, 55-hour power reserve; COSC-certified chronometer
Functions: hours, minutes, sweep seconds; date
Case: red gold, ø 40.8 mm, height 9.5 mm; sapphire crystal; water-resistant to 3 atm
Band: reptile skin, buckle
Price: $22,300

Bugatti Type 390
Reference number: PFH390-1201401-HA1442
Movement: manually wound, Parmigiani Caliber PF390; 25 × 37.5 mm, height 2.6 mm; 32 jewels; 28,800 vph; cylindrical layered movement construction with 1-minute tourbillon on left side, skeletonized hands mechanism; 80-hour power reserve
Functions: hours, minutes; power reserve indicator (roller-shaped)
Case: white gold, 42.2 × 57.7 mm, height 18.4 mm; sapphire crystal; water-resistant to 3 atm
Band: reptile skin, folding clasp
Remarks: 2-part hinged case, can be folded to 12° to better fit wrist
Price: $295,000

Kalpagraphe
Reference number: PFC128-1003200-X01441
Movement: automatic, Parmigiani Caliber PF334; ø 30.3 mm, height 6.8 mm; 68 jewels; 28,800 vph; 50-hour power reserve
Functions: hours, minutes, subsidiary seconds; chronograph; date
Case: rose gold, 39.2 × 44.45 mm, height 12.8 mm; sapphire crystal; water-resistant to 3 atm
Band: rubber, buckle
Price: $46,000

Kalpagraphe Chronometer
Reference number: PFC193-3044100-X01442
Movement: automatic, Parmigiani Caliber PF362; 31.9 × 39.7 mm, height 7 mm; 42 jewels; 36,000 vph; 65-hour power reserve; COSC-certified chronometer
Functions: hours, minutes, subsidiary seconds; chronograph; date
Case: titanium, 40.9 × 48.2 mm, height 14 mm; sapphire crystal; water-resistant to 3 atm
Band: rubber, folding clasp
Price: $36,700

PARMIGIANI

Tonda 1950 Rainbow
Reference number: PFC288-1063302-HA4021
Movement: automatic, Parmigiani Caliber PF701; ø 30 mm, height 2.6 mm; 21,600 vph; 42-hour power reserve
Functions: hours, minutes, subsidiary seconds
Case: rose gold, ø 39 mm, height 8.3 mm; bezel set with 36 precious stones; sapphire crystal; water-resistant to 3 atm
Band: reptile skin, buckle
Remarks: mother-of-pearl dial
Price: $55,700

Tonda Métropolitaine Galaxy
Reference number: PFC273-0060601-XA3121
Movement: automatic, Parmigiani Caliber PF310; ø 23.9 mm, height 3.9 mm; 28 jewels; 28,800 vph; double spring barrel, 50-hour power reserve
Functions: hours, minutes, subsidiary seconds; date
Case: stainless steel, ø 33.1 mm, height 8.65 mm; bezel set with 72 diamonds; sapphire crystal; transparent case back; water-resistant to 3 atm
Band: reptile skin, buckle
Remarks: aventurine dial
Price: $12,300

Tonda Métropolitaine
Reference number: PFC273-0063300-B00002
Movement: automatic, Parmigiani Caliber PF310; ø 23.9 mm, height 3.9 mm; 28 jewels; 28,800 vph; double spring barrel; finely finished with côtes de Genève; 50-hour power reserve
Functions: hours, minutes, subsidiary seconds; date
Case: stainless steel, ø 33.1 mm, height 8.65 mm; bezel set with 72 diamonds; sapphire crystal; transparent case back; water-resistant to 3 atm
Band: stainless steel, folding clasp
Remarks: mother-of-pearl dial
Price: $10,900
Variations: without diamonds

Tonda Métropolitaine
Reference number: PFC273-1063300-B10002
Movement: automatic, Parmigiani Caliber PF310; ø 23.9 mm, height 3.9 mm; 28 jewels; 28,800 vph; double spring barrel; finely finished with côtes de Genève; 50-hour power reserve
Functions: hours, minutes, subsidiary seconds; date
Case: rose gold, ø 33.1 mm, height 8.6 mm; bezel set with 72 diamonds; sapphire crystal; transparent case back; water-resistant to 3 atm
Band: rose gold, folding clasp
Remarks: mother-of-pearl dial
Price: $41,800
Variations: without diamonds, with leather strap

Kalparisma Agenda
Reference number: PFC123-1000700-HA2421
Movement: automatic, Parmigiani Caliber PF331; ø 25.6 mm, height 3.5 mm; 32 jewels; 28,800 vph; double spring barrel, 55-hour power reserve
Functions: hours, minutes, sweep seconds; date
Case: rose gold, 31.2 × 37.5 mm, height 8.4 mm; sapphire crystal; water-resistant to 3 atm
Band: calfskin, buckle
Remarks: ivory-colored dial with sunray guilloché
Price: $18,600

Kalpa Donna
Reference number: PFC160-0020501-B00002
Movement: quartz
Functions: hours, minutes
Case: stainless steel, 24.8 × 34.8 mm, height 6.8 mm; sapphire crystal; water-resistant to 3 atm
Band: stainless steel, folding clasp
Remarks: case with 43 diamonds
Price: $9,400
Variations: various dials

Caliber PF361

Manually wound; control by 2 column wheels; skeletonized movement; rose gold mainplate and bridges; single spring barrel, 65-hour power reserve
Functions: hours, minutes, subsidiary seconds; flyback chronograph; large date
Diameter: 30.6 mm
Height: 8.5 mm
Jewels: 25
Frequency: 36,000 vph
Remarks: 317 parts

Caliber PF702

Automatic; platinum microrotor; single spring barrel, 48-hour power reserve
Functions: hours, minutes, subsidiary seconds
Diameter: 30 mm
Height: 2.6 mm
Jewels: 29
Frequency: 21,600 vph

Caliber PF362

Automatic; column wheel control of chronograph functions; single spring barrel, 65-hour power reserve; COSC-certified chronometer
Functions: hours, minutes, subsidiary seconds; chronograph; date
Measurements: 31.9 × 39.7 mm
Height: 7 mm
Jewels: 42
Frequency: 36,000 vph
Remarks: 332 parts

Caliber PF110

Manually wound; double spring barrel, 192-hour power reserve
Functions: hours, minutes, subsidiary seconds; power reserve indicator; date
Measurements: 29.3 × 23.6 mm
Height: 4.9 mm
Jewels: 28
Frequency: 21,600 vph

Caliber PF390

Manually wound; cylindrical movement design, with 1-minute tourbillon on left-hand side, skeletonized mechanism driving the hands; single spring barrel, 80-hour power reserve
Functions: hours, minutes; power reserve indicator (cylindrical)
Measurements: 25 × 37.5 mm
Height: 2.6 mm
Jewels: 32
Frequency: 28,800 vph
Remarks: 302 parts; mainplate and bridges with black PVD coating

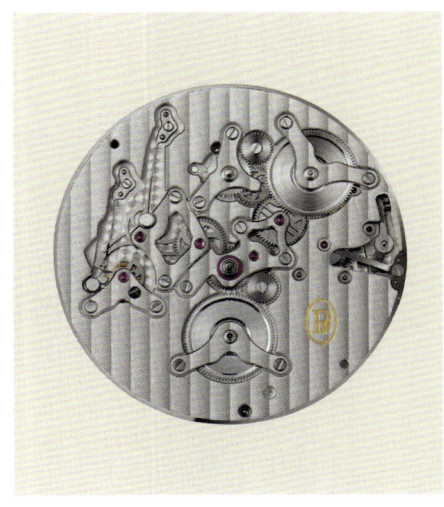

Caliber PF317

Automatic; rose gold microrotor; double spring barrel, 50-hour power reserve
Functions: hours, minutes, subsidiary seconds; additional 12-hour display (2nd time zone) with day/night indicator; date (retrograde)
Diameter: 35.6 mm
Height: 5.4 mm
Jewels: 28
Frequency: 28,800 vph
Remarks: 316 parts

PATEK PHILIPPE

In the Swiss watchmaking landscape, Patek Philippe has a special status as the last independent family-owned business. The company originated in 1839 with two Polish emigrés to Switzerland, Count Norbert Antoine de Patek and Frantiszek Czapek. In 1845, following the natural end of their contract, Patek sought another partner in the master watchmaker Jean Adrien Philippe, who had developed a keyless winding and time-setting mechanism. Ever since, Patek Philippe has been known for creating high-quality mechanical watches, some with extremely sophisticated complications. Even among its competition, the *manufacture* enjoys the greatest respect.

In 1932, Charles-Henri Stern took over the *manufacture*. His son Henri and grandson Philippe continued the tradition of solid leadership, steering the company through the notorious quartz crisis without ever compromising quality. The next in line, also Henri, heads the enterprise these days.

In 1997, Patek Philippe moved into new quarters, based on the most modern standards. The facility boasts the world's largest assembly of watchmakers under one roof, and yet production figures are comparatively modest. A small section of the building is reserved for restoring old watches either using parts from a large and valuable collection of components or rebuilding them from scratch.

The company opened a highly industrialized second branch between La Chaux-de-Fonds and Le Locle, where case components are manufactured, cases are polished, and gem setting is done. Patek Philippe's main headquarters remain in Geneva, but the *manufacture* no longer has a need for that city's famed seal: All of its mechanical watches now feature the "Patek Philippe Seal," the criteria for which far exceed the requirements of the *Poinçon de Genève* and include specifications for the entire watch, not just the movement. Among the most recent creations to make that grade is the World Time Chronograph, a masterful extension of the company's large range of chronographs. To make space, there is no second hand and only a thirty-minute counter. A moving city ring and twenty-four-hour ring have a place on the dial as well, and the whole piece is just over 12 millimeters high.

Patek Philippe SA
Chemin du pont-du-centenaire 141
CH-1228 Plan-les-Ouates
Switzerland

Tel.:
+41-22-884-20-20

Website:
www.patek.com

Founded:
1839

Number of employees:
approx. 2,000 (estimated)

Annual production:
approx. 60,000 watches worldwide per year

U.S. distributor:
Patek Philippe USA
45 Rockefeller Center, Suite 401
New York, NY 10111
212-218-1240

Most important collections:
Aquanaut, Calatrava, Ellipse, Gondolo, Nautilus / ladies' timepieces

Alarm Travel Time
Reference number: 5520P-001
Movement: automatic, Patek Philippe Caliber AL 30-660 S C FUS; ø 31 mm, height 6.6 mm; 52 jewels; 28,800 vph; silicon Spiromax hairspring, gold rotor; 42-hour power reserve
Functions: hours, minutes, sweep seconds; additional 12-hour display (2nd time zone), day/night indicator, alarm; date
Case: platinum, ø 42.2 mm, height 11.6 mm; sapphire crystal; transparent case back; water-resistant to 3 atm
Band: calfskin, buckle
Remarks: wake-up time (in separate window) based on local time, setting in 5-minute increments
Price: $226,805

Chronograph
Reference number: 5172G-001
Movement: manually wound, Patek Philippe Caliber CH 29-535 PS; ø 29.6 mm, height 5.35 mm; 33 jewels; 28,800 vph; Breguet hairspring, column wheel control of chronograph functions; 65-hour power reserve
Functions: hours, minutes, subsidiary seconds; chronograph
Case: white gold, ø 41 mm, height 11.45 mm; sapphire crystal; transparent case back; water-resistant to 3 atm
Band: calfskin, folding clasp
Price: $66,316

Annual Calendar Chronograph
Reference number: 5905R-001
Movement: automatic, Patek Philippe Caliber CH 28-520 QA 24H; ø 33 mm, height 7.68 mm; 37 jewels; 28,800 vph; silicon Spiromax hairspring, gold rotor; 45-hour power reserve
Functions: hours, minutes; flyback chronograph; annual calendar with date, weekday, month
Case: rose gold, ø 42 mm, height 14.3 mm; sapphire crystal; transparent case back; water-resistant to 3 atm
Band: reptile skin, buckle
Price: $65,774

PATEK PHILIPPE

Regulator Annual Calendar
Reference number: 5235/50R-001
Movement: automatic, Patek Philippe Caliber 31-260 REG QA; ø 33 mm, height 5.08 mm; 31 jewels; 23,040 vph; Pulsomax escapement and silicon Spiromax hairspring, microrotor; 38-hour power reserve
Functions: hours (off-center), minutes, subsidiary seconds; annual calendar with date, weekday, month
Case: rose gold, ø 40.5 mm, height 10 mm; sapphire crystal; transparent case back; water-resistant to 3 atm
Band: reptile skin, buckle
Price: $51,825

Calatrava Weekly Calendar
Reference number: 5212A-001
Movement: automatic, Patek Philippe Caliber 26-330 S C J SE; ø 27 mm, height 4.82 mm; 50 jewels; 28,800 vph; silicon Spiromax hairspring, gold rotor; 35-hour power reserve
Functions: hours, minutes, sweep seconds; date, weekday, calendar week
Case: stainless steel, ø 40 mm, height 10.79 mm; sapphire crystal; transparent case back; water-resistant to 3 atm
Band: calfskin, buckle
Price: $33,454

Nautilus Annual Calendar
Reference number: 5726/1A-014
Movement: automatic, Patek Philippe Caliber 324 S QA LU 24H; ø 33.3 mm, height 5.78 mm; 34 jewels; 28,800 vph; silicon Spiromax hairspring, gold rotor; 35-hour power reserve
Functions: hours, minutes, sweep seconds; additional 24-hour display; annual calendar with date, weekday, month, moon phase
Case: stainless steel, ø 40.5 mm, height 11.3 mm; sapphire crystal; transparent case back; screw-in crown; water-resistant to 12 atm
Band: stainless steel, folding clasp
Price: $45,928

Aquanaut
Reference number: 5168G-010
Movement: automatic, Patek Philippe Caliber 324 S C; ø 27 mm, height 3.3 mm; 29 jewels; 28,800 vph; silicon Spiromax hairspring, gold rotor; 35-hour power reserve
Functions: hours, minutes, sweep seconds; date
Case: white gold, ø 42.2 mm, height 8.25 mm; sapphire crystal; transparent case back; screw-in crown; water-resistant to 12 atm
Band: rubber, folding clasp
Price: $39,691

Nautilus
Reference number: 7118/1R-010
Movement: automatic, Patek Philippe Caliber 324 S C; ø 27 mm, height 3.3 mm; 29 jewels; 28,800 vph; silicon Spiromax hairspring, gold rotor; 35-hour power reserve
Functions: hours, minutes, sweep seconds; date
Case: rose gold, ø 35.2 mm, height 8.62 mm; sapphire crystal; transparent case back; water-resistant to 6 atm
Band: rose gold, folding clasp
Price: $47,629
Variations: set with diamonds ($57,999)

Nautilus
Reference number: 7118/1200A-011
Movement: automatic, Patek Philippe Caliber 324 S C; ø 27 mm, height 3.3 mm; 29 jewels; 28,800 vph; silicon Spiromax hairspring, gold rotor; 35-hour power reserve
Functions: hours, minutes, sweep seconds; date
Case: stainless steel, ø 35.2 mm, height 8.62 mm; bezel set with 56 diamonds; sapphire crystal; transparent case back; water-resistant to 6 atm
Band: stainless steel, folding clasp
Price: $34,021
Variations: without diamonds ($24,836)

PATEK PHILIPPE

Twenty4 Automatic
Reference number: 7300/1200R-010
Movement: automatic, Patek Philippe Caliber 324 S C; ø 27 mm, height 3.3 mm; 29 jewels; 28,800 vph; silicon Spiromax hairspring, gold rotor; 35-hour power reserve
Functions: hours, minutes, sweep seconds; date
Case: rose gold, ø 36 mm, height 10.05 mm; bezel set with 160 diamonds; sapphire crystal; transparent case back; water-resistant to 3 atm
Band: rose gold, folding clasp
Price: $26,083
Variations: various cases and straps (starting at $26,000)

World Time Watch with Minute Repeater
Reference number: 5531R-001
Movement: automatic, Patek Philippe Caliber R 27 HU; ø 32 mm, height 8.5 mm; 45 jewels; 21,600 vph; chime with traditional gong; microrotor winding; 43-hour power reserve
Functions: hours, minutes; world time display, minute repeater (chimes local time, can be set using the pusher)
Case: rose gold, ø 40.2 mm, height 11.49 mm; sapphire crystal; transparent case back
Band: reptile skin, folding clasp
Remarks: dial center with cloisonné enamel motif
Price: on request

Chronograph Perpetual Calendar with Tourbillon and Minute Repeater
Reference number: 5208R-001
Movement: automatic, Patek Philippe Caliber R CH 27 PS QI; ø 32 mm, height 10.35 mm; 63 jewels; 21,600 vph; 1-minute tourbillon; monopusher control of chronograph functions; microrotor winding; 38-hour power reserve
Functions: hours, minutes, subsidiary seconds; minute repeater; chronograph; perpetual calendar with date, weekday, month, moon phase, leap year
Case: rose gold, ø 42 mm, height 15.11 mm; sapphire crystal; transparent case back
Band: reptile skin, folding clasp
Price: on request

Chronograph Perpetual Calendar
Reference number: 5270/1R-001
Movement: manually wound, Patek Philippe Caliber CH 29 535 PS Q; ø 32 mm, height 7 mm; 33 jewels; 28,800 vph; 55-hour power reserve
Functions: hours, minutes, subsidiary seconds; day/night indicator; chronograph; perpetual calendar with date, weekday, month, moon phase, leap year
Case: rose gold, ø 41 mm, height 12.4 mm; sapphire crystal; transparent case back; water-resistant to 3 atm
Band: rose gold, folding clasp
Price: $198,454
Variations: platinum with reptile skin band ($187,114)

Perpetual Calendar
Reference number: 5320G-001
Movement: automatic, Patek Philippe Caliber 324 S Q; ø 32 mm, height 4.97 mm; 29 jewels; 28,800 vph; gold rotor; 35-hour power reserve
Functions: hours, minutes, sweep seconds; day/night indicator; perpetual calendar with date, weekday, month, moon phase, leap year
Case: white gold, ø 40 mm, height 11.1 mm; sapphire crystal; transparent case back; water-resistant to 3 atm
Band: reptile skin, folding clasp
Remarks: comes with additional white gold case back
Price: $87,320

Annual Calendar
Reference number: 5205G-013
Movement: automatic, Patek Philippe Caliber 324 S QA LU 24H; ø 32.6 mm, height 5.78 mm; 34 jewels; 28,800 vph; 35-hour power reserve
Functions: hours, minutes, sweep seconds; additional 24-hour display; annual calendar with date, weekday, month, moon phase
Case: white gold, ø 40 mm, height 11.36 mm; sapphire crystal; transparent case back; water-resistant to 3 atm
Band: reptile skin, buckle
Price: $47,970

Exclusively Designed and Assembled by the Detroit Watch Company

42mm case, Swiss automatic self-winding
Eta 2893-2. Exhibition caseback.

DETROIT WATCH COMPANY

PONTCHARTRAIN

EXPLORE THE COLLECTION AT
WWW.DETROITWATCHCO.COM

Copyright © 2020, Detroit Watch Company, LLC, All Rights Reserved

PATEK PHILIPPE

Calatrava Pilot Travel Time
Reference number: 5524R-001
Movement: automatic, Patek Philippe Caliber 324 S C FUS; ø 31 mm, height 4.9 mm; 29 jewels; 28,800 vph; silicon Spiromax hairspring; 35-hour power reserve
Functions: hours, minutes, sweep seconds; additional 12-hour display (2nd time zone), day/night indicator; date
Case: rose gold, ø 42 mm, height 10.78 mm; sapphire crystal; transparent case back; water-resistant to 6 atm
Band: calfskin, buckle
Price: $47,600
Variations: white gold ($47,600)

Ladies' Chronograph
Reference number: 7150/250R-001
Movement: manually wound, Patek Philippe Caliber CH 29-535 PS; ø 29.6 mm, height 5.35 mm; 33 jewels; 28,800 vph; column wheel control of chronograph functions, Breguet hairspring; 65-hour power reserve
Functions: hours, minutes, subsidiary seconds; chronograph
Case: rose gold, ø 38 mm, height 10.59 mm; bezel set with 72 diamonds; sapphire crystal; transparent case back; water-resistant to 3 atm
Band: reptile skin, buckle set with 27 diamonds
Price: $83,918

World Time
Reference number: 5230G-014
Movement: automatic, Patek Philippe Caliber 240 HU; ø 27.5 mm, height 3.88 mm; 33 jewels; 21,600 vph; silicon Spiromax hairspring; 48-hour power reserve
Functions: hours, minutes; world time display (2nd time zone)
Case: white gold, ø 38.5 mm, height 10.23 mm; pusher-activated inner bezel with city references; sapphire crystal; transparent case back; water-resistant to 3 atm
Band: reptile skin, folding clasp
Price: $47,629

Ellipse d'Or
Reference number: 5738R-001
Movement: automatic, Patek Philippe Caliber 240; ø 27.5 mm, height 2.53 mm; 27 jewels; 21,600 vph; gold microrotor; 48-hour power reserve
Functions: hours, minutes
Case: rose gold, 34.5 × 39.5 mm, height 5.9 mm; sapphire crystal
Band: reptile skin, buckle
Price: $31,980

Nautilus Perpetual Calendar
Reference number: 5740/1G-001
Movement: automatic, Patek Philippe Caliber 240 Q; ø 27.5 mm, height 3.88 mm; 27 jewels; 21,600 vph; 38-hour power reserve
Functions: hours, minutes; additional 24-hour display; perpetual calendar with date, weekday, month, moon phase, leap year
Case: white gold, ø 40 mm, height 8.42 mm; sapphire crystal; transparent case back; screw-in crown; water-resistant to 6 atm
Band: white gold, folding clasp
Price: $119,073

Aquanaut Chronograph
Reference number: 5968A-001
Movement: automatic, Patek Philippe Caliber CH 28-520 C; ø 30 mm, height 6.63 mm; 32 jewels; 28,800 vph; 45-hour power reserve
Functions: hours, minutes; chronograph; date
Case: stainless steel, ø 42.2 mm, height 11.9 mm; sapphire crystal; transparent case back; screw-in crown; water-resistant to 12 atm
Band: rubber, folding clasp
Price: $43,774

PATEK PHILIPPE

Caliber R 27 HU

Automatic; gold microrotor, chime with traditional gong activated by lateral slider; single spring barrel, 43-hour power reserve
Functions: hours, minutes; world time display, minute repeater (chimes local time, set by pusher)
Diameter: 32 mm
Height: 8.5 mm
Jewels: 45
Balance: Gyromax
Frequency: 21,600 vph
Balance spring: Spiromax
Remarks: 462 parts

Caliber R TO 27 PS QI

Manually wound; 1-minute tourbillon; chime with traditional gong; single spring barrel, 38-hour power reserve
Functions: hours, minutes, subsidiary seconds; minute repeater; perpetual calendar with date, weekday, month, moon phase
Diameter: 32 mm
Height: 9.33 mm
Jewels: 37
Balance: Gyromax
Frequency: 21,600 vph
Balance spring: Breguet
Remarks: 549 parts

Caliber CH 29-535 PS

Manually wound; column wheel control of chronograph functions, precisely jumping 30-minute totalizer; single spring barrel, 65-hour power
Functions: hours, minutes, subsidiary seconds; flyback chronograph
Diameter: 29.6 mm
Height: 7.1 mm
Jewels: 34
Balance: Gyromax, 4-armed, with 4 regulating weights
Frequency: 28,800 vph
Balance spring: Breguet
Shock protection: Incabloc
Remarks: 312 parts

Caliber CHR 29-535 PS Q

Manually wound; 2 column wheels for control of chronograph functions, flyback mechanism with isolator; single spring barrel, 65-hour power reserve
Functions: hours, minutes, subsidiary seconds; day/night indicator; flyback chronograph; perpetual calendar with date, weekday, month, moon phase, leap year
Diameter: 32 mm; **Height:** 8.7 mm
Jewels: 34
Balance: Gyromax, 4-armed, with 4 regulating weights
Frequency: 28,800 vph
Balance spring: Breguet
Remarks: 496 parts: 182 for perpetual calendar, 42 for flyback mechanism with an isolator

Caliber 324 S Q

Automatic; gold rotor; single spring barrel, 35-hour power reserve
Functions: hours, minutes, sweep seconds; day/night indicator; perpetual calendar with date, weekday, month, moon phase, leap year
Diameter: 32 mm
Height: 4.97 mm
Jewels: 29
Frequency: 28,800 vph

Caliber 324 S C

Automatic; gold rotor; single spring barrel, 35-hour power reserve
Functions: hours, minutes, sweep seconds; date
Diameter: 27 mm
Height: 3.3 mm
Jewels: 29
Balance: Gyromax
Frequency: 28,800 vph
Balance spring: Breguet

PATEK PHILIPPE

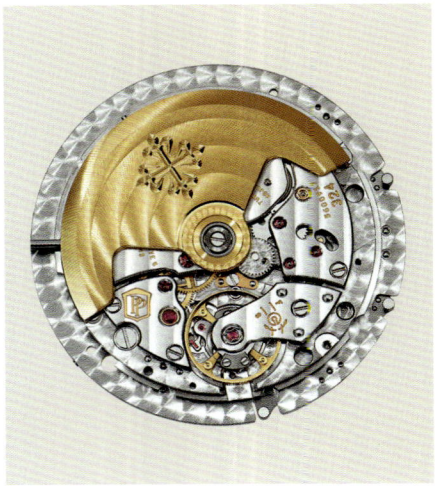

Caliber 324 S C FUS
Automatic; gold rotor; single spring barrel, 35-hour power reserve
Functions: hours, minutes, sweep seconds; additional 12-hour display (2nd time zone), day/night indicator; date
Diameter: 31 mm
Height: 4.82 mm
Jewels: 29
Balance: Gyromax
Frequency: 28,800 vph
Balance spring: silicon Spiromax
Remarks: 294 parts

Caliber 324 S QA LU 24H-303
Automatic; central rotor in 21-kt gold; single spring barrel, 45-hour power reserve
Functions: hours, minutes, sweep seconds; additional 24-hour display (2nd time zone); annual calendar with date, weekday, month, moon phase
Diameter: 32.6 mm
Height: 5.78 mm
Jewels: 34
Balance: Gyromax
Frequency: 28,800 vph
Balance spring: silicon Spiromax
Remarks: silicon escape wheel; 347 parts

Caliber 240 HU
Automatic; off-center, ball bearing–mounted, unidirectional gold microrotor in 22-kt gold; single spring barrel, 48-hour power reserve
Functions: hours, minutes; world time display (2nd time zone)
Diameter: 27.5 mm
Height: 3.88 mm
Jewels: 33
Balance: Gyromax
Frequency: 21,600 vph
Remarks: 239 parts

Caliber 240 Q
Automatic; gold microrotor; single spring barrel, 48-hour power reserve
Functions: hours, minutes; additional 24-hour display (2nd time zone); perpetual calendar with date, weekday, month, moon phase, leap year
Diameter: 30 mm
Height: 3.75 mm
Jewels: 27
Balance: Gyromax, with 8 massebotte regulating weights
Frequency: 21,600 vph
Balance spring: flat hairspring
Shock protection: Kif

Caliber AL 30-660 S C FUS
Automatic; gold rotor; single spring barrel, 42-hour power reserve
Functions: hours, minutes, sweep seconds; additional 12-hour display (2nd time zone), day/night indicator, alarm; date
Diameter: 31 mm
Height: 6.6 mm
Jewels: 52
Frequency: 28,800 vph
Balance spring: silicon Spiromax

Caliber 26-330 S C J SE
Automatic; gold rotor; single spring barrel, 35-hour power reserve
Functions: hours, minutes, sweep seconds; date, weekday, calendar week
Diameter: 27 mm
Height: 4.82 mm
Jewels: 50
Frequency: 28,800 vph
Balance spring: silicon Spiromax

Caliber CH 28-520 QA 24H
Automatic; gold rotor; single spring barrel, 45-hour power reserve
Functions: hours, minutes; flyback chronograph; annual calendar with date, weekday, month
Diameter: 33 mm
Height: 7.68 mm
Jewels: 37
Frequency: 28,800 vph
Balance spring: silicon Spiromax

Caliber 31-260 REG QA
Automatic; Pulsomax escapement, microrotor; single spring barrel, 38-hour power reserve
Functions: hours (off-center), minutes, subsidiary seconds; annual calendar with date, weekday, month
Diameter: 33 mm
Height: 5.08 mm
Jewels: 31
Frequency: 23,040 vph
Balance spring: silicon Spiromax

Caliber 240
Automatic; gold microrotor; single spring barrel, 48-hour power reserve
Functions: hours, minutes
Diameter: 27.5 mm
Height: 2.53 mm
Jewels: 27
Balance: Gyromax
Frequency: 21,600 vph
Balance spring: silicon Spiromax
Remarks: 161 parts

Caliber CH 28-520 C
Automatic; single spring barrel, 45-hour power reserve
Functions: hours, minutes; chronograph; date
Diameter: 30 mm
Height: 6.63 mm
Jewels: 32
Balance: Gyromax
Frequency: 28,800 vph
Balance spring: silicon Spiromax
Remarks: 308 parts

Caliber R 27 PS
Automatic; gold microrotor, chime with traditional gong activated by slide in flank; single spring barrel
Functions: hours, minutes, subsidiary seconds; minute repeater
Diameter: 28 mm
Height: 5.05 mm
Jewels: 39
Frequency: 21,600 vph

Caliber R TO 27 PS QR
Manually wound; 1-minute tourbillon; single spring barrel, 48-hour power reserve; COSC-certified chronometer
Functions: hours, minutes, subsidiary seconds; minute repeater; perpetual calendar with date (retrograde), weekday, month, leap year (in separate window); moon phase
Diameter: 28 mm
Height: 8.61 mm
Jewels: 28
Balance: Gyromax
Frequency: 21,600 vph
Balance spring: Breguet
Remarks: 336 parts

PAUL GERBER

Watchmaker Paul Gerber has already developed mechanisms and complications, including calendar movements, alarms, and tourbillons, for numerous renowned watchmakers over the decades. Time and again, this genial watchmaker has astonished the horological world with outrageously complicated mechanisms, which he somehow manages to create by fitting hundreds of additional tiny parts into filigree movements. Gerber is the one who designed the complicated calendar mechanism for the otherwise minimalist MIH watch conceived by Ludwig Oechslin, curator of the International Museum of Horology (MIH) in La Chaux-de-Fonds and himself a watchmaker. To avoid cluttering a dial for a special customer, he recently devised a battery-run moon phase that fits in the watch strap. His work has twice appeared in *Guinness World Records*.

When his daily work for others lets up, Gerber gets around to building watches bearing his own name with such marvelous features as a retrograde second hand in an elegant thin case and a synchronously, unidirectional rotor system with miniature oscillating weights for his self-winding Retro Twin model. Gerber's works are all limited editions.

After designing a tonneau-shaped manually wound wristwatch with a three-dimensional moon phase display, Gerber created a simple three-hand watch with an automatic movement conceived and produced completely in-house. It features a 100-hour power reserve and is wound by three synchronically turning gold rotors. Gerber also offers the triple rotor and large date features in a watch with an ETA movement and lightweight titanium case as a classic pilot watch design or in a version with a more modern dial (the Synchron model). The Model 41 has an optional complication that switches the second hand from sweep to dead-beat motion by way of a pusher at 2 o'clock.

Gerber is allegedly retired. But a watchmaker never really does. Besides continuing to produce outstanding pieces, he occasionally gives three-day workshops for people wanting to get a real feel for the work.

Paul Gerber
Uhren-Konstruktionen
Bockhornstrasse 69
CH-8047 Zürich
Switzerland

Tel.:
+41-44-401-4569

E-mail:
info@gerber-uhren.ch

Website:
www.gerber-uhren.ch

Founded:
1976

Annual production:
up to 50 watches

U.S. distributor:
Intro Swiss—Michael Schmutz
7615 Estate Circle
Niwot, CO 80503
303-652-1520
introswiss@q.com

Most important collections/price range:
mechanical watches / from approx. $4,900 to $60,000; tourbillon desk clocks / from approx. $48,000 to $70,000

Retro Twin
Reference number: 155
Movement: automatic, Gerber Caliber 15 (base ETA 7001); ø 28 mm, height 5.2 mm; 27 jewels; 21,600 vph; automatic winding with 2 synchronically rotating platinum rotors
Functions: hours, minutes, subsidiary seconds (retrograde)
Case: yellow gold, ø 36 mm, height 10.8 mm; sapphire crystal; transparent case back; water-resistant to 3 atm
Band: reptile skin, buckle
Price: $16,430
Variations: rose gold ($16,430) or white gold ($16,880); with platinum rotors set with brilliants (plus $3,000)

Modell 42
Reference number: 420 pilot (blue dial)
Movement: automatic, Gerber Caliber 42 (base ETA 2824); ø 36 mm, height 6.1 mm; 25 jewels; 28,800 vph; automatic winding with 3 synchronically rotating gold rotors
Functions: hours, minutes, sweep seconds; large quick-set date
Case: titanium, ø 42 mm, height 12 mm; sapphire crystal; transparent case back; screw-in crown; water-resistant to 10 atm
Band: calfskin, buckle
Price: $4,900
Variations: anthracite or synchron ($4,900); pilot's/synchron DaN (day and night) ($5,830); pilot's/synchron DT (Dual Time) ($5,785)

Modell 33
Reference number: 336-D
Movement: manually wound, Paul Gerber Caliber 33 with patented escapement; 28 × 34 × 5 mm; 20 jewels; 21,600 vph; 36-hour power reserve
Functions: hours, minutes, seconds; 3D moon phase (6-mm moon, corrected for 128 years), date
Case: white gold, 34 × 40 × 10.2 mm; sapphire crystal; transparent case back; water-resistant to 3 atm
Remarks: 1 moon hemisphere with 54 diamonds and 1 hemisphere (the dark side) of lapis
Band: reptile skin, gold buckle
Price: $44,690
Variations: rose gold ($44,690); platinum ($48,760)

PIAGET

One of the oldest watch manufacturers in Switzerland, Piaget began making watch movements in the secluded Jura village of La Côte-aux-Fées in 1874. For decades, those movements were delivered to other watch brands. The *manufacture* itself, strangely enough, remained in the background. It wasn't until the 1940s that the Piaget family began to offer complete watches under their own name.

Even today, Piaget, which long ago moved the business side of things to Geneva, still makes its watch movements at its main facility high in the Jura mountains.

In the late fifties, Piaget began investing in the design and manufacturing of ultrathin movements. This lends these watches the kind of understated elegance that became the company's hallmark. In 1957, Valentin Piaget presented the first ultrathin men's watch, the Altiplano, with the manual caliber 9P, which was 2 millimeters high. Shortly after, it came out with the 12P, an automatic caliber that clocked in at 2.3 millimeters.

The Altiplano has faithfully accompanied the brand for sixty years now. The movement has evolved over time. The recent 900P measures just 3.65 millimeters and is inverted to enable repairs, making the case back the mainplate with the dial set on the upper side. Striving for the thinnest watch produced the Altiplano Ultimate Concept in 2018, a 2-millimeter, manually wound watch, released—but not for sale—after four years of R&D.

Worthy of note, too, is Piaget's concept watch that combines mechanical and quartz technology. The spring barrel, wound by hand or microrotor, drives a miniature generator that turns at a constant 5.33 rpm and replaces the escapement and balance wheel. It supplies the regulating quartz with power, which in turn regulates the movement. This inverted caliber is just 5.5 millimeters high. All the basic parts are on the dial side and partly visible thanks to skeletonized plates.

Piaget SA
CH-1228 Plan-les-Ouates
Switzerland

Tel.:
+41-32-867-21-21

E-mail:
info@piaget.com

Website:
www.piaget.com

Founded:
1874

Number of employees:
900

Annual production:
about 25,000 watches

U.S. distributor:
Piaget North America
645 5th Avenue, 6th Floor
New York, NY 10022
212-909-4362
www.piaget.com

Most important collection/price range:
Altiplano / approx. $13,500 to $22,000

Altiplano
Reference number: G0A44051
Movement: automatic, Piaget Caliber 1203P; ø 29.9 mm, height 3 mm; 25 jewels; 21,600 vph; rose gold microrotor; côtes de Genève; 44-hour power reserve
Functions: hours, minutes; date
Case: rose gold, ø 40 mm, height 6.36 mm; sapphire crystal; water-resistant to 3 atm
Band: reptile skin, folding clasp
Remarks: dial made of meteorite
Price: $24,600

Altiplano
Reference number: G0A44052
Movement: automatic, Piaget Caliber 1203P; ø 29.9 mm, height 3 mm; 25 jewels; 21,600 vph; rose gold microrotor; côtes de Genève; 44-hour power reserve
Functions: hours, minutes; date
Case: rose gold, ø 40 mm, height 6.36 mm; bezel set with 72 diamonds; sapphire crystal; water-resistant to 3 atm
Band: reptile skin, folding clasp
Remarks: dial made of meteorite
Price: $32,700

Altiplano
Reference number: G0A44060
Movement: manually wound, Piaget Caliber 430P; ø 20.5 mm, height 2.1 mm; 18 jewels; 21,600 vph; côtes de Genève; 44-hour power reserve
Functions: hours, minutes
Case: rose gold, ø 34 mm, height 6.5 mm; bezel set with 72 diamonds; sapphire crystal; water-resistant to 3 atm
Band: reptile skin, folding clasp
Remarks: dial made of meteorite
Price: $23,100

Altiplano Ultimate Automatic
Reference number: G0A43120
Movement: automatic, Piaget Caliber 910P; ø 41 mm, height 4.3 mm (case with movement); 30 jewels; 21,600 vph; inverted movement with case and hubless peripheral rotor; 50-hour power reserve
Functions: hours, minutes (off-center)
Case: rose gold, ø 41 mm, height 4.3 mm; sapphire crystal
Band: reptile skin, buckle
Price: $27,300

Altiplano Ultimate Automatic
Reference number: G0A43121
Movement: automatic, Piaget Caliber 910P; ø 41 mm, height 4.3 mm (case with movement); 30 jewels; 21,600 vph; inverted movement with case, hubless peripheral rotor; 50-hour power reserve
Functions: hours, minutes (off-center)
Case: white gold, ø 41 mm, height 4.3 mm; sapphire crystal
Band: reptile skin, buckle
Price: $28,400

Altiplano Ultimate Concept
Reference number: G0A43900
Movement: manually wound, Piaget Caliber 900P-UC; ø 41 mm, height 2 mm (case with movement); 13 jewels; 28,800 vph; inverted movement construction integrated in the case, flying gearwheels mounted (one-sided); 44-hour power reserve
Functions: hours, minutes (off-center)
Case: carbon and cobalt-based alloy, ø 41 mm, height 2 mm; sapphire crystal
Band: reptile skin, buckle
Remarks: concept watch, thinnest mechanical wristwatch ever made; probably not for serial production
Price: not for sale

Polo S
Reference number: G0A44001
Movement: automatic, Piaget Caliber 1110P; ø 25.58 mm, height 4 mm; 25 jewels; 28,800 vph; mainplate with perlage, blued screws, finely finished with côtes de Genève; 50-hour power reserve
Functions: hours, minutes, sweep seconds; date
Case: stainless steel, ø 42.4 mm, height 9.4 mm; sapphire crystal; transparent case back; water-resistant to 10 atm
Band: reptile skin, folding clasp
Price: $8,400

Polo S
Reference number: G0A41002
Movement: automatic, Piaget Caliber 1110P; ø 25.58 mm, height 4 mm; 25 jewels; 28,800 vph; mainplate with perlage, blued screws, finely finished with côtes de Genève; 50-hour power reserve
Functions: hours, minutes, sweep seconds; date
Case: stainless steel, ø 42 mm, height 9.4 mm; sapphire crystal; transparent case back; water-resistant to 10 atm
Band: stainless steel, folding clasp
Price: $9,900

Polo S Chronograph
Reference number: G0A41006
Movement: automatic, Piaget Caliber 1160P; ø 25.58 mm, height 5.72 mm; 35 jewels; 28,800 vph; mainplate with perlage, blued screws, finely finished with côtes de Genève; 50-hour power reserve
Functions: hours, minutes; chronograph; date
Case: stainless steel, ø 42 mm, height 11.2 mm; sapphire crystal; transparent case back; water-resistant to 10 atm
Band: stainless steel, folding clasp
Price: $14,400
Variations: black dial; reptile skin band

PIAGET

Polo S
Reference number: G0A43010
Movement: automatic, Piaget Caliber 1110P; ø 25.58 mm, height 4 mm; 25 jewels; 28,800 vph; mainplate with perlage, blued screws, finely finished with côtes de Genève; 50-hour power reserve
Functions: hours, minutes, sweep seconds; date
Case: rose gold, ø 42 mm, height 9.4 mm; sapphire crystal; transparent case back; water-resistant to 10 atm
Band: reptile skin, folding clasp
Price: $21,000

Polo S Chronograph
Reference number: G0A43011
Movement: automatic, Piaget Caliber 1160P; ø 25.58 mm, height 5.72 mm; 35 jewels; 28,800 vph; mainplate with perlage, blued screws, finely finished with côtes de Genève; 50-hour power reserve
Functions: hours, minutes; chronograph; date
Case: rose gold, ø 42 mm, height 11.2 mm; sapphire crystal; transparent case back; water-resistant to 10 atm
Band: reptile skin, folding clasp
Price: $27,700

Limelight Stella
Reference number: G0A44123
Movement: automatic, Piaget Caliber 584P; ø 26 mm; 21,600 vph; 42-hour power reserve
Functions: hours, minutes, sweep seconds; moon phase
Case: rose gold, ø 36 mm, height 9.9 mm; bezel set with 126 diamonds; sapphire crystal; transparent case back; water-resistant to 3 atm
Band: reptile skin, buckle
Remarks: dial set with 14 diamonds
Price: $37,200
Variations: white gold ($38,700)

Limelight Stella
Reference number: G0A44124
Movement: automatic, Piaget Caliber 584P; ø 26 mm; 21,600 vph; 42-hour power reserve
Functions: hours, minutes, sweep seconds; moon phase
Case: white gold, ø 36 mm, height 9.9 mm; bezel set with 126 diamonds; sapphire crystal; transparent case back; water-resistant to 3 atm
Band: reptile skin, buckle
Remarks: dial set with 173 diamonds
Price: $38,700

Limelight Gala
Reference number: G0A43391
Movement: quartz
Functions: hours, minutes
Case: rose gold, ø 32 mm, height 7.4 mm; bezel set with 62 diamonds; sapphire crystal; water-resistant to 3 atm
Band: reptile skin, buckle
Price: $33,900

Limelight Gala Milanaise
Reference number: G0A44212
Movement: quartz
Functions: hours, minutes
Case: white gold, ø 26 mm, height 7 mm; bezel set with 62 diamonds; sapphire crystal; water-resistant to 3 atm
Band: white gold Milanese mesh, sliding clasp
Price: $26,600

PIAGET

Caliber 910P

Automatic; inverted movement construction as single unit with watch case; hubless peripheral rotor on movement edge; single spring barrel, 50-hour power reserve
Functions: hours, minutes (off-center)
Diameter: 41 mm
Height: 4.3 mm
Jewels: 30
Balance: glucydur
Frequency: 21,600 vph
Balance spring: flat hairspring
Remarks: finely finished movement; 238 parts

Caliber 1110P

Automatic; single spring barrel, 50-hour power reserve
Functions: hours, minutes, sweep seconds; date
Diameter: 25.58 mm
Height: 4 mm
Jewels: 25
Frequency: 28,800 vph
Remarks: perlage on mainplate, blued screws, finely finished with côtes de Genève; 180 parts

Caliber 1160P

Automatic; single spring barrel, 50-hour power reserve
Functions: hours, minutes; chronograph; date
Diameter: 25.58 mm
Height: 5.72 mm
Jewels: 35
Frequency: 28,800 vph
Remarks: perlage on mainplate, blued screws, finely finished with côtes de Genève; 262 parts

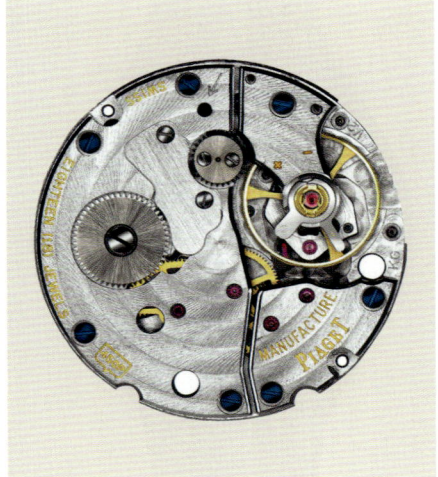

Caliber 450P

Manually wound; single spring barrel, 43-hour power reserve
Functions: hours, minutes, subsidiary seconds
Diameter: 20.5 mm
Height: 2.1 mm
Jewels: 18
Balance: glucydur
Frequency: 21,600 vph
Balance spring: flat hairspring
Remarks: finely finished movement; 131 parts

Caliber 1205P

Automatic; microrotor; single spring barrel, 44-hour power reserve; Geneva Seal
Functions: hours, minutes, subsidiary seconds; date
Diameter: 29.9 mm
Height: 3 mm
Jewels: 27
Balance: glucydur
Frequency: 21,600 vph
Balance spring: flat hairspring
Shock protection: Incabloc
Remarks: world's thinnest automatic movement with date from current production; 221 parts

Caliber 1208P

Automatic; microrotor; single spring barrel, 42-hour power reserve; Geneva Seal
Functions: hours, minutes, subsidiary seconds
Diameter: 29.9 mm
Height: 2.35 mm
Jewels: 27
Balance: glucydur
Frequency: 21,600 vph
Balance spring: flat hairspring
Shock protection: Incabloc

PORSCHE DESIGN

Porsche Design has always made sure it was partnering with the best to manufacture its products. In 1978, it was the Schaffhausen-based brand IWC that produced watches under the name Porsche Design through a license agreement with the F.A. Porsche design firm. When the IWC license expired in 1998, Eterna, purchased by Porsche in 1995, took over manufacturing. In March 2014, Eterna and Porsche Design separated. Since then, all Porsche Design watches have been developed by the company subsidiary Porsche Design Timepieces in Solothurn, Switzerland, in collaboration with the well-established design studio in Zell-am-See, Austria.

Porsche Design was founded by Professor Ferdinand Alexander Porsche in 1972—the fountainhead of numerous objects in daily use beyond just watches. The Professor—a title bestowed by the Austrian government—who died in April 2012, created a string of classic objects at his "Studio," but sports car fans will always remember him for the Porsche 911.

In 2003, the Professor decided to found his own company, which is separate from the carmaker. The brand is proud not only of its unusual designs but also of its use of light metals: In the 1970s already, it was using black PVD-coated aluminum and titanium for its watches and cases. The Chronotimer collection harked back to this very avant-garde esthetic statement. The streamlined and rigorous design is also visible in the new 1919 collection, named for the foundation year of the Bauhaus movement.

Porsche Design engineers obviously inspire themselves from the automobile industry when it comes to materials and functionality. The innovative rocker arm that activates the chronograph of the new Monobloc Actuator was inspired from the valve control of high-powered race cars using tappets. It improves ease of use and increases the mechanism's durability. A milestone was the release of the Caliber 01.200, in 2017, which featured a complex flyback mechanism. In 2019 came the Caliber 04.110, with a very clever GMT switching mechanism that could become a new industry standard.

Porsche Design Group
Groenerstrasse 5
D-71636 Ludwigsburg
Germany

Tel.:
+49-711-911-0

E-mail:
timepieces@porsche-design.us

Website:
www.porsche-design.com

Founded:
1972

U.S. distributor:
Porsche Design of America, Inc
Plaza Tower
600 Anton Blvd., Suite 1280
Costa Mesa, CA 92626
770-290-7500
timepieces@porsche-design.us
www.porsche-design.com

Most important collections/price range:
Chronotimer Series 1, 1919 Datetimer Eternity, 1919 Globetimer, 1919 Chronotimer, Monobloc Actuator / $3,150 to $7,450

Chronotimer Flyback Special Edition

Movement: automatic, Porsche Design Caliber Werk 01.200 (base ETA 7750); ø 30 mm, height 7.9 mm; 25 jewels; 28,800 vph; 48-hour power reserve; COSC-certified chronometer
Functions: hours, minutes; rate control; flyback chronograph; date
Case: titanium with black titanium carbide coating, ø 42 mm, height 14.62 mm; sapphire crystal; transparent case back; screw-in crown; water-resistant to 10 atm
Band: calfskin, folding clasp
Price: $6,700

Chronotimer Series 1 Deep Blue

Reference number: 4046901408770
Movement: automatic, ETA Caliber 7750; ø 30 mm, height 7.9 mm; 25 jewels; 28,800 vph; 48-hour power reserve
Functions: hours, minutes, subsidiary seconds; chronograph; date
Case: titanium, ø 42 mm, height 14.62 mm; sapphire crystal; transparent case back; screw-in crown; water-resistant to 5 atm
Band: textile, folding clasp
Price: $4,200

Monobloc Actuator Chronotimer Flyback Limited Edition

Reference number: 4046901810504
Movement: automatic, Porsche Design Caliber Movement 01.200 (base ETA 7750); ø 30 mm, height 7.9 mm; 25 jewels; 28,800 vph; 48-hour power reserve; COSC-certified chronometer
Functions: hours, minutes; rate control; flyback chronograph; date; **Case:** titanium with black titanium carbide coating, ø 45.5 mm, height 15.6 mm; sapphire crystal; transparent case back; screw-in crown; water-resistant to 10 atm
Band: rubber with leather overlay, folding clasp
Remarks: large rocker pusher integrated into right case side
Price: $8,500; limited to 251 pieces

PORSCHE DESIGN

Monobloc Actuator
GMT-Chronotimer All Titanium
Reference number: 4046901564124
Movement: automatic, ETA Caliber 7754; ø 30 mm, height 7.9 mm; 25 jewels; 28,800 vph; 48-hour power reserve
Functions: hours, minutes; radio control; additional 24-hour display (2nd time zone); chronograph; date
Case: titanium, ø 45.5 mm, height 15.6 mm; sapphire crystal; transparent case back; screw-in crown; water-resistant to 10 atm
Band: titanium, folding clasp
Remarks: large rocker pusher integrated into right case side
Price: $6,900

Monobloc Actuator
24H-Chronotimer Black & Rubber
Reference number: 4046901568047
Movement: automatic, ETA Caliber 7754; ø 30 mm, height 7.9 mm; 25 jewels; 28,800 vph; 48-hour power reserve
Functions: hours, minutes; rate control; additional 24-hour display (2nd time zone); chronograph; date
Case: titanium with black titanium carbide coating, ø 45.5 mm, height 15.6 mm; sapphire crystal; transparent case back; screw-in crown; water-resistant to 10 atm
Band: rubber, folding clasp
Remarks: large rocker pusher integrated into right case side
Price: $6,700

911 Chronograph
Timeless Machine Limited Edition
Reference number: 4046901133931
Movement: automatic, ETA Caliber 7750; ø 30 mm, height 7.9 mm; 25 jewels; 28,800 vph; 48-hour power reserve
Functions: hours, minutes; rate control; chronograph; date
Case: titanium, ø 42 mm, height 14.9 mm; sapphire crystal; transparent case back; screw-in crown; water-resistant to 10 atm
Band: calfskin, folding clasp
Price: $5,411; limited to 911 pieces

1919 Chronotimer Flyback
Black & Leather
Reference number: 4046901978983
Movement: automatic, Porsche Design Caliber Movement 01.200 (base ETA 7750); ø 30 mm, height 7.9 mm; 25 jewels; 28,800 vph; 48-hour power reserve; COSC-certified chronometer
Functions: hours, minutes; rate control; flyback chronograph; date
Case: titanium, ø 42 mm, height 14.9 mm; sapphire crystal; transparent case back; screw-in crown; water-resistant to 10 atm
Band: calfskin, folding clasp
Price: $7,450

1919 Globetimer UTC
Titanium & Black
Reference number: 4046901979133
Movement: automatic, Porsche Design Caliber Movement 04.110; ø 28.5 mm, height 6.94 mm; 26 jewels; 28,800 vph; 38-hour power reserve; COSC-certified chronometer
Functions: hours, minutes, sweep seconds; additional 24-hour display (2nd time zone), day/night indicator; date
Case: titanium, ø 42 mm, height 14.9 mm; sapphire crystal; screw-in crown; water-resistant to 10 atm
Band: calfskin, folding clasp
Price: $6,350

1919 Datetimer Eternity
Brown Alligator Leather
Reference number: 4046901986117
Movement: automatic, Sellita Caliber SW200-1; ø 25.6 mm, height 4.6 mm; 26 jewels; 28,800 vph; 38-hour power reserve
Functions: hours, minutes, sweep seconds; date
Case: titanium, ø 42 mm, height 11.92 mm; sapphire crystal; screw-in crown; water-resistant to 10 atm
Band: reptile skin, folding clasp
Price: $4,200

PRAMZIUS

Whatever their political affiliations or leanings, no one can deny that Eastern Europe, the Baltic states, and Russia, in particular, exert a considerable fascination on people. It may be the extreme quality of everything that comes from that part of the world that appeals to our need for drama—the long and troubled history; the brutal leaders; the staggeringly talented people, from musicians to chess players; the brooding novels about adultery, complex love, suicide, war, dark morality; the antics of modern-day Russians caught on smartphones and dashcams. That may explain the success of Détente Group and its boisterous watches celebrating Big Mechanics—not for the limp-wristed, by any stretch.

In 2017, Craig Hester, distributor of Vostok-Europe, Sturmanskie, and other brands, parlayed over 20 years' experience in the watch business into the launch of a series of watches that would continue paying tribute to this wild, dangerous, creative, and at times sincerely eccentric part of the world. The name of the brand, Pramzius, is a reference to the Baltic Ruler of Time, an ancient and, appropriately, pagan god. Funding for the project came from a brief but successful Kickstarter campaign.

The first series of Pramzius was devoted to the renowned Trans-Siberian Railway and was inspired by a correspondingly themed pocket watch from back in the day. The modern version is, accordingly, big—48 millimeters in diameter—made of high-grade steel instead of brass. The second in the series celebrates the thirtieth anniversary of the fall of the Berlin Wall (2019) with a dial featuring graffiti from the last stretch of the Wall, the open-air East Side Gallery in Berlin, and a bit of the Wall in the crown as a souvenir of the ghastly frontier. The latest stroke is named the Iron Wolf, after the legend behind the founding of the Lithuanian capital, Vilnius. It has become the official watch of a Lithuanian NATO brigade and its vehicle. Their insignia, a wolf's head, appears on the dial with the word *vilkas*, wolf.

Pramzius Watches
31 Halls Hill Road
Colchester, CT 06415

Website:
www.pramzius.com

E-mail:
info@pramzius.com

Founded:
2017

Number of employees:
4

Annual production:
2,500

Distribution:
direct sales

Most important collections/price range:
Trans-Siberian Railroad / $479; Berlin Wall Watch / $649 to $949; Military Iron Wolf Watch / $699

Military Iron Wolf Chronograph
Reference number: P715303
Movement: quartz, 6S21 Miyota Caliber; ø 34.6 mm, height 4.9 mm
Functions: hours, minutes, subsidiary seconds; 24-hour indicator
Case: stainless steel, ø 44 mm, height 14 mm; bezel with 0-120 scale; sapphire crystal; screw-down crown; water-resistant to 10 atm
Band: stainless steel, clasp
Remarks: full lume sandwich dial; bezel with "wolf teeth" indicators; comes with NATO nylon strap and bund strap
Price: $699

Military Iron Wolf
Reference number: P712302
Movement: automatic, 82S7 Miyota Caliber; ø 27.4 mm, height 5.67 mm; 21 jewels; 21,600 vph; bidirectional rotor; 42-hour power reserve
Functions: hours, minutes, subsidiary seconds; 24-hour indicator
Case: stainless steel, ø 44 mm, height 14 mm; bezel with 0-120 scale; sapphire crystal; screw-down crown; water-resistant to 10 atm
Band: stainless steel, clasp
Remarks: full lume sandwich dial; bezel with "wolf teeth" indicators; comes with NATO nylon strap and bund strap
Price: $699

Berlin Wall Watch
Movement: automatic, Seiko Caliber NH35; ø 27.4 mm, height 5.32 mm; 24 jewels; 21,600 vph; bidirectional rotor; 41-hour power reserve
Functions: hours, minutes, sweep seconds; date
Case: stainless steel, ø 42 mm, height 14 mm, K1 mineral glass; screw-down crown; 3D rendering of Brandenburg Gate on case back; water-resistant to 10 atm
Band: calfskin strap, buckle
Remarks: genuine marble dial featuring original graffiti from Berlin Wall; bits of Berlin Wall in crown; comes with extra leather-nylon strap
Price: $649 leather; $699 bracelet
Variations: ETA 2824 movement ($899–$949); 48-millimeter case ($649–$699)

Rado Uhren AG
Bielstrasse 45
CH-2543 Lengnau
Switzerland

Tel.:
+41-32-655-6111

E-mail:
info@rado.com

Website:
www.rado.com
store.us.rado.com

Founded:
1957

Number of employees:
approx. 470

U.S. distributor:
Rado
The Swatch Group (U.S.), Inc.
703 Waterford Way, Suite 450
Miami, FL 33126
786-725-5393

Most important collections/price range:
Hyperchrome / from approx $1,100; Diamaster / from approx. $1,500; Integral / from approx. $2,000; True / from approx. $1,400; Centrix / from approx. $800; Coupole Classic / from approx. $1,000; Tradition / from approx. $2,000

RADO

Rado is a relatively young brand, especially for a Swiss one. The company, which grew out of the Schlup clockwork factory, launched its first watches in 1957, but it achieved international fame only five years later, in 1962, when it surprised the world with a revolutionary invention. Rado's oval DiaStar was the first truly scratch-resistant watch ever, sporting a case made of the impervious alloy hardmetal. In 1985, its parent company, the Swatch Group, decided to put Rado's know-how and extensive experience in developing materials to good use, and from then on the brand intensified its research activities at its home in Lengnau, Switzerland, and continued to produce only watches with extremely hard cases. A record of sorts was even set in 2004, when they managed to create a 10,000-Vickers material, which is as hard as natural diamonds.

Rado also made jewel watches, but over time it was the high-tech watches and pioneering spirit of the brand's ceramic researchers and engineers that won out. The company already holds more than thirty patents arising from research and production of new case materials. In 2011, for example, they produced the ultra-light Ceramos, which went into the D-Star collection. It has returned in a series of slim automatics branded DiaMaster. This innovative material is made up of 90 percent ceramic and 10 percent of a special metal alloy. It is scratch-resistant and comes in a rosy gold or steely hue. Rado also uses a plasma-ceramic process to produce a material in warm metallic tones that keeps its sheen. Finally, there's the HyperChrome, which offers more resilience than regular ceramic, while weighing far less.

Coupole Classic Automatic
Reference number: R22894153
Movement: automatic, ETA Caliber C07.631; ø 25.6 mm, height 4.74 mm; 25 jewels; 21,600 vph; partially skeletonized mainplate and dial; 80-hour power reserve
Functions: hours, minutes, sweep seconds
Case: stainless steel, ø 41 mm, height 11.7 mm; sapphire crystal; water-resistant to 5 atm
Band: stainless steel, folding clasp
Price: $1,600

Golden Horse Automatic
Reference number: R33101204
Movement: automatic, ETA Caliber C07.611; ø 25.6 mm, height 5.2 mm; 25 jewels; 21,600 vph; 80-hour power reserve
Functions: hours, minutes, sweep seconds; date
Case: stainless steel, ø 42 mm, height 10.4 mm; sapphire crystal; water-resistant to 5 atm
Band: stainless steel, triple folding clasp
Price: $2,000

HyperChrome Automatic Chronograph
Reference number: R32042205
Movement: automatic, ETA Caliber A05.H21; ø 30 mm, height 7.9 mm; 25 jewels; 21,600 vph; 54-hour power reserve
Functions: hours, minutes, subsidiary seconds; chronograph; date
Case: stainless steel, ø 44 mm, height 15.1 mm; ceramic bezel; sapphire crystal; water-resistant to 10 atm
Band: calfskin, triple folding clasp
Price: $2,400

RESERVOIR

One of the most logical inspirations for watches is the humble gauge, and for good reason. It usually has a similar shape to a watch (round), and it serves to depict a certain event or action using a pointing device and numerals. It must also be legible at a glance. In addition, gauges tend to be found where a mechanical process is taking place, and that excites the imagination of any person who appreciates engineering.

While gauges and meters are used fairly frequently as elements in watchmaking, only a few brands have actually made them the centerpiece of their esthetic strategy. A recent and rare one is Reservoir, a French brand founded in 2017 by François Moreau. Connoisseurs of vintage British cars will easily spot the resemblance of many models to the odometers in the Mini Morrises: a big round dial with a fuel gauge at the lower end. This basic dial serves as a visual touchstone for three separate lines, namely air, land, and sea. Automobile, for example, is composed of three collections: GT Tour, Supercharged, and Longbridge. The latter even includes the oil and ignition lamps, a reminder of the original Smiths odometers used in, among others, the Morris Minor. The other lines are Airfight, with gauges from airplanes, and Marine, with the Tiefenmesser (depth gauge) and a real diver's watch, the Hydrosphere.

Care was given to the authenticity of the look. Gauges usually have a single pointer. On the Reservoir models it becomes a retrograde minute hand. The hours are jumping and appear in a separate window below the center. The fuel gauge at 6 o'clock is used for the power reserve. The movements are based on an ETA 2824-2 with a special patented module made by the company. By reducing the variations in the movements, the company has been able to offer excellent value.

Reservoir Watch SAS
138, rue du Faubourg Saint-Honoré
F-75008 Paris
France

Tel:
+41-32-967-97-97

E-mail:
contact@reservoir-watch.com

Website:
www.reservoir-watch.com

Founded:
2017

Number of employees:
4

Distributor:
Online sales
contact@reservoir-watch.com
+33-1-47-48-80-77

Most important collections/price range
Cars, Aeronautics, Marine / from $3,900

Longbridge British Racing
Reference number: RSV01.LB/130-62s
Movement: automatic, ETA Caliber 2824-2 with special in-house module; ø 25.60 mm, height 4.60 mm; 25 jewels; 28,800 vph; 37-hour power reserve
Functions: jumping hours, retrograde minutes; power reserve indicator
Case: stainless steel, ø 39 mm, height 11.5 mm; screw-in crown; sapphire crystal; transparent case back; water-resistant to 5 atm
Band: leather, folding clasp
Remarks: British racing green dial; additional NATO strap
Price: $4,900; **Variations:** 41.5-mm rose gold case ($13,400); palladium case ($14,900)

Airfight Propeller
Reference number: RSV02.AF/231-15
Movement: automatic, ETA Caliber 2824-2 with special in-house module; ø 25.60 mm, height 4.60 mm; 25 jewels; 28,800 vph; 37-hour power reserve
Functions: jumping hours, retrograde minutes; power reserve indicator
Case: stainless steel with black PVD, ø 43 mm, height 12.8 mm; screw-in crown; sapphire crystal; transparent case back; water-resistant to 5 atm
Band: canvas strap, folding clasp with black PVD
Remarks: comes with additional NATO strap
Price: $3,900
Variations: black PVD ($3,900); titanium case ($4,250)

Tiefenmesser Bronze
Reference number: RSV03.TM/330-23
Movement: automatic, ETA Caliber 2824-2 with special in-house module; ø 25.60 mm, height 4.60 mm; 25 jewels; 28,800 vph; 37-hour power reserve
Functions: jumping hours, retrograde minutes; power reserve indicator
Case: bronze, ø 43 mm, height 12.8 mm; screw-in crown; sapphire crystal; transparent titanium case back; water-resistant to 5 atm
Band: leather, folding clasp with black PVD
Remarks: comes with additional NATO strap
Price: $4,250
Variations: stainless steel case and black PVD ($3,900)

RESSENCE

Ressence Watches
Meirbrug 1
2000 Antwerp
Belgium

Tel.:
+32-3-446-0060

E-mail:
hello@ressence.be

Website:
www.ressencewatches.com

Founded:
2011

U.S. distributor:
Totally Worth It, LLC
76 Division Avenue
Summit, NJ 07901-2309
201-894-4710
724-263-2286
info@totallyworthit.com

Most important collections/price range:
Type 1 / from $20,600; Type 3 / from $42,200; Type 5 / from $35,800

Belgian Benoit Mintiens had the luck of the newcomer at Baselworld 2010. He showed up at the last minute and found some space to show a strange watch with an almost two-dimensional dial. . . . He returned in 2011 with the Type 1001. It consisted of a large rotating dial carrying a hand that pointed to a minute track on the bezel. Hours, small second, and a day/night indication rotated on dedicated subsidiary dials. The ballet on the dial mesmerized those who saw it, so he sold all his fifty models off the bat.

The mechanics behind the Ressence watches—the name is a compounding of Renaissance of the Essential—are basically simple: A stripped-down and rebuilt ETA 2824 leaves the minute wheel as the main driver of the other wheels. Mintiens, however, was about to go further.

In 2012 came the Type 0 series, which included a few design changes. Then, in a successful bid to improve readability, he immersed the dial section in oil, giving the displays a very contemporary two-dimensional look, much like an electronic watch. The movement had to be kept separate from the oil, and was connected to the dial using magnets and a set of superconductors and a Faraday cage to protect the movement from magnetism. A series of baffles compensated for the expanding and contracting of the oil due to temperature shifts. The Type 3 also lost the crown, the only obstacle to making a perfectly smooth watch, in favor of a clever setting and winding mechanism controlled by the case back. The watch was an automatic, of course. Not surprisingly, it won the Revelation Prize at the Grand Prix d'Horlogerie in Geneva in 2013.

The variations on the theme have been emerging from the Ressence studio at a regular pace. Several watches came with slightly different design. One was a diver's watch. The latest innovation is the e-Crown, which allows the wearer to reset the time electronically.

Type 2A
Movement: automatic, Ressence Orbital Convex System (ROCS) 2 (module base ETA 2892A); ø 32 mm; 45 jewels; 28,800 vph; case back for winding and time setting; gear train with 37 gearwheels; e-Crown module activated by tapping the sapphire crystal; 36-hour power reserve
Functions: hours, minutes, subsidiary seconds; orbiting minute dial with rotating satellites for additional displays; e-Crown functions (2nd time zone, energy-saving mode, automatic time setting)
Case: titanium with dark gray PVD coating, ø 45 mm, height 12 mm; sapphire crystal; **Band:** calfskin, buckle
Remarks: e-Crown function monitors and controls mechanical movement; up to 3 months dark power reserve; **Price:** $48,800

Type 1B Slim
Movement: automatic, Ressence Orbital Convex System (ROCS) 1.3 (module base ETA 2892A); ø 32 mm; 40 jewels; 28,800 vph; case back for winding and time setting; 27 gearwheels; 36-hour power reserve
Functions: hours, minutes, subsidiary seconds; orbiting minute dial with rotating satellites for additional displays; weekday (off-center, orbiting)
Case: titanium, ø 42 mm, height 11 mm; sapphire crystal
Band: reptile skin, buckle
Price: $20,600
Variations: white, blue, or silver dial

Type 3W
Movement: automatic, Ressence Orbital Convex System (ROCS) 3 (module base ETA 2824-2); ø 32 mm; 41 jewels; 28,800 vph; case back for winding and time setting; 25 gearwheels; 36-hour power reserve
Functions: minutes, hours, 180-second "runner" (orbiting minute dial with rotating satellites), oil temperature gauge; date, weekday
Case: titanium, ø 44 mm, height 15 mm; sapphire crystal; water-resistant to 10 atm
Band: textile, buckle
Remarks: 2 separate, sealed case chambers; dial-side chamber filled with oil; magnetic drive for display disks
Price: $42,200
Variations: black dial

RGM

The old Puritan values of hard work and persistence are alive and well in Roland Murphy, founder of RGM, one of the U.S.'s most famous and exclusive watch companies. Murphy, born in Maryland, went through the watchmaker's drill, studying at the Bowman Technical School, then in Switzerland, and finally working with Swatch before launching his own business in 1992 in Pennsylvania, which could be considered a kind of "watch valley."

The secret to his success, however, has been always to stay in touch with fundamental American values and icons. His first watch, the Signature, resurrected vintage pocket watch movements developed by Hamilton. His second big project was the Caliber 801, the first "high-grade mechanical movement made in series in America since Hamilton stopped production of the 992 B in 1969," Murphy grins. The next goal was to manufacture an all-American-made watch, the Pennsylvania Tourbillon.

And so, model by model, Murphy continues to expand his "Made in U.S.A." portfolio. "You cannot compare us to the big brands," says Murphy. "We are small and specialized, the needs are different. We work directly with the customer." This may account for the brand's diversity. There are retro-themed watches, sports-themed watches (honoring baseball or chess), a diver water-resistant to 70 atm, and the series 400 chronograph with a pulsometer and extra-large subdials for visibility.

One of the brand's main creations is the Caliber "20," using the motor barrel, a system by which the watch is wound by the barrel and the barrel arbor then drives the gear train. Less friction and wear and a slimmer chance of damage to the watch if the mainspring breaks are the two main advantages. Of late, Murphy has turned to crafts, with, for example, a fine cloisonné dial and woman's watch with a painted mother-of-pearl dial.

RGM Watch Company
801 W. Main Street
Mount Joy, PA 17552

Tel.:
717-653-9799

E-mail:
sales@rgmwatches.com

Founded:
1992

Number of employees:
12

Annual production:
200–300 watches

Distribution:
RGM deals directly with customers.

Most important collection/price range:
Pennsylvania Series (completely made in the U.S.) / $2,500 to $125,000

Pennsylvania Tourbillon
Reference number: MM2
Movement: manually wound, in-house movement; ø 37.22; 19 jewels; 18,000 vph; German silver and rose gold finish with perlage and côtes de Genève; 42-hour power reserve
Functions: hours, minutes; 1-minute tourbillon
Case: stainless steel, ø 43.5 mm, height 13.5 mm; guilloché dial; sapphire crystal; transparent case back
Band: reptile skin, buckle
Remarks: blued-steel minute and hour hands
Price: $95,000
Variations: rose gold ($125,000); platinum (price on request)

Classic Enamel
Reference number: PS 801 CE
Movement: manually wound, RGM Caliber 801; ø 37 mm; 19 jewels; lever escapement; screw balance; hand-engraved balance bridge with swan-neck regulator; U.S.-made bridges, mainplate, settings, 7-tooth winding click; circular côtes de Genève; 42-hour power reserve
Functions: hours, minutes, 3-armed second hand
Case: stainless steel, ø 43.3 mm, height 12.3 mm; sapphire crystal
Band: reptile skin, buckle
Remarks: grand-feu white glass double sunk enamel dial
Price: $11,900; limited edition
Variations: rose gold ($24,700)

Skeletonized 801
Reference number: PS 801 SK
Movement: manually wound, RGM Caliber 801; ø 37 mm; 19 jewels; lever escapement; screw balance; U.S.-made bridges, mainplate, settings, 7-tooth winding click; circular côtes de Genève; 42-hour power reserve
Functions: hours, minutes, seconds
Case: stainless steel, ø 43.3 mm, height 12.3 mm; sapphire crystal
Band: reptile skin, buckle
Remarks: skeleton dial with gold plaques
Price: $21,400
Variations: rose gold ($34,200)

Cloisonné Model 25
Reference number: Model 25
Movement: automatic, RGM/Swiss movement with solid gold rotor; ø 25.6 mm; 21 jewels; 28,800 vph; rhodium finish with perlage and côtes de Genève; 42-hour power reserve
Functions: hours, minutes, sweep second
Case: stainless steel, ø 40 mm, height 11.2 mm; sapphire crystal; transparent case back; water-resistant to 5 atm
Band: leather, buckle
Remarks: custom cloisonné dial
Price: $13,900
Variations: custom dial design encouraged

Lady RGM Hand Painted Mother of Pearl
Reference number: Lady RGM
Movement: manually wound, RGM/ETA Peseux 7001; ø 23.3 mm; 17 jewels; 21,600 vph; rhodium finish with côtes de Genève; 42-hour power reserve
Functions: hours, minutes
Case: rose gold with diamond bezel and lugs, ø 28 mm, height 7.7 mm; sapphire crystal; transparent case back
Band: leather, buckle
Remarks: custom hand-painted dial on natural mother-of-pearl
Price: $24,900
Variations: stainless steel, gold without diamonds; custom dial design encouraged

Wood Marquetry Model 25
Reference number: Model 25
Movement: automatic, RGM/Swiss movement with solid gold rotor; ø 25.6 mm; 21 jewels; 28,800 vph; rhodium finish with perlage and côtes de Genève; 42-hour power reserve
Functions: hours, minutes, sweep second
Case: stainless steel, ø 40 mm, height 11.2 mm; sapphire crystal; transparent case back; water-resistant to 5 atm
Band: Hirsch leather, buckle
Remarks: custom wood marquetry dial
Price: $13,900

222 Railroad Series—Boxcar Dial
Reference number: 222 RR
Movement: manually wound, restored Hamilton 923; ø 38.1 mm; 23 jewels; lever escapement; screw balance; U.S.-made bridges, mainplate, settings, 7-tooth winding click; circular côtes de Genève; 42-hour power reserve
Functions: hours, minutes, subsidiary seconds
Case: stainless steel, ø 41 mm, height 12 mm; sapphire crystal; transparent case back; water-resistant to 5 atm
Band: leather, buckle
Remarks: grand-feu white glass enamel "boxcar" dial
Price: $7,900
Variations: Hamilton 921 ($5,900)

Professional Diver
Reference number: 300 Mother of Pearl
Movement: automatic, modified ETA Caliber 2892; ø 25.6 mm, height 3.6 mm; 21 jewels; 28,800 vph; bridges and plates with perlage and côtes de Genève; 42-hour power reserve
Functions: hours, minutes, sweep seconds; date
Case: brushed stainless steel, ø 43.5 mm, height 17 mm; sapphire crystal (5 mm thick); unidirectional bezel with 0-60 scale (240 clicks); screw-down back; screw-in crown; water-resistant to more than 70 atm
Band: rubber strap, buckle
Remarks: classic natural mother-of-pearl dial, blue ceramic bezel
Price: $4,650; limited to 75 pieces
Variations: rubber strap, buckle ($3,900)

Enamel Corps of Engineers
Reference number: 801 COE
Movement: manually wound, RGM Caliber 801; ø 37 mm; 19 jewels; lever escapement; screw balance; U.S.-made bridges, mainplate, settings, 7-tooth winding click; circular côtes de Genève; 42-hour power reserve
Functions: hours, minutes, subsidiary seconds
Case: stainless steel, ø 42 mm, height 10.5 mm; sapphire crystal; transparent case back; water-resistant to 5 atm
Band: leather, buckle
Remarks: grand-feu white glass enamel dial with aged luminous numbers
Price: $9,700
Variations: stainless steel bracelet ($10,450)

RICHARD MILLE

Mille never stops delivering the wow to the watch world with what he calls his "race cars for the wrist." He is not an engineer, however, but rather a marketing expert who earned his first paychecks in the watch division of the French defense, automobile, and aerospace concern Matra in the early 1980s. "I have no historical relationship with watchmaking whatsoever," says Mille, "and so I have no obligations either. The mechanics of my watches are geared towards technical feasibility."

His early work was with the wizards at Audemars Piguet Renaud & Papi (APRP) in Le Locle, who would take on the Mille challenge. Audemars Piguet even tested some of those scandalous innovations—materials, technologies, functions—in a Richard Mille watch before daring to use them in its own collections (Tradition d'Excellence).

In 2007, Audemars Piguet finally became a shareholder in Richard Mille, and so the three firms are now closely bound. The assembly of the watches is done in the Franches-Montagnes region in the Jura, where Richard Mille opened the firm Horométrie.

To keep its fans happy, the brand never ceases to explore the lunatic fringe of the technically possible, like the collaboration with Airbus Corporate Jets, which gave rise to a case made of a lightweight titanium-aluminum alloy used in turbines. Then there is the superlight and tough material called graphene developed at the University of Manchester and used by McLaren. The 2018 watch for polo star Pablo Mac Donough features a unique, reinforced sapphire crystal. Formula One champion Alain Prost, who is a cycling fan, got a watch with a pusher-activated kilometer totalizer, and for action star Sylvester Stallone, Mille conceived an adventure watch with a tourbillon, a chronograph, and a detachable compass including a water level.

Richard Mille
c/o Horométrie SA
11, rue du Jura
CH-2345 Les Breuleux
Switzerland

Tel.:
+41-32-959-4353

E-mail:
info@richardmille.ch

Website:
www.richardmille.com

Founded:
2000

Annual production:
approx. 4,600 watches

U.S. distributor:
Richard Mille Americas
8701 Wilshire Blvd.
Beverly Hills, CA 90211
310-205-5555

Tourbillon Chronograph Adventure
Reference number: RM 25-01
Movement: manually wound, Richard Mille Caliber RM25-01; ø 38.95 mm, height 8.37 mm; 35 jewels; 21,600 vph; 1-minute tourbillon; skeletonized titanium plates and bridges; chronograph mechanism with titanium levers; 72-hour power reserve
Functions: hours, minutes, subsidiary seconds; torque indicator, function indicator; chronograph
Case: carbon fiber (TPT carbon), 23.65 × 50.85 mm; changeable bezels of titanium or TPT carbon with 0-360 scale and cardinal directions, detachable transparent compass module with level and mirrored cover; sapphire crystal; transparent case back; water-resistant to 10 atm; **Band:** rubber, folding clasp
Price: $982,000; limited to 75 pieces

Automatic Skeleton
Reference number: RM 023
Movement: automatic, Richard Mille Caliber 005-S (base Vaucher 331); 28.6 × 30.2 mm, height 4.43 mm; 31 jewels; 28,800 vph; skeletonized titanium plates and bridges, winding rotor, adjustable inertia and winding performance; 2 spring barrels, 55-hour power reserve
Functions: hours, minutes, sweep seconds; large date
Case: white gold, 37.8 × 45 mm, height 11.45 mm; sapphire crystal; transparent case back; water-resistant to 5 atm
Band: reptile skin, folding clasp
Price: $105,500; limited to 75 pieces

Tourbillon Alain Prost
Reference number: RM 70-01
Movement: manually wound, Richard Mille Caliber RM70; 29.7 × 37.1 mm, height 10.7 mm; 32 jewels; 21,600 vph; 1-minute tourbillon; 5 pusher-activated number rollers; distance tracker; 69-hour power reserve.
Functions: hours, minutes; kilometer counter
Case: TPT carbon; sapphire crystal; transparent case back; crown with torque limiter; water-resistant to 5 atm
Band: silicon, folding clasp
Remarks: homage to passionate cyclist Alain Prost; price includes custom-made Colnago racing bike
Price: $840,000; limited to 30 pieces

RICHARD MILLE

Dizzy Hands
Reference number: RM 63-01
Movement: automatic, Richard Mille Caliber CRMA3; ø 31 mm, height 6.67 mm; 35 jewels; 28,800 vph; skeletonized titanium plates and bridges, red gold winding rotor; 50-hour power reserve
Functions: hours, minutes; "dizzy hands" with indicator
Case: red gold and titanium, ø 42.7 mm, height 11.7 mm; sapphire crystal; transparent case back; crown activates "dizzy hands" function; water-resistant to 5 atm; **Band:** rubber, folding clasp
Remarks: dizzy hands function involves rotating sapphire crystal dial and hands that turn in opposite directions and essentially stop time
Price: $124,500

Tourbillon Flyback Chronograph "Aviation E6-B"
Reference number: RM 39-01
Movement: manually wound, Richard Mille Caliber RM039-01; ø 38.95 mm, height 7.95 mm; 58 jewels; 21,600 vph; 1-minute tourbillon, function selelector (W=Winding), Zero reset (N), handsetting (H=Hands), and rapid setting (S=Speed); 70-hour power reserve
Functions: hours, minutes; power reserve indicator, function indicator; flyback chronograph; date, weekday
Case: titanium, ø 50 mm, height 19.4 mm; bidirectional bezel, with tachymeter and conversion tables; sapphire crystal; transparent case back
Band: rubber, folding clasp
Price: $1,012,000

Worldtimer
Reference number: RM 63-02
Movement: automatic, Richard Mille Caliber CRMA4; ø 33.8 mm, height 7.73 mm; 37 jewels; 28,800 vph; titanium base plate; skeletonized movement; 50-hour power reserve
Functions: hours, minutes; world time display (2nd time zone), crown function indicator; large date
Case: titanium, ø 47 mm, height 13.85 mm; bidirectional bezel to set 2nd time zone; sapphire crystal; transparent case back; pushers and crown for function selection
Band: rubber, folding clasp
Price: $150,000

Automatic Extra-Thin
Reference number: RM 67-01
Movement: automatic, Richard Mille Caliber CRMA6; 29.1 × 31.25 mm, height 3.6 mm; 25 jewels; 28,800 vph; titanium plates and bridges; platinum rotor; 50-hour power reserve
Functions: hours, minutes; crown-activated function indicator; date
Case: plasma-coated titanium, 38.7 × 47 mm, height 7.75 mm; sapphire crystal; transparent case back
Band: rubber, folding clasp
Price: $92,500

Tourbillon Split Seconds Chronograph McLaren F1
Reference number: RM 50-03
Movement: manually wound, Richard Mille Caliber RM52-03; 31.1 × 32.15 mm, height 9.92 mm; 43 jewels; 21,600 vph; 1-minute tourbillon; titanium and TPT carbon plates and bridges; 70-hour power reserve
Functions: hours, minutes, subsidiary seconds; power reserve, torque and crown position indicator; split-second chronograph
Case: composite material, Graph TPT, 44.5 × 49.65 mm, height 16.1 mm; sapphire crystal; transparent case back; **Band:** rubber, folding clasp
Remarks: cooperation with McLaren F1
Price: $1,061,000; limited to 75 pieces

Automatic
Reference number: RM 016
Movement: automatic, Richard Mille Caliber RM 005-S (base Vaucher 331); 28.6 × 30.2 mm, height 6.35 mm; 31 jewels; 28,800 vph; skeletonized titanium mainplate and bridges, 2 spring barrels, winding with adjustable rotor geometry and winding power
Functions: hours, minutes; large date
Case: pink gold, 38 × 49.8 mm, height 8.25 mm; sapphire crystal; transparent case back; water-resistant to 5 atm
Band: rubber, folding clasp
Price: on request

ROGER DUBUIS

Roger Dubuis has always been a *manufacture* committed to luxury and "très haute horlogerie." The brand makes some outstanding movement components—parts that, because of their quality and geographical origins, bear the coveted Seal of Geneva. Founder Roger Dubuis, who passed away in 2017, was steeped in watchmaking and the business. In 2008, he sold 60 percent of the company shares to Richemont Group, which benefited from the resulting synergies, especially Cartier, which gets its skeletonized movements from the Roger Dubuis *manufacture*. In early 2016, Richemont went all the way and acquired the remaining 40 percent of the Genevan brand.

Roger Dubuis was founded in 1995 as SOGEM SA (Société Genevoise des Montres) by name-giver Roger Dubuis and financier Carlos Dias, who came up with timepieces with unheard-of dimensions and incomparable complications. The meteoric development of this *manufacture* and the incredible frequency of its new introductions—even technical ones—continue to amaze colleagues and consumers alike. Today, Roger Dubuis develops all of its own movements, currently numbering more than thirty different mechanical calibers. In addition, it produces almost all components in-house, from base plates to escapements and balance springs. With this heavy-duty technological know-how in its quiver, the brand has been able to build some remarkable movements, like the massive RD101, with four balance springs and all manner of differentials and gear works to drive the Excalibur Quatuor, the equivalent in horology to a monster truck. Even in their more delicate versions, like the Brocéliande, featuring colored ivy leaves embracing the movement, Roger Dubuis watches always seem ready to jump off your wrist.

Recently, the brand has rubbed elbows with car racing. Its partnership with Pirelli has produced models using genuine Formula One rubber as straps on the crowns. The rubber has the original tire color coding for different driving options: wet, medium, soft, supersoft, ultrasoft, and hypersoft. Another partnership, with Lamborghini's motor sports division, Lamborghini Squadra Corse, has produced models inspired by the design of such cars as the Aventador and the Huracàn.

Manufacture Roger Dubuis
2, rue André-De-Garrini - CP 149
CH-1217 Meyrin 2 (Geneva)
Switzerland

Tel.:
+41-22-783-2828

E-mail:
info@rogerdubuis.com

Website:
www.rogerdubuis.com

Founded:
1995

Annual production:
over 5,000 watches (estimated)

U.S. distributor:
Roger Dubuis New York
545 Madison Ave.
New York, NY 10022
212-651-3773
Roger Dubuis Beverly Hills
9490C Brighton Way
Beverly Hills, CA 90210
310-734-1855

Most important collections/price range:
Excalibur, Velvet / $12,000 to $1,100,000

Excalibur Huracán
Reference number: RDDBEX0749
Movement: automatic, Roger Dubuis Caliber RD630; ø 36.1 mm, height 7.78 mm; 29 jewels; 28,800 vph; 2 spring barrels; 60-hour power reserve
Functions: hours, minutes, sweep seconds; date
Case: titanium, ø 45 mm, height 13.3 mm; sapphire crystal; water-resistant to 5 atm
Band: rubber with leather inlay, folding clasp
Price: $47,000

Excalibur Huracán
Reference number: RDDBEX0750
Movement: automatic, Roger Dubuis Caliber RD630; ø 36.1 mm, height 7.78 mm; 29 jewels; 28,800 vph; 2 spring barrels; 60-hour power reserve
Functions: hours, minutes, sweep seconds; date
Case: rose gold, ø 45 mm, height 13.3 mm; titanium bezel; sapphire crystal; water-resistant to 5 atm
Band: rubber with leather inlay, folding clasp
Price: $68,000

Excalibur Huracán
Reference number: RDDBEX0748
Movement: automatic, Roger Dubuis Caliber RD630; ø 36.1 mm, height 7.78 mm; 29 jewels; 28,800 vph; 2 spring barrels; 60-hour power reserve
Functions: hours, minutes, sweep seconds; date
Case: titanium, ø 45 mm, height 13.3 mm; sapphire crystal; water-resistant to 5 atm
Band: rubber with leather inlay, folding clasp
Price: $47,000

Excalibur Spider Skeleton Pirelli
Reference number: RDDBEX0747
Movement: automatic, Roger Dubuis Caliber RD820SQ; ø 36.1 mm, height 6.38 mm; 35 jewels; 28,800 vph; skeletonized movement, microrotor; 60-hour power reserve; Geneva Seal
Functions: hours, minutes
Case: titanium with black DLC coating, partially coated in rubber, ø 45 mm, height 14.02 mm; sapphire crystal; transparent case back; water-resistant to 5 atm
Band: rubber with leather inlay, folding clasp
Price: $72,000; limited to 88 pieces
Variations: various colors

Excalibur Spider Skeleton Automatic
Reference number: RDDBEX0647
Movement: automatic, Roger Dubuis Caliber RD820SQ; ø 36.1 mm, height 6.38 mm; 35 jewels; 28,800 vph; skeletonized movement, microrotor; 60-hour power reserve; Geneva Seal
Functions: hours, minutes
Case: rose gold with titanium inner case, partially rubber-coated, ø 45 mm, height 14.02 mm; sapphire crystal; transparent case back; water-resistant to 5 atm
Band: rubber with leather inlay, folding clasp
Price: $94,500
Variations: in carbon ($87,000)

Excalibur Skeleton Automatic
Reference number: RDDBEX0777
Movement: automatic, Roger Dubuis Caliber RD820SQ; ø 36.1 mm, height 6.38 mm; 35 jewels; 28,800 vph; skeletonized movement, microrotor; 60-hour power reserve; Geneva Seal
Functions: hours, minutes
Case: carbon fiber, ø 42 mm, height 11.9 mm; sapphire crystal; transparent case back; water-resistant to 3 atm
Band: rubber, folding clasp
Price: $65,500

Excalibur 45 Automatic
Reference number: RDDBEX0602
Movement: automatic, Roger Dubuis Caliber RD830; ø 29.21 mm, height 4 mm; 27 jewels; 28,800 vph; 48-hour power reserve
Functions: hours, minutes, subsidiary seconds; date
Case: titanium, ø 45 mm, height 14.7 mm; sapphire crystal; transparent case back; water-resistant to 5 atm
Band: rubber, folding clasp
Price: $16,700
Variations: various straps, cases, and dials

Excalibur 45 Automatic
Reference number: RDDBEX0566
Movement: automatic, Roger Dubuis Caliber RD830; ø 29.21 mm, height 4 mm; 27 jewels; 28,800 vph; 48-hour power reserve
Functions: hours, minutes, subsidiary seconds; date
Case: rose gold, ø 45 mm, height 14.7 mm; sapphire crystal; transparent case back; water-resistant to 3 atm
Band: reptile skin, folding clasp
Price: $32,100
Variations: various straps, cases, and dials

Excalibur 45 Automatic
Reference number: RDDBEX0567
Movement: automatic, Roger Dubuis Caliber RD830; ø 29.21 mm, height 4 mm; 27 jewels; 28,800 vph, 48-hour power reserve
Functions: hours, minutes, subsidiary seconds; date
Case: titanium with black DLC coating, ø 45 mm, height 14.7 mm; sapphire crystal; transparent case back; water-resistant to 5 atm
Band: rubber, folding clasp
Price: $16,700
Variations: various straps, cases, and dials

ROGER DUBUIS

Caliber RD630
Automatic; skeletonized movement; winding rotor shaped like a tire rim; double spring barrel, 60-hour power reserve
Functions: hours, minutes, sweep seconds; date
Diameter: 36.1 mm
Height: 7.78 mm
Jewels: angled at 12°
Frequency: 28,800 vph
Remarks: bead-blasted plates and bridges, NAC-coated; 233 parts

Caliber RD 103SQ
Manually wound; double sprung balance with angled balance wheels, 28,800 vph each; power transmission and synchronization via planetary gears; skeletonized movement; single spring barrel, 40-hour power reserve; Geneva Seal
Functions: hours, minutes, sweep seconds (jumping); power reserve indicator
Diameter: 36.1 mm
Height: 7.8 mm
Jewels: 48
Frequency: 57,600 vph

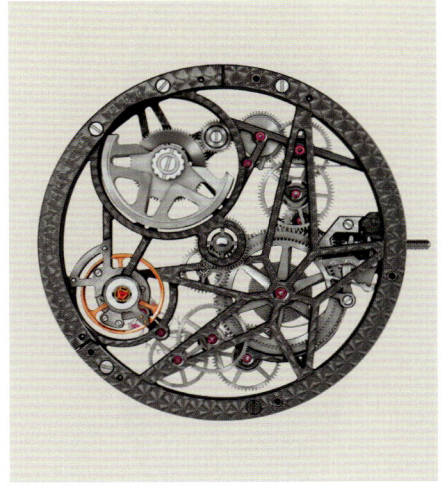

Caliber RD820SQ
Automatic; skeletonized movement; microrotor; single spring barrel, 60-hour power reserve; Geneva Seal
Functions: hours, minutes
Diameter: 36.1 mm
Height: 6.38 mm
Jewels: 35
Frequency: 28,800 vph
Remarks: rhodium-plated movement, finely finished with perlage; 167 parts

Caliber RD01SQ
Manually wound; 2 flying 1-minute tourbillons with equalizing differential skeletonized movement; single spring barrel, 48-hour power reserve; Geneva Seal, COSC-certified chronometer
Functions: hours, minutes
Diameter: 37.8 mm
Height: 7.67 mm
Jewels: 28
Balance: glucydur variable inertia balance
Frequency: 21,600 vph
Remarks: 319 components

Caliber RD101
Manually wound; 4 radially assembled lever escapements, synchronized with 3 balancing differentials; additional planetary gears for winding and power reserve indicator; skeletonized movement; double spring barrel, 40-hour power reserve; Geneva Seal
Functions: hours, minutes; power reserve indicator
Diameter: 37.9 mm
Height: 10.6 mm
Jewels: 113
Balance: glucydur (4 ×)
Frequency: 28,800 vph
Balance spring: flat hairspring
Remarks: galvanic black movement, beveled and with perlage; 590 parts

Caliber RD830
Automatic; rotor in rose gold; single spring barrel, 48-hour power reserve
Functions: hours, minutes, subsidiary seconds; date
Diameter: 29.21 mm
Height: 4 mm
Jewels: 27
Frequency: 28,800 vph
Remarks: finely finished with côtes de Genève; 183 parts

QUILL & PAD
KEEPING WATCH ON TIME

Make **time** for **a unique watch experience**

Breaking Stories
Unique Photography
Interesting Angles and Subjects

Quill & Pad is an online platform combining decades of excellence and experience in watch journalism, bringing **you** original stories and photography.

Ian Skellern

Elizabeth Doerr

twitter.com/QuillandPad
facebook.com/QuillandPad
quillandpad.tumblr.com
instagram.com/quillandpad

www.QuillandPad.com

ROLEX

Essentially, the Rolex formula for success has always been "what you see is what you get"—and plenty of it. For over a century now, the company has made wristwatch history without a need for *grandes complications*, perpetual calendars, tourbillons, or exotic materials. And its output in sheer quantity is phenomenal, at not quite a million watches per year. But make no mistake about it: The quality of these timepieces is legendary.

For as long as anyone can remember, this brand has held the top spot in the COSC's statistics, and year after year Rolex delivers just about half of all of the official institute's successfully tested mechanical chronometer movements. The brand has also pioneered several fundamental innovations: Rolex founder Hans Wilsdorf invented the hermetically sealed Oyster case in the 1920s, which he later outfitted with a screwed-in crown and an automatic movement wound by rotor. Shock protection, water resistance, the amagnetic Parachrom hairspring, and automatic winding are some of the virtues that make wearing a Rolex timepiece much more comfortable and reliable. As for movements, the automatic caliber 3255 features new materials (nickel-phosphorus), special micromanufacturing technology (LIGA) to make the pallet fork and balance wheel of the Chronergy escapement, and a barrel spring that can store up more energy than ever.

Rolex watches are produced in four different locations in Switzerland. Headquarters in Geneva handles final assembly and quality control and sales. All development, manufacturing, and quality control is done a few miles away in new premises in Plan-les-Ouates. Jewel-setting and dials are made in the Chêne-Bourg district of Geneva, and movements come from a factory in Bienne/Biel.

Meanwhile the company has built up representation in nearly one hundred countries in the world, with over thirty subsidiaries with customer service centers. The network also includes around four thousand watchmakers trained according to Rolex standards.

Rolex SA
Rue François-Dussaud 3
CH-1211 Geneva 26
Switzerland

Website:
www.rolex.com

Founded:
1908

Number of employees:
over 2,000 (estimated)

Annual production:
approx. 1,000,000 watches (estimated)

U.S. distributor:
Rolex Watch U.S.A., Inc.
Rolex Building
665 Fifth Avenue
New York, NY 10022-5358
212-758-7700
www.rolex.com

Oyster Perpetual GMT-Master II
Reference number: 126710BLNR
Movement: automatic, Rolex Caliber 3285; ø 28.5 mm, height 6.4 mm; 31 jewels; 28,800 vph; Parachrom hairspring, Paraflex shock absorber, Chronergy escapement; 70-hour power reserve; COSC-certified chronometer
Functions: hours (switched via crown), minutes, sweep seconds; additional 24-hour display (2nd time zone); date
Case: stainless steel, ø 40 mm, height 13 mm; bidirectional bezel with ceramic insert, with 0-24 scale; sapphire crystal; screw-in crown; water-resistant to 10 atm; **Band:** Jubilee stainless steel, folding clasp with safety lock, with extension link
Price: $9,250

Oyster Perpetual GMT-Master II
Reference number: 126710BLRO
Movement: automatic, Rolex Caliber 3285; ø 28.5 mm, height 6.4 mm; 31 jewels; 28,800 vph; Parachrom hairspring, Paraflex shock absorber, Chronergy escapement; 70-hour power reserve; COSC-certified chronometer
Functions: hours (switched via crown), minutes, sweep seconds; additional 24-hour display (2nd time zone); date
Case: Oystersteel, ø 40 mm, height 13 mm; bidirectional bezel with ceramic inlay, with 0-24 scale; sapphire crystal; screw-in crown; water-resistant to 10 atm; **Band:** Jubilee, Oystersteel, folding clasp, with safety lock and extension link
Price: $9,250

Oyster Perpetual GMT-Master II
Reference number: 126711CHNR
Movement: automatic, Rolex Caliber 3285; ø 28.5 mm, height 6.4 mm; 31 jewels; 28,800 vph; Parachrom hairspring, Paraflex shock absorber, Chronergy escapement; 70-hour power reserve; COSC-certified chronometer; **Functions:** hours (switched via crown), minutes, sweep seconds; additional 24-hour display (2nd time zone); date
Case: stainless steel, ø 40 mm, height 13 mm; bidirectional bezel in rose gold with ceramic insert, with 0-24 scale; sapphire crystal; screw-in crown; water-resistant to 10 atm
Band: Oyster stainless steel with rose gold elements, folding clasp with safety lock, with extension link
Price: $14,050; **Variations:** rose gold ($36,750)

ROLEX

Oyster Perpetual Deepsea
Reference number: 126660
Movement: automatic, Rolex Caliber 3235; ø 29.1 mm; 31 jewels; 28,800 vph; Parachrom hairspring, Paraflex shock absorber, Chronergy escapement, glucydur balance with microstella regulating bolts; 70-hour power reserve; COSC-certified chronometer
Functions: hours, minutes, sweep seconds; date
Case: stainless steel, ø 44 mm; unidirectional bezel with ceramic insert, with 0-60 scale; sapphire crystal; screw-in crown; helium valve; water-resistant to 390 atm
Band: Oystersteel, folding clasp, with safety lock, with extension link
Price: $12,250; **Variations:** D-blue dial ($12,550)

Oyster Perpetual Sea-Dweller
Reference number: 126603
Movement: automatic, Rolex Caliber 3235; ø 29.1 mm; 31 jewels; 28,800 vph; Parachrom hairspring, Paraflex shock absorber, Chronergy escapement, glucydur balance with microstella regulating bolts; 70-hour power reserve; COSC-certified chronometer
Functions: hours, minutes, sweep seconds; date
Case: stainless steel, ø 43 mm, height 13.8 mm; unidirectional, yellow gold bezel with ceramic insert, 0-60 scale; sapphire crystal; screw-in crown; helium valve; water-resistant to 122 atm
Band: Oyster stainless steel with yellow gold elements, folding clasp with extension link
Price: $16,050; **Variations:** stainless steel ($11,350)

Oyster Perpetual Submariner
Reference number: 114060
Movement: automatic, Rolex Caliber 3130; ø 28.5 mm; 31 jewels; 28,800 vph; Parachrom hairspring; 48-hour power reserve; COSC-certified chronometer
Functions: hours, minutes, sweep seconds
Case: stainless steel, ø 40 mm, height 12.5 mm; unidirectional bezel with ceramic insert, with 0-60 scale; sapphire crystal; screw-in crown; water-resistant to 30 atm
Band: Oystersteel, folding clasp, with extension link
Price: $7,500
Variations: with date display ($7,500)

Oyster Perpetual Air-King
Reference number: 116900
Movement: automatic, Rolex Caliber 3131; ø 28.5 mm; 31 jewels; 28,800 vph; Parachrom hairspring, glucydur balance with microstella regulating bolts; soft-iron cap for amagnetic protection; 48-hour power reserve; COSC-certified chronometer
Functions: hours, minutes, sweep seconds
Case: stainless steel, ø 40 mm; sapphire crystal; screw-in crown; water-resistant to 10 atm
Band: Oystersteel, folding clasp, with safety lock, with extension link
Price: $6,200

Oyster Perpetual Explorer
Reference number: 214270
Movement: automatic, Rolex Caliber 3132; ø 28.5 mm; 31 jewels; 28,800 vph; Parachrom hairspring, Paraflex shock protection, glucydur balance with microstella regulating bolts; 48-hour power reserve; COSC-certified chronometer
Functions: hours, minutes, sweep seconds
Case: stainless steel, ø 39 mm; sapphire crystal; screw-in crown; water-resistant to 10 atm
Band: Oystersteel, folding clasp, with extension link
Price: $6,550

Oyster Perpetual Cosmograph Daytona
Reference number: 116500LN
Movement: automatic, Rolex Caliber 4130; ø 30.5 mm, height 6.5 mm; 44 jewels; 28,800 vph; Parachrom hairspring, glucydur balance with microstella regulating bolts; 72-hour power reserve; COSC-certified chronometer
Functions: hours, minutes, subsidiary seconds; chronograph
Case: stainless steel, ø 40 mm, height 12.8 mm; Cerachrom bezel; sapphire crystal; screw-in crown and pusher; water-resistant to 10 atm
Band: Oystersteel, folding clasp, with safety lock, with extension link
Price: $12,400; **Variations:** black dial

ROLEX

Oyster Perpetual Yacht-Master II
Reference number: 116680
Movement: automatic, Rolex Caliber 4161 (base Caliber 4130); ø 31.2 mm, height 8.05 mm; 42 jewels; 28,800 vph; Parachrom hairspring; 72-hour power reserve; COSC-certified chronometer
Functions: hours, minutes, subsidiary seconds; programmable regatta countdown with memory
Case: stainless steel, ø 44 mm, height 13.8 mm; bidirectional bezel with ceramic insert to control functions; sapphire crystal; screw-in crown; water-resistant to 10 atm
Band: Oystersteel, folding clasp, with safety lock, with extension link
Price: $18,750; **Variations** yellow gold ($18,750); stainless steel/rose gold ($25,150)

Oyster Perpetual Yacht-Master 42
Reference number: 116659
Movement: automatic, Rolex Caliber 3135; ø 28.5 mm, height 6 mm; 31 jewels; 28,800 vph; Parachrom hairspring, glucydur balance with microstella regulating bolts; 48-hour power reserve; COSC-certified chronometer
Functions: hours, minutes, sweep seconds; date
Case: white gold, ø 42 mm, height 11.9 mm; bidirectional bezel with ceramic insert, 0-60 scale; sapphire crystal; screw-in crown; water-resistant to 10 atm
Band: Oysterflex (elastomer with a titanium blade inside), folding clasp
Price: $27,800

Oyster Perpetual Yacht-Master 40
Reference number: 126655
Movement: automatic, Rolex Caliber 3135; ø 28.5 mm, height 6 mm; 31 jewels; 28,800 vph; Parachrom hairspring, glucydur balance with microstella regulating bolts; 48-hour power reserve; COSC-certified chronometer
Functions: hours, minutes, sweep seconds; date
Case: Everose gold, ø 40 mm, height 11.7 mm; bidirectional bezel with ceramic insert, with 0-60 scale; sapphire crystal; screw-in crown; water-resistant to 10 atm
Band: Oysterflex (elastomer with titanium blade inside), folding clasp
Price: $26,200

Oyster Perpetual Sky-Dweller
Reference number: 326934
Movement: automatic, Rolex Caliber 9001; ø 33 mm, height 8 mm; 40 jewels; 28,800 vph; 72-hour power reserve; COSC-certified chronometer
Functions: hours, minutes, sweep seconds; additional 24-hour display (2nd time zone); annual calendar with date, month
Case: stainless steel, ø 42 mm, height 14.1 mm; bidirectional white gold bezel to control functions; sapphire crystal; screw-in crown; water-resistant to 10 atm; **Band:** Oysterflex (elastomer with titanium blade inside), folding clasp with extension link
Price: $14,400
Variations: stainless steel/yellow gold ($17,150); yellow gold ($46,150); Everose gold ($48,850)

Oyster Perpetual Day-Date 40
Reference number: 228239
Movement: automatic, Rolex Caliber 3255; ø 29.1 mm, height 5.4 mm; 31 jewels; 28,800 vph; Parachrom hairspring, Paraflex shock protection, Chronergy escapement, glucydur balance with microstella regulating bolts; 70-hour power reserve; COSC-certified chronometer
Functions: hours, minutes, sweep seconds; date, weekday
Case: white gold, ø 40 mm, height 11.6 mm; sapphire crystal; screw-in crown; water-resistant to 10 atm
Band: President white gold, folding clasp
Price: $37,550
Variations: yellow gold ($34,850); Everose gold ($37,550); platinum ($62,500)

Oyster Perpetual Day-Date 36
Reference number: 128238
Movement: automatic, Rolex Caliber 3255; ø 29.1 mm, height 5.4 mm; 31 jewels; 28,800 vph; 31 jewels; 28,800 vph; Parachrom hairspring, Paraflex shock protection, Chronergy escapement, glucydur balance with microstella regulating bolts; 70-hour power reserve; COSC-certified chronometer
Functions: hours, minutes, sweep seconds; date, weekday
Case: yellow gold, ø 36 mm, height 11.1 mm; sapphire crystal; screw-in crown; water-resistant to 10 atm; **Band:** President yellow gold, folding clasp
Remarks: dial with diamond indices
Price: $34,550
Variations: white gold ($37,250); rose gold ($37,250)

ROLEX

Oyster Perpetual Datejust 41
Reference number: 126334
Movement: automatic, Rolex Caliber 3235; ø 29.1 mm; 31 jewels; 28,800 vph; Parachrom hairspring, Paraflex shock protection, Chronergy escapement, glucydur balance with microstella regulating bolts; 70-hour power reserve; COSC-certified chronometer
Functions: hours, minutes, sweep seconds; date
Case: stainless steel, ø 41 mm, height 11.6 mm; bezel of white gold; sapphire crystal; screw-in crown; water-resistant to 10 atm
Band: Oystersteel, folding clasp, with extension link
Price: $9,350
Variations: with Jubilee bracelet ($9,450)

Oyster Perpetual Datejust 36
Reference number: 126231
Movement: automatic, Rolex Caliber 3235; ø 29.1 mm; 31 jewels; 28,800 vph; Parachrom hairspring, Paraflex shock protection, Chronergy escapement, glucydur balance with microstella regulating bolts; 70-hour power reserve; COSC-certified chronometer
Functions: hours, minutes, sweep seconds; date
Case: stainless steel, ø 36 mm, height 11.3 mm; bezel in Everose gold; sapphire crystal; screw-in crown, in Everose gold; water-resistant to 10 atm
Band: Oyster steel and Everose gold, folding clasp, with extension link
Price: $10,950
Variations: Jubilee bracelet ($11,600)

Oyster Perpetual Datejust 31
Reference number: 278289RBR
Movement: automatic, Rolex Caliber 2236; ø 20 mm, height 5.95 mm; 31 jewels; 28,800 vph; Syloxi hairspring, glucydur balance with microstella regulating bolts; 55-hour power reserve; COSC-certified chronometer
Functions: hours, minutes, sweep seconds; date
Case: white gold, ø 31 mm, height 11 mm; bezel with 46 diamonds; sapphire crystal; screw-in crown; water-resistant to 10 atm
Band: President white gold, folding clasp
Price: $40,100

Cellini Moonphase
Reference number: 50535
Movement: automatic, Rolex Caliber 3195; ø 28.5 mm; 31 jewels; 28,800 vph; Parachrom hairspring, Paraflex shock protection; 48-hour power reserve; COSC-certified chronometer
Functions: hours, minutes, sweep seconds; date, moon phase
Case: Everose gold, ø 39 mm; sapphire crystal; screw-in crown; water-resistant to 5 atm
Band: calfskin, folding clasp
Remarks: blue enameled disk with rhodium-plated full moon
Price: $26,750

Cellini Date
Reference number: 50519
Movement: automatic, Rolex Caliber 3165 (base Rolex Caliber 3187); ø 28.5 mm; 31 jewels; 28,800 vph; Parachrom Breguet hairspring; 48-hour power reserve; COSC-certified chronometer
Functions: hours, minutes, sweep seconds; date
Case: white gold, ø 39 mm; sapphire crystal; screw-in crown; water-resistant to 5 atm
Band: calfskin, buckle
Price: $17,800
Variations: various dials; Everose gold

Cellini Dual Time
Reference number: 50525
Movement: automatic, Rolex Caliber 3180 (base Rolex Caliber 3187 with module); 28,800 vph; Parachrom hairspring; 48-hour power reserve; COSC-certified chronometer
Functions: hours, minutes, sweep seconds; additional 12-hour display (2nd time zone), day/night indicator
Case: Everose gold, ø 39 mm; sapphire crystal; screw-in crown; water-resistant to 5 atm
Band: leather, buckle
Price: $19,400
Variations: various dials

ROLEX

Caliber 3255
Automatic; optimized Chronergy escapement, nickel phosphorus pallet lever and escape wheel made using LIGA process; single spring barrel, 70-hour power reserve; COSC-certified chronometer
Functions: hours, minutes, sweep seconds; date, weekday
Diameter: 29.1 mm
Height: 5.4 mm
Jewels: 31
Balance: glucydur with microstella regulating bolts
Frequency: 28,800 vph
Balance spring: Parachrom Breguet hairspring
Shock protection: Paraflex
Remarks: used in the Day-Date 40

Caliber 3235
Automatic; optimized Chronergy escapement, nickel phosphorus pallet lever and escape wheel made using LIGA process; single spring barrel, 70-hour power reserve; COSC-certified chronometer
Functions: hours, minutes, sweep seconds; date
Diameter: 28.5 mm
Height: 6 mm
Jewels: 31
Balance: glucydur with microstella regulating bolts
Frequency: 28,800 vph
Balance spring: Parachrom Breguet hairspring
Shock protection: Paraflex
Remarks: used in the Datejust

Caliber 2236
Automatic; single spring barrel, 55-hour power reserve; COSC-certified chronometer
Functions: hours, minutes, sweep seconds; date
Diameter: 20 mm
Height: 5.95 mm
Jewels: 31
Balance: glucydur with microstella regulating bolts
Frequency: 28,800 vph
Balance spring: Parachrom flat hairspring
Shock protection: Kif
Remarks: used in the Lady Datejust

Caliber 4130
Automatic; single spring barrel, 72-hour power reserve; COSC-certified chronometer
Functions: hours, minutes, subsidiary seconds; chronograph
Diameter: 30.5 mm
Height: 6.5 mm
Jewels: 44
Balance: glucydur with microstella regulating bolts
Frequency: 28,800 vph
Balance spring: Parachrom Breguet hairspring
Shock protection: Kif
Remarks: used in the Daytona

Caliber 4161
Automatic; single spring barrel, 72-hour power reserve; COSC-certified chronometer
Base caliber: Caliber 4130
Functions: hours, minutes, subsidiary seconds; programmable regatta countdown with memory
Diameter: 31.2 mm
Height: 8.05 mm
Jewels: 42
Balance: glucydur with microstella regulating bolts
Frequency: 28,800 vph
Balance spring: Parachrom Breguet hairspring
Shock protection: Kif
Remarks: used in the Yacht-Master II

Caliber 9001
Automatic; single spring barrel, 72-hour power reserve; COSC-certified chronometer
Functions: hours, minutes, sweep seconds; additional 24-hour display (2nd time zone); annual calendar with date, month
Diameter: 33 mm
Height: 8 mm
Jewels: 40
Balance: glucydur with microstella regulating bolts
Frequency: 28,800 vph
Balance spring: Parachrom Breguet hairspring
Shock protection: Kif
Remarks: used in the Sky-Dweller

SCHAUMBURG WATCH

Frank Dilbakowski is the owner of this small watchmaking business in Rinteln, Westphalia, which has been producing very unusual yet affordable timepieces since 1998. The name Schaumburg comes from the surrounding region. The firm has gained a reputation for high-performance timepieces for rugged sports and professional use. The chronometer line Aquamatic, with water resistance to 1,000 meters, and the Aquatitan models, secure to 2,000 meters, confirm the company's maxim that form, function, and performance are inseparable from one another.

By the same token, traditional watchmaking is also high on the agenda. The Rinteln workbenches produce the plates and bridges and provide all the finishing as well (perlage, engraving, skeletonizing). Some of the bracelets, cases, and dials are even manufactured here, but the base movements come from Switzerland. Besides unadorned one-hand watches, the current portfolio of timepieces includes such outstanding creations as a special moon phase, which, rather than simply showing a moon, has a "shadow" crossing over an immobile photo-like reproduction of the moon. Coming at the time of writing is a stunning skeletonized watch called the Steel Flower in a tonneau case and with blue bridges. And, of course, the Schaumburg workshop also produces unique pieces.

Riding the vintage movement, the company has created an unusual line involving the artificial aging of cases, movements, and components. The Steam Punk collection looks as if it had been buried in someone's garden and has now been unearthed, cleaned up, but not restored. The watches work, of course.

Schaumburg Watch
Lindburgh & Benson
Kirchplatz 5 and 6
D-31737 Rinteln
Germany

Tel.:
+49-5751-923-351

E-mail:
info@lindburgh-benson.com

Website:
www.schaumburgwatch.com

Founded:
1998

Number of employees:
7

Annual production:
not specified

Distribution:
retail

U.S. distributor:
Schaumburg Watch
About Time Luxury Group
210 Bellevue Avenue
Newport, RI 02840
401-846-0598
nicewatch@aol.com

Most important collections/price range:
mechanical wristwatches / approx. $1,500 to $13,000

Urbanic Galaxy Limited Edition
Reference number: SWURLE19
Movement: automatic, Caliber SW-7750 (base ETA 7750); ø 30 mm, height 7.9 mm; 25 jewels; 28,800 vph; skeletonized and decorated movement, blued screws; 42-hour power reserve
Functions: hours, minutes, subsidiary seconds; chronograph; date
Case: stainless steel, ø 45 mm, height 15 mm; sapphire crystal; transparent case back; screw-in crown; water-resistant to 10 atm
Band: calfskin, buckle
Remarks: skeletonized dial
Price: $4,900; limited to 99 pieces

Steam Punk II
Reference number: SWSTEM2
Movement: manually wound, SW Caliber 08 (base ETA 6498); ø 36.6 mm, height 4.5 mm; 17 jewels; 21,600 vph; 48-hour power reserve
Functions: hours, minutes
Case: stainless steel, ø 42 mm, height 11.8 mm; sapphire crystal; transparent case back; water-resistant to 5 atm
Band: calfskin, buckle
Remarks: dial is circle of indices made of artficially aged metal in typical steampunk style
Price: $2,200

Classoco Edition
Reference number: SWCLE1
Movement: automatic, SW Caliber 20A (base ETA 2824-2); ø 25.6 mm, height 4.6 mm; 25 jewels; 28,800 vph; 38-hour power reserve
Functions: hours, minutes, sweep seconds; date
Case: stainless steel, ø 42 mm, height 11 mm; sapphire crystal; transparent case back; water-resistant to 5 atm
Band: calfskin, buckle
Price: $1,500
Variations: various cases and dials

SCHWARZ ETIENNE

Schwarz Etienne SA
Route de L'Orée-du-Bois 5
CH-2300 La Chaux-de-Fonds
Switzerland

Tel.:
+41-32-967-9420

E-mail:
info@schwarz-etienne.ch

Website:
www.schwarz-etienne.com

Founded:
1902

Number of employees:
20

Annual production:
300 to 500

Distribution:
Contact main office in Switzerland.

Most important collections:
La Chaux-de-Fonds, Roma, Roswell

When Raffaello Radicchi, who hails from Perugia, Italy, talks about his business, you might think he was talking about a little shop he set up in Neuchâtel. Ask him why he went into watchmaking, he answers, "I was allergic to the metal and could only wear a gold watch." Subtext: He could not afford a gold watch, so he founded a watch company.

Radicchi is a genuine maverick and a lone figure in this somewhat hermetic industry. He arrived in Switzerland at 18, a mason. Unable to continue his work, he retrained as a carpenter and started renovating homes, then buying and renovating, and soon he was earning some serious money. Easy-peasy. In the early aughts, an acquaintance bought up a watch brand in La Chaux-de-Fonds and suggested that Radicchi buy the building that came with it. The brand, once a big name in the industry and a supplier of movements (to Chanel, among others), had originally been founded by Paul Schwarz and Olga Etienne.

By 2008, Radicchi owned the whole package. He understood that the company needed independence to survive. Having a number of outstanding suppliers locally to partner with was a good start. But Schwarz Etienne needed movements. By 2013, he had two, and a third came in 2015. These calibers drive a series of watches, including a tourbillon, that are classical in look, yet very modern-technical, thanks to the inverted movement construction that puts the off-center microrotor on the dial. They've recently started appearing in the watches of other brands.

For all its traditionalism, the brand still maintains a feeling of youthful creativity. The Roswell's case, for example, is shaped like a comic-book UFO. And if you have seven figures to spend, you can purchase a special box of seven watches honoring the days of the week, their planets, and their astrological sign. Not surprisingly, Schwarz Etienne came up with a particularly distinctive ladies' watch called Fiji. The dials are in various colors, with droplet indices, and the subsidiary seconds dial is cut out in such a way as to create a floral animation with the underlying dial.

Fiji
Reference number: WFI15MA08SS04AA
Movement: automatic, Schwarz Etienne Caliber ASE 200.00; ø 30.40 mm, height 5.35 mm; 33 jewels; 21,600 vph; inverted movement, irreversible engraved microrotor; visible date module; 86-hour power reserve
Functions: hours, minutes, subsidiary seconds
Case: stainless steel, ø 38 mm, height 10.74 mm; sapphire crystal; water-resistant to 5 atm
Remarks: salmon-colored dial; comes with additional ruby-red strap
Band: calfskin, folding clasp
Price: $7,150
Variations: various dials

La Chaux-de-Fonds Tourbillon Petite Seconde Rétrograde
Reference number: WCF09TSE06RB21AA
Movement: automatic, Schwarz Etienne Caliber TSE PSR 122.00; ø 30.40 mm, height 7.05 mm; 40 jewels; 21,600 vph; inverted movement, microrotor on dial side; 1-minute flying tourbillon; plate/bridges sandblasted and chamfered; 72-hour power reserve
Functions: off-center hours, minutes, subsidiary seconds (retrograde)
Case: stainless steel, ø 44 mm, height 13.70 mm; sapphire crystal; transparent case back; water-resistant to 5 atm
Remarks: lapis lazuli numeral track
Band: reptile skin, folding clasp
Price: $69,995

Roma Manufacture Small Second
Reference number: WRO15MA25SS01AA
Movement: automatic, Schwarz Etienne Caliber ASE 100.00; ø 30.4 mm, height 5.35 mm; 34 jewels; 21,600 vph; 96-hour power reserve
Functions: hours, minutes, subsidiary seconds
Case: stainless steel, ø 42 mm, height 12.13 mm; sapphire crystal; transparent case back; water-resistant to 5 atm
Band: reptile skin, buckle
Remarks: silver-colored dial with rhodium-blue hands
Price: $9,995
Variations: various dials

SEIKO

The Japanese watch giant is a part of the Seiko Holding Company, but the development and production of its watches are fully self-sufficient. Seiko makes every variety of portable timepiece and offers mechanical watches with both manual and automatic winding, quartz watches with battery and solar power or with the brand's own mechanical "Kinetic" power generation, as well as the groundbreaking "Spring Drive" hybrid technology. This intelligent mix of mechanical energy generation and electronic regulation is reserved for Seiko's top models.

Also in the top segment of the brand is the Grand Seiko line, a group of watches that enjoys cult status among international collectors. Only recently did the Tokyo-based company offer a large collection to the global market. Today, there are several watches with the Spring Drive technology, but most new Grand Seikos (see page 160) are conventional, mechanical hand-wound and automatic watches.

Classic Seikos are designed for tradition-conscious buyers. The Astron, however, with its automatic GPS-controlled time setting, suggests the watch of the future. In its second incarnation, the Astron is 30 percent more compact, and the energy required by the GPS system inside is supplied by a high-tech solar cell on the dial. As for the new Prospex collection, released for the fiftieth anniversary of the first Seiko diver's watches, it has an unmistakably modern look. The old protective case of the Marinemaster is now made of ceramic instead of plastic.

Seiko Holdings
Ginza, Chuo, Tokyo
Japan

Website:
www.seikowatches.com

Founded:
1881

U.S. distributor:
Seiko Corporation of America
1111 MacArthur Boulevard
Mahwah, NJ 07430
201-529-5730
custserv@seikousa.com
www.seikousa.com

Most important collections/price range:
Astron / approx. $1,850 to $3,400; Presage / approx. $425 to $4,500; Prospex / approx. $395 to $6,000

Astron GPS Solar Dual Time
Reference number: SSH021J1
Movement: quartz, Seiko Caliber 5X53; autonomous energy from solar cells on dial
Functions: hours, minutes, sweep seconds; additional 12-hour display (2nd time zone), world time function (39 time zones), flight mode, signal reception indication, daylight saving time indication; perpetual calendar, date, weekday
Case: stainless steel (with hard coating), ø 41.4 mm, height 13.3 mm; sapphire crystal with super-clear coating; water-resistant to 10 atm
Band: stainless steel with hard coating, folding clasp
Price: $2,000

Astron GPS Solar Dual Time
Reference number: SSH001J1
Movement: quartz, Seiko Caliber 5X53; autonomous energy from solar cells on dial
Functions: hours, minutes, sweep seconds; additional 12-hour display (2nd time zone), world time function (39 time zones), flight mode, signal reception display, daylight saving time indication; perpetual calendar with date, weekday
Case: titanium (with hard coating), ø 42.9 mm, height 12.2 mm; ceramic bezel; sapphire crystal with clear coating; water-resistant to 10 atm
Band: titanium, folding clasp
Price: $2,100

Prospex LX Line Spring Drive GMT
Reference number: SNR033J1
Movement: Spring Drive (manual and automatic winding), Seiko Caliber 5R66; ø 30 mm, height 5.8 mm; 30 jewels; 32,768 vph; electromagnetic Tri-synchro regulator with a glide wheel; amagnetic protection to 4,800 A/m; 72-hour power reserve
Functions: hours, minutes, sweep seconds; additional 24-hour display (2nd time zone), power reserve indicator; date; **Case:** titanium (with hard coating), ø 45 mm, height 15 mm; bidirectional bezel, with 0-24 scale; sapphire crystal with clear coating; screw-in crown; water-resistant to 10 atm
Band: titanium with hard coating, folding clasp
Price: $5,500

Prospex Diver's 1970 Limited Edition

Reference number: SLA033J1
Movement: automatic, Seiko Caliber 8L35; ø 28.4 mm, height 5.3 mm; 26 jewels; 28,800 vph; amagnetic protection to 4,800 A/m; 50-hour power reserve
Functions: hours, minutes, sweep seconds; date
Case: stainless steel (hard coating), ø 45 mm, height 13 mm; unidirectional bezel, 0-60 scale; sapphire crystal; screw-in crown; water-resistant to 20 atm
Band: silicone, buckle
Remarks: re-creation of the second Prospex automatic-diver's watch from 1970, worn by Captain Willard in *Apocalypse Now*
Price: $4,250; limited to 2,500 pieces

Prospex Automatic Diver's "Sumo"

Reference number: SPB103J1
Movement: automatic, Seiko Caliber 6R35; ø 27.4 mm, height 4.95 mm; 24 jewels; 21,600 vph; 70-hour power reserve
Functions: hours, minutes, sweep seconds; date
Case: stainless steel, ø 45 mm, height 13 mm; unidirectional bezel, 0-60 scale; sapphire crystal; screw-in crown; water-resistant to 20 atm
Band: stainless steel, folding clasp with safety lock, with extension link
Price: $850

Prospex Solar Analog Digital Diver's

Reference number: SNJ025P1
Movement: solar quartz, Seiko Caliber H851
Functions: hours, minutes, sweep seconds; additional 12-hour display (2nd time zone), alarm; remaining energy display; chronograph; date, weekday
Case: stainless steel with matte black outer case, black PVD coating, ø 48 mm, height 14 mm; unidirectional bezel, 0-60 scale; Hardlex crystal; screw-in crown and pushers; water-resistant to 20 atm
Band: silicon, buckle
Price: $525

Presage Automatic Multifunction

Reference number: SPB091J1
Movement: automatic, Seiko Caliber 6R27; ø 27.4 mm, height 6 mm; 29 jewels; 28,800 vph; 45-hour power reserve
Functions: hours, minutes, sweep seconds; power reserve indicator; date
Case: stainless steel, ø 41 mm, height 13 mm; dual curved sapphire crystal; transparent case back; water-resistant to 10 atm
Band: stainless steel, folding clasp
Remarks: enamel dial
Price: $1,450

Presage Automatic

Reference number: SSA395J1
Movement: automatic, Seiko Caliber 4R57; ø 27.4 mm, height 6.48 mm; 29 jewels; 21,600 vph; 41-hour power reserve
Functions: hours, minutes, sweep seconds; power reserve indicator; date
Case: stainless steel, ø 42 mm, height 14 mm; dual curved sapphire crystal; transparent case back; water-resistant to 5 atm
Band: stainless steel, dual folding clasp
Price: $675

Presage Automatic

Reference number: SRPD37J1
Movement: automatic, Seiko Caliber 4R35; ø 27 mm, height 4.95 mm; 23 jewels; 21,600 vph; 41-hour power reserve
Functions: hours, minutes, sweep seconds; date
Case: stainless steel, ø 41 mm, height 12 mm; Hardlex crystal; transparent case back; water-resistant to 5 atm
Band: calfskin, folding clasp
Price: $425

SINN

Pilot and flight instructor Helmut Sinn began manufacturing watches in Frankfurt am Main because he thought the pilot's watches on the market were too expensive. The resulting combination of top quality, functionality, and a good price-performance ratio turned out to be an excellent sales argument. Sinn Spezialuhren zu Frankfurt am Main is a brand with origins in technology. There is hardly another source that offers watch lovers such a sophisticated and reasonable collection of sporty watches, many conceived to survive in extreme conditions by conforming to German DIN industrial norms.

In 1994, Lothar Schmidt took over the brand, and his product developers began looking for inspiration in other industries and the sciences. They did so out of a practical technical impulse without any plan for launching a trend. Research and development are consistently aimed at improving the functionality of the watches. This includes application of special Sinn technology such as moisture-proofing cases by pumping in an inert gas like argon. Other Sinn innovations include the Diapal (a lubricant-free lever escapement), the Hydro (an oil-filled diver's watch), and tegiment processing (for hardened steel and titanium surfaces). Having noticed a lack of norms for aviator watches, Schmidt negotiated a partnership with the Aachen Technical University to create the *Technischer Standard Fliegeruhren* (TESTAF, or Technical Standard for Pilot's Watches), which is housed at the Eurocopter headquarters.

Sinn recently joined forces with two German watch companies, the Sächsische Uhrentechnologie Glashütte (SUG) and the Uhren-Werke-Dresden (UWD). The latter produced the outstanding UWD 33.1 caliber with Sinn as chaperone. That movement was then used to drive the Meisterbund I, which translates as "master alliance."

All these moves have brought the company enough wherewithal to open new headquarters in the Sossenheim district of Frankfurt. The building offers nearly 25,000 square feet of space, most of which is devoted to assembly and manufacturing. At the heart of the two-story construction is a grandiose atrium with a skylight offering lots of natural light. The roof was also turned into an open-air terrace.

Sinn Spezialuhren GmbH
Wilhelm-Fay-Strasse 21
D-65936 Frankfurt / Main
Germany

Tel.:
+49-69-9784-14-200

E-mail:
info@sinn.de

Website:
www.sinn.de

Founded:
1961

Number of employees:
approx. 120

Annual production:
approx. 14,000 watches

U.S. distributor:
WatchBuys
888-333-4895
www.watchbuys.com

Most important collections/price range:
Financial District, U-Models, Diapal / from approx. $1,000 to $17,000

6012 Rose Gold Jubilee

Reference number: 6012.021
Movement: automatic, Sinn Caliber SZ06 (base ETA 7751); ø 30.4 mm, height 7.9 mm; 25 jewels; 28,800 vph; amagnetic according to German Industrial Norm (DIN), lubrication-free escapement (Diapal); 42-hour power reserve
Functions: hours, minutes, subsidiary seconds; chronograph; full calendar with date, weekday, month, moon phase
Case: rose gold, ø 41.5 mm, height 14.5 mm; sapphire crystal; transparent case back; water-resistant to 10 atm; **Band:** reptile skin, buckle
Remarks: comes with reptile skin strap
Price: $14,950; limited to 50 pieces
Variations: stainless steel unlimited ($4,670)

1800 Damaszener

Reference number: 1800.040
Movement: automatic, ETA Caliber 2892-A2; ø 25.6 mm, height 3.6 mm; 21 jewels; 28,800 vph; amagnetic according to German Industrial Norm (DIN); 42-hour power reserve
Functions: hours, minutes, sweep seconds; date
Case: tegimented Damascus steel, ø 43 mm, height 10.4 mm; sapphire crystal; screw-in crown; water-resistant to 10 atm
Band: calfskin, buckle
Remarks: Damascus steel dial; comes with calfskin strap
Price: $8,580; limited to 100 pieces

206 Arktis II

Reference number: 206.012
Movement: automatic, ETA Caliber 7750 (modified); ø 30 mm, height 8.4 mm; 25 jewels; 28,800 vph; amagnetic according to German Industrial Norm (DIN), 46-hour power reserve
Functions: hours, minutes, subsidiary seconds; chronograph; date, weekday
Case: stainless steel, ø 43 mm, height 17 mm; unidirectional bezel, 0-60 scale; sapphire crystal; transparent case back; water-resistant to 30 atm
Band: stainless steel, folding clasp with safety lock, with extension link
Remarks: certified according to European diving norm, dehumidifying technology (protective gas)
Price: $3,760; **Variations:** calfskin band ($3,570)

SINN

EZM 12
Reference number: 112.010; **Movement:** automatic, ETA Caliber 2836-2; ø 25.6 mm, height 5.05 mm; 25 jewels; 28,800 vph; protected from magnetic fields up to 80,000 A/m; 38-hour power reserve; **Functions:** hours, minutes, sweep seconds; date, weekday; **Case:** tegimented stainless steel, black hard coating, ø 44 mm, height 14 mm; bidirectional bezel with 0-60 scale (counting downward); crown-activated inner ring with 0-60 scale (counting upward); sapphire crystal; water-resistant to 20 atm **Band:** silicon, folding clasp with extension link **Remarks:** developed for emergency medical professionals; comes with pocketknife; dehumidifying technology (protective gas)
Price: $3,560

EZM 10 TESTAF
Reference number: 950.011
Movement: automatic, Sinn Caliber SZ 01 (base ETA 7750); ø 30 mm, height 7.9 mm; 29 jewels; 28,800 vph; sweep minute counter, lubrication-free escapement (Diapal), shockproof and amagnetic
Functions: hours, minutes, subsidiary seconds; 2nd 24-hour display; chronograph; date
Case: tegimented titanium, ø 46.5 mm, height 15.6 mm; bidirectional bezel with 0-60 scale; sapphire crystal; screw-in crown; water-resistant to 20 atm **Band:** calfskin, buckle
Remarks: certified according to Technical Standard for Pilot's Watches (TESTAF); dehumidifying technology (protective gas)
Price: $5,480; **Variations:** titanium bracelet ($5,910)

3006 Hunting Watch
Reference number: 3006.010
Movement: automatic, ETA Caliber 7751; ø 30 mm, height 7.9 mm; 25 jewels; 28,800 vph; shock-resistant and amagnetic according to German Industrial Norm (DIN); 42-hour power reserve
Functions: hours, minutes, subsidiary seconds; additional 24-hour display (2nd time zone); chronograph; date, weekday, month, moon phase
Case: tegimented stainless steel, ø 44 mm, height 15.5 mm; sapphire crystal; transparent case back; screw-in crown; water-resistant to 20 atm
Band: calfskin, buckle
Remarks: dehumidifying technology (special gas)
Price: $3,980; **Variations:** stainless steel bracelet ($4,340); silicon strap ($4,100)

910 SRS
Reference number: 910.020
Movement: automatic, modified ETA Caliber 7750; ø 30 mm, height 8.4 mm; 25 jewels; 28,800 vph; column wheel control of chronograph functions; shock-resistant and amagnetic according to German Industrial Norm (DIN); 46-hour power reserve
Functions: hours, minutes, subsidiary seconds; flyback chronograph; date
Case: stainless steel, ø 41.5 mm, height 15.5 mm; sapphire crystal; transparent case back; water-resistant to 10 atm
Band: calfskin, buckle
Price: $3,980
Variations: stainless steel bracelet ($4,260)

U1 B
Reference number: 1010.0102
Movement: automatic, Sellita Caliber SW200-1; ø 25.6 mm, height 4.6 mm; 26 jewels; 28,800 vph; shock-resistant and amagnetic according to German Industrial Norm (DIN); 38-hour power reserve
Functions: hours, minutes, sweep seconds; date
Case: stainless steel (U-boat steel), ø 44 mm, height 14.7 mm; unidirectional bezel, 0-60 scale; sapphire crystal; screw-in crown; water-resistant to 100 atm
Band: silicon, folding clasp with extension link
Remarks: certified according to European diving norm
Price: $2,080
Variations: with hard black coating ($2,530)

U212 (EZM 16)
Reference number: 212.040
Movement: automatic, Sellita Caliber SW300-1; ø 25.6 mm, height 3.6 mm; 25 jewels; 28,800 vph; shock-resistant and amagnetic according to German Industrial Norm (DIN); 42-hour power reserve
Functions: hours, minutes, sweep seconds; date
Case: stainless steel (U-boat steel), ø 47 mm, height 14.5 mm; unidirectional bezel, 0-60 scale; sapphire crystal; screw-in crown; water-resistant to 100 atm
Band: stainless steel, folding clasp with extension link
Remarks: certified according to European diving norm, dehumidifying technology (protective gas)
Price: $2,950; **Variations:** silicon strap ($2,870); textile strap ($2,750)

SINN

T1
Reference number: 1014.010
Movement: automatic, ETA Caliber 2892-A2; ø 25.6 mm, height 3.6 mm; 21 jewels; 28,800 vph; shock-resistant and amagnetic according to German Industrial Norm (DIN); 42-hour power reserve
Functions: hours, minutes, sweep seconds; date
Case: bead-blasted titanium, ø 45 mm, height 12.5 mm; unidirectional bezel, 0-60 scale; sapphire crystal; screw-in crown; water-resistant to 100 atm
Band: titanium, folding clasp with safety lock, with extension link
Remarks: certified according to European diving norm, dehumidifying technology (protective gas)
Price: $3,440; **Variations:** blue dial ($3,440); 41-mm case ($3,240)

103 St
Reference number: 103.031
Movement: automatic, ETA Caliber 7750; ø 30 mm, height 7.9 mm; 25 jewels; 28,800 vph; amagnetic according to German Industrial Norm (DIN); 42-hour power reserve
Functions: hours, minutes, subsidiary seconds; chronograph; date, weekday
Case: stainless steel, ø 41 mm, height 15.5 mm; bidirectional bezel, 0-60 scale; Plexiglas; screw-in crown; water-resistant to 20 atm
Band: calfskin, buckle
Price: $1,890
Variations: stainless steel bracelet ($2,130)

104 St Sa A
Reference number: 104.011
Movement: automatic, Sellita Caliber SW220-1; ø 25.6 mm, height 5.05 mm; 26 jewels; 28,800 vph; shock-resistant and amagnetic according to German Industrial Norm (DIN); 38-hour power reserve
Functions: hours, minutes, sweep seconds; date, weekday
Case: stainless steel, ø 41 mm, height 11.5 mm; bidirectional bezel, 0-60 scale; sapphire crystal; transparent case back; screw-in crown; water-resistant to 20 atm
Band: stainless steel, folding clasp with safety lock, with extension link
Price: $1,560
Variations: without Arabic numerals ($1,560)

6200 WG Meisterbund I
Reference number: 6200.020
Movement: manually wound, Caliber UWD 33.1; ø 33 mm, height 4.2 mm; 19 jewels; 21,600 vph; weighted balance; flying spring barrel, amagnetic according to German Industrial Norm (DIN); 55-hour power reserve
Functions: hours, minutes, subsidiary seconds
Case: white gold, ø 40 mm, height 9.3 mm; sapphire crystal; transparent case back; water-resistant to 10 atm
Band: calfskin, buckle
Price: $16,460; limited to 55 pieces

104 St Sa I A
Reference number: 104.014
Movement: automatic, Sellita Caliber SW220-1; ø 25.6 mm, height 5.05 mm; 26 jewels; 28,800 vph; amagnetic up to 80,000 A/m according to German Industrial Norm (DIN); 38-hour power reserve
Functions: hours, minutes, sweep seconds; date, weekday
Case: stainless steel, ø 41 mm, height 11.5 mm; bidirectional bezel, 0-60 scale; sapphire crystal; transparent case back; screw-in crown; water-resistant to 20 atm
Band: Alcantara leather, buckle
Price: $1,330
Variations: blue or white dial ($1,330)

556 I B
Reference number: 556.0104
Movement: automatic, ETA Caliber 2824-2; ø 25.6 mm, height 4.6 mm; 25 jewels; 28,800 vph; shock-resistant and amagnetic according to German Industrial Norm (DIN); 38-hour power reserve
Functions: hours, minutes, sweep seconds
Case: stainless steel, ø 38.5 mm, height 11 mm; sapphire crystal; transparent case back; screw-in crown; water-resistant to 20 atm
Band: calfskin, buckle
Price: $1,160
Variations: black dial ($1,080); mocha-colored dial ($1,160)

SPEAKE-MARIN

Speake-Marin
Avenue de Miremont 33C
1206 Geneva
Switzerland

Tel.:
+41-21-695-26-55

E-mail:
info@speake-marin.com

Website:
www.speake-marin.com

Founded:
2002

Number of employees:
9

Annual production:
400 watches

Most important collections:
One & Two, Art Series, Vintage, Haute Horlogerie

Peter Speake-Marin brings realism, genius, and a sense of romance to his work. As a horological innovator, he could have been a poet or adventurer. He has an outstanding reputation for originality, virtuosity, and being a very friendly and helpful colleague in a highly competitive field. He has also had his skilled fingers in a number of iconic timepieces, like the HM1 of MB&F, the Chapter One for Maîtres du Temps, and the Harry Winston Excenter Tourbillon.

Born in Essex in 1968, Speake-Marin attended Hackney College, London, and WOSTEP in Switzerland, before earning his spurs restoring antique watches at a Somlo in Piccadilly. In 1996, he moved to Le Locle, Switzerland, to work with Renaud et Papi, when he also set about making his own pieces. A dual-train tourbillon (the Foundation Watch) opened the door to the prestigious AHCI.

Peter Speake-Marin is a profoundly creative watchmaker, one willing to give a hand even to his competitors. In 2017, he decided to leave the brand he had given birth to and shaped for sixteen years. In a brief letter, CEO Christelle Rosnoblet promised to continue the brand's characteristic "British elegance and impertinence." Whether this mission is accomplished remains to be seen. What the "new" Speake-Marin has produced, though, is very high-end, notably the double tourbillon with a special mechanism to regulate and even out the rate of the two tourbillons. Long-time Speake-Marin fans might recognize the boldness in the technical concepts, but they will also recognize the famous Piccadilly case, though remodeled, and the conical crown.

One & Two Openworked
Reference number: 424207150
Movement: automatic, SMA01 Caliber; ø 32 mm, height 4.2 mm; 33 jewels; 28,000 vph; open-worked dial, COSC-certified; 52-hour power reserve
Functions: hours, minutes, subsidiary seconds
Case: red gold, ø 42 mm, height 10.5 mm; sapphire crystal; water-resistant to 3 atm
Band: reptile skin, buckle
Price: $33,925; limited to 10 pieces
Variations: with 38-mm case ($31,625, limited to 10 pieces)

One & Two Openworked Dual Time
Reference number: 424209250
Movement: automatic, SMA02 Caliber; ø 34 mm, height 6.65 mm; 31 jewels; 28,000 vph; open-worked dial, 52-hour power reserve
Functions: hours, minutes, subsidiary seconds; 2nd 24-hour time zone; retrograde date
Case: red gold, ø 42 mm, height 10.5 mm; sapphire crystal; water-resistant to 3 atm
Band: reptile skin, buckle
Price: $41,400; limited to 20 pieces
Variations: with 38-mm case ($39,100, limited to 20 pieces)

Double-Tourbillon Openworked
Reference number: 934681150
Movement: automatic, SMA-HH06 Caliber; ø 38.4 mm, height 8.75 mm; 56 jewels; 21,600 vph; two 1-minute tourbillons, patented rate equalizer for the two regulators; double barrel springs; open-worked dial, 72-hour power reserve
Functions: hours, minutes, subsidiary seconds
Case: red gold, ø 46 mm, height 10.5 mm; sapphire crystal; water-resistant to 3 atm
Band: reptile skin, buckle
Price: $305,000; unique piece

STOWA

When a watch brand organizes a museum for itself, it is usually with good reason. The firm Stowa may not be the biggest fish in the horological pond, but it has been around for more than eighty years, and its products are well worth taking a look at as expressions of German watchmaking culture. Stowa began in Pforzheim, then moved to the little industrial town of Rheinfelden, and now operates in Engelsbrand, a "suburb" of Pforzheim. After a history as a family-owned company, today the brand is headed by Jörg Schauer, who has maintained the goal and vision of original founder Walter Storz: delivering quality watches at a reasonable price.

Stowa is one of the few German brands to have operated without interruption since the start of the twentieth century, albeit with a new owner as of 1990. Besides all the political upheavals, it survived the quartz crisis of the 1970s, during which Europe was flooded with cheap watches from Asia and many traditional German watchmakers were put out of business. Storz managed to keep Stowa going, but even a quality fanatic has to pay a price during times of trouble: With huge input from his son, Werner, Storz restructured the company so that it was able to begin encasing reasonably priced quartz movements rather than being strictly an assembler of mechanical ones.

Schauer bought the brand in 1996. Spurred on by the success of his own eponymous line, he also steered Stowa back toward mechanical watches, taking inspiration from older Stowa timepieces but using Swiss ETA movements. But the way out of the retro trap was about to become apparent: In 2015, Schauer joined forces with Hartmut Esslinger to create the Rana (frog) model, with an almost ethereal case and a modern dial, whose dot markers (DynaDots they are called) grow larger by the hour. These new shapes are above all expressed in the new Flieger (pilot) watches.

Stowa GmbH & Co. KG
Gewerbepark 16
D-75331 Engelsbrand
Germany

Tel.:
+49-7082-942630

E-mail:
info@stowa.com

Website:
www.stowa.com

Founded:
1927

Number of employees:
20

Annual production:
around 4,500 watches

Distribution:
direct sales; please contact company in Germany; orders taken by phone Monday through Friday 9 a.m. to 5 p.m. European time. Note: prices are determined according to daily exchange rate.

Flieger Verus 40

Reference number: FliegerVerus40
Movement: automatic, ETA Caliber 2824-2; ø 25.6 mm, height 4.6 mm; 25 jewels; 28,800 vph; 40-hour power reserve
Functions: hours, minutes, sweep seconds; date
Case: stainless steel, ø 40 mm, height 10.2 mm; sapphire crystal; water-resistant to 5 atm
Band: calfskin, buckle
Price: $753
Variations: high-end movement ($895)

Flieger Classic 40

Reference number: FliegerKlassik40
Movement: automatic, ETA Caliber 2824-2; ø 25.6 mm, height 4.6 mm; 25 jewels; 28,800 vph; 40-hour power reserve
Functions: hours, minutes, sweep seconds
Case: stainless steel, ø 40 mm, height 10.2 mm; sapphire crystal; transparent case back; water-resistant to 5 atm
Band: calfskin, buckle
Price: $1,145
Variations: manually wound movement ($1,167)

Flieger Classic Chrono

Reference number: FliegerKlassikChrono
Movement: automatic, ETA Caliber 7753; ø 30 mm, height 7.9 mm; 27 jewels; 28,800 vph; 48-hour power reserve
Functions: hours, minutes; chronograph
Case: stainless steel, ø 41 mm, height 13.7 mm; sapphire crystal; transparent case back; water-resistant to 5 atm
Band: calfskin, buckle
Price: $2,127
Variations: manually wound movement ($2,455)

STOWA

Marine Classic 40 Roman White
Reference number: MarineKlassik40Römisch
Movement: automatic, ETA Caliber 2824-2; ø 25.6 mm, height 4.6 mm; 25 jewels; 28,800 vph; 40-hour power reserve
Functions: hours, minutes, sweep seconds
Case: stainless steel, ø 40 mm, height 10.3 mm; sapphire crystal; water-resistant to 5 atm
Band: calfskin, buckle
Price: $753
Variations: high-end movement (895); manually wound movement ($916)

Marine Original
Reference number: MarineOriginalpolweissarabisch
Movement: manually wound, ETA Caliber 6498-1; ø 36.6 mm, height 4.5 mm; 17 jewels; 18,000 vph; screw balance, swan-neck fine adjustment, côtes de Genève, blued screws; 46-hour power reserve
Functions: hours, minutes, subsidiary seconds
Case: stainless steel, ø 41 mm, height 12 mm; sapphire crystal; transparent case back; water-resistant to 5 atm
Band: calfskin, buckle
Price: $1,505
Variations: silver dial ($1,669)

Antea 390 with Date "Back to Bauhaus"
Reference number: Antea390b2bdatumweiss
Movement: automatic, ETA Caliber 2824-2; ø 25.6 mm, height 4.6 mm; 25 jewels; 28,800 vph; blued screws, handmade rotor; 40-hour power reserve
Functions: hours, minutes, sweep seconds; date
Case: stainless steel, ø 39 mm, height 9.2 mm; sapphire crystal; transparent case back; water-resistant to 5 atm
Band: calfskin, buckle
Price: $1,069

Chronograph 1938 Black
Reference number: chronograph1938schwarz
Movement: automatic, ETA Caliber 7753; ø 30 mm, height 7.9 mm; 27 jewels; 28,800 vph; 48-hour power reserve
Functions: hours, minutes, subsidiary seconds; chronograph
Case: stainless steel, ø 41 mm, height 13.7 mm; sapphire crystal; transparent case back; water-resistant to 5 atm
Band: calfskin, buckle
Price: $2,171
Variations: manually wound movement ($2,498)

Partitio Black with Red Second Hand
Reference number: PartitioschwarzroteSek
Movement: manually wound, ETA Caliber 2804-2; ø 25.6 mm, height 3.35 mm; 17 jewels; 28,800 vph; 42-hour power reserve
Functions: hours, minutes, sweep seconds
Case: stainless steel, ø 37 mm, height 9.8 mm; sapphire crystal; transparent case back; water-resistant to 5 atm
Band: calfskin, buckle
Price: $1,004
Variations: white dial; with automatic movement ($840)

Prodiver Grey Limited
Reference number: Prodivergreylimited
Movement: automatic, ETA Caliber 2824-2; ø 25.6 mm, height 4.6 mm; 25 jewels; 28,800 vph; 40-hour power reserve
Functions: hours, minutes, sweep seconds; date
Case: titanium, ø 42 mm, height 15.6 mm; unidirectional bezel, 0-60 scale; sapphire crystal; screw-in crown; water-resistant to 100 atm
Band: rubber, double folding clasp with safety lock and extension link
Price: $1,625; limited to 100 pieces

TAG HEUER

Measuring speed accurately in ever greater detail was always the goal of TAG Heuer. The brand also established numerous technical milestones, including the first automatic chronograph caliber with a microrotor (created in 1969 with Hamilton-Büren, Breitling, and Dubois Dépraz). Of more recent vintage is the fascinating mechanical movement V4 with its belt-driven transmission, unveiled in a limited edition. At the same time TAG Heuer released its first chronograph with an in-house movement, Caliber 1887, the basis of which was an existing chronograph movement by Seiko. Some of the components are made by the company itself in Switzerland, while assembly is done entirely in-house.

Lately, TAG Heuer has increased its manufacturing capacities to meet the strong and growing demand and to maintain its independence. In addition, it serves as an extended workbench for companion brands Zenith and Hublot, also part of the LVMH Group.

TAG Heuer has continued to break world speed records for mechanical escapements. The Caliber 360 combined a standard movement with a 360,000-vph (50-Hz) chronograph mechanism able to measure hundredths of a second. In 2011, the Mikrograph 1/100th brought time display and measurement on a single plate. Shortly after, the Mikrotimer Flying 1000 broke the thousandth-of-a-second barrier. A year later, the Mikrogirder 2000 doubled the frequency using a vibrating metal strip instead of a balance wheel. The MikrotourbillonS features a separate chronograph escapement driven at a record-breaking 360,000 vph.

The new LVMH coordinator, Jean-Claude Biver, decided to cut back on the top end of the pricing scale. CEO Guy Sémon, a scientist with a PhD in physics, also heads the company's Research Institute. He has experimented with electromagnetic, hairspring-less pendulum watches and new materials, like graphene, a synthetic material that does not need to be processed as a blank but can be easily shaped right from the drawing board. The research was used in the new Autovia Caliber 5 Isograph, which has a hairspring made of carbon nanotubes.

TAG Heuer
Branch of LVMH SA
6a, rue L.-J.-Chevrolet
CH-2300 La Chaux-de-Fonds
Switzerland

Tel.:
+41-32-919-8164

E-mail:
info@tagheuer.com

Website:
www.tagheuer.com

Founded:
1860

Number of employees:
1,600 employees internationally

U.S. distributor:
TAG Heuer/LVMH Watch & Jewelry USA
966 South Springfield Avenue
Springfield, NJ 07081
973-467-1890

Most important collections/price range:
TAG Heuer Formula 1, Aquaracer, Link, Carrera, Connected, Monaco, Heritage / from approx. $1,300 to $20,000

Formula 1 Calibre 16

Reference number: CAZ2010.BA0876
Movement: automatic, TAG Heuer Calibre 16 (base ETA 7750); ø 30.4 mm, height 7.9 mm; 25 jewels; 28,800 vph
Functions: hours, minutes, subsidiary seconds; chronograph; date
Case: stainless steel, ø 44 mm, height 15 mm; sapphire crystal; screw-in crown; water-resistant to 20 atm
Band: stainless steel, folding clasp
Price: $2,850

Aquaracer 300M Calibre 5

Reference number: WAY2013.BA0927
Movement: automatic, TAG Heuer Calibre 5 (base ETA 2824-2); ø 26 mm, height 4.6 mm; 25 jewels; 28,800 vph
Functions: hours, minutes, sweep seconds; date
Case: stainless steel, ø 43 mm; unidirectional bezel, 0-60 scale; sapphire crystal; screw-in crown; water-resistant to 30 atm
Band: stainless steel, folding clasp
Price: $2,300

Aquaracer 300M Calibre 5

Reference number: WAY201A.FT6142
Movement: automatic, TAG Heuer Calibre 5 (base ETA 2824-2); ø 26 mm, height 4.6 mm; 25 jewels; 28,800 vph
Functions: hours, minutes, sweep seconds; date
Case: stainless steel, ø 41 mm; unidirectional ceramic bezel, 0-60 scale; sapphire crystal; screw-in crown; water-resistant to 30 atm
Band: rubber, folding clasp
Price: $2,500

TAG HEUER

Link Calibre 5
Reference number: WBC2111.BA0603
Movement: automatic, TAG Heuer Calibre 5 (base ETA 2824-2); ø 26 mm, height 4.6 mm; 25 jewels; 28,800 vph
Functions: hours, minutes, sweep seconds; date
Case: stainless steel, ø 41 mm; sapphire crystal; water-resistant to 10 atm
Band: stainless steel, folding clasp
Price: $2,900

Link Calibre 17
Reference number: CBC2110.BA0603
Movement: automatic, TAG Heuer Calibre 17 (base ETA 2894-2); ø 28.6 mm, height 6.1 mm; 37 jewels; 28,800 vph; 42-hour power reserve
Functions: hours, minutes, subsidiary seconds; chronograph; date
Case: stainless steel, ø 41 mm; sapphire crystal; transparent case back; water-resistant to 10 atm
Band: stainless steel, folding clasp
Price: $4,500
Variations: blue dial

Carrera Calibre 5
Reference number: WAR211A.BA0782
Movement: automatic, TAG Heuer Calibre 5 (base ETA 2824-2); ø 26 mm, height 4.6 mm; 25 jewels; 28,800 vph
Functions: hours, minutes, sweep seconds; date
Case: stainless steel, ø 39 mm, height 12 mm; sapphire crystal; transparent case back; water-resistant to 10 atm
Band: stainless steel, folding clasp
Price: $2,500
Variations: various dial colors; reptile skin strap ($2,500)

Carrera Calibre 5 Day-Date
Reference number: WAR201E.FC6292
Movement: automatic, TAG Heuer Calibre 5 (base ETA 2836-2); ø 26 mm, height 5.05 mm; 25 jewels; 28,800 vph
Functions: hours, minutes, sweep seconds; date, weekday
Case: stainless steel, ø 41 mm, height 13 mm; sapphire crystal; transparent case back; water-resistant to 10 atm
Band: reptile skin, folding clasp
Price: $2,700
Variations: various dials; stainless steel bracelet ($2,700)

Carrera Calibre 16
Reference number: CBM2110.BA0651
Movement: automatic, TAG Heuer Calibre 16 (base ETA 7750); ø 30.4 mm, height 7.9 mm; 25 jewels; 28,800 vph
Functions: hours, minutes, subsidiary seconds; chronograph; date
Case: stainless steel, ø 41 mm; ceramic bezel; sapphire crystal; screw-in crown; water-resistant to 10 atm
Band: stainless steel, folding clasp
Price: $4,450

Carrera Calibre Heuer 02 Automatic
Reference number: CBG2010.FT6143
Movement: automatic, TAG Heuer Calibre Heuer 02; ø 31 mm, height 6.9 mm; 33 jewels; 28,800 vph; 80-hour power reserve
Functions: hours, minutes, subsidiary seconds; chronograph; date
Case: stainless steel, ø 43 mm; ceramic bezel; sapphire crystal; transparent case back; water-resistant to 10 atm
Band: rubber, folding clasp
Price: $5,350

TAG HEUER

Carrera Calibre Heuer 02
Reference number: CBG2A10.FT6168
Movement: automatic, TAG Heuer Calibre Heuer 02; ø 31 mm, height 6.9 mm; 33 jewels; 28,800 vph; 80-hour power reserve
Functions: hours, minutes, subsidiary seconds; chronograph; date
Case: stainless steel, ø 45 mm; ceramic bezel; sapphire crystal; transparent case back; water-resistant to 10 atm
Band: rubber, folding clasp
Price: $5,450

Carrera Calibre Heuer 02
Reference number: CBG2A10.BA0654
Movement: automatic, TAG Heuer Calibre Heuer 02; ø 31 mm, height 6.9 mm; 33 jewels; 28,800 vph; 80-hour power reserve
Functions: hours, minutes, subsidiary seconds; chronograph; date
Case: stainless steel, ø 45 mm; ceramic bezel; sapphire crystal; transparent case back; water-resistant to 10 atm
Band: stainless steel, folding clasp
Price: $5,600

Carrera Calibre Heuer 02
Reference number: CBG2A90.BH0653
Movement: automatic, TAG Heuer Calibre Heuer 02; ø 31 mm, height 6.9 mm; 33 jewels; 28,800 vph; 80-hour power reserve
Functions: hours, minutes, subsidiary seconds; chronograph; date
Case: ceramic, ø 45 mm; sapphire crystal; transparent case back; water-resistant to 10 atm
Band: ceramic, double folding clasp
Price: $6,550

Carrera Calibre Heuer 02 GMT
Reference number: CBG2A1Z.BA0658
Movement: automatic, TAG Heuer Calibre Heuer 02; ø 31 mm, height 6.9 mm; 33 jewels; 28,800 vph; 80-hour power reserve
Functions: hours, minutes, subsidiary seconds; additional 24-hour display (2nd time zone); chronograph; date
Case: stainless steel, ø 45 mm; bezel with ceramic insert; sapphire crystal; transparent case back; water-resistant to 10 atm
Band: stainless steel, folding clasp
Price: $6,150
Variations: rubber strap ($5,950)

Carrera Calibre Heuer 02 Tourbillon C.O.S.C. Black Titanium
Reference number: CAR5A8Y.FC6377
Movement: automatic, TAG Heuer Calibre Heuer 02 T; ø 31 mm, height 6.9 mm; 33 jewels; 28,800 vph; 1-minute tourbillon; COSC-certified chronometer
Functions: hours, minutes; chronograph; date
Case: titanium with black titanium carbide coating, ø 45 mm; sapphire crystal; water-resistant to 10 atm
Band: reptile skin strap, folding clasp
Price: $17,000

TAG Heuer Monaco Calibre 11
Reference Number: CAW211P.FC6356
Movement: automatic, base Sellita SW300 with 2006 Dubois Dépraz module; ø 30 mm, height 7.3 mm; 59 jewels; 28,800 vph
Functions: hours, minutes, subsidiary seconds; chronograph; date
Case: stainless steel, 39 × 39 mm, height 14.5 mm; sapphire crystal; transparent case back; water-resistant to 10 atm
Band: calfskin, folding clasp
Price: $5,900

TAG HEUER

Heuer Heritage Autavia Calibre Heuer 02
Reference number: CBE2110.BA0687
Movement: automatic, TAG Heuer Calibre Heuer 02; 59 jewels; 28,800 vph
Functions: hours, minutes, subsidiary seconds; chronograph; date
Case: 42-mm bidirectional polished steel turning bezel; water-resistant up to 100 meters
Band: polished steel
Price: $5,450
Variations: leather strap ($5,300)

Formula 1 Quartz
Reference Number: CAZ101N.FC8243
Movement: quartz
Functions: hours, minutes, subsidiary seconds; chronograph; date
Case: 43-mm fine-brushed and polished steel
Band: blue calfskin
Price: $1,600

Monaco Calibre 11 Special Edition Gulf
Reference number: CAW211R.FC6401
Movement: automatic, TAG Heuer Calibre 11 (base Sellita SW300 with 2006 Dubois Dépraz module); ø 30 mm, height 7.3 mm; 59 jewels; 28,800 vph
Functions: hours, minutes, subsidiary seconds; chronograph; date
Case: stainless steel, 39 × 39 mm, height 14.5 mm; sapphire crystal; transparent case back; water-resistant to 10 atm
Band: calfskin, folding clasp
Price: $5,900

Aquaracer Calibre 7 GMT
Reference Number: WAY201F.BA0927
Movement: Calibre 7 Twin Time
Functions: hours, minutes, seconds; 2nd time zone, date
Case: 43-mm unidirectional turning bezel, polished steel and aluminum
Band: polished steel, folding clasp
Price: $2,850

Aquaracer Calibre 16
Reference Number: CAY2112.BA0927
Movement: Calibre 16
Functions: hours, minutes, seconds at 9; chronograph: ¼-second, 30-minute counter, 12-hour counter; 2nd time zone, date
Case: 43-mm unidirectional turning bezel, polished steel and aluminum
Band: polished steel, folding clasp
Price: $2,850

Connected Modular 45
Reference number: SBF8A8013.32FT6079
Movement: quartz, Intel Core Duo microprocessor; Android OS; near-field communication with smartphone for data sharing and reciprocal function control
Functions: hours, minutes, sweep seconds; special application for use on golf course; other displays and functions through smartphone connection; chronograph; date
Case: titanium, ø 45 mm, height 13.2 mm; unidirectional ceramic bezel; sapphire crystal; water-resistant to 5 atm
Band: calfskin and rubber, folding clasp
Price: $3,300

TEMPTION

Temption has been operating under the leadership of Klaus Ulbrich since 1997. Ulbrich is an engineer with special training in the construction of watches and movements, and right from the start, he intended to develop timekeepers that were modern in their esthetics but not subject to the whims of zeitgeist. Retro watches would have no place in his collections. The design behind all Temption models is inspired more by the Bauhaus or the Japanese concept of wabi sabi. Reduction to what is absolutely necessary is the golden rule here. Beauty emerges from clarity, or in other words, less is more.

Ulbrich sketches all the watches himself. Some of the components are even made in-house, but all the pieces are assembled in the company facility in Herrenberg, a town just to the east of the Black Forest. The primary functions are always easy to read, even in low light. The company logo is discreetly included on the dial.

Ulbrich works according to a model he calls the "information pyramid." Hours and minutes are at the tip, with all other functions subordinated. To maintain this hierarchy, the dials are dark, the date windows are in the same hue, and all subdials are not framed in any way. The most unimportant information for reading time comes at the end of the "pyramid"; it is shiny black on black: the logo can only be identified in lateral light.

The Cameo rectangular model is a perfect example of Ulbrich's esthetic ideas and his consistent technological approach: Because rectangular sapphire crystals can hardly be made water-resistant, the Cameo's crystal is chemically bonded to the case and water-resistant to 10 atm. The frame for the sapphire was metalized inside to hide the bonded edge. The overall look is one of stunning simplicity and elegance. With the CGK205 chronograph, Ulbrich took the concept out of the case. Whether it be the leather strap or the stainless steel bracelet, the watch's attachment is seamlessly integrated into the case, without any visible split.

Temption GmbH
Raistinger Str. 46
D-71083 Herrenberg
Germany

Tel.:
+49-7032-977-954

E-mail:
ftemption@aol.com

Website:
www.temption.info

Founded:
1997

Number of employees:
4

Annual production:
700 watches

U.S. distributor:
TemptionUSA
Debby Gordon
2053 North Bridgeport Drive
Fayetteville, AR 72704
888-400-4293
temptionusa@sbcglobal.net

Most important collections/price range:
automatics (three-hand), GMT, chronographs, and chronographs with complications / approx. $1,900 to $4,200

CM05

Reference number: CM05A10SST
Movement: automatic, Temption Caliber T15.1 (base Soprod A10, or on request with a Caliber ETA 2892-A2); ø 25.6 mm, height 3.6 mm; 21 jewels; 28,800 vph; finely finished movement; 42-hour power reserve
Functions: hours, minutes, sweep seconds; date
Case: stainless steel, ø 42 mm, height 10.8 mm; sapphire crystal; transparent case back; screw-in crown; water-resistant to 10 atm
Band: stainless steel, double folding clasp with safety lock
Price: $2,400

Chronograph CGK205 V2

Reference number: 205V2316BSST
Movement: automatic, Temption Caliber T18.1 (base ETA 7751); ø 30 mm, height 7.8 mm; 25 jewels; 28,800 vph; finely finished movement; 42-hour power reserve
Functions: hours, minutes; second 24-hour display; chronograph; full calendar with date, weekday, month, moon phase
Case: stainless steel, ø 43 mm, height 14 mm; sapphire crystal; transparent case back; screw-down crown and pusher with colored cabochons; water-resistant to 10 atm
Band: stainless steel, double folding clasp
Remarks: comes with additional textile strap
Price: $3,540

Cameo-B

Reference number: CAMBLBFS151
Movement: automatic, Temption Caliber T15.1 (base Soprod A10); ø 25.6 mm, height 3.6 mm; 21 jewels; 28,800 vph; finely finished movement; 42-hour power reserve
Functions: hours, minutes, sweep seconds; date
Case: stainless steel, 37 × 41 mm, height 9.9 mm; sapphire crystal; transparent case back; screw-in crown; water-resistant to 10 atm
Band: calfskin, double folding clasp
Price: $1,750

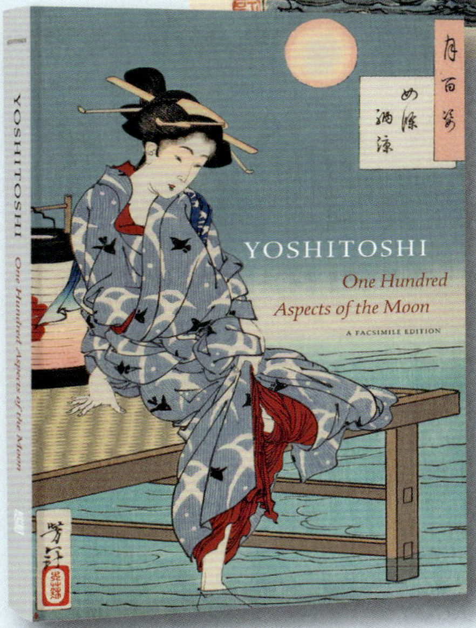

Yoshitoshi
One Hundred Aspects of the Moon

By John Stevenson

A magnificent facsimile edition of the final masterpiece of ukiyo-e—*strictly limited to 3,000 numbered copies*

Yoshitoshi (1839–1892) was the last virtuoso of the Japanese woodblock print, and the One Hundred Aspects of the Moon, published between 1885 and 1892, were his crowning achievement. This series—illustrating scenes from history, legend, and contemporary life, unified by the motif of the moon—abounds with stylistic innovations, drawn from Western art and the artist's own fertile imagination.

ISBN 978-0-7892-1355-6 · $175

Available wherever fine books are sold

TISSOT

Tissot SA
Chemin des Tourelles, 17
CH-2400 Le Locle
Switzerland

Tel.:
+41-32-933-3111

E-mail:
info@tissot.ch

Website:
www.tissot.ch

Founded:
1853

U.S. distributor:
Tissot
The Swatch Group (U.S.), Inc.
703 Waterford Way
Suite 450
Miami, FL 33126
www.us.tissotshop.com

Most important collection/price range:
Ballade / from $925; T-Touch / from $575; NBA Collection / from $395; Chemin des Tourelles / from $795; Seastar from $695; Swissmatic from $395

The Swiss watchmaker Tissot was founded in 1853 in the town of Le Locle in the Jura mountains. In the century that followed, it gained international recognition for its Savonnette pocket watch. And even when the wristwatch became popular in the early twentieth century, time and again Tissot managed to attract attention to its products. To this day, the Banana Watch of 1916 and its first watches in the art deco style (1919) remain design icons of that epoch. The watchmaker has always been at the top of its technical game as well: The first amagnetic watch (1930), the first mechanical plastic watch (Astrolon, 1971), and its touch-screen T-Touch (1999) all bear witness to Tissot's remarkable capacity for finding unusual and modern solutions.

Today, Tissot belongs to the Swatch Group and, with its wide selection of quartz and inexpensive mechanical watches, serves as the group's entry-level brand. Within this price segment, Tissot offers something special for the buyer who values traditional watchmaking but is not of limitless financial means. The brand has been cultivating a sportive image of late, expanding into everything from basketball to superbike racing, from ice hockey to fencing—and water sports, of course. Partnerships with several NBA teams have been signed, notably with the Houston Rockets, Chicago Bulls, and Washington Wizards in October 2018. The chronograph Couturier line is outfitted with the new ETA chronograph caliber C01.211. This caliber features a number of plastic parts: another step in simplifying, and lowering the cost of, mechanical movements.

Increasingly, in addition, a number of Tissot models are being equipped with silicon hairsprings, which are notorious for outstanding isochronous oscillation as well as imperviousness to magnetic fields and changes in temperature. And for the buyer, it means only a slight increase in price.

Heritage 1973

Reference number: T124.427.16.031.00
Movement: automatic, ETA Caliber 7753; ø 30 mm, height 7.9 mm; 25 jewels; 28,800 vph; 42-hour power reserve
Functions: hours, minutes subsidiary seconds; chronograph; date
Case: stainless steel, ø 43 mm, height 14.8 mm; sapphire crystal; transparent case back; water-resistant to 10 atm
Band: calfskin, folding clasp
Price: $2,100; limited to 1,973 pieces

T-Touch Expert Solar II

Reference number: T110.420.44.051.00
Movement: quartz, multifunctional movement with LCD display and separate solar energy supply
Functions: hours, minutes; additional 12-hour display (2nd time zone), barometer, height altimeter and altitude difference meter, compass, regatta function, 2 alarms; chronograph with countdown timer; perpetual calendar with date, weekday, calendar week
Case: titanium, ø 45 mm, height 13.1 mm; ceramic bezel; sapphire crystal; water-resistant to 10 atm
Band: titanium, folding clasp
Remarks: sapphire crystal touch screen to access functions and displays
Price: $1,275

Gentleman Automatic

Reference number: T927.407.41.031.00
Movement: automatic, Tissot Powermatic 80 (base ETA Caliber 2824-2); ø 25.6 mm, height 4.6 mm; 25 jewels; 21,600 vph; 80-hour power reserve
Functions: hours, minutes, sweep seconds; date
Case: stainless steel, ø 40 mm, height 10.64 mm; rose gold bezel; sapphire crystal; transparent case back; water-resistant to 5 atm
Band: stainless steel, folding clasp
Price: $1,350

Everytime Swissmatic

Reference number: T109.407.36.031.00
Movement: automatic, ETA Caliber C15.111; ø 31.9 mm, height 5.77 mm; 19 jewels; 21,600 vph; 72-hour power reserve
Functions: hours, minutes, sweep seconds; date
Case: stainless steel with rose gold PVD coating, ø 40 mm, height 11.62 mm; sapphire crystal; transparent case back; water-resistant to 3 atm
Band: calfskin, buckle
Price: $495
Variations: without PVD coating ($390)

Carson Automatic Gent

Reference number: T122.407.11.051.00
Movement: automatic, Tissot Powermatic 80 (base ETA Caliber 2824-2); ø 25.6 mm, height 4.6 mm; 25 jewels; 21,600 vph; 80-hour power reserve
Functions: hours, minutes, sweep seconds; date
Case: stainless steel, ø 40 mm, height 10.3 mm; sapphire crystal; transparent case back; water-resistant to 5 atm
Band: stainless steel, folding clasp
Price: $650

Heritage Visodate Automatic

Reference number: T019.430.11.041.00
Movement: automatic, ETA Caliber 2836-2; ø 25.6 mm, height 5.05 mm; 25 jewels; 28,800 vph; 38-hour power reserve
Functions: hours, minutes, sweep seconds; date, weekday
Case: stainless steel, ø 40 mm, height 11.6 mm; sapphire crystal; transparent case back; water-resistant to 3 atm
Band: stainless steel Milanese mesh, folding clasp with safety lock
Price: $675

Chemin des Tourelles GMT

Reference number: T099.429.16.058.00
Movement: automatic, Tissot Powermatic 80 (base ETA Caliber 2824-2); ø 25.6 mm, height 4.6 mm; 23 jewels; 21,600 vph; 80-hour power reserve
Functions: hours, minutes, sweep seconds; additional 24-hour display (2nd time zone); date
Case: stainless steel, ø 42 mm, height 12.52 mm; sapphire crystal; transparent case back; water-resistant to 5 atm
Band: calfskin, double folding clasp
Price: $875
Variations: rose gold PVD coating ($975)

Seastar Automatic

Reference number: T120.407.17.041.00
Movement: automatic, Tissot Powermatic 80 (base ETA Caliber 2824-2); ø 25.6 mm, height 4.6 mm; 23 jewels; 21,600 vph; 80-hour power reserve
Functions: hours, minutes, sweep seconds; date
Case: stainless steel, ø 43 mm, height 12.7 mm; unidirectional bezel with ceramic insert, 0-60 scale; sapphire crystal; water-resistant to 30 atm
Band: rubber, buckle
Price: $695

T-Race MotoGP 2019 Automatic Chronograph Limited Edition

Reference number: T115.427.37.051.00
Movement: automatic, ETA Caliber C01.211; ø 31 mm, height 8.44 mm; 15 jewels; 21,600 vph; 45-hour power reserve
Functions: hours, minutes, subsidiary seconds; chronograph; date
Case: stainless steel with rose gold PVD coating, ø 45 mm, height 16.6 mm; bezel set with black PVD coating; sapphire crystal; transparent case back; water-resistant to 10 atm
Band: calfskin, buckle
Price: $1,295; limited to 3,333 pieces

TOURBY WATCHES

Tourby Watches from the town of Wetter in Westphalia, Germany, manufactures mechanical wristwatches whose design is inspired by classic models. The story began when Erdal Yildiz inherited a pocket watch from his grandfather. The Unitas movement inside was in need of serious revision. So he looked around for a proper watchmaker, and was soon enamored with the craft itself. The world of mechanical watches became a genuine passion during his studies. He then contacted a number of suppliers in Germany and Switzerland, and in 2007 founded his own brand. The name Tourby has nothing to do with tourbillons, which his company does not manufacture. Rather, it is his nickname, it is short and memorable, and the domain name was still available!

All raw materials are purchased from top-notch suppliers in Germany and Switzerland. Some of the parts are ready to use on delivery; others need to be reworked in the company's own workshops in the cities of Bochum and Hagen. The cases are finished by hand, for example, as are the movements—all Swiss ETA calibers—which are extensively decorated, and the dials, in part at least. The leather straps are stitched by hand, as well. Final assembly, quality control, and after-sales service are all done by the company.

Tourby Watches produces series, but also does made-to-order pieces. The customer can choose his or her case, dial, hands, strap, and even the movement with its decoration. Another option is skeletonization. It's a good way to get hold of a unique piece.

This little brand has already quite a following in the U.S., notably. A pilot's watch was made especially for the dangerous deployments of the Strike Fighters Weapons School Pacific, a U.S. Navy training school for fighter pilots.

Tourby Watches
Königstr. 78
D-58300 Wetter an der Ruhr
Hagen in Westfalen
Germany

Tel:
+49 176 83118382

E-mail:
info@tourbywatches.com

Website:
www.tourbywatches.com

Founded:
2007

Number of employees:
5

Annual production:
500

Distribution:
Tourby deals directly with customers.

Most important collections/price range:
Lawless Diver / from $1,400; Art Deco Classic from / $1,800; Ottoman / from $1,575; Planetarium / $9,000

Lawless Vintage 42
Reference number: 6121.1
Movement: automatic, ETA Caliber 2824-2; 25.6 mm; 25 jewels; 28,800 vph; adjusted in 5 positions; 36-hour power reserve
Functions: hours, minutes, sweep second; date
Case: brushed stainless steel, 42 mm, height 13 mm; sapphire crystal; 3D deep engraved case back; unidirectional bezel with 0-60 scale (120 clicks), ceramic bezel inlay; screw-in crown; water-resistant to more than 50 atm
Band: stainless steel bracelet, rubber strap
Price: $1,650
Variations: JNT Edition ($2,075)

Lawless 42 Black
Reference number: 6120.1
Movement: automatic, ETA Caliber 2824-2; 25.6 mm; 25 jewels; 28,800 vph; adjusted in 5 positions; 36-hour power reserve
Functions: hours, minutes, sweep second; date
Case: brushed stainless steel, 42 mm, height 13 mm; sapphire crystal; 3D deep engraved case back; unidirectional bezel with 0-60 scale (120 clicks), ceramic bezel inlay; screw-in crown; water-resistant to more than 50 atm
Band: stainless steel bracelet, rubber strap
Price: $2,050
Variations: blue limited edition ($1,850)

Lawless GMT Blue 40
Reference number: 6230
Movement: automatic, ETA Caliber 2893-2; 25.6 mm; 21 jewels; 28,800 vph; adjusted in 5 positions; 42-hour power reserve
Functions: hours, minutes, sweep second; GMT, date
Case: brushed stainless steel, 40 mm, height 11.8 mm; sapphire crystal; bidirectional bezel with 24h scale (120 clicks), sapphire bezel inlay; screw-in crown; water-resistant to more than 20 atm
Band: stainless steel bracelet
Price: $2,000
Variations: black ($2,050)

TOURBY WATCHES

Lawless Blue 40
Reference number: 6220.2
Movement: automatic, ETA Caliber 2824-2; 25.6 mm; 25 jewels; 28,800 vph; adjusted in 5 positions; 36-hour power reserve
Functions: hours, minutes, sweep second; date
Case: brushed stainless steel, 40 mm, height 11.8 mm; sapphire crystal; unidirectional bezel with 0-60 scale (120 clicks), sapphire bezel inlay; screw-in crown; water-resistant to more than 20 atm
Band: stainless steel bracelet
Price: $1,650
Variations: in black ($1,400)

Art Deco Marine Arabic 40
Reference number: 2002.2
Movement: manually wound, ETA Caliber 6498-1; 37 mm; 17 jewels; 18,000 vph; adjusted in 5 positions; côtes de Genève; sunburst wheels; blue screws; 48-hour power reserve
Functions: hours, minutes, subsidiary seconds
Case: stainless steel, 40.5 mm, height 10.6 mm; arched sapphire crystal; transparent case back; water-resistant to 5 atm
Band: reptile skin, buckle
Remarks: 925/000 sterling silver dial
Price: $1,575
Variations: skeletonized and modified movement ETA 6498-2 ($2,925)

Art Deco Rose 43
Reference number: 2040.2
Movement: manually wound, ETA Caliber 6498-1; 37 mm; 17 jewels; 18,000 vph; adjusted in 5 positions; côtes de Genève; sunburst wheels; blue screws; 48-hour power reserve
Functions: hours, minutes, subsidiary seconds
Case: stainless steel, rose gold plated, 43 mm, height 10.4 mm; arched sapphire crystal; transparent case back; water-resistant to 5 atm
Band: reptile skin, buckle
Remarks: 925/000 sterling silver dial
Price: $2,030
Variations: skeletonized and modified movement ETA 6498-2 ($3,375); different size (40, 43, 45 mm) and different dial colors (silver, black, anthracite)

Ottoman Enamel 40
Reference number: 2091
Movement: manually wound, ETA Caliber 6498-1; 37 mm; 17 jewels; 18,000 vph; adjusted in 5 positions; côtes de Genève; sunburst wheels; blue screws; 48-hour power reserve
Functions: hours, minutes, subsidiary seconds
Case: stainless steel, 40.5 mm, height 10.6 mm; arched sapphire crystal; transparent case back; water-resistant to 5 atm
Band: reptile skin, buckle
Remarks: enamel-coated dial with old Ottoman numbers
Price: $1,575
Variations: skeletonized and modified movement ETA 6498-2 ($2,925)

Old Military Vintage 45
Reference number: 1404
Movement: manually wound, ETA Caliber 6498-1; 37 mm; 17 jewels; 18,000 vph; adjusted in 5 positions; côtes de Genève; sunburst wheels; blue screws; 48-hour power reserve
Functions: hours, minutes, subsidiary seconds
Case: stainless steel, 45 mm, height 13.35 mm; arched sapphire crystal; transparent case back; water-resistant to 5 atm
Band: Vintage cordovan strap, buckle
Price: $1,400
Variations: enamel dial and 43-mm case

Pilot Automatic Dark Blue 40
Reference number: 1330
Movement: automatic, ETA Caliber 2824-2; 25.6 mm; 25 jewels; 28,800 vph; adjusted in 5 positions; 36-hour power reserve
Functions: hours, minutes, sweep second
Case: stainless steel, 40.5 mm, height 10.6 mm; arched sapphire crystal; transparent case back; water-resistant to 5 atm
Band: Vintage cordovan strap, buckle
Price: $1,525
Variations: different-sized cases

TOWSON WATCH COMPANY

After over forty years repairing high-grade watches, repeaters, and chronographs, and making his own tourbillons, George Thomas, a master watchmaker, met Hartwig Balke, a graduate in mechanical engineering and also a talented watchmaker, by chance in a bar in Annapolis. The two men, each well on his way to retirement, decided to turn their passion into a business and, in 2000, founded the Towson Watch Company. Thomas's first tourbillon pocket watches are displayed at the National Watch and Clock Museum in Columbia, Pennsylvania. In 1999, Balke made his first wrist chronograph, the STS-99 Mission, for a NASA astronaut and mission specialist. It was worn during the first shuttle mission in the new millennium, in the year 2000. The two also restored one of the world's oldest watches, one belonging to Philip Melanchton. In 2009, Thomas was invited to open up a pocket watch belonging to President Lincoln and revealed a secret message engraved by a servicing watchmaker and Union supporter working in Maryland: "Jonathan Dillon April 13-1861 Fort Sumpter [sic] was attacked by the rebels on the above date J Dillon." Towson timepieces pay tribute to local sites, like the Choptank and Potomac rivers. The timepieces are imaginative, a touch retro, a bit nostalgic perhaps, and very personal—not to mention affordable. A number of chronographs give the brand a sportive look. For the Dress Chronograph, Towson recruited the German watchmaker and dial specialist Jochen Benzinger.

Their local commitment is also shared by entrepreneur and former University of Maryland football captain Kevin Plank, who launched the technological sports apparel company Under Armour. In early 2016, the company announced it had bought a 25 percent stake in Towson, to boost its market presence and ensure its future. The two founders had been thinking of succession. Those concerns have now been laid to rest: "The brand will continue to grow and thrive for a long time to come," they told the *Baltimore Sun*.

Towson Watch Co.
502 Dogwood Lane
Towson, MD 21286

Tel.:
410-823-1823

E-mail:
towsonwatchco@aol.com

Website:
www.twcwatches.com

Founded:
2000

Number of employees:
4

Annual production:
200 watches

Distribution:
retail

Most important collections/price range:
Skipjack GMT / approx. $2,950; Mission / approx. $2,500; Potomac / approx. $2,000; Choptank / approx. $4,500; Martin / approx. $3,950 / custom design / $10,000 to $35,000

Dress Chronograph
Reference number: BCH 25
Movement: automatic, Caliber 7750 Valjoux; diameter ø 30 mm, height 7.9 mm; 21 jewels; 28,800 vph; finely finished with côtes de Genève
Functions: hours, minutes, subsidiary seconds; chronograph; date
Case: stainless steel, ø 42 mm, height 15.8 mm; sapphire crystal; screw-down transparent case back; water-resistant to 5 atm
Band: reptile skin, folding clasp
Remarks: elaborate silver dial with guilloché by Jochen Benzinger
Price: $8,100

Mission Moon SC
Reference number: MM250-CS
Movement: automatic ETA Caliber 7751; ø 25.6 mm, height 3.6 mm; 21 jewels; 28,800 vph; fine finishing with côtes de Genève
Functions: hours, minutes, subsidiary seconds; weekday, month, date; moon phase; 24-hour display; chronograph
Case: stainless steel, 40 mm, height 13.5 mm; sapphire crystal; screw-down back with engraving; water-resistant to 5 atm
Band: calfskin, orange stitching, folding clasp
Price: $4,160
Variations: stainless steel bracelet ($4,460)

Choptank Moon Chrono Special
Reference number: CT025-G
Movement: automatic, ETA Caliber 7751 Valjoux; ø 30 mm, height 7.9 mm; 25 jewels; 28,800 vph; fine finishing with côtes de Genève
Functions: hours, minutes, subsidiary seconds; weekday, month, date; moon phase; 24-hour display; chronograph
Case: stainless steel, 40 mm × 44 mm, height 13.5 mm; sapphire crystal at front; transparent screw-down back; water-resistant to 5 atm
Band: reptile skin with folding clasp
Price: $8,500
Variations: mesh stainless steel bracelet ($8,850)

TOWSON WATCH COMPANY

Sagamore (Three-Diamond Watch)
Reference number: SAG100
Movement: manually wound, Soprod Unitas Caliber 6498; ø 36.6 mm, height 4.5 mm; 17 jewels; 18,000 vph; 46-hour power reserve
Functions: hours, minutes, subsidiary seconds
Case: stainless steel, ø 42 mm, height 12.5 mm; sapphire crystal; transparent case back; water-resistant to 5 atm
Remarks: silver and rhodium-plated dial, 3 diamonds at 3 o'clock
Band: reptile skin, 14-kt rose gold buckle
Price: $1,550

North.er
Reference number: NP100
Movement: automatic, ETA Caliber 2893-2; ø 25.6 mm, height 4.1 mm; 21 jewels; 28,800 vph; 38-hour power reserve
Functions: hours, minutes, sweep seconds; date; 2nd time zone hand
Case: stainless steel, 42 mm, height 13.5 mm; sapphire crystal; transparent case back; water-resistant to 5 atm
Band: calfskin, folding clasp
Price: $2,500

14-kt Gold Potomac
Reference number: GP 001-14K
Movement: manually wound, Soprod Unitas Caliber 6497; ø 37.2 mm, height 4.5 mm; 17 jewels; 18,000 vph; swan-neck fine adjustment; barley and solar guilloché on dial, rhodium-plated dial; skeletonized movement
Functions: hours, minutes, subsidiary seconds
Case: 14-kt rose gold, ø 42 mm, height 12.5 mm; sapphire crystal; transparent case back; water-resistant to 3 atm
Band: reptile skin, 14-kt rose gold buckle
Price: $23,500

Martin M-130
Reference number: CC100
Movement: automatic, ETA Caliber 7750 Valjoux; ø 30 mm, height 7.9 mm; 25 jewels; 28,800 vph; fine finishing with côtes de Genève
Functions: hours, minutes, subsidiary seconds; chronograph, date
Case: stainless steel, ø 42 mm, height 13.5 mm; sapphire crystal; screw-down back with engraving; water-resistant to 5 atm
Band: leather, folding clasp
Price: $3,950
Variations: mesh stainless steel bracelet ($4,250)

Potomac
Reference number: PO250-S
Movement: manually wound, Soprod Unitas Caliber 6498; ø 37.2 mm, height 4.5 mm; 17 jewels; 18,000 vph
Functions: hours, minutes, subsidiary seconds
Case: stainless steel, ø 42 mm, height 12.5 mm; domed sapphire crystal; screw-down transparent back; water-resistant to 3 atm
Band: calfskin, buckle
Price: $1,995
Variations: black dial with gold numerals and black calfskin strap; stainless steel mesh bracelet ($2,345)

Skipjack GMT
Reference number: SKJ100-S
Movement: Automatic Caliber ETA 2893-2; ø 25.6 mm, height 4.1 mm; 21 jewels; 28,800 vph; fine finish with côtes de Genève
Functions: hours, minutes, sweep seconds; date; 24-hour adjustable hand
Case: stainless steel, cannelage; ø 41.5 mm; sapphire crystal; screw-down transparent back with sapphire crystal; water-resistant to 5 atm
Band: calfskin, folding clasp
Price: $2,950
Variations: black dial with rhodium-plated numerals and leather strap with deployment clasp; stainless steel bracelet ($3,250)

TUDOR

The Tudor brand came out of the shadow cast by its "big sister" Rolex in 2007 and worked hard to develop its own personality. The strategy focuses on distinctive models that draw inspiration from the brand's rich past but remain in the "affordable quality watch segment."

Rolex founder Hans Wilsdorf started Tudor in 1946 as a second brand in order to offer the legendary reliability of his watches to a broader public at a more affordable price. To this day, Tudor still benefits from the same industrial platform as Rolex, especially in the area of cases and bracelets, assembly, and quality assurance, not to mention distribution and after-sales. However, the movements themselves are usually delivered by ETA and "Tudorized" according to the company's own esthetic and technical criteria.

After the Heritage Black Bay diver's watch, based on a 1954 model, came the blue-highlighted 1973 Chronograph Montecarlo. In 2014, Tudor completed the Heritage collection with the Ranger, a sports watch with an urban-adventurer feel, inspired by the same "tool watch" from the 1960s. For 2019 it was the turn of the diver's project "Commando," a 1960s prototype that finally saw the light of day under the name Black Bay P-01, whose rotating bezel is held in place with a clip. The original watch's bezel could be removed for cleaning, but risked getting lost.

Tudor has also been in the movement business. The MT-5621 made its debut in the simple North Flag and was built as a three-hander (MT-5612) for the Pelagos models. Two other caliber iterations are used for the new Black Bay models.

The M5601/5602 calibers, with three hands and a date, were followed by an attractive automatic chronograph using Breitling's B01 Caliber in exchange for the three-hand MT5912. Meanwhile, the Tudor engineers came up with the automatic MT5652, which powers a brand-new GMT. These exchanges between the two brands give both of them independence from the large suppliers of movements.

Montres Tudor SA
Rue François-Dussaud 3-5-7
1211 Geneva 26
Switzerland

Tel.:
+41-22-302-2200

Website:
www.tudorwatch.com

Founded:
1946

U.S. distributor:
Tudor Watch U.S.A., LLC
665 Fifth Avenue
New York, NY 10022
212-897-9900
www.tudorwatch.com

Most important collections/price range:
Black Bay / $2,475 to $6,800; Heritage / $2,675 to $6,175; Pelagos / $4,450; 1926 / $1,725 to $3,475

Black Bay P01
Reference number: 70150
Movement: automatic, Tudor Caliber MT5612; ø 31.8 mm, height 6.5 mm; 26 jewels; 28,800 vph; silicon hairspring, balance with variable inertia; 70-hour power reserve; COSC-certified chronometer
Functions: hours, minutes, sweep seconds; date
Case: stainless steel, ø 42 mm; bidirectional bezel, 0-12 scale, with stop system (hinged element on upper lug); sapphire crystal; screw-in crown; water-resistant to 20 atm
Band: calfskin with rubber coating, folding clasp with safety lock
Remarks: release of a 1960s prototype for the U.S. Navy that was never manufactured serially
Price: $3,950

Black Bay GMT
Reference number: 79830RB
Movement: automatic, Tudor Caliber MT5652; ø 31.8 mm, height 7.52 mm; 28 jewels; 28,800 vph; silicon hairspring; approx. 70-hour power reserve; COSC-certified chronometer
Functions: hours (crown-activated jumping GMT hand), minutes, sweep seconds; additional 24-hour display (2nd time zone); date
Case: stainless steel, ø 41 mm; bidirectional bezel with 0-24 scale; sapphire crystal; screw-in crown; water-resistant to 20 atm
Band: stainless steel, folding clasp, with safety lock
Price: $3,950
Variations: calfskin or textile strap ($3,625)

Black Bay Fifty-Eight
Reference number: 79030N
Movement: automatic, Tudor Caliber MT5402; ø 26 mm, height 4.99 mm; 27 jewels; 28,800 vph; silicon hairspring; approx. 70-hour power reserve; COSC-certified chronometer
Functions: hours, minutes, sweep seconds
Case: stainless steel, ø 39 mm; unidirectional bezel with aluminum insert, with 0-60 scale; sapphire crystal; screw-in crown; water-resistant to 20 atm
Band: textile, buckle
Price: $3,300
Variations: stainless steel bracelet ($3,625); calfskin strap ($3,300)

TUDOR

Heritage Black Bay 41
Reference number: 79540
Movement: automatic, Tudor Caliber 2824 (base ETA 2824-2); ø 25.6 mm, height 4.6 mm; 25 jewels; 28,800 vph; approx. 38-hour power reserve
Functions: hours, minutes, sweep seconds
Case: stainless steel, ø 41 mm; sapphire crystal; screw-in crown; waterproof to 150 m
Band: calfskin, folding clasp
Price: $2,675
Variations: stainless steel bracelet ($3,000); textile strap ($2,675)

Black Bay 41 S&G
Reference number: 79543
Movement: automatic, Tudor Caliber 2824 (base ETA 2824-2); ø 25.6 mm, height 4.6 mm; 25 jewels; 28,800 vph; 38-hour power reserve
Functions: hours, minutes, sweep seconds
Case: stainless steel, ø 41 mm; yellow gold bezel; sapphire crystal; screw-in crown; water-resistant to 15 atm
Band: stainless steel with yellow gold elements, folding clasp with safety lock
Price: $4,150
Variations: champagne-colored dial; 36-mm case ($4,050); 32-mm case ($3,950)

Black Bay S&G
Reference number: 79733N
Movement: automatic, Tudor Caliber MT5612; ø 31.8 mm, height 6.5 mm; 26 jewels; 28,800 vph; silicon hairspring, variable inertia balance; approx. 70-hour power reserve; COSC-certified chronometer
Functions: hours, minutes, sweep seconds; date
Case: stainless steel, ø 41 mm; unidirectional yellow gold bezel, with 0-60 scale; sapphire crystal; screw-in crown in yellow gold; water-resistant to 20 atm
Band: stainless steel with yellow gold elements, folding clasp with safety lock
Price: $5,075
Variations: aged-leather strap ($3,875)

Black Bay Bronze
Reference number: 79250BA
Movement: automatic, Tudor Caliber MT5601; ø 33.8 mm, height 6.5 mm; 25 jewels; 28,800 vph; silicon hairspring; approx. 70-hour power reserve; COSC-certified chronometer
Functions: hours, minutes, sweep seconds
Case: bronze, ø 43 mm; unidirectional bezel, with 0-60 scale; sapphire crystal; screw-in crown; water-resistant to 20 atm
Band: calfskin, buckle
Price: $4,050
Variation: textile strap ($4,050)

Black Bay Chrono S&G
Reference number: 79363N
Movement: automatic, Tudor Caliber MT5813; ø 30.4 mm, height 7.23 mm; 41 jewels; 28,800 vph; silicon hairspring, balance with variable inertia; 70-hour power reserve; COSC-certified chronometer
Functions: hours, minutes, subsidiary seconds; chronograph; date
Case: stainless steel, ø 41 mm; yellow gold bezel; sapphire crystal; screw-in crown and pushers; water-resistant to 20 atm
Band: stainless steel with yellow gold elements, folding clasp with safety lock
Price: $6,800
Variations: textile or calfskin strap ($5,600)

Black Bay Chrono
Reference number: 79350
Movement: automatic, Tudor Caliber MT5813; ø 30.4 mm, height 7.23 mm; 41 jewels; 28,800 vph; silicon hairspring, balance with variable inertia; 70-hour power reserve; COSC-certified chronometer
Functions: hours, minutes, subsidiary seconds; chronograph; date
Case: stainless steel, ø 41 mm; sapphire crystal; screw-in crown and pushers; water-resistant to 20 atm
Band: stainless steel, folding clasp
Remarks: comes with textile band
Price: $5,100
Variations: calfskin strap ($4,775)

TUDOR

Heritage Advisor
Reference number: 79620TC
Movement: automatic, Tudor Caliber 2892 with module (base ETA 2892-A2); ø 25.6 mm; 21 jewels; 28,800 vph; 42-hour power reserve
Functions: hours, minutes, sweep seconds; alarm; date
Case: stainless steel, titanium, ø 42 mm; sapphire crystal; water-resistant to 10 atm
Band: reptile skin, folding clasp with safety lock
Price: $5,950
Variations: stainless steel bracelet ($6,175); silk strap ($5,850)

Heritage Chrono
Reference number: 70330N
Movement: automatic, Tudor Caliber 2892 with module (base ETA 2892-A2); ø 25.6 mm; 21 jewels; 28,800 vph; approx. 42-hour power reserve
Functions: hours, minutes, subsidiary seconds; chronograph; date
Case: stainless steel, ø 42 mm; bidirectional 12-hour bezel; sapphire crystal; screw-in crown; water-resistant to 150 m
Band: textile, buckle
Price: $4,150
Variations: stainless steel bracelet ($4,475)

Heritage Ranger
Reference number: 79910
Movement: automatic, Tudor Caliber 2824 (base ETA 2824-2); ø 25.6 mm, height 4.6 mm; 25 jewels; 28,800 vph; approx. 38-hour power reserve
Functions: hours, minutes, sweep seconds
Case: stainless steel, ø 41 mm; sapphire crystal; screw-in crown; water-resistant to 15 atm
Band: stainless steel, folding clasp with safety lock
Price: $3,000
Variations: textile strap ($2,675); leather bund strap ($2,675)

Caliber MT5601
Automatic; single spring barrel, 70-hour power reserve; COSC-certified chronometer
Functions: hours, minutes, sweep seconds
Diameter: 33.8 mm
Height: 6.5 mm
Jewels: 25
Balance: glucydur with weighted screws
Frequency: 28,800 vph
Balance spring: silicon
Related caliber: MT5602 (with smaller encasement diameter: 31.8 mm)

Caliber MT5402
Automatic; single spring barrel, 70-hour power reserve; COSC-certified chronometer
Functions: hours, minutes, sweep seconds
Diameter: 26 mm
Height: 4.99 mm
Jewels: 27
Balance: glucydur with weighted screws
Frequency: 28,800 vph
Balance spring: silicon

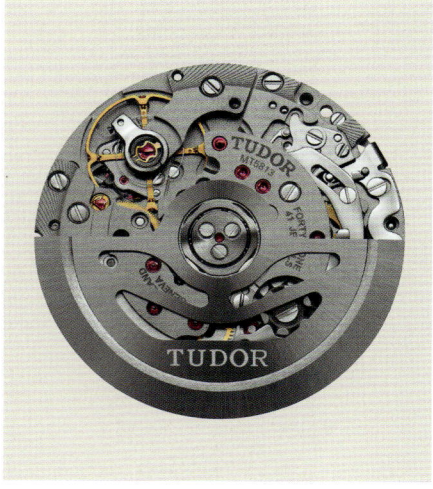

Caliber MT5813
Automatic; single spring barrel, 70-hour power reserve; COSC-certified chronometer
Functions: hours, minutes, subsidiary seconds; chronograph; date
Diameter: 30.4 mm
Height: 7.23 mm
Jewels: 41
Balance: glucydur with weighted screws
Frequency: 28,800 vph
Balance spring: silicon

Tutima Uhrenfabrik GmbH Ndl. Glashütte
Altenberger Strasse 6
D-01768 Glashütte
Germany

Tel.:
+49-35053-320-20

E-mail:
info@tutima.com

Website:
www.tutima.com

Founded:
1927

Number of employees:
approx. 60

U.S. distributor:
Tutima USA, Inc.
P.O. Box 983
Torrance, CA 90508
1-TUTIMA-1927
info@tutimausa.com
www.tutima.com

Most important collections/price range:
Patria, Saxon One, M2, Grand Flieger, Hommage / approx. $1,650 to $29,500

TUTIMA

The name Glashütte is synonymous with watches in Germany. The area, also known for precision engineering, already had quite a watchmaking industry going when World War I closed off markets, followed by the hyperinflation of the early twenties. To rebuild the local economy, a conglomerate was created to produce finished watches, under the leadership of jurist Dr. Ernst Kurtz, consisting of the movement manufacturer UROFA Glashütte AG and UFAG. The top watches were given the name Tutima, derived from the Latin *tutus*, meaning whole, sound. Among the brand's most famous timepieces was a pilot's watch that set standards in terms of esthetics and functionality.

A few days before World War II ended, Kurtz left Glashütte and founded Uhrenfabrik Kurtz in southern Germany. A young businessman and former employee of Kurtz by the name of Dieter Delecate is credited with keeping the manufacturing facilities and the name Tutima going even as the company sailed through troubled waters. In founding Tutima Uhrenfabrik GmbH in Ganderkesee, this young, resolute entrepreneur prepared the company's strategy for the coming decades.

Delecate has had the joy of seeing Tutima return to its old home and vertically integrated operations, meaning it is once again a genuine *manufacture*. Under renowned designer Rolf Lang, it has developed an in-house minute repeater. In 2013, Tutima proudly announced a genuine made-in-Glashütte movement (at least 50 percent must be produced in the town), Caliber 617.

In addition to technically advanced and sportive watches, Tutima Glashütte has started reviving the great watchmaking crafts that have made the region world famous. There is the Hommage minute repeater and the three-hand Patria. In 2017, the brand introduced the Tempostopp, a flyback chronograph run on the Caliber 659, a replica of the legendary Urofa Caliber 59 from the 1940s with a few necessary improvements in the details. And then there are the models for everyday usage based on military watches, like the M2 Coastline, of lightweight titanium but with soft edges that will not ruin a silk shirt cuff.

Saxon One Chronograph Royal Blue
Reference number: 6420-06
Movement: automatic, Tutima Caliber 521 (base ETA 7750); ø 30 mm, height 7.9 mm; 25 jewels; 28,800 vph; sweep minute counter, rotor with gold seal; 48-hour power reserve
Functions: hours, minutes, subsidiary seconds; additional 24-hour display (2nd time zone); chronograph; date
Case: stainless steel, ø 43 mm, height 15.7 mm; bidirectional bezel with reference markers; sapphire crystal; transparent case back; screw-in crown; water-resistant to 20 atm
Band: reptile skin, folding clasp
Price: $6,100

Saxon One M
Reference number: 6121-05
Movement: automatic, Tutima Caliber 330 (base ETA 2836-2); ø 25.6 mm, height 5.05 mm; 25 jewels; 28,800 vph; rotor with gold seal; 38-hour power reserve
Functions: hours, minutes, sweep seconds; date, weekday
Case: stainless steel, ø 40 mm, height 13 mm; sapphire crystal; transparent case back; screw-in crown; water-resistant to 10 atm
Band: stainless steel, folding clasp
Price: $2,350
Variations: calfskin band ($1,950)

Saxon One Lady Diamonds
Reference number: 6701-03
Movement: automatic, Tutima Caliber 340 (base ETA 2892-A2); ø 25.6 mm, height 3.6 mm; 21 jewels; 28,800 vph; rotor with gold seal; 42-hour power reserve
Functions: hours, minutes, sweep seconds; date
Case: stainless steel, ø 36 mm, height 10.7 mm; bezel set with 48 diamonds; sapphire crystal; transparent case back; screw-in crown; water-resistant to 10 atm
Band: reptile skin, folding clasp
Remarks: mother-of-pearl dial
Price: $6,100

TUTIMA

M2 Pioneer
Reference number: 6451-02
Movement: automatic, Tutima Caliber 521 (base ETA 7750); ø 30 mm, height 7.9 mm; 25 jewels; 28,800 vph; sweep minute counter; rotor with gold seal; 48-hour power reserve
Functions: hours, minutes, subsidiary seconds; additional 24-hour display; chronograph; date
Case: titanium, ø 46.5 mm, height 16 mm; bidirectional bezel, 0-60 scale; sapphire crystal; screw-in crown; water-resistant to 30 atm
Band: textile, folding clasp
Remarks: soft-iron inner case for amagnetic protection
Price: $6,100

M2 Seven Seas
Reference number: 6151-02
Movement: automatic, Tutima Caliber 330 (base ETA 2836-2); ø 25.6 mm, height 5.05 mm; 25 jewels; 28,800 vph; rotor with gold seal; 38-hour power reserve
Functions: hours, minutes, sweep seconds; date, weekday
Case: titanium, ø 44 mm, height 13 mm; unidirectional bezel, 0-60 scale; sapphire crystal; screw-in crown; water-resistant to 50 atm
Band: titanium, folding clasp
Price: $2,300

M2 Coastline
Reference number: 6150-02
Movement: automatic, Tutima Caliber 330 (base ETA 2836-2); ø 25.6 mm, height 5.05 mm; 25 jewels; 28,800 vph; rotor with gold seal; 38-hour power reserve
Functions: hours, minutes, sweep seconds; date, weekday
Case: titanium, ø 43 mm, height 13 mm; sapphire crystal; screw-in crown; water-resistant to 30 atm
Band: titanium, folding clasp
Price: $1,950

Grand Flieger Classic Chronograph
Reference number: 6402-01
Movement: automatic, Tutima Caliber 320 (base ETA 7750); ø 30 mm, height 7.9 mm; 25 jewels; 28,800 vph; rotor with gold seal; 48-hour power reserve; chronometer certified by German Industrial Norm (DIN)
Functions: hours, minutes, subsidiary seconds; chronograph; date
Case: stainless steel, ø 43 mm, height 16 mm; bidirectional bezel, with reference mark; sapphire crystal; transparent case back; screw-in crown; water-resistant to 20 atm; **Band:** calfskin, folding clasp
Price: $5,100
Variations: stainless steel bracelet ($5,500)

Flieger
Reference number: 6105-02
Movement: automatic, Tutima Caliber 330 (base ETA 2836-2); ø 25.6 mm, height 5.05 mm; 25 jewels; 28,800 vph; rotor with gold seal; 38-hour power reserve
Functions: hours, minutes, sweep seconds; date
Case: stainless steel, ø 41 mm, height 13 mm; sapphire crystal; transparent case back; screw-in crown; water-resistant to 10 atm
Band: stainless steel, folding clasp
Price: $1,950

Flieger
Reference number: 610-29
Movement: automatic, Tutima Caliber 330 (base ETA 2836-2); ø 25.6 mm, height 5.05 mm; 25 jewels; 28,800 vph; rotor with gold seal; 38-hour power reserve
Functions: hours, minutes, sweep seconds; date
Case: stainless steel, ø 41 mm, height 13 mm; sapphire crystal; transparent case back; screw-in crown; water-resistant to 10 atm
Band: calfskin, folding clasp
Price: $1,650

TUTIMA

Patria
Reference number: 6610-01
Movement: manually wound, Tutima Caliber 617; ø 31 mm, height 4.78 mm; 20 jewels; 21,600 vph; screw balance with weighted screws and Breguet hairspring; Glashütte three-quarter plate; winding wheels with click; gold-plated and finely finished movement; 65-hour power reserve
Functions: hours, minutes, subsidiary seconds
Case: stainless steel, ø 43 mm, height 11.2 mm; sapphire crystal; transparent case back; water-resistant to 5 atm
Band: reptile skin, buckle
Price: $6,500
Variations: rose gold

Tempostopp
Reference number: 6650-01
Movement: manually wound, Tutima Caliber 659; ø 33.7 mm, height 6.6 mm; 28 jewels; 21,600 vph; screw balance with gold weight screws and Breguet hairspring; winding wheels with click; hand-engraved balance cock, gold-plated and finely finished movement; 65-hour power reserve
Functions: hours, minutes, subsidiary seconds; flyback chronograph
Case: rose gold, ø 43 mm, height 12.95 mm; sapphire crystal; transparent case back
Band: reptile skin, buckle
Remarks: optimized replica of legendary UROFA Caliber 59 from 1940s
Price: $29,500

Hommage
Reference number: 6800-02
Movement: manually wound, Tutima Caliber 800; ø 32 mm, height 7.2 mm; 42 jewels; 21,600 vph; screw balance with gold weight screws and Breguet hairspring; Glashütte three-quarter plate; winding wheels with click; gold-plated and finely finished movement; hand-engraved balance cock; 65-hour power reserve
Functions: hours, minutes, subsidiary seconds; minute repeater
Case: rose gold, ø 43 mm, height 13.4 mm; sapphire crystal; transparent case back
Band: reptile skin, buckle
Price: on request

Caliber Tutima 618
Manually wound; 3 screw-mounted gold chatons, Glashütte three-quarter plate; winding wheels with click; single spring barrel, 65-hour power reserve
Functions: hours, minutes, subsidiary seconds; power reserve indicator
Diameter: 31 mm
Height: 4.78 mm
Jewels: 27
Balance: screw balance with gold weight screws
Frequency: 21,600 vph
Balance spring: Breguet hairspring
Remarks: gold-plated and finely finished movement

Caliber Tutima 659
Manually wound; column wheel control of chronograph functions; single spring barrel, 65-hour power reserve
Functions: hours, minutes, subsidiary seconds; flyback chronograph
Diameter: 33.7 mm
Height: 6.6 mm
Jewels: 28
Balance: screw balance with gold weight screws
Frequency: 21,600 vph
Balance spring: Breguet hairspring
Remarks: optimized replica of the legendary UROFA Caliber 59; gold-plated and finely finished movement

Caliber Tutima 800
Manually wound; 4 screw-mounted gold chatons, Glashütte three-quarter plate, 2 gongs, winding wheels with click; single spring barrel, 65-hour power reserve
Functions: hours, minutes, subsidiary seconds; minute repeater
Diameter: 32 mm
Height: 7.2 mm
Jewels: 42
Balance: screw balance with gold weight screws
Frequency: 21,600 vph
Balance spring: Breguet hairspring
Remarks: gold-plated and finely finished movement

ULYSSE NARDIN

At the beginning of the 1980s, following the infamous quartz crisis, Rolf Schnyder revived the venerable Ulysse Nardin brand, which once upon a time had a reputation for marine chronometers and precision watches. He had the luck to meet the multitalented Dr. Ludwig Oechslin, who developed a host of innovations for Ulysse Nardin, from intelligent calendar movements to escapement systems. He was the first to use silicon and synthetic diamonds. In fact, just about every Ulysse Nardin has become famous for some spectacular technical innovation, be it the Moonstruck with its stunning moon phase accuracy or the outlandish Freak series that more or less does away with the dial.

After Schnyder's death in 2011, the brand developed a strategy of partnerships and acquisitions, notably of the enameler Donzé Cadrans SA, which gave rise to the Marine Chronometer Manufacture, powered by the Caliber UN-118.

In 2014, the French luxury group Kering, owner of Girard-Perregaux, purchased Ulysse Nardin. The two companies are neighbors in La Chaux-de-Fonds, Switzerland, and this has created synergies. Ulysse Nardin's creative power remains strong, with such innovations as a new blade-driven anchor escapement and the regatta countdown watch with a second hand that runs counterclockwise first before running clockwise like a conventional chronograph once the race has started.

A joint venture with Sigatec in Sion and its sister company, Mimotec, which specialize in lithogalvanics (LIGA) and processing silicon, allowed Ulysse Nardin to continue developing its advanced technologies, producing, among others, the dual Ulysse escapement in the recent Freaks and the "Anchor Escapement" for the Caliber 178 with tourbillon.

Ulysse Nardin SA
3, rue du Jardin
CH-2400 Le Locle
Switzerland

Tel.:
+41-32-930-7400

Website:
www.ulysse-nardin.com

Founded:
1846

U.S. distributor:
Ulysse Nardin Inc.
7900 Glades Rd., Suite 200
Boca Raton, FL 33434
561-988-8600
usa@ulysse-nardin.com

Most important collections:
Marine chronometers and diver's watches; Dual Time (also ladies' watches); complications (alarm clocks, perpetual calendar, tourbillons, minute repeaters, jacquemarts, astronomical watches)

Marine Mega Yacht
Reference number: 6319-305
Movement: manually wound, Caliber UN-631; ø 37 mm, height 9.36 mm; 53 jewels; 21,600 vph; flying 1-minute tourbillon, winding mechanism deviated over windlass at 12 o'clock; 80-hour power reserve
Functions: hours, minutes; power reserve indicator (linear), tide display with tidal coefficients; moon phase and age
Case: platinum, ø 44 mm, height 14.77 mm; sapphire crystal; transparent case back; water-resistant to 5 atm
Band: reptile skin, folding clasp
Price: $310,000; limited to 30 pieces

Skeleton X Carbonium Gold
Reference number: 3715-260/CARB
Movement: manually wound, Caliber UN-371; ø 37 mm, height 5.86 mm; 23 jewels; 18,000 vph; skeletonized movement; double spring barrel; silicon escape wheel and hairspring; 96-hour power reserve
Functions: hours, minutes
Case: carbon fiber with gold sprinklings, ø 43 mm, height 10.85 mm; sapphire crystal; transparent case back; water-resistant to 5 atm
Band: reptile skin, buckle
Price: $21,000
Variations: titanium

Skeleton X Titanium
Reference number: 3713-260-3/03
Movement: manually wound, Caliber UN-371; ø 37 mm, height 5.86 mm; 23 jewels; 18,000 vph; skeletonized movement; double spring barrel; silicon escape wheel and hairspring; 96-hour power reserve
Functions: hours, minutes
Case: titanium, ø 42 mm, height 10.85 mm; bezel with blue PVD coating; sapphire crystal; transparent case back; water-resistant to 5 atm
Band: rubber, buckle
Price: $17,500
Variations: black bezel; carbonium gold ($21,000); rose gold ($29,000)

ULYSSE NARDIN

Executive Tourbillon Free Wheel
Reference number: 1766-176
Movement: manually wound, Caliber UN-176; ø 37 mm; 18,000 vph; 1-minute tourbillon, Ulysse anchor escapement, silicon escape wheel and hairspring; double spring barrel, 168-hour power reserve
Functions: hours, minutes; power reserve indicator
Case: rose gold, ø 44 mm, height 12.45 mm; sapphire crystal; water-resistant to 3 atm
Band: reptile skin, folding clasp
Remarks: inverted movement construction with moving sections spread out on dial
Price: $96,000
Variations: white gold ($99,000)

Freak Vision
Reference number: 2502-250LE
Movement: automatic, Caliber UN-250; ø 31 mm; 19 jewels; 18,000 vph; flying 1-minute tourbillon on rotating carousel, automatic "grinder" winding system with pawl and flexible control, constant force lever escapement; silicon escapement and hairspring, movement components used as hands, time-setting via bezel; 50-hour power reserve
Functions: hours, minutes
Case: rose gold, ø 45 mm, height 14.1 mm; bidirectional hand-setting bezel with rubber insert; sapphire crystal; transparent case back
Band: reptile skin, folding clasp
Price: $95,000; limited to 99 pieces

Freak Out
Reference number: 2053-132/03.1
Movement: automatic, Caliber UN-250; ø 31 mm; 19 jewels; 18,000 vph; flying 1-minute tourbillon on rotating carousel, automatic "grinder" winding system with pawl and flexible control, constant force lever escapement; silicon escapement and hairspring, movement parts serve as hands, time-setting via bezel; 50-hour power reserve
Functions: hours, minutes
Case: titanium, ø 45 mm, height 13.5 mm; bidirectional hand-setting bezel; sapphire crystal; transparent case back
Band: textile, folding clasp
Price: $48,000

Freak X
Reference number: 2303-270/03
Movement: automatic, Caliber UN-230; ø 31 mm; 19 jewels; 28,800 vph; baguette movement on peripheral carousel; silicon escapement and hairspring, movement parts serve as hands; time-setting via bezel, conventional winding and time-setting by crown; 72-hour power reserve
Functions: hours, minutes
Case: titanium, ø 43 mm, height 13.5 mm; sapphire crystal; transparent case back
Band: calfskin, folding clasp
Price: $21,000

Marine Tourbillon Manufacture
Reference number: 1283-181/E3
Movement: manually wound, Caliber UN-128; ø 31 mm, height 6.45 mm; 50 jewels; 28,800 vph; flying 1-minute tourbillon; silicon escapement and hairspring; 60-hour power reserve
Functions: hours, minutes; power reserve indicator
Case: stainless steel, ø 43 mm, height 12.2 mm; sapphire crystal; transparent case back; screw-in crown, with rubber overlay; water-resistant to 10 atm
Band: reptile skin, double folding clasp
Remarks: enamel dial
Price: $28,000
Variations: rubber strap ($27,900); stainless steel bracelet ($28,700)

Marine Chronograph Manufacture Regatta
Reference number: 1553-155-3/43
Movement: automatic, Caliber UN-155; ø 34 mm, height 8.28 mm; 67 jewels; 28,800 vph; silicon escapement and hairspring
Functions: hours, minutes, subsidiary seconds; chronograph with integrated 10-minute countdown function; date
Case: stainless steel, ø 44 mm; sapphire crystal; transparent case back; screw-in crown; water-resistant to 10 atm
Band: rubber and titanium, folding clasp
Remarks: countdown totalizer; second hand turns counterclockwise, then clockwise when reaching 0
Price: $15,900

ULYSSE NARDIN

Marine Torpilleur
Reference number: 1182-310-3/42
Movement: automatic, Caliber UN-118; ø 31.6 mm, height 6.45 mm; 50 jewels; 28,800 vph; DIAMonSIL escapement, silicon hairspring; 60-hour power reserve; COSC-certified chronometer
Functions: hours, minutes, subsidiary seconds; power reserve indicator; date
Case: rose gold, ø 42 mm, height 13 mm; sapphire crystal; transparent case back; screw-in crown; water-resistant to 10 atm
Band: reptile skin, folding clasp
Price: $17,900
Variations: white dial; reptile skin strap ($17,900); stainless steel ($6,900)

Diver Chronometer
Reference number: 1185-170-3/BLACK
Movement: automatic, Caliber UN-118; ø 31.6 mm, height 6.45 mm; 50 jewels; 28,800 vph; DIAMonSIL escapement, silicon hairspring; 60-hour power reserve; COSC-certified chronometer
Functions: hours, minutes, subsidiary seconds; power reserve indicator; date
Case: titanium with black PVD coating, ø 44 mm, height 13.1 mm; unidirectional rose gold bezel with rubber insert, 0-60 scale; sapphire crystal; transparent case back; screw-in crown; water-resistant to 30 atm
Band: rubber, buckle
Price: $12,000
Variations: titanium ($7,900)

Diver Chronometer
Reference number: 1183-170-3/93
Movement: automatic, Caliber UN-118; ø 31.6 mm, height 6.45 mm; 50 jewels; 28,800 vph; DIAMonSIL escapement, silicon hairspring; 60-hour power reserve; COSC-certified chronometer
Functions: hours, minutes, subsidiary seconds; power reserve indicator; date
Case: titanium, ø 44 mm, height 13.1 mm; unidirectional bezel set with rubber insert, 0-60 scale; sapphire crystal; transparent case back; screw-in crown; water-resistant to 30 atm
Band: rubber, buckle
Price: $7,900
Variations: rose gold bezel ($12,000)

Caliber UN-118
Automatic; DIAMonSIL escapement (patented); single spring barrel, approx. 60-hour power reserve
Functions: hours, minutes, subsidiary seconds; power reserve indicator; date
Diameter: 31.6 mm
Height: 6.45 mm
Jewels: 50
Balance: with variable inertia
Frequency: 28,800 vph
Balance spring: silicon
Shock protection: Incabloc
Remarks: perlage on mainplate, bridges with concentric côtes de Genève ("côtes circulaires")

Caliber UN-334
Automatic; silicon escapement; single spring barrel, 48-hour power reserve
Functions: hours, minutes, subsidiary seconds; additional 24-hour display (2nd time zone); large date
Jewels: 49
Balance: with variable inertia
Frequency: 28,800 vph
Balance spring: silicon
Shock protection: Incabloc
Remarks: patented rapid time adjustment for 2nd time zone; perlage on mainplate, bridges with concentric côtes de Genève ("côtes circulaires")

Caliber UN-155
Automatic; silicon escapement; column wheel control of chronograph functions; single spring barrel, 52-hour power reserve
Functions: hours, minutes, subsidiary seconds; chronograph with integrated 10-minute backward countdown; date
Diameter: 34 mm
Height: 8.28 mm
Jewels: 67
Frequency: 28,800 vph
Balance spring: silicon
Remarks: for regatta countdown, second hand runs backward first, then reverses when it reaches its target time (can be set accurately to the minute); 650 parts

Urban Jürgensen
Route Boujean 77
CH-2502 Biel-Bienne
Switzerland

Tel.:
+41-32-365-1526

E-mail:
info@urbanjurgensen.com

Website:
www.urbanjurgensen.com

Founded:
1773

Annual production:
several hundred watches

U.S. distributor:
Martin Pulli
4337 Main Street
Philadelphia, PA 19127
215-508-4610
martin@martinpulli.com
www.martinpulli.com

Most important collections:
High-end references with in-house movements; some are sold exclusively from the workshop with a private pickup visit arrangement.

URBAN JÜRGENSEN & SØNNER

For all aficionados and collectors of fine timekeepers, the name Urban Jürgensen & Sønner is synonymous with outstanding watches. The company was founded in 1773 and has always strived for the highest rungs of the horological art. Technical perfection consistently combines with imaginative cases. A lot of attention is given to dials and hands.

Today, Urban Jürgensen & Sønner—originally a Danish firm—manufactures watches in Switzerland, where a team of eight superbly qualified watchmakers do the work in three ateliers. For over a quarter century now, they have been making highly complicated unique pieces and very upmarket wristwatches in small editions of 50 to 300 pieces. The series were based mostly on *ébauches* by Frédéric Piguet. Like all keen watchmakers, those at Urban Jürgensen have also sought to make their own movements, which would meet the highest standards of precision and reliability and not require too much servicing.

In 2003, a team began collaborating with a well-known external design engineer to construct a base movement. The new UJS-P8 was conceived with both a traditional Swiss lever escapement and in a special variation featuring a pivoting chronometer escapement, available for the first time in a wristwatch.

The esthetic concept behind the brand's watches is clearly vintage. Urban Jürgensen & Sønner timepieces have the broad open face of old pocket watches and classic hands, including a Breguet-type hour hand. The lugs on the 1741 recall the link to the watch chain. CEO Søren Jenry Petersen, an industrialist and watch lover, has kept up that watchmaking concept. The 1140 series is composed of classical watches with a modernized eighteenth-century feel. A detail worth noting is the complex "grenage" technique used to create that grainy look on the dial.

Reference 1741
Reference number: 1741 PT
Movement: manually wound, Urban Jürgensen Caliber P4 base with special module; ø 32 mm, height 5.2 mm; 35 jewels; 21,600 vph, double spring barrel, 72-hour power reserve
Functions: hours, minutes, sweep seconds; perpetual calendar with date, weekday, month, moon phase, leap year
Case: platinum, ø 41 mm, height 12.3 mm; sapphire crystal; transparent case back; water-resistant to 3 atm
Band: reptile skin, buckle
Price: $98,600
Variations: on request

The Alfred
Reference number: 1142 SS
Movement: manually wound, Urban Jürgensen Caliber P4; ø 32 mm, height 5.2 mm; 23 jewels; 21,600 vph; 2 spring barrels, 72-hour power reserve
Functions: hours, minutes, subsidiary seconds
Case: stainless steel, ø 42 mm, height 11.5 mm; sapphire crystal; transparent case back; water-resistant to 3 atm
Band: calfskin, buckle
Remarks: solid silver handmade "grenage" dial
Price: $15,800

Jürgensen One
Reference number: 5241
Movement: automatic, Urban Jürgensen Caliber F5; ø 32 mm, height 6.6 mm; 34 jewels; 21,600 vph; 2 spring barrels, 72-hour power reserve
Functions: hours, minutes, subsidiary seconds
Case: stainless steel, 41 mm, height 12.1 mm at bezel; sapphire crystal; transparent case back; water-resistant to 12 atm
Band: stainless steel, integrated, double folding clasp with security lock
Price: $27,200
Variations: gray or blue dial; as GMT ($37,200)

URWERK

Felix Baumgartner and designer Martin Frei count among the living legends of innovative horology. They founded their company Urwerk in 1997 with a name that is a play on the words *Uhrwerk*, for movement, and *Urwerk*, meaning a sort of primal mechanism. Their specialty is inventing surprising time indicators featuring digital numerals that rotate like satellites and display the time in a relatively linear depiction on a small "dial" at the front of the flattened case, which could almost—but not quite—be described as oval. Their inspiration goes back to the so-called night clock of the eighteenth-century Campanus brothers, but the realization is purely *2001: A Space Odyssey*.

Urwerk's debut was with the Harry Winston Opus 5. Later, they created the Black Cobra, which displays time using cylinders and other clever ways to recoup energy for driving rather heavy components. The Torpedo is another example of high-tech watchmaking, again based on the satellite system of revolving and turning hands. These pieces remind one of the frenetic engineering that has transformed the planet since the eighteenth century. And with each return to the drawing board, Baumgartner and Frei find new ways to explore what has now become an unmistakable form, using high-tech materials, like aluminum titanium nitride (AlTiN), or finding new functions for the owner to play with.

Urwerk is continually pushing the envelope, even by its own standards. The "Transformator" adds a rotatable, pivotable case to the watch. If you're not interested in the time, you can turn the watch around and admire the automatic mechanism through the back. The latest model UR-105 CT Maverick is like the older Kryptonite, but now with a bronze case that will age along with the wearer. In 2019, the brand came up with a watch that can be reset by placing it in a case carrying a seventy-pound atomic clock. Far more portable is the 111C, where time is given more fluidly on wheels, including the digital seconds.

Urwerk SA
114, rue du Rhône
CH-1204 Geneva
Switzerland

Tel:
+41-22-900-2027

E-mail:
info@urwerk.com

Website:
www.urwerk.com

Founded:
1995

Annual production:
150 watches

U.S. distributor:
Ildico Inc.
8701 Wilshire Blvd.
Beverly Hills, CA 90211
310-205-5555

UR-105 CT Maverick

Movement: automatic, Caliber UR 5.03; 52 jewels; winding system steered by 2 turbines; 28,800 vph; wandering hour satellites with Geneva Cross control and planetary transmission (all numerals always remain in vertical position), winding system regulated by fluid dynamics decoupling; 48-hour power reserve
Functions: hours (digital, rotating), minutes (segment display), digital seconds; power reserve indicator
Case: bronze, 39.5 × 53 mm, height 17.8 mm; sapphire crystal; water-resistant to 3 atm
Band: reptile skin, buckle
Price: $69,000

UR-111C

Movement: automatic, Caliber UR 7.10; 51 jewels; 28,800 vph; 37 jewels; 48-hour power reserve
Functions: jumping hours; retrograde linear minutes; digital seconds on 2 wheels
Case: stainless steel with gunmetal finish coated steel, 46 × 42 mm, height 15 mm; sapphire crystal; water-resistant to 3 atm
Remarks: digital seconds carried by network of optical fibers, 2 wheels cut by LIGA
Band: textile, buckle
Price: $135,000; limited to 25 pieces
Variations: polished steel

UR-T8 Transformer

Movement: automatic, Caliber UR 8.01; 28,800 vph; wandering hour satellites with Maltese Cross control and planetary transmission (all numerals always remain in vertical position), winding system regulated by fluid dynamics decoupling; 50-hour power reserve
Functions: hours (digital, rotating), minutes
Case: titanium with black PVD coating, 48.3 × 60.2 mm, height 20 mm; sapphire crystal; water-resistant to 3 atm
Band: reptile skin, buckle
Remarks: case on carrier frame can be pivoted and turned 180 degrees
Price: $100,000

UTS Watches, Inc.
P.O. Box 6293
Los Osos, CA 93412

Tel.:
877-887-0123 or 805-528-9800

E-mail:
info@utswatches.com

Website:
www.utswatches.com

Founded:
1999

Number of employees:
2

Annual production:
fewer than 500

Distribution:
direct sales only

Most important collections/price range:
sports and diver's watches, chronographs / from $2,500 to $7,000

UTS

UTS, or "Uhren Technik Spinner," was the natural outgrowth of a company based in Munich and manufacturing CNC tools and machines for the watch industry. Nico aus Spinner, a mechanical engineer and aficionado in his own right, learned the nitty-gritty of watchmaking by the age-old system of taking watches apart. From there to making robust diver's watches was just a short step. The collection has grown considerably since he started production in 1999. The watches are built mainly around ETA calibers. Some, like the new 4000M, feature a unique locking bezel using a stem, a bolt, and a ceramic ball bearing system invented by Spinner. Another specialty is the 6-mm sapphire crystal, which guarantees significant water resistance. Spinner's longtime friend and business partner, Stephen Newman, is the owner of the UTS trademark in the United States. He not only has worked on product development, but has also contributed his own design ideas and handles sales and marketing for the small brand. A new watch released in 2014, the 4000M Diver, boasts an extreme depth rating even without the need for a helium escape valve and is available in a GMT version. The collection is small, but UTS has a faithful following in Germany and the United States. The key for the fan club is a unique appearance coupled with mastery of the technology. These are pure muscle watches with no steroids.

Diver 4000M GMT
Movement: automatic, ETA Caliber 2893-2; ø 25.6 mm, height 4.6 mm; 25 jewels; 28,800 vph; 42-hour power reserve
Functions: hours, minutes, sweep seconds; date; 2nd time zone
Case: stainless steel, ø 45 mm, height 17.5 mm; bidirectional bezel with 0-60 scale; 6-mm sapphire crystal, antireflective on back; screwed-down case back; screw-in crown and buttons; locking bezel; water-resistant to 400 atm
Band: stainless steel with diver's extension folding clasp or rubber or leather strap
Price: $6,800

2000M
Movement: automatic, ETA Caliber 2824-2; ø 25.6 mm, height 4.6 mm; 25 jewels; 28,800 vph; 42-hour power reserve
Functions: hours, minutes, sweep seconds; date
Case: stainless steel, ø 44 mm, height 16.5 mm; unidirectional bezel with 0-60 scale; automatic helium escape valve; sapphire crystal, antireflective on back; screwed-down case back; screw-in crown and buttons; water-resistant to 200 atm
Band: stainless steel with diver's extension folding clasp, comes with rubber leather strap
Price: $3,950

Adventure Manual Wind
Movement: manually wound, ETA Unitas Caliber 6497; ø 36.6 mm, height 5.4 mm; 18 jewels; 18,000 vph; 48-hour power reserve
Functions: hours, minutes, subsidiary seconds
Case: stainless steel, ø 46 mm, height 14 mm; screw-in crown; antireflective sapphire crystal; screwed-down sapphire crystal case back; water-resistant to 50 atm
Band: leather, buckle
Price: $3,400
Variations: rubber strap

VACHERON CONSTANTIN

The origins of this oldest continuously operating watch *manufacture* can be traced back to 1755 when Jean-Marc Vacheron opened his workshop in Geneva. His highly complex watches were particularly appreciated by clients in Paris. The development of such an important outlet for horological works there had a lot to do with the emergence of a wealthy class around the powerful French court. The Revolution put an end to all the financial excesses of that market, however, and the Vacheron company suffered as well . . . until the arrival of marketing wizard François Constantin in 1819.

Fast-forward to the late twentieth century: The brand with the Maltese cross logo had evolved into a tradition-conscious keeper of *haute horlogerie* under the aegis, starting in the mid-1990s, of the Vendôme Luxury Group (today's Richemont SA).

Vacheron Constantin is one of the last luxury brands to have abandoned the traditional way of dividing up labor. Today, most of its basic movements are made in-house at the production facilities and headquarters in Plan-les-Ouates and the workshops in Le Brassus in Switzerland's Jura region.

Products range from the world's most complicated watch, the 57260, and the finely crafted Les Cabinotiers collection of unique pieces, to the rejuvenated Overseas models, and the entry-level collection, the Fiftysix, with a basic movement and no Geneva Seal. In 2019, the brand's competence in movements produced a genuine novelty: a perpetual calendar driven by the "Twin Beat" escapement. It runs at 36,000 vph on the wearer's arm, and can be switched to 8,640 vph when stored, giving it a 65-day power reserve.

Vacheron Constantin
Chemin du Tourbillon
CH-1228 Plan-les-Ouates
Switzerland

Tel.:
+41-22-930-2005

E-mail:
info@vacheron-constantin.com

Website:
www.vacheron-constantin.com

Founded:
1755

Number of employees:
approx. 800

Annual production:
over 20,000 watches (estimated)

U.S. distributor:
Vacheron Constantin
Richemont North America
645 Fifth Avenue
New York, NY 10022
877-701-1755

Most important collections:
Harmony, Patrimony, Traditionnelle, Historiques, Métiers d'Art, Malte, Overseas, Quai de l'Île

Traditionnelle Twin Beat Perpetual Calendar

Reference number: 3200T/000P-B578
Movement: manually wound, Vacheron Constantin Caliber 3610; ø 32 mm, height 6 mm; 64 jewels; 36,000 or 8,640 vph; movement with Twin-Beat escapement system, switchable between active and passive mode (for storage in a safe, for ex.), 96-hour or up to 65-day power reserve; Geneva Seal
Functions: hours, minutes; mode indicator, double power reserve indicator for active and passive mode; perpetual calendar with date, month, leap year
Case: platinum, ø 42 mm, height 12.3 mm; sapphire crystal; transparent case back; water-resistant to 3 atm
Band: reptile skin, buckle
Price: $241,000

Les Cabinotiers Celestia Astronomica Grande Complication 3600

Reference number: 9720C/000G-B281
Movement: manually wound, Vacheron Constantin Caliber 3600; ø 36 mm, height 8.7 mm; 64 jewels; 18,000 vph; 1-minute tourbillon; 6 spring barrels, 21-day power reserve; Geneva Seal
Functions: hours, minutes, sweep seconds; power reserve indicator; perpetual calendar with date, weekday, month, moon phase, season, moon age, sunrise/sunset; day/night duration; solar system conjunctions; celestial map of northern hemisphere
Case: white gold, ø 45 mm, height 13.6 mm; sapphire crystal; transparent case back; water-resistant to 3 atm
Remarks: opal dial; **Price:** on request

Les Cabinotiers Minute Repeater Perpetual Calendar

Reference number: 6610C/000G-B511
Movement: manually wound, Vacheron Constantin Caliber 1731QP; ø 32.8 mm, height 5.7 mm; 36 jewels; 21,600 vph; 65-hour power reserve; Geneva Seal
Functions: hours, minutes; minute repeater; perpetual calendar with date, weekday, month, moon phase, leap year
Case: white gold, ø 42 mm, height 10.44 mm; sapphire crystal; transparent case back
Band: reptile skin, buckle
Price: on request

VACHERON CONSTANTIN

Fiftysix Automatic
Reference number: 4600E/000A-B442
Movement: automatic, Vacheron Constantin Caliber 1326; ø 26.2 mm, height 4.3 mm; 25 jewels; 28,800 vph; 48-hour power reserve
Functions: hours, minutes, sweep seconds; date
Case: stainless steel, ø 40 mm, height 9.6 mm; sapphire crystal; transparent case back; water-resistant to 3 atm
Band: reptile skin, folding clasp
Price: $17,900
Variations: pink gold ($19,900)

Fiftysix Day/Date
Reference number: 4400E/000A-B437
Movement: automatic, Vacheron Constantin Caliber 2475 SC/2; ø 26.2 mm, height 5.7 mm; 27 jewels; 28,800 vph; 40-hour power reserve; Geneva Seal
Functions: hours, minutes, sweep seconds; power reserve indicator; date, weekday
Case: stainless steel, ø 40 mm, height 11.6 mm; sapphire crystal; transparent case back; water-resistant to 3 atm
Band: reptile skin, folding clasp
Price: $17,900
Variations: pink gold ($33,400)

Fiftysix Complete Calendar
Reference number: 4000E/000R-B438
Movement: automatic, Vacheron Constantin Caliber 2460 QCL/1; ø 29 mm, height 5.4 mm; 27 jewels; 28,800 vph; 40-hour power reserve; Geneva Seal
Functions: hours, minutes, sweep seconds; full calendar with date, weekday, month
Case: pink gold, ø 40 mm, height 11.6 mm; sapphire crystal; transparent case back; water-resistant to 3 atm
Band: reptile skin, folding clasp
Price: $36,800
Variations: stainless steel ($23,500)

Fiftysix Full Calendar
Reference number: 4000E/000A-B548
Movement: automatic, Vacheron Constantin Caliber 2460QCL/1; ø 29 mm, height 5.4 mm; 27 jewels; 28,800 vph; 40-hour power reserve; Geneva Seal
Functions: hours, minutes, sweep seconds; full calendar with date, weekday, month, moon phase
Case: stainless steel, ø 40 mm, height 11.6 mm; sapphire crystal; transparent case back; water-resistant to 3 atm
Band: reptile skin, folding clasp
Price: $21,700
Variations: rose gold ($33,800)

Historique American 1921
Reference number: 1100S/000R-B430
Movement: manually wound, Vacheron Constantin Caliber 4400 AS; ø 28.6 mm, height 2.8 mm; 21 jewels; 28,800 vph; 65-hour power reserve; Geneva Seal
Functions: hours, minutes, subsidiary seconds
Case: pink gold, ø 36.5 mm, height 8 mm; sapphire crystal; transparent case back; water-resistant to 3 atm
Band: reptile skin, buckle
Remarks: modeled after a 1921 watch
Price: $35,700

Historique 1942
Reference number: 3110V/000A-B426
Movement: manually wound, Vacheron Constantin Caliber 4400 QC; ø 29 mm, height 4.6 mm; 21 jewels; 28,800 vph; 65-hour power reserve; Geneva Seal
Functions: hours, minutes, subsidiary seconds; full calendar with date, weekday, month
Case: stainless steel, ø 40 mm, height 10.35 mm; sapphire crystal; transparent case back; water-resistant to 3 atm
Band: reptile skin, buckle
Price: $19,700

VACHERON CONSTANTIN

Overseas Perpetual Calendar Extra-Thin

Reference number: 4300V/000R-B064
Movement: automatic, Vacheron Constantin Caliber 1120 QP/1; ø 29.6 mm, height 4.05 mm; 36 jewels; 19,800 vph; 40-hour power reserve; Geneva Seal
Functions: hours, minutes; perpetual calendar with date, weekday, month, moon phase, leap year
Case: rose gold, ø 41.5 mm, height 8.1 mm; sapphire crystal; transparent case back; water-resistant to 5 atm
Band: rubber, triple folding clasp
Remarks: amagnetic soft-iron cage; comes with additional reptile skin strap
Price: $73,500

Overseas Tourbillon

Reference number: 6000V/110A-B544
Movement: automatic, Vacheron Constantin Caliber 2160; ø 31 mm, height 5.65 mm; 30 jewels; 18,000 vph; 1-minute tourbillon; double spring barrel; 80-hour power reserve; Geneva Seal
Functions: hours, minutes, subsidiary seconds (on tourbillon cage)
Case: stainless steel, ø 42.5 mm, height 10.39 mm; sapphire crystal; transparent case back; water-resistant to 5 atm
Band: stainless steel, triple folding clasp
Remarks: amagnetic soft-iron cage; comes with additional reptile skin strap and rubber strap
Price: $98,500

Overseas World Time Watch

Reference number: 7700V/110A-B172
Movement: automatic, Vacheron Constantin Caliber 2460 WT; ø 36.6 mm, height 7.55 mm; 27 jewels; 28,800 vph; 40-hour power reserve; Geneva Seal
Functions: hours, minutes, sweep seconds; world time indicator (2nd time zone), day/night indicator
Case: stainless steel, ø 43.5 mm, height 12.6 mm; sapphire crystal; transparent case back; screw-in crown; water-resistant to 15 atm
Band: reptile skin, buckle
Remarks: amagnetic soft-iron cage comes with stainless steel bracelet and rubber strap
Price: $37,500

Overseas Chronograph

Reference number: 5500V/110A-B481
Movement: automatic, Vacheron Constantin Caliber 5200; ø 30.6 mm, height 6.6 mm; 54 jewels; 28,800 vph; column wheel control of chronograph functions; gold rotor; 52-hour power reserve; Geneva Seal
Functions: hours, minutes, subsidiary seconds; chronograph; date
Case: stainless steel, ø 42.5 mm, height 13.7 mm; sapphire crystal; transparent case back; screw-in crown and pushers; water-resistant to 15 atm
Band: rubber, double folding clasp
Price: $27,800
Variations: reptile skin band

Overseas Small Model

Reference number: 2305V/100R-B077
Movement: automatic, Vacheron Constantin Caliber 5300; ø 22.6 mm, height 4 mm; 31 jewels; 28,800 vph; gold rotor; 44-hour power reserve; Geneva Seal
Functions: hours, minutes, subsidiary seconds
Case: rose gold, ø 37 mm, height 10.8 mm; with 84 diamonds; sapphire crystal; transparent case back; water-resistant to 15 atm
Band: rose gold, double folding clasp
Price: $25,400
Variations: reptile skin and rubber strap; stainless steel

Overseas Automatic

Reference number: 4500V/110A-B128
Movement: automatic, Vacheron Constantin Caliber 5100; ø 30.6 mm, height 4.7 mm; 37 jewels; 28,800 vph; gold rotor; 60-hour power reserve; Geneva Seal
Functions: hours, minutes, sweep seconds; date
Case: stainless steel, ø 41 mm, height 11 mm; sapphire crystal; transparent case back; water-resistant to 15 atm
Band: stainless steel, double folding clasp
Price: $20,400
Variations: reptile skin strap; rubber strap

VACHERON CONSTANTIN

Traditionnelle Tourbillon
Reference number: 6000T/000R-B346
Movement: manually wound, Vacheron Constantin Caliber 2160; ø 31 mm, height 5.65 mm; 30 jewels; 18,000 vph; 1-minute tourbillon; 80-hour power reserve; Geneva Seal
Functions: hours, minutes, subsidiary seconds (on tourbillon cage)
Case: rose gold, ø 41 mm, height 10.4 mm; sapphire crystal; transparent case back; water-resistant to 3 atm
Band: reptile skin, folding clasp
Price: on request

Traditionnelle Full Calendar
Reference number: 4010T/000R-B344
Movement: manually wound, Vacheron Constantin Caliber 2460 QCL; ø 29 mm, height 5.4 mm; 27 jewels; 28,800 vph; 40-hour power reserve; Geneva Seal
Functions: hours, minutes, sweep seconds; full calendar with date, weekday, month, moon phase
Case: rose gold, ø 41 mm, height 10.7 mm; sapphire crystal; transparent case back; water-resistant to 3 atm
Band: reptile skin, folding clasp
Price: $39,300

Traditionnelle Moon Phase
Reference number: 83570/000G-9916
Movement: manually wound, Vacheron Constantin Caliber 1410 AS; ø 26 mm, height 4.2 mm; 22 jewels; 28,800 vph; 40-hour power reserve; Geneva Seal
Functions: hours, minutes, subsidiary seconds; power reserve indicator; moon phase
Case: white gold, ø 36 mm, height 9.1 mm; bezel and lugs set with 81 diamonds; sapphire crystal; transparent case back; crown with diamond; water-resistant to 3 atm
Band: reptile skin, buckle
Remarks: mother-of-pearl dial
Price: $40,200

Patrimony Automatic
Reference number: 85180/000R-B515
Movement: automatic, Vacheron Constantin Caliber 2450 Q6; ø 26.2 mm, height 3.6 mm; 27 jewels; 28,800 vph; 40-hour power reserve; Geneva Seal
Functions: hours, minutes, sweep seconds; date
Case: rose gold, ø 40 mm, height 8.55 mm; sapphire crystal; water-resistant to 3 atm
Band: reptile skin, buckle
Price: $25,600

Patrimony Retrograde Date and Weekday
Reference number: 4000U/000R-B516
Movement: automatic, Vacheron Constantin Caliber 2460 R31R7/2; ø 27.2 mm, height 5.4 mm; 27 jewels; 28,800 vph; 40-hour power reserve; Geneva Seal
Functions: hours, minutes; date weekday (retrograde)
Case: rose gold, ø 42.5 mm, height 9.7 mm; sapphire crystal; water-resistant to 3 atm
Band: reptile skin, folding clasp
Price: $42,500

Patrimony Automatic
Reference number: 4100U/000G-B181
Movement: automatic, Vacheron Constantin Caliber 2450 Q6; ø 26.2 mm, height 3.6 mm; 27 jewels; 28,800 vph; 40-hour power reserve; Geneva Seal
Functions: hours, minutes, sweep seconds; date
Case: white gold, ø 36 mm, height 8.1 mm; sapphire crystal; transparent case back; water-resistant to 3 atm
Band: reptile skin, buckle
Price: $24,100

VACHERON CONSTANTIN

Caliber 3610
Manually wound; movement with Twin-Beat escapement system, switchable between active and passive mode (for storage in a safe, for ex.), 96-hour or up to 65-day power reserve; Geneva Seal
Functions: hours, minutes; perpetual calendar with date, month, leap year; mode indicator, double power reserve indicator for active and passive mode
Diameter: 32 mm
Height: 6 mm
Jewels: 64
Balance: glucydur
Frequency: 36,000 or 8,460 vph
Remarks: 480 parts

Caliber 2460 QCL/1
Automatic; stop-seconds mechanism; single spring barrel, 40-hour power reserve; Geneva Seal
Functions: hours, minutes, sweep seconds; full calendar with date, weekday, month
Diameter: 29 mm
Height: 5.4 mm
Jewels: 27
Balance: glucydur
Frequency: 28,800 vph
Remarks: gold rotor; 308 parts

Caliber 5110 DT
Automatic; single spring barrel, 60-hour power reserve; Geneva Seal
Functions: hours, minutes, sweep seconds; additional 12-hour display (2nd time zone), day/night indicator; date
Diameter: 30.6 mm
Height: 6 mm
Jewels: 37
Balance: glucydur
Frequency: 28,800 vph
Remarks: gold rotor; 234 parts

Caliber 2160
Manually wound; 1-minute tourbillon; double spring barrel, 80-hour power reserve; Geneva Seal
Functions: hours, minutes, subsidiary seconds (on tourbillon cage)
Diameter: 31 mm
Height: 5.65 mm
Jewels: 30
Balance: glucydur
Frequency: 18,000 vph
Remarks: 188 parts

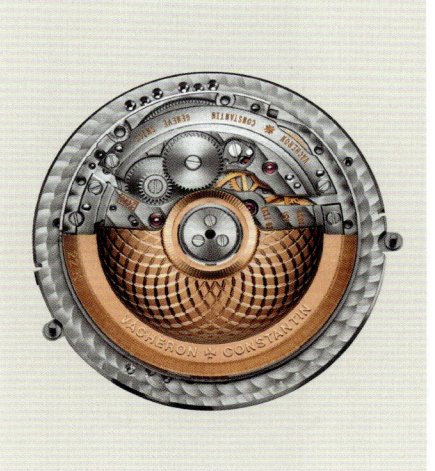

Caliber 2460 G4/1
Automatic; single spring barrel, 40-hour power reserve; Geneva Seal
Functions: disk display for hours, minutes; disk display for date, weekday
Diameter: 31 mm
Height: 6.05 mm
Jewels: 27
Balance: glucydur
Frequency: 28,800 vph
Remarks: gold rotor; 237 parts

Caliber 3300
Manually wound; column wheel control of chronograph functions, horizontal clutch; single spring barrel, 65-hour power reserve; Geneva Seal
Functions: hours, minutes, subsidiary seconds; power reserve indicator; chronograph with crown pusher
Diameter: 32.8 mm
Height: 6.7 mm
Jewels: 35
Balance: glucydur
Frequency: 21,600 vph
Remarks: 252 parts

VACHERON CONSTANTIN

Caliber 5200
Automatic; column wheel control of chronograph functions; single spring barrel, 52-hour power reserve; Geneva Seal
Functions: hours, minutes, subsidiary seconds; chronograph; date
Diameter: 30.6 mm
Height: 6.6 mm
Jewels: 54
Balance: glucydur
Frequency: 28,800 vph
Remarks: gold rotor; 263 parts

Caliber 1120 QP
Automatic; extra-thin construction; winding rotor with supporting ring; single spring barrel, 40-hour power reserve; Geneva Seal
Functions: hours, minutes; perpetual calendar with date, weekday, month, moon phase, leap year
Diameter: 29.6 mm
Height: 4.05 mm
Jewels: 36
Balance: glucydur
Frequency: 19,800 vph
Remarks: skeletonized rotor with gold oscillating mass; 276 parts

Caliber 1731
Manually wound; single spring barrel, 65-hour power reserve; Geneva Seal
Functions: hours, minutes, subsidiary seconds; hour, quarter-hour, and minute repeater
Diameter: 32.8 mm
Height: 3.9 mm
Jewels: 36
Balance: glucydur
Frequency: 21,600 vph
Remarks: perlage on mainplate, beveled edges, bridges with côtes de Genève

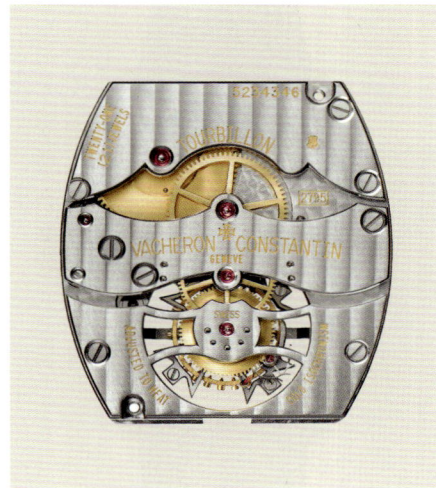

Caliber 2795
Automatic; 1-minute tourbillon; single spring barrel, 45-hour power reserve; Geneva Seal
Functions: hours, minutes, subsidiary seconds (on tourbillon cage)
Dimensions: 27.37 × 29.3 mm
Height: 6.1 mm
Jewels: 27
Balance: glucydur
Frequency: 18,000 vph
Remarks: tonneau-shaped

Caliber 2260
Manually wound; 1-minute tourbillon; quadruple spring barrel, 336-hour power reserve; Geneva Seal
Functions: hours, minutes, subsidiary seconds (on tourbillon cage); power reserve indicator
Diameter: 29.1 mm
Height: 6.8 mm
Jewels: 31
Balance: glucydur
Frequency: 18,000 vph
Remarks: 231 parts

Caliber 1003
Manually wound; single spring barrel, 31-hour power reserve; Geneva Seal
Functions: hours, minutes
Diameter: 21.1 mm
Height: 1.64 mm
Jewels: 18
Balance: glucydur
Frequency: 18,000 vph
Remarks: thinnest movement currently being made

VAN CLEEF & ARPELS

Van Cleef & Arpels
2, rue du Quatre-Septembre
F-75002 Paris
France

Tel.:
+33-1-70-70-36-56

Website:
www.vancleefarpels.com

Founded:
1906

U.S. distributor:
1-877-VAN-CLEEF

Most important collections:
Charms; Pierre Arpels; Poetic Complications

In 1999, while shopping around for more companies to add to its roster of high-end jewelers, Richemont Group decided to purchase Van Cleef & Arpels. The venerable jewelry brand had a lot of name recognition, thanks in part to a host of internationally known customers, like Jacqueline Kennedy Onassis, whose two marriages each involved a Van Cleef & Arpels ring. It also had a reputation for the high quality of its workmanship. It was Van Cleef & Arpels that came up with the mystery setting using a special rail and cut totally hidden from the casual eye.

Van Cleef & Arpels was a family business that came to be when a young stonecutter, Alfred van Cleef, married Estelle Arpels in 1896, and ten years later opened a business on Place Vendôme in Paris with Estelle's brother Charles. More of Estelle's brothers joined the firm, which was soon booming and serving, quite literally, royalty.

Watches were always a part of the portfolio. But after joining Richemont, Van Cleef now had the support of a very complete industrial portfolio that would allow it to make stunning movements that could bring dials to life. A collaboration with Jean-Marc Wiederrecht and Agenhor produced outstanding combinations of artistry in design and crafts, with horological excellence that made the watch-loving public take notice. The brand has come up with some genuine innovations: The Midnight Nuit Lumineuse lights up six diamonds with a pusher using a ceramic band and the phenomenon of piezoelectricity. The Lady Arpels Planétarium won the Ladies' Complication Prize at the prestigious GPHG in 2018. The watch features an extraordinary complication: Mercury, Venus, and Earth rotating in real time around the sun, with the Moon rotating around Earth, and a shooting star fulfilling wishes all day long on an aventurine sky.

Lady Arpels Planétarium
Reference number: VCAROAR500
Movement: automatic, Valfleurier Q020 with exclusive module (van der Klaauw); 34 jewels; 40-hour power reserve
Functions: retrograde hours and minutes
Case: white gold, ø 38 mm, height 11.8 mm; white gold bezel with round diamonds; sculpted bridge; diamond on crown
Band: reptile skin, white gold buckle
Remarks: planetarium with aventurine dial, pink gold sun and white gold shooting star, pink mother-of-pearl Mercury, green enamel Venus, turquoise Earth, diamond Moon; planets rotate at actual speed
Price: $245,000
Variation: on diamond bracelet ($330,000)

Midnight Nuit Lumineuse
Reference number: VCARO5YB00
Movement: automatic, Valfleurier Q020, exclusive caliber developed for Van Cleef & Arpels; 50 jewels; 40-hour power reserve
Functions: retrograde hours; minutes
Case: white gold, ø 42 mm, height 12.1 mm; white gold bezel set with diamonds; round diamond on crown; water-resistant up to 3 atm
Remarks: six LEDs backlight diamonds on the dial to form the Unicorn constellation on the dial, lit by piezoelectricity
Band: reptile skin, buckle
Remarks: aventurine dial with miniature painting and diamonds
Price: on request

Pierre Arpels Heure d'ici & Heure d'ailleurs
Reference number: VCARO4II00
Movement: automatic, exclusive Agenhor caliber; 48-hour power reserve
Functions: double jumping hours and retrograde minutes; dual time zone
Case: rose gold, ø 42 mm, height 7.97 mm; white gold bezel; crown with round diamond; sapphire case back; water-resistant up to 3 atm
Remarks: black lacquer dial with sunburst motif on the edge
Band: reptile skin, white gold buckle
Price: $28,300
Variations: in white gold and white lacquer dial with "piqué" motif ($40,900)

Vortic Watch Co.
517 N. Link Lane, Unit A
Fort Collins, CO 80524

Tel.:
855-285-7884

E-mail:
info@vorticwatches.com

Website:
www.vorticwatches.com

Founded:
2013

Number of employees:
5

Most important collections/price range:
American Artisan Series, Railroad Edition, Military Edition, "Convert Your Watch" service / $1,495 to $7,495

VORTIC WATCH COMPANY

The U.S. watch industry produced some very fine timepieces back in the nineteenth century like Ball, Elgin, Hamilton, and Waltham. So where did the millions of pocket watches go?

Enter R. T. Custer from Pennsylvania. He heard about companies gathering cases of old pocket watches for their gold and silver, and throwing out the movements, dials, hands, and anything deemed worthless. So he took some classes in industrial design, learned all about 3D printing, graduated, and moved out to Colorado. With crowd-funded seed money, and a few friends, he started printing simple cases.

In the meantime, the business has been transformed and expanded, not without some resistance from a modern watchmaker bearing one of the old names. RT had to fend off a rather nasty injunction. . . . But it didn't dampen his enthusiasm.

Today, 3D printed titanium cases are made for the American Artisan series, which features a crystal of Corning's very robust Gorilla Glass. Potential customers also have the option of sending in their old inherited pocket watches for a reconditioning and wrist conversion. Or, thanks to a large store of components, they can more or less order a personal configuration. The Railroad Edition offers vintage railroad watches featuring a lever under the removable bezel, a system that prevents the watches from being accidentally reset.

The latest family of watches, the Military Edition, comes from a stock of pocket watches originally manufactured for the United States Army Air Corps. RT is now successful enough to "give back": Five hundred dollars from the sale of each watch will go to the Veterans Watchmaker Initiative, which provides training for U.S. military veterans who wish to become professional watchmakers. So it's not all altruism: If the company continues to grow the way it has, it will need more watchmakers!

American Artisan Series "The Springfield"
Movement: manually wound, antique Illinois Watch Company movement (built 1926); 12size (ø 20.32 mm); 17 jewels; 36-hour power reserve
Functions: hours, minutes, seconds
Case: titanium, ø 46 mm, height 12 mm; Gorilla Glass crystal; transparent case back; water-resistant to 1 atm
Band: distressed leather, titanium
Remarks: unique patina on dial; original antique dial and hands
Price: $1,495 to $2,995 (all unique pieces)
Variations: cases in 3D-printed titanium, machined titanium, black DLC titanium, and machined bronze

The Railroad Edition
Movement: antique Rockford Watch Co. railroad-grade pocket watch movement; 16size (ø 16.93 mm); 21 jewels
Functions: hours, minutes, seconds; power reserve
Case: CNC machined titanium, ø 51 mm, height 15 mm; special bezel system allows access to railroad lever setting mechanism; Gorilla Glass crystal; transparent case back; water-resistant to 1 atm
Band: Horween Shell Cordovan Leather in "Oxblood," machined titanium buckle
Remarks: unique; original dial and hands
Price: $2,495 to $7,495 (all unique pieces)
Variations: machined titanium, black DLC titanium, and machined bronze

The Military Edition (First Edition)
Movement: antique Hamilton movement (from 1938–1950); 16size (ø 20.32 mm); 22 jewels; 36-hour power reserve
Functions: hours, minutes, dead-beat seconds
Case: titanium with black PVD, ø 49 mm, height 15 mm; domed German glass; transparent case back (Gorilla glass); water-resistant to 5 atm
Band: canvas strap, buckle
Remarks: original antique hands; comes with 2 additional straps
Price: $4,995 (50-piece limited edition)

VOSTOK-EUROPE

Vostok-Europe is a young brand with old roots. In 2014, it celebrated its tenth anniversary.

What started as a joint venture between the original Vostok company—a wholly separate entity—deep in the heart of Russia and a start-up in the newly minted European Union member nation of Lithuania has grown into something altogether different over the years. Originally, every Vostok model had a proprietary Russian engine, a 32-jewel automatic built by Vostok in Russia. Over the years, demand and the need for alternative complications expanded the portfolio of movements to include Swiss and Japanese ones. While the heritage of the eighty-year Russian watch industry is still evident in the inspirations and designs of Vostok-Europe, the watches built today have become favorites of extreme athletes the world over.

"Real people doing real things," is the mantra that Igor Zubovskij, managing director of the company, often repeats. "We don't use models to market our watches. Only real people test our watches in many different conditions."

That community of "real people" includes cross-country drivers in the Dakar Rally, one of the most famous aerobatic pilots in the world, a team of spelunkers who literally went to the bottom of the world in the Krubera Cave, and world free-diving champions. Much of the Vostok-Europe line is of professional dive quality. For illumination, some models incorporate tritium tube technology, which offers about twenty-five years of constant lighting. The Lunokhod 2, the current flagship of the brand, incorporates vertical tubes in a "candleholder" design for full 360-degree illumination.

The watches are assembled in Vilnius, Lithuania, and Zubvoskij still personally oversees quality control operations. The Mriya, named after the world's largest cargo airplane, was the first watch in the world to carry the new Seiko NE88 column wheel chronograph movement.

Koliz Vostok Co. Ltd.
Naugarduko 41
LT-03227 Vilnius
Lithuania

Tel.:
+370-5-2106342

E-mail:
info@vostok-europe.com

Website:
www.vostok-europe.com

Founded:
2003

Number of employees:
24

Annual production:
30,000 watches

U.S. distributor:
Vostok-Europe
Détente Watch Group
244 Upton Road, Suite 4
Colchester, CT 06415
877-486-7865
www.detentewatches.com

Most important collections/price range:
Anchar collection / from $759; Mriya / from $649

Expedition Everest Underground Automatic

Reference number: YN84-597A543
Movement: automatic, Seiko Epson YN84; ø 29.36 mm; 22 jewels; 21,600 vph; 40-hour power reserve; **Functions:** hours, minutes, sweep seconds; power reserve indication, 24-hour display
Case: stainless steel, ø 48 mm, height 17.5 mm; unidirectional bezel with 0-60 scale, hardened antireflective K1 mineral glass; screw-in crown; water-resistant to 20 atm; **Band:** leather, buckle
Remarks: "Trigalight" constant tritium illumination; comes with additional silicon strap, changing tool, and dry box
Price: $769; limited and numbered edition of 3,000 pieces

Expedition Everest Underground

Reference number: YM8J-597E546
Movement: quartz, Seiko Epson YM8J
Functions: hours, minutes, sweep seconds; world time with city references; weekday, date, 24-hour chronograph, 24-hour countdown, 24-hour sound alarm
Case: stainless steel, ø 47 mm, height 17.5 mm; unidirectional bezel with 0-60 scale, hardened antireflective K1 mineral glass; screw-in crown; water-resistant to 20 atm; **Band:** leather, buckle
Remarks: "Trigalight" constant tritium illumination; comes with additional silicon strap, changing tool, and dry box
Price: $599; limited and numbered edition of 3,000 pieces

Lunokhod 2 Chrono & Alarm & Perpetual Calendar "Tritium Gaslight"

Reference number: YM86-620A506
Movement: S. Epson YM86; ø 27 mm, height 3.7 mm
Functions: hours, minutes, subsidiary seconds; 24-hour chronograph; 24-hour sound alarm; perpetual calendar; days of the week
Case: stainless steel, ø 49 mm, height 17.5 mm; unidirectional bezel with 0-60 scale, hardened antireflective K1 mineral glass; water-resistant to 30 atm, helium release valve
Band: calfskin, buckle
Remarks: with 2nd silicon strap, screwdriver, and dry box; "Trigalight" constant tritium illumination
Price: $899

VOSTOK-EUROPE

Ekranoplan Automatic "Tritium Gaslight"
Reference number: NH35-546H515
Movement: automatic, Seiko Caliber NH35A; ø 27.4 mm, height 5.32 mm; 24 jewels; 21,600 vph; 40-hour power reserve
Functions: hours, minutes, sweep seconds; date
Case: titanium, ø 47 mm, height 16 mm; unidirectional bezel with 0-60 scale, K1 hardened antireflective mineral glass; screw-in crown; water-resistant to 20 atm
Band: leather, buckle
Price: $759
Variations: silicon strap, nylon strap

N-1 Rocket
Reference number: NE57-225A562/B
Movement: automatic, Seiko Caliber NH57; ø 29.36 mm, height 5.32 mm; 29 jewels, 21,600 vph; 41-hour power reserve
Functions: hours, minutes, sweep seconds; sweep power reserve; date
Case: stainless steel, ø 46 mm, height 17 mm; unidirectional bezel with 0-120 scale, K1 hardened antireflective mineral glass; water-resistant to 20 atm
Band: leather, buckle
Price: $799

Energia 2
Reference number: YN84/5750540
Movement: automatic, Seiko Caliber YN84; ø 26.6 mm, height 5.32 mm; 22 jewels; 21,600 vph; 41-hour power reserve
Functions: hours, minutes, sweep seconds; power reserve indicator; 24-hour indication
Case: bronze, ø 48 mm, height 17 mm; unidirectional bezel with 0-60 scale, K1 hardened antireflective mineral glass; water-resistant to 30 atm; helium release valve
Band: leather, buckle
Remarks: with 2nd silicon strap, screwdriver, and dry box; "Trigalight" constant tritium illumination
Price: $1,079; limited and numbered edition of 3,000 pieces

Anchar Men's Diver Watch
Reference number: NH35A-510C530
Movement: automatic, Seiko Caliber NH35; ø 26.6 mm, height 5.32 mm; 24 jewels; 21,600 vph; 41-hour power reserve
Functions: hours, minutes, sweep seconds; date
Case: stainless steel, ø 48 mm, height 16 mm; unidirectional bezel with 0-60 scale, hardened antireflective K1 mineral glass; screw-in crown; water-resistant to 30 atm
Band: calfskin, buckle
Remarks: comes with 2nd silicon band, screwdriver, and dry box; "Trigalight" constant tritium illumination
Price: $639
Variations: various dial colors

Expedition North Pole
Movement: automatic, Seiko Caliber SII NH35; ø 29.36 mm, height 5.32 mm; 24 jewels; 21,600 vph; bidirectional winding; 41-hour power reserve
Functions: hours, minutes, sweep seconds; date
Case: stainless steel, ø 43 mm, height 15.5 mm; hardened antireflective K1 mineral crystal; screw-in crown; transparent case back; water-resistant to 20 atm
Band: calfskin, buckle
Price: $439

Limousine
Reference number: YN84-565E550
Movement: automatic, Seiko Epson YN84; ø 27.4 mm, height 5.77 mm; 22 jewels; 21,600 vph; 40-hour power reserve
Functions: hours, minutes, sweep seconds; 24-hour indicator; power reserve; date
Case: bicolor stainless steel and rose gold, ø 45 mm, height 14 mm; hardened antireflective K1 mineral crystal; water-resistant to 5 atm
Remarks: "Trigalight" constant tritium illumination; open balance
Band: calfskin, buckle
Price: $859
Variations: yellow gold, blue PVD bezel

WEMPE GLASHÜTTE I/SA

Ever since 2005, the global jewelry chain Gerhard D. Wempe KG has been putting out watches under its own name again. It was probably inevitable: Gerhard D. Wempe, who founded the company in the late nineteenth century in Oldenburg, was himself a watchmaker. And in the 1930s, the company also owned the Hamburg chronometer works that made watches for seafarers and pilots.

Today, while Wempe remains formally in Hamburg, its manufacturing is done in Glashütte. The move to the fully renovated and expanded Urania observatory in the hills above town was engineered by Eva-Kim Wempe, great-granddaughter of the founder. There, the company does all its after-sales service and tests watches using the strict German Industrial Norm (DIN 8319), with official blessings from the Saxon and Thuringian offices for measurement and calibration, and according to international norms paid out by the German Calibration Service.

The move to Glashütte coincided with a push to verticalize by creating a line of in-house movements for the exclusive Chronometerwerke models, like the very retro Chronometerwerke Power Reserve, or the eminently noticeable Tonneau Tourbillon. The calibers, bearing the initials CW, are made in partnership with companies like Nomos in Glashütte or the Swiss workshop MHVJ. In 2016, Wempe released the CW4, an automatic that had its first "outing" in a classic three-hander. It has a promising future ahead of it.

The second Wempe line is called Zeitmeister, or Master of Time. This collection uses more standard, but reworked, ETA or Sellita calibers. It meets all the requirements of the high art of watchmaking and, thanks to its accessible pricing, is attractive for budding collectors. All models are in the middle price range, which the luxury watch industry has long shunned.

Gerhard D. Wempe KG
Steinstrasse 23
D-20095 Hamburg
Germany

Tel.:
+49-40-334-480

E-mail:
info@wempe.de

Website:
www.wempe.com

Founded:
1878

Number of employees:
820 worldwide; 65 at Wempe Glashütte I/SA

Annual production:
5,000 watches

U.S. distributor:
Wempe
700 Fifth Avenue
New York, NY 10019
212-397-9000
www.wempe.com

Most important collections/price range:
Wempe Zeitmeister / approx. $1,000 to $4,500;
Wempe Chronometerwerke / approx. $6,000 to $56,500

Chronometerwerke Power Reserve

Reference number: WG 080003
Movement: manually wound, Wempe Caliber CW3; ø 32 mm, height 6.1 mm; 40 jewels; 28,800 vph; three-quarter plate, 3 screw-mounted gold chatons, hand-engraved balance cock; 42-hour power reserve; DIN-certified chronometer
Functions: hours, minutes, subsidiary seconds; power reserve indicator
Case: stainless steel, ø 43 mm, height 12.5 mm; sapphire crystal; transparent case back; water-resistant to 3 atm
Band: reptile skin, buckle
Price: $6,300
Variations: yellow gold ($13,800)

Chronometerwerke Small Seconds

Reference number: WG 070001
Movement: manually wound, Wempe Caliber CW3.1; ø 32.8 mm, height 6.1 mm; 40 jewels; 28,800 vph; three-quarter plate, 3 screw-mounted gold chatons, swan-neck fine adjustment, hand-engraved balance cock; 42-hour power reserve; DIN-certified chronometer
Functions: hours, minutes, subsidiary seconds
Case: yellow gold, ø 41 mm, height 12.5 mm; sapphire crystal; transparent case back; water-resistant to 3 atm
Band: reptile skin, buckle
Price: $11,500
Variations: stainless steel ($5,700)

Chronometerwerke Automatic

Reference number: WG 090003
Movement: automatic, Wempe Caliber CW4; ø 32.8 mm, height 6 mm; 35 jewels; 28,800 vph; 2 spring barrels, three-quarter plate, hand-engraved balance cock, 6 gold chatons, tungsten microrotor, finely finished with Glashütte ribbing; 92-hour power reserve; ISO 3159-certified chronometer; 90-hour power reserve
Functions: hours, minutes, sweep seconds; date
Case: stainless steel, ø 41 mm, height 11.7 mm; sapphire crystal; transparent case back; water-resistant to 3 atm
Band: reptile skin, buckle
Price: $6,900
Variations: yellow gold ($14,950)

WEMPE GLASHÜTTE I/SA

Zeitmeister World Time
Reference number: WM 340001
Movement: automatic, ETA Caliber 2893-2; ø 25.6 mm, height 4.1 mm; 21 jewels; 28,800 vph; ISO 3159-certified chronometer; 42-hour power reserve
Functions: hours, minutes, sweep seconds; world time display (2nd time zone); date
Case: stainless steel, ø 42 mm, height 11 mm; sapphire crystal; water-resistant to 5 atm
Band: reptile skin, buckle
Price: $2,135

Zeitmeister Moon Phase Full Calendar
Reference number: WM 350001
Movement: automatic, ETA Caliber 2892-A2 with module; ø 25.6 mm, height 5.35 mm; 21 jewels; 28,800 vph; ISO 3159-certified chronometer; 42-hour power reserve
Functions: hours, minutes, sweep seconds; full calendar with date, weekday, month, moon phase
Case: stainless steel, ø 42 mm, height 14.1 mm; sapphire crystal; water-resistant to 5 atm
Band: reptile skin, folding clasp
Price: $2,890

Zeitmeister Large Date
Reference number: WM 370001
Movement: automatic, ETA Caliber 2892-A2 with module; ø 25.6 mm, height 5.35 mm; 21 jewels; 28,800 vph; ISO 3159-certified chronometer; 42-hour power reserve
Functions: hours, minutes, sweep seconds; additional 12-hour display (2nd time zone); large date
Case: stainless steel, ø 42 mm, height 13.65 mm; sapphire crystal; water-resistant to 5 atm
Band: reptile skin, folding clasp
Price: $2,890

Zeitmeister Ceramic Chronograph Camouflage
Reference number: WM 690018
Movement: automatic, ETA Caliber 7753; ø 30 mm, height 7.9 mm; 27 jewels; 28,800 vph; ISO 3159-certified chronometer; 42-hour power reserve
Functions: hours, minutes, subsidiary seconds; chronograph; date
Case: ceramic, ø 44 mm, height 16 mm; sapphire crystal; water-resistant to 5 atm
Band: calfskin, folding clasp
Price: $4,160; limited to 50 pieces

Zeitmeister Ceramic Chronograph Black
Reference number: WM 690019
Movement: automatic, ETA Caliber 7753; ø 30 mm, height 7.9 mm; 27 jewels; 28,800 vph; ISO 3159-certified chronometer; 42-hour power reserve
Functions: hours, minutes, subsidiary seconds; chronograph; date
Case: ceramic, ø 44 mm, height 16 mm; sapphire crystal; water-resistant to 5 atm
Band: textile, folding clasp
Price: $4,160; limited to 50 pieces

Zeitmeister Ceramic Chronograph Khaki
Reference number: WM 690020
Movement: automatic, ETA Caliber 7753; ø 30 mm, height 7.9 mm; 27 jewels; 28,800 vph; ISO 3159-certified chronometer; 42-hour power reserve
Functions: hours, minutes, subsidiary seconds; chronograph; date
Case: ceramic, ø 44 mm, height 16 mm; sapphire crystal; water-resistant to 5 atm
Band: textile, folding clasp
Price: $4,160; limited to 50 pieces

ZEITWINKEL

Zeitwinkel turned ten in 2016, but that is not really important for this small, independent company based in St.-Imier, one of the hubs of the watch industry in Switzerland. The key attributes of the brand, ones that many watch manufacturers aspire to endow their creations with, are "timeless, simple, and sustainable." What are ten years compared to timelessness?

The models produced by Zeitwinkel (the name means "time angle") are deceptively classical: The simplest exemplar is a two-hand watch; the most complicated, the 273°, a three-hand timepiece with power reserve display and large date. The most decoration one will find on the dials is a spangling of stylized Ws, for Winkel (angle). With cases designed by Jean-François Ruchonnet (TAG Heuer V4, Cabestan), the watches look fairly "German," which comes as no surprise, because Zeitwinkel's founders, Ivica Maksimovic and Peter Nikolaus, hail from there. Some details will catch the eye, notably the extra-large subsidiary seconds dial or the large date aperture, found beside the 11 o'clock marker.

The most valuable part of the watches is their veritable *manufacture* movements, the likes of which are very rare in the business. The calibers were developed by Laurent Besse and his *artisans horlogers*, or watchmaking craftspeople. All components come courtesy of independent suppliers—Zeitwinkel balance wheels, pallets, escape wheels, and Straumann spirals, for example, are produced by Precision Engineering, a company associated with watch brand H. Moser & Cie. The 273° comes with a smoked sapphire crystal dial; the new 083° is smaller (39 millimeters) as an epitome of discreetness.

In keeping with the company's ideals, you won't find any alligator in Zeitwinkel watch straps. Choices here are exclusively rubber, calfskin, or calfskin with an alligator-like pattern. Gold cases were also once taboo for the brand, but thanks to a partnership with the Alliance for Responsible Mining, the watches now come in "fair-mined" gold cases.

Zeitwinkel Montres SA
Rue Pierre-Jolissaint 35
CH-2610 Saint-Imier
Switzerland

Tel.:
+41-32-940-17-71

E-mail:
info@zeitwinkel.ch

Website:
www.zeitwinkel.ch

Founded:
2006

Annual production:
approx. 800 watches

U.S. distributor:
Tourneau
510 Madison Avenue
New York, NY 10022
212-758-5830
Right Time
7110 E. County Line Road
Highlands Ranch, CO 80126
303-862-3900

Most important collections/price range:
mechanical wristwatches / starting at around $7,500

082° Email Grand Feu
Reference number: 082-3.S02-01-23
Movement: automatic, Caliber ZW0102; ø 30.4 mm, height 5.7 mm; 30 jewels; 28,800 vph; German silver three-quarter plate and bridges, côtes de Genève, polished screws and edges; 72-hour power reserve
Functions: hours, minutes, sweep seconds
Case: stainless steel, ø 39 mm, height 11.6 mm; sapphire crystal; transparent case back; water-resistant to 5 atm
Band: calfskin, folding clasp
Remarks: white enamel dial, grand feu
Price: $10,500
Variations: different straps

273° Saphir Fumé
Reference number: 273-4.S01-01-21
Movement: automatic, Caliber ZW0103; ø 30.4 mm, height 8 mm; 49 jewels; 28,800 vph; German silver three-quarter plate and bridges, côtes de Genève, polished screws and edges; perlage on dial side; 72-hour power reserve
Functions: hours, minutes, subsidiary seconds; power reserve indicator; patented big date mechanism
Case: stainless steel, ø 42.5 mm, height 13.8 mm; sapphire crystal; transparent back; water-resistant to 5 atm
Band: calfskin, folding clasp
Remarks: smoky black sapphire crystal dial
Price: $15,500
Variations: various dial colors; different straps

188° Galvano-blue
Reference number: 188-23-01-23
Movement: automatic, Caliber ZW0102; ø 30.4 mm, height 5.7 mm; 28 jewels; 28,800 vph; German silver three-quarter plate and bridges, côtes de Genève, polished screws and edges; 72-hour power reserve
Functions: hours, minutes, subsidiary seconds; date
Case: stainless steel, ø 39 mm, height 11.6 mm; sapphire crystal; transparent case back; water-resistant to 5 atm
Band: calfskin, folding clasp
Price: $7,490
Variations: various dial colors

Zenith SA
34, rue des Billodes
CH-2400 Le Locle
Switzerland

Tel.:
+41-32-930-6262

Website:
www.zenith-watches.com

Founded:
1865

Number of employees:
over 330 employees worldwide

U.S. distributor:
Zenith Watches
966 South Springfield Avenue
Springfield, NJ 07081
866-675-2079
contact.zenith@lvmhwatchjewelry.com

Most important collections/price range:
Academy / from $80,900; Elite / from $4,700; Chronomaster / from $6,700; Pilot / from $5,700; Defy / from $5,900

ZENITH

The tall, narrow building in Le Locle, with its closely spaced high windows to let in daylight, is a testimony to Zenith's history as a self-sufficient *manufacture* in the entrepreneurial spirit of the Industrial Revolution. The company, founded in 1865 by Georges Favre-Jacot as a small watch reassembly workshop, has produced and distributed every type of watch from the simple pocket watch to the most complicated calendar. But it remains primarily linked with the El Primero caliber, the first wristwatch chronograph movement boasting automatic winding and a frequency of 36,000 vph, allowing for measurements of a tenth of a second. That was the year 1969, and only a few watch manufacturers had risked such a high oscillation frequency—and none of them with such complexity as the integrated chronograph mechanism and bilaterally winding rotor of the El Primero.

Purchase of the brand by LVMH Group in 1999 gave the company new technical possibilities. Zenith was dusted off and modernized—perhaps a little too much for some at the time, but the recession of 2009 did bring sobriety back. Also dusted off was the historic complex in Le Locle, which was put on UNESCO's World Heritage list in 2009. Over eighty different crafts are practiced here, from watchmaking to design, from art to prototyping. Synergies with the Group companion Hublot and TAG Heuer produced the Defy 21, a complex chronograph movement based on the 36,000-vph El Primero. It features two separate gear trains and escapements for time and chronograph functions, respectively. The chronograph movement beats at 360,000 vph, allowing the hundredths of a second to be displayed. The other technical feat is the Zero G that keeps the escapement system in the horizontal position. To keep lovers of classical watches happy, though, Zenith also offers a growing collection of classic-nostalgic pilots' watches.

Defy El Primero 21
Reference number: 95.9000.9004/78.R782
Movement: automatic, Zenith Caliber 9004 "El Primero"; ø 32 mm, height 7.9 mm; 53 jewels; 36,000 vph; independent chronograph mechanism with separate escapement (360,000 vph) and power management; COSC-certified chronometer
Functions: hours, minutes, subsidiary seconds; power reserve indicator (for chronograph functions); chronograph (1/100th of a second display)
Case: ceramic, ø 44 mm, height 14.5 mm; sapphire crystal; transparent case back; water-resistant to 10 atm
Band: rubber, double folding clasp
Price: $11,200

Defy El Primero 21
Reference number: 95.9002.9004/78.M9000
Movement: automatic, Zenith Caliber 9004 "El Primero"; ø 32 mm, height 7.9 mm; 53 jewels; 36,000 vph; independent chronograph mechanism with separate escapement (360,000 vph) and power management; COSC-certified chronometer
Functions: hours, minutes, subsidiary seconds; power reserve indicator (for chronograph functions); chronograph (1/100th of a second display)
Case: titanium, ø 44 mm, height 14.5 mm; sapphire crystal; transparent case back; water-resistant to 10 atm
Band: titanium, double folding clasp
Price: $12,200

El Primero A384 Revival
Reference number: 03.A384.400/21.C815
Movement: automatic, Zenith Caliber 400 "El Primero"; ø 30 mm, height 6.6 mm; 31 jewels; 36,000 vph; 50-hour power reserve
Functions: hours, minutes, subsidiary seconds; chronograph; date
Case: stainless steel, ø 37 mm, height 12.6 mm; sapphire crystal
Band: reptile skin, double folding clasp
Remarks: perfect replica of the first "El Primero" from 1969
Price: $7,600

ZENITH

Defy El Primero 21
Reference number: 22.9003.9004/72.R585
Movement: automatic, Zenith Caliber 9004 "El Primero"; ø 32 mm, height 7.9 mm; 53 jewels; 36,000 vph; independent chronograph mechanism with separate escapement (360,000 vph); Timelab-certified chronometer; 50-hour power reserve
Functions: hours, minutes, subsidiary seconds; power reserve indicator (for chronograph functions); chronograph (1/100th of a second display)
Case: rose gold, set with 288 diamonds, ø 44 mm, height 14.5 mm; bezel set with 44 baguette diamonds; sapphire crystal; transparent case back; water-resistant to 10 atm; **Band:** rubber with reptile skin layer, double folding clasp
Price: $64,900

Defy El Primero 21
Reference number: 22.9000.9004/71.R585
Movement: automatic, Zenith Caliber 9004 "El Primero"; ø 32 mm, height 7.9 mm; 53 jewels; 36,000 vph; independent chronograph mechanism with separate escapement (360,000 vph) and power management; Timelab-certified chronometer; 50-hour power reserve; **Functions:** hours, minutes, subsidiary seconds; power reserve indicator (for chronograph functions); chronograph (1/100th of a second display)
Case: rose gold, set with 288 diamonds, ø 44 mm, height 14.5 mm; bezel set with 44 baguette diamonds; sapphire crystal; transparent case back; water-resistant to 10 atm; **Band:** rubber with reptile skin layer, double folding clasp
Price: $59,900

Defy El Primero 21
Reference number: 10.9000.9004/96.R921
Movement: automatic, Zenith Caliber 9004 "El Primero"; ø 32 mm, height 7.9 mm; 53 jewels; 36,000 vph; independent chronograph mechanism with separate escapement (360,000 vph) and power management; 50-hour power reserve; Timelab-certified chronometer
Functions: hours, minutes, subsidiary seconds; power reserve indicator (for chronograph functions); chronograph (1/100th of a second display)
Case: carbon fiber, ø 44 mm, height 14.5 mm; sapphire crystal; transparent case back; water-resistant to 10 atm
Band: rubber, double folding clasp
Price: $17,800

Defy Zero G
Reference number: 18.9000.8812/79.R584
Movement: manually wound, Zenith Caliber 8812 "El Primero"; ø 38.5 mm, height 7.85 mm; 41 jewels; 36,000 vph; gyroscopic "gravity control" module keeps regulating organ horizontal irrespective of watch's position; skeletonized movement; 50-hour power reserve
Functions: hours, minutes, subsidiary seconds; power reserve indicator
Case: rose gold, ø 44 mm, height 14.85 mm; sapphire crystal; transparent case back; water-resistant to 10 atm
Band: rubber with reptile skin overlay, double folding clasp
Price: $115,900; **Variations:** titanium ($99,800)

Fusee Tourbillon
Reference number: 40.9000.4805/75.R582
Movement: manually wound, Zenith Caliber 4805 SK "El Primero"; ø 37 mm, height 5.9 mm; 34 jewels; 36,000 vph; 1-minute tourbillon, fusée and chain escapement mechanism, skeletonized movement; 50-hour power reserve
Functions: hours, minutes; power reserve indicator
Case: platinum, ø 44 mm, height 13.35 mm; sapphire crystal; transparent case back; water-resistant to 10 atm
Band: reptile skin, double folding clasp
Price: $103,500; limited to 10 pieces

Defy Inventor
Reference number: 95.9001.9100/78.R584
Movement: automatic, Zenith Caliber 9100; ø 32.8 mm, height 8.13 mm; 18 jewels; 129,600 vph; silicon monolithic regulating organ without ball bearings or turning parts; amagnetic according to ISO 764; Timelab-certified chronometer; 50-hour power reserve
Functions: hours, minutes, sweep seconds
Case: titanium, ø 44 mm, height 14.5 mm; Aeronith bezel; sapphire crystal; transparent case back; water-resistant to 5 atm
Band: rubber with reptile skin overlay, double folding clasp
Remarks: comes with rubber strap
Price: $17,800

Defy Classic
Reference number: 95.9000.670/78.M9000
Movement: automatic, Zenith Caliber 670 SK "Elite"; ø 25.6 mm, height 3.88 mm; 27 jewels; 28,800 vph; skeletonized movement; 48-hour power reserve
Functions: hours, minutes, sweep seconds; date
Case: titanium, ø 41 mm, height 10.75 mm; sapphire crystal; transparent case back; water-resistant to 10 atm
Band: titanium, double folding clasp
Price: $7,500
Variations: reptile skin strap ($6,500); rubber strap ($6,500)

Defy Classic
Reference number: 49.9000.670/77.R782
Movement: automatic, Zenith Caliber 670 SK "Elite"; ø 25.6 mm, height 3.88 mm; 27 jewels; 28,800 vph; skeletonized movement; 48-hour power reserve
Functions: hours, minutes, sweep seconds; date
Case: ceramic, ø 41 mm, height 10.75 mm; sapphire crystal; transparent case back; water-resistant to 10 atm
Band: rubber, double folding clasp
Price: $7,500

Defy Classic
Reference number: 87.9001.670/79.R589
Movement: automatic, Zenith Caliber 670 SK "Elite"; ø 25.6 mm, height 3.88 mm; 27 jewels; 28,800 vph; skeletonized movement; 48-hour power reserve
Functions: hours, minutes, sweep seconds; date
Case: titanium, ø 41 mm, height 10.75 mm; rose gold bezel; sapphire crystal; transparent case back; water-resistant to 10 atm
Band: reptile skin, double folding clasp
Price: $9,900

Chronomaster El Primero
Reference number: 51.2150.400/69.C713
Movement: automatic, Zenith Caliber 400 "El Primero"; ø 30 mm, height 6.6 mm; 31 jewels; 36,000 vph; 50-hour power reserve
Functions: hours, minutes, subsidiary seconds; chronograph; date
Case: stainless steel, ø 38 mm, height 12.45 mm; rose gold bezel; sapphire crystal; transparent case back; water-resistant to 10 atm
Band: reptile skin, triple folding clasp
Price: $7,600

Chronomaster El Primero
Reference number: 03.2040.400/69.M2040
Movement: automatic, Zenith Caliber 400 "El Primero"; ø 30 mm, height 6.6 mm; 31 jewels; 36,000 vph; 50-hour power reserve
Functions: hours, minutes, subsidiary seconds; chronograph; date
Case: stainless steel, ø 38 mm, height 12.45 mm; sapphire crystal; transparent case back; water-resistant to 10 atm
Band: stainless steel, double folding clasp
Price: $7,100

Chronomaster El Primero Open
Reference number: 03.2040.4061/52.C700
Movement: automatic, Zenith Caliber 4061 "El Primero"; ø 30 mm, height 6.6 mm; 31 jewels; 36,000 vph; partially skeletonized under regulating organ; 50-hour power reserve
Functions: hours, minutes; chronograph
Case: stainless steel, ø 42 mm, height 14.05 mm; sapphire crystal; transparent case back; water-resistant to 10 atm
Band: reptile skin, triple folding clasp
Price: $8,600

ZENITH

Chronomaster El Primero Grande Date Full Open
Reference number: 03.2530.4047/78.C813
Movement: automatic, Zenith Caliber 4047B "El Primero"; ø 30.5 mm, height 9.05 mm; 32 jewels; 36,000 vph; partially skeletonized movement; 50-hour power reserve
Functions: hours, minutes, subsidiary seconds; chronograph; large date, moon phase
Case: stainless steel, ø 45 mm, height 15.6 mm; sapphire crystal; transparent case back; water-resistant to 10 atm
Band: calfskin, double folding clasp
Price: $10,600

Pilot Cronometro Tipo CP-2 Flyback
Reference number: 29.2240.405/18.C801
Movement: automatic, Zenith Caliber 405 B "El Primero"; ø 30 mm, height 6.6 mm; 31 jewels; 36,000 vph; column wheel control of chronograph functions; 50-hour power reserve
Functions: hours, minutes, subsidiary seconds; flyback chronograph
Case: bronze, ø 43 mm, height 12.85 mm; unidirectional bezel, 0-60 scale; sapphire crystal; water-resistant to 10 atm
Band: calfskin, double folding clasp
Price: $7,700

Pilot Type 20 Extra Special
Reference number: 29.2430.679/21.C753
Movement: automatic, Zenith Caliber 679 "Elite"; ø 25.6 mm, height 3.85 mm; 27 jewels; 28,800 vph; 50-hour power reserve
Functions: hours, minutes, sweep seconds
Case: bronze, ø 45 mm, height 14.25 mm; sapphire crystal; water-resistant to 10 atm
Band: calfskin, buckle
Price: $6,700

Pilot Type 20 Chronograph Adventure
Reference number: 29.2430.4069/63.I002
Movement: automatic, Zenith Caliber 4069 "El Primero"; ø 30 mm, height 6.6 mm; 35 jewels; 36,000 vph; 50-hour power reserve
Functions: hours, minutes, subsidiary seconds; chronograph
Case: bronze, ø 45 mm, height 14.25 mm; sapphire crystal; water-resistant to 10 atm
Band: calfskin, buckle
Remarks: comes with reptile skin strap
Price: $7,700

Pilot Type 20 Adventure
Reference number: 29.2430.679/63.I001
Movement: automatic, Zenith Caliber 679 "Elite"; ø 25.6 mm, height 3.85 mm; 27 jewels; 28,800 vph; 50-hour power reserve
Functions: hours, minutes, sweep seconds
Case: bronze, ø 45 mm, height 14.25 mm; sapphire crystal; water-resistant to 10 atm
Band: calfskin, buckle
Remarks: comes with reptile skin strap
Price: $7,100

Elite Classic
Reference number: 03.2290.679/51.C700
Movement: automatic, Zenith Caliber 679 "Elite"; ø 25.6 mm, height 3.85 mm; 27 jewels; 28,800 vph; 50-hour power reserve
Functions: hours, minutes, sweep seconds
Case: stainless steel, ø 39 mm, height 9.45 mm; sapphire crystal; transparent case back; water-resistant to 5 atm
Band: reptile skin, buckle
Price: $4,700
Variations: folding clasp

Caliber 9004 El Primero
Automatic; independent chronograph mechanism with separate escapement (360,000 vph) and power management; COSC-certified chronometer; two hairsprings of nanotube carbon matrix, impervious to magnetic fields and temperature fluctuations; single spring barrel, 50-hour power reserve; Timelab-certified chronometer
Functions: hours, minutes, subsidiary seconds; power reserve indicator (for chronograph functions); chronograph displays 1/100th of a second
Diameter: 32.8 mm; **Height:** 7.9 mm
Jewels: 53
Balance: glucydur
Frequency: 36,000 vph
Remarks: côtes de Genève; 293 parts

Caliber 670 Elite
Automatic; skeletonized movement; single spring barrel, 50-hour power reserve
Functions: hours, minutes, sweep seconds; date
Diameter: 25.6 mm
Height: 3.88 mm
Jewels: 27
Balance: glucydur
Frequency: 28,800 vph
Balance spring: flat hairspring
Shock protection: Kif
Remarks: 187 parts

Caliber 679 Elite
Automatic; single spring barrel, 50-hour power reserve
Functions: hours, minutes, sweep seconds
Diameter: 25.6 mm
Height: 3.85 mm
Jewels: 27
Balance: glucydur
Frequency: 28,800 vph
Balance spring: flat hairspring
Shock protection: Kif
Remarks: perlage on the plate, rotor (removed for the image above) and bridges finely finished with côtes de Genève; 126 parts

Caliber 400 El Primero
Automatic; column wheel control of chronograph functions; single spring barrel, 50-hour power reserve
Functions: hours, minutes, subsidiary seconds; chronograph; date
Diameter: 30 mm
Height: 6.5 mm
Jewels: 31
Balance: glucydur
Frequency: 36,000 vph
Balance spring: flat hairspring
Shock protection: Kif
Remarks: 278 parts

Caliber 400B El Primero
Automatic; single spring barrel, 50-hour power reserve
Functions: hours, minutes, subsidiary seconds; chronograph; date
Diameter: 30 mm
Height: 6.6 mm
Jewels: 31
Balance: glucydur
Frequency: 36,000 vph
Balance spring: flat hairspring
Shock protection: Kif

Caliber 4047 El Primero
Automatic; single spring barrel, 50-hour power reserve
Functions: hours, minutes; chronograph; large date; sun and moon phase (integrated day/night indicator)
Diameter: 30.5 mm
Height: 9.05 mm
Jewels: 41
Balance: glucydur
Frequency: 36,000 vph
Balance spring: flat hairspring
Shock protection: Kif

CONCEPTO

The Concepto Watch Factory, founded in 2006 in La Chaux-de-Fonds, is the successor to the family-run company Jaquet SA, which changed its name to La Joux-Perret a little while ago and then moved to a different location on the other side of the hub of watchmaking. In 2008, Valérien Jaquet, son of the company founder Pierre Jaquet, began systematically building up a modern movement and watch component factory on an empty floor of the building.

Today, the Concepto Watch Factory employs eighty people in various departments, such as Development/Prototyping, Decoparts (partial manufacturing using lathes, machining, or wire erosion), Artisia (production of movements and complications in large series), as well as Optimo (escapements). In addition to the standard family of calibers, the C2000 (based on the Valjoux) and the vintage chronograph movement C7000 (the evolution of the Venus Caliber), the company's product portfolio includes various tourbillon movements (Caliber C8000) and several modules for adding onto ETA movements (Caliber C1000). A brand-new caliber series, the C3000, features a retrograde calendar and seconds, a power reserve indicator, and a chronograph. The C4000 chronograph caliber with automatic winding is currently in pre-series testing.

One of Concepto's greatest assets is its flexibility. Most of the company's movements are not sold off the shelf, as it were, but rather designed according to the specific requirements of the customer with regard to form or technical DNA. Complicated movements are assembled entirely and tested by the company's watchmakers, while others are sold as kits for assembly by the watchmakers. Annual production is somewhere between 30,000 and 40,000 units, with additional hundreds of thousands of components made for contract manufacturing.

Caliber 1053
Automatic; inverted construction with dial-side escapement; bidirectional off-center winding rotor; single spring barrel; 42-hour power reserve
Functions: hours, minutes, subsidiary seconds (all off-center)
Diameter: 33 mm
Height: 3.75 mm
Jewels: 31
Balance: glucydur
Frequency: 28,800 vph
Balance spring: flat hairspring
Remarks: black finishing on movement

Caliber 2904 (dial side)
Inverted construction with dial-side escapement; single spring barrel; 48-hour power reserve
Functions: hours, minutes, subsidiary seconds
Diameter: 30.4 mm
Height: 4.6 mm
Jewels: 31
Balance: screw balance
Frequency: 28,800 vph
Balance spring: flat hairspring

Caliber 3041 Skeleton (dial side)
Manually wound; skeletonized symmetrical construction; single spring barrel; 48-hour power reserve
Functions: hours, minutes
Diameter: 32.6 mm
Height: 5.5 mm
Jewels: 21
Balance: screw balance
Frequency: 28,800 vph
Balance spring: flat hairspring
Remarks: extensive personalization options for finishing and accessories

CONCEPTO

Caliber 2000-RAC

Automatic; column wheel control of chronograph functions; stop-second system; single spring barrel; 48-hour power reserve
Functions: hours, minutes, subsidiary seconds; chronograph
Diameter: 30.4 mm; **Height:** 8.4 mm
Jewels: 26; **Balance:** screw balance
Frequency: 28,800 vph
Balance spring: flat hairspring
Shock protection: Incabloc
Remarks: related calibers: 2000 (without control wheel); with two or three totalizers ("tricompax") with or without date; various additional displays (moon phase, retrograde date hand, additional 24-hour sweep hand, power reserve indicator)

Caliber 8500

Manually wound; 1-minute tourbillon; column wheel control of chronograph functions; single spring barrel; 50-hour power reserve
Functions: hours, minutes, subsidiary seconds; split-seconds chronograph
Diameter: 31.3 mm
Height: 7.2 mm
Jewels: 31
Balance: screw balance
Frequency: 21,600 vph
Balance spring: flat hairspring
Remarks: very fine movement finishing

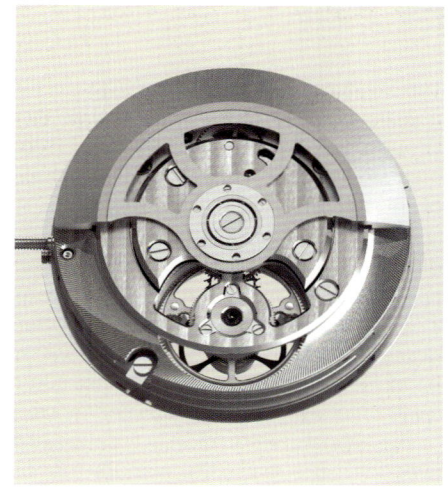

Caliber 8950-A

Automatic; 1-minute tourbillon; single spring barrel; 60-hour power reserve
Functions: hours, minutes
Diameter: 30.4 mm
Height: 6.7 mm
Jewels: 27
Balance: glucydur
Frequency: 28,800 vph
Balance spring: flat hairspring
Remarks: related caliber: 8950-M (manual winding); extensive personalization options for the finishing, accessories, and functions

Caliber 8000 (dial side)

Manually wound; 1-minute tourbillon; single spring barrel; 72-hour power reserve
Functions: hours, minutes
Diameter: 32.6 mm
Height: 5.7 mm
Jewels: 19
Balance: screw balance
Frequency: 21,600 vph
Balance spring: flat hairspring
Remarks: extensive personalization options for the finishing, accessories, and functions

Caliber 8152

Automatic; 1-minute tourbillon; bridges and plate made of sapphire crystal; off-center, bidirectional rotor; single spring barrel; 72-hour power reserve
Functions: hours, minutes
Diameter: 32.6 mm
Height: 8.5 mm
Jewels: 25
Balance: screw balance
Frequency: 21,600 vph
Balance spring: flat hairspring
Remarks: extensive personalization options for the finishing, accessories, and functions

Caliber 8908-M (dial side)

Manually wound; flying 1-minute tourbillon; single spring barrel; 42-hour power reserve
Functions: hours, minutes
Diameter: 34.6 mm
Height: 6.6 mm
Jewels: 21
Balance: screw balance
Frequency: 28,800 vph
Balance spring: flat hairspring
Remarks: extensive personalization options for the finishing, accessories, and functions

ETA

This Swatch Group movement manufacturer produces more than five million movements a year. And after the withdrawal of Richemont's Jaeger-LeCoultre as well as Swatch Group sisters Nouvelle Lémania and Frédéric Piguet from the business of selling movements on the free market, most watch brands can hardly help but beat down the door of this full-service manufacturer.

ETA offers a broad spectrum of automatic movements in various dimensions with different functions, chronograph mechanisms in varying configurations, pocket watch classics (Calibers 6497 and 98), and manually wound calibers of days gone by (Calibers 1727 and 7001). This company truly offers everything that a manufacturer's heart could desire—not to mention the sheer variety of quartz technology from inexpensive three-hand mechanisms to highly complicated multifunctional movements and futuristic ETA-quartz featuring autonomous energy creation using a rotor and generator.

The almost stereotypical accusation of ETA being "mass goods" is not justified, however, for it is a real art to manufacture filigreed micromechanical technology in consistently high quality. This is certainly one of the reasons why there have been very few movement factories in Europe that can compete with ETA, or that would want to. Since the success of Swatch—a pure ETA product—millions of Swiss francs have been invested in new development and manufacturing technologies. ETA today owns more than twenty production locales in Switzerland, France, Germany, Malaysia, and Thailand.

In 2002, ETA's management announced it would discontinue providing half-completed component kits for reassembly and/or embellishment to specialized workshops, and from 2010 only offer completely assembled and finished movements for sale. The Swiss Competition Commission, however, studied the issue, and a new deal was struck in 2013, phasing out sales to customers over a period of six years. ETA is already somewhat of a competitor of independent reassemblers such as Soprod, Sellita, La Joux-Perret, Dubois Dépraz, and others thanks to its diversification of available calibers, which has led the rest to counter by creating their own base movements.

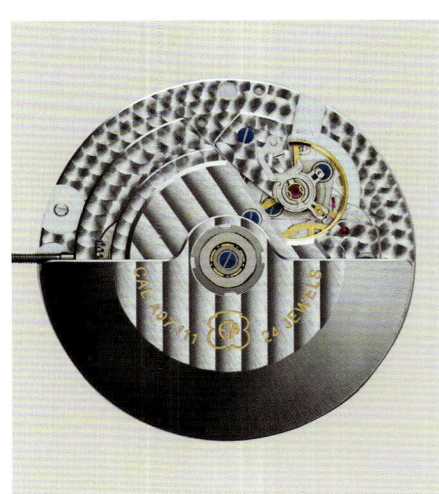

Caliber A07.111
Automatic; ETACHRON regulating system with fine-timing device, rotor on ball bearings, stop-second system; single spring barrel; 48-hour power reserve
Functions: hours, minutes, sweep seconds
Diameter: 37.2
Height: 7.9 mm
Jewels: 24
Frequency: 28,800 vph
Balance spring: flat hairspring
Shock protection: Incabloc
Remarks: related calibers: A07.161 (with power reserve display)

Caliber A07.171 (dial side)
Automatic; ETACHRON regulating system with fine-timing device, rotor on ball bearings, stop-second system; single spring barrel; 48-hour power reserve
Functions: hours, minutes, sweep seconds; 2nd time zone, additional 24-hour display (2nd time zone); quick-set date window
Diameter: 37.2 mm
Height: 7.9 mm
Jewels: 24
Frequency: 28,800 vph
Balance spring: flat hairspring
Shock protection: Incabloc

Caliber A07.211 (dial side)
Automatic; ETACHRON regulating system with fine-timing device, rotor on ball bearings, stop-second system; single spring barrel; 48-hour power reserve
Functions: hours, minutes, subsidiary seconds; chronograph; quick-set date window
Diameter: 37.2 mm
Height: 7.9 mm
Jewels: 25
Frequency: 28,800 vph
Balance spring: flat hairspring
Shock protection: Incabloc

ETA

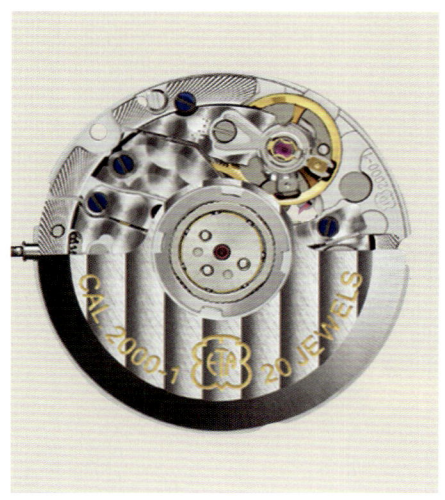

Caliber 2000-1
Automatic; ball bearing–mounted rotor; stop-seconds, ETACHRON regulating system; single spring barrel; 40-hour power reserve
Functions: hours, minutes, sweep seconds; quick-set date window
Diameter: 20 mm
Height: 3.6 mm
Jewels: 20
Balance: glucydur
Frequency: 28,800 vph
Balance spring: flat hairspring
Shock protection: Incabloc

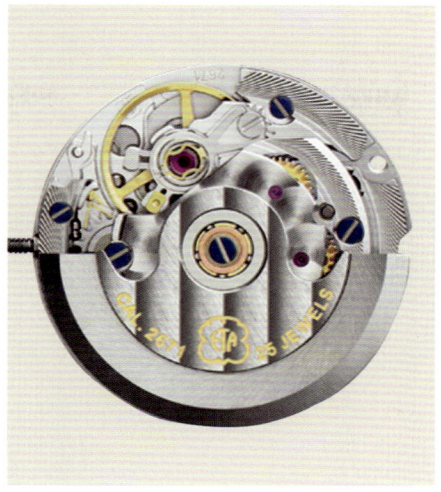

Caliber 2671
Automatic; ball bearing–mounted rotor; stop-seconds, ETACHRON regulating system; single spring barrel; 38-hour power reserve
Functions: hours, minutes, sweep seconds; date window
Diameter: 17.5 mm
Height: 4.8 mm
Jewels: 25
Balance: glucydur
Frequency: 28,800 vph
Balance spring: flat hairspring
Shock protection: Incabloc
Remarks: related calibers: 2678 (additional weekday window, height 5.35 mm)

Caliber 2681 (dial side)
Automatic; ball bearing–mounted rotor; stop-seconds, ETACHRON regulating system; single spring barrel; 38-hour power reserve
Functions: hours, minutes, sweep seconds; quick-set date window
Diameter: 20 mm
Height: 4.8 mm
Jewels: 25
Balance: glucydur
Frequency: 28,800 vph
Balance spring: flat hairspring
Shock protection: Incabloc

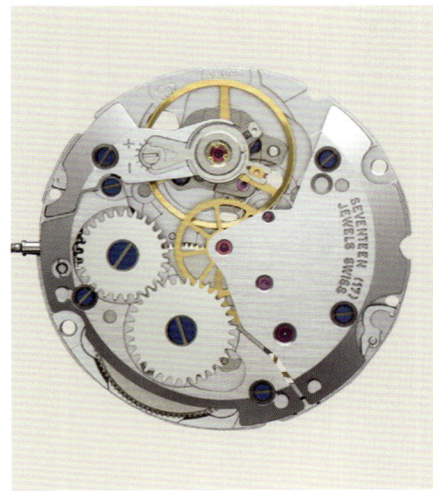

Caliber 2801-2
Manually wound; ETACHRON regulating system; 42-hour power reserve
Functions: hours, minutes, sweep seconds
Diameter: 26 mm
Height: 3.35 mm
Jewels: 17
Frequency: 28,800 vph
Related caliber: 2804-2 (with date window and quick set)

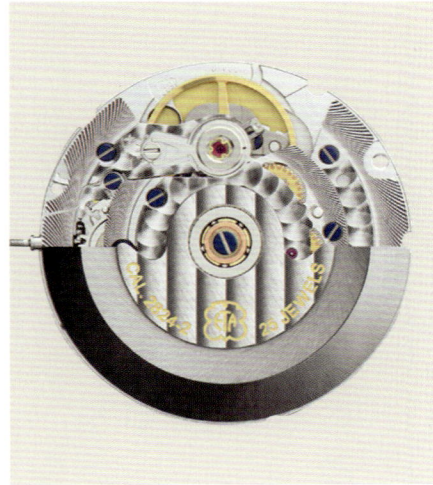

Caliber 2824-2
Automatic; ball bearing–mounted rotor; stop-seconds, ETACHRON regulating system; 38-hour power reserve
Functions: hours, minutes, sweep seconds; quick-set date window at 3 o'clock
Diameter: 26 mm
Height: 4.6 mm
Jewels: 25
Frequency: 28,800 vph
Related calibers: 2836-2 (additional day window at 3 o'clock, height 5.05 mm); 2826-2 (with large date, height 6.2 mm)

Caliber 2834-2 (dial side)
Automatic; ball bearing–mounted rotor; stop-seconds, ETACHRON regulating system; single spring barrel; 38-hour power reserve
Functions: hours, minutes, sweep seconds; quick-set date window, quick-set weekday
Diameter: 29.4 mm
Height: 5.05 mm
Jewels: 25
Balance: glucydur
Frequency: 28,800 vph
Balance spring: flat hairspring
Shock protection: Incabloc

ETA

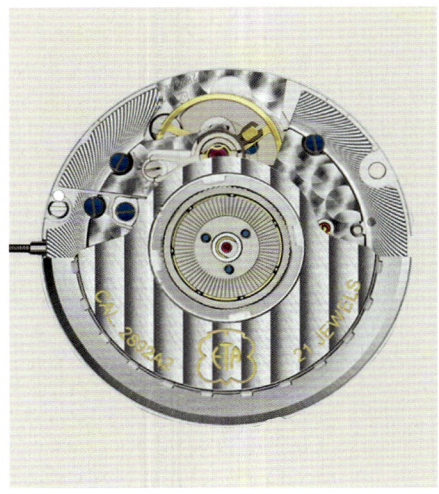

Caliber 2892-A2

Automatic; ball bearing–mounted rotor; stop-seconds, ETACHRON regulating system; single spring barrel; 42-hour power reserve
Functions: hours, minutes, sweep seconds; quick-set date window
Diameter: 26.2 mm
Height: 3.6 mm
Jewels: 21
Balance: glucydur
Frequency: 28,800 vph
Balance spring: flat hairspring
Shock protection: Incabloc

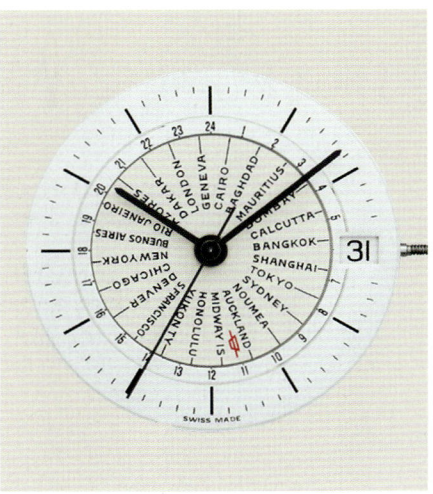

Caliber 2893-1 (dial side)

Automatic; ball bearing rotor; stop-seconds, ETACHRON regulating system; 42-hour power reserve
Functions: hours, minutes, sweep seconds; quick-set date window at 3 o'clock; world time display via central disk
Diameter: 25.6 mm
Height: 4.1 mm
Jewels: 21
Frequency: 28,800 vph
Related calibers: 2893-2 (24-hour hand; 2nd time zone instead of world time disk); 2893-3 (only world time disk without date window)

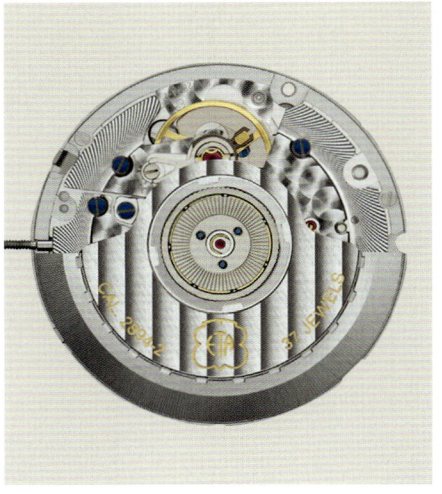

Caliber 2894-2

Automatic; ball bearing–mounted rotor; stop-seconds, ETACHRON regulating system; single spring barrel; 42-hour power reserve
Functions: hours, minutes, subsidiary seconds; chronograph; quick-set date window
Diameter: 28.6 mm
Height: 6.1 mm
Jewels: 37
Balance: glucydur
Frequency: 28,800 vph
Balance spring: flat hairspring
Shock protection: Incabloc
Related caliber: 2094 (diameter 23.9 mm, height 5.5 mm, 33 jewels)

Caliber 2895-2 (dial side)

Automatic; ball bearing–mounted rotor; stop-seconds, ETACHRON regulating system; single spring barrel; 42-hour power reserve
Functions: hours, minutes, subsidiary seconds, at 6 o'clock; quick-set date window
Diameter: 26.2 mm
Height: 4.35 mm
Jewels: 27
Balance: glucydur
Frequency: 28,800 vph
Balance spring: flat hairspring
Shock protection: Incabloc

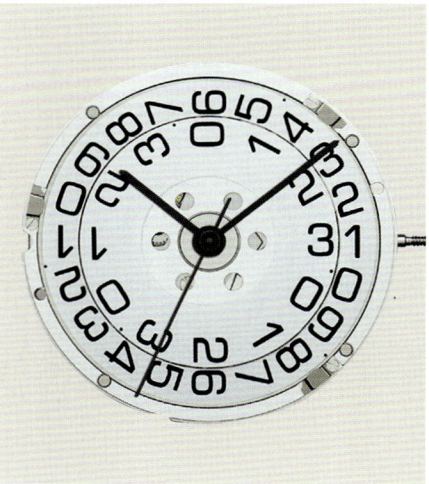

Caliber 2896 (dial side)

Automatic; ball bearing rotor; stop-seconds, ETACHRON regulating system; 42-hour power reserve
Functions: hours, minutes, sweep seconds; power reserve display at 3 o'clock
Diameter: 25.6 mm
Height: 4.85 mm
Jewels: 21
Frequency: 28,800 vph

Caliber 2897 (dial side)

Automatic; ball bearing–mounted rotor; stop-seconds, ETACHRON regulating system; single spring barrel; 42-hour power reserve
Functions: hours, minutes, sweep seconds; power reserve indicator; quick-set date window
Diameter: 26.2 mm
Height: 4.85 mm
Jewels: 21
Balance: glucydur
Frequency: 28,800 vph
Balance spring: flat hairspring
Shock protection: Incabloc

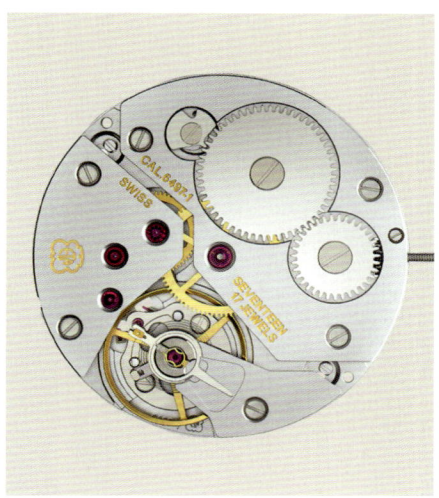

Caliber 6497-1
Manually wound; ETACHRON regulating system; single spring barrel; 46-hour power reserve
Functions: hours, minutes, subsidiary seconds
Diameter: 37.2 mm
Height: 4.5 mm
Jewels: 17
Frequency: 18,000 vph
Balance spring: flat hairspring
Remarks: pocket watch movement (Unitas model) in Lépine version with subsidiary seconds extending from the winding stem); as Caliber 6497-2 with 21,600 vph and 53-hour power reserve

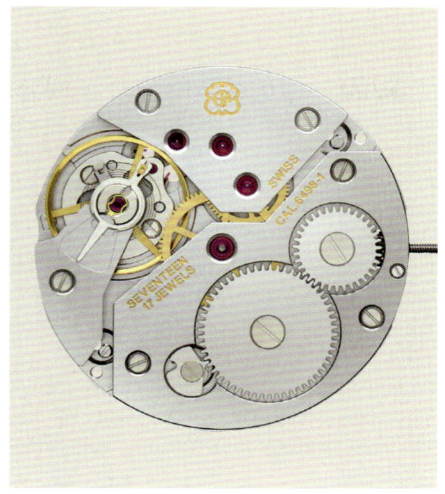

Caliber 6498-1
Manually wound; ETACHRON regulating system; single spring barrel; 46-hour power reserve
Functions: hours, minutes, subsidiary seconds
Diameter: 37.2 mm
Height: 4.5 mm
Jewels: 17
Frequency: 18,000 vph
Balance spring: flat hairspring
Remarks: pocket watch movement (Unitas model) in savonette version (subsidiary seconds at right angle to the winding stem); as Caliber 6498-2 with 21,600 vph and 53-hour power reserve

Caliber 7001
Manually wound; ultrathin construction; single spring barrel; 42-hour power reserve
Functions: hours, minutes, subsidiary seconds
Diameter: 23.7 mm
Height: 2.5 mm
Jewels: 17
Frequency: 21,600 vph
Balance spring: flat hairspring

Caliber 7750 (dial side)
Automatic; stop-second system; single spring barrel; 42-hour power reserve
Functions: hours, minutes, subsidiary seconds; chronograph; quick-set date and weekday window
Diameter: 30.4 mm
Height: 7.9 mm
Jewels: 25
Balance: glucydur
Frequency: 28,800 vph
Balance spring: flat hairspring
Shock protection: Incabloc

Caliber 7751 (dial side)
Automatic; stop-second system; single spring barrel; 42-hour power reserve
Functions: hours, minutes, subsidiary seconds; additional 24-hour display; chronograph; full calendar with date, weekday, month, moon phase
Diameter: 30.4 mm
Height: 7.9 mm
Jewels: 25
Balance: glucydur
Frequency: 28,800 vph
Balance spring: flat hairspring
Shock protection: Incabloc
Remarks: related caliber: 7754 with sweep 24-hour hand (2nd time zone)

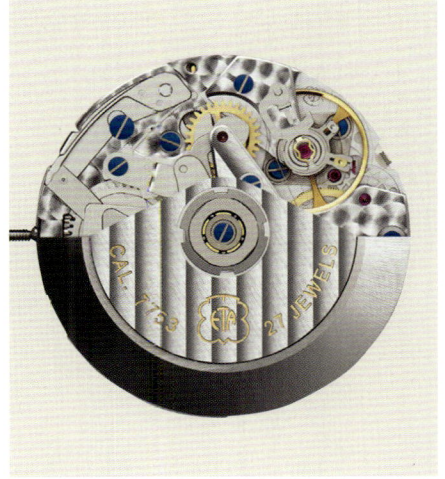

Caliber 7753
Automatic; stop-second system; single spring barrel; 42-hour power reserve
Functions: hours, minutes, subsidiary seconds; chronograph; quick-set date window with pusher
Diameter: 30.4
Height: 7.9 mm
Jewels: 25
Balance: glucydur
Frequency: 28,800 vph
Balance spring: flat hairspring
Shock protection: Incabloc
Remarks: variation of the Valjoux chronograph caliber with symmetrical "tricompax" layout of the totalizers

RONDA

Ronda is a Swiss company with a long tradition. It was founded by William Mosset, born in 1909 in the village of Hölstein, a man whose gift for micro-engineering declared itself early on when he invented a way to drill thirty-two holes in a metal plate in one operation and with great accuracy. The company was founded in 1946 in Lausen, a little town in the hinterlands of German-speaking Switzerland near Basel, where the first factory was built.

In the meantime the company has turned into a group with five subsidiaries: There are two production sites in Ticino, one in the Jura mountains, one operation in Thailand, and sales offices in Hong Kong. Overall, Ronda employs around 1,800 people in Switzerland and Asia.

The shareholders of the family enterprise, which is now in its second generation, value the company's absolute independence. This is undoubtedly a key advantage for the customer, since Ronda can continue defining its own strategy and can react decisively to customer needs.

That is why the company, which had already made a name for itself with quartz movements, decided to add a portfolio of automatic mechanical movements. The first product batches arrived on the market in early 2017; in the medium term, the mechanical Ronda Caliber R150 is to be produced in batches of six figures per year.

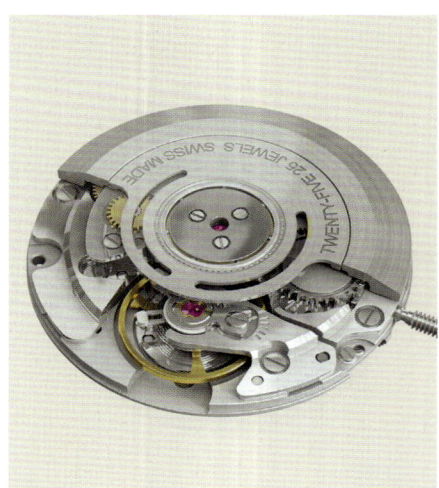

Caliber R150
Automatic; ball bearing–mounted rotor; stop-seconds, index for fine adjustment; single spring barrel; 40-hour power reserve
Functions: hours, minutes, sweep seconds; quick-set date
Diameter: 25.6 mm
Height: 4.4 mm
Jewels: 25
Frequency: 28,800 vph
Balance spring: flat hairspring
Shock protection: Incabloc

Caliber 5040.B
Quartz; 54-month power reserve; single spring barrel
Functions: hours, minutes, subsidiary seconds; chronograph, with add and split function; large date
Diameter: 28.6 mm
Height: 4.4 mm
Jewels: 13

Caliber 7004.P
Quartz; 48-month power reserve; single spring barrel
Functions: hours, minutes, subsidiary seconds; large date and weekday (retrograde)
Diameter: 34.6 mm
Height: 5.6 mm
Jewels: 6

BATTLE FIELDS

BY YAN MORVAN
FOREWORD BY ADRIAN GOLDSWORTHY

A monumental photo book documenting the scenes of more than 3,000 years of human conflict
ISBN 978-0-7892-1307-5 · $125.

"Striking . . . a new view of the history of war." —*Publishers Weekly*

"*Battlefields* is a singular achievement . . . a military history journey to nearly every corner of the globe." —John C. McManus, Curators' Distinguished Professor, Missouri S&T

"Winston Churchill would surely have devoured this magnificent volume." —Alan Axelrod, author of *The Battle of the Somme*

ABBEVILLE PRESS
Visit us at www.abbeville.com

Available wherever fine books are sold

SELLITA

Sellita, founded in 1950 by Pierre Grandjean in La Chaux-de-Fonds, is one of the biggest reassemblers and embellishers in the mechanical watch industry. On average, Sellita embellishes and finishes about one million automatic and hand-wound movements annually—a figure that represents about 25 percent of Switzerland's mechanical movement production, according to Miguel García, Sellita's president.

Reassembly can be defined as the assembly and regulation of components to make a functioning movement. This is the type of work that ETA loved to give to outside companies back in the day in order to concentrate on manufacturing complete quartz movements and individual components for them.

Reassembly workshops like Sellita refine and embellish components purchased from ETA according to their customers' wishes and can even successfully fulfill smaller orders made by the company's estimated 350 clients.

When ETA announced that it would only sell ébauches to companies outside the Swatch Group until the end of 2010, García, who has owned Sellita since 2003, reacted by shifting production to the development and manufacturing of new in-house products.

He planned and implemented a new line of movements based on the dimensions of the most popular ETA calibers, whose patents had expired. The company now has a line of manually wound or automatic movements with little complications, like a date, weekday, GMT. or a second time zone, as well as chronographs with different display constellations. The new design types are all based on mature models. A whole new line of automatic movements was launched, the Caliber SW1000, which has no ETA parts at all. The way to identify these movements will simply be the four digits. The price range will be similar to that of other products offered by the company.

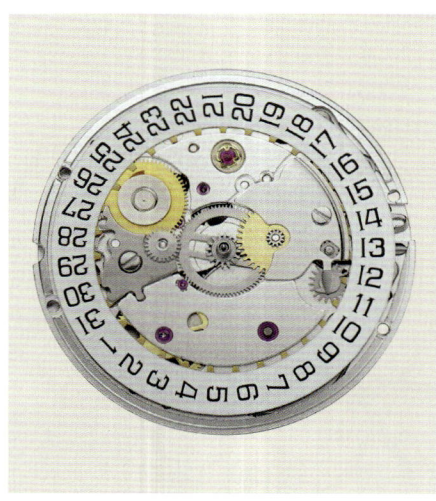

Caliber SW200-1

Automatic; ball bearing–mounted rotor; stop-second system; single spring barrel; 38-hour power reserve
Functions: hours, minutes, sweep seconds; quick-set date
Diameter: 25.6 mm
Height: 4.6 mm
Jewels: 26
Balance: nickel or glucydur
Frequency: 28,800 vph
Balance spring: Nivaflex
Shock protection: Novodiac or Incabloc

Caliber SW210-1

Manually wound; stop-second system; single spring barrel; 42-hour power reserve
Functions: hours, minutes, sweep seconds
Diameter: 25.6 mm
Height: 3.35 mm
Jewels: 19
Balance: nickel
Frequency: 28,800 vph
Balance spring: Nivaflex
Shock protection: Novodiac or Incabloc
Remarks: related caliber: SW215 (with window date)

Caliber SW220-1

Automatic; ball bearing–mounted rotor; stop-second system; single spring barrel; 38-hour power reserve
Functions: hours, minutes, sweep seconds; quick-set date and weekday
Diameter: 25.6 mm
Height: 5.05 mm
Jewels: 26
Balance: nickel or glucydur
Frequency: 28,800 vph
Balance spring: flat hairspring, Nivaflex
Shock protection: Novodiac or Incabloc
Remarks: related calibers: SW221-1 (with hand date); SW240-1 with larger mainplate (ø 29 mm)

SELLITA

Caliber SW260-1

Automatic; ball bearing–mounted rotor; stop-second system; single spring barrel; 38-hour power reserve
Functions: hours, minutes, subsidiary seconds at 6 o'clock; quick-set date
Diameter: 25.6 mm
Height: 5.6 mm
Jewels: 31
Balance: nickel or glucydur
Frequency: 28,800 vph
Balance spring: flat hairspring, Nivaflex
Shock protection: Novodiac or Incabloc
Remarks: related caliber: SW290-1 (subsidiary seconds at 9 o'clock)

Caliber SW300-1

Automatic; ball bearing–mounted rotor; stop-second system; single spring barrel; 42-hour power reserve
Functions: hours, minutes, sweep seconds; quick-set date
Diameter: 25.6 mm
Height: 3.6 mm
Jewels: 25
Balance: glucydur
Frequency: 28,800 vph
Balance spring: flat hairspring, Nivaflex
Shock protection: Incabloc
Remarks: related caliber: SW360-1 (with subsidiary seconds, height 4.35 mm, 31 jewels)

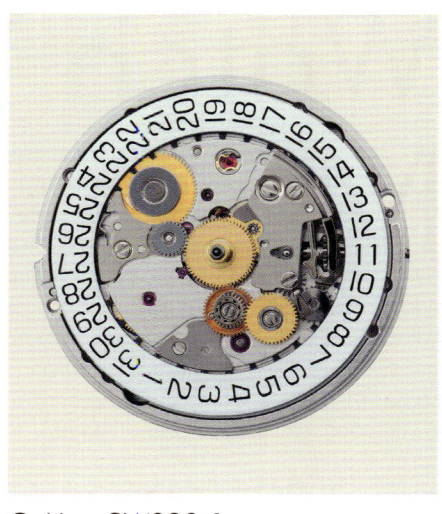

Caliber SW330-1

Automatic; ball bearing–mounted rotor; stop-second system; single spring barrel, 42-hour power reserve
Functions: hours, minutes, sweep seconds; additional 24-hour display (2nd time zone); quick-set date
Diameter: 25.6 mm
Height: 4.1 mm
Jewels: 25
Balance: glucydur
Frequency: 28,800 vph
Balance spring: flat hairspring, Nivaflex
Shock protection: Incabloc

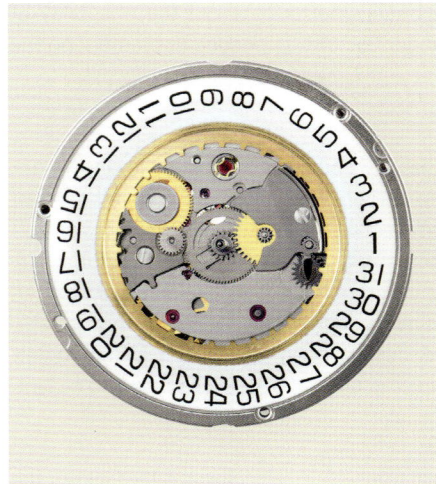

Caliber SW400-1

Automatic; ball bearing–mounted rotor; stop-second system; single spring barrel; 38-hour power reserve
Functions: hours, minutes, sweep seconds; quick-set date
Diameter: 31 mm
Height: 4.67 mm
Jewels: 26
Balance: nickel or glucydur
Frequency: 28,800 vph
Balance spring: Nivaflex
Shock protection: Novodiac or Incabloc

Caliber SW500-1

Automatic; ball bearing–mounted rotor; stop-second system; single spring barrel; 48-hour power reserve
Functions: hours, minutes, subsidiary seconds; chronograph quick-set date and weekday
Diameter: 30 mm
Height: 7.9 mm
Jewels: 25
Balance: nickel or glucydur
Frequency: 28,800 vph
Balance spring: Nivaflex
Shock protection: Incabloc

Caliber SW1000-1

Automatic; ball bearing–mounted rotor; stop-second system; single spring barrel; 38-hour power reserve
Functions: hours, minutes, sweep seconds; quick-set date
Diameter: 20 mm
Height: 3.9 mm
Jewels: 18
Balance: nickel or glucydur
Frequency: 28,800 vph
Balance spring: Nivaflex
Shock protection: Incabloc

Watch Your Watch

Mechanical watches are not only by and large more expensive and complex than quartzes, they are also a little high-maintenance, as it were. The mechanism within does need servicing occasionally—perhaps a touch of oil and an adjustment. Worse yet, the complexity of all those wheels and pinions engaged in reproducing the galaxy means that a user will occasionally do something perfectly harmless like wind his or her watch up only to find everything grinding to a halt. Here are some tips for dealing with these mechanical beauties for new watch owners and reminders for the old hands.

1. DATE CHANGES

Do not change the date manually (via the crown or pusher) on any mechanical watch—whether manual wind or automatic—when the time indicated on the dial reads between 10 and 2 o'clock. Although some better watches are protected against this horological quirk, most mechanical watches with a date indicator are engaged in the process of automatically changing the date between the hours of 10 p.m. and 2 a.m. Intervening with a forced manual change while the automatic date shift is engaged can damage the movement. Of course, you can make the adjustment between 10 a.m. and 2 p.m. in most cases—but this is just not a good habit to get into. When in doubt, roll the time past 12 o'clock and look for an automatic date change before you set the time and date. The Ulysse Nardin brand is notable, among a very few others, for in-house mechanical movements immune to this effect.

2. CHRONOGRAPH USE

On a simple chronograph, start and stop are almost always the same button. Normally located above the crown, the start/stop actuator can be pressed at will to initiate and end the interval timing. The reset button, normally below the crown, is only used for resetting the chronograph to zero, but only when the chronograph is stopped—never while engaged. Only a "flyback" chronograph allows safe resetting to zero while running. With the chronograph engaged, you simply hit the reset button and all the chronograph indicators (seconds, minutes, and hours) snap back to zero and the chronograph begins to accumulate the interval time once again. In the early days of air travel this was a valuable complication as pilots would reset their chronographs when taking on a new heading—without having to fumble about with a three-step procedure with gloved hands.

Nota bene: Don't actuate or reset your chronograph while your watch is submerged—even if you have one of those that are built for such usage, like Omega, IWC, and a few other brands. Feel free to hit the buttons before submersion and jump in and swim while they run; just don't push anything while in the water.

3. CHANGING TIME BACKWARD

Don't adjust the time on your watch in a counterclockwise direction—especially if the watch has calendar functions. A few watches can tolerate the abuse, but it's better to avoid the possibility of damage altogether. Change the dates as needed (remembering the 10 and 2 rule above).

4. SHOCKS

Almost all modern watches are equipped with some level of shock protection. Best practices for the Swiss brands allow for a three-foot fall onto a hard wood surface. But if your watch is running poorly—or even worse has stopped entirely after an impact—do not shake, wind, or bang it again to get it running; take it to an expert for service as you may do even more damage. Sports like tennis, squash, or golf can have a deleterious effect on your watch, including flattening the pivots, overbanking, or even bending or breaking a pivot.

5. OVERWINDING

Most modern watches are fitted with a mechanism that allows the mainspring to slide inside the barrel—or stops it completely once the spring is fully wound—for protection against overwinding. The best advice here is just don't force it. Over the years, a winding crown may start to get "stickier" and more difficult to turn even when unwound. That's a sure sign it is due for service.

6. JACUZZI TEMPERATURE

Don't jump into the Jacuzzi—or even a steaming hot shower—with your watch on. Better-built watches with a deeper water-resistance rating typically have no problem with this scenario. However, take a 3 or 5 atm water-resistant watch into the Jacuzzi, and there's a chance the different rates of expansion and contraction of the metals and sapphire or mineral crystals may allow moisture into the case.

Bovet's barrier to pressing the wrong pusher.

WATCH YOUR WATCH

Panerai makes sure you think before touching the crown.

Do it yourself at your own risk.

7. SCREW THAT CROWN DOWN (AND THOSE PUSHERS)!

Always check and double-check to ensure a watch fitted with a screwed-down crown is closed tightly. Screwed-down pushers for a chronograph—or any other functions—deserve the same attention. This one oversight has cost quite a few owners their watches. If a screwed-down crown is not secured, water will likely get into the case and start oxidizing the metal. In time, the problem can destroy the watch.

8. MAGNETISM

If your watch is acting up, running faster or slower, it may have become magnetized. This can happen if you leave your timepiece near a computer, cell phone, or some other electronic device. Many service centers have a so-called degausser to take care of the problem. A number of brands also make watches with a soft iron core to deflect magnetic fields, though this might not work with the stronger ones.

9. TRIBOLOGY

Keeping a mechanical timepiece hidden away in a box for extended lengths of time is not the best way to care for it. Even if you don't wear a watch every day, it is a good idea to run your watch at regular intervals to keep its lubricating oils and greases viscous. Think about a can of house paint: Keep it stirred and it stays liquid almost indefinitely; leave it still for too long and a skin develops. On a smaller level the same thing can happen to the lubricants inside a mechanical watch.

10. SERVICE

Most mechanical watches call for a three- to five-year service cycle for cleaning, oiling, and maintenance. Some mechanical watches can run twice that long and have functioned within acceptable parameters, but if you're not going to have your watch serviced at regular intervals, you do run the risk of having timing issues. Always have your watch serviced by a qualified watchmaker (see box), not at the kiosk in the local mall. The best you can expect there is a quick battery change.

Gary Girdvainis is the founder of Isochron Media LLC, publishers of WristWatch *and* AboutTime *magazines.*

WATCH REPAIR SERVICE CENTERS

RGM
www.rgmwatches.com/repair

Stoll & Co.
www.americaswatchmaker.com

Swiss Watchmakers & Company
www.swisswatchland.com

Universal Watch Repair
www.universalwatch.net

Watch Repairs USA
www.watchrepairsusa.com

Glossary

ANNUAL CALENDAR

The automatic allowances for the different lengths of each month of a year in the calendar module of a watch. This type of watch usually shows the month and date, and sometimes the day of the week (like this one by Patek Philippe) and the phases of the moon.

ANTIMAGNETIC

Magnetic fields found in common everyday places affect mechanical movements, hence the use of anti- or non-magnetic components in the movement. Some companies encase movements in antimagnetic cores such as Sinn's Model 756, the Duograph, shown here.

ANTIREFLECTION

A film created by steaming the crystal to eliminate light reflection and improve legibility. Antireflection functions best when applied to both sides of the crystal, but because it scratches, some manufacturers prefer to have it only on the interior of the crystal. It is mainly used on synthetic sapphire crystals. Dubey & Schaldenbrand applies antireflection on both sides for all of the company's wristwatches, such as this Aquadyn model.

AUTOMATIC WINDING

A rotating weight set into motion by moving the wrist winds the spring barrel via the gear train of a mechanical watch movement. Automatic winding was invented during the pocket watch era in 1770, but the breakthrough automatic winding movement via rotor began with the ball bearing Eterna-Matic in the late 1940s. Today we speak of unidirectional winding and bidirectionally winding rotors, depending on the type of gear train used. Shown is IWC's automatic Caliber 50611.

BALANCE

The beating heart of a mechanical watch movement is the balance. Fed by the energy of the mainspring, a tirelessly oscillating little wheel, just a few millimeters in diameter and possessing a spiral-shaped balance spring, sets the rhythm for the escape wheel and pallets with its vibration frequency. Today the balance is usually made of one piece of antimagnetic glucydur, an alloy that expands very little when exposed to heat.

BEVELING

To uniformly file down the sharp edges of a plate, bridge, or bar and give it a high polish. The process is also called *anglage*. Edges are usually beveled at a 45° angle. As the picture shows, this is painstaking work that needs the skilled hands and eyes of an experienced watchmaker or *angleur*.

BAR OR COCK

A metal plate fastened to the base plate at one point, leaving room for a gear wheel or pinion. The balance is usually attached to a bar called the balance cock. Glashütte tradition dictates that the balance cock be decoratively engraved by hand like this one by Glashütte Original.

GLOSSARY

BRIDGE
A metal plate fastened to the base plate at two points leaving room for a gear wheel or pinion. This vintage Favre-Leuba movement illustrates the point with three individual bridges.

CARBON FIBER
A very light, tough composite material, carbon fiber is composed of filaments comprised of several thousand seven-micron carbon fibers held together by resin. The arrangement of the filaments determines the quality of a component, making each unique. Carbon fiber is currently being used for dials, cases, and even movement components.

CALIBER

A term, similar to type or model, that refers to different watch movements. Pictured here is Heuer's Caliber 11, the legendary automatic chronograph caliber from 1969. This movement was a coproduction jointly researched and developed for four years by Heuer-Leonidas, Breitling, and Hamilton-Büren. Each company gave the movement a different name after serial production began.

CHAMPLEVÉ
A dial decoration technique, whereby the metal is engraved, filled with enamel, and baked, as in this cockatoo on a Cartier Tortue, enhanced with mother-of-pearl slivers.

CERAMIC
An inorganic, nonmetallic material formed by the action of heat and practically unscratchable. Pioneered by Rado, ceramic is a high-tech material generally made from aluminum and zirconia oxide. Today, it is used generally for cases and bezels and now comes in many colors.

CHRONOGRAPH
From the Greek *chronos* (time) and *graphein* (to write). Originally a chronograph literally wrote, inscribing the time elapsed on a piece of paper with the help of a pencil attached to a type of hand. Today this term is used for watches that show not only the time of day, but also certain time intervals via independent hands that may be started or stopped at will. Stopwatches differ from chronographs because they do not show the time of day. This exploded illustration shows the complexity of a Breitling chronograph.

CHRONOMETER
Literally, "measurer of time." As the term is used today, a chronometer denotes an especially accurate watch (one with a deviation of no more than 5 seconds a day for mechanical movements). Chronometers are usually supplied with an official certificate from an independent testing office such as the COSC. The largest producer of chronometers in 2008 was Rolex, with 769,850 officially certified movements. Chopard came in sixth with more than 22,000 certified L.U.C mechanisms, like the 4.96 in the Pro One model shown here.

COLUMN WHEEL
The component used to control chronograph functions within a true chronograph movement. The presence of a column wheel indicates that the chronograph is fully integrated into the movement. In the modern era, modules are generally used that are attached to a base caliber movement. This particular column wheel is made of blued steel.

345

Glossary

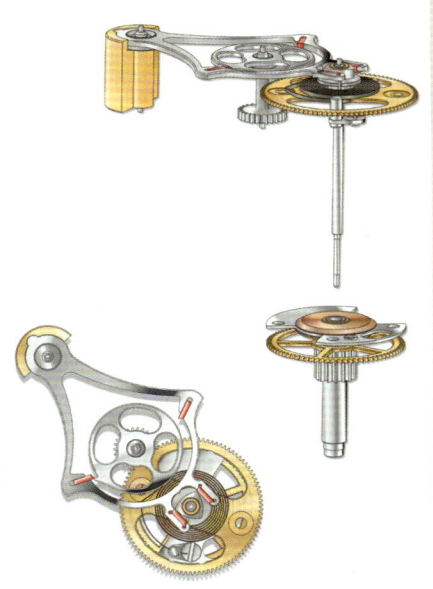

CONSTANT FORCE MECHANISM

Sometimes called a constant force escapement, it isn't really: in most cases this mechanism is "simply" an initial tension spring. It is also known in English by part of its French name, the *remontoir*, which actually means "winding mechanism." This mechanism regulates and portions the energy that is passed on through the escapement, making the rate as even and precise as possible. Shown here is the constant force escapement from A. Lange & Söhne's Lange 31—a mechanism that gets as close to its name as possible.

COSC

The Contrôle Officiel Suisse de Chronomètrage, the official Swiss testing office for chronometers. The COSC is the world's largest issuer of so-called chronometer certificates, which are only otherwise given out individually by certain observatories (such as the one in Neuchâtel, Switzerland). For a fee, the COSC tests the rate of movements that have been adjusted by watchmakers. These are usually mechanical movements, but the office also tests some high-precision quartz movements. Those that meet the specifications for being a chronometer are awarded an official certificate as shown here.

CÔTES DE GENÈVE

Also called *vagues de Genève* and Geneva stripes. This is a traditional Swiss surface decoration comprising an even pattern of parallel stripes, applied to flat movement components with a quickly rotating plastic or wooden peg. Glashütte watchmakers have devised their own version of *côtes de Genève* that is applied at a slightly different angle, called Glashütte ribbing.

CROWN

The crown is used to wind and set a watch. A few simple turns of the crown will get an automatic movement started, while a manually wound watch is completely wound by the crown. The crown is also used for the setting of various functions, almost always including at least the hours, minutes, seconds, and date. A screwed-down crown like the one on the TAG Heuer Aquagraph pictured here can be tightened to prevent water entering the case or any mishaps while performing extreme sports such as diving.

EQUATION OF TIME

The mean time that we use to keep track of the passing of the day (24 hours evenly divided into minutes and seconds) is not equal to true solar time. The equation of time is a complication devised to show the difference between the mean time shown on one's wristwatch and the time the sun dictates. The Équation Marchante by Blancpain very distinctly indicates this difference via the golden sun-tipped hand that also rotates around the dial in a manner known to watch connoisseurs as *marchant*. Other wristwatch models, such as the Boreas by Martin Braun, display the difference on an extra scale on the dial.

GLOSSARY

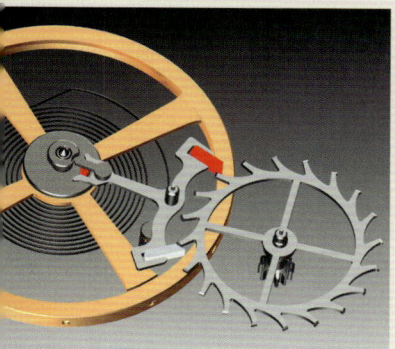

ESCAPEMENT

The combination of the balance, balance spring, pallets, and escape wheel, a subgroup which divides the impulses coming from the spring barrel into small, accurately portioned doses. It guarantees that the gear train runs smoothly and efficiently. The pictured escapement is one newly invented by Parmigiani, containing pallet stones of varying colors, though they are generally red synthetic rubies. Here one of them is a colorless sapphire, or corundum, the same geological material that ruby is made of.

FLINQUÉ

A dial decoration in which a guilloché design is given a coat of enamel, softening the pattern and creating special effects, as shown here on a unique Bovet.

FLYBACK CHRONOGRAPH

A chronograph with a special dial train switch that makes the immediate reuse of the chronograph movement possible after resetting the hands. It was developed for special timekeeping duties such as those found in aviation, which require the measurement of time intervals in quick succession. A flyback may also be called a *retour en vol*. An elegant example of this type of chronograph is Corum's Classical Flyback Large Date shown here.

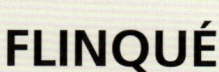

GEAR TRAIN

A mechanical watch's gear train transmits energy from the mainspring to the escapement. The gear train comprises the minute wheel, the third wheel, the fourth wheel, and the escape wheel.

GUILLOCHÉ

A surface decoration usually applied to the dial and the rotor using a grooving tool with a sharp tip, such as a rose engine, to cut an even pattern onto a level surface. The exact adjustment of the tool for each new path is controlled by a device similar to a pantograph, and the movement of the tool can be controlled either manually or mechanically. Real *guillochis* (the correct term used by a master of guilloché) are very intricate and expensive to produce, which is why most dials decorated in this fashion are produced by stamping machines. Breguet is one of the very few companies to use real guilloché on every one of its dials.

GLUCYDUR

Glucydur is a functional alloy of copper, beryllium, and iron that has been used to make balances in watches since the 1930s. Its hardness and stability allow watchmakers to use balances that were poised at the factory and no longer required adjustment screws.

INDEX

A regulating mechanism found on the balance cock and used by the watchmaker to adjust the movement's rate. The index changes the effective length of the balance spring, thus making it move more quickly or slowly. This is the standard index found on an ETA Valjoux 7750.

JEWEL

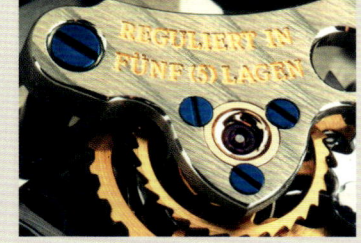

To minimize friction, the hardened steel tips of a movement's rotating gear wheels (called pinions) are lodged in synthetic rubies (fashioned as polished stones with a hole) and lubricated with a very thin layer of special oil. These synthetic rubies are produced in exactly the same way as sapphire crystal using the same material. During the pocket watch era, real rubies with hand-drilled holes were still used, but because of the high costs involved, they were only used in movements with especially quickly rotating gears. The jewel shown here on a bridge from A. Lange & Söhne's Double Split is additionally embedded in a gold chaton secured with three blued screws.

LIGA

The word LIGA is actually a German acronym that stands for lithography (*Lithografie*), electroplating (*Galvanisierung*), and plastic molding (*Abformung*). It is a lithographic process exposed by UV or X-ray light that literally "grows" perfect micro components made of nickel, nickel-phosphorus, or 23.5-karat gold in a plating bath. The components need no finishing or trimming after manufacture.

347

GLOSSARY

LUMINOUS SUBSTANCE

Tritium paint is a slightly radioactive substance that replaced radium as a luminous coating for hands, numerals, and hour markers on watch dials. Watches bearing tritium must be marked as such, with the letter *T* on the dial near 6 o'clock. It has now for the most part been replaced by nonradioactive materials such as Superluminova. Traser technology (as seen on these Ball timepieces) uses tritium gas enclosed in tiny silicate glass tubes coated on the inside with a phosphorescing substance. The luminescence is constant and will hold around twenty-five years.

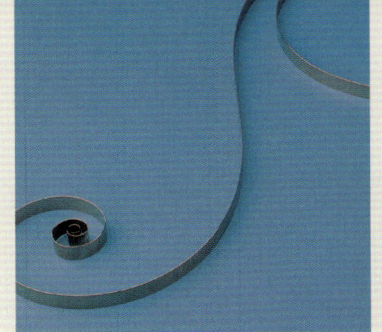

MAINSPRING

The mainspring, located in the spring barrel, stores energy when tensioned and passes it on to the escapement via the gear train as the tension relaxes. Today, mainsprings are generally made of Nivaflex, an alloy invented by Swiss engineer Max Straumann at the beginning of the 1950s. This alloy basically comprises iron, nickel, chrome, cobalt, and beryllium.

MINUTE REPEATER

A striking mechanism with hammers and gongs for acoustically signaling the hours, quarter hours, and minutes elapsed since noon or midnight. The wearer pushes a slide, which winds the spring. Normally a repeater uses two different gongs to signal hours (low tone), quarter hours (high and low tones in succession), and minutes (high tone). Some watches have three gongs, called a carillon. The Chronoswiss Répétition à Quarts is a prominent repeating introduction of recent years.

PERPETUAL CALENDAR

The calendar module for this type of timepiece automatically makes allowances for the different lengths of each month as well as leap years until the next secular year, which will occur in 2100. A perpetual calendar usually shows the date, month, and four-year cycle, and may show the day of the week and moon phase as well, as does this one introduced by George J von Burg at Baselworld 2005. Perpetual calendars need much skill to complete.

PERLAGE

Surface decoration comprising an even pattern of partially overlapping dots, applied with a quickly rotating plastic or wooden peg, as shown here on the plates of Frédérique Constant's *manufacture* Caliber FC 910-1.

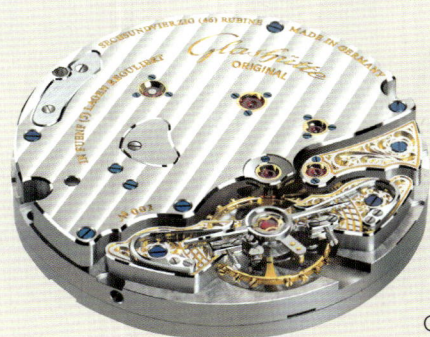

PLATE

A metal platform having several tiers for the gear train. The base plate of a movement usually incorporates the dial and carries the bearings for the primary pinions of the "first floor" of a gear train. The gear wheels are made complete by tightly fitting screwed-in bridges and bars on the back side of the plate. A specialty of the so-called Glashütte school, as opposed to the Swiss school, is the reverse completion of a movement not via different bridges and bars, but rather with a three-quarter plate. Glashütte Original's Caliber 65 (shown) displays a beautifully decorated three-quarter plate.

GLOSSARY

POWER RESERVE DISPLAY

A mechanical watch contains only a certain amount of power reserve. A fully wound modern automatic watch usually possesses between 36 and 42 hours of energy before it needs to be wound again. The power reserve display keeps the wearer informed about how much energy his or her watch still has in reserve, a function that is especially practical on manually wound watches with several days of possible reserve. The Nomos Tangente Power Reserve pictured here represents an especially creative way to illustrate the state of the mainspring's tension. On some German watches the power reserve is also displayed with the words "auf" and "ab."

QUALITÉ FLEURIER

This certification of quality was established by Chopard, Parmigiani Fleurier, Vaucher, and Bovet Fleurier in 2004. Watches bearing the seal must fulfill five criteria, including COSC certification, passing several tests for robustness and precision, top-notch finishing, and being 100 percent Swiss-made (except for the raw materials). The seal appears here on the dial of the Parmigiani Fleurier Tonda 39.

PULSOMETER

A scale on the dial, flange, or bezel that, in conjunction with the second hand, may be used to measure a pulse rate. A pulsometer is always marked with a reference number—if it is marked with *gradué pour 15 pulsations*, for example, then the wearer counts fifteen pulse beats. At the last beat, the second hand will show what the pulse rate is in beats per minute on the pulsometer scale. The scale on Sinn's World Time Chronograph (shown) is marked simply with the German world *Puls* (pulse), but the function remains the same.

RETROGRADE DISPLAY

A retrograde display shows the time linearly instead of circularly. The hand continues along an arc until it reaches the end of its scale, at which precise moment it jumps back to the beginning instantaneously. This Nienaber model not only shows the minutes in retrograde form, it is also a regulator display.

ROTOR

The rotor is the component that keeps an automatic watch wound. The kinetic motion of this part, which contains a heavy metal weight around its outer edge, winds the mainspring. It can either wind unilaterally or bilaterally (to one or both sides) depending on the caliber. The rotor from this Temption timepiece belongs to an ETA Valjoux 7750.

SAPPHIRE CRYSTAL

Synthetic sapphire crystal is known to gemologists as aluminum oxide (Al_2O_3) or corundum. It can be colorless (corundum), red (ruby), blue (sapphire), or green (emerald). It is virtually scratchproof; only a diamond is harder. The innovative Royal Blue Tourbillon by Ulysse Nardin pictured here features not only sapphire crystals on the front and back of the watch, but also actual plates made of both colorless and blue corundum within the movement.

SCREW BALANCE

Before the invention of the perfectly weighted balance using a smooth ring, balances were fitted with weighted screws to get the exact impetus desired. Today a screw balance is a subtle sign of quality in a movement due to its costly construction and assembly utilizing minuscule weighted screws.

GLOSSARY

SEAL OF GENEVA

Since 1886 the official seal of this canton has been awarded to Genevan watch *manufactures* who must follow a defined set of high-quality criteria that include the following: polished jewel bed drillings, jewels with olive drillings, polished winding wheels, quality balances and balance springs, steel levers and springs with beveling of 45 degrees and *côtes de Genève* decoration, and polished stems and pinions. The list was updated in 2012 to include the entire watch and newer components. Testing is done on the finished piece. The Seal consists of two, one on the movement, one on the case. The pictured seal was awarded to Vacheron Constantin, a traditional Genevan *manufacture*.

SILICIUM/SILICON

Silicon is an element relatively new to mechanical watches. It is currently being used in the manufacture of precision escapements. Ulysse Nardin's Freak has lubrication-free silicon wheels, and Breguet has successfully used flat silicon balance springs.

SKELETONIZATION

The technique of cutting a movement's components down to their weight-bearing basic substance. This is generally done by hand in painstaking hours of microscopic work with a small handheld saw, though machines can skeletonize parts to a certain degree, such as the version of the Valjoux 7750 that was created for Chronoswiss's Opus and Pathos models. This tourbillon created by Christophe Schaffo is additionally—and masterfully—hand-engraved.

SONNERIE

A variety of minute repeater that—like a tower clock—sounds the time not at the will of the wearer, but rather automatically (*en passant*) every hour (*petite sonnerie*) or quarter hour (*grande sonnerie*). Gérald Genta designed the most complicated sonnerie back in the early nineties. Shown is a recent model from the front and back.

SPLIT-SECONDS CHRONOGRAPH

Also known in the watch industry by its French name, the *rattrapante* (exploded view at left). A watch with two second hands, one of which can be blocked with a special dial train lever to indicate an intermediate time while the other continues to run. When released, the split-seconds hand jumps ahead to the position of the other second hand. The PTC by Porsche Design illustrates this nicely.

Glossary

SPRING BARREL

The spring barrel contains the mainspring. It turns freely on an arbor, pulled along by the toothed wheel generally doubling as its lid. This wheel interacts with the first pinion of the movement's gear train. Some movements contain two or more spring barrels for added power reserve.

SWAN-NECK FINE ADJUSTMENT

A regulating instrument used by the watchmaker to adjust the movement's rate in place of an index. The swan neck is especially prevalent in fine Swiss and Glashütte watchmaking (here, Lang & Heyne's Moritz model). Mühle Glashütte has varied the theme with its woodpecker's neck.

TACHYMETER

A scale on the dial, flange, or bezel of a chronograph that, in conjunction with the second hand, gives the speed of a moving object. A tachymeter takes a value determined in less than a minute and converts it into miles or kilometers per hour. For example, a wearer could measure the time it takes a car to pass between two mile markers on the highway. When the car passes the marker, the second hand will be pointing to the car's speed in miles per hour on the tachymetric scale.

TOURBILLON

A technical device invented by Abraham-Louis Breguet in 1801 to compensate for the influence of gravity on the balance of a pocket watch. The entire escapement is mounted on an epicyclic train in a "cage" and rotated completely on its axis over regular periods of time. This superb horological highlight is seen as a sign of technological know-how in the modern era. Harry Winston's Histoire de Tourbillon 4 is a spectacular example.

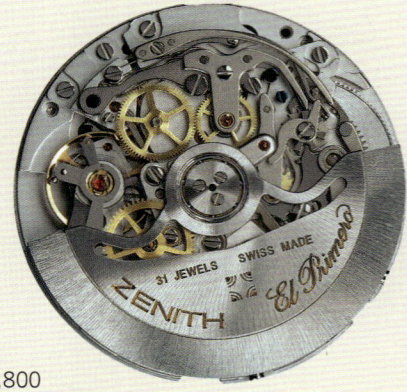

VIBRATION FREQUENCY (VPH)

The spring causes the balance to oscillate at a certain frequency measured in hertz (Hz) or vibrations per hour (vph). Most of today's wristwatches tick at 28,800 vph (4 Hz) or 21,600 vph (3 Hz). Less usual is 18,000 vph (2.5 Hz). Zenith's El Primero was the first serial movement to beat at 36,000 vph (5 Hz), and the Breguet Type XXII runs at 72,000 vph.

WATER RESISTANCE

Water resistance is an important feature of any timepiece and is usually measured in increments of one atmosphere (atm or bar, equal to 10 meters of water pressure) or meters and is often noted on the dial or case back. Watches resistant to 100 meters are best for swimming and snorkeling. Timepieces resistant to 200 meters are good for scuba diving. To deep-sea dive there are various professional timepieces available for use in depths of 200 meters or more. The Hydromax by Bell & Ross (shown) is water-resistant to a record 11,000 meters.

Copyright © 2020 HEEL Verlag GmbH, Königswinter, Germany

English-language translation copyright © 2020 Abbeville Press,
655 Third Avenue, New York, NY 10017

Editor-in-chief: Peter Braun
Editor: Marton Radkai
Production manager: Louise Kurtz
Copy editor: Virginia Carroll
Composition: Madeline Brubaker
Project management: North Market Street Graphics

For more information about advertising, please contact:
Gary Girdvainis
Isochron Media, LLC
25 Gay Bower Road, Monroe, CT 06468
203-485-6276, garygeorgeg@gmail.com

All rights reserved under international copyright conventions.
No part of this book may be reproduced or utilized in any form or by any means, electronic or mechanical,
including photocopying, recording, or by any information retrieval system,
without permission in writing from the publisher.
Inquiries should be addressed to Abbeville Press, 655 Third Avenue, New York, NY 10017.
Printed and bound in South Korea.

ISBN 978-0-7892-1352-5

Twenty-second edition
10 9 8 7 6 5 4 3 2 1

Library of Congress Cataloging-in-Publication Data available upon request

For bulk and premium sales and for text adoption procedures, write to Customer Service Manager,
Abbeville Press, 655 Third Avenue, New York, NY 10017, or call 1-800-Artbook.

Visit Abbeville Press online at www.abbeville.com.